INTERNATIONAL COPYRIGHT
LAW AND POLICY

INTERNATIONAL COPYRIGHT LAW AND POLICY

Silke von Lewinski

OXFORD
UNIVERSITY PRESS

OXFORD

UNIVERSITY PRESS

Great Clarendon Street, Oxford ox2 6DP

Oxford University Press is a department of the University of Oxford.
It furthers the University's objective of excellence in research, scholarship,
and education by publishing worldwide in

Oxford New York

Auckland Cape Town Dar es Salaam Hong Kong Karachi
Kuala Lumpur Madrid Melbourne Mexico City Nairobi
New Delhi Shanghai Taipei Toronto

With offices in

Argentina Austria Brazil Chile Czech Republic France Greece
Guatemala Hungary Italy Japan Poland Portugal Singapore
South Korea Switzerland Thailand Turkey Ukraine Vietnam

Oxford is a registered trade mark of Oxford University Press
in the UK and in certain other countries

Published in the United States
by Oxford University Press Inc., New York

British Library Cataloguing in Publication Data

Data available

Library of Congress Cataloging in Publication Data

Data available

Typeset by Cepha Imaging Private Ltd, Bangalore, India
Printed in Great Britain
on acid-free paper by
Biddles Ltd., King's Lynn

ISBN 978–0–19–920720–6

1 3 5 7 9 10 8 6 4 2

PREFACE

This book is one of those very few in a lifetime with which one is secretly pregnant for many years, a book which grows slowly and continuously with experience and knowledge, and in which every relevant detail observed throughout the years is absorbed and quietly inserted into the emerging picture, until the last remaining pieces have completed the picture and the magic moment arrives when the result vigorously forces the author to release it from her mind, into the outside world. Thus this book (and consequently also this preface) is more 'autobiographical' or personal than all the others written by the undersigned, since it has travelled with her for most of her professional life.

Carrying a seed for a book within oneself and letting it grow for more than ten years seems to be a luxury these days, when current mainstream tendencies (whether in economies, research, or other areas) point towards short-term thinking and action, as well as fast production (sometimes followed by an equally fast descent into oblivion), possibly to 'occupy' a certain topic or to fulfil an apparent need for 'selling' research. Yet, such luxury is essential to fundamental research. I am more than grateful that my work at the Max Planck Institute has allowed me to pursue such a long-term approach.

This book is truly international—not only in its content, but also in the underlying experiences, the 'delivery phase' and even the choice of its 'birthplace'—a choice made upon the recommendation of two British gentlemen who were by chance sitting next to me at a seminar lunch in Manila, and recommended OUP in particular for its intellectual property law editor-in-chief Chris Rycroft, who by chance had worked with a different publisher as an excellent language editor on one of my earlier books in English (a fact which of course did not, rightly, make OUP's anonymous book proposal procedure obsolete). This was certainly one of the best possible recommendations; working with professionals of that high level of quality is more than satisfactory and seems to be exceptional rather than—as desirable—the standard generally practised. The 'delivery phase' of the book has been quite international too—I worked on it not only in Munich, but during spare moments in many places in the world where my tasks took me, such as at places in the USA or France where I was teaching, or during long phone calls with my language editor, between California and Geneva before and after WIPO meetings, or wherever we were when time pressure dictated that the calls should happen; proofs were corrected on a flight to Buenos Aires, in airport lounges, and in some free minutes at a conference hotel in Uruguay; and last but not least, this preface was developed on a mission to UNMIK (Kosovo) between nightly power cuts, and amidst KFOR soldiers—a place where I had the unique experience of advising a Ministry of what could be called (in an analogy to the international negotiation term 'non-paper') a 'non-country'.

My international experiences likewise have had a strong influence on this book. Teaching at least five master classes per year for many years, specifically on international and European copyright law in different countries, such as France, the USA, or Australia, with students from countries of different legal systems, cultures, and different development levels, necessitated careful attention to the specific needs of varied audiences. The same attention to specific needs is reflected in this book, which equally aims at reaching a diverse readership. Accordingly, the way in which certain concepts are presented may seem superfluous or self-evident to certain groups of readers while being essential to other groups of readers. Implicitly, this method of presentation may at the same time sensitize readers to those aspects which are vulnerable to potential misunderstandings in cross-cultural communication on copyright and related rights, and may thereby especially serve those who move from a background of national work to the international context.

Teaching students with different backgrounds (which might be in science, rather than law) also requires the use of clear and simple expressions, which are (as under comparative law) most useful when detached from any specific legal system—a requirement which presupposes a deep understanding and perception of the underlying issues, and their presentation in the manner of an X-ray picture. Yet, such simple means of expression as I have intended to use in this book may well obscure the inherent complexity. To repeat what a German judge once stated: it is easier to express simple thoughts in complicated words than complicated concepts in clear and simple words; or, to quote Arthur Schopenhauer: 'Und doch ist nichts leichter, als so zu schreiben, daß kein Mensch es versteht; wie hingegen nichts schwerer, als bedeutende Gedanken so auszudrücken, daß Jeder sie verstehn muß'.

Another important international experience reflected in this book is my diverse involvement in law-making, both nationally through legislative and infrastructural advice to governments of former socialist countries and developing countries in Asia and Africa, and internationally in treaty-making and preparation—an experience which has changed my perception of international copyright law, and which has given me a sense of responsibility and a desire to pass this experience on to a broader audience. Therefore, this book is deliberately not limited to research-based results alone, but enriches these results by discussion of policy; it explains the (often non-legal) background of provisions through the general policies underlying such provisions, or the treaty itself and, as the case may be, as reflected in similar treaties, in order to enhance the understanding of not only the individual provisions but also the overall context of other treaties. The author would be glad if this book thereby conveyed to the reader some sparks of the fascination which may strike those who, with a strong sense of observation and analysis, closely follow international dynamics.

Since the policy aspect seemed sufficiently important to appear in the title of the book, another aspect had to be kept out of the title while still being a fundamental subject of the book, namely related rights or neighbouring rights (used synonymously). One may justify this decision not only by a wish to keep the title suitably brief, but also by the fact that the term 'copyright' is frequently used with a broad meaning, so as to include 'related rights' or 'neighbouring rights'; in the copyright system, this term in any case covers most of what is classified as related or neighbouring rights in the author's rights system.

In this context, some notes on language are important. This book was written in English because this is the predominant international language today. Yet it has gained from and refers to many publications in other languages, as the book is also intended to be read by non-native English readers, and as the use of English is a chance to make important thoughts from non-English literature accessible to a broader readership. The choice of English inevitably also brings about the general use of the term 'copyright', while terms corresponding to 'author's rights' would have been used generally had the book been written in another language. It may be worthwhile studying whether the prevalence of the English language has had an impact on the perception of this field of law, or given rise to a possibly enhanced influence of 'copyright thinking'. With regard to a different aspect of language, a non-native English author, even with the best editor, will always have a competitive disadvantage when compared with a native speaker, never feeling as much in control of all the nuances as she would in her native language.

The structure of the book largely, though not slavishly, follows the historical developments through to the current situation, while taking into account further structural elements, such as the distinction between copyright and related rights, and the shift from 'classical', non-trade treaties to the trade arena and back to the WIPO. This approach intends to facilitate and maximize the understanding of current international copyright law, which can only be fully understood against the background of its roots and past dynamics. Having delineated the contents of the book and clarified the essential reasons for the need for international protection in this field, the pre-Berne historical developments are presented in chapter 2.

Before chapter 4 summarizes the further development of the Berne and other classical pre-TRIPS Conventions, not only for copyright but also for related rights, those readers who are not as familiar with the author's rights system (including the concept of related rights) should benefit from the insertion of a chapter on the copyright and author's rights systems—a chapter which is in any case indispensable in gaining a proper understanding of the existing international treaties and continuous international initiatives.

While the overview in chapter 4 must suffice for those classical pre-TRIPS Conventions, which are less important today, separate chapters are devoted to the Berne and Rome Conventions which have remained cornerstones of international copyright and related rights protection, if not by themselves alone then through their incorporation into subsequent treaties. Chapter 7 then highlights some examples of challenges to the interpretation of these Conventions, such as computer programs. These examples give justification for recalling the general rules of interpretation under international law and for showing, in chapter 8, the consequences of divergences in interpretation by Member countries and violations of the Conventions, taking into account all relevant aspects of public international law, including the internal applicability of treaties and dispute settlement under the Conventions. These two chapters show the deficiencies of the Berne and Rome Conventions and thereby build up smoothly to chapter 9 on the reasons for the shift to the trade arena in the late 1980s and, more generally, to Part II on the trade arena.

The TRIPS Agreement is then, to enable a more comprehensive understanding, presented against the background of general trade law of the GATT and WTO rather than in an isolated manner. Following on naturally from chapter 10, NAFTA is presented as the first TRIPS-plus treaty, followed by relevant provisions in other regional trade agreements worldwide (chapter 11), and in the closely connected bilateral trade and investment treaties, which are often based on the same pattern; also less well-known treaties, including those between countries other than the USA, are described here. Additionally, unilateral trade measures regarding copyright are analysed (chapter 13). An overall assessment of the trade approach in chapter 14 concludes Part II.

The most appropriate way to introduce Part III on post-TRIPS developments in WIPO is to briefly present the WIPO as a UN organization (chapter 15). Chapter 16 on the unrealised WIPO Dispute Settlement Treaty has been included to show the international dynamics and strategies at the time when the success of the TRIPS negotiations became a realistic prospect, and the interplay between the different 'competitors' involved. Chapter 17 on the WCT and WPPT not only illustrates the actual making of the treaties, but explains in detail the contents of these treaties which have become the milestones of modern international copyright law with answers (though in part criticized by some) to the challenges of digital technology including the internet, and which are integrated in most of the recent trade agreements.

Chapters 18 to 22 cover other recent initiatives within WIPO, including those which have been stalled for the time being (such as the planned treaties on the protection of audiovisual performances and broadcasting organisations as well as on database protection) or those ongoing (such as on folklore and the development agenda).

Part IV supplements the previous presentation of the most important treaties in copyright and related rights in historical order with comparative tables, in order to illustrate the contents of these treaties in a horizontal way and thereby also to make visible the continuous changes from one to another treaty. Chapter 24 deals with the obviously resulting question of how the different treaties in the same field relate to one other. The book concludes with an overall presentation of the 'grandes lignes' of international copyright law development from its inception, and with an outlook which, at the end, places the copyright developments into the broader current context of general political, economic and societal developments.

For the book to be as comprehensive as possible while remaining within a reasonably-sized volume, the author had to resist the temptation to include other interesting details; instead, she decided to point out problematic issues and indicate references for further study. Also, many cross-references to EC developments analysed in the forthcoming twin volume of this book, on European copyright law, are made to show the interplay between EC law and influence as well as international law and developments. Indeed, this book is meant to be more than a reference book alone; rather, one of its strengths is meant to be its 'plot'—a story to be read from the beginning, in which a puzzle of many pieces will continuously assemble and finally result in a captivating picture, and which in the best possible case will leave the reader thrilled.

Many thanks go to Dagmar Liesegang who tirelessly transcribed the text and took care of the formal requirements—things I tend to overlook; and to John Glover, who had taken my class on international copyright law at Franklin Pierce Law Center, and was ready to apply his wisdom from his student editing to this book with lots of enthusiasm and inexhaustible patience; when we discussed the nuances of his suggestions to modify style or expression—ultimately on the night before delivery, when he kept me awake on the phone from 4 a.m. to 7 a.m.—a moment when it turned out to be ideal to have an editor in California. Finally, this book could hardly have been written without my time at the Max Planck Institute, which allowed me to focus my research on this quite specific yet rich area of international copyright law—an opportunity which does not exist for most university professors—and to gain all the experiences outside the Institute which I could then condense in this book. Aside from its support, its outstanding library deserves to be mentioned, even in the age of the internet; indeed, although the internet is very valuable in many respects, no one should believe it alone is sufficient for sound research, and everyone should be aware that an essential part of knowledge is still to be found exclusively in books—including books in languages other than English, as reflected in the literature quoted in this book.

To end on a personal note, the Institute's creative ambiance has been inspiring, be it when in innumerable long nights in the office, in sole company with the spirits, my heartbeat, and the book, suddenly Latin-American piano sounds played by our Chilean fellow might enter from the lobby hall into the deep silence, say at 3:30 in the morning, enchanting the ascetic atmosphere and consolingly reminding me of another world; or be it when—in the tense period shortly before the due delivery date—Mendelssohn and Bruckner, performed open-air by Kent Nagano and the Orchestra of the Bavarian State Opera right outside my office, powerfully broke into my frantically book-focused life and inevitably conquered my discipline for two wonderful hours, nourishing me with what is so enriching in life: music.

Silke von Lewinski
Munich
20 December 2007

CONTENTS—SUMMARY

CONTENTS

3. Comparison of the Copyright System and the Author's Rights *(Droit d'auteur)* System

4. Overview of the Main 'Classical' Copyright and Neighbouring Rights Conventions before the TRIPS Agreement

7. **New Phenomena as a Challenge to the Interpretation of the Berne and Rome Conventions**

PART II THE INCLUSION OF COPYRIGHT AND NEIGHBOURING RIGHTS IN TRADE TREATIES AND TRADE MEASURES

PART III DEVELOPMENTS IN THE WORLD INTELLECTUAL PROPERTY ORGANIZATION (WIPO) AFTER THE ADOPTION OF THE TRIPS AGREEMENT

15. Presentation of the WIPO

16. Dispute Settlement Draft Treaty

TABLE OF CASES

A. ALPHABETICAL LIST BY CASE NAME

B. ALPHABETICAL LIST BY COUNTRY/EC

TABLES OF LEGISLATION, TREATIES, AND CONVENTIONS

E. MULTILATERAL TREATIES
INCLUDING FREE TRADE
AGREEMENTS

LIST OF ABBREVIATIONS

ACP	African, Caribbean, and Pacific
ACTA	Anti-Counterfeiting Trade Agreement
ADR	Alternative Dispute Resolution
AFTA	ASEAN Free Trade Area
ALAI	International Literary and Artistic Association
APEC	Asia-Pacific Economic Cooperation Forum
ARIPO	African Regional Intellectual Property Organization
ASEAN	Association of South East Asian Nations
AU	African Union
BC	Berne Convention
BGH	Bundesgerichtshof (Supreme Court of Germany)
BIT	Bilateral Investment Treaty
BIRPI	Bureaux Internationaux Réunis pour la Protection de la Propriété Intellectuelle
CAFTA-DR	Central American Free Trade Agreement—Dominican Republic
CAN	Comunidad Andina
CARICOM	Caribbean Community
CDPA	Copyright, Designs and Patents Act (United Kingdom)
CEFTA	Central European Free Trade Agreement
CER	Closer Economic Relations (FTA between Australia and New Zealand)
CISAC	International Confederation of Societies of Authors and Composers
CMLRev	Common Market Law Review
CMO	collective management organization
COMECON	Council for Mutual Economic Assistance
DMCA	Digital Millennium Copyright Act (USA)
DSB	Dispute Settlement Body
DSU	Dispute Settlement Understanding
EAEC	European Atomic Energy Community
EBU	European Broadcasting Union
EC	European Community
EEA	European Economic Area
EEC	European Economic Community

EFTA	European Free Trade Agreement
EIPR	European Intellectual Property Review
ENP	European Neighbourhood Policy
EPA	economic partnership agreement
EU	European Union
FAO	Food and Agriculture Organization
FIM	International Federation of Musicians
FTA	free trade agreement
FTAA	Free Trade Area of the Americas
GATS	General Agreement on Trade in Services
GATT	General Agreement on Tariffs and Trade
GCC	Gulf Cooperation Council
GRULAC	Group of Latin American and Caribbean Countries
GRUR	Gewerblicher Rechtsschutz und Urheberrecht
GRUR Int	Gewerblicher Rechtsschutz und Urheberrecht, Internationaler Teil
GSP	Generalized System of Preferences
IAB	International Association of Broadcasting
ICJ	International Court of Justice
IFAC	Industry Functional Advisory Committee
IFPI	International Federation of the Phonographic Industry
IIC	International Review of Industrial Property and Copyright Law (until 2004); International Review of Intellectual Property and Competition Law (from 2005)
IIPA	International Intellectual Property Alliance
ILM	International Legal Materials
ILO	International Labour Organization
IP	intellectual property
ISP	internet service provider
ITAC	Industry Trade Advisory Committee
ITO	International Trade Organization
ITU	International Telecommunication Union
J Copyright Soc USA	Journal of the Copyright Society of the USA
JCP	Juris Classeur Périodique
LDC	least developed country

MAI	Multilateral Agreement on Investment
MERCOSUR	Mercado Común del Sur
MFN	most favoured nation
NAFTA	North American Free Trade Agreement
NCPI	New Commercial Policy Instrument
OAPI	Organisation Africaine de la Propriété Intellectuelle
OAU	Organization of African Unity
OGH	Oberster Gerichtshof (Austrian Supreme Court)
OIR	Organisation internationale de radiodiffusion
OLG	Oberlandesgericht
phr	phrase
PLR	public lending right
pma	*post mortem auctoris*
RC	Rome Convention
RDBP	Revised Draft Basic Proposal
RGZ	Decisions of Reichsgericht (Germany) in civil law
RIDA	Revue Internationale du Droit d'Auteur
RT	Rome Treaty (synonymous with 'Rome Convention')
RTA	regional trade agreement
SAA	stabilization and association agreement
SACU	Southern African Customs Union
SAFTA	Singapore–Australia Free Trade Agreement
SCCR	Standing Committee on Copyright and Related Rights
SME	small to medium-sized enterprise
TA	trade agreement
TAFTA	Thailand–Australia Free Trade Agreement
TBR	Trade Barriers Regulation
TGI	Tribunal de Grande Instance (French first instance court)
TIFA	Trade and Investment Framework Agreement
TRIPS	Trade-Related Aspects of Intellectual Property Rights
UAE	United Arab Emirates
UCC	Universal Copyright Convention
UNCTAD	United Nations Conference on Trade and Development
UNEP	United Nations Environment Programme
UNESCO	United Nations Educational and Scientific Organization
UNMiK	United Nations Interim Administration Mission in Kosovo

UNO	United Nations Organization
UNTS	United Nations Treaty Series
USC	United Stated Code
USTR	United States Trade Representative
WCT	WIPO Copyright Treaty
WIPO	World Intellectual Property Organization
WIPR	World Intellectual Property Report
WPPT	WIPO Performances and Phonograms Treaty
WTO	World Trade Organization

PART I

THE LAW OF THE 'CLASSICAL' CONVENTIONS

1

INTRODUCTION TO INTERNATIONAL COPYRIGHT AND NEIGHBOURING RIGHTS LAW

A. The notion of 'international law'

(1) Delineation from foreign national laws

What is international law and why is it needed at all in the field of copyright and **1.01** neighbouring rights law? The answers to these questions are essential for understanding the fundamentals of international copyright and neighbouring rights law. First, the notion of 'international law' is often misconceived as referring to foreign, national laws or to comparative law. As the Latin origin of the word reveals, however, international law refers to the law governing relations *inter nationes*, ie between nation-states—it refers to the regulation of relationships between states.[1] This traditional concept has been modernized to also include

---

[1] In this book, the notion 'states' is used as it is understood in international law, which qualifies a state by a territory, a population, a government, and the capacity to engage in diplomatic or foreign relations. Therefore, individual states of a federation, such as the individual states of the USA or the *Länder* of the Federal Republic of Germany, are hereinafter not referred to by 'states'.

'the conduct of states and of international organisations and . . . their relations *inter se* as well as . . . some of their relations with persons, whether natural or juridical'.[2] In the field of copyright and neighbouring rights law, the most important rules of international law are those regarding the law of treaties, which addresses in particular treaty-making, application, revision, and interpretation (see Chapters 8 and 7) and the relationship between different treaties that cover the same or similar subject matter (see Chapter 24). Notably, the relevant interpretation rules show important distinctions from rules that typically govern the interpretation of national laws—a fact often overlooked by those whose main task is national copyright law interpretation in light of treaty language. Most of these rules are part of customary international law as codified in the Vienna Convention on the Law of Treaties (Vienna Convention).[3]

1.02 Since this book focuses on international law, it does not provide a detailed presentation of individual national laws, or of comparative law. Nevertheless, international law has mostly developed on the basis of national laws, and therefore should be understood against the background of leading national law systems and particular national laws that had an influence on the drafting of specific treaty provisions.[4] Thus, national laws are discussed in the context of comparing the copyright and *droit d'auteur* systems (Chapter 3) and at places where necessary or helpful as a background for understanding particular treaty provisions.

(2) Delineation from international private law

1.03 Secondly, international law, often called 'public international law', has to be distinguished from 'private international law', which is also called 'international private law', 'applicable law', 'conflict of laws', or 'choice of law'. Despite the word 'international', it is national law which regulates the application of a particular foreign or domestic law as the *lex causae* in private law cases involving elements from foreign jurisdictions. This nature of international private law does not exclude the possibility of adopting treaties or treaty provisions in order to harmonize domestic rules on international private law. So far, however, international private law has not been regulated at the international level specifically for copyright and neighbouring rights.[5] Further exploration of this topic would require

---

[2] American Law Institute, Restatement of the Foreign Relations Law of the United States (Third) s 101 (1987).

[3] UN Doc A/CONF 39/27(1969); 8 ILM 679 (1969).

[4] International law is not, however, to be interpreted on the basis of national laws, but autonomously, as implied in Art 31(1) of the Vienna Convention; on rules of interpretation in general, see paras 7.02 ff, 7.07 ff below.

[5] The Hague Conference on Private International Law has adopted many conventions in the area of international private law, but none specifically regarding copyright or neighbouring rights. Some scholars, though, understand the principle of territoriality, as codified in the *lex loci protectionis* rule of

analysis of specific national laws, an approach that diverges from the international focus of this book. Moreover, international private law rules may be highly complicated and their interpretation controversial even under one national law, specifically in the fields of copyright and neighbouring rights law, such that serious analysis would require more extensive discussion than possible in the limited scope of this book. This is illustrated, for example, by the detailed studies mandated by the World Intellectual Property Organization (WIPO) on international private law questions related to the transfer of rights by performers to audiovisual producers.[6] Therefore, and although international private law is an important field, it is largely excluded from this book.

(3) Delineation from transnational law

Finally, international law as discussed throughout this book is distinguished from **1.04** the concept of 'transnational law', which Jessup first proposed to embrace 'all law which regulates actions or events that transcend national frontiers'.[7] Accordingly, this term covers not only public international law, but also private international law; international procedural, criminal, or administrative law; and other norms concerning international economic relations. Transnational law, as far as it is considered a legitimate concept, is thus too broad a concept for meaningful discussion in this book.

B. The need for international protection in the fields of copyright and neighbouring rights

Why do we need international protection in the field of copyright and neigh- **1.05** bouring rights laws? An answer is not self-evident, particularly given that there was a time with exclusively national as opposed to international protection, and that even after the first treaties were adopted, many countries did not adhere to

---

national treatment under the Berne Convention and subsequent treaties, also as a rule of international private law (see n 11 below). The Hague Agreement on Choice of Court Agreements of 30 June 2005 only concerns international jurisdiction. For a general presentation of the issues at stake and solutions based on different national laws, see the voluminous work of J Fawcett and P Torremans, *Intellectual Property and Private International Law* (1998), which deals with jurisdiction, choice of law, and recognition and enforcement of foreign judgments.

6 See the main study by J Ginsburg and A Lucas, WIPO Doc AVP/IM/03/04 Add of 12 May 2004 following a 2003 version with the same document number; and paras 18.23–18.24 below. See also related studies on Mexico by JR Obón Léon, WIPO Doc AVP/IM/03/4A Rev; on the United Kingdom by H MacQueen and C Waelde, WIPO Doc AVP/IM/03/4B; on Egypt by H Bodrawi, WIPO Doc AVP/IM/03/4C; on Germany by S von Lewinski and D Thum, WIPO Doc AVP/IM/03/4D Rev; on India by P Anand, WIPO Doc AVP/IM/03/4E; and on Japan by M Dogouchi and T Ueno, WIPO Doc AVP/IM/03/4F.

7 P Jessup, *Transnational Law* (1956) 2.

them for quite some time. A combination of factors explains the need for international law in this field: the prevailing principle of territoriality; the regular discrimination of foreigners (permitted in the absence of international obligations); and, even where foreigners were not entirely excluded from protection, the difficulties in fulfilling the conditions for equal treatment particularly in context with material reciprocity and diverse standards of protection among the different countries, especially at the beginning of copyright history.

(1) Territoriality

1.06 Under the principle of territoriality, the effects of national copyright and neighbouring rights legislation are limited to the territory of the legislating state; national copyright and neighbouring rights laws do not have extraterritorial effect.[8] As a consequence, an author or neighbouring rights holder does not enjoy a uniform, worldwide copyright or neighbouring right; rather, he or she owns a bundle of national, independent rights, for which the conditions for protection, contents, and effects are governed by each of the relevant legislations within their territories—and this only if he or she is eligible for protection in the other countries at all. Due to the territorially limited effect of copyright and neighbouring rights, the principle of territoriality has also been understood as a rule of private international law, which refers to the law of the country for which protection is sought (*lex loci protectionis*).[9]

1.07 The principle of territoriality is not explicitly laid down in any legal text.[10] Historical development, however, has resulted in its acceptance in legal practice and theory. Also, the principle is reflected in the leading international conventions on copyright and neighbouring rights.[11] Historically, the principle of territoriality has its roots in the predecessor of modern copyright—the medieval system of privileges that were granted by sovereigns such as kings, princes, and churches to individual publishers or, later, also to authors. Such privileges were necessarily limited to the territory governed by the relevant sovereign. When the system of privileges was replaced by modern copyright as a part of private law, the territorial nature of copyright endured.[12] The principle of territoriality is further

---

[8] eg G Boytha, 'Some Private International Law Aspects of the Protection of Authors' Rights' [1988] Copyright 399, 400; E Ulmer, *Intellectual Property Rights and the Conflict of Laws* (1978) 9; P Goldstein, *International Copyright* (2001) § 3.1.2.

[9] P Katzenberger, 'vor §§ 120 ff' in G Schricker (ed), *Urheberrecht* (3rd edn, 2006) no 124, with further references.

[10] G Koumantos, 'Private International Law and the Berne Convention' [1988] Copyright 415, 417.

[11] Boytha (n 8 above) 399; Katzenberger (n 9 above) no 120; E Ulmer, *Urheber- und Verlagsrecht* (3rd edn, 1980) § 13 II. 4.

[12] MM Boguslawski, *Urheberrecht in den internationalen Beziehungen* (1977) 23; Boytha (n 8 above) 401.

justified by state sovereignty: any state has an interest in regulating copyright and neighbouring rights protection for all works and other subject matter in its territory.[13] Not least, the principle of territoriality is justified by the interests of users. For example, users who want to exploit works on the domestic market in a given state only need to know and follow the domestic rules, irrespective of whether the relevant work is domestic or foreign.[14]

The principle of territoriality is often delineated from the principle of universality. Yet, a delineation between the principle of the country of protection (*lex loci protectionis*) and the principle of the country of origin would be more accurate. The first principle is followed in current international copyright and neighbouring rights law. The only international copyright treaty that contains the principle of country of origin is the Convention of Montevideo on Literary and Artistic Property of 11 January 1889.[15] According to its Article 2, an author of a work and her successors shall enjoy, in the signatory states, the rights accorded to her by the law of the state in which the first publication or production of the work took place. In other words, national copyright rules of the country of origin of the work in principle 'follow' the work in other signatory states where it is exploited. For example, a work that originates in Argentina would in principle be protected in all other signatory states under Argentinian law. **1.08**

This Latin American treaty had the potential to become universally accepted, as it was open to third countries if accepted by its members.[16] Indeed, several European states have acceded to it.[17] Yet, this treaty was not successful in 'competing' against the Berne Convention and the Universal Copyright Convention, both of which integrated the principle of *lex loci protectionis*. The latter two treaties prevail over the Convention of Montevideo,[18] which no longer finds application today, given the wide membership of the Berne and Universal Copyright Conventions.[19] **1.09**

---

[13] Goldstein (n 8 above) § 3.1; Katzenberger (n 9 above) no 123.

[14] ibid.

[15] See the text in S Ladas, *The International Protection of Literary and Artistic Property* (1938) Vol II, 1175; W Nordemann, K Vinck, P Hertin, and G Meyer, *International Copyright* (1990) 604; (1889) Droit d'auteur, 52.

[16] Art 6 of the Additional Protocol of 1889.

[17] Between 1896 and 1931: France, Spain, Italy, Belgium, Austria, Germany, and Hungary, Ladas (n 15 above) 636.

[18] Art XIX of the Universal Copyright Convention, Art 20 of the Berne Convention. On the relation between treaties, see ch 24 below; on the Convention of Montevideo, see paras 4.29–4.31 below.

[19] It still has to be taken into account in the context of transitional provisions and effectiveness of well-acquired rights, see Katzenberger (n 9 above) no 67.

1.10   Those who (especially in the context of the internet) advocate applying the principle of country of origin in connection with the extraterritorial operation of the law of the country of origin of the work[20] should consider why this principle has not enjoyed more success. Although the country of origin principle may look promising for authors at first sight, since the copyright in their works would be governed by domestic law in all contracting states of a treaty, the enforcement of their rights in foreign countries would meet considerable obstacles. Users, attorneys, judges, and enforcement authorities would need to get acquainted with the multiplicity of foreign laws governing the protection of foreign works exploited in any given domestic market. Even the obligation of the contracting states to submit the texts of their laws to other governments would not be sufficiently helpful, given that a proper and comprehensive understanding of foreign laws cannot be expected solely on the basis of legislative texts.[21]

(2) Discrimination

1.11   Another reason international copyright and neighbouring rights law is needed is the fact that public international law in general (as opposed to specific treaties) does not oblige states to recognize or provide protection for foreign works and subject matter of neighbouring rights,[22] and that most states, since copyright protection has existed, have shown a strong tendency to discriminate against foreign works and subject matter of neighbouring rights.[23] In principle, by the mid-nineteenth century such discrimination was not self-evident since national treatment of foreigners regarding their legal status in general, including their capacity to enjoy property rights, was recognized as a necessary corollary to the principle of territoriality. Yet, when the system of privileges was replaced by private rights, national treatment was not extended to authors' rights mainly because of opposition by countries whose printing industries relied on reprinting and translating foreign works. The only exception was France,[24] followed by Belgium, both of which unilaterally applied national treatment to foreign authors. Yet, since these countries remained the only ones giving protection without

---

[20] Koumantos (n 10 above) 423 ff; further references in Katzenberger (n 9 above) no 122.

[21] Boytha (n 8 above) 406 in the context of the Montevideo Convention and its inefficiency.

[22] Boguslawski (n 12 above) 26.

[23] eg before 1886, nationality alone made authors eligible for protection in Greece, Portugal, Spain, Sweden, Finland, and the USA, see S Ricketson and J Ginsburg, *International Copyright and Neighbouring Rights: The Berne Convention and Beyond* (2006) 1.26.

[24] For the context with the principle of fraternity under the French Revolution, see Boytha (n 8 above) 401; see, however, B Lindner, 'Rechtsvergleichender Überblick über die vertraglichen Beziehungen zwischen Felix Mendelssohn Bartholdy und seinen europäischen Verlegern' (1998) 136 UFITA 233, 250 f, referring to inconsistent case law that sometimes required first publication or deposit of the work in France, so that first publication in France was actually necessary to acquire protection with certainty.

receiving reciprocal protection, they discontinued the practice in 1921 and 1964, respectively.[25]

(3) Conditions for equal treatment and diversity of standards

Even in countries where works of foreign authors were not fully excluded from **1.12** protection, the conditions to obtain equal treatment were often difficult to fulfil. For example, under the German laws of 1870 and 1876, foreign works were protected in Germany if they were published by a German publisher.[26] In other countries, it was somewhat easier to obtain protection for foreign works, since they only needed to be published within the territory of the relevant state, irrespective of the publisher's (or author's) nationality.[27] In certain countries, protection was granted to authors domiciled in those countries, irrespective of the country of first publication.[28] In some countries, foreign works were protected under the national law, on condition of either formal or material reciprocity.[29]

Formal reciprocity is tantamount to national treatment. It means that foreign **1.13** works (or works by foreign citizens) are assimilated to domestic works (or works by domestic authors) on condition that the converse is also true, namely that domestic works or authors enjoy a local's status in the foreign country. For example, under Article 578 of the Civil Code of 1 July 1867 of Portugal, foreign writers were assimilated to Portuguese authors if the relevant foreign country assimilated Portuguese authors to nationals. Yet, formal reciprocity was often subject to various conditions. For example, under Article 1270 of the Mexican Civil Code of 1884, the authors who were residents of other nations were assimilated to Mexicans if the latter were assimilated to the former at the place where the work was published.[30]

Material reciprocity is the assimilation of foreign authors or works on condition **1.14** that the domestic authors or works are protected in the foreign country either in exactly the same way as under the domestic law (ie, complete reciprocity), or receive substantially equivalent protection. Material reciprocity was chosen by most of those states that provided for a relatively high level of protection. An example of complete reciprocity is Article 50 of the Spanish law on intellectual property of 10 January 1879, under which foreign authors enjoyed protection

---

[25] Boytha (n 8 above), 401; on the widespread practice of exploiting foreign works (legally) without securing protection to them, see Ricketson/Ginsburg (n 23 above) 1.20–1.21.

[26] ibid 1.26 with further examples.

[27] ibid.

[28] Art 10(1) Swiss Law on Literary and Artistic Property of 23 April 1883 (repr (1888) Droit d'auteur, 14 ff).

[29] Ricketson/Ginsburg (n 23 above) 1.27 with further examples.

[30] These and further examples are listed in Anon, 'Les Dispositions légales concernant la réciprocité dans les divers pays' (1907) Droit d'auteur 42, 43.

under the Spanish law in Spain if their legislation provided Spanish authors with the same protection as established under the substantive law provisions of the Spanish law of 1879.[31] An example of substantial equivalence is Article 44(2) of the Italian Copyright Act of 19 October 1882, under which the protection in the foreign country was not to be 'essentially different' from that recognized under the Italian law.[32] To detail, legislative provisions on the conditions for reciprocity were quite diverse. For example, in Bolivia,[33] foreign authors enjoyed the same protection as that granted to Bolivian authors resident in the foreign country. In Colombia, protection was granted under the condition of material reciprocity only to authors from Spanish-speaking countries. Finnish law explicitly stated that foreigners not residing or publishing their works in Finland could be protected in Finland under the condition of reciprocity only if agreed in a treaty.[34]

1.15 Since it was not always easy to establish whether or not the conditions of reciprocity were fulfilled, particularly with material reciprocity, some countries chose the so-called 'diplomatic reciprocity' by stating in a formal declaration by the relevant authority, such as in a royal decree, whether the conditions of reciprocity were fulfilled in relation to a particular country.[35] Other countries chose the so-called 'legal reciprocity' which applied *ipso jure*—courts were to determine whether or not the conditions of reciprocity were fulfilled.[36]

1.16 Especially in cases of material reciprocity, authors had to invest considerable time and effort in order to find out how, if at all, they were protected in different foreign countries. They had to take into account the various conditions for material reciprocity and, if these were fulfilled, the substantive laws of the relevant countries. To do so was particularly cumbersome in the nineteenth century because the contents of national laws were much more diverse than today, when the worldwide adoption of the prevailing international treaties has resulted in similar levels of protection in most countries of the world. For example, in the first half of the nineteenth century, when protection in some states was still granted in the form of privileges, only literary or certain other kinds of works were protected. It was only around the time when the Berne Convention was adopted that most kinds of works were protected in most countries, except for

---

[31] Other examples are the Costa Rican law of 1896 and the Greek Criminal Code of 1833, ibid.
[32] Other examples were Austria, Denmark, Britain, Iceland, Norway, and Sweden, ibid 44.
[33] Art 9 of the Bolivian Decree on Literary and Artistic Works of 13 August 1879, ibid.
[34] Art 25(1) of the law on literary and artistic property of 26 October 1886 of Colombia and Art 32(2) of the law on the right of the author and artist in the product of his work of 15 March 1880 of Finland, ibid 45.
[35] In 1907, these countries were Austria, Denmark, United States, Finland, Great Britain, Iceland, Italy, Norway, and Sweden, ibid 42.
[36] In 1907, the relevant countries were Bolivia, Colombia, Costa Rica, Spain, Greece, Italy, Mexico, Monaco, Nicaragua, Portugal, Romania, and Switzerland, ibid.

differences regarding architectural, photographic, choreographic, and oral works.[37] Substantial differences also existed for the rights granted, the limitations of protection, the duration thereof, formalities, and enforcement measures.[38] In addition to the diversity of protection standards under national laws, lack of clarity within many laws[39] constituted a further obstacle for the smooth enforcement of copyright at that time.

The following example illustrates the efforts necessary to secure protection in **1.17** several countries in the mid-nineteenth century. The composer Felix Mendelssohn Bartholdy wanted to secure protection of his music for the play *A Midsummer Night's Dream* in Germany, France, and England. He could do so only by first publication in these countries, which meant publication on the same day. In principle, one way of achieving this goal was to choose one single publisher who would exercise the rights for the different countries and organize the simultaneous publication in these countries. Since Mendelssohn could however gain more income from the grant of national publishing rights to different publishers, he preferred to choose one publisher per country and to ask them to coordinate the publication on the same day in the three countries. Mostly though, the composer would undertake coordination himself rather than relying on such independent coordination. With the transportation and communication facilities of the mid-nineteenth century, publishing in three countries on the same day required great effort at great risk. For the *Midsummer Night's Dream*, Mendelssohn had to warn his publishers in France and Germany at short notice to postpone the publication because arrival of the manuscript designated for England was delayed due to the ship getting stuck in the frozen Channel.[40] To some extent, such problems were avoided through a general practice of replacing the actual publication in a country with an announcement of its publication in a musical journal as long as the announcement was made on the same day as the simultaneous publication in the other countries—a practice that was, however, not based on the law.[41]

---

[37] Ricketson/Ginsburg (n 23 above) 1.09.

[38] A highly comprehensive analysis of these aspects of national laws during the second half of the nineteenth century can be found in A Darras, *Du Droit des auteurs et des artistes dans les rapports internationaux* (1887) nos 303–427; the relevant national provisions including decrees, regulations, mandates, and other forms of legal norms dealing with the protection of literary and artistic works in the middle of the nineteenth century in the German states, France, and England are reprinted in CF Eisenlohr, *Sammlung der Gesetze und internationalen Verträge zum Schutze des literarisch-artistischen Eigenthums in Deutschland, Frankreich und England* (1856) 1–155; a synopsis of different national provisions in the second part of the nineteenth century is contained in Ricketson/Ginsburg (n 23 above) 1.07–1.19 and J Cavalli, *La Genèse de la Convention de Berne pour la protection des œuvres littéraires et artistiques du 9 September 1886* (1986) 28–68 (analyses of national laws of the Signatory States of the Berne Convention of 9 September 1886).

[39] Darras (n 38 above) eg nos 256, 257.

[40] Lindner (n 24 above) 251–4, quoting from the letters of Mendelssohn Bartholdy.

[41] ibid 254–5.

1.18 Mendelssohn's efforts to achieve protection for works in foreign countries and to overcome related obstacles demonstrated the need for a consistent, more stable, and more easily obtainable protection of works abroad. Authors began to call for such protection, especially against the background of the growing distribution of works beyond national borders in the nineteenth century. These calls finally resulted in the adoption of international treaties that addressed the international protection of literary and artistic works.

1.19 Although this analysis on the need for international copyright and neighbouring rights protection has been carried out mainly against the historical background, in principle it also holds true today. Indeed, a country that is not a member of any international treaty in the field (or to the extent the relevant treaties do not apply) will mostly not grant protection to foreigners or, if at all, only upon the fulfilment of certain conditions and, often, to a limited extent. It is also likely that standards of protection would be much more diverse today if countries had not accepted being bound by international treaties.

2

HISTORICAL DEVELOPMENT OF INTERNATIONAL COPYRIGHT LAW

A. Early individual claims for international protection

Long before the first treaties addressed the international protection of authors' **2.01** rights in their works, legal experts and other individuals had advocated the introduction of such protection. One of the earliest examples was the proposal for an international treaty on the protection of authors' rights by the law professor Johann Rudolf Thurneysen of the University of Basel who published his book *De recursione librorum fortiva* in 1738.[1] This was only twenty-eight years after the adoption of the first copyright act ever enacted, the English Statute of Anne of 1709.[2] Soon after, the Dutch lawyer and librarian Elie Luzac presented a legislative proposal against piracy to the Peace Conference of Aix-la-Chapelle of 1745 for approval by all present states and inclusion into the

---

[1] Anon, 'Publication nouvelle: Die geschichtliche Entwicklung der Urheberrechtsgesetzgebung auf dem Gebiete der Schweizerischen Eidgenossenschaft' (1943) Droit d'auteur 132; J Cavalli, *La Genèse de la Convention de Berne pour la protection des œuvres littéraires et artistiques du 9 Septembre 1886* (1986) 69.

[2] 8 Anne c19, 1710.

peace treaty as an agreement.[3] This proposal was apparently ahead of its time. Diplomats considered it 'one of these nice dreams based on the unachieved ideal of general fraternity of the Abbot of St.-Pierre', as reported by the German lawyer Johannes Stephan Pütter in his book on piracy of books.[4] Nevertheless, Pütter considered Luzac's proposal as important and advocated for equal protection of foreigners and nationals.[5]

2.02   In the nineteenth century, the desire to have copyright protection recognized beyond national borders was expressed more frequently. For example, Jobard wrote in 1837: 'What a magnificent era of progress will open up before us, when an international law will regulate the property of thoughts, when the work of genius will receive its worldwide passport and will be submitted to the protection of countries, whether friends or allied, as stated in the passports.'[6] Two years later, Viscount Siméon urged the French Chamber of Peers not to deviate in national law too much from laws of other countries, 'on the assumption of an international law of which the possibility smiles to the friends of literature'.[7] Also Lamartine spoke in front of the Chamber of Deputies in Paris in 1841 on piracy: 'Everybody complains, everybody asks for an international law which must be established for all.'[8]

B. Bilateral treaties

(1) Development of bilateral treaties

2.03   The need for protection beyond national borders became particularly relevant in states where the same language was spoken, such as in German states in the early nineteenth century. For example, the German writer Johann Wolfgang von Goethe needed to approach thirty-nine sovereigns in order to obtain the

---

[3] F Ruffini, *De la protection internationale des droits sur les œuvres littéraires et artistiques* (1927) 62; Cavalli (n 1 above) 70; E Röthlisberger, *Die Berner Übereinkunft zum Schutze von Werken der Literatur und Kunst und die Zusatzabkommen* (1906) 2, instead refers to the conference of Aachen in 1748.

[4] JS Pütter, *Der Büchernachdruck nach ächten Grundsätzen des Rechts geprüft* (1774) 117, as also quoted in Ruffini (n 3 above) 62, Cavalli (n 1 above) 70 and Röthlisberger (n 3 above) 2 (translation by the author).

[5] Ruffini (n 3 above) 62–3, Cavalli (n 1 above) 70.

[6] M Jobard, *De la propriété de la pensée et de la contrefaçon, considérée comme droit d'aubaine et de détraction* (1837) 10, as quoted in Cavalli (n 1 above) 89 (translation by the author).

[7] Quoted in Ruffini (n 3 above) 63, Cavalli (n 1 above) 89, and Röthlisberger (n 3 above) 2 (translation by the author).

[8] Quoted in Ruffini (n 3 above) 63, Cavalli (n 1 above) 89 referring to Cluné (translation by the author).

privileges for his works in all German Federal States.[9] His claim before the Federal Diet in 1825 to grant an overall privilege in the name of all German sovereigns was unsuccessful.[10] Nevertheless, most sovereigns (except those of Bavaria and Württemberg) at least did not insist that Goethe should apply separately to each of them.[11] Although the Federal Diet was charged by Federal Act of 8 June 1815 to provide for uniform measures in favour of authors and publishers against illicit reproduction of works, it remained inactive for a long time. Recognizing the need to protect domestic works in the other German states also, Prussia concluded with the other thirty-one German states, between 1827 and 1829, bilateral agreements which provided protection on the basis of formal reciprocity.[12] This Prussian strategy may have encouraged the Federal Diet to accelerate its work and finally adopt resolutions in 1832, 1837, and later by which any distinction between nationals of the different states of the Federation was abolished in respect of counterfeiting, and by which certain, common minimum standards of protection were introduced.[13]

The series of intra-German treaties was followed by the first bilateral treaty **2.04** between countries of different languages, namely between Austria and Sardinia of 22 May 1840.[14] One of its most notable features was its openness to the adherence of specific third states, an aspect that could have potentially qualified it as a multilateral treaty of limited reach. This aspect is best understood against the geopolitical background of the time. In 1840, Austria occupied Lombardy-Venetia and exercised its influence in Parma, Modena, and Tuscany. The kingdom of Sardinia extended to large areas including Piedmont and Savoy. Given the large overlap of the respective language areas, it seemed natural to open the bilateral treaty to 'the other governments of Italy and those of the Canton Ticino' to accede to this treaty by mere consent.[15] In the end, the states of Modena, Lucca, Parma, Rome, and Tuscany adhered to the treaty.[16] Thereafter, more than eighty bilateral or limited multilateral treaties were concluded between different European states,

---

[9] At the time, the basis for the protection of authors' works was still the system of privileges.

[10] The Federal Diet did not have any competences of its own. See the reprint of Goethe's claim of 11 January 1825, in M Tietzel, 'Goethes Strategien bei der wirtschaftlichen Verwertung seiner Werke', Börsenblatt no 22 of 19 March 1999, Buchhandelsgeschichte 1999/1, B15.

[11] ibid B 2, B16.

[12] S Ricketson and J Ginsburg, *International Copyright and Neighbouring Rights: The Berne Convention and Beyond* (2006) 1.29; Cavalli (n 1 above) 70; Ruffini (n 3 above) 63. A list of the 31 treaties between Prussia and other German states is reprinted in CSM Eisenlohr, *Sammlung der Gesetze und internationalen Verträge zum Schutz des literarisch-artistischen Eigenthums in Deutschland, Frankreich und England* (1856) Supplement 50–1.

[13] Cavalli (n 1 above) 29–30.

[14] As repr in Eisenlohr (n 12 above) 239–43 and in 31 British and Foreign State Papers 117.

[15] Art 27 of the Austro-Sardinian treaty ibid.

[16] Eisenlohr (n 12 above) 243; Ricketson/Ginsburg (n 12 above) 1.29.

Salvador, and Colombia.[17] The high number of bilateral treaties, declarations, or other agreements was in part due to the need of non-German states to conclude separate treaties with the thirty-two individual German states; after 1868 these separate treaties were replaced by treaties with the North German Federation and later the German Empire. Similarly, the earlier treaties with Sardinia and Tuscany were later replaced by new ones negotiated by Italy. Consequently, when the Berne Convention was adopted in 1886, only thirty-three bilateral treaties remained among fifteen countries.[18]

(2) Contents of bilateral treaties in the nineteenth century

(a) National treatment

2.05 **(i) General observations** The contents of the bilateral treaties in the nineteenth century showed many differences as well as a number of similar, basic features.[19] The general rule for reciprocal protection was national treatment, yet it was formulated in different ways and often subject to different conditions or restrictions. For example, national treatment was sometimes understood as the treatment granted to works first published in one state, to be granted to authors of works first published in the other state.[20] In other treaties, national treatment was defined as the treatment granted to nationals of a state to be granted to the nationals of the other state.[21]

2.06 Mostly, legal representatives and successors in title of the author were also protected.[22] Some treaties also protected the publishers of works published in the territory of either contracting state if the authors were nationals of other states.[23]

2.07 A common restriction of national treatment was a reference back to the level of protection in the country of origin or the home country of the author. For example, an author could not claim rights which would be more extensive than those

---

[17] cf the chronological list of treaties with their signature dates up to 1886 in Cavalli (n 1 above) 73–5; cf also Ricketson/Ginsburg (n 12 above) 1.30; a list according to countries may be found in S Ladas, *The International Protection of Literary and Artistic Property* (1938) Vol I, 49–50.

[18] Cavalli (n 1 above) 75; Ladas (n 17 above) 49.

[19] For comparative summaries of the contents of the bilateral treaties, cf Ladas (n 17 above) 50–67; Ricketson/Ginsburg (n 12 above) 1.32–1.42; Cavalli (n 1 above) 76–83.

[20] eg Art 1 of the Treaty between Hanover and France of 20 October 1851, repr in Eisenlohr (n 12 above) 156, 158.

[21] eg Art 1 of the Treaty between Hesse and France of 18 September 1852, repr in Eisenlohr (n 12 above) 166.

[22] eg Art 1(2) of the Treaty between Hanover and France of 20 October 1851 (n 20 above); Ricketson/Ginsburg (n 12 above) 1.33.

[23] ibid.

enjoyed in his own country,[24] or he could enjoy national treatment only for the duration for which his work was protected in the country of origin, of his nationality, or of first publication.[25] In addition, its scope was usually limited to certain rights as specified in the treaties.[26] Accordingly, national treatment was much more restricted than later under the Berne Convention.

(ii) Rights and limitations   National treatment usually covered only the repro-   **2.08** duction or reprinting rights (often even with a reference to the interpretation and scope of the reproduction right under national law)[27] and, less often, the public performance right regarding musical, dramatic, and dramatico-musical works. The public performance right, if granted under a bilateral agreement at all, was often subject to different conditions, such as its recognition under the national laws of both contracting parties[28] or prior publication of the work, if done after the entry into force of the bilateral treaty. Often, the treaties also referred back to the national law regarding the conditions of exercise of the public performance right which, under some laws, had to be expressly reserved on the copies of the work.[29]

The translation right was contained in most treaties but was often subject to con-   **2.09** ditions, such as the express reservation of the translation right by the author on the front page of the work, the use of the translation right within a short period (eg three years from publication of the original work), deposit and registration of the original work in the country of protection within three years from the publication in the country of origin, and publication of the authorized translation within a short period (eg three years after deposit and registration of the original work in one of the contracting states).[30] Often, several of such conditions were applied cumulatively. Along with the rights of reproduction, public perform-ance, and translation, many bilateral treaties also prohibited acts of distribution

---

[24] eg Art 1(2) of the Convention between France and the Netherlands of 29 March 1855, repr in Eisenlohr (n 12 above) 284f ('. . . ne plus étendus que . . . '); Ladas (n 17 above) 57; A Darras, *Du droit des auteurs et des artistes dans les rapports internationaux* (1887) 603.

[25] This rule of 'comparison of terms' survived as an option in the Berne Convention; it was very common, see Anon, 'Les Arrangements particuliers entre pays de l'Union littéraire et artistique', (1892) Droit d'auteur 106; Art 1(2) of the Treaty between France and Switzerland of 1882; Darras (n 24 above) 612 no 492.

[26] See paras 2.08, 2.09 below.

[27] eg Art 5(2) of the Treaty between Hanover and France (n 20 above). These rights were often described as 'exclusive rights' or the 'property rights' of reproduction.

[28] Art 2 of the Treaty between Hanover and France (n 20 above).

[29] Cavalli (n 1 above) 81–2.

[30] See in particular Art III of the Additional Convention between twelve German states and Great Britain of 14 June 1855, repr in Eisenlohr (n 12 above) 219. For the shorter duration of the transla-tion right as compared to other rights, see para 2.11 below.

of copies for example by sale or importation, where the copies were illegally reproduced.[31]

2.10 Limitations of all these rights were allowed according to specific provisions under the bilateral treaties, such as the copying of extracts of works for educational or scientific purposes, and of articles in newspapers.[32]

2.11 **(iii) Duration** The general duration was often fixed at different lengths in different treaties, such as ten, twenty, or fifty years after the author's death or another event[33] and, in respect of translation rights, mostly at shorter lengths, namely between five and ten years from first publication.[34] In other cases, the duration was determined according to the law of the country where protection was sought. More often, however, the duration was subject to the comparison of terms[35] and anyway could not exceed that accorded to nationals in the country of protection.[36]

2.12 **(iv) Works** The works covered in principle by the bilateral treaties were described in different ways. Often, general terms such as 'works of the mind or of the art' (*ouvrages d'esprit ou d'art*)[37] or 'works or products of the human mind or the art'[38] were used, either exclusively or supplemented by lists of examples such as 'books, writings, dramatic works, musical compositions . . . '[39] or by specific provisions on individual kinds of works such as dramatic works, translations, musical arrangements, individual articles in encyclopedias or periodicals, and specific works of art.[40] Some treaties were limited, from the outset, to certain categories of works such as literary and scientific works[41] or published versus published and unpublished works,[42] while others explicitly excluded specific kinds of works

---

[31] eg Art 4 of the Treaty between Hanover and France (n 20 above); Art 5 of the Treaty between France and the Netherlands of 29 March 1855 (n 24 above). Ladas (n 17 above) 65–6.

[32] Ricketson/Ginsburg (n 12 above) 1.37.

[33] Ladas (n 17 above) 61–2.

[34] See in particular Art III of the Additional Convention between 12 German states and Great Britain of 14 June 1855, repr in Eisenlohr (n 12 above) 219.

[35] Above n 25 and accompanying text.

[36] On duration, see Ricketson/Ginsburg (n 12 above) 1.38; Ladas (n 17 above) 61; L Rivière, *Protection internationale des œuvres littéraires et artistiques* (1897) 136.

[37] Art 1 of the Treaty between Hanover and France (n 20 above).

[38] Art 1 of the Treaty between Austria and Sardinia of 22 May 1840, Eisenlohr (n 14 above).

[39] Art 1 of the Treaty between Hanover and France (n 20 above).

[40] Arts 2, 3, 9, 10, 12 of the above Treaty between Austria and Sardinia (n 14 above).

[41] Treaty between France and the Netherlands of 29 March 1855 (n 24 above); in 1884, it was extended by a declaration to musical works, Ladas (n 17 above) 54.

[42] Unpublished works were covered less often, eg Art 1 of the Treaty between France and Italy of 9 July 1884; Ladas (n 17 above) 54.

such as photographic works.[43] Such limitations often reflected the level of protection granted in the national laws of the contracting states; there was no will to grant further-reaching protection to foreigners than to nationals. For example, the treaties concluded by the Netherlands with France and Belgium, respectively in 1855 and 1858, did not cover works of art, thereby following the Dutch law.[44]

Yet, even those works covered in principle by the bilateral treaties were not pro- **2.13** tected *iure conventionis*. Their protection was not guaranteed by the treaty but only under national treatment, which meant that they had to be protected under the law of the country of protection. In addition, the enjoyment of national treatment was often dependent on the existence of protection in the country of origin of the work or the home country of the author.[45]

(b) Formalities and censorship

Another frequent restriction of full enjoyment of protection was the requirement **2.14** to fulfil certain formalities for the rights to be recognized and enforced in the other country. Such formalities included the deposit or registration of the work in the country of origin and, at the same time, in the country where protection was sought.[46] In other countries it was sufficient to prove the existence of protection and the fulfilment of formalities in the country of origin.[47] Only a few treaties did not require the fulfilment of formalities.[48]

Apart from such formalities, most bilateral treaties also included provisions **2.15** allowing for national provisions on censorship and similar restrictions on the exploitation of works.[49]

(c) Most-favoured-nation clause

Many bilateral treaties on copyright contained a most-favoured-nation clause. **2.16** This clause has always been a standard element of trade treaties. Its concept can be traced back to the twelfth century; the clause gained importance with the

---

[43] Protocol to the Treaty between Germany and Belgium of 1883; Ladas (n 17 above) 54. Art 6 Final Protocol of the Treaty between Germany and France of 19 April 1883, cf Rivière (n 36 above) 133.

[44] Cavalli (n 1 above) 79; Ladas (n 17 above) 54. Also the exclusion of photographic works under the German treaties of 1883 (preceding note) reflected German law, Rivière (n 36 above) 133.

[45] para 2.07 above.

[46] All treaties of Great Britain concluded between 1846 and 1860 and the treaties between Belgium and Portugal of 11 October 1866 and between Austria and France of 11 December 1866; Cavalli (n 1 above) 82.

[47] Treaties between France and the Netherlands of 29 March 1855, between Belgium and the Netherlands of 30 August 1858, between France and Spain of 16 June 1880, and between Italy and Spain of 28 June 1880; Cavalli (n 1 above) 82.

[48] Treaties between Belgium and France of 26 June 1880, Germany and Italy of 20 June 1884, and Germany and France of 19 April 1883; Cavalli (n 1 above) 82.

[49] eg Art 8 of the Treaty between Hanover and France (n 20 above).

increase of world commerce in the fifteenth and sixteenth centuries and with the decline of mercantilism.[50] Bilateral treaties on copyright were often linked to broader trade treaties, from which they borrowed a most-favoured-nation clause. In principle, the clause obliges each contracting state to extend to the other contracting state any privilege or advantage that it grants to a third country. It constitutes a form of non-discrimination by a contracting state between the other contracting state and any third country. For example, in a case where Belgium, in its treaty with France of 1861, allowed the public performance of a dramatic work without the author's consent, and where the treaties of Belgium with Portugal (1866) and Switzerland (1867) required the author's authorization for this kind of exploitation, the French authors Zola, Busnach, and Gastineau could successfully claim that the most-favoured-nation clause gave them a right of public performance for the work *L'Assomoir*.[51]

2.17 In bilateral copyright treaties as in general trade treaties, the most-favoured-nation clause appeared in different forms. It could be unconditional or conditional on such aspects as reciprocity, equal conditions, or provisions in the national law.[52] In the case of an unconditional clause, the contracting state grants most-favoured-nation treatment irrespective of any compensation by the other contracting state. For example, where a contracting state X grants most-favoured-nation treatment to contracting state Y and X grants more favourable treatment to Z than under the treaty between X and Y, then X has to grant this more favourable treatment to Y without having the right to claim any compensation from Y.

2.18 In the case of a conditional clause, the following examples show its operation. (1) Reciprocity: where, in the above case, X grants most-favoured-nation treatment to Y subject to reciprocity and X grants more favourable treatment to Z than under the treaty between X and Y, then X needs to grant this more favourable treatment to Y only if Y grants to X reciprocal advantages. (2) Equal conditions: where in the above case, X has granted the more favourable treatment to Z only under a specific condition,[53] Y can claim most-favoured-nation treatment in X

---

[50] On its history in general, see Subcomm on Int'l Trade, Senate Comm on Finance, 93rd Congress, 2nd Sess, Executive Branch GATT Studies no 9, 133–5 (1973) as quoted in J Jackson, W Davey, and A Sykes, *Legal Problems of International Economic Relations* (3rd edn, 1995) 440.

[51] Decision of Court of Appeals of Brussels of 17 May 1880, (1881) Sirey, part IV, 9 and as referred to in Cavalli (n 1 above) 78–9, with further references, and in Rivière (n 36 above) 130–1 n 3.

[52] Anon, 'La Clause de la nation la plus favorisée dans les traités et accords concernant la protection du droit d'auteur', 2nd pt (1908) Droit d'auteur 17–20 with excerpts from different treaties as examples. In general, the clause was used in the unconditional form until the eighteenth century and again, in Europe, in the second half of the nineteenth century, when free trade and liberalism prevailed. The conditional form was common in Europe in the second half of the nineteenth century, see Subcomm on Int'l Trade (n 50 above).

[53] In the example of the treaty between France and Brazil of 1893, the condition was that France had to reduce its tariff on coffee, see Ladas (n 17 above) 175.

only if it fulfils the same conditions as Z. (3) National law—when the clause is subject to the law of each contracting party (as in the following real example, under the Treaty of 14 March 1908 between Switzerland and Colombia): Colombia had granted translation rights in its treaty with Spain of 1885, but its national law provided that free translation of works published in a foreign language was allowed and translation rights were not to be granted unless the works were printed in a country where Spanish was the prevailing language. Therefore, Switzerland could not claim translation rights on the basis of the most-favoured-nation clause.[54]

Aside from the unconditional or conditional forms, the most-favoured-nation **2.19** clause in bilateral copyright treaties showed further diversity. In particular, under some treaties only advantages granted in future treaties, and under others also those in pre-existing treaties were taken into account for most-favoured-nation treatment.[55] In addition, the clause was not always applied generally but sometimes only to particular rights or kinds of works.[56]

The most-favoured-nation clause was controversial as an element of copyright **2.20** treaties for quite some time.[57] On one side, it has been praised (in particular by the Association Littéraire et Artistique Internationale) for its capacity to lead directly to the overall aim and ideal in international law of treating authors from all nations equally; it was said that it had rendered nothing else but a service to authors who could thereby best benefit from the existing treaties. Proponents believed that legal consultants could solve whatever practical problems arose in applying the clause.[58]

On the other side, the clause was criticized for a number of reasons. A principal **2.21** objection was that the clause was inappropriate for the area of copyright because the kind of competition known from the domain of tariffs (where third countries could be prejudiced by a privilege given to another one) would not arise.[59] Another objection was the perceived negative effect on the otherwise governing principle of reciprocity: where country A first concluded, on the basis of reciprocity, a treaty with country B which granted a lower level of protection, and later

---

[54] ibid.
[55] A table indicating this difference in the then existing treaties is published in Anon (n 52 above) 17, 18.
[56] Ricketson/Ginsburg (n 12 above) 1.42; Ladas (n 17 above) 66.
[57] See, eg, a discussion in Bulletin de l'Association Littéraire et Artistique Internationale (Congrès d'Anvers 1894) 2nd series no 22, pp 19 ff. At the end of this Congress, the participants rejected the conclusion of the report proposed by Mr Darras, according to which it was desirable not to include any longer the most-favoured-nation clause in copyright treaties, for reasons of simplicity and clarity; see also Anon (n 52 above) 17, 18.
[58] ibid. Also positive: Rivière (n 36 above) 129–30.
[59] Darras (n 24 above) 555.

granted larger advantages to a country C, the application of the most-favoured-nation clause in favour of B disrupted the balance of the treaty between A and B because A also had to grant such advantages to B, which itself could continue to provide its low level of protection to A.[60] This criticism, however, has been rejected on the basis that the more generous country could choose not to give the advantage to the third country, or to provide from the beginning that the most-favoured-nation treatment would be given only on condition of reciprocity.[61]

2.22 A better reasoned criticism referred to the practical consequences of the most-favoured-nation clause: authors, in order to know what rights they enjoyed in another country at a given point in time, would have to analyse not only the bilateral treaty with the other country at stake, but also all treaties and commercial relations of the other country with any third state to which a greater privilege could have been granted. This task was made even more difficult by the fact that 'each day new conventions [were] signed . . .'.[62]

(d) Duration of treaties

2.23 Very often bilateral copyright treaties of the nineteenth century were subject to instability. First, they were limited to a short time of validity, such as five or ten years with a tacit prolongation subject to denunciation by one of the contracting states.[63] Secondly, since many of the copyright treaties were linked to broader trade treaties, and trade treaties were often renegotiated, the effect of the copyright treaties was essentially controlled by the dynamic trade arena. For example, the treaty between France and the Netherlands of 29 March 1855 was valid until 25 July 1859 and its fate thereafter was linked to that of the treaty on commerce and navigation of 25 July 1840. Accordingly, the denunciation of the latter treaty automatically resulted in the denunciation of the former.[64] Thirdly, the situation of war resulted in the nullity of treaties.[65] Finally, treaties could be modified by common agreement between the parties.[66] As a consequence of all these factors, legal certainty suffered.

---

[60] ibid 563–4.

[61] Rivière (n 24 above) 130.

[62] Darras (n 24 above) 556.

[63] eg Art 15(2) of the Treaty between Belgium and Great Britain of 12 August 1854 (Eisenlohr (n 12 above) 287, 294) stipulated a duration of ten years after coming into force and an automatic prolongation for one year each, subject to denunciation by one party at one year's notice.

[64] Art 11(2) of the Treaty between France and the Netherlands of 29 March 1855, (n 24 above).

[65] Rivière (n 36 above) 117.

[66] eg Art 11(3) of the Treaty between France and the Netherlands of 29 March 1855 (n 24 above) and Art 15(3) of the Treaty between Belgium and Great Britain of 12 August 1854 (n 63 above).

(3) Résumé of bilateral treaties

The disadvantages of the most-favoured-nation clause, the short duration and **2.24** frequent denunciation of bilateral treaties, the high number of bilateral treaties, the high diversity of their contents, and the frequent conditions of material reciprocity and formalities created a highly complex, uncertain legal environment.[67] Given these weaknesses, it became clear that bilateral treaties could be only one step towards promoting international copyright law, but not an ideal solution.[68]

C. Development towards the first multilateral treaty

(1) Overview of first steps

Dissatisfaction with the system of bilateral treaties was one reason behind the **2.25** further development towards the first multilateral treaty on the protection of copyright. Another reason was the often expressed recognition of the universal character of works and the consequential need for a universal protection.[69] First steps towards the first treaty involved a number of international congresses that were convened in order to discuss the possibilities and ways of an international, universal protection of copyright—an approach that corresponded to the general phenomenon of organizing international meetings, which had become common by the mid-nineteenth century.[70] The relevant congresses were the Congress of Brussels 1858,[71] the Congresses of Antwerp 1861 and 1877 dealing with artistic works,[72] as well as in the framework of the Universal Exhibition 1878 in Paris, the International Literary Congress in June, organized by the Société des Gens de

---

[67] eg, Cavalli (n 1 above) 83–5.

[68] Anon (n 52 above) 19; Rivière (n 36 above) 117 (who speaks of a way towards 'universal legislation') and 136–7 (also mentioning the positive effect of bilateral treaties providing for the international recognition of authors' rights ('it is from imperfection itself that progress is born', translation by the author)).

[69] Cavalli (n 1 above) 89; E Romberg, *Comptes rendues des travaux du Congrès de la Propriété Littéraire et Artistique* (1859) Vol I, 2, referring to the proposal of the organizers of the Congress of 1858.

[70] Ricketson/Ginsburg (n 12 above) 2.05.

[71] Congress of Literary and Artistic Property of 27–30 September 1858, cf the records of the conference: Romberg (n 69 above) (2 vols including further documentations and an appendix with the then valid national copyright laws); paras 2.26–2.29 below.

[72] cf the records of the 1861 Congress, E Gressin Dumoulin, *Comptes rendues des travaux du Congrès Artistique d'Anvers* (1862). The second Congress 1877 was in part prepared by the preceding Congress of Bremen 1876 organized by the Association for the Codification and Reform of the Law of Nations. It mandated a commission to deal with international norms in the field. Its results regarding common principles of the laws of Germany, England, and North America were presented in 1877 in Antwerp (Röthlisberger (n 3 above) 5); paras 2.30–2.31 below.

Lettres de France (Society of Writers of France),[73] and the International Congress on Artistic Property in September, just following a congress on industrial property.[74] At the Literary Congress, the International Literary Association was founded and soon thereafter became instrumental in promoting an international union for the protection of literary property—the later Berne Union—to be established by a conference of states.[75] Additional activities by private associations, often at a national level but with a view to improving the international copyright protection, took place during the same time.[76] Eventually, three diplomatic conferences led to the adoption of the Berne Convention in 1886.[77]

(2) The Brussels Congress 1858

2.26   Notably, the first of these congresses took place at a time when an initial wave of around thirty bilateral treaties (in addition to the intra-German treaties) had already been concluded and had revealed their weaknesses.[78] Belgium as a host country for the initial international congresses on universal copyright is remarkable given that it was one of the leading piracy countries, not least since its own nationals enjoyed a much lower protection than foreigners would enjoy in Belgium. The choice of Belgium may reflect the wish of Belgian representatives to improve the reputation of Belgium in this field, and to influence the Belgian government to improve national legislation in favour of their own nationals.[79] This congress and the other pre-Berne congresses were initiated and run by 'distinguished men'[80] and organized by well-known representatives of politics, the judiciary, and the arts.[81] The congresses were attended by participants who would today be called interested parties. For example, the Brussels Congress was attended by around 300 delegates of eighty-one associations from fourteen countries; namely sixty-two writers, fifty-four delegates from learned societies, forty-seven delegates from universities, forty civil servants and representatives of authorities, twenty-nine lawyers, twenty-nine booksellers, twenty-four artists, twenty-one

---

[73] The Société des Gens de Lettres de France had already—unsuccessfully—tried to convene such a Congress in 1867 at another Universal Exhibition in Paris, Cavalli (n 1 above) 117.

[74] ibid 116–31 on the literary congress and 132–40 on the artistic congress of 18–21 September; for both, see paras 2.32–2.34 below.

[75] Ricketson/Ginsburg (n 12 above) 2.09, 2.10; paras 2.35–2.38 below.

[76] eg Röthlisberger (n 3 above) 4–5 on the German Book Traders' Association requesting, in 1871, to replace the bilateral treaties involving German states by a treaty involving the German Reich and third states.

[77] paras 2.39–2.45 below.

[78] For the weaknesses, see para 2.24 and preceding paras above.

[79] Cavalli (n 1 above) 91–2.

[80] Romberg (n 69 above) Vol I, 1: 'hommes distingués'.

[81] eg the list of organizers of the Congress of Brussels 1858 in Romberg (n 69 above) Vol I, 3–4 and Cavalli (n 1 above) 90–1; for the Congress of Antwerp 1861 Cavalli (n 1 above) 108 referring to Gressin Dumoulain (n 72 above) 1 ff.

economists, and sixty journalists.[82] Accordingly, civil society itself was at the roots of the Berne Convention.[83]

The aims of the Brussels Congress reflected the problematic legal situation of copyright law at that time: given the lack of protection in a number of countries and, where protection existed, the diversity of national norms, the Congress viewed its task as preparing 'general elements of a universal law of intellectual property'[84]—elements to become part of all national laws that, once developed in a similar way, could lead to a universal law. The working programme of the Congress thus included detailed questions not only on mechanisms of international protection, but also on substantive law provisions with the aim of approximating national laws. These questions had been commented on by the Organizing Committee before their submission to the Congress.[85] On substantive copyright law, the overall eighteen questions covered, for example, the rights of translation, reproduction, public performance and adaptation of musical works, and problems of artworks. One of the most controversial questions was the appropriate duration of protection and, more basically, the question whether protection should be perpetual or limited in time; the latter question was decided by the relevant section of the Congress by fifty-six to thirty-six votes in favour of limited duration for protection.[86]

2.27

Eventually, the Congress adopted its answers to the questions in the form of resolutions,[87] and it mostly followed the views of the Organizing Committee.[88] The resolutions on international protection claimed the international recognition of literary and artistic property even in the absence of reciprocity, full national treatment, no requirement of formalities in the country of protection, and the adoption of national legislation on a uniform basis. The resolutions on substantive law included the exclusive rights of publication, reproduction, distribution, translation (subject to restrictions), musical arrangement, public performance of dramatic and musical works, a general duration of fifty years *pma* (*post mortem auctoris*) or after the death of the surviving spouse and special durations, as well as particular provisions on artworks.

2.28

---

[82] Röthlisberger (n 3 above) 3 (in n 1); Ricketson/Ginsburg (n 12 above) 2.05.

[83] This may be worth highlighting today where associations of consumers seem to suggest that copyright protection goes against the interests of civil society (for more detail, see paras 25.27–25.32 below).

[84] Romberg (n 69 above) Vol I, 2.

[85] The questions are repr in (the original) French in Cavalli (n 1 above), 94–5 and Romberg (n 69 above) Vol I, 4-6.

[86] ibid 126; discussion on 100–26. For the discussion on the duration of anonymous and pseudonymous works, see ibid 135–7.

[87] ibid 175–8; the resolutions are repr in (the original) French in Cavalli (n 1 above) 104–7 and largely in Ricketson/Ginsburg (in English) (n 12 above) 2.05.

[88] Cavalli (n 1 above) in particular 100–4 on the different issues.

2.29 The President of the Congress seemed to anticipate its importance when he addressed the participants with the words '. . . you will thereby have the honour of having been, in some way, the authors of the code of intellectual property.'[89] He also predicted: 'These resolutions will spread with a new authority in the intellectual world.'[90] It was indeed at this Congress that interested parties took basic decisions with a strong impact on the further development of national copyright laws and that the basic principles of the later Berne Convention emerged.[91]

(3) The Antwerp Congresses 1861 and 1877

2.30 The first Antwerp Congress of 1861 worked in a similar way, but with fewer questions and specifically regarding rights of authors of artworks.[92] In respect of international protection, the question regarding the best way to achieve an agreement among governments to generalize protection of artistic property could not be properly discussed, due to lack of time; only a general recommendation to use all kinds of permitted measures was adopted. Nevertheless, the first three resolutions of the 1858 Brussels Congress in favour of the international recognition of the protection of works and full national treatment were adopted specifically in respect of artworks.[93]

2.31 The second Antwerp Congress of 1877 on artworks had the task, among others, of seeking a basis for international legislation on property rights in artistic works. In the end this Congress only adopted a resolution encouraging work towards a 'law with an international character',[94] combined with a request to the Institute for International Law to prepare a draft universal law on artistic works.[95] This request, however, was not realized, and later became obsolete when the International Literary Association, founded in 1878 and enlarged to the International Literary and Artistic Association (ALAI) in 1884, played the leading role in the preparation of the Berne Convention.

(4) The International Literary and Artistic Congresses 1878

2.32 The foundation of the International Literary Association was indeed one of the main successes of the 1878 International Literary Congress in Paris. Towards the end of the Literary Congress, it was decided under the presidency of Victor Hugo

---

[89] Romberg (n 69 above) Vol 8. I, 173–4 (translation by the author).
[90] ibid 94 (translation by the author).
[91] Cavalli (n 1 above) 108.
[92] The questions by the Organization Committee are repr in Cavalli (n 1 above) 109–10 n 67.
[93] ibid 113; in respect of the entire discussion at the 1861 Congress, see ibid 110–13.
[94] Röthlisberger (n 3 above) 5.
[95] Darras (n 24 above) 523; Röthlisberger (n 3 above) 5. The Institute for International Law had been founded only four years earlier in Geneva.

to found the International Literary Association, which should 'spread and defend in all countries the principles of intellectual property, to examine the international treaties and to work towards their completion'[96]—a role which it took over vigorously.[97]

In addition, the International Literary Congress adopted the wish (*vœu*) that the **2.33** French government should take the initiative to convene an international meeting of representatives of the different governments in order to elaborate a uniform convention on the use of literary property according to the ideas as adopted by this Congress in its resolutions, which included, in particular, the principle of national treatment.[98]

A similarly important step was taken by the Artistic Congress of 1878 which pro- **2.34** posed, for the first time in international copyright history, the idea of a 'general Union' to be established among the different European and overseas countries in order to adopt a uniform legislation in the field of artistic property. The treaty establishing this Union was to be inspired by the resolutions adopted by the 1878 Congress (including national treatment) and spearheaded through the French competent Minister.[99] This proposal for a Union followed up on a similar request in the field of industrial property made only some days earlier at the relevant International Congress of Paris.[100] It seems, though, that the general political situation was not very favourable for the convocation of an international conference for the establishment of such a Union; in addition, France was already busy preparing the upcoming 1879 diplomatic conference on an international treaty on industrial property (the result was the Paris Convention of 1883).[101] Five years after this proposal at the 1878 Congress, another country, Switzerland, fulfilled this task.

(5) The work of the International Literary Association

After its establishment in 1878, the International Literary Association[102] annu- **2.35** ally organized an international congress on questions of copyright, the writers'

---

[96] Röthlisberger (n 3 above) 6 (translation by the author) referring to the sessions of the Third Commission of 21 and 25 June and the final session of 29 June 1878; Ricketson/Ginsburg (n 12 above) 2.08 indicate as the date of decision 27 June, and Ladas (n 17 above) 74, 28 June.
[97] paras 2.35–2.38 below.
[98] Cavalli (n 1 above) 131; Röthlisberger (n 3 above) 6.
[99] Resolutions nos 20 and 21, repr in Cavalli (n 1 above) 138; Röthlisberger (n 3 above) 7. Resolution no 21 mandated the Congress to take steps with the Minister of Education and Arts with a view to taking the initiative for the convocation of an official, international commission with the aim of establishing such a Union.
[100] Röthlisberger (n 3 above) 7.
[101] ibid 8–9.
[102] It was extended in 1884 to become the International Literary and Artistic Association, known as ALAI to date; also paras 2.31–2.32 above.

situation, and literature.[103] Among the most important legal questions discussed during the years preceding the diplomatic conferences for the Berne Convention were the right of translation and its duration; the right of adaptation and musical arrangements; the duration of authors' rights; the definition of literary, scientific, and artistic works; the extensive literary piracy in Brazil and in Russia; and national treatment.[104]

2.36 One annual congress, the Congress of Rome 1882, is particularly noteworthy because the lawyer De Marchi had proposed a project with more than 130 articles for the codification of the rights of literary property. De Marchi considered that the uniformity of laws would be difficult but not impossible to achieve since it was a direct consequence of the unity of the human mind (*esprit humain*).[105] He suggested that 'despite the differences in races and civilisation', one should have the aim of a complete unification of the laws on literary property.[106] Given the length and vagueness of his proposal, however, it was not even examined.

2.37 In contrast, the proposal by Paul Schmidt, General Secretary of the German Book Traders' Association, was unanimously adopted at the same Congress.[107] He revived the idea of a union of literary property upon the model of the already existing Postal Union, to be based on ideas of all interested parties in literature and music. He proposed to provoke a thorough discussion on such a union in the press of all countries and to fix a date and place for a conference of interested parties on the creation of a union of literary property. It was immediately decided this conference would be held in 1882 in Berne—on the neutral territory of Switzerland where the international bureaux of organizations, such as the Postal and Telegraph Unions, already had their headquarters, and where the Bureau of the International Union for the Protection of Industrial Property was about to be established.[108]

2.38 The envisaged Conference of the International Literary Association eventually took place in 1883. It was supported by the Swiss government, which also showed its readiness to initiate a diplomatic conference with a view to adopt an international

---

[103] Cavalli (n 1 above) 142; eg at the Congress of Vienna 1881, a proposal for a resolution demanding the liberation of a Russian writer who had been detained in Siberia for 18 years was discussed but rejected, ibid 150.

[104] For a more detailed summary of the contents of the congresses of London (1879), Lisbon (1880), Vienna (1881), and Rome (1882), cf Cavalli (n 1 above) 141–55, referring to the relevant bulletins of 'ALAI'.

[105] ibid 151.

[106] ibid.

[107] ibid 153; Röthlisberger (n 3 above) 9–10.

[108] Cavalli (n 1 above) 152–4.

convention, if necessary.[109] The 1883 Conference was attended by around twenty-five representatives of interested parties.[110] On the basis of preparatory work done, in particular by the Swiss national committee and three national commissions, after only three days of discussion the Conference adopted a draft convention of ten articles; most of these were finally taken over by the delegates of the three diplomatic conferences 1884–6 into the final text of the Berne Convention.[111] The draft convention was submitted to the Swiss Federal Council as a basis for further elaboration of a draft treaty on a Union to be submitted to the governments and dealt with by a diplomatic conference.[112]

(6) The diplomatic conferences preceding the Berne Convention

The draft convention of the 1883 Conference was limited in its scope, even in comparison with many of the existing bilateral treaties. For example, it neither dealt with the duration of rights, nor with a list of precise kinds of rights to be recognized, nor with limitations of them. What was included was in particular the principle of national treatment and related issues, a definition of 'literary and artistic works', the recognition of exclusive translation and adaptation rights and the protection of translations, the 'retroactive' application, the permission for Union states to enter into special agreements between themselves, and the establishment of an International Office of the proposed Union (in particular for supply of information on the copyright laws of Member States).[113] **2.39**

Despite its narrow scope, the draft inspired the Swiss government to take the next step towards a multilateral treaty, namely by addressing a circular note to the governments of 'all civilised nations' that elaborated on the need for multilateral protection of literary and artistic property, given the deficiencies of the bilateral treaties and the lack of uniform protection. The Swiss government also announced that it would hold a diplomatic conference if the addressed states would be favourable to agree, in principle, with the idea that the 'natural right should be proclaimed, that the author of a literary or artistic work, no matter what may be his nationality or the place of reproduction, ought to be protected everywhere equally with the natives of each state'—a principle to be realized through a Union **2.40**

---

109 Ricketson/Ginsburg (n 12 above) 2.10; on the Conference also Cavalli (n 1 above) 158–62 and Röthlisberger (n 3 above) 10–11.

110 ibid 11.

111 Ricketson/Ginsburg (n 12 above) 2.11, 2.12; Cavalli (n 1 above) 160–2; on 162 see also the quote from the concluding speech of the President of the Association, showing that he was aware of the importance of this Conference (in particular: '. . . we have only made an ascent, but no one had done it before us, and no one can do it again unless in our footsteps' (translation by the author).

112 Röthlisberger (n 3 above) 11.

113 For more details on the draft convention, see Ricketson/Ginsburg (n 12 above) 2.13–2.17. The text of the draft convention is reprinted in Bulletin ALAI no 18, November 1883 p 19 and in (1883) Journal du droit international privé 563–4.

between states.[114] The positive reaction by many states[115] was considered by the Swiss government important enough to convene a first diplomatic conference in 1884 for which, however, the adoption of binding resolutions was not yet envisaged.

2.41 At the first diplomatic conference in 1884,[116] eleven countries[117] discussed a Draft Convention on the basis of a Swiss proposal, which was itself based on the proposal adopted by the International Literary Association in 1883.[118] A study on the common features (*concordance*) of the most important provisions in laws and treaties on literary and artistic property, published by the Swiss government, had been submitted to facilitate the work at the conference. After twelve days, the countries adopted in particular a Draft Convention with a Draft Additional Article and Draft Final Protocol (*protocol de clôture*) to be submitted for study by interested governments. Only France made counter-proposals to the results of the 1884 Conference. The Draft Convention brought about major advances; though inspired by the Swiss proposal, it went much further.[119]

2.42 At the second conference in 1885, additional countries were represented, resulting in broader discussions. In the light of this and in order to enable the highest number of governments to sign the final agreement, more time was conceded to governments before a treaty would be adopted. Therefore, twelve of sixteen countries signed the Draft Convention, Additional Article and Final Protocol (*protocol de clôture*) without binding effect at the 1885 Conference, and mandated the Swiss government to prepare a diplomatic conference where the Draft Convention could only be rejected or adopted en bloc. Finally, at the third conference, the Berne Convention was signed by Belgium, France, Germany, Great Britain, Haiti, Italy, Liberia, Spain, Switzerland, and Tunisia on 9 September 1886.[120] With the exception of Liberia, all other signatory states ratified the Convention on 5 September 1887.[121]

---

[114] The circular note is repr in part in Ricketson/Ginsburg (n 12 above) 2.18 and Cavalli (n 1 above) 163, n 18.

[115] For the positive and negative responses, see Cavalli (n 1 above) 163 and, regarding the US objections based on commercial reasons, ibid 163–4; Ricketson/Ginsburg (n 12 above) 2.19.

[116] On this Conference and its results, see in detail Cavalli (n 1 above) 162–6; Ricketson/Ginsburg (n 12 above) 2.19–2.37 with further refs; Röthlisberger (n 3 above) 12–16.

[117] Germany, Austria-Hungary, Belgium, Costa Rica, France, Great Britain, Haiti, the Netherlands, Sweden, Norway, and Switzerland; Italy and Spain were prevented from being represented by an epidemic of cholera, Cavalli (n 1 above) 164.

[118] para 2.39 above.

[119] Cavalli (n 1 above) 165–6; Ricketson/Ginsburg (n 12 above) 2.37, quoting delegate Adams who referred to the 'moderate program' transformed 'into a draft Convention of considerable dimensions'.

[120] Cavalli (n 1 above) 166–8.

[121] Anon, 'La Constitution de l'Union (III.)' (1888) Droit d'auteur 23.

A detailed discussion on the debates about the individual provisions[122] is beyond **2.43** the scope of this book. However, some features of the debates are highlighted here: at the 1884 Conference, the discussions were strongly influenced by the German delegation, which was instrumental in the success achieved.[123] First, it submitted a questionnaire that sought clarification and amendment of, as well as supplements to, the submitted Swiss draft. Thereby, it brought focus to discussions and advanced them. France (the usual leaders) and Britain only exercised an enhanced influence on the contents of the future convention at the 1885 Conference.[124] In particular, the French delegation advocated for stronger copyright protection, while Great Britain often took the opposite role and preferred to rely on the national treatment principle 'pure and simple'.[125] The final text, therefore, necessitated a compromise to also allow the accession of those countries that were only ready to provide for a lower level of protection—a compromise only seen as a first step on the way to a complete and uniform international protection (as reflected in Art 17 on regular revisions of the Convention).[126]

Secondly, the German delegation, in accordance with the authors' and artists' **2.44** societies and many privately expressed opinions, provoked discussion on the basic approach to international protection. It proposed a universal codification of authors' rights by way of regulating all copyright provisions in a uniform manner for the entire union of states.[127] In other words, the ultimate form of protection was seen, as by many others earlier, to be a uniform law that would directly apply in all contracting states. Other delegations, however, objected to this proposal because they believed it was unrealistic to simply clear away the existing differences among national copyright laws.[128] Therefore, the Conference of 1884 finally adopted a pragmatic approach, namely by maintaining different national laws as a basis of international protection, combined with the principle of national treatment and minimum rights. This approach was laid down in 1884 in the final records (*procès verbal*), which contained a number of principles indicating the discrepancy between the diversity of existing laws as an obstacle to widely accepted

---

122 On those, cf Ricketson/Ginsburg (n 12 above) 2.21–2.37; 2.42–2.49.
123 ibid 2.37, 2.24.
124 ibid 2.24–2.26 and 2.40.
125 ibid 2.40, 2.49.
126 ibid 2.49.
127 The proposal was put in the form of the following question: 'Instead of concluding a convention based on the principle of national treatment, would it not be preferable to aim for a codification, in the framework of a convention, regulating in a uniform manner for the whole projected Union, and in the framework of a convention, the totality of provisions relating to the protection of copyright?', Actes de la conférence internationale pour la protection des droits d'auteur réunie à Berne du 8 au 19 Septembre 1884, 24; Ricketson/Ginsburg (n 12 above) 2.24.
128 ibid.

unification, and the continuing desirability of unification and international codification of copyright law.[129]

2.45 Like an earlier compromise motion proposed by the Swiss government at the 1884 Conference on this latter issue, the *procès verbal* reflected the overall view that the universal codification of a uniform law would be the better, ideal solution and that the chosen solution was only second best, but selected as the only realistic solution to be immediately adopted by the largest possible number of states, at least as an interim step to future development towards the desired uniformity.[130] This basic choice also helped ensure maximum accession throughout the future development of the Berne Convention: if only twelve countries were not already able to agree on one uniform law, then it was much less likely that in the future more countries interested in acceding to such a convention would be ready to do so. Indeed, absolute uniformity of laws of different countries has never been achieved to date, even if certain developments of more recent copyright history have brought about a quite far-reaching approximation of the contents of national laws worldwide—at least on the surface.[131]

---

129 ibid 2.36.
130 Actes de la conférence 1884 (n 127 above) 29; the motion is repr in Ricketson/Ginsburg (n 12 above) 2.24. On the disappointment of this outcome, cf ibid 2.37 with further references.
131 eg paras 14.24 and 25.34 below.

3

COMPARISON OF THE COPYRIGHT SYSTEM AND THE AUTHOR'S RIGHTS (*DROIT D'AUTEUR*) SYSTEM

A. Introduction

(1) The different systems

Today, two major systems of protection govern most national copyright laws of **3.01** the world: the Anglo-Saxon or Anglo-American 'copyright system' and the Continental European 'author's rights' or '*droit d'auteur*' system. They are rooted in different philosophies, as reflected in distinctive features of laws under each system. The differences of these systems have proved to be a major source of problems for initiating and adopting international agreements or even regional harmonization, especially from the mid-1980s when the increased economic importance of copyright resulted in more competition and countries' more aggressive pursuit of protection for the benefit of their domestic industries through international trade law. In addition, not least since its accession to the Berne Convention in 1989, the USA has exercised increased influence on international copyright law and strongly pushed for recognition of elements of the copyright system,[1] thereby accentuating the 'competition' between the systems. Strategies of minimizing the differences in order to 'bridge the gap' were mostly discerned as tools to introduce elements of the copyright system into the international framework.[2]

3.02 Since the systems of protection are often understood as expressing the underlying cultures and identities rather than as only neutral tools to regulate a situation by law, fights to influence regional or international solutions tend to be particularly fierce and sometimes emotional; they have even been characterized as 'religious wars'[3] or a 'big battle'.[4] Traces of this battle may be observed particularly in the TRIPS Agreement (Trade-Related Aspects of Intellectual Property Rights), the WCT (WIPO Copyright Treaty), and the WPPT (WIPO Performances and Phonograms Treaty). Therefore, an explanation of the basic approaches and differences under both systems is essential as a background for understanding international copyright law.

3.03 Although discussions on this topic in general and within this book focus on the copyright and author's rights system, a third system, the so-called 'socialist system', is briefly mentioned here for completeness. It existed mainly in the Soviet Union and affiliated Eastern and Central European countries during their socialist periods. Individual property rights did not match well with concepts of socialist community and state control; the interests of society as a whole often prevailed in case of conflict, and the exploitation of works was performed and controlled by state enterprises.[5] Former socialist countries in Central and Eastern Europe and the ex-Soviet Union follow the author's rights system today.

3.04 Before concentrating on the copyright and author's rights systems, another notable aspect is mentioned for enhanced understanding. In contrast to the copyright and the author's rights systems, which have their origins in Europe and have spread to other parts of the world as Western concepts, a different approach

---

[1] eg the inclusion of phonograms in the ambit of the Berne Convention, see para 17.05 below; recent activities in this regard take place mainly in bilateral trade agreements, see paras 12.11, 12.32–12.35, 12.40, and 12.64 below; A Françon, *Cours de propriété littéraire et artistique* (1999) 114f; S von Lewinski, 'Copyright in Modern International Trade Law' (1994) 171 RIDA 5, 57–9.

[2] Allusion to this is made, eg in S von Lewinski, 'Intervention' in J Rosén and PJ Nordell (eds), *Copyright, Related Rights and Media Convergence in the Digital Context: ALAI Nordic Study Days, June 18–20, 2000, Stockholm* (2001) 59; also in R Kreile, 'Bericht über die WIPO Sitzungen zum möglichen Protokoll zur Berner Konvention und zum "Neuen Instrument" im September 1995' (1995) ZUM 815 and 824.

[3] N Turkewitz, 'Authors' Rights are Dead' (1990) 38 J Copyright Soc USA 41, 45.

[4] 'Une bataille de grande envergure', see B Edelman, 'Entre copyright et droit d'auteur: l'intégrité de l'œuvre de l'esprit' (1990) Recueil Dalloz, Chronique 295.

[5] S Stewart, *International Copyright and Neighbouring rights* (2nd edn, 1989) n 1.17 and, on the law of the USSR, ibid ch 19.

towards creation has remained alive for a long time in some parts of the world and in particular in Asia:[6] an author mainly strived for recognition in society as a master of his art; copying of his works showed his popularity and his authority as a master. Such status in society was more important than direct earnings from the work, all the more so since artists were usually employees; in this regard, the situation recalls that in the Middle Ages in Europe. Furthermore, aggressive Western-style enforcement may be perceived as incompatible with Asian tradition.[7] Yet, Asian societies are dramatically changing; artists need to live on the exploitation of their works and therefore have an interest in seeing them protected by copyright.[8] Along with Western-style markets and individualism, Western concepts of copyright are also continuously integrated not only in Asian laws, but also in culture.[9] Still, the argument that Western concepts are imposed and do not correspond to Asian culture is continuously used against international endeavours to improve intellectual property protection in Asia.[10]

(2) Geographical spreading

Both the copyright and the author's rights systems emerged in Europe in the **3.05** eighteenth century and spread from there across the world through colonization and, most recently, economic pressure by powerful nations. Consequently, the copyright system has been adopted not only in the United Kingdom, but also in its former colonies and Commonwealth countries such as the USA, New Zealand, Australia, former African colonies, Sri Lanka, and India. The author's rights system has been adopted in countries of the European Continent and, consequently, in their former colonies, such as Latin American countries, former French colonies in Africa, and a number of Asian countries such as Indonesia and Vietnam.

Countries that are or have been subject to different influences show mixed **3.06** systems, such as Canada with the French influence in Quebec and the otherwise dominant English influence, or the Philippines and Panama where a strong US influence followed the original Spanish (and therefore author's rights system) approach. Some non-colonized—in particular Asian—countries such as Thailand have conceived their own systems, often with elements both from the

---

6 For a particular perspective of Islam, see M Amanullah, 'Author's Copyright: An Islamic Perspective' (2006) 9/3 Journal of World Intellectual Property 301 ff.

7 C Antons, 'Legal Culture and its Impact on Harmonisation' in C Antons, M Blakeney, and C Heath (eds), *Intellectual Property Harmonisation within ASEAN and APEC* (2004) 35; however, he also mentions other deficiencies, such as corruption, as sources for enforcement problems.

8 On these developments, see in more detail Antons ibid 29, 32 f. However, creation in indigenous communities remains largely subject to approaches that are fundamentally different from Western views, see paras 20.02–20.04 below.

9 In many Asian countries, protection had already been introduced by the end of the nineteenth century, but often with little relevance in practice, ibid 34.

10 ibid.

copyright and the author's rights system.[11] Similarly, the first modern Chinese Copyright Act of 1990 largely follows the author's rights system, but integrates certain elements from the copyright system especially as regards practical implementation.[12]

3.07   Although former socialist countries adhere to the author's rights system, many, especially ex-Soviet countries (like many developing countries) have recently integrated elements of the copyright system into their laws, not least due to US pressure to conclude bilateral treaties with specific contents modelled on the copyright system.[13] At the same time, countries of the copyright system, before adhering to the Berne Convention or any subsequent copyright convention based thereon, have to implement elements of the author's rights system that characterize the Berne Convention. Accordingly, through these varying influences most countries today no longer follow entirely one or the other system but have admitted certain elements of the opposite system.

3.08   Moreover, the following comparative presentation of the copyright and author's rights systems must not create the wrong impression that countries' laws of the same system would essentially be homogeneous among themselves. For example, Germany and France—both author's rights system countries—show basic systematic differences in their laws,[14] and copyright system countries, such as the USA, Canada, and the United Kingdom, have different approaches to issues such as originality or limitations and exceptions (including concepts such as fair use or fair dealing).

B. Development of the basic approaches under both systems

(1) Beginnings in the eighteenth century

3.09   Modern copyright started to replace the European system of privileges in the eighteenth century, beginning with the English Statute of Anne in 1710, laws of the first American states after 1783, the US Constitution of 1787, and the post-Revolution French laws of 1791 and 1793.[15] While the earlier privileges were

---

[11] ibid 34–5; most consider the Thai system as Continental European.

[12] See A Dietz, 'The Chinese Copyright Law: Copyright or "Droit d'auteur"?' (2004) Auteurs & Media 14 ff; P Ganea, 'Copyright' in C Heath (ed), *Intellectual Property Law in China* (2005) 205, 211, also on the more recent versions of this Act.

[13] paras 12.09 ff, in particular 12.11 below.

[14] In particular, the monistic and dualistic approaches, see E Adeney, *The Moral Rights of Authors and Performers* (2006) 8.24 and 9.12 for a short explanation for France and Germany in the context of moral rights.

[15] eg Françon (n 1 above) 116–19; for France: A Lucas and H-J Lucas, *Traité de la propriété littéraire et artistique* (3rd edn, 2006) 9 ff.

granted by sovereigns and therefore could even be a tool for censorship, modern copyright is based on several philosophical ideas mainly developed in the seventeenth and eighteenth centuries in Europe, that were then supplemented in the nineteenth century. Among these ideas were, in particular, the new justification of law and property against the background of the modern notion of freedom, as expressed during the French Revolution. Property was conceived as a tool for the individual person to guarantee his freedom. These basic thoughts were characteristic for the period of so-called 'enlightenment'; they had first been expressed by John Locke and later by Rousseau, Kant, Fichte, and Hegel.

For example, Locke considered that each person was sovereign of himself and also **3.10** owned every product of his labour as property.[16] Also, many philosophers from the last third of the eighteenth century followed the natural law theory that was generally established by Hugo de Groot and Pufendorf and used as a basis to justify a property right in works of the mind. Such right, unlike the earlier privileges granted by sovereigns, would realize the freedom of the right owners. Accordingly, anyone who created a work would automatically enjoy a property right in this product of his mind.[17] Consequently, the rights of publishers who, rather than authors, were regularly beneficiaries of privileges, had to be explained by contracts between publishers and authors. In a contract, an author would grant licences to the publisher but in principle remain the owner of his work and thus keep his fundamental right of freedom.

(2) Clear division in the nineteenth century

(a) Main approaches to protection under both systems

Philosophy has often influenced the development of law, even if not always **3.11** immediately. The early English and American copyright laws granted limited exclusive reproduction rights for authors, while highlighting the public benefit as a rationale for protection: copyright was seen as an incentive to creation, leading to an enrichment of the public.[18] It is controversial in detail whether one can interpret the early English and American laws as predominantly utilitarian and the first French laws as protecting the author simply because he has created a work to which he remains linked, or whether one should view more common

---

[16] J Locke, *Second Treatise of Government* (1689) §§ 27, 31.

[17] Similarly, JS Pütter, *Der Büchernachdruck nach ächten Grundsätzen des Rechts geprüft* (1774) 25.

[18] This rationale is reflected, eg, in the title and preamble of the Statute of Anne, and in the US Constitution, according to which 'The Congress shall have power . . . to promote the progress of science and useful arts, by securing for limited times to authors and inventors the exclusive right to their respective writings and discoveries' (Art I s 8 (8)).

elements of these laws.[19] In any case, it is clear that the English and American laws on the one hand and the French (as well as other author's rights system) laws on the other hand developed in different directions during the nineteenth century.

3.12   The English, American, and later also other laws of the copyright system were characterized by the utilitarian approach under which copyright protection is justified because it is necessary to stimulate creation and thereby enhance the general well-being of societies. Logically, copyright is only justified as long as it can fulfil this role. Under this approach, property rights function as a tool to enhance creation and its dissemination to the public. Accordingly, publishing and other disseminating industries in principle play an equally important role as authors; the economic efficiency of the copyright to reach the overall aim of supplying the society with new works is essential.[20]

3.13   By contrast, author's rights on the European Continent since the nineteenth century have been predominantly influenced by the natural law theory and personalist doctrines. Accordingly, the author's creation naturally belongs to him and the protection is justified simply as a matter of justice. The simple fact of creation establishes a bond between the author and his work, which must be protected as his property irrespective of any utility of the protection for the society. Personalist doctrines justified the protection of both the author's personal and economic interests in the work on the basis of a personality right rather than a property right;[21] even if these doctrines have not survived, all laws under the author's rights system give the author—as a human being who creates works—the central place in the system of protection. For example, as expressed in the German Copyright Act, 'the author's right protects the author in his intellectual and personal relations to the work and in the exploitation of the work'.[22]

3.14   Even if the laws of the author's rights system are not based on natural law,[23] they are rooted in it and reflect many aspects of the natural law theory;[24] this theory also shows a strong influence in their interpretation, at least in the absence of contrary legal provisions. For example, the German Supreme Court referred to the author's control over his work as the 'natural consequence of his intellectual property which itself is simply recognised by legislation in a more precise

---

[19] J Ginsburg, 'A Tale of Two Copyrights: Literary Property in Revolutionary France and America' (1991) 147 RIDA 125 ff (more common features), Lucas/Lucas (n 15 above) 10–11, with further refs (in part disagreeing in relation to the French laws).

[20] On the utilitarian justification, see a detailed analysis by A Strowel, *Droit d'auteur et copyright* (1993) 191, 234.

[21] eg for Germany O von Gierke, *Deutsches Privatrecht I* (1895) 762 ff.

[22] Art 11 phr 1 of the German Copyright Act 1965 as amended.

[23] Strowel invokes as a reason the territorial restriction of protection, Strowel (n 20 above) 140–2.

[24] Details are shown under paras 3.20 ff below.

formulation';[25] from this the Supreme Court concluded that the author's exclusive rights covered new kinds of exploitation and thus entitled the author to obtain remuneration for each use of his work even in absence of explicit provisions in the law.[26]

Despite the separate development of both systems, mutual influences between the systems have been ascertained. In particular, an influence of natural law on the US Copyright Act, and a positivist logic in French law may be observed to a certain extent.[27] **3.15**

(b) Reflections of the approaches in terminology and structure of laws

The different focus of the copyright and author's rights systems—the focus on the utility of copyright for the society versus the focus on the author who must be protected in his work as a matter of justice—is reflected in the respective terminology of some laws. For instance, laws of the author's rights system acknowledge 'rights' as a form of protection in favour of the author. Instead, many laws of the copyright system, such as the UK Copyright, Designs and Patents Act 1988 (CDPA), use phrases such as 'acts restricted by copyright'.[28] This terminology reflects the different viewpoints of the relevant laws: a 'right' designates the protection from the author's point of view, while the same phenomenon is seen as a 'restricted act' from the user's point of view. Not surprisingly, author's rights laws use the words 'limitations' and 'exceptions' representing the author's point of view, while laws of the copyright system usually employ words such as 'acts permitted', 'fair dealing', 'fair use', or 'free use' in order to designate the same phenomenon from the user's point of view for whom these acts are permitted by law, fair, or free.[29] **3.16**

Even more importantly, the overall terms 'copyright' and 'author's rights' reflect the differences, namely the focus on the copy of a work which itself is protected against copying on the one hand, and the focus on the human being who created the work, the author on the other hand. The copy which is a means for distribution of the work for the benefit of the public seems to be particularly important **3.17**

---

[25] *Tonband v Grundig-Reporter*, German Supreme Court (BGH) 18 May 1955, BGHZ 17, 266.

[26] For this case and French cases showing the influence of the natural law theory in interpretation of author's rights laws, see Strowel (n 20 above) 142–4.

[27] ibid 139–42.

[28] In particular, ss 16–21 of the CDPA; the title of the respective ch II, as well as the beginning of s 16(1), however, also use the word 'rights' and 'exclusive right', respectively.

[29] eg the title of ch III and ss 29, 30 of the CDPA; such use of terminology is not consistent in all laws of the copyright system but is symptomatic for the different philosophies behind both systems; for an example of a copyright act using the terms 'exclusive rights' rather than (also) 'restricted acts', and 'limitations' instead of 'acts permitted', see ss 106 and 110 US Copyright Act (Title 17 USC).

in the copyright system while the right of the author is in the centre of attention in the author's rights system.

3.18 Countries of the author's rights system use terms like *droit d'auteur, Urheberrecht, auteursrecht, diritto d'autore, derecho d'autor, Avtorskoe pravo,* all meaning 'author's right' rather than anything like 'copyright'. Not only the designation of laws, but also the language of the opening articles of copyright acts reveal the different focus on the copy or work in the copyright system and the author in the author's rights system. For example, the first article of the French Code of Intellectual Property reads: 'The author of a work of the mind enjoys an exclusive right . . . of intangible property in this work, on the basis of the mere fact of its creation'.[30] Similarly, other laws place 'the author' at the beginning of their respective introductory articles according to which the author enjoys protection or rights in his works.[31] By contrast, the UK CDPA starts by stating 'copyright is a property right which subsists . . . in the following descriptions of work . . .'.[32] Similarly, US law states that 'copyright protection subsists . . . in original works of authorship . . .'.[33] Accordingly, it seems that copyright countries' laws focus on the object rather than the creator, while laws of the author's rights system are primarily concerned about the author in his relation to the work.[34]

3.19 Since this book is in the English language, the term 'copyright' is generally used, while 'author's right' is mainly used in the specific context of laws of countries with the author's rights system.

C. Main differences between the copyright and the author's rights systems

(1) General remarks

(a) Description of systems in pure form

3.20 The following description of differences presents the typical elements of the copyright and the author's rights systems in their pure forms, in order to facilitate an understanding of the differences. As shown above, though, many contemporary laws no longer strictly follow only one of the systems. In particular, countries of the copyright system, most of which have adhered to the Berne Convention, the TRIPS Agreement, or the WCT have incorporated in their laws elements from

---

[30] Art L111-1 of the French Code of Intellectual Property.
[31] eg Art 1 of the German Copyright Act 1965.
[32] s 1 of the CDPA.
[33] s 102(a) of the US Copyright Act (Title 17 USC).
[34] Scholarly writing confirms this view; for an overview, see Strowel (n 20 above) 20–3.

these treaties that are part of the author's rights system. Vice versa, many countries of the author's rights system have integrated elements of the copyright system due to obligations under bilateral agreements, particularly with the USA.[35]

(b) General differences rooted in common law and civil law

A general difference between copyright acts under both systems is rooted in characteristics of legislation in common law versus civil law countries. Under common law, statutes are regularly considered as a merely secondary means with the task of specifying the principles established by case law; accordingly, they are interpreted restrictively. As a consequence, each and every detail must be spelled out in statutes; consequently, copyright acts of countries adhering to the copyright system are usually very long.[36] In part though, the length of such copyright acts in recent times may also be due to particular mechanisms of lobbying and the resulting influence by those who have individual circumstances in mind.   **3.21**

By contrast, legislation in the civil law tradition is principle-based and situated at a more abstract level, so that it can afford to be less detailed and shorter while easily offering solutions to a broad range of current and future problems. At the same time, judges might be more challenged by the need to interpret abstract terms in these laws. The tools for doing so, namely the methods of statutory interpretation, are therefore instrumental in civil law countries. Those educated in the civil law system are thus usually more at ease with treaty interpretation for which similar methods as under national law are used.   **3.22**

One of the symptoms for these fundamental differences is the typical absence of definitions in laws of the author's rights system[37] as opposed to usually long lists of definitions in laws of the copyright system.[38] Admittedly, definitions have also been widely introduced in the laws of ex-Soviet (and some Central and Eastern European) countries after 1991, although they adhere to the author's rights system; while this recent development is mainly due to influence by technical assistance offered by countries where definitions are common and by WIPO,[39] which has been using a non-official model law for these countries that contains   **3.23**

---

[35] paras 12.11, 12.32–12.35, 12.40, and 12.64 below.

[36] See, in particular, the UK CDPA; the US Copyright Act (Title 17 USC); the Irish Copyright Act 2000, and the Australian Copyright Amendment Act 2006 (no 158/2006), which alone was more than 200 pages long.

[37] Yet, these laws often contain a few, selected definitions directly in the context of the term to be defined, or also in a separate article, eg Arts 15(3) ('public') and 17(3) ('rental') of the German Copyright Act (1965, as amended), and Art 3 of the Croatian Copyright Act of 2003 ('public').

[38] See, eg, ss 172–8 and an index of defined expressions in s 179 of the UK CDPA; ss 2 and 202 of the Irish Copyright and Related Rights Act 2000; s 101 of Title 17 of the USC of more than six pages.

[39] S von Lewinski, 'Américanisation' in M Vivant, *Propriété intellectuelle et mondialisation: la propriété intellectuelle est-elle une marchandise?* (2004) 13, 20 f.

definitions, one may discern an even more recent development back to the roots of the original system, including the abolition of lists of definitions.[40] Definitions in these countries, however, might have been considered useful by those providing technical assistance especially where copyright acts during the socialist period were rarely subject to legal proceedings and experience with this field of law is lacking. Another symptom in particular of the difference between the litigation-oriented common law system and the civil law system with its methodical, systematic approach to law is the importance of the notion 'infringement' in the copyright law of common law countries. For example, the titles of sections 16 to 26 of the UK CDPA refer to 'infringement' when describing, in particular, the scope of rights granted; the major treatises on copyright law in copyright system countries include in their chapters on infringement the elements to establish a claim, such as ownership of a right, a protected work, or part of a work affected by an unauthorized act, etc. In countries of the civil law system, articles on infringement are mainly restricted to subjective conditions (such as knowledge or intent) for infringement and available remedies, while other aspects, such as authorship and the contents of rights, logically follow from the articles on these aspects.

3.24 Those who give legal advice to persons from countries of the other system, or those who have to interpret such foreign laws, should recall these fundamental differences of a generally restrictive interpretation of laws of the copyright system and a much more flexible, yet rule-oriented statutory interpretation of laws of the author's rights system.[41] For example, contrary to certain practices mainly in the framework of unilateral measures and negotiations of bilateral treaties, it is not necessary for the *demandeur* country to insist on the introduction of exact wording of provisions where the content of such provisions is clearly covered by the law, as interpreted in accordance with the particular (civil law) legal system; rather, such behaviour results in unwanted inconsistencies of the local system, leading to new interpretation problems.

---

[40] eg Art 4 of the Armenian Copyright Act of 8 December 1999, and the new Act of 15 June 2006, which does not contain a list of definitions; the situation is similar in Russia, where also the new copyright law (Civil Code, Part IV) of 18 December 2006 (Official Gazette no 289 (4255) of 22 December 2006) no longer contains such a list, which was contained in Art 4 of the preceding Copyright Act of 9 July 1993, as amended; see, however, the list of definitions in Art 4 of the Albanian Copyright Act of 28 April 2005; by contrast, the Croatian Copyright Act no 173/2003, in force from 30 October 2003 (Official Gazette 167/2003) as amended in 2007, does not include a list of definitions.

[41] On these fundamental differences and more reflections thereof, see also Strowel (n 20 above) 147–9; for British law in context with transformed international law, see W Cornish and D Llewelyn, *Intellectual Property: Patents, Copyright, Trade Marks and Allied Rights* (5th edn, 2003) 1-25, also referring to tendencies towards taking into account other methods than only literal interpretation.

(2) Genesis of protection

(a) *Formalities*

(i) **Author's rights system**   In countries of the author's rights system, works are **3.25** protected by the mere fact of creation; no formality needs to be fulfilled in order to obtain protection. This is nicely expressed, for example, in Article L111-1(1) of the French Intellectual Property Code according to which 'the author of a work of the mind enjoys an exclusive right . . . of intangible property in this work *on the basis of the mere fact of its creation*'. Similarly, under Article 9(2) of the Croatian Copyright Act, 'The author's right in a work belongs to its author by the mere act of creation of the work.' The absence of formalities as a condition for protection reflects the natural law philosophy according to which the author obtains property in his work as a natural consequence of creating the work by his own mind; thereby, the author is no longer dependent on any state action such as the medieval grant of privileges by a sovereign. Rather, this natural property guarantees him freedom from the state or any sovereign. Where countries of the author's rights system require the deposit of publications with a central library or other institution, as they usually do, such obligations are of a public law nature and have no relation to author's rights.

(ii) **Copyright system**   In the copyright system, the requirement of formalities **3.26** corresponds to that system's focus on the interests of the society, because it leads to the absence of protection where the authors do not make intentional efforts to achieve protection by fulfilling the formalities, and because it enhances legal security by establishing at least a prima facie evidence in respect of different aspects of protection of a work. Already under the early laws of England and the USA, formalities, such as registration with the Stationers' Company or the copyright notice, were a constitutive requirement for copyright protection. England modified the requirement in its 1842 Copyright Act from a mandatory, constitutive requirement to a requirement for infringement actions only; after the Berlin Revision of the Berne Convention in 1908 prohibited formalities, it completely abolished any formalities from its Copyright Act 1911 and established the 'no formalities' principle.[42] The 1911 Act also governed the situation in most of His Majesty's dominions and territories, such as Canada, Australia, and African territories like the Northern and Southern Nigeria Protectorates.[43]

---

[42] On this principle, see paras 5.54–5.61 below.

[43] Arts 25–8 of the 1911 Copyright Act, see *Copinger and Skone James on Copyright* (13th edn, 1991) 17–122 ff. For Nigeria, see J Asein, *Nigerian Copyright Law & Practice* (2004) 28–9; the 1911 Act was repealed in Nigeria only by the Copyright Act 1970.

3.27   The USA deleted the constitutive requirement of a copyright notice only upon its adherence to the Berne Convention in 1989, and this initially just in favour of foreign works, as required by the Berne Convention.[44] Today, countries of the copyright system usually no longer require any formalities for the enjoyment of copyright, in particular due to the influence of the Berne Convention.

3.28   (iii) **Voluntary fulfilment of formalities**   Many countries of the copyright system have maintained the possibility for authors voluntarily to fulfil formalities, such as registration, particularly to gain prima facie evidence or to claim statutory damages.[45] The continuance of formalities in a non-mandatory form in countries of the copyright system is reflected in the existence of copyright offices, while such offices usually do not exist in countries of the author's rights system, with the exception mainly of former Soviet countries, where, however, the main tasks of copyright offices are of a political, norm-setting nature.

3.29   Recently, non-mandatory registration has raised interest as an option in particular in the digital environment; yet, the advantages and disadvantages of this option still need to be analysed in depth.[46]

(b) Fixation

3.30   (i) **Author's rights system**   Unlike for formalities, the Berne Convention allows Union countries to require fixation of the work in some material form as a condition for protection.[47] Author's rights system countries do not require fixation, so that works expressed without prior fixation are protected from the moment of expression, for example by improvisation of music, dance, or speeches. Consequently, anyone who records, otherwise fixes, or communicates such improvisation infringes the author's right, if done without his authorization. This is again in line with the natural law philosophy, under which rights in a work automatically exist once a work is created and expressed in whatever form.

3.31   (ii) **Copyright system**   In contrast, fixation is regularly required in countries of the copyright system.[48] Authors who improvise works typically can be protected only by contract, or indirectly, namely as performers who enjoy a fixation

---

[44] On the amendments in detail see W Patry, *Patry on Copyright* (2007) § 6:75–6:77; also § 23:21 fn 5 regarding s 411(a) Title 17 USC.

[45] eg s 39 Copyright Act of 17 May 2005 of Ghana; ss 408 ff Title 17 USC; on the situation in the USA, see in detail Strowel (n 20 above) 299–309, also on the situation under the 1909 and 1976 Copyright Acts.

[46] In particular, WIPO has offered this topic for discussion and published a questionnaire with answers by some Member States, para 22.13 below and WIPO Doc SCCR/13/2 of 9 November 2005; see also para 5.61 below.

[47] Art 2(2) of the Berne Convention; paras 5.71–5.73 below.

[48] eg s 3(2), (3) UK CDPA; s 102(a) Title 17 USC: s 1(2)(b) Copyright Act 2005 of Ghana.

right.[49] In the USA, authors may be protected for their improvisations under common law.[50] The question whether the person who expresses a work or who first fixes it is recognized as the author has been regularly answered in favour of the person who expresses the work.[51] The fixation requirement is usually seen as a corollary of the expression–idea dichotomy under the assumption that expression can only occur in a permanent form, namely through fixation. Yet, as the real and quite common example of improvisations shows, expression in fact does not necessitate fixation.

(3) Protected works

(a) Author's rights system

The laws under the author's rights system often describe protected works in sim- **3.32** ple words such as 'personal intellectual creations' or 'works of the mind whatever may be the kind, form of expression, merit, or destination'.[52] While these abstract words usually have been specified in detail through case law and doctrine, they all reflect the natural law thought that a work is a creation by the human mind,[53] and they are understood to require an element of subjective novelty or creativity. Case law has required different levels of creativity for a work to be protected, such as the imprint of the personality or a certain degree of individuality. Although a detailed, comparative analysis of the required level of creativity in author's rights countries is beyond the scope of this book,[54] suffice it to say that the level of creativity or individuality required for protection in author's rights countries is higher than that in copyright countries. Consequently, fewer works are protected.

(b) Copyright system

Laws of the copyright system countries usually do not mention the 'creation' or **3.33** personal, intellectual activity but simply describe the protected work as 'original'.[55] The term 'original' is differently interpreted in the individual copyright

---

[49] Cornish/Llewelyn (n 41 above) 10-33; for the fixation right of performers, see Art 7(1) of the Rome Convention, Art 14(1) of the TRIPS Agreement, and Art 6(i) of the WPPT, and paras 6.39, 10.91, and 17.125 below.

[50] M Leaffer, *Understanding Copyright Law* (4th edn, 2005) § 2.06.

[51] For the UK, see Cornish/Llewelyn (n 41 above) 10-34; s 101 Title 17 USC defines the work as 'fixed' by requiring that fixation occur 'by or under the authority of the author'; consequently, a non-authorized recording of an improvisation by a third person does not make the pirate the author of the improvisation.

[52] Art 2(2) of the German Copyright Act, and Art L112-1(1) of the French Intellectual Property Code.

[53] For an exception to this principle, ie the concept of 'collective works', see para 3.37 below.

[54] For a comparison of French, Belgian, and German law as opposed to US and UK law, see Strowel (n 20 above) 401–80.

[55] eg s 1(1)(a) UK CDPA; s 102(a) Title 17 USC; s 1(2)(a) Copyright Act 2005 of Ghana.

system countries. Mostly, the very low level of originality under British law applies, ie that what is not copied is original. 'Original' in this sense simply means that the work must originate from the author, from his skill, labour, and judgment. Logically, this precondition allows for the protection of anyone who invests in labour and capital in order to produce a work. As a consequence, many works that are protected under the copyright system do not reach the necessary level of creativity under the author's right system and remain unprotected there.[56]

3.34 This very low level of originality was not followed in the famous *Feist* case of the US Supreme Court in 1991.[57] In that decision, the Supreme Court did not consider the 'sweat of the brow' as sufficient to protect a compilation of addresses in a telephone book, but required at least a 'modicum' of originality; yet, the Court failed to see any trace of even the smallest level of creativity.[58] This important decision has been followed not only by lower courts in the USA but also by the Canadian Supreme Court regarding a similar work; namely a Yellow Pages Directory.[59] In contrast, the Australian Federal Court did not follow *Feist* but continued to apply the British approach.[60]

(c) Phonograms and similar objects of protection

3.35 From this comparison it logically follows that certain kinds of products cannot be protected as works under the author's rights system while they are protected under the copyright system, namely phonograms, broadcasts, and the like industrial products. Under the author's rights system, a work must be a creation of the mind and reach a certain level of creativity—these conditions are not fulfilled where the activity is mainly an industrial, investment-related one. In order to nevertheless protect such products that were considered valuable and in need of protection, author's rights countries developed the notion of 'neighbouring rights'.[61]

3.36 By contrast, originality of works under the copyright system is regularly fulfilled, if the product originates from the author, so that investment in labour and capital is usually sufficient for protection. Accordingly, there is no obstacle to protect phonograms and broadcasts as works. The United Kingdom, though, has differentiated between entrepreneurial copyrights for which originality is not required and the 'classical' copyright in literary and artistic works in the meaning of the

---

[56] Cornish/Llewlyn (n 41 above) 10-08–10-10.
[57] *Feist Publications v Rural Telephone* 499 US 340, 111 S Ct 1282 (1991); D Gervais, 'Feist Goes Global: A Comparative Analysis of the Notion of Originality in Copyright Law' (2002) 49 J Copyright Soc USA 949, 951; Strowel (n 20 above) 448–50.
[58] ibid 449.
[59] *Tele-Direct Publications v American Business Information* (1997) 76 CPR (3d) 296 (FC).
[60] *Desktop Marketing Systems v Telstra* (2002) 119 FCR 491.
[61] paras 3.39 and 3.68 below.

Berne Convention that require originality.[62] Since copyright in these products protects investments, it has been considered as a disguised neighbouring right.[63] In countries of the copyright system, such entrepreneurial copyrights may enjoy lesser protection than 'classical' copyrights.

(4) Authorship

(a) Author's rights system

Not surprisingly, the principle under the author's rights system is that only a nat- **3.37** ural person rather than a legal person or corporation can be an author, since a natural person alone has a mind and is capable of intellectual creation. In addition, only the natural person who created the work rather than, for example, a person who commissioned the work can be an author. This principle corresponds to the personalist concept of author's rights and may be considered as an immediate consequence of natural law philosophy, as nicely expressed, for example, in the Croatian Copyright Act: 'The author's right shall belong, *by its nature*, to a natural person who has created a work.'[64] It is in line with the concept of a work as a personal, intellectual creation. This principle is usually stated in clear and simple words, such as: 'The author is the creator of the work,'[65] or 'The author of the work is a natural person who has created the work.'[66] Admittedly, some countries of the author's rights system also recognize an exception from this principle in the concept of 'collective work' where the promoter of a collective project enjoys the copyright in the product, even if he is a legal person and does not make a creative contribution.[67] Yet, this concept is often considered alien to the author's rights system and is quite restricted in its application.[68]

As a consequence of this principle, authorship logically vests in anyone who is the **3.38** actual creator, including, for example, an employed author, a film director and any other creative contributors to a film, an assistant to a professor, and a ghost writer. If an employer, film producer, or other party that did not create the work needs rights from such authors, he has to acquire them on the basis of a contract.

---

[62] Ss 3 and 4 UK CDPA for 'classical' works and ss 5–8 for phonograms, films, broadcasts or cable programs, and typographical arrangements of published works, for which no originality is required; see also s 1(1)(a) versus (b) and (c).

[63] Cornish/Llewelyn (n 41 above) 10-29; on all entrepreneurial copyrights ibid, 10-26–10-31; on the concept of neighbouring rights, see paras 3.39 and 3.68 below.

[64] Art 2(1) of the Act of 8 December 2003; emphasis added.

[65] Art 7 of the German Copyright Act.

[66] Art 9(1) of the Croatian Copyright Act of 2003.

[67] eg Art L113-2(3) French Intellectual Property Code for the definition of collective work under French law. After 1991, many Eastern and Central European as well as ex-Soviet countries introduced this concept, since they mostly followed a WIPO model law for countries in transition.

[68] For a critical appreciation and call for restrictive interpretation of the French provision, see Lucas/Lucas (n 15 above) 170–80, in particular 175–7 and n 219.

In certain cases, the law supports the employer or film producer by presuming that such a contract, if not drafted clearly, brings about the assignment of all or at least some specified rights to the employer or film producer; yet, such presumption usually can be rebutted.

3.39 A second consequence of this principle—authorship of creators only—is the exclusion of all others who only perform achievements in context with creations rather than create by themselves. In particular, performers who only perform existing works are not authors in the author's rights system. The same applies to different investors, such as phonogram producers, film producers, and broadcasting organizations, which help works become available to the public; their main activities are the organization of productions or broadcasts, including the rental of recording studios and hiring of staff or the conclusion of contracts with artists; the investment in technical facilities; and financial investment. These activities are not creative. Since they are, however, generally considered important for the dissemination of works, laws under the author's rights system usually protect them as so-called neighbouring rights or related rights—literally, rights that are 'neighbours of' or 'related to' author's rights. This concept allows author's rights countries to vest protection in legal persons without distorting the system of protection; protection for neighbouring rights is usually more restricted than author's rights protection.[69]

3.40 A third consequence of the principle relates to terminology: laws of the author's rights system only use the term 'author' and thereby automatically cover any successor in title. Where an author enjoys a right under the law, it logically follows that this right vests in a successor in title where a valid succession has occurred; no mention of the successor in title is needed in the text of the law. The same approach is taken by the Berne Convention, which clarifies that the protection of the Convention applies to authors and successors in title,[70] but otherwise only uses the term 'author'. Therefore, and because no other right owner than the author or his successor in title are protected under the author's rights system, laws under this system do not use terms such as 'or other right owner' or just 'right owner'.

(b) Copyright system

3.41 Since countries of the copyright system protect works that may be the simple result of investment and labour, there is no obstacle to vesting copyright not only in those natural persons who create a work but also in others, including legal persons that make investments in context with works. For example, in accordance with their stronger orientation towards industry rather than towards the creator,

---

[69] On neighbouring rights, see para 3.68 below.
[70] Art 2(6) of the Berne Convention.

laws under the copyright system usually provide that the economic rights of a work shall in principle vest in the employer or even commissioner of a work, subject to further conditions;[71] a notable exception is the Nigerian Copyright Act which attributes first ownership of copyright in the employee or author who has been commissioned, unless otherwise stipulated in a written contract.[72] In respect of makers of sound recordings and of similar objects, many laws simply designate such makers as 'authors'; however, the UK CDPA distinguishes between the author who creates a work and a person taken to be the author, who makes the necessary arrangements for a sound recording or similar object.[73] Accordingly, the title of the relevant provision distinguishes between the terms 'authorship' and 'ownership' of copyright.[74]

Copyright system countries do not need the concept of neighbouring rights **3.42** because their concept of copyright also allows them to cover legal persons that invest in phonograms and the like products; yet, performers usually are not recognized as authors or first owners of copyright in these countries, but instead are afforded separate protection.[75]

In respect of terminology, laws of the copyright system often use terms such as **3.43** 'right owner', 'first right owner', or 'right holder'; this use may reflect the attitude that protection does not primarily envisage the author, but mainly the object of protection irrespective of who is the right owner, whether a natural or legal person. At the international level, an influence of the copyright system is notable in the TRIPS Agreement, where the rental right is provided for the 'authors and successors in title'—a specification not considered necessary under laws of the author's rights system—and where the legitimate interests of the 'right holder' (rather than author) are referred to.[76] By contrast, the WCT is consistent with the

---

71 eg the famous 'work-made-for-hire' theory set out in ss 101 and 201(b) Title 17 USC s 11(2) UK CDPA, which describes the employer as the 'first owner of any copyright in the work'; s 7 Copyright Act 2005 of Ghana, where the economic rights are vested directly in an employer or person who commissions the work.

72 S 9(2) of the Nigerian Copyright Act 1988 as amended; see also J Asein, 'Redefinition of First Ownership under Nigerian Copyright Law: Lessons from Inchoate Mutation' (2007) 38/3 IIC 299 ff.

73 S 9(1) versus (2) and (3) UK CDPA.

74 By contrast, the corresponding terms under the author's rights system are the 'author' and the 'neighbouring rights holder', or 'authorship' and 'ownership of a neighbouring right'.

75 eg Part II of the UK CDPA, which follows Part I on copyright and precedes Part III on the design right; while this performer's right may be considered as a form of neighbouring right (Cornish/Llewelyn (n 41 above) 13-32), it was originally protected under a separate act, namely the Musical Performers' Protection Act 1925, followed by the Performers' Protection Acts 1958–1972. For the USA, see s 1101 Title 17 USC—although it is based on the Commerce Clause rather than the Copyright Clause, it was included in the Copyright Act for administrative convenience, see W Patry, *Copyright and the GATT: An Interpretation and Legislative History of the Uruguay Round Agreements Act* (1995) 10. For Australia, see Part XIA of the Copyright Act 1968, as amended.

76 Arts 11 and 13 of the TRIPS Agreement.

Berne Convention, which both more closely follows the author's rights system and uses the term 'authors'.

(5) Rights

(a) Moral rights

3.44 **(i) General background and current importance** Moral rights were first developed by French case law during the nineteenth century, when personalist doctrines influenced the emerging author's rights system.[77] Irrespective of different theories of moral rights, the essential idea underlying these rights is to protect the author beyond his mere economic interests namely, in his intellectual, artistic, and similar non-economic interests. This holistic view of the relation between the author and his work is reflected, for example, in the French law under which the author's right 'includes attributes of an intellectual and moral nature and also attributes of an economic nature',[78] and in the German law according to which the author is protected 'in his intellectual and personal relationship with his work, and also in respect of the utilisation of the work'.[79]

3.45 Accordingly, moral rights do not refer to issues of morality but simply to the non-economic, intellectual, and artistic interests of the author in the work. This approach fully corresponds to the focus of the author's rights system on the individual creator who is not just perceived as someone who produces goods that can be exploited on the market, but as a human being working in the delicate and personality-focused area of cultural creation.

3.46 Those who might suggest that moral rights would be an outdated, romantic idea of the nineteenth century[80] are disproved by the abundant case law and disputes settled out of court in author's rights countries. For example, before legal proceedings were necessary, the 1972 Olympic stadium in Munich was 'rescued' from a planned, distorting transformation into a soccer stadium; as a consequence, a new stadium was constructed for the 2006 World Soccer Championships.

---

[77] O von Gierke and J Kohler are mentioned as the leading representatives of the personalist doctrine who analysed the moral rights from a legal rather than philosophical point of view; I Kant developed the idea that the author's right remains attached to the person who is the intellectual creator and influenced in particular A Morillot, who is seen as the creator of the theory of moral rights and a personalist author's right in France, see Strowel (n 20 above) 491–2, 516–21; on early case law in both France and Germany ibid 482–9 and 522–7; on early French law also Lucas/Lucas (n 15 above) 12–13.

[78] Art L111-1(2) of the French Intellectual Property Code.

[79] Art 11 of the German Copyright Act 1965.

[80] The increased focus of attention mainly in academic writing on the economic importance of copyright and on the impact of digital technology, together with (mostly US) cliché arguments on the 'romantic author' may have (mis)led to such suggestions.

Other noteworthy cases include the pending dispute between the architect of the spectacular, new central station in Berlin against German Railways, and a decision of a Swedish appeal court holding that the insertion of commercial breaks in certain movies on television was a violation of moral rights of the film directors because the continuity and dramaturgy of his films were interrupted and the transition from one to the next scene was lost. In another noteworthy case, the Hungarian composer G Ligeti was offended when film director Stanley Kubrick incorporated three of his compositions into the soundtrack of the movie *2001: A Space Odyssey* in 1968—particularly because his music was placed close to works by Johannes Strauss II and Richard Strauss.[81]

(ii) **The three basic rights** Most author's rights countries provide, in different **3.47** variations, at least for the following three moral rights: the right of divulgation; the right of authorship or paternity; and the right of integrity of the work. The right of divulgation allows the author to determine whether his work should be published at all, and if so, under what circumstances—for example, at what point of time; in which country, city, and even particular theatre or other location; and by which publishing house or record company. Such decisions may be essential for the first impression of the work with the public and thus for its subsequent chances for success. In principle, such decisions are part of the author's prerogative and irrespective of public views or interests. For example, where the public might be interested in reading unpublished works by a famous author who himself, however, did not consider them worth publishing (as was the case for Kafka), the divulgation right gives priority to the author's decision.

The right of authorship or paternity, which is recognized in the Berne Convention, **3.48** includes the right of the author to claim that his own name or a pseudonym be used in connection with his work, or that he remain anonymous. While this right may have important economic consequences for the author, it primarily aims at protecting the author in his desire to be (or not to be) publicly identified with his work, so that the intellectual relationship between him and his work is (or is not) visible.[82]

The right of integrity, also covered by the Berne Convention, likewise protects **3.49** the author's intellectual and artistic decisions regarding his work, irrespective of any preferences or tastes of the general public and the potential on the market; nevertheless, many laws allow for some form of balancing of the different interests involved, mainly in the fields of film production and architecture, where major economic interests of film producers and commissioners of buildings are involved.

---

[81] Anon, work description 'Lontano', New York Philharmonic Concert Program (October 2006) at 34.
[82] For more, see paras 5.98–5.99 below.

The integrity right covers the distortion of the work itself and any derogatory action that indirectly affects rather than modifies the work, for example where it is presented in a context that changes its impression. Some countries require (in line with the minimum standard of the Berne Convention) that any modifications are prejudicial to the author's honour or reputation, while in other countries, this is not even necessary for a violation of the integrity right.[83]

3.50 The question whether the integrity right also covers protection against destruction is differently answered in different countries; often, destruction is regarded as not affecting the author's interest in the integrity of the work, because a destroyed work can no longer generate any impression to which the author would not like to be connected.[84]

3.51 **(iii) Additional moral rights and reflections thereof under national laws** Beyond these three principal moral rights, many laws (mainly of author's rights countries) also provide for the right of withdrawal of economic rights for change of conviction or for lack of exercise by a licensee. Where, for example, an author has changed his opinion and no longer wants to be confronted with his earlier work, he can withdraw the publication rights from the publisher (subject to payment of damages, as the case may be) in order to prevent his work being published anew.[85] The right to withdraw licences where the publisher does not exercise the publication right corresponds to the personal interest of the author to see his work made accessible to the public. Where a publisher has obtained an exclusive right from the author, the publisher could otherwise prevent any publication even by other publishers, and thereby act like a censor.[86]

3.52 Finally, many additional provisions in copyright laws of author's rights countries reflect the aim of protecting intellectual and personal interests of the author, even if they do not refer to 'moral rights'. Examples are provisions on contracts, such as the legal impossibility to assign rights in yet unknown uses, the requirement for the author to give his consent to a subsequent transfer of an assigned right, and the right of the author to have access to the original or a copy of his work in order to make a copy for himself.[87]

---

[83] For more detail in context with the Berne Convention, see paras 5.100–5.104 below.

[84] For German law, see references in Adeney (n 14 above) 9.97 (n 198); for Dutch case law, see Dutch Supreme Court (Hoge Raad) no C02/282HR of 6 February 2004, *Jelles v Municipality of Zwolle* (reasoning mainly on the basis of the wording and intent of the legislator to implement Art 6bis of the Berne Convention without going beyond its scope), <http://www.rechtspraak.nl/ljn.asp?ljn=AN7830> and (2004) EIPR N-155 (annotation by J Krikke).

[85] eg Art 42 of the German Copyright Act.

[86] eg Art 41 ibid. Also this right is subject to a number of conditions and, potentially, to payment of damages.

[87] For these and additional reflections of such protection of moral rights in a broader sense under German law, eg A Dietz, in G Schricker (ed), *Urheberrecht* (3rd edn, 2006) vor §§ 12 ff nn 8–10.

(iv) Duration and transfer of moral rights   Many countries (essentially, but **3.53** not necessarily those of the author's rights system) provide that moral rights have an unlimited duration rather than the same duration as economic rights.[88] Likewise, moral rights in many (mainly author's rights system) countries are inalienable, non-waivable, imprescriptible, and non-transferable, because they are conceived as inherently linked to the personality of the author. These characteristics render moral rights very strong and they often make them the last resort for an author, especially if he has transferred (where possible) all economic rights. Where an author has an interest in not exercising his moral rights, for example because of the financial gain to be made as a ghost writer, pragmatic solutions have been found in these countries, such as a contractual obligation not to exercise the right of authorship; this solution is different from a waiver (which is generally not possible in author's rights countries) because the author retains his moral right and can still exercise it, even if he would thereby breach the contract.[89]

(v) Moral rights in countries of the copyright system[90]   In the copyright sys- **3.54** tem, which focuses on the protection of the work for the benefit of the general public rather than on the author, the concept of moral rights always has been alien. Even if today most countries of the copyright system have integrated moral rights into their laws in order to implement international obligations under the Berne Convention and the WCT, moral rights still seem to be perceived as an imposed element of protection, which does not have a place in the philosophy of the copyright system; moral rights are often looked upon with astonishment or even regarded as an evil that hinders unrestricted exploitation of works as merchandise by film producers and other businesses, or as an undue, indirect restriction of freedom of contract, namely a restriction over freely negotiated assignments of economic rights.[91] Respect of author's choices seems to have less value in the copyright system than the best possible, easiest commercialization. Not surprisingly, moral rights, where provided in copyright system countries as statutory rights, are usually waivable or transferable. The general attitude towards moral rights in these countries generally remains sceptical.[92]

Long before countries of the copyright system introduced (if at all) statutory **3.55** moral rights, many of them covered certain aspects of moral rights by different legal instruments, such as under common law, rules of unfair competition,

---

[88] eg Art L121-1 of the French Intellectual Property Code.

[89] eg Adeney (n 14 above) 8.148 ff for France, 9.178 ff for Germany.

[90] For a detailed analysis regarding Canada, the UK, and the USA, ibid 10.01 ff for an introduction, and 11.01 ff, 13.01 ff, and 15.01 ff.

[91] For this aspect, see Cornish/Llewelyn (n 41 above) 12-02.

[92] eg ibid 11-89; Adeney (n 14 above) 10.07, 16.03–04, 17.01–02.

defamation, or contract interpretation.[93] Since copyright under the copyright system is only a property right,[94] it cannot possibly cover aspects of moral rights that are therefore clearly separated from provisions on copyright protection. The typical placement of moral rights in copyright acts in these countries may be seen to reveal the level of importance acknowledged to moral rights: mostly, they only appear (if at all) after provisions on protected works, authorship, duration of copyright, economic rights, secondary infringement, and limitations and exceptions ('acts permitted').[95] By contrast, moral rights in author's rights countries are often mentioned at the beginning of the copyright acts and, in addition, mostly appear before provisions on the economic rights, only following the fundamental questions on works and authorship.[96]

(b) Economic rights

3.56 **(i) Exclusive rights: broad versus specific rights** As regards economic rights, the differences between both systems seem less pronounced. Existing differences in defining rights usually do not follow the distinction between both systems of protection; for example, sale and other transfer of ownership is covered in some countries by a 'distribution right' (eg Germany), in others by a 'right to issue copies to the public' (eg the UK), a *droit de destination* developed on the basis of the reproduction right (eg France), or other rights, and may or may not include rental and other transfer of possession; also the term 'communication to the public' is used in different ways, irrespective of the system of protection. As regards the nature of rights, exclusive rights are the classical and still basic form of protection in both systems. A difference in principle between both systems though can be ascertained as regards the scope of rights: many laws of the author's rights system provide for a broad right of exploitation in material and non-material form, specified by examples. For instance, French law provides for the basic rights of *représentation* (exploitation in immaterial form) and of *reproduction* (exploitation in material form).[97] Both terms are then very broadly defined and specified by examples, such as public performance and broadcasting for the right of *représentation*.[98] Similarly, the broad right of exploitation in material form under German law covers 'in particular' the rights of reproduction, distribution, and

---

[93] For the UK, Cornish/Llewelyn (n 41 above) 11-66–11-89; for the USA and the UK, Strowel (n 20 above) 538–82.

[94] eg s 1(1) of the UK CDPA.

[95] eg UK CDPA 1988 (ch IV on moral rights); Irish Copyright Act of 2004 (ch 7 on moral rights); in Australia (1968 Copyright Act, as amended), they even appear much later (Part IX), only before miscellaneous and transitional provisions and performers' protection.

[96] eg Art L 111(1), Art L121-1 ff of the French Intellectual Property Code (on moral rights); Arts 11 and 12–14 of the German Copyright Act.

[97] Art L122-1 of the French Intellectual Property Code.

[98] Arts L122-2 and 122-3 ibid for both rights respectively.

exhibition, while the broad right of communication to the public is specified by five examples, such as the broadcasting right.[99]

This approach corresponds to the natural law concept of author's rights, accord- **3.57** ing to which, as a matter of principle, the author enjoys a right to fully control the work's exploitation, irrespective of the way of exploitation. It logically follows that any newly emerging ways of exploitation, such as digital uses, are automatic- ally covered by the existing protection, if such uses are within the very broad scope of the basic rights of exploitation in material and non-material form; accord- ingly, legislative amendments to adapt the rights to new technical developments are often unnecessary. This principle also means that the explicit recognition of a new right, such as the right of making available works on the internet, usually does not represent an extension of rights, but simply corresponds to the principle that the author enjoys an exclusive right in the material and non-material exploit- ation of his work.

This principle is not part of the copyright system, under which the granted exclu- **3.58** sive rights are comprehensively listed and precisely defined.[100] As a consequence, any newly appearing kind of use not covered by the comprehensive list usually requires an act by the legislator to explicitly amend the law. This approach corres- ponds to the underlying thought that copyright is granted by the state rather than being a natural consequence of creation. Accordingly, the state must seriously consider and separately limit the scope of copyright protection for each kind of use—all the more where legislators must take account of the utility of copyright for the general public, such as under US law.

(ii) Statutory remuneration rights   Statutory remuneration rights are much **3.59** more frequent in countries of the author's rights system than of the copyright sys- tem.[101] They may be self-standing, such as the resale right (*droit de suite*) and public lending right, or provided in context with restrictions of rights. They mostly benefit authors as opposed to publishers or similar entrepreneurs. For example, the resale right—a right to remuneration for the commercial reselling of artworks in galleries or auction houses[102]—usually cannot be waived, and therefore directly benefits the author rather than a publisher or other business. Similarly, authors usually receive a considerable percentage, if not all revenues,

---

99   Art 15(1), (2) of the German Copyright Act. Similarly, the Croatian Copyright Act of 2003 provides two separate articles on exclusive rights of exploitation in material and non-material form, both of which explicitly include a mere list of examples, see Arts 18 and 21 and the detailed explana- tion of the individual rights in Arts 19, 20, 22–3.

100   eg s 16 of the UK CDPA 1988; s 37 of the Irish Copyright Act 2000, s 106 Title 17 USC.

101   Note, however, that author's rights countries with a particularly strong author's rights tradi- tion, such as France, may not have many of such remuneration rights.

102   See also on Art 14[ter] of the Berne Convention, in the context of reciprocity, para 5.48 below.

from public lending right—a remuneration right for the lending of literary and artistic works in public libraries.[103]

3.60　An eminent example for remuneration rights provided for in context with limitations is the statutory remuneration right for private reproduction. It is often called 'private copy levy'—a misleading term that hides the justification of the right, namely the compensation of the author for an important use, and suggests that the payment of the remuneration would be a tax.[104] Many countries (mainly of the author's rights system) provide a limitation of the exclusive reproduction right for private reproduction; at the same time, in order to compensate the author for the important, thereby legal use, they offer a statutory remuneration right for private reproduction to be paid by manufacturers, sellers, or operators of copying devices or blank copying media. The remuneration is usually collected by collective management organizations that represent authors and often also publishers. Such remuneration rights often benefit right holders better than exclusive rights, which in practice can hardly be enforced, unless effective technical protection measures are employed. In addition, through the system of collective management organizations, authors *versus* entrepreneurs may best benefit from a remuneration right administered by a collective management organization, because there they usually have a stronger position to assert their adequate share in the remuneration than if they had an exclusive right, assigned under an individual contract with the entrepreneur.

3.61　Other examples include statutory remuneration rights for authors in context with limitations for the use by disabled persons or the use of works for school books.[105] These remuneration rights seem of special benefit to the individual author, in line with the focus of the author's rights system.

(6) Exceptions and limitations

(a) Author's rights system

3.62　In principle, protection under the author's rights system leaves a rather narrow scope of limitations and exceptions that is usually subject to restrictive interpretation, while the utilitarian approach of the copyright system seems to leave more room for limitations and exceptions. This scenario seems to correspond to the respective ideas underlying both systems—the focus on author's protection versus the well-being of society. In fact, one may recognize such tendencies in many laws. For example, the French copyright law was bare of any compulsory

---

[103] On this right, see eg S von Lewinski, 'Public Lending Right: General and Comparative Survey of Existing Systems in Law and Practise' (1992) 154 RIDA 3 ff.

[104] For criticism of this term, see S von Lewinski, 'Stakeholder Consultation on Copyright Levies in a Converging World' (2007) IIC 65 (nn 1, 2).

[105] eg Arts 49(1), 52(1), 52a(4) of the German Copyright Act.

licence until 1985, and until recently included just one article with four short paragraphs on limitations and exceptions.[106] Admittedly, many other author's rights countries provide for more limitations and exceptions; yet, as a matter of principle, they are still usually precisely defined and subject to restrictive interpretation.[107] Especially in respect of limitations and exceptions, the differences among countries of the author's rights system are somewhat bigger than for other elements of protection. In Europe, countries such as France and southern countries show a tendency towards fewer limitations and exceptions as compared with countries towards the north, such as Germany, the Netherlands, and in particular Scandinavian countries where the interests of the general public are strongly taken into account.

(b) Copyright system

At least some countries of the copyright system incorporate broader concepts to restrict rights, such as 'fair dealing' and, in particular, 'fair use' in the USA, which leaves judges more flexibility in taking account of the needs of the general public. Yet, it is notable that Australia has recently discussed but rejected the idea to introduce 'fair use' provisions according to the US model, not least due to problems of legal certainty.[108] Also, limitations in these countries may be quite specific and restrictive, such as in UK law. Differences regarding limitations and exceptions among countries of the copyright system and even between laws of the different systems seem not to follow clear-cut categories. **3.63**

(7) Duration of protection

Before the Berne Convention (which is based on the author's rights system) influenced national laws of the world, early laws under the copyright system protected works from publication only—hence, from the moment the work became useful to the public and protection was needed to recoup investments.[109] In addition, short terms of protection could be extended by renewal upon certain conditions. In particular, the Statute of Anne provided for a duration of fourteen years after publication; thereafter, protection could be renewed for another fourteen years, if the author was still alive at the expiry of the first fourteen years; in 1814, the **3.64**

---

106 Art L122-5; Art L122-6 was introduced in order to implement the EC Computer Software Directive, and several additional limitations in Art L122-5 to implement the EC Information Society Directive.

107 eg for Germany, S von Lewinski, 'News from Germany: Developements in Germany from mid-1997 to Spring 2005' (2005) 206 RIDA 235, 247 ff on recent case law confirming this principle, even if some authors seem to recognize a deviation from this principle.

108 For a discussion, see Australian Copyright Council, *Fair Use: Issues & Perspectives: A Discussion Paper* (2006).

109 On the Statute of Anne in England and the American law before the Copyright Act 1976, see Strowel (n 20 above) 608–9 and 615.

statutory duration was prolonged to an initial term of twenty-eight years after publication and, if the author was still alive at this time, until the end of his life.[110]

3.65 Similarly, the American Copyright Act of 1790 provided for an initial term of fourteen years after fulfilment of formalities, and if the author was alive at this time, a renewal for another fourteen years. Later, this duration was extended to twenty-eight years plus renewal for fourteen years under certain conditions, and later also the renewal period was extended to twenty-eight years after publication.[111] The termination right under Section 203 of the US Copyright Act 1976, which was a non-transferable right of the author to terminate a licence contract after twenty-five years, replaced the system of renewal for duration and took over the idea that the author should have another chance after a certain period of time to own the rights himself.[112]

3.66 The protection from publication and for a short, renewable period of time reflected the focus of the copyright system on the utility of the work's protection for society. With this focus the author should not enjoy a right for longer than necessary to fulfil the purpose of copyright protection, namely, to stimulate creation as well as public benefits.

3.67 By contrast, the author under the author's rights system is protected from creation until a long time after his death—fifty years *pma* were in principle already provided under the 1908 Berlin Revision Act of the Berne Convention. The approach of protecting the work from its creation reflects the natural law philosophy underlying the author's rights system and has always been applied within this system. The longer duration also reflects the stronger focus on the author and the non-utilitarian justification for protection, as compared to the copyright system.[113] Today, these differences are largely eliminated, due to the influence of relevant international law.

(8) Neighbouring rights

3.68 Since author's rights do not protect anything other than creations of a human mind, certain products that have been considered valuable enough to merit protection are excluded from author's rights protection. The purpose of neighbouring rights is to serve the protection needs of such products. Since the concept of

---

[110] ibid 608–9.

[111] ibid 615–16.

[112] ibid 619.

[113] For the background of duration under both systems, see S Ricketson and J Ginsburg, *International Copyright and Neighbouring Rights: The Berne Convention and Beyond* (2006) 9.09, 9.10.

neighbouring rights is not rooted in the natural law philosophy, protection is usually more limited than that of author's rights. While authors in principle enjoy a broad right of exploitation for their works so as easily to cover future kinds of exploitation, neighbouring rights owners are only granted specified rights, which must be considered necessary against the background of justification of their protection. Accordingly, where new kinds of uses become possible due to new economic or technical circumstances, they are not automatically covered by a broad right but must be newly covered by protection, if at all, upon a conscious decision of the legislature. Neighbouring rights are also more limited than author's rights in other respects, such as for the duration of protection and the rights of communication and broadcasting.

In the copyright system, the concept of neighbouring rights is not needed, since **3.69** copyright is broad enough to cover products that are covered by neighbouring rights. One may even discern a certain lack of understanding for this concept in some countries of the copyright system, where copyright industries are suspicious about neighbouring rights being 'second-class' rights and wish to 'improve' this situation in countries of the author's rights system without acknowledging the independent legal justification for this system.[114]

(9) Contract law

The strong focus on the author in the author's rights system is also expressed **3.70** through so-called 'copyright contract law', namely, statutory provisions restricting the freedom of contract or influencing the interpretation of contracts in favour of the author. Such provisions typically are part of copyright acts and apply in addition to general contract law; they may contain obligatory rules on the interpretation of copyright licensing contracts or rules directly restricting the freedom of contract in order to strengthen the weaker party to a contract.[115] Examples are provisions on a restrictive interpretation of assignment of rights if the contract is not clear, and interpretative rules under which the assignment of rights that are not explicitly mentioned only extends to those rights that are absolutely necessary for the fulfilment of the purpose of the contract.[116] Other provisions

---

114 See also paras 3.41–3.42 above; on such views of the US industry, see IFAC-3-CAFTA, 2004, 10, <http://www.ustr.gov/assets/Trade_Agreements/Regional/CAFTA/CAFTA_Reports/asset_upload_file571_5945.pdf> and para 12.31 n 94 below.

115 For some examples, see P Katzenberger, 'Protection of the Author as the Weaker Party to a Contract under International Copyright Contract Law' (1988) IIC 731 ff. See also, with a special focus on the German rules regarding remuneration (n 118 below) but also on the notion of 'copyright contract law' in general, A Dietz, 'International and European Aspects of Copyright Contract Law' (2004) Auteurs & Media 527 ff.

116 eg Art 31(5) of the German Copyright Act; Art L 131-3(1) of the French Intellectual Property Code (so-called 'specification rule').

may voluntarily limit the duration of assignment, so that the author has a second chance to seek a better return for an assignment. Under another rule, assignments cannot cover any uses yet unknown at the time of the contract, so that, for example, the assignment of a reproduction right before the digital age did not cover reproduction on CD-ROMs and similar digital reproductions.[117]

3.71 A notable example regarding the establishment of an equitable remuneration is the 2002 Amendment to the German Copyright Act, under which the author enjoys a right to obtain an equitable remuneration for the grant of licences, irrespective of the contents of the contract; the law also regulates the establishment of such equitable remuneration.[118] Another way of guaranteeing an equitable remuneration has been realized in Article 4 of the EC Rental Rights Directive, which was also taken as a model for the cable retransmission right in Germany.[119]

3.72 In contrast, the principle of 'freedom of contract' prevails in the copyright system as in common law in general.[120] Statutory provisions restricting the freedom of contract in principle are alien to that system. Under common law, only case law has assisted the author in balancing his weak position in specific circumstances compared to the relatively stronger position of businesses, such as a publisher or other company.[121] In order to spread this tradition with its industry-oriented approach to other countries, the US industry and government continuously strive for inclusion into US trade agreements (as demonstrated in the trade-related chapters of this book) of provisions on the free and separate transferability of rights and the full enjoyment of rights and their benefits by persons acquiring or holding any economic rights by contract—provisions directed against the

---

[117] eg Art 31(4) of the German Copyright Act, to be modified in 2007. For case law, see A Dietz, 'Chronique d'Allemagne' (1998) 176 RIDA 167, 214 ff.

[118] A Dietz 'Amendment of German Copyright Law in Order to Strengthen the Contractual Position of Authors and Performers' (2002) IIC 828–48 (including the amendment).

[119] For Art 4 of the EC Rental Rights Dir, see Vol II ch 6; Arts 27(1), (3) and 20b(2) of the German Copyright Act.

[120] Cornish/Llewelyn (n 41 above) 12-02.

[121] For British law, especially the doctrines of restraint of trade and undue influence, see W Cornish, 'UK Report' in G Roussel (ed), *ALAI Conference Montebello 97, Conference Proceedings: Protection of Authors and Performers through Contracts* (1998) 226, 230–3; similarly, Cornish/Llewelyn (n 41 above) 12-28–12-34 and, on collective action in trade unions and Minimum Term Agreements 12-35–12-50; on the difference between the copyright and author's rights systems in this respect, ibid 12-02–12-03. For the USA, see the quite specific Supreme Court decision of 25 June 2001 *New York Times Co, Inc v Tasini*, 206 F 3d 161, based on s 201(c) of the US Copyright Act. It held that the involved publishers had infringed the copyright of freelance authors by including their articles in a database without authorization and could not rely on s 201(c) of the Copyright Act. For an analysis, see eg P Jaszi, 'Tasini and Beyond' (2001) EIPR 595 ff; H Abrams, *The Law of Copyright* (2004, Release 10/06) § 4:39.

above-mentioned protective provisions recognized in countries of the author's rights system.

(10) Collective management of rights

Collective management of rights occurs in particular where individual exercise is **3.73** not possible or too costly, and where it is rendered obligatory by law. Among the most important differences between the systems is the low level of regulation of activities of collective management organizations (CMOs) in copyright system countries, where usually only questions regarding the establishment of tariffs (ie user-related questions) are regulated by law. The control of CMOs under the aspect of their usual character as monopolies is usually left to general competition or antitrust law. By contrast, the typically much higher level of regulation in author's rights countries covers not only the relation of CMOs with users (including the establishment of tariffs), but also their relation with right owners; in addition, laws often provide a specific control that prevails over a general antitrust or competition control.[122]

Moreover, authors generally have a better position and representation in CMOs **3.74** in author's rights countries—in some countries CMOs are even designated as 'authors societies' (*sociétés d'auteurs*), and some do not include owners of derived rights as members, such as publishers; relevant rules are often meant to guarantee an appropriate position of authors versus entrepreneurs within the collecting society, for example by particular group voting procedures. By contrast, entrepreneurs such as publishers seem to have a much stronger role in countries of the copyright system.[123]

Furthermore, the functions of CMOs differ: in the copyright system, CMOs in **3.75** principle exercise the mere economic function of collectively administering rights so as to reflect the property of the individual rights owners whose works are used. In the author's rights system, CMOs usually have additional social and cultural functions that are sometimes even mandated by law.[124] Within a CMO it may be a legal obligation or simply an acknowledged practice to agree on establishing social funds to assist authors in circumstances of social need, or cultural funds in

---

[122] P Katzenberger, 'Les Divers Systèmes du droit de contrôle de la gestion collective de droits d'auteurs dans les États Européens' in R Hilty (ed), *La Gestion collective du droit d'auteur en Europe* (1995) 17 ff.

[123] For a collection of articles on CMOs in different countries, see D Gervais, *Collective Management of Copyright and Related Rights* (2006).

[124] The European Parliament has stressed this function and recommended that it be maintained, see 'Report on the Commission Recommendation of 18 October 2005 on collective cross-border management of copyright and related rights for legitimate online music services' (2005/737/EC), (2006/2008(INI) <http://www.europarl.europa.eu/oeil/file.jsp?id=5303682>.

order to promote the publication of works, to grant awards or scholarships, or to otherwise promote young artists or other eligible persons. Apart from such funds, cultural evaluations may serve to promote particular categories of works that may be of a high cultural value but not be extensively used, as with poetry. Such basic differences between categories of works may be taken into account through systems of distribution, under which a higher number of points than earned on the mere basis of frequency of use is awarded to certain categories of works. In countries of the author's rights system, CMOs are generally also seen as cultural organizations, for which the principle of solidarity among authors is important, rather than as entities fulfilling a mere economic task, like in the copyright system.

3.76 Accordingly, also in the context of CMOs, the author's rights system primarily seems to take care of needs of authors rather than those of entrepreneurs, and to follow a comprehensive approach—including economic, social, and cultural aspects—rather than a purely market-based approach; the copyright system on the other hand focuses on the property aspect of copyright. These differences are also reflected in terminology: the so far prevailing term in English language, 'collecting societies', reflects the purely economic approach and is even wrongly limited to the aspect of 'collection' of fees from users rather than distribution to authors.[125] Terms used in other languages in author's rights countries, such as 'societies of authors', and 'societies for the protection (or safeguard) of rights', reflect the more comprehensive approach under this system.

(11) Structure of copyright acts

3.77 The preceding comparative overview of individual elements of protection under both systems is completed here by a presentation of these elements within the typical structures of copyright acts. After all, the different basic approaches of the author's rights and copyright systems are to some extent reflected in the structure of their representative copyright acts.

(a) Author's rights system

3.78 Modern copyright acts in the author's rights system are usually based on five main pillars: the contents of protection of author's rights, the contents of protection of neighbouring rights, statutory rules on copyright (and neighbouring rights) contracts, rules on CMOs, and special provisions on enforcement.[126] In the sections on the contents of protection both for authors and neighbouring right owners, general

---

[125] More recently however, general usage tends towards terms such as 'collective management (or administration) organisations' in the English language.

[126] A Dietz, 'Die fünf Säulen des Urheberrechtssystems und ihre Gefährdungen' in A Dümling (ed), *Musik hat ihren Wert: 100 Jahre musikalische Verwertungsgesellschaft in Deutschland* (2003) 336 ff.

provisions are usually followed by provisions on the work or object of neighbouring rights, on the author (rather than 'first right owner') or neighbouring rights owner, on moral rights, on economic rights, on limitations and exceptions, and on duration of protection; the order of these matters may vary slightly in the different laws.

(b) Copyright system

Copyright acts of the copyright system often start with definitions and usually **3.79** continue with protected works (including certain subject matter that would be covered by neighbouring rights under the author's rights system, such as phonograms and broadcasts), authorship and first ownership of copyright, duration of copyright, economic rights (or acts restricted by copyright), provisions on secondary infringement, limitations and exceptions ('acts permitted'), and moral rights. The rights of performers are not protected under copyright but as a separate category of right.[127]

(12) Résumé

Given the far-reaching approximation of copyright laws through multilateral **3.80** treaties and, quite strongly, bilateral agreements, it may seem at first glance that differences between the systems are minimal. Indeed, many similarities between copyright acts of the world exist today. Yet, beneath the surface, as often reflected in the understanding, interpretation, and application of laws, major differences become visible. Since such legal differences are often linked to fundamental cultural differences, they may subsist well into the future. Those who have strongly advocated 'bridging the gap' between both systems[128] may have overlooked this fact or simply meant that their own system should prevail. The most 'sustainable' way in dealing with these differences would certainly be to exercise basic respect for the existing differences, which are so closely related to fundamental concepts and cultural views.[129]

---

[127] eg Part II on rights and performances (following Part I on copyright) of the UK CDPA 1988; similarly: Part III on performances following Part II on copyright in the Irish Copyright Act 2000; for the USA and Australia, see also n 75 above.

[128] Von Lewinski (n 2 above) 59.

[129] For the same reason, the author of this book does not consider appropriate a unification of EC copyright law through an EC regulation, see Vol II ch 25.

4

OVERVIEW OF THE MAIN 'CLASSICAL' COPYRIGHT AND NEIGHBOURING RIGHTS CONVENTIONS BEFORE THE TRIPS AGREEMENT

A. The main copyright conventions

(1) The Berne Convention of 1886 and its revision acts up to 1971

(a) The Berne Convention and bilateral treaties: the situation in the early Berne years

The adoption of the Berne Convention aimed at improving international copy-   **4.01**
right protection by remedying the deficiencies of the pre-existing bilateral treaties with their instability, high degree of complexity, legal uncertainty, and insufficient protection.[1] At the same time, the Berne Convention upon its adoption neither automatically and fully replaced the existing bilateral treaties, nor did it hinder governments of Berne Union countries from concluding new bilateral treaties, subject, however, to the following condition: such treaties had to confer on authors and their representatives more extended rights than those granted by

---

[1] More details on these deficiencies above, paras 2.05 ff, in particular 2.24.

the Berne Union, or they had to contain other provisions not contrary to the Berne Convention.[2] Indeed, some of the existing bilateral treaties provided for a higher level of protection than the original Berne Convention, and the relevant countries had an interest in preserving that higher level in their mutual relationships.[3]

4.02 In order to avoid new legal uncertainty, the first Revision Conference of 1896 adopted a resolution requiring Union countries to determine those provisions of bilateral treaties which would still be considered in force, and to communicate them to the Union's International Bureau.[4] After 1886, most of the existing bilateral treaties were denounced, and only a very limited number of new bilateral treaties were concluded—eg those of Germany with Belgium, France, and Italy of 1907 which provided greater protection than the then most recent version of the Berne Convention. Even these three bilateral treaties, however, became obsolete (except for their most-favoured-nation clauses) when the revision of the Berlin Conference 1908 came into force in 1910.[5] Thereafter, Berne Union countries concluded few bilateral treaties between themselves, most of which were not, or not for long, of major importance.[6] Yet, in relations between countries outside the Berne Union, or between a member and a non-member, bilateral treaties continued to be concluded and to be of primary importance.[7] In certain cases, bilateral treaties between Berne Union countries, too, continued to be of considerable importance for a long time;[8] also, since the 1980s they have regained importance through the conclusion of new free trade agreements.[9]

---

[2] Art 15 of the Berne Convention 1886 regarding future treaties; the Additional Article adopted at the first Berne Conference in respect of existing treaties between Contracting States. The original version of the Berne Convention is reprinted, eg in W Nordemann, K Vinck, P Hertin, and G Meyer, *International Copyright and Neighbouring Rights Law* (1990) 519 ff. The conditions for special agreements between Berne countries are today contained in Art 20 of the Berne Convention (1971) which has fulfilled new functions in particular in connection with bilateral free trade agreements (cf ch 12 below) and the WCT (para 17.158 below).

[3] eg France in respect of the translation right, cf SP Ladas, *The International Protection of Literary and Artistic Property* Vol I (1938) 151–2. This right was provided in some of France's bilateral treaties for the general copyright duration (ibid 59), while the Berne Convention of 1886 (Art 5(1)) provided it only for the shorter term of 10 years from publication in a Union country.

[4] Ladas (n 3 above) 152–3.

[5] ibid 153.

[6] ibid 154–6 on subsequent bilateral agreements up to the 1930s.

[7] Such conventions up to 1937 are presented ibid 163–73.

[8] eg the German–US Treaty of 15 January 1892 which did not allow for the comparison of terms governed the German–US relations earlier and again between the US accession to the Berne Convention in 1989 and its prolongation of duration some years later, cf in detail J Drexl, 'Duration of Copyright Protection Accorded U.S. Authors in the Federal Republic of Germany: Changes due to the U.S. Accession to the Berne Convention' (1991) IIC 27–47 and 204–18.

[9] cf ch 12 below.

(b) Administrative Organization of the Berne Union

After the Berne Convention entered into force on 5 December 1887, the admin- **4.03**
istrative organ of the Union, the so-called 'International Bureau' (or 'International
Office'), was established on the basis of Article 16 and began to operate on
1 January 1888. By 1 January 1893, it was combined with the already existing
International Bureau of the Paris Union for the Protection of Industrial Property
law. The Bureaux worked under a common Director and Secretary General under
whom two Secretaries were charged with industrial property and with literary
and artistic works, respectively.[10] These united Bureaux were referred to as
'Bureaux Internationaux Réunis pour la Protection de la Propriété Intellectuelle',
abbreviated as BIRPI, only in the late 1950s, and only unofficially.[11] The functions
of the Berne Bureau were mainly to collect and to publish any kind of information
on the protection of authors' rights, to undertake studies in the field, to deliver
information on requests of Member States, to assist in the preparation of revision
conferences, and to edit a periodical publication in French regarding Berne Union
matters.[12] In fact, from January 1888 on, the Bureau published the journal
Le Droit d'auteur, which was supplemented by a parallel English edition not
before 1965. These primary functions served the aims of the Berne Convention
as recited in its preamble: 'to protect, in as effective and uniform a manner as
possible, the rights of authors. . .'. The Bureau was under the supervision of the
Swiss government, which had a number of tasks, in particular of supervising the
Bureau's finances and appointing its staff, but which otherwise did not influence
the Bureau.[13]

The Bureau served the 'Union', a notion frequently used since the mid- **4.04**
nineteenth century in order to refer to an association of states pursuing a common goal on the basis of an agreement. Examples for other such unions established
in the nineteenth century are the International Telegraph Union of 1865 and the
Universal Postal Union of 1874.[14] It seems however that in public international
law, the concept of a 'union' was used without being defined; controversial legal
discussion on this concept followed only later.[15]

---

[10] Ladas (n 3 above) 128.
[11] S Ricketson and J Ginsburg, *International Copyright and Neighbouring Rights: The Berne
Convention and Beyond* (2006) 16.30.
[12] Final Protocol no 5 on Art 16 of the Berne Convention (1886), corresponding to Art 22 of the
Berne Convention (1971).
[13] Ladas (n 3 above) 130.
[14] For a list of existing unions in 1901, cf L Poinsard, *Les Unions et ententes internationales* (1901) 4-5.
[15] F Ruffini, *De la protection internationale des droits sur les œuvres littéraires et artistiques* (1927)
93, and, for the discussion of the legal nature of unions, 93–113; on this concept also Ricketson/
Ginsburg (n 11 above) 5.60–5.82; Ladas (n 3 above) 108–9.

(c) Revision conferences and interim steps

4.05 **(i) Paris 1896** Many participants of the 1886 Berne Conference perceived that the Berne Convention of 1886 was only a compromise and a first step towards greater protection, possibly even through a universal law.[16] Their perception was reflected in the openness of the 1886 Berne Convention for the dynamics of future revisions,[17] and in the concrete provision that the first Revision Conference should take place in Paris within four to six years after entry into force of the Berne Convention.[18] While, consequently, this Revision Conference should have taken place at the latest in 1893, the general political situation during these years did not seem favourable for a Revision Conference. French protectionist measures at the beginning of the 1890s led to tensions in general commercial relations, to the extent that some countries denounced their bilateral treaties on authors' rights with France. The Conference eventually took place in 1896.[19] The French government took a realistic approach and proposed for this Conference only limited amendments to the existing Berne Convention text, in particular regarding the translation right.

4.06 Even with this limited approach, the Conference still had to cope with the following challenges: while the great majority could agree on a specific text amending the Berne Convention of 1886, two countries were not ready to do so: Norway and Great Britain. Norway did not want to change its recent law of 1893. Great Britain faced internal problems—it had introduced a new, liberal copyright act in accordance with the Berne Convention in 1886 and had received approval from its colonies for this act; through an amendment thereof in 1896, it could have unintentionally provoked a principal debate on the affiliation to the Union of certain colonies with separatist tendencies (such as Canada).[20] In this situation, a revision was not possible, since the Berne Convention, in accordance with customary international law, required unanimity for any revision of the Convention.[21]

4.07 One solution could have been to adopt the new Convention (the 1886 text with amendments) only by the majority of countries, and thereby constitute a new, restricted union that would replace the old one. The other solution, which was finally chosen, could better realize the aim of continuing the 1886 Union while

---

[16] cf para 2.45 above; W Briggs, *The Law of International Copyright* (1906) 464 saw this aim of a universal law to be achieved through continuous approximation of national laws according to Conventional minimum protection.

[17] Art 17 of the Berne Convention 1886.

[18] Final Protocol no 6.

[19] E Röthlisberger, *Die Berner Übereinkunft zum Schutze von Werken der Literatur und Kunst und die Zusatzabkommen* (1906) 18–19.

[20] ibid 19.

[21] Art 17 of the Berne Convention 1886; Ladas (n 3 above) 138.

not restricting its membership: the adoption of a so-called 'Additional Act' which did not require the adoption by all countries and still left the Berne Convention of 1886 unaffected.[22] Accordingly, the 1896 Conference did not result in a revision, but the amendments of substantive law were adopted in the form of the Additional Act, and a separate Interpretative Declaration regarding three provisions of the Berne Convention was adopted—again without unanimity. Besides Norway and Great Britain, even newly acceding countries were free to accede only to the 1886 Berne Convention without being bound by the Additional Act or the Interpretative Declaration. As a result, before the subsequent Revision Conference in Berlin 1908, the following fragmentation had taken place: twelve Member States were party not only to the Berne Convention but also to the Additional Act and the Interpretative Declaration, while Great Britain with its colonies was a party only to the Berne Convention and the Additional Act, and Norway and Sweden were parties only to the Berne Convention and the Interpretative Declaration.[23]

4.08 Such fragmentation certainly was not ideal for the future of the Berne Convention; in fact, one of the (non-binding) resolutions also adopted at the Paris Conference of 1896 called for deliberations at the next Conference to result in a single text of the Convention.[24] Like the 1886 Berne Conference, the Paris Conference determined where and when the next Revision Conference should take place—namely, in Berlin within six to ten years after 1896.[25] However, before the ten-year period elapsed, a number of Union countries successfully expressed their preference for postponing the Conference. Particularly Great Britain, a key member, asked for a postponement for another one to two years since it had not had a chance to amend its internal copyright law after the 1896 Conference.[26]

4.09 **(ii) Berlin 1908** The Berlin Revision Conference of 1908 was more important than that of 1896: many more countries and delegates were present, including observer delegations from twenty-one non-Union countries; and the pressure and plans for additional minimum standards was high. In particular, the International Literary and Artistic Association (ALAI) drafted in 1900 a model law for the unification of national laws on literary and artistic property and proposed reforms to the Berne Convention.[27] In fact, this Conference succeeded in adopting a fair number of additional minimum standards to be granted to authors.

---

[22] Actes de la Conférence réunie à Paris du 15 avril au 4 mai 1896 (1897) 179.

[23] Ladas (n 3 above) 140.

[24] L Rivière, *Protection internationale des œuvres littéraires et artistiques* (1897) 211 and the text of the relevant resolution no V, 266; Röthlisberger (n 19 above) 21.

[25] Actes de la Conférence (n 22 above) 146; Röthlisberger (n 19 above) 20.

[26] ibid 20–1.

[27] Ricketson/Ginsburg (n 11 above) 3.08. The model law is repr in Briggs (n 16 above) 798–801.

Finally, the wish of the 1896 Paris Conference to adopt one single text of the Convention was also fulfilled, although the situation was similar to that of the Paris Conference in that some countries could not agree to all amendments. While the previous texts of the Berne Convention 1886 and of the Paris Conference 1896 were merged into one single text, it became necessary, in order to reach the required unanimity, to offer a number of reservations. Consequently, it became possible to adopt a revision, but only because countries were allowed to remain bound by the text of 1886 only, or by that text as amended in 1896, if they could not immediately ratify the entire text of 1908. To promote ratification, countries were also allowed to adhere to the 1908 text while at the same time declaring that they wished to be bound by the earlier text in respect of specific points only. A similar possibility to substitute provisions from earlier Acts for the 1908 text was provisionally granted to newly acceding countries.[28]

4.10   Accordingly, for those countries which did not ratify the Berlin Act of 1908 or which did so but declared a reservation regarding specific points, the respective earlier Acts continued to govern their relationships with the other Berne countries, even if those other countries had ratified the 1908 Act. Hence, the Berlin Conference resulted in one single revision text which constituted the first actual revision of the Berne Convention (subsequently designated as the 'Revised Berne Convention'). Nevertheless, fragmentation still remained: at the time of the Rome Conference in 1928, nineteen countries had ratified the Convention of 1908 without any reservation, and eighteen countries had made different reservations to Articles 2, 8, 9, 11, or 18 of the Convention of 1908, so as to be bound by one of the earlier texts instead. This complex situation did not seem to be an ideal solution either; at the same time, it showed that restricted Unions with different texts governing the different Union countries had to be accepted in order to preserve the Berne Union as a whole.

4.11   **(iii) Additional Protocol 1914 and the First World War**   Before the next Revision Conference, an Additional Protocol was signed in 1914 in Berne on the proposal of Great Britain and supported by a resolution of ALAI. Great Britain, after having ratified in 1912 the Berne Convention of 1908, was confronted with an inequitable situation: authors of the British Empire were mostly prevented from obtaining protection in the United States (not a Berne Union member at the time), while American authors could easily obtain protection in the British Empire and the entire Berne Union on the basis of national treatment under the Berne Convention, in particular through first publication in a

---

[28] Arts 27 and 25 of the Berlin Act 1908 for Union countries and acceding countries respectively; Ladas (n 3 above) 140; Ricketson/Ginsburg (n 11 above) 3.19.

Berne Union country.[29] As a remedy, reservations were proposed at the Imperial Copyright Conference 1910, but they would not clearly have complied with the Berne Convention.[30] After the British Empire ratified the 1908 Berne Convention, Canada refused its ratification for itself and requested Great Britain to propose the Additional Protocol.[31] This Protocol was to re-establish an equitable situation by allowing for retaliation under certain conditions (contained today in Article 6 of the Berne Convention 1971).[32] Given the risk of losing the British Empire from the Berne Union unless this Protocol were signed, all Member Countries signed, and most of them later ratified the Additional Protocol of Berne 1914.[33]

The Berne Convention survived the First World War largely because it was considered to be of a legal rather than political nature and to be adopted in the interest of private persons rather than of states; therefore, no country contended that the convention had to be deemed abrogated by the war, even if its full application was hampered or suspended.[34] The continued viability of the Berne Convention was also supported by a decision of the Hanseatic Supreme Court in 1917.[35] That decision held that the Berne Convention applied in Germany although Great Britain did not apply the Convention in favour of nationals of enemy countries under its Act of 10 August 1916. **4.12**

(iv) Rome 1928   After 1908, revision conferences took place every twenty years. While the Conference following the Berlin Revision was supposed to take place in Rome between 1915 and 1918, the First World War obviously rendered this goal impossible.[36] When finally held in 1928, thirty-four Union countries[37] and twenty-one observer countries[38] attended—again more than before. Not surprisingly, the higher number of countries made obtaining unanimity more difficult than at earlier conferences. At the same time, it became more important to avoid additional fragmentation and complexity by enhanced **4.13**

---

[29] For more details, cf paras 5.49–5.50 below. Anon, 'Le Nouveau Protocol Additionnel à la Convention de Berne Révisée 1908' (1914) Droit d'auteur 79 ff, 93 ff.

[30] ibid 80; Ladas (n 3 above) 95-6

[31] ibid; Ricketson/Ginsburg (n 11 above) 3.21.

[32] On the contents of that provision in the 1971 version, cf paras 5.51–5.52 below.

[33] Ladas (n 3 above) 94–7.

[34] Anon, 'Les Unions internationales et la guerre' (1914) Droit d'auteur 118 f; Ladas (n 3 above) 102, and 103–7 on the interpretation of the relevant provisions of the Treaty of Versailles and other peace treaties in respect of the Berne Convention. On the copyright provisions on the Treaty of Versailles, cf also M Seligsohn, 'Die Bestimmungen des Friedensvertrages über den Schutz der Werke der Literatur und Kunst' (1919) GRUR 229 ff.

[35] Decision of 14 July 1917, OLG Hamburg (1918) GRUR 79; the case *Ricordi* was also reported in (1918) Droit d'auteur 9; Ladas (n 3 above) 102–3.

[36] ibid 97.

[37] In 1928, the Union membership had grown to 36.

[38] Actes de la Conférence réunie à Rome du 7 mai au 2 juin 1928 (1929) 131 ff.

possibilities for reservations. In the end, agreement was reached on relatively few amendments that increased the minimum standards for authors, but the Conference achieved at least one major success: restriction on the possibilities for reservation. In particular, newly acceding countries could make a reservation only in respect of the translation right with a view to applying Article 5 of the 1886 Act instead of Article 8 of the Rome Act.[39] In addition, Union countries were not allowed to make any reservations to the new text adopted at the Rome Conference. They could, however, decide not to ratify the Rome Act and remain bound by the relevant earlier text. Also, Union countries could maintain prior reservations if they made a declaration to this effect when ratifying the Rome Act, whether they signed the Rome text, or did not sign it but only later adhered to it.[40] A further proliferation of reservation possibilities was at least avoided by that solution.

4.14 In addition, a notable achievement of the Rome Conference was the adoption of a *vœu* to work on the unification of the Berne Convention and the Conventions of Buenos Aires/Havana.[41] The latter had developed separately; they excluded non-American membership and were preferred by American countries over the Berne Convention. This development contradicted the Berne aim towards universal protection.[42]

4.15 (v) **Brussels 1948** Like the Rome Conference, the following Revision Conference, originally planned for 1935 in Brussels, also had to be postponed—first because the Rome Act was ratified by Union countries hesitantly, and, secondly, because the preparation of a draft agreement to ensure copyright protection between Berne Union countries and parties of the Buenos Aires/Havana Conventions[43] took more time than anticipated.[44] When in 1936 such draft agreements were prepared, the Belgian government was asked to organize a special conference open to all states of the world (rather than just a revision conference of the Berne Convention) in order to explore possibilities for a universal agreement. This conference was then envisaged for 1939. The Second World War interrupted both the plans for the special conference and for the revision conference. After the war, these plans were clearly split: the Brussels Revision Conference took place in 1948, while the plan of a universal agreement was pursued by

---

[39] Art 27(3) of the Rome Act of the Berne Convention.
[40] Art 27 ibid; Ricketson/Ginsburg (n 11 above) 3.26.
[41] Actes (n 38 above) 350; in English: Ladas (n 3 above) 650.
[42] On further developments, cf paras 4.32–4.35 below.
[43] cf para 4.14 above.
[44] Ricketson/Ginsburg (n 11 above) 3.33.

the United Nations Educational and Scientific Organization (UNESCO) after 1947, resulting in the Universal Copyright Convention in 1952.[45]

At the time of the 1948 Conference, the Berne Union had only four more Members States than in 1928—not least because it also lost some members through denunciation and through loss of the status of an independent national entity.[46] The situation regarding reservations had improved, since only seven countries had retained reservations.[47] The Brussels Conference did not achieve any fundamental progress regarding the minimum standards for authors, possibly due to the following new tendencies that began to appear. The demands for greater protection of authors' rights according to the European tradition were confronted with interests of strong user industries (which had grown not least due to new technical developments), and of the general public in access to works, as well as with similar demands by developing countries. Also, the diversity of Union countries was greater than in 1928. Finally, the beginning of a change from French to English as the dominant language may have indicated a subtle shift from the overall agreed ideal of a strong, universal law for authors to a more diverse approach.[48]

4.16

(vi) **Stockholm 1967**   The 1967 Stockholm Revision Conference was different from all its predecessors in that it was the first Conference where developing countries played a major role.[49] This was because decolonization had taken place mainly after the 1948 Conference. The result was a number of new states free to exercise their independence from the colonizing powers. While most of them had already been subject to the Berne Convention as dependent territories of Berne Union countries, they were now, as sovereigns, able to decide to withdraw from the Berne Convention or to remain bound by it. Most chose to remain bound, while demanding that their particular concerns would have to be better taken into account.[50]

4.17

At the Stockholm Conference more than one-third (twenty-one out of fifty-seven Members) of the Berne Union countries were developing countries—a setting that changed the character and focus of debates. Accordingly, the adoption of the Protocol regarding developing countries was one of the major outcomes of the

4.18

---

[45] ibid 3.33 and 18.18; on the Universal Copyright Convention, cf paras 4.33–4.48 below.

[46] eg Estonia and Latvia, cf Ricketson/Ginsburg (n 11 above) 3.34.

[47] ibid.

[48] ibid 3.48, 3.36.

[49] Another important feature was the concurrent negotiation on several issues of the Paris Convention and related agreements on industrial property and on the new Treaty establishing the WIPO.

[50] Ricketson/Ginsburg (n 11 above) 14.05.

Stockholm Conference.[51] The Protocol provided for privileges for developing countries, such as the possibility to shorten the term of protection, as well as the possibility to grant compulsory licences for translation and reproduction rights and for any uses for the purpose of teaching, study, and research under further conditions.[52] These quite far-reaching privileges were adopted by the Stockholm Conference not least to avoid a possible decline in membership through withdrawal from the Convention by developing countries.[53]

4.19 Yet, developed countries rather reluctantly agreed to these privileges. Also, their interested parties, in particular authors and publishers, rejected the Protocol inter alia on the argument that the more appropriate way to help developing countries was by technical and economic assistance rather than by reducing international copyright protection; they argued that otherwise, exactly those would suffer who often did not enjoy the best living conditions even in developed countries, namely authors and publishers.[54] In addition, the USA stated that the Protocol, if in force, would be a major obstacle for it to adhere to the Berne Convention.[55] It soon became clear that entry into force would not be reached regarding the substantive provisions (including the protocol for developing countries) of the Stockholm text, and could not be expected in the nearer future.[56]

4.20 This situation was probably the greatest challenge which the Berne Convention had faced until then. The threat was that developing countries would leave the Berne Union, and instead choose to adhere to the Universal Copyright Convention (UCC) with its lower level of protection,[57] to conclude bilateral agreements despite all their negative consequences,[58] or even to stay outside the international protection system.

4.21 (vii) **Paris 1971** Soon after the deadlock of the Stockholm Revision, negotiations for an overall acceptable solution resumed as early as December 1967 in the

---

[51] For other results cf para 4.27 below and Ricketson/Ginsburg (n 11 above) 3.57–3.63.

[52] On more detail cf ibid 14.18–14.32.

[53] ibid 3.64.

[54] Resolution of 23 April 1968 by ALAI pts (2), (3), recommending governments of developed countries suspend their decisions on ratification and accession at least until intentions of developing countries are revealed, (1968) Copyright 146; the Resolution and Recommendation of the International Publishers' Association pointing at technical assistance as an alternative, (1968) Copyright 188 f, and of CISAC, (1968) Copyright 189 f.

[55] Ricketson/Ginsburg (n 11 above) 14.34.

[56] Berne Union countries could choose to ratify or accede to the Stockholm Act either entirely, including the substantive provisions and the revised administrative and final clauses, or to ratify only one or the other. Indeed, only the administrative provisions were ratified by a sufficient number of countries.

[57] This would, however, not have been useful due to the Berne safeguard clause of the UCC, cf para 4.38 below.

[58] para 2.24 above.

frameworks of the Berne Convention, the UCC, and through joint efforts, and led to simultaneous Revision Conferences of the Berne Convention and the UCC 1971 in Paris.[59] The Conferences took place on the basis of drafts adopted by committees of the Berne Convention and of the UCC.[60] These drafts included provisions to raise minimum standards under the UCC, grant privileges for developing countries under both Conventions, and newly regulate the relationship between both Conventions regarding developing countries.[61] The drafts were considered to be a 'package deal', an overall compromise between developing and developed countries that could only be adopted as a single package or be rejected.[62] The results regarding the Berne Convention were twofold.[63] First, the new provisions in favour of developing countries were adopted as the Appendix (rather than 'Protocol'), which became an integral part of the Paris Act.[64] As compared to the Stockholm Protocol, the Appendix provided for fewer privileges in favour of developing countries, namely compulsory licences for the translation and reproduction rights only, and this only subject to complicated procedural rules and a number of conditions. Secondly, the Paris Act included the substantive provisions and the administrative provisions of the Berne Convention as amended by the Stockholm Act;[65] it had been decided to adopt these provisions of the Stockholm Act as part of an entirely new Act rather than leave them as part of the Stockholm Act and limit the Paris Act to the Protocol.[66]

This compromise gained acceptance by unanimity, and the Paris Act entered into force only three years later[67]—the Berne Convention survived its first major crisis.[68] At the same time, the Stockholm and Paris Conferences had shown the impact of the newly arisen North–South conflict and the extreme difficulty in reaching the unanimity required for the revision of the Berne Convention. After that experience, the WIPO hesitated to prepare and convene any new revision conference, instead preferring a different, smoother way to promote the **4.22**

---

[59] On the individual meetings from 1967 on cf Ricketson/Ginsburg (n 11 above) 14.36–14.45 and E Ulmer, 'The Revision of the Copyright Conventions in the Light of the Washington Recommendation' (1970) IIC 235 ff. Notably, the Paris Conference was the first revision conference of the Berne Convention convened not on the invitation by a Member Country, but by the newly established International Bureau of WIPO.

[60] E Ulmer, 'The Revisions of the Copyright Conventions' (1971) 4 IIC 345, 346.

[61] The preceding one under the Berne safeguard clause of the UCC 1952 was quite harsh on developing countries, cf para 4.38 below.

[62] ibid.

[63] On the results regarding the UCC and its relation to the Berne Convention cf paras 4.39–4.42 below.

[64] Art 21 of the Berne Convention.

[65] Arts 1–20 and 22–6 respectively.

[66] Ulmer (n 59 above) 348.

[67] On 10 October 1974, cf (1974) Copyright 156.

[68] Many considered the situation after 1967 as a 'crisis', eg Ulmer (n 59 above) 235.

international copyright law development, the so-called 'guided development'.[69] Although the 1971 Paris Act therefore constitutes the latest revision of the Berne Convention to date,[70] it does not represent the end of multilateral treaty-making in the field of copyright; indeed, exactly twenty years after the Paris Revision, another important multilateral text was provisionally agreed and, at the same time, preparations started for a new multilateral copyright treaty, the WCT.[71]

(d) Development of the contents of the Berne Convention from 1886 to 1971

4.23 Regarding the contents of the Berne Convention, the main steps of development are introduced here. The 1886 Berne Convention provided for national treatment for citizens of the other Union countries in respect of the right of public performance of dramatic or dramatico-musical works and musical works that were unpublished or published but with the author's reservation of his right on the title-page, as well as the right of adaptation.[72] It also provided, as a minimum standard, a translation right for ten years from publication. For the enjoyment of protection under the Convention, the conditions and formalities under the law of the country of origin of the work had to be fulfilled. The Convention included a list of examples for 'literary and artistic works'; separately named translations to be protected as original works; contained some rudimentary exceptions from protection; and included provisions on the seizure of pirated works, the prima facie proof of authorship, the governments' right to provide for censorship and the like, rules on so-called 'retroactive' application, the right to conclude special agreements between Union countries, revisions by unanimity, and administrative and final clauses. The language and structure of the 1886 Berne Convention was much less developed and systematic than modern multilateral copyright treaties.

4.24 The 1908 Berlin Revision brought about major amendments to the substantive protection requirements. In particular, the list of works was explicitly supplemented by architectural, choreographic, and pantomime works as well as adaptations and collections, and (with restrictions) works of applied art and photographic works. Translations found their systematically correct place in the list.

---

[69] A Bogsch, 'The First Hundred Years of the Berne Convention for the Protection of Literary and Artistic Works' (1986) Copyright 291, 327; M Ficsor, *The Law of Copyright and the Internet* (2002) n 1.02 ff.

[70] Only an amendment of the administrative provisions was adopted by the Assembly of the Berne Union on 2 October 1979 (in force from 19 November 1984 according to Art 26(3) of the Berne Convention) by which WIPO's triannual budget was changed into a biannual one.

[71] The Dunkel Draft 1991 for the TRIPS Agreement and the first WIPO Committee of Experts on a Possible Berne Protocol, cf on the developments towards the TRIPS Agreement ch 9 and towards the WIPO Copyright Treaty paras 17.01 ff below.

[72] Art 9 of the Berne Convention 1886 referred to its Art 2 on national treatment.

The way in which national treatment worked was amended, the principle of minimum rights was explicitly recognized,[73] the principle of 'no formalities' was introduced, and the protection was made fully independent from the conditions and formalities in the country of origin of the work (except for the duration). For the first time, a general, non-mandatory minimum duration of fifty years *pma* was established, together with the comparison of terms for photographic and other works. The duration regarding translation rights was assimilated to that of other rights. The advent of new technologies was reflected in provisions on the mechanical reproduction of musical works combined with the possibility of compulsory licences and similar conditions, and on rights regarding the cinematographic adaptation. Overall, the 1908 Berlin Conference shaped the basic structure and major parts of the contents of the Convention; these are still reflected in its latest version of 1971.

Much less progress was achieved by the Rome Conference 1928. The most **4.25** important additions regarding substantive law included the recognition of moral rights, the introduction of the exclusive rights of broadcasting and similar communication, and the inclusion of lectures and other oral works in Article 2 of the Berne Convention. Also, the possibility of retorsion, as agreed under the Berne Additional Protocol of 1914,[74] was included as a new Article 6 of the Berne Convention.

The 1948 Brussels Conference mainly brought about refinements and clarifica- **4.26** tions of existing provisions and the establishment of the fifty years' duration as a mandatory minimum standard, the introduction of public performance and communication rights in respect of literary works, the extension of the existing broadcasting and communication rights, and (though not as a minimum right) the basic recognition of the resale right (*droit de suite*).

The 1967 Stockholm Conference also added only relatively minor changes,[75] **4.27** apart from the Stockholm Protocol for Developing Countries, which never entered into force. Noteworthy examples are the explicit recognition of the exclusive reproduction right with permitted exceptions as a minimum right, the fixation of special minimum durations for cinematographic and photographic works as well as for works of applied art, the reference to national law as regards any potential fixation requirement for the protection of works, Article 14[bis] on cinematographic works, the protection of folklore,[76] and amendments to the eligibility criteria and

---

[73] Art 4(1) last half phr, corresponding to Art 5(1) last half phr of the Berne Convention 1971; also, the public performance and adaptation rights were slightly amended.

[74] cf paras 4.11–4.12 above.

[75] They came into force later as part of the Paris Act 1971.

[76] Art 15(4) of the Berne Convention. This approach to protection of folklore, however, was not successful, cf paras 20.27–20.29 below.

to the terms of 'country of origin' and 'published works'. In addition, the administrative and final clauses were fundamentally amended as a consequence of the simultaneous adoption of the Convention Establishing the World Intellectual Property Organization which was to administer the Berne Union in the future.[77]

4.28 Finally, the Paris Act brought to life the Stockholm Revision regarding the substantive law provisions, included the administrative and final clauses of the Stockholm Revision, and added the revised Appendix for Developing Countries.[78]

(2) Other early multilateral conventions

(a) Convention of Montevideo

4.29 Only three years after the adoption of the Berne Convention in 1886, the first Latin American copyright convention was adopted: the Convention of Montevideo of 11 January 1889 on the Protection of Literary and Artistic Works.[79] The reason for the perceived need to adopt a second treaty covering the same subject matter (ie copyright protection) was similar to that in the later case of the Universal Copyright Convention: a number of Latin American countries had participated in the preparatory work for the Berne Convention but did not consider its provisions as appropriate for them, given their status of development.

4.30 The Convention of Montevideo was partly modelled on the text of the Berne Convention, but showed also a number of differences. The most important one was the principle of universality under which the law of the country of origin applied to works first published in a Contracting State regarding uses in the other Contracting States.[80] Also, the Convention of Montevideo did not protect unpublished works, did not apply to existing subject matter, and did not create a union with an office. At the same time, it provided for stronger protection than the 1886 Berne Convention, such as regarding the protection of photographic and choreographic works, the full recognition of translation rights, and a strict principle of 'no formalities'.

4.31 Among the possible reasons why the Convention of Montevideo could not, in the long term, become a strong 'competitor' of the Berne Convention was the

---

[77] On the WIPO, cf ch 15, in particular paras 15.02 ff below.

[78] The texts of the versions of the Berne Convention from 1886 to 1948 are repr, eg in Nordemann/Vinck/Hertin/Meyer (n 2 above) 519–83; for a résumé of the initial and the revision conferences, cf Ricketson/Ginsburg (n 11 above) 2.50–3.67.

[79] Text repr in (1889) Droit d'auteur 52 ff and, in English, eg in Nordemann/Vinck/Hertin/ Meyer (n 2 above) 604 (with Additional Protocol of 13 February 1889).

[80] By contrast, the Berne Convention is governed by the principle of the country of protection, cf paras 1.06–1.08 above.

hardly practical principle of universality. Also, only five of seven signatory states ratified the Convention,[81] which did not even gain membership after the first International American Conference in Washington in 1889 adopted a resolution encouraging all American governments to accede to the Montevideo Convention.[82] In addition, non-signatory states could not automatically become members, but had to be accepted individually by each member.[83] As a result, a number of European states were accepted, but in most cases only by one or two and, in some cases, also three countries; Uruguay and Peru refused the accession of European countries which therefore had no relations with these two countries under the Convention. Today, the Convention may have to be taken into account in the context of transitional provisions and effectiveness of acquired rights[84] but is otherwise of no current importance.

(b) Other American conventions

After the adoption of the Convention of Montevideo, additional conventions **4.32** were concluded in the Americas in the first half of the twentieth century: the Convention of Caracas of 17 July 1911; a number of Central American conventions, including the Treaty of Peace and Amity (Washington Treaty of 20 December 1907); and a number of Pan-American conventions, namely the Convention of Mexico City of 1902, the Convention of Rio de Janeiro of 1906 which incorporated and supplemented the Mexico Convention, the Convention of Buenos Aires of 1910, the Convention of Havana of 1928 which revised the Buenos Aires Convention and, finally, the Convention of Washington of 1946.[85] None of them obtained complete membership of all the American states. Their contents and membership differed in many ways, thereby creating a complex network of relationships between the American states.[86] This result has been attributed to a lack of comparative studies of the national laws involved as a preparation for the adoption of multilateral conventions, and a lack of entities such as the Berne Bureau or ALAI able to carry out or promote such studies.[87] This unsatisfactory situation together with the fact that the American treaties, except the Convention of Montevideo, were not open to non-American states finally led to the first

---

[81] The signatory states were: Argentina, Bolivia, Brazil, Chile, Paraguay, Peru, Uruguay; all except Chile and Brazil also ratified the Convention, Ladas (n 3 above) 635 f.

[82] ibid 639; Minutes of the International American Conference (Washington, 1890) 81, 92, 220, 227, 235.

[83] Arts 13, 16 of the Montevideo Convention and Art 6 of the Additional Protocol; on the individual policy of the members towards accession of non-signatory states, cf Ladas (n 3 above) 636.

[84] Katzenberger, 'vor §§ 120 ff' in G Schricker (ed), *Urheberrecht* (3rd edn, 2006) no 67.

[85] cf a description of these conventions except that of 1946 in Ladas (n 3 above) 654–66; for their history and interim Conferences, cf 635–53; Ricketson/Ginsburg (n 11 above) 18.03–18.11.

[86] The complexity of inter-American copyright relations in 1937 is impressively illustrated by Ladas (n 3 above) 648 f.

[87] ibid 649–50.

attempts to combine the international protection of the Berne Convention and of the Pan-American conventions. In 1952, these attempts resulted in the adoption of the Universal Copyright Convention.[88]

(3) The Universal Copyright Convention

(a) Reasons for the adoption of the Universal Copyright Convention

4.33 The above developments in Latin America explain the need perceived in the mid-1940s for another multilateral treaty on authors' rights in addition to the Berne Convention—a need perceived although the Berne Convention had just proved its dynamics by its then latest revision of 1948. Indeed, international relations in the field of copyright in the first half of the twentieth century were not truly universal but split between major parts of the world. While the Berne Convention was centred around Europe, other multilateral treaties had developed in parallel in the Americas[89] to govern relations among most North and South American countries.[90] Most American treaties excluded the accession of non-American countries.[91] At the same time, most American countries were not members of the Berne Convention[92] because they were not ready to comply with its comparatively high level of minimum standards. The USA had the additional obstacle of its national copyright system, which partly remained at odds with the authors' rights system embodied in Berne. In particular, US law required the fulfilment of formalities for the enjoyment of copyright protection. Also, the duration was twenty-eight years from publication, with the possibility of one renewal for another twenty-eight years. Furthermore, moral rights were fundamentally alien to its system of protection. This development towards a split into two separate international protection systems contradicted the fundamental aim of the Berne Convention to achieve international protection universally. The idea of a convention that should overcome this split was born.

(b) The way towards the adoption of the Universal Copyright Convention

4.34 In order to advance work on a more universal approach by reconciling the different multilateral conventions, the Rome Revision Conference 1928 of the Berne Convention adopted a *vœu* to take measures towards the preparation of a general agreement on the basis of the similar rules of the Berne and the Buenos

---

[88] cf paras 4.33–4.35 below.

[89] On these treaties, cf para 4.32 above.

[90] cf in particular the inter-American Conventions of Buenos Aires (1910), Havana (1928), and Washington (1946) which was adopted with the leadership of the USA.

[91] E Ulmer, 'Der Entwurf eines Welturheberrechtsabkommens' (1952) GRUR Auslands- und Internationaler Teil 16; para 4.32 above.

[92] On 1 January 1952, Brazil and Canada were the only Berne Union members from the Americas (1952) Droit d'auteur 1, 2.

Aires/Havana Conventions with the aim of worldwide unification of laws.[93] In addition, the General Assembly of the League of Nations in 1935 mandated two International Institutes[94] with the relevant work.[95] Many options were explored at the time, such as one universal convention replacing the existing ones, or a roof convention under which the existing Conventions of Berne and Buenos Aires/ Havana would be maintained but linked.[96] The Second World War interrupted this and other preparatory work.[97] After the Second World War, these plans were no longer pursued in the framework of the Berne Convention[98] but by the newly established UNESCO.[99]

When UNESCO started work on these plans in initial meetings of its copyright **4.35** expert committee in 1947 and 1949 in Paris, it became clear to the experts that the existing conventions should not be replaced, and that even a roof convention should not be adopted. Instead, all countries, irrespective of their membership in the existing unions and treaties, were to be able to sign and ratify the envisaged new treaty, even if they were not members of UNESCO. On this basis, the Universal Copyright Convention was adopted on 6 September 1952 and came into force on 16 September 1955 after ratification by twelve countries.[100] Its historical background—the aim of avoiding a lasting split into the Berne and the American protection systems—was reflected in the attendance at the Conference: most of the Berne Union countries and American countries signed it.[101]

(c) Main contents of the Universal Copyright Convention of 1952

To approach the aim of universal membership and thus to include countries with **4.36** a need for low protection, such as developing countries (more than in the pre-existing conventions), the USA, and the Soviet Union, the contents of the 1952 Universal Copyright Convention had to follow a relatively minimalist approach.[102]

---

93 Actes de la Conférence (n 38 above) 350; in English: Ladas (n 3 above) 650.
94 The International Institute for Intellectual Cooperation and the International Institute of Rome for the Unification of Private Law.
95 Ricketson/Ginsburg (n 11 above) 3.33.
96 Ulmer (n 91 above) 16–17.
97 cf para 4.15 above.
98 On the Berne context, cf para 4.16 above.
99 UNESCO's first programme in the field of copyright which included a universal convention reflected its focus on education and science and the view that copyright would be an obstacle to free circulation of information—a view that was later revised, Anon, 'La Première Conférence Générale de l'UNESCO' (1947) Droit d'auteur 4–5.
100 Since the UCC was adopted in Geneva, it is also often referred to as 'the Geneva Convention'.
101 Ricketson/Ginsburg (n 11 above) 18.20.
102 The text of the UCC 1952 is integrated in the commentary by Nordemann/Vinck/Hertin/ Meyer (n 2 above) 213 ff.

4.37 For example, the Preamble, unlike that of the Berne Convention, did not introduce the aim of protecting the rights of authors 'in as effective and uniform a manner as possible', but only intended to 'assure in all countries copyright protection'. The principle of minimum rights was hardly realized in the 1952 text; there was only a very limited translation right in addition to the very general obligation to 'provide for the adequate and effective protection of the rights . . . '.[103] Instead of Berne's principle of 'no formalities', Article III(1) of the UCC permitted formalities for foreign works, but only those specified in this provision. This compromise allowed countries such as the USA to continue their requirements for domestic works, while enabling works from other UCC countries to enjoy copyright protection in the USA or other countries if they only fulfilled the limited requirements of the UCC. Article IV of the UCC provided for a general minimum duration of only twenty-five years *pma* and of ten years for photographic works and works of applied art. A transitional provision even allowed any Contracting State which, at the date of entry into force of the UCC in that state, provided for certain classes of works such duration only to be computed after the first publication of the work, to maintain such duration and even extend it to all classes of works. Reciprocity was introduced, given the diversity of national laws on the duration.

4.38 The principle of national treatment was drafted in a slightly different way from that under the Berne Convention. The UCC in the version of 1952 also contained a definition of 'publication',[104] a rule on application in time,[105] final and administrative clauses, and framework provisions,[106] in particular the so-called Berne safeguard clause.[107] This clause was to discourage Berne Union countries from leaving the Berne Convention in order to adhere (only) to the Universal Copyright Convention; if they did so, their works would not be protected in the remaining Berne countries. More precisely, if a Berne country which was country of origin of a work under the Berne Convention withdrew from the Berne Convention after 1 January 1951, the respective work would not be protected by the Universal Copyright Convention in the Berne countries. In addition, this provision stipulated that among Berne Union countries which were also

---

[103] Arts V and I of the Geneva text 1952; the General Report noted that this clause referred to the rights 'generally granted to authors in civilized countries', Actes de la Conférence Intergouvernementale du Droit d'Auteur (1954) 77 (translation by the author). The US delegate at the committee preparing the basic negotiation text in 1951 rejected any concrete stipulation of minimum rights, Ulmer (n 91 above) 18.

[104] Art VI of the UCC 1952.

[105] No application of the UCC to works that are already in the public domain in the country where protection is claimed (Art VII of the UCC 1952).

[106] Arts VIII–XVI and XVIII–XXI ibid.

[107] Art XVII ibid and the related Declaration.

Contracting States of the Universal Copyright Convention, the latter was not applicable in respect of works whose country of origin was a Berne country.

(d) 1971 Paris Revision

At the 1971 Paris Revision Conference which took place in combination with the **4.39** Paris Revision Conference of the Berne Convention,[108] a number of major amendments were made to the UCC. The Paris Revision was adopted on 24 July 1971 and came into force on 10 July 1974.[109] First, some basic economic minimum rights in addition to the existing translation right were introduced for works in their original form and derived therefrom: the rights of reproduction, public performance, and broadcasting. At the same time, Contracting States were allowed to introduce exceptions to these rights, as long as a 'reasonable degree of effective protection' was reached.[110] These amendments accommodated the needs of developed countries with a high standard of protection, because they were not ready to grant national treatment while not receiving any guaranteed, comparable protection in other Contracting States.[111]

By contrast, the other substantive law amendments generally favoured develop- **4.40** ing countries. In particular, the new Articles V^{bis}, V^{ter}, and V^{quater} of the UCC provided for a number of privileges corresponding to those laid down in the Appendix to the Berne Convention. These provisions allowed developing countries to provide for compulsory licences in respect of the rights of translation and reproduction under specific conditions and subject to procedural requirements. The length and high degree of complexity of these provisions reflected the need to conclude a compromise between the opposite groups of countries and to realize a balance between their diverging interests in each and every detail.[112] In practice, little use has been made of the compulsory licences.[113]

Another provision that favoured developing countries was a loosening of the **4.41** strict Berne safeguard clause of the 1952 version whereby they could withdraw from the Berne Union without losing the protection of the Universal Copyright

---

[108] cf paras 4.21–4.22 above.

[109] cf the commentary by Nordemann/Vinck/Hertin/Meyer (n 2 above) 214 ff; Ulmer (n 60 above) 350–71.

[110] Art IVbis of the UCC 1971.

[111] cf on the same situation in 1952 para 4.37 above, in n 103.

[112] cf Ulmer (n 60 above) 356–70.

[113] Ricketson/Ginsburg (n 11 above) 14.106 for the corresponding provisions of the Berne Convention.

Convention, on condition of deposit of a specific notification.[114] Most developing countries chose, however, not to withdraw from the Berne Convention.[115]

4.42   The relation between the texts of 1952 and 1971 was regulated as follows: both were separate conventions; accession to the 1971 text would also constitute accession to the 1952 text; after entry into force of the 1971 text, no country could adhere only to the 1952 text; where only one of two UCC members adhered to the 1952 text, that text applied exclusively between them.[116]

(e) Development of the Universal Copyright Convention after 1971

4.43   For some forty years, the UCC fulfilled its purpose to establish international copyright protection beyond the membership of the Berne Convention. In particular, most of those countries which were not ready to accede to the Berne Convention joined the UCC, namely most Latin American countries and the USA. Another important country that had largely stayed outside international copyright relations[117] was Russia, which joined the UCC as part of the Soviet Union in 1973. In 2007, the UCC has 100 members.

4.44   The UCC has, however, lost importance to the extent that its Contracting States also adhered to the Berne Convention, because the UCC does not apply to Berne works between UCC countries which are also Berne Members.[118] Mainly since the end of the 1980s, many UCC countries also adhered to the Berne Union, as in particular the USA in 1989, the Russian Federation in 1995, as well as many other former Soviet countries and some Central and Eastern European countries since the early 1990s. Others that had not been a member of the UCC directly adhered to the Berne Convention, such as China in 1992. Another wave of accessions to the Berne Convention was indirectly due to the bilateral agreements initiated by the USA since the end of the 1980s by which countries were mostly obliged or at least encouraged to accede to the Berne Convention if they were not yet members.[119] Also, the TRIPS Agreement 1994 had a similar effect: although it did not oblige its Members to accede to the Berne Convention, it required

---

[114] Appendix Declaration relating to Art XVII (version of 1971).

[115] Nordemann/Vinck/Hertin/Meyer (n 2 above) Art XVII UCC n 4; Ricketson/Ginsburg (n 11 above) 18.39.

[116] Art IX of the UCC 1971 with further specifications.

[117] On Russia's few, not very long-lasting bilateral treaties, cf M Boguslawski, *Urheberrecht in den internationalen Beziehungen* (1977) 89–96.

[118] Art XVII of the UCC and the related Declaration.

[119] cf para 12.09 below. Less strict obligations were contained in bilateral agreements by the EC, cf paras 12.48–12.49 below.

compliance with the Berne substantive standards, so that countries which had to comply with them anyway usually decided also to become Berne Members.[120]

In 2007, only Laos remains as a party to the UCC but not to the Berne Convention **4.45** for the TRIPS Agreement. This country, however, has begun measures to accede to the WTO/TRIPS Agreement and the Berne Convention, such that the UCC will no longer apply to Laos in the foreseeable future.

In the future, other countries might bring life back to the UCC, namely, those **4.46** countries which are not yet parties to any multilateral instrument covering copyright protection (Eritrea, Ethiopia, Iran, Iraq, Samoa, San Marino, Sao Tomé and Principe, Seychelles, Somalia, and Yemen). For the same reasons that the UCC originally attracted acceptance, these countries might adhere to the UCC as an initial step towards international copyright protection. Yet, it is more likely that if they embrace international copyright protection, then they will directly adhere to the Berne Convention (as did China in 1992), the WTO/TRIPS Agreement, or both. Indeed, all of the above countries except Eritrea, San Marino, and Somalia have already applied for WTO membership.

Even if no country in the future will be a party of the UCC without also being a **4.47** member of the Berne Convention or more recent treaties, the UCC remains applicable in a number of (probably rare) situations. In particular, the UCC applies between two countries which are both Contracting States to the UCC and parties to either the Rome Act or the Brussels Act of the Berne Convention, if the country of origin (under the rules of the Rome or Brussels Act of the Berne Convention) is a country outside the Berne Union and the work is created by a citizen of the other Berne Union country; of course, the criteria of eligibility under Article II of the UCC must still be fulfilled. The UCC also applies where the scenario is the same except that one of the two Berne Union countries has adhered to the Paris Act and the other one only to the Rome or Brussels Act.[121] Since, in 2007, there are no more than five countries each which are Members only of the Rome and Brussels Acts of the Berne Convention,[122] the UCC will not apply very often in such scenarios.

Other scenarios of possible UCC application have been discussed, but are subject **4.48** to controversy and would not lead to any substantial applicability in any case.[123]

---

[120] eg the Berne Convention had seventy-seven members on 1 January 1988 ((1988) Copyright 6), on 1 January 1995 111 members ((1995) Copyright 14), and in July 2007 163 members.

[121] Art 32 of the Berne Convention.

[122] These are Lebanon, New Zealand, Malta, Pakistan, Zimbabwe (Rome Act), and Bahamas, Chad, Fiji, Madagascar, and South Africa (Brussels Act).

[123] A Bogsch, *The Law of Copyright under the Universal Convention* (3rd edn, 1968) 120–2; cf also S von Lewinski, 'The Role and Future of the Universal Copyright Convention' (2006) October e-Copyright Bulletin UNESCO 1, 6–10.

Even where the UCC is not applicable today, it remains important where it is necessary to know whether a specific work is still protected in the relationship between particular countries. In such cases, one has to chronologically verify the status of protection of the work in the relation between such countries.[124] Yet, given its overall limited importance today, this concludes detailed discussion of the UCC in this book.

B. The main neighbouring rights conventions

(1) The Rome Convention of 1961

(a) Early steps towards the introduction of neighbouring rights

4.49 The International Convention for the Protection of Performers, Producers of Phonograms and Broadcasting Organisations of 26 October 1961 (Rome Convention), was the first multilateral convention covering selected neighbouring rights. Several reasons show why the first neighbouring rights convention was adopted a long time (namely 75 years) after the first important multilateral copyright convention. First, the need to protect performers, phonogram producers, and broadcasting organizations primarily emerged as a consequence of technical progress, which brought about the possibility of recording performances and other sounds and broadcasting programmes. In the field of copyright, the comparable technical progress triggering the need for protection was the possibility of printing works. While the printing press had been invented in 1492 by Johannes Gutenberg, Edison's sound recording invention followed only in 1877 and became widely used at the beginning of the twentieth century. Radio broadcasting started a little later (eg, in Germany in 1923) and television broadcasting even later, in the mid-1930s.[125]

4.50 Early instances of recognition and favourable consideration of protection for performing artists include a 1900 case before the Regional Court Berlin, recognizing protection to an opera singer against reproduction of phonographs incorporating his singing,[126] and a favourable ALAI debate in 1903 regarding the protection of solo performers.[127] In the early 1930s academic literature on the subject discussed protection mainly for performing artists, but also phonogram

---

[124] The UCC played a role, eg in recent court cases in Germany: OLG Frankfurt/M of 7 October 2003, (2004) ZUM-RD 349 (on the question whether a particular work first published in the USA in 1939 was protected in Germany in 2000), and BGH (Supreme Court) of 29 March 2001, 'Lepo Sumera', (2001) GRUR 1134.

[125] BGH of 13 May 1982, (1982) GRUR 727, 730–1.

[126] LG Berlin (1900) GRUR 131–2. The court based its decision on the consideration that the interpretation of music by a singer reflected his originality.

[127] C Masouyé, *Guide to the Rome Convention and to the Phonograms Convention* (1981) 7.

producers and broadcasting organizations began to blossom, after the very early pledge for performers' protection by Joseph Kohler in 1909.[128] During the same time, in 1933, the International Federation of the Phonographic Industry (IFPI) was founded and started to claim protection for the phonographic industry; similarly, organizations such as the International and European Broadcasting Unions claimed the need for their members' protection.

Early legislative attempts to address the protection of neighbouring rights, in **4.51** particular of performers and phonogram producers, include the 1910 amendment of the German Literary Authors' Rights Law of 1901 which created in its Article 2(2) a legal fiction to the effect that the performer was recognized as the author of an adaptation because and to the extent that he caused a transformation of works on 'devices for instruments which serve the mechanical communication for the hearing'; such transformation was assimilated to an adaptation. This approach of granting performers in such circumstances the rights of an author of an adaptation was also followed in the Swiss, Austrian, Czech, and Hungarian Copyright Acts. Yet, this right was usually considered to be transferred to the phonogram producer, as explicitly stated in the 1920 amendment to the Austrian Copyright Act 1895.[129] A number of other early laws provided for a similar kind of protection. In contrast, the British Dramatic and Musical Performer's Protection Act of 31 July 1925 provided for a mere criminal law protection of performers instead of exclusive rights, in addition to copyright protection for phonogram producers.[130] A number of laws followed from the mid-1930s, but they still provided only a fragmentary and also diverse protection mainly for performers and phonogram producers.

(b) Early steps at the international level in the context of the Berne Convention

At the international level, it was as early as at the Berlin Revision Conference of **4.52** the Berne Convention of 1908 that Great Britain questioned 'whether it would not be desirable to include in the Convention a provision specifically giving international copyright protection, in suitable cases, to gramophone disks, pianola roles and so on'. This suggestion was, however, opposed because 'this subject was on the borderline between industrial property and copyright and might conceivably be held to belong more properly to the former category'.[131]

---

128 J Kohler, 'Autorschutz des reproduzierenden Künstlers' (1909) GRUR 230–2; references to European literature in the field in the 1930s are given in A Baum, 'Über den Rom-Entwurf zum Schutze der vortragenden Künstler, der Hersteller von Phonogrammen und des Rundfunks' (1953) GRUR International 197–8.
129 ibid 199.
130 ibid 189 f; also the Danish and Polish laws recognized copyright protection for phonograms, ibid.
131 ibid 199.

4.53   At the following Revision Conference of the Berne Convention in Rome 1928, proposals were made to grant performing artists an exclusive right of broadcasting and, in the case of mechanical recording, an author's right in such an 'adaptation'.[132] Also, Great Britain again proposed protection for phonograms.[133] Yet, the relevant commission rejected such provisions because these matters were considered (in particular by France) to be outside the scope of the Berne Convention and to be premature for the international level, considering that even at the national level, legislation in the field had hardly been adopted yet.[134] Only the *vœu* was expressed that the Union countries should envisage the possibility of measures for the safeguard of the rights of performing artists.[135]

(c) A separate initiative outside the Berne context

4.54   The next step took place outside the context of the Berne Union and related only to the protection of phonograms. In 1935, the Italian government took the initiative to convoke an international diplomatic conference for the adoption of a convention on the protection of phonograms to take place in Rome in 1936. Italy wanted to respond to the claims of the phonographic industry in a separate framework outside authors' rights protection and therefore outside the Berne Convention. Yet, only a few governments responded positively to the invitation. In particular, the United Kingdom whose phonographic industry at the time played a leading role in Europe rejected the invitation, possibly due to the then tension between the United Kingdom and Italy resulting from the Abyssinian War. In the end, the Italian government had to renounce organizing the conference.[136]

(d) The Conference of Samaden 1939: Draft Annexes to the Berne Convention

4.55   Soon thereafter, but now under the auspices of the Berne Union and the International Institute for the Unification of Private Law, a committee of copyright experts, excluding any representatives of interested parties, was convoked in July 1939 in Samaden (Switzerland). Its task was to consider, on the basis of a Draft Treaty elaborated by the former director of the Bureau of the Berne Union, Dr Ostertag, a possible international treaty for the protection of performers, phonogram producers, and broadcasting organizations as well as other subject matter such as the resale right and protection of letters. It was based on the

---

[132]   This proposal corresponded to earlier national law where performers were regarded as authors of adaptations, cf para 4.51 above; cf proposals on Arts 11[bis](2) and 13 (1bis), Actes de la conférence (n 38 above) 260, 262–4.

[133]   Actes (n 38 above) 263.

[134]   ibid 262–4.

[135]   cf *Vœu* V, (1928) Droit d'auteur 85.

[136]   Baum (n 128 above) 199.

principle of national treatment and a number of minimum rights, even including a moral right for performing artists. It was conceived as an agreement connected to the Berne Convention, and thus to be open for accession only by Berne Union countries.[137]

Regarding the neighbouring rights, the committee of experts elaborated proposals **4.56** for two treaties (rather than one, as under the Draft), namely one on performers and phonogram producers, and a separate one on broadcasting organizations, albeit both as annexes to the Berne Convention. The proposals also deviated in substance from the Draft by Ostertag.[138] These Draft Annexes to the Berne Convention were intended to be adopted at the next revision conference of the Berne Convention planned to take place in Brussels later in 1939.[139] This plan was obviously frustrated by the outbreak of the Second World War.

(e) A new start at the Brussels Conference of the Berne Convention

When the Brussels Revision Conference finally took place in 1948, it did not **4.57** adopt these Annexes, since the chances for an agreement were low from the outset, and negotiations soon after the end of the war were difficult in general. Instead, the Brussels Revision Conference concentrated on issues within the scope of the Berne Convention. However, in respect of performers, phonogram producers, and broadcasting organizations, there was at least one point which was clarified by the Conference: according to the majority of delegates, the protection of such subject matter (which had been proposed to be included in the Berne Convention by Great Britain) did not belong in the framework of the Berne Convention and therefore had to be regulated elsewhere. The Conference adopted a *vœu* according to which Berne Union countries should study the protection of performers, phonogram producers, and broadcasting organizations, taking into account that such protection should not affect authors' rights.[140]

(f) Subsequent work leading to the Rome Convention

As a consequence of the 1948 Brussels Conference, the Standing Committee of **4.58** the Berne Union was created and convened regularly from September 1949. In the following years, continuous and important work on the way to the future international convention on the protection of neighbouring rights was

---

[137] cf the Draft and its presentation in F Ostertag, 'Nouvelles Propositions pour la Conférence de Bruxelles' (1939) Droit d'auteur 71 ff, 62 ff.

[138] cf the proposals in Anon, 'La Protection internationale des droits voisins du droit d'auteur' (1940) 109 ff, 125, 134; Baum (n 128 above) 202.

[139] Ricketson/Ginsburg (n 11 above) 19.05.

[140] *Vœu* VI–VIII, Documents of the Conference of Brussels, 428, 587; Masouyé (n 127 above) 8.

accomplished in this Committee.[141] Likewise, intensive work was carried out by the associations of interested parties, such as CISAC (International Confederation of Societies of Authors and Composers) and ALAI (which adopted a joint draft, which included primacy of authors' rights over the exercise of related rights, in 1956),[142] IFPI, the OIR (Organisation Internationale de Radiodiffusion, practically a predecessor of the European Broadcasting Union (EBU)) and the International Federation of Musicians (FIM). At the 1950 Session of the Berne Standing Committee, the delegate of the International Labour Organization (ILO) made it clear that the protection of performing artists had long since been among its areas of activities[143] and that it had to preserve the right to proceed further with its own work. The potential split of performers' rights in a separate convention under the auspices of the ILO, however, carried the danger that the provisions in different treaties would be incompatible. The participants, including the interested parties, agreed that the conflicting interests could best be balanced in a common convention for all three groups of right owners. In fact, the OIR and IFPI presented to the 1950 Committee a commonly elaborated draft convention including the three groups; the FIM had not participated merely because it was founded only in August 1948. Consequently, the ILO was invited to participate in the future work and agreed to do so. This cooperation cleared the way towards the Rome Convention.

4.59 A number of drafts for an international treaty preceded the Rome Convention: the draft of November 1951 (Rome Draft)[144] elaborated by a Sub-commission of the Standing Committee of the Berne Union together with delegations of the ILO and UNESCO[145] and representatives of performing artists, phonogram producers, broadcasting organizations as well as of ALAI and CISAC; the 1956 draft of the ILO (Geneva Draft);[146] a 1957 draft prepared by experts from twelve governments upon invitation of the Berne Union and UNESCO in Monaco

---

[141] Baum (n 128 above) 204–9; the reports of the sessions are published in the journal Droit d'auteur, eg (1949) Droit d'auteur 132; (1950) Droit d'auteur 127; (1951) Droit d'auteur 70, 122, 137; (1952) Droit d'auteur 100.

[142] Anon, 'Sixième Session du Comité permanent de l'Union internationale pour la protection des œuvres littéraires et artistiques' (1956) Droit d'auteur 69, 71–3.

[143] The ILO had begun such work already in 1926—at a time when the upcoming mechanical recording started to threaten employment opportunities for performers and therefore their standard of living, Masouyé (n 127 above) 8.

[144] (1951) Droit d'auteur 140. According to the mandate of the Berne Bureau, the drafts were not based on the drafts of Samaden and of OIR/IFPI.

[145] Since UNESCO had already started to work in the field of copyright in the context of the planned UCC from 1947 (cf paras 4.34–4.35 above), it was logical that it became involved in the plans on neighbouring rights, too.

[146] (1956) Droit d'auteur 93.

(Monaco Draft);[147] and, given the differences of the drafts by the ILO on the one hand and the Berne Union/UNESCO on the other hand, the Hague Draft adopted by a joint committee of governmental experts of the Berne Union, UNESCO, and the ILO.[148] This latter common draft was the basis for the Rome Convention, which was adopted one year later and signed by eighteen countries.[149]

(g) The development of the Rome Convention after 1961

The Rome Convention came into force on 18 August 1964, after ratification by six countries.[150] To date, it has not been revised. Its membership initially grew slowly; as of 31 December 1976, only nineteen countries were Contracting States to the Rome Convention.[151] Later, the 'Model Law concerning the protection of performers, producers of phonogram and broadcasting organisations' drafted by the Intergovernmental Committee of the Rome Convention in 1974 on the basis of the Rome Convention helped promote national legislation in the field.[152]   **4.60**

The Convention indirectly gained new influence as a model for more recent international treaties, in particular the TRIPS Agreement and the WPPT.[153] It has also influenced regional harmonization in the European Community.[154] As of August 2007, it has eighty-six Contracting States.   **4.61**

Like the copyright conventions, the Rome Convention is based on the principles of national treatment (though with a controversial, potentially different scope from that of the Berne Convention),[155] minimum standards of protection for the three groups of right owners, and the principle that only specified formalities can be required in respect of phonograms. Since this Convention is—directly or indirectly—still of major importance in the field of neighbouring rights, it will be discussed in more detail below.[156]   **4.62**

---

147 On the session, see (1957) Droit d'auteur 72; see also ibid 245 for consultations of governments, and the Monaco Draft.

148 (1960) Droit d'auteur 161.

149 Argentina, Austria, Belgium, Brazil, Cambodia, Chile, Denmark, Federal Republic of Germany, France, Great Britain, Iceland, India, Italy, Mexico, Spain, Sweden, Vatican, Yugoslavia.

150 Masouyé (n 127 above) 75.

151 Nordemann/Vinck/Hertin/Meyer (n 2 above) Art 25 RC n 2; for a number of reasons, cf also paras 4.63–4.64 below.

152 cf (1974) Copyright 163 ff; Masouyé (n 127 above) 12.

153 On Art 14(1)–(3) and (6) of the TRIPS Agreement and comments, cf paras 10.89–10.96 and 10.100–10.102 below; on the WPPT, see ch 17 below.

154 It has particularly influenced provisions in the 1992 Dir, eg Arts 8(2) and 10 EC Rental Rights Dir, cf Vol II ch 6.

155 cf para 6.27 below and further references; on the WPPT, cf paras 17.45–17.46 below.

156 cf ch 6.

(2) The Geneva Phonograms Convention of 1971

(a) Reasons for the adoption of the Geneva Phonograms Convention

4.63 Why was a new treaty on the protection of phonogram producers considered necessary only a few years after the Rome Convention had entered into force in 1964 and already provided for such protection? Limited membership of the Rome Convention (only 11 Contracting States in 1971)[157] seemed to show that this Convention did not meet the needs of many countries. Countries of the author's rights system with a strong authors' rights tradition were principally reluctant to introduce neighbouring rights. Countries of the copyright system at first sight would have been natural candidates for membership, since they used to grant copyright protection for phonograms; yet, in 1971 they were only represented in the Rome Convention by the United Kingdom. The main obstacle preventing countries of the copyright system joining the Rome Convention was its protection of performers and broadcasting organizations—a protection not usually granted by these countries.[158] Accordingly, while many copyright system countries were ready to protect phonograms not only domestically but also internationally, they were reluctant to introduce protection for the other two groups of right owners. This was certainly true for the USA as one important country where piracy of phonograms was widespread.[159] The Rome Convention with its coverage of the three groups of right owners therefore did not appeal to a large number of countries.

4.64 Another reason may have been the obligation under Article 24(2) of the Rome Convention also to adhere to the Berne or Universal Copyright Conventions.[160] In addition, the remuneration right for secondary uses for performers and phonogram producers may have been, for many countries, an obstacle to their adherence to the Rome Convention, even if this article is subject to reservations.[161] While these requirements may have been too demanding for some, other provisions seemed unsatisfactory for an efficient protection. In particular, the mere exclusive right of reproduction for phonogram producers[162] alone was not considered sufficient for a successful fight against piracy; an additional exclusive importation or distribution right would have been necessary for this purpose. Accordingly, the phonographic industry, pointing at the immense extent of

---

[157] (1971) Copyright 12.

[158] The United Kingdom provided only criminal protection for performers. This was, however, accepted as part of a compromise under the Rome Convention since it was considered very important to gain the United Kingdom (with its powerful phonographic industry) as a party of the Convention.

[159] E Ulmer, 'The Convention for the Protection of Producers of Phonograms against Unauthorised Duplication of their Phonograms' (1972) IIC 317, 320.

[160] cf Masouyé (n 127 above) 93.

[161] Arts 12 and 16 of the Rome Convention.

[162] Art 10 ibid.

piracy, strongly called for the adoption of an international treaty with the aim of fighting phonogram piracy.[163]

(b) Preparation for the Geneva Phonograms Convention

The call for such an anti-piracy treaty was then brought to the international level by **4.65** the United Kingdom, which presented the issue before the Intergovernmental Committee of the Universal Copyright Convention and the Permanent Committee of the Berne Union in 1970. These committees expressed their desires that the Directors General of UNESCO and WIPO establish a committee of governmental experts for the preparation of an international treaty in the field. Their desires quickly gained momentum as by May 1971 this plan was realized and the Committee of Experts adopted a Draft Convention on the basis of a working paper drafted by American, British, French and German experts, and recommended a Diplomatic Conference to be held within the same year.[164] The Diplomatic Conference was indeed held in October 1971; it resulted in the adoption of the Convention for the Protection of Producers of Phonograms against Unauthorized Duplication of their Phonograms (Geneva Phonograms Convention) on 29 October 1971 in Geneva. The Convention was signed by twenty-three states and entered into force on 18 April 1973. As of August 2007 it has seventy-six Members. The impressive speed with which the Convention was created—within thirteen months from the official initiative up to adoption—may be explained by the will of a sufficient number of countries to adopt such a treaty in conjunction with the limited focus on a very specific problem—the piracy of phonograms—and the flexibility regarding implementation. The narrow focus and the flexibility for member countries also served the goal of attracting the widest possible membership in the shortest possible time.[165]

(c) Main contents of the Geneva Phonograms Convention

The narrow focus of the Convention is reflected in its provisions, which are rather **4.66** basic and limited in number and scope. There is no national treatment obligation. The central obligation is the provision of protection of producers of phonograms against reproduction and importation made for the purpose of distribution to the public, and against distribution itself.[166] The Convention offers flexibility regarding the means for implementation of this provision. In particular, Contracting States may provide protection by a copyright or neighbouring right, by unfair competition, or by criminal sanctions.[167] The protection needs only to be granted to

---

163 cf Masouyé (n 127 above) 93.
164 (1971) Copyright 54 (report on the meeting: 54 ff, Draft Convention: 62 ff).
165 Masouyé (n 127 above) III (n 9.4).
166 Art 2 of the Geneva Phonograms Convention; for definitions of 'phonogram', 'producers of phonograms', 'duplicate', and 'distribution to the public', cf Art 1 of the Convention.
167 Art 3 ibid.

nationals of other Contracting States; under certain conditions, other existing criteria may be applied instead of the nationality of the producer.[168] Limitations of protection are only regulated where a Contracting State chooses the means of copyright, another specific right, or criminal sanctions as a form of protection. In these instances, states may provide the same kinds of limitations as those permitted with respect to the protection of authors' rights; compulsory licences for reproduction are, however, allowed only for the purpose of teaching or scientific research, are valid only within the territory of the Contracting State whose competent authority has granted the licence, and are subject to an equitable remuneration.[169] This provision on limitations was partly inspired by Article 15 of the Rome Convention. Its part on compulsory licences was promoted by the special interests of developing countries, and may be considered as a strongly simplified form of the compulsory licences adopted in the Paris Revisions of the Berne and Universal Copyright Conventions in the same year, though with the difference that the provisions of the Geneva Convention apply to all rather than only developing countries.

4.67 Contracting States are free to provide for a specific duration or not; if they do so, it must not be less than twenty years from the end of the year of first fixation or first publication.[170] Formalities possibly required under domestic law are deemed to be fulfilled if the formalities specified in Article 5 of the Geneva Phonograms Convention are fulfilled—an approach similar to that of the Rome Convention. There is no obligation to apply the Convention to phonograms fixed before its entry into force in the relevant country.[171] Unlike in the Rome Convention, adherence to a copyright convention or another neighbouring rights convention is not required, because negotiating parties preferred to keep the Geneva Phonograms Convention as open as possible. Accordingly, any adhering country need only be a country that is a Member of the United Nations, any Specialized Agency brought into relationship with the United Nations, the International Atomic Energy Agency, or that is a party to the Statute of the International Court of Justice.[172]

4.68 The protection of performers is explicitly left to the Contracting States. Existing protection of authors, performers, producers of phonograms, or broadcasting organizations under other international or under domestic law must not be limited or prejudiced by the Geneva Phonograms Convention.[173]

---

168 Art 7(4) ibid.
169 Art 6 ibid.
170 Art 4 ibid.
171 Art 7(3) ibid.
172 Art 9(1), (2) ibid.
173 Art 7(2), (1) ibid.

(d) Administrative and framework provisions

Although the Geneva Conference had been prepared by WIPO together with **4.69**
UNESCO, the governments decided that the administration of the Convention
would be simpler and more efficient if carried out through one organization only;
they voted for the International Bureau of WIPO as the administrative body.
However, as a compromise with a view to UNESCO, it was decided that the
deposit of the Convention and the instruments of ratification, acceptance, and
accession should take place with the Secretary General of the United Nations
who will notify the Directors General of WIPO, UNESCO, and the ILO.[174] The
International Bureau of WIPO has to assemble and publish relevant information, conduct studies, and provide services to facilitate the protection of phonograms, but it has no function in respect of revisions that are not even provided in
the Convention. The participating governments considered the object of the
Convention as permanent and modifications of the Convention as inappropriate, given the need for urgently achieving the aim of fighting piracy.[175] Also,
unlike under the Rome Convention, the establishment of an intergovernmental
committee has not been provided in the Geneva Phonograms Convention.[176]

(3) The Brussels Satellite Convention of 1974

(a) Reasons for the adoption of the Convention

In many respects, the reasons for the adoption of the Brussels Satellite Conven- **4.70**
tion and the approach taken for its adoption were comparable to those in the case
of the Geneva Phonograms Convention.[177] First, international piracy of programme-carrying signals transmitted by satellites had become a major problem
for broadcasting organizations, which therefore started to urge for international
protection from the late 1960s.[178] Secondly, the already existing Rome Convention, which covered the protection of broadcasting organizations, was not
considered to be satisfactory for a number of reasons:[179] its low number of members and little prospects for rapid, enhanced membership; its condition of
membership in the Berne Convention or the Universal Copyright Convention;
and its deficiency in not clearly covering protection against unauthorized
interception and transmission of signals broadcast by distribution satellites.

---

174 Arts 9 and 13(3) ibid; the WIPO is also addressee of notifications of denunciations.
175 Masouyé (n 127 above) 91.
176 On the background of the contents of the individual provisions of the Geneva Phonograms
Convention, cf Ulmer (n 159 above) 317, 323–34.
177 cf above paras 4.63–4.64.
178 G Straschnov, 'Comments on the Draft Convention against Unauthorised Distribution of
Program-Carrying Signals Transmitted by Satellites' (1972) 19/6 Bulletin of the Copyright Society
of the USA 429 ff; he explains the interests of broadcasting organizations in this respect.
179 cf paras 4.63–4.64 above on the weaknesses of the Rome Convention.

Even if most Contracting States represented in the Intergovernmental Committee of the Rome Convention and most delegations at the Brussels Satellite Conference thought that the Rome Convention applied to satellite broadcasting,[180] strong doubts were expressed mainly in academic literature because, in the case of distribution satellites and point-to-point transmissions, signals from the satellites were not directly received by the public.[181] In addition, national broadcasting organizations and their associations exercised their influence in many countries to argue against the ratification of the Rome Convention,[182] possibly due to the conflicting interests with performers and phonogram producers also covered by that Convention; they might have preferred a separate treaty for their interests only.[183] Broadcasting organizations also did not enjoy sufficient protection under the Berne Convention on the basis of rights derived from authors against unauthorized retransmission of direct satellite broadcasts because, at the time, direct satellite broadcasting was employed mainly for 'space travel projects' or sports and news broadcasts, rather than programmes including protected works.[184]

(b) Preparation of the Brussels Satellite Convention

4.71   Like the Geneva Phonograms Convention, the Brussels Satellite Convention was prepared in parallel and, later, jointly by UNESCO and WIPO.[185] The 1974

---

[180] More specifically: broadcasting by distribution satellites, point-to-point satellites, and the illicit broadcasting of broadcasts via direct satellites; Report on the Third Session of the Intergovernmental Committee of the Rome Convention of November 1971, (1971) Copyright 207 (no 18); report re the session of September 1972, (1972) Copyright 221 (no 12); General Report of the Brussels Conference, (1974) Copyright 267 ff (no 37).

[181] G Straschnov, 'Legal Protection of Television Broadcasts Transmitted via Satellite against their Use without the Permission of the Originating Organization' (1969) 17 no 1 Bulletin of the Copyright Society of the USA 27, 35; J von Ungern-Sternberg, *Die Rechte der Urheber an Rundfunk- und Drahtfunksendungen* (1973) 159–61.

[182] E Steup and E Bungeroth, 'Die Brüsseler Konferenz zum Schutz der durch Satelliten übertragenen Sendungen' (1975) GRUR Int 124, 130.

[183] Since the option of a separate treaty for broadcasters could even have strengthened their opposition to the ratification of the Rome Convention, and since the Rome members wanted to avoid the resulting detriment to the protection of performers and phonogram producers, most Rome members claimed to include into the Brussels Convention the protection of performers and phonogram producers, yet without success. At least, they successfully insisted on the adoption of a model law on neighbouring rights with a balance of interests also satisfying the European Broadcasting Organization, which then declared it would give up its opposition to the Rome Convention. The Model Law (cf (1974) Copyright 163 ff) was adopted by the Intergovernmental Committee of the Rome Convention during the Diplomatic Conference for the Brussels Convention 1974, cf Steup/ Bungeroth (n 182 above) 130–1.

[184] E Ulmer, 'Protection of Authors in Relation to the Transmission via Satellite of Broadcast Programs' (1977) LXXXXIII Revue internationale du droit d'auteur 4, 6.

[185] The predecessor of WIPO, BIRPI, convened the first working group of experts on this topic in 1968, (1968) Copyright 230; for the report of the UNESCO Committee of Governmental Experts' Meeting in 1969, cf (1970) Copyright 57; for the joint meetings of governmental experts of both organizations in Lausanne 1971, Paris 1972, and Nairobi 1973, cf (1971) Copyright 102, (1972) Copyright 142, and (1973) Copyright 147.

Diplomatic Conference in Brussels adopted the Convention Relating to the Distribution of Program-Carrying Signals Transmitted by Satellite.[186] It was signed by fifteen states and entered into force on 25 August 1979. As of August 2007, it has thirty Contracting States. Its basic approach is comparable to that of the Geneva Phonograms Convention: it is very limited in scope, it leaves a considerable degree of flexibility to the Contracting States, and it includes a number of similar provisions.

(c) Main contents of the Brussels Satellite Convention

First, the scope of the Brussels Satellite Convention is limited to the protection of **4.72** broadcasting organizations against the distribution of their programme-carrying satellite signals[187] by anyone to whom they were not intended. The Convention does not apply to the distribution of signals derived from a preceding legal redistribution by another organization.[188] Likewise, it does not apply to satellite broadcasts intended for direct reception by the general public,[189] since they are already protected by the Rome Convention. Similarly to the Geneva Phonograms Convention, Contracting States have a considerable amount of flexibility as to the implementation of such protection. They simply need to 'take adequate measures to prevent the distribution . . .',[190] be it through protection by a neighbouring right, copyright, criminal, administrative, telecommunication, or other law.[191] The broadcasting organizations which are eligible for protection in a Contracting State are nationals of another Contracting State. Limitations of protection are permitted under specified conditions for purposes of reporting on current events, quotations and—only in developing countries—teaching and research.[192]

In respect of the duration of protection, the Brussels Satellite Convention is even **4.73** more flexible than the Geneva Phonograms Convention: where a duration applies at all, it shall be fixed by domestic law.[193] The Convention does not even indicate a required minimum, although the draft texts of Lausanne and Paris provided for a minimum duration of twenty years (as in the Geneva Phonograms Convention). This duration then appeared in the Conference Report as one which could be considered adequate.[194]

---

[186] cf the General Report of the Diplomatic Conference, (1974) Copyright 267 ff.

[187] For definitions in relation to 'signal', 'satellite'/'program', 'distribution', etc. cf Art 1 of the Brussels Satellite Convention.

[188] Art 2(3) ibid.

[189] Art 3 ibid.

[190] Art 2(1) ibid.

[191] cf the General Report (n 186 above) 277 (no 79).

[192] Art 4 of the Brussels Satellite Convention; cf also Art 6 of the Geneva Phonograms Convention, which is not limited to developing countries.

[193] Art 2(2) of the Brussels Satellite Convention.

[194] Steup/Bungeroth (n 182 above) 128–9.

4.74 The Brussels Satellite Convention has even more in common with the Geneva Phonograms Convention: it does not apply retroactively;[195] it prohibits any interpretation to limit or prejudice the protection for authors, performers, producers of phonograms, and broadcasting organizations under any domestic law or international agreement;[196] no intergovernmental committee is established; and no provision is made for the revision of the Convention. In addition, the Secretary General of the United Nations rather than the Director General of WIPO functions as the depositary of the Convention and instruments of ratification, acceptance or accession, and notifications, and has to notify thereof, in particular, UNESCO, the WIPO, ILO, and ITU.[197] Moreover, it is open for accession to the same broad range of states as the Geneva Phonograms Convention.

C. Résumé

4.75 As this chapter shows, the Berne and Rome Conventions today are the most widely adopted and influential treaties on copyright and neighbouring rights among the treaties covered by this chapter. Therefore, two additional chapters are devoted to these conventions. By contrast, other treaties under this chapter, such as the UCC, today hardly apply any more, or are limited in membership and scope and therefore are not further discussed. For the last-mentioned reasons, other treaties are not even considered in this book.[198]

---

[195] Art 5 of the Brussels Satellite Convention.

[196] Art 6 ibid. Originally, a number of countries had even urged the inclusion of provisions protecting the authors, performers, and others whose achievements were contained in the broadcasts and obliging broadcasting organizations to inform authors and neighbouring right owners about the satellite broadcasts of their contributions in order to facilitate the exercise of their rights. Yet, the majority of countries rejected such proposals with varying arguments, cf Steup/Bungeroth (n 182 above) 129–30.

[197] Art 12 of the Brussels Satellite Convention

[198] eg the European Agreement on the Protection of Television Broadcasts of 22 June 1960, the European Agreement for the Prevention of Broadcasts Transmitted from Stations outside National Territories of 22 January 1965, the European Convention Relating to Questions on Copyright Law and Neighbouring Rights in the Framework of Trans-Frontier Broadcasting by Satellite of 11 May 1994, the European Convention on the Legal Protection of Services Based on, or Consisting of, Conditional Access of 24 January 2001, the Treaty on the International Registration of Audiovisual Works of 20 April 1989, and the Convention on Cyber-crime of 23 November 2001.

5

THE BERNE CONVENTION FOR THE PROTECTION OF LITERARY AND ARTISTIC WORKS (PARIS ACT 1971)

A. Principles of protection

(1) National treatment and minimum rights

(a) Origins, aim, and solutions in earlier versions

(i) Basic choices in the 1886 version The Berne Convention did not emerge **5.01** from nowhere, but against the background of the then existing network of bilateral agreements that had proved unsatisfactory for authors' needs, so that the next step of a multilateral agreement was needed to improve the situation.[1] The basic aim of both the bilateral treaties and the Berne Convention was to protect foreign works in the contracting states. The bilateral treaties achieved this aim in most cases by the principle of national treatment in different variations, for example, limited in its scope to specified rights or subject to material reciprocity; only in

---

[1] cf para 2.24 above.

some cases did specific rights stipulated in the bilateral treaties have to be guaranteed.[2]

5.02 The principle of national treatment alone proved insufficient for an adequate protection of foreign works because it could not guarantee more than the level of protection in the country for which protection was sought; such level could be very low and therefore not satisfy the authors' needs. Accordingly, the Berne Convention added the principle of minimum rights as a second pillar of a satisfactory international protection. This principle would guarantee to foreign works a certain level of protection laid down in the treaty, irrespective of the national law of the country for which the protection was sought. When the preparatory work for the Berne Convention showed that the primary goal of a universal law could not be achieved, the combination of the principles of national treatment and minimum rights was chosen as the second best solution.[3]

5.03 The drafters of the Berne Convention 1886 were faced with different models of national treatment under the existing bilateral treaties and different proposals submitted during the treaty preparation.[4] They decided to grant national treatment to nationals of Berne Union countries and to their successors in title, regarding their unpublished works as well as their works published in one of the Berne Union countries. Where the author was not a national of a Union country, the work was nevertheless protected in favour of the publisher of the work if published in one of the Union countries.[5] The scope of national treatment in countries where protection was sought included all rights granted under national law to domestic authors, whether these rights already existed or would be granted in the future. This extension to future rights had not been common in preceding bilateral treaties and was a decision favourable to authors.[6]

5.04 Another decision to be made was whether material reciprocity, which was quite common in bilateral treaties, should be provided for in the Berne Convention. The decision was again made in favour of authors: material reciprocity was in principle not admitted, except for the duration of protection, which was to be no

---

[2] S Ladas, *The International Protection of Literary and Artistic Property* (1938) Vol I, 57–61.

[3] para 2.45 above; yet, the principle of minimum rights as such was not explicitly expressed in the 1886 Act, but only referred to in Art 15 (Art 20 of the Paris Act), see S Ricketson and J Ginsburg, *International Copyright and Neighbouring Rights: The Berne Convention and Beyond* (2006) 6.81.

[4] See paras 2.05 ff above for the bilateral treaties. For the development of the provision on national treatment and the different drafts from 1883 to 1886, cf Ricketson/Ginsburg (n 3 above) 6.74–6.75; for minimum rights, whose development is not dealt with here, see ibid 6.81–6.82.

[5] Art 3 of the Berne Convention of 1886.

[6] Among the bilateral treaties that included future rights were those between Germany and Belgium of 1883, and France and Italy of 1884, cf Ladas (n 2 above) 57.

longer than that in the country of origin.[7] Less favourably for authors though, national treatment was made subject to the fulfilment of conditions and formalities in the country of origin; this choice largely corresponded to that of the ones prevailing in the pre-existing bilateral treaties.

Since duration and formalities had to be determined according to the laws of the **5.05** country of origin, the country of origin had to be defined. In respect of unpublished works, the Berne Union country to which the author 'belonged' was considered the country of origin; in respect of published works, the Union country of first publication was chosen to be the country of origin, thereby following the British proposal made on the model of British law. Where the first publication was simultaneous in several Union countries, the country of origin was determined to be the one with the shortest duration.[8]

(ii) **Amendments in subsequent versions** The revision conferences of the **5.06** Berne Convention brought about a number of clarifications and additions. The term 'published' was clarified to mean 'published for the first time'; in the case of simultaneous publication in a Union and a non-Union country, only the Union country was determined as the country of origin; and the 'simultaneity' (undefined in the 1886 Act and, hence, left to interpretation by national laws)[9] was defined as a period of thirty days in the Brussels Revision 1948.[10] Additional criteria were introduced at the Brussels Conference to determine the country of origin of works of architecture, and of graphic or plastic art that were a part of a building. In 1908, in addition to the minimum rights laid down in the Berne Convention of 1886 the principle of minimum rights was explicitly expressed in the context of the principle of national treatment.[11]

The Stockholm Revision Conference finally brought about the merit of **5.07** systemizing the provisions on national treatment including those on the country of origin and the eligibility of authors;[12] it also added further criteria of eligibility for authors and amended the definitions of 'published work'

---

[7] Material reciprocity regarding duration was controversial; given the diversity of national laws in this respect and the inability to agree on a mandatory minimum duration, the majority finally opted for material reciprocity in order to avoid any inconveniences of full national treatment in such a case, cf Ricketson/Ginsburg (n 3 above) 6.74.

[8] Art 2 of the Berne Convention of 1886; Ricketson/Ginsburg (n 3 above) 6.75, on the model of British law.

[9] National laws indeed defined 'simultaneous' by different periods, see Ricketson/Ginsburg (n 3 above) 6.77.

[10] It was previously discussed at the Rome Revision Conference, Ricketson/Ginsburg (n 3 above) 6.78.

[11] The Berlin Act also transferred the principle of national treatment from Art 2 to the new Art 4.

[12] This merit has been attributed to the president of the Commission I, Professor Dr E Ulmer, then director of the Max Planck Institute; D Reimer, 'Anknüpfungspunkte und Ursprungsland (Art 3–6)' (1967) GRUR Int 435–6.

and of 'country of origin'.[13] These amendments were reintroduced in Paris and adopted as part of the Paris Act 1971.[14]

(b) Conditions of application and mode of operation under the Paris Act 1971

5.08   The principles of national treatment[15] and minimum rights are laid down in Article 5(1) of the Berne Convention and apply in connection with its Articles 3 and 4 on the eligibility for protection and Article 5(4) on the country of origin. The following hypothetical case with its variations illustrates how these principles operate.[16]

5.09   Author A, a national and habitual resident of Laos (not a Berne Union Member) published a novel on 8 March 2004 in Laos and on 28 March 2004 in Mexico (a Berne Union Member). The novel is later exploited without the author's consent in the USA (a Berne Union Member). Can the author claim protection for his novel in the USA on the basis of national treatment under Article 5(1) of the Berne Convention? The proffered solution to this hypothetical case is presented in a series of methodical steps and is directly based on international norms, irrespective of questions of their internal applicability.[17]

5.10   (i) **Criteria of eligibility for protection of the author**   Article 5(1) of the Berne Convention begins with the beneficiary of national treatment and minimum rights, 'the author'. Apart from the meaning of authorship, including the question whether only natural persons or also legal entities can be authors under the Berne Convention,[18] it is the question of eligibility of authors for protection under the Berne Convention that matters here. This question is generally dealt with in Article 3, and specifically in Article 4 for cinematographic works, works of architecture, and artistic works incorporated in a building. Article 3 of the Berne Convention offers three criteria of eligibility as alternative options: nationality of a Berne Union country, habitual residence in such a country, and first publication in a Union country (or simultaneous publication in a country outside and a country inside the Berne Union). In addition, Article 4 offers the following criteria: for authors of cinematographic works, the headquarters or habitual residence of the maker of the works in a Union country; for authors of

---

[13] Reimer (n 12 above) 436–9.

[14] On the fate of the Stockholm Act, cf paras 4.19–4.21 above.

[15] Following the French designation (*principe d'assimilation*), national treatment is also referred to as the 'principle of assimilation'.

[16] A very specific problem of interpretation of these principles will be analysed in paras 7.27–7.30 below.

[17] In respect of the protection of foreigners, most national laws (where they apply) simply refer to the 'international treaties that apply' and thereby require the application of national treatment.

[18] cf paras 5.84–5.86 below.

works of architecture, the construction of their works in a Union country; and for authors of other artistic works incorporated in a building or other structure, the location of the building or other structure in a Union country.

Nationality   In the hypothetical case, the author is a national of Laos (not a Berne Union member) and therefore not eligible for protection under Article 3(1)(a) of the Berne Convention.   **5.11**

In general, the definition of 'nationality'[19] and the question of loss of citizenship are left to the national law of the Union country for which protection is claimed. Stateless persons and refugees are not covered by the term 'nationals' under the Berne Convention, even if some national laws assimilate them to nationals.[20] Where an author's heir or other successor in title is the beneficiary of protection,[21] the nationality of the successor in title is irrelevant.   **5.12**

Where an author changes nationality so as to become a national of a non-Union country at the time when her eligibility under the Berne Convention is already established, she remains eligible for protection; by contrast, where the author becomes a national of a Union country only after first publication outside the Union, the work has already been in the public domain in the Union and will remain so.[22] For unpublished works, it is controversial whether the nationality of a Union country is required at the time when the work is created, when the rights are asserted, or according to the leading opinion when the infringement occurs, in particular through unauthorized making available of the work to the public;[23] the question must be decided by the national law of the country for which protection is claimed.   **5.13**

Habitual residence   In the hypothetical case, the author from Laos also does not have her habitual residence in a Union country and therefore is not eligible for protection under Article 3(2) of the Berne Convention.   **5.14**

This criterion was proposed (but rejected) for the 1886 Act of the Berne Convention and finally introduced in 1967/1971. Its proponents argued that authors of non-Union countries living in a Union country also established a close link to the Union, such as the Italian composer Rossini who lived in France.   **5.15**

---

[19] This English term was only introduced in the Rome Act 1928; before, the French term 'ressortissants à' was translated as 'subjects or citizens' and used by BIRPI, while the United Kingdom used 'authors of any countries of the Union', cf Ricketson/Ginsburg (n 3 above) 6.04.

[20] W Nordemann, K Vinck, P Hertin, and G Meyer, *International Copyright* (1990) Art 3/4 BC n 6.

[21] cf Art 2(6) phr 2 of the Berne Convention.

[22] Reimer (n 12 above) 436, in respect of the habitual residence.

[23] For the change of nationality, cf Nordemann/Vinck/Hertin/Meyer (n 20 above) Art 3/4 BC n 11, with further references; Ricketson/Ginsburg (n 3 above) 6.08, pointing at the particular weight of the moment of first making available to the public, mentioned in the final report of the 1967 Conference.

The opponents were afraid that such a rule could discourage non-Union countries from adhering to the Union, since their authors could obtain Union protection by simply establishing their habitual residence in a Union country.[24]

5.16 The proposal at the 1967 Conference to employ the word 'domiciled' raised controversies which showed widely varying interpretations of this term. Finally, the term 'habitual residence' was chosen in order to stress the factual *versus* legal character of the residence,[25] in accordance with the reasoning behind all Berne criteria of eligibility, namely, to protect those who establish strong ties to a Union country. For the time at which the habitual residence must be in a Union country and the effects of its change, the same principles as those mentioned in connection with the change of nationality apply.[26] Where an author has habitual residences in several countries including a Union country, the question whether the residence in the Union country suffices for eligibility is left to the country for which protection is claimed; the Union countries did not reach agreement on this question.[27]

5.17 *First or simultaneous publication in a Union country*   Since the author in the hypothetical case is neither a national of a Union country nor has her habitual residence in one of them, her only chance to be eligible for protection under the Berne Convention is Article 3(1)(b). Accordingly, her work must have been first published[28] in a Union country, or simultaneously published in a country outside and a country inside the Union. Her novel was first published in a non-Union country (Laos), and twenty days later in a Union country (Mexico). Since 'simultaneous' publication is defined as a publication within thirty days of the first publication,[29] the criteria of Article 3(1)(b) of the Berne Convention are fulfilled, so that the author in this case is eligible for protection under Article 5(1) of the Berne Convention.

5.18 (ii) **Protected work**   As the second requirement under Article 5(1) of the Berne Convention, the author must claim protection in respect of a 'work protected under this Convention'. Articles 2 and 2[bis] of the Berne Convention determine which works are protected. A novel is without doubt a literary work covered by Article 2(1) of the Berne Convention.[30]

---

[24] Ricketson/Ginsburg (n 3 above) 6.05. The same argument was used in the negotiations on the treaty on audiovisual performances, cf para 18.21 below.

[25] Ricketson/Ginsburg (n 3 above) 6.06.

[26] cf the preceding text; Ricketson/Ginsburg (n 3 above) 6.07–6.08; Nordemann/Vinck/Hertin/Meyer (n 20 above) Art 3/4 BC n 11.

[27] Ricketson/Ginsburg (n 3 above) 6.09.

[28] On 'publication', see paras 5.32–5.34 below.

[29] Art 3(4) of the Berne Convention.

[30] For a deeper analysis of works under the Berne Convention, cf paras 5.62 ff below.

(iii) Union country other than country of origin

Overview　As the third requirement, the author must claim protection in a **5.19** country of the Union—the 'country of protection'. In the hypothetical case, the author does so in the USA, which is a Union country.

This country must be a country 'other than the country of origin'. In other words, **5.20** national treatment and minimum rights are not granted in the country of origin, but only in other Union countries. This rule reflects the restriction of the Berne Convention to international situations; domestic protection is left to domestic law. The country of origin is regarded as the 'home country' of the work where only domestic law applies in principle.[31] It is determined in Article 5(4) of the Berne Convention for five situations: (i) first publication in a Union country; (ii) simultaneous publication in several Union countries; (iii) simultaneous publication in a country outside and a country inside the Union; (iv) publication only in a country outside the Union; or (v) no publication at all.

In the hypothetical case, the author simultaneously (namely, within thirty days **5.21** after first publication[32]), published the novel in a non-Union country (Laos) and a Union country (Mexico), so that Mexico is the country of origin under Article 5(4)(b) of the Berne Convention. This means for the basic rule in Article 5(1) of the Berne Convention that she seeks protection in a Union country (USA) which is not ('other than') the country of origin (Mexico). Therefore, the author fulfils the conditions to claim national treatment and minimum rights under the Berne Convention.

Country of origin　Basically, Article 5(4) of the Berne Convention considers the **5.22** Union country of first publication as the country of origin, supplemented by the Union country of the author's nationality where no (first or simultaneous) publication takes place in a Union country. Accordingly, where first publication takes place in a Union country, that country is the country of origin. Where simultaneous publication (publication within thirty days of the first publication) takes place in several Union countries, the country of origin is the Union country with the shortest term of protection.[33] Where the work is simultaneously (within thirty days) published in a Union country and a non-Union country, the country of origin is the Union country.[34]

---

[31] See, however, Art 5(3) of the Berne Convention and paras 5.35–5.36 below.
[32] Art 3(4) of the Berne Convention.
[33] Art 5(4)(a) ibid. The choice of the country with the shortest term of protection was already part of the Berne Act 1886 and of earlier bilateral treaties, see above.
[34] Art 5(4)(b) ibid.

5.23   Where first publication does not (even simultaneously) take place in a Union country—namely in the case of unpublished works and works first published in a non-Union country without simultaneous publication in a Union country—the basic determining factor for the country of origin is the author's nationality.[35] However, instead of the author's nationality, other criteria apply to particular kinds of works: in the case of cinematographic works, the country of origin is the Union country where the maker of the work has his headquarters or habitual residence. In the case of works of architecture, it is the Union country where the work is erected; where other artistic works are incorporated in a building or other structure, it is the Union country where the building or other structure is located.

5.24   *Determining the country of origin in unregulated cases*   Some cases are not explicitly regulated; in all of them, the Union country for which protection is claimed will have to determine the country of origin. In particular, Article 5(4)(a) of the Berne Convention does not specify the country of origin where several Union countries grant the same, shortest term of protection. In this case, several solutions are suggested, such as the recognition of all those countries as countries of origin;[36] the country of the author's nationality; or the country with the most author-favourable national law.[37]

5.25   Where nationality of the author determines the country of origin,[38] several cases are not regulated, such as the case of co-authors with different nationalities. Here, an analogous application of Article 5(4)(a) of the Berne Convention has been proposed. Accordingly, the country of origin would be the country of the co-author's nationality with the shortest term of protection (in the case of several countries with the same, shortest term of protection, they would all be countries of origin).[39] In another unregulated case where the author is a national of several countries including only one Union country, the Union country will be the country of origin; where the author is a national of several Union countries, it has been proposed to again apply Article 5(4)(a) of the Berne Convention by analogy and to consider the country with the shortest term of protection as the country of origin.[40]

---

[35] Art 5(4)(c) ibid.

[36] Nordemann/Vinck/Hertin/Meyer (n 20 above) Art 5 BC n 8 (c); S Ricketson, *The Berne Convention 1886–1986* (1987) 5.72.

[37] Ricketson/Ginsburg (n 3 above) 6.57 (ii).

[38] ie in the case of an unpublished work or a work first published outside the Union without simultaneous publication in a Union country.

[39] Ricketson/Ginsburg (n 3 above) 6.57 (iii); Nordemann/Vinck/Hertin/Meyer (n 20 above) Art 5 BC n 8 (d).

[40] Ricketson/Ginsburg (n 3 above) 6.68.

In a third case, where the author is not a national of a Union country but has her 5.26
habitual residence in such country, the country of origin will have to be considered as the Union country of the habitual residence because authors with a habitual residence in a Union country are assimilated to nationals of a Union country
'for the purposes of this Convention'.[41] Where in such a case the author is simultaneously a national of one Union country and has her habitual residence in
another Union country, the country of nationality in the narrow sense will have
to be considered the country of origin, since the assimilation under Article 3(2)
of the Berne Convention is not required.[42] In a fourth unregulated case, where
the author changes nationality between different Union countries, the nationality at the time of first publication in a non-Union country may be considered to
determine the country of origin.[43] Where her work instead is unpublished, different approaches seem possible; this matter would have to be decided by the
country for which protection is claimed.[44]

The country of origin may change, in particular where a Union author of an 5.27
unpublished work later publishes it in another Union country; in this case, the
country of origin is the Union country of first publication from the time of publication.[45] Where a Union author first publishes a work in a non-Union country
that later accedes to the Berne Convention, the country of origin changes with
the accession from that of nationality to that of first publication.[46] The country
of origin also changes where an unpublished cinematographic or architectural
work is later published in a Union country other than the country of the headquarters of the producer or of the construction of the building, respectively.[47]

(iv) Contents of principles of national treatment and minimum rights 5.28
Article 5(1) of the Berne Convention describes national treatment as the grant of
'the rights which their [the Union countries'] respective laws do now or may
hereafter grant to their nationals'. This wording refers to the protection of nationals under the domestic laws of the Union countries for which protection is
claimed. The author in the hypothetical case may therefore claim the protection
granted to US citizens under US law.

---

[41] Art 3(2) of the Berne Convention.
[42] Ricketson/Ginsburg (n 3 above) 6.58.
[43] ibid 6.66; for works first published in a Union country, that country remains the country of
origin, ibid.
[44] For a detailed analysis, see ibid 6.66 and, regarding the unlikely case of change of nationality
from a Union to a non-Union country, ibid 6.67.
[45] Nordemann/Vinck/Hertin/Meyer (n 20 above) Art 5 BC n 8 (a); for an analysis of the question whether the country of nationality remains an additional country of origin (a suggestion not
followed by the author of this book), see Ricketson/Ginsburg (n 3 above) 6.57.
[46] For further details, see ibid 6.69; for the unlikely case of a Union author whose country leaves
the Berne Union, see ibid 6.70.
[47] Nordemann/Vinck/Hertin/Meyer (n 20 above) Art 5 BC n 8 (e).

5.29   In general, the scope of national treatment includes not only the level of protection granted in the country of protection at the time of its accession to the Berne Convention, but automatically also includes any further amendment of the national law ('do now or hereafter grant').[48] The 'respective laws' are usually copyright acts, but may also be any other national norms dealing with rights of authors in their works, or even established case law in this field.[49] The label of a law as a 'copyright act' alone is not the decisive criterion for a 'respective law'. Copyright acts may contain provisions not covered by national treatment, and laws other than copyright acts (such as library laws) may contain provisions falling under national treatment. The issue of 'respective law' is further analysed in Chapter 7.

5.30   The fulfilment of the requirements under Article 5(1) of the Berne Convention entitles authors not only to national treatment, but also to the enjoyment of minimum rights, as is expressed by the words 'the rights specially granted by this Convention'. These rights are specified in a number of articles of the Berne Convention.[50] Like national treatment, they need to be granted only in the international context, namely to 'foreign works' as further specified in Article 5 of the Berne Convention. The Berne Convention does not regulate any purely domestic situations; these are left to national law. Accordingly, it does not oblige Union countries to introduce the Berne minimum rights in favour of domestic works. Nevertheless, most countries have chosen to do so because they usually prefer not to discriminate against domestic in favour of foreign works.[51] Accordingly, the principle of minimum rights, despite its restriction to international situations, has in fact indirectly achieved a certain degree of approximation of the laws of the Berne Union countries.

5.31   Under Article 5(2) of the Berne Convention, the extent of protection and means of redress are governed by the laws of 'the country where protection is claimed'.

---

[48] This broad and dynamic concept of national treatment was taken over from some of the bilateral treaties preceding the Berne Convention, cf para 5.03 above.

[49] Nordemann/Vinck/Hertin/Meyer (n 20 above) Art 5 BC n 2.

[50] cf paras 5.94 ff below for a detailed presentation.

[51] A different problem arises where a country does not fulfil the obligation to introduce a certain minimum right in favour of foreign works and does not allow their authors to directly rely on the Berne Convention. For example, in the hypothetical case, the author may not obtain the full protection of moral rights as laid down in Article 6[bis] of the Berne Convention, to the extent that these rights may be considered not to have been fully implemented into US law (cf J Ginsburg and J Kernochan, 'One Hundred and Two Years Later: The US Joins the Berne Convention' [1988] 13/1 Columbia-VLA Journal of Law & the Arts 1, 31–7). This problem relates to the internal applicability of treaties and international dispute settlement, cf paras 8.11 ff and 8.16 ff below.

What is meant by this country is not the *lex fori* or the country where the claim is made, but the country for which protection is sought.[52]

(v) Particular problems: definition of 'publication' The following variation **5.32**
of the hypothetical case[53] focuses on the important term 'publication'. In this variation, the author (a national of Laos residing there) has composed and first performed a song in Mexico. She then claims protection against subsequent exploitation in the USA (a Union country). In this case, the author is not even eligible for protection and therefore enjoys no national treatment and no minimum rights: she is neither a national nor a habitual resident of a Union country, nor (unlike in the basic hypothetical case) has the work been 'published' in the Union country Mexico[54] because the performance of a musical work does not constitute 'publication'.[55]

The definition of a 'published work' in Article 3(3) of the Berne Convention **5.33**
reflects the function of the term 'first publication' in the Berne Convention. This term in particular serves to establish a point of attachment to the Berne Union in favour of those authors who are not otherwise attached thereto (namely, by nationality or habitual residence). As the basic hypothetical case shows, authors from non-Union countries may enjoy protection in all Berne Union countries by simply first (or simultaneously) publishing their works in a Union country. Article 3(3) of the Berne Convention envisages avoiding too easy enjoyment of the broad and strong Berne protection for 'outsiders' by requiring a relatively strong attachment to a Union country.[56] Otherwise, non-Union countries might see little need and motivation to adhere to the Berne Convention.

Such strong attachment is considered to exist where, in particular, copies in a suf- **5.34**
ficient number to satisfy the reasonable requirements of the public have been published with the author's consent.[57] To the contrary, the performance of a dramatic, dramatico-musical, musical, or cinematographic work, the public recitation of a literary work, the communication by wire, or the broadcasting of works each represent intangible ways of exploitation that are, in general, ephemeral. Therefore, they are not considered important enough to constitute 'publication' for the purpose of protecting 'outsiders' under the Berne Union.[58] Against this

---

[52] For arguments, see Ricketson/Ginsburg (n 3 above) 6.100, also with references to dissenting opinions.

[53] para 6.09 above.

[54] Art 3(1)(b) of the Berne Convention.

[55] Art 3(3) phr 2 ibid.

[56] Ricketson/Ginsburg (n 3 above) 6.44.

[57] An analysis of the individual conditions of Art 3(3) of the Berne Convention is beyond the scope of this book; see instead Ricketson/Ginsburg (n 3 above) 6.27–6.42.

[58] In addition, they were considered to be difficult to prove, Ricketson/Ginsburg (n 3 above) 6.45. For the exclusion of the exhibition of an artwork and the construction of a work of architecture, see ibid.

background, it may be challenging to determine whether or not making available on the internet constitutes 'publication' in the meaning of the Berne Convention.[59]

5.35   **(vi) Particular problems: protection in the country of origin**   In another variation of the hypothetical case, the author from Laos seeks protection in Mexico rather than in the USA. As established above, Mexico is the country of origin, so that the condition that the author must seek protection in a Union country 'other than the country of origin'[60] is not fulfilled. Accordingly, the author in principle is left to the Mexican provisions on the status of foreigners, irrespective of the Berne Convention. This is confirmed in Article 5(3) phrase 1 of the Berne Convention: it is only the domestic (Mexican) law which governs this situation. On the surface, this would mean that the author from Laos could not enjoy protection in Mexico (unless Mexican law protected foreign works in the described situation, but countries rarely do so).[61] However, Article 5(3) phrase 2 of the Berne Convention provides for non-discrimination where the author is not a national of the country of origin. Accordingly, the author from Laos may enjoy the same protection in Mexico as do Mexican citizens under Mexican law.[62]

5.36   At the same time, the author cannot enjoy the minimum rights of the Berne Convention in Mexico. Yet, the factual consequences of this provision are minimal, since the Union countries have regularly implemented the minimum rights in favour of domestic works too.[63] Consequently, the assimilation to nationals in the country of origin will mostly have the same effect as if that country also recognized minimum rights in the country of origin. Accordingly, although the Convention does not apply in the country of origin, in fact works are usually well enough protected there.

5.37   **(vii) Summary**   In summary, the systematic approach to protection under the Berne Convention is as follows: first, the author must be protected in respect of her work. The Convention itself lays down the criteria of eligibility of authors and determines the kinds of works covered by its protection. The author is covered by the Convention if one of the criteria of eligibility is fulfilled, namely nationality of a Union country, habitual residence in a Union country, or first publication in a Union country (or publication therein within thirty days after first publication in a non-Union country). Authors of cinematographic works, works of architecture, and artistic works incorporated in a building benefit from

---

[59] cf paras 7.31–7.33 below.
[60] Art 5(1) of the Berne Convention.
[61] Most countries discriminate between foreign and domestic works unless they are obliged by international law to grant protection to foreign works, cf para 1.11 above.
[62] Her work still must be covered by the Convention.
[63] cf para 5.30 above.

additional criteria. This broad openness of the Berne Convention even to protect works by non-national and non-resident authors, provided they otherwise strongly connect with a Union country, aims at stimulating the accession of non-Union countries, whose authors can experience the advantages of Union protection through first publication. Whether this system indeed produces these desired effects is difficult to ascertain.

In addition, the Berne Convention only provides for protection in international **5.38** situations, rather than in the 'home country' of the work. 'At home', namely in domestic situations, the Berne Convention in principle does not apply.[64] In order to determine the 'home country' of the work (called in this Convention the 'country of origin'), where the author would only be protected under domestic law, the drafters of the Convention have not chosen the most obvious criterion, namely, the author's nationality. Instead, they have primarily chosen the criterion of first publication in a Union country; the nationality criterion only applies where no publication or a publication outside the Union takes place.

This system has the effect of encouraging authors to first publish their works in a **5.39** Union country with a higher level of protection because, where material reciprocity applies, the work may then benefit from this level in Union countries with at least the same level of protection.[65] Indeed, a Swiss proposal at the 1967 Stockholm Conference to simplify the system by determining the country of the author's nationality as the country of origin was rejected, partly because of problems expected in the case of co-authors of different nationalities or authors of dual nationality, and partly because Union countries wanted to enable their authors to choose the country with the longer term of protection in order to secure better protection in many other Union countries.[66] In addition, the system has the effect of strengthening the publishing industry in countries with higher levels of protection.

(c) Exceptions to national treatment

Exceptions to national treatment by way of material reciprocity were introduced **5.40** into the Berne Convention in large part because the national laws of Union countries were so diverse that national treatment would have created unreasonable imbalances. Those granting stronger protection would have needed to grant their full protection to foreign works, while their own works would not have benefited from a comparatively strong protection.

---

[64] However, non-discrimination is guaranteed, see para 5.35 above.
[65] For material reciprocity, cf paras 5.40 ff below.
[66] Ricketson/Ginsburg (n 3 above) 5.70; Reimer (n 12 above) 438.

5.41 **(i) Duration of protection** The most important exception to national treatment applies to the duration of protection.[67] It is also called 'comparison of terms' or 'the rule of the shorter term' and constitutes a case of material reciprocity. It has been part of the Berne Convention in various versions since 1886, when the differences of the duration provided in the then ten Union countries were much greater than today: they varied between twenty and eighty years *pma*.[68] This diversity made an agreement on a minimum duration impossible, which easily explains the preference by the majority of the negotiating parties for material reciprocity—a model which had already prevailed under most bilateral treaties that preceded the Berne Convention.[69]

5.42 Article 7(8) of the Berne Convention first repeats the general rule—the country for which protection is claimed governs the duration—and then makes this rule subject to a shorter term in the country of origin[70] and thereby to material reciprocity where a country so chooses. Reciprocity can possibly apply only where the duration in the country of origin is shorter than that in the country for which protection is claimed. This may occur, for example, where the country of origin provides for the minimum term under the Berne Convention and the other country for a longer term, or where both countries provide for longer, but different terms. Accordingly, where country A (country of origin) provides for fifty years *pma* and country B (country for which protection is claimed) provides for seventy years *pma*, B may protect works from A for only fifty years *pma*. Also, where A provides for sixty and B for eighty years *pma*, B may protect the work from A for only sixty years *pma*. If in the above cases the country of origin were B and the country for which protection is claimed were A, material reciprocity could not apply, because country A only provides fifty and sixty years *pma* respectively, so that in no case could national treatment result in stronger protection than available under national law. Accordingly, in these cases, the work from B would be protected in A only for fifty and sixty years *pma*, respectively, but not for seventy or eighty years.

5.43 An important aspect of Article 7(8) of the Berne Convention is that the application of material reciprocity is voluntary. Accordingly, Union countries can be more generous than required and provide for full national treatment even in respect of works whose country of origin provides for a shorter duration. In the above initial cases, B could therefore protect works from A for seventy or eighty

---

[67] Art 7(8) of the Berne Convention.

[68] Ricketson/Ginsburg (n 3 above) 9.14.

[69] ibid; for discussion at revision conferences and various versions under revision acts, cf ibid 9.16 ff.

[70] Art 5(4) of the Berne Convention defines the country of origin; cf also paras 5.22–5.27 above.

years instead of fifty or sixty years. Article 7(8) of the Berne Convention is drafted so as to presume that countries apply material reciprocity, as shown by the wording 'unless . . . that country otherwise provides'. Most often, national legislation does not explicitly provide for a deviation from material reciprocity under Article 7(8) of the Berne Convention. Where it only contains a general reference to national treatment according to the relevant international treaties, it is doubtful whether such a non-specific reference can be interpreted as an intended deviation from the rule of material reciprocity; it seems that more specific provisions would be necessary to clearly show the intent of deviating from this reciprocity rule.[71]

Material reciprocity, where applied throughout an important economic area with **5.44** a longer duration than in other countries, may have the effect of encouraging other countries to extend their own durations in order to benefit from the longer duration in the economic area. These dynamics became visible when the European Community (EC) harmonized the duration at seventy years *pma* and rendered obligatory the application of material reciprocity under Article 7(8) of the Berne Convention.[72] Consequently, other countries with a shorter duration than seventy years *pma* could only benefit from the seventy years' term in the EC if they prolonged their own terms up to at least seventy years *pma*. Indeed, the USA for example amended its law (also) against this background.[73] Similar effects of material reciprocity have been observed regarding the resale right and the *sui generis* protection for databases after their harmonization in the EC.[74]

(ii) Works of applied art/industrial designs and models Even more than for **5.45** the duration of protection, considerable differences in the protection of works of applied art already existed in national laws of the Berne Union countries before 1886 and continuously thereafter. To mention only the basic differences of approaches, some countries granted copyright protection according to the general rules; other countries, given the utilitarian purpose and (often) industrial production or application of such works, instead provided for a special design or model protection outside copyright, usually with lower requirements and a lower

---

[71] In the USA, despite the lack of a specific provision on deviating from reciprocity, national treatment applies to the duration, since the Berne Convention is not self-executing and the Copyright Act does not distinguish between foreign and domestic works, see E Schwartz and D Nimmer, 'United States' in P Geller (ed), *International Copyright Law and Practice*, Vol II (looseleaf release 17), § 3[3], in particular n 49.

[72] Arts 1 and 7 of Dir 93/83 (as amended) harmonizing the duration of protection, cf for further details Vol 2 Part II ch 7.

[73] W Patry, *Patry on Copyright* (2006) 23-4.

[74] Material reciprocity under the EC Dirs on the Resale Right (2001/84) and Databases (1996/9) are analysed in Vol 2 Part II chs 9, 11. Unlike for the duration, US initiatives to provide a comparable protection under national law in order to benefit from the resale right and the *sui generis* database protection in the EC have so far not been successful.

scope of protection; and even other countries provided for both copyright and design protection, either applying them cumulatively or not.[75]

5.46 The fate of works of applied art under the Berne Convention changed throughout the revision conferences.[76] The continuing diversity of national approaches has prevented agreement on an unrestricted protection, even in the most recent version of the Berne Convention. Although these works are included in the list of Article 2(1) of the Berne Convention, Union countries are permitted to determine the extent and conditions of protection.[77] Accordingly, countries may choose to protect works of applied art by copyright law only, by a specific designs and models law only, or by both. Full national treatment in such a case would have created an imbalance where some countries granted only a design protection and others also copyright protection. Therefore, a number of countries insisted on the introduction of material reciprocity in this case.[78]

5.47 Accordingly, where the country of origin (A) protects works of applied art only as designs and models, and the country for which protection is claimed (B) provides for both a special design protection and copyright protection, B may refuse copyright protection to A but is obliged to grant design and model protection. Only where B does not provide for any design and model protection but exclusively for copyright protection must the work from A be protected in B as an artistic work under copyright.[79] Where, instead, B is the country of origin and A the country for which protection is claimed, the situation of material reciprocity does not arise at all: in this case, the work anyway could never obtain more than the level of protection granted in A, namely the designs and models protection.

5.48 **(iii) Resale right** The reasons for the introduction of material reciprocity regarding the resale right in 1948 were similar to those in the above cases: only a few Berne Union countries provided for the right, and those that did so offered a different scope or even did not consider it as a matter of copyright.[80] Also, the lack of interest in this right and the high diversity of its regulation have hindered its establishment as a minimum right, so that Berne countries may decide not to provide this right at all.[81] Given this situation, countries providing for the resale right expressed an interest in material reciprocity in order to avoid imbalances in relation with other countries; this concession alone would permit inclusion of the

---

[75] Ricketson/Ginsburg (n 3 above) 8.60.

[76] On the details of discussions and versions adopted at the different revision conferences, cf ibid 8.60–8.68.

[77] Art 2(7) phr 1 of the Berne Convention.

[78] Ricketson/Ginsburg (n 3 above) 11.64 on these dynamics in general.

[79] Art 2(7) phr 2 of the Berne Convention.

[80] Ricketson/Ginsburg (n 3 above) 11.59–11.61 on the development of this right.

[81] Art 14ter(2) of the Berne Convention; Ricketson/Ginsburg (n 3 above) 11.61.

right in the Berne Convention.[82] Accordingly, the Berne Convention provides for material reciprocity in the meaning of 'substantial equivalence', so that a country may reject, for example, protection in respect of manuscripts where the country to which the author belongs only provides a resale right for artworks but not for manuscripts.[83] The 'country to which the author belongs' is generally understood as the country of origin.[84]

(iv) Retaliation against nationals from non-Union countries Article 6 of the **5.49** Berne Convention has its roots in a specific, historical situation before 1914 when this case of material reciprocity was introduced on the basis of an Additional Protocol to the Berne Convention. The USA (then not a member of the Berne Union) protected foreign authors who were not resident in the USA in respect of their works written in the English language only under the condition of the manufacturing clause. This clause required that the copies intended for deposit and sale in the USA had to be printed from typeset within the USA.[85] At the same time, Berne Union countries such as Great Britain with its dominions and colonies (including an important neighbour of the USA, namely Canada) had to protect works from foreign (including US) authors resident in any Union country on the mere condition of first publication in a Union country, or simultaneous publication in a non-Union country such as the USA and a Union country like Canada. The imbalance of the situation is evident: US authors could easily obtain the protection of the Berne Convention in the entire Berne Union, while authors of Union countries were mostly prevented from obtaining protection in the USA.

In face of the danger of losing the British Empire as a Berne Union Member, its **5.50** proposal to introduce material reciprocity towards nationals of non-Union countries was accepted by all Union countries and, after its adoption in the Additional Protocol of 1914, incorporated in Article 6 of the Berne Convention at the 1928 Rome Conference.[86] Retaliation to date has only been applied by Canada, which imposed restrictions on specific rights of American authors under the Canadian Copyright Act 1921 in accordance with the Protocol upon its accession to the Protocol on 7 January 1924.[87] Today, Article 6 of the Berne Convention has lost

---

[82] Ricketson/Ginsburg (n 3 above) 11.64.
[83] For an analysis of the peculiar, unclear formulation of Art 14ter(2) of the Berne Convention, cf Ricketson/Ginsburg (n 3 above) 11.64–11.66, also on 'substantial equivalence'.
[84] Art 14ter(2) of the Berne Convention; Ricketson/Ginsburg (n 3 above) 11.64; see, however, Art 7(1) of the EC Resale Right Dir, which refers to nationality.
[85] The Chase Act of 1891 provided for this condition even in respect of books in any language, photographs, chromo- or lithographs; after the Act of 4 March 1909, these conditions were retained only in respect of works written in the English language; cf on more detail Ladas (n 2 above) 95.
[86] cf paras 4.11 ff above.
[87] (1924) Droit d'auteur 13.

most of its importance since most countries of the world are Berne Union members.

5.51 Under Article 6(1) of the Berne Convention, any Union country whose authors are not adequately protected in a non-Union country may retaliate against such non-Union country. It is up to the affected country to determine whether the non-Union country fails to protect its authors in an 'adequate manner', and if so, to decide on retaliation. Retaliation may only consist of restrictions rather than a complete denial of protection. The retaliating country has discretion to specify the kind of restriction, such as a denial of specific rights or a restriction of the term of protection. Retaliation is directed to works by non-Union authors without a habitual residence in a Union country. Initially, retaliation may be exclusively applied by the Union country where the work was first published. Only if this country retaliates may the other Union countries apply the same measures as the Union country of first publication; such retaliation is voluntary.

5.52 Article 6(2) of the Berne Convention excludes any retroactive effects of retaliatory measures; previously acquired rights remain unaffected. Retaliating countries must give notice of the retaliation and its specifications by a written declaration to the Director General of WIPO who then shall communicate the declaration to all Union countries in order to enable them to take their own positions towards the non-Union country.[88] The requirement of giving notice has not been considered as a condition for validity of the retaliatory measure.[89]

5.53 **(v) Privileges for developing countries** Material reciprocity in the context of privileges for developing countries[90] is a response to a permitted reservation. Developing countries that accede to the Berne Convention can, at least temporarily, declare that they apply, in respect of the translation right, Article 5 of the Berne Convention in the versions of 1886 or 1896 instead of Article 8 of the Paris text 1971.[91] Accordingly, they may grant the exclusive translation right for only ten years from the publication of the original work in a Union country. This reservation is permitted where translations are made into languages in general use in the relevant country. Where a developing country makes such a reservation, the other countries may apply material reciprocity in relation to works for which the country of origin is that developing country. This case of material reciprocity seems to be largely insignificant as of today. In 2007, only slightly more than ten countries have made this reservation to which countries may respond by material reciprocity.

---

[88] Art 6(3) of the Berne Convention.
[89] Ricketson/Ginsburg (n 3 above) 6.20 (in n 70).
[90] Art 30(2)(b) phr 2 of the Berne Convention.
[91] Art 30(2)(b) phr 1 ibid.

(2) Principle of 'no formalities'

(a) Historical background

Under many bilateral treaties preceding the Berne Convention, protection was **5.54** only granted upon fulfilment of formalities required by the law of the country of origin, and in some cases also by the law of the country for which protection was claimed.[92] The Berne Convention of 1886 considered it sufficient for a work to fulfil the formalities in the country of origin, as clarified by the so-called Interpretative Declaration at the Paris Conference 1896.[93] Yet, even this requirement resulted in many practical problems; the requirement was not well enough facilitated by the evidentiary presumptions under Article 11 of the Berne Act of the Berne Convention.[94] Therefore, the Berlin Revision Act of 1908 completely abolished any requirement to fulfil formalities.[95]

(b) Contents of the principle

Under the first half of Article 5(2) phrase 1 of the Berne Convention, authors **5.55** must enjoy and exercise their rights under the Berne Convention irrespective of the fulfilment of any formalities. This principle of 'no formalities', like the principles of national treatment and minimum rights, only applies in the international context, namely when protection is claimed in a Union country other than the country of origin. Accordingly, domestic legislation may impose formalities for domestic works (only)—a choice made by the USA upon its accession to the Berne Convention as regards registration as a condition for initiation of infringement actions.[96]

The absence of formalities for the 'enjoyment' of authors' rights means that the **5.56** genesis of authors' rights under the Berne Convention must not depend on formalities; accordingly, these rights must come into existence and be recognized without fulfilment of formalities.[97] In addition, the 'exercise' of the authors' rights must not be subject to any formalities, as already specified in the 1908 Berlin Act. Thus, formalities must not be a prerequisite for the bringing of proceedings to enforce authors' rights under the Convention.[98] 'Formalities' must be understood in a wide sense so as to include any formal conditions, as confirmed

---

[92] para 2.14 above.
[93] Ricketson/Ginsburg (n 3 above) 6.84, 6.85.
[94] eg the infringer had to prove failure to comply with formalities in the country of origin, see ibid 6.86.
[95] ibid 6.87.
[96] S 411 of the US Copyright Act (Title 17 USC); for details, see Ginsburg/Kernochan (n 51 above) 13.
[97] Ricketson/Ginsburg (n 3 above) 6.103, referring to the historical interpretation.
[98] ibid 6.104 with examples.

by historical interpretation.[99] Examples are registration, deposit, or filing of copies with an authority, placement of a copyright notice on the work, the payment of fees for registration, or the submission of any declarations. Prohibited formalities only relate to copyright-specific requirements rather than to general procedural prerequisites, such as the payment of general court fees.[100] They do not cover facilitation measures such as those to facilitate proof of authorship.[101] Formalities must be distinguished from the substantive law conditions for the protection of a work (eg, originality), and from the fixation requirement that is permitted under Article 2(2) of the Berne Convention; neither are formalities under the Berne Convention.[102]

5.57 For some conditions under national law, one may doubt whether they are permitted under the Convention. In particular, the requirement of registration as a condition to claim statutory damages[103] or the public assertion of moral rights under the UK CDPA[104] might require careful scrutinizing. Registration requirements regarding assignments and licences may raise doubts under certain conditions.[105] Mandatory collective administration is usually recognized as permitted,[106] as are mandatory rules for copyright contracts in written form or specification requirements, for example; such rules protect the author and therefore do not contradict the prohibition of formalities that protects the public.[107]

---

[99] ibid 6.103.

[100] ibid 6.105.

[101] ibid 6.108.

[102] WIPO Doc SCCR/13/2 p 3.

[103] S 412 of the US Copyright Act; although statutory damages are generally sought, since they only are invaluable and the actual damage is often difficult to prove, and although, therefore, they are necessary to fully enjoy the value of the author's rights, commentators so far do not seem to have put into question the compatibility of this rule with the 'no formalities' principle; see Ginsburg/Kernochan (n 51 above) 14–15; Nordemann/Vinck/Hertin/Meyer (n 20 above) Art 5 BC n 7; Ricketson/Ginsburg (n 3 above) 6.108 in n 324 who, at the same time, admit that the distinction between a formality and the means of redress that is subject to national law (Art 5(2) phr 2 of the Berne Convention) may be delicate, ibid 6.108.

[104] ibid 6.104.

[105] eg Art 45(1) of the Albanian Copyright Act no 9380 of 28 April 2005 requires deposit, registration with, and certification by the Albanian Copyright Office of the publishing contract for it to become effective. Although this rule may to some extent serve the interest of authors and publishers in transparency, it mainly protects the public (potential future licensees) and hinders the exercise of rights by contract without deposit, registration, and certification; on the distinction between author-protective and public-protective rules, see below in the following text and at n 107. For various national rules regarding registration of contracts, see WIPO Doc SCCR/13/2 at 10 and Annexes.

[106] Nordemann/Vinck/Hertin/Meyer (n 20 above) Art 5 BC n 7; S von Lewinski, 'Mandatory Collective Administration of Exclusive Rights: A Case Study on its Compatibility with International and EC Copyright Law' (2004) 1 e.Copyright Bulletin of UNESCO, 1, 14–15; Ricketson/Ginsburg (n 3 above) 6.105 in n 322.

[107] ibid 6.105.

(c) Rationale of the principle

The principle of 'no formalities' is crucial for the realization of an effective inter-national protection of authors' rights. Its rationale is rooted in the natural rights theory according to which the mere creation of the mind naturally results in the creator's (ie author's) right therein. The rationale also becomes evident when considering a situation with formality requirements: if an author had to fulfil national formality requirements in other Berne Union countries in order to enjoy and exercise protection there, he would rarely do so, and this for different reasons. For example, he might be unaware of such obligation, especially where his domes-tic law does not require formalities; even if he were aware thereof, he might not have the energy, means, or time to find out what formalities have to be fulfilled and what has to be done in order to do so, especially if information is available only in a foreign language; often, too, an author may not be able or willing to pay the relevant fees. **5.58**

Reality shows that most authors are interested in creation rather than administration, and thus tend to neglect such administrative efforts, even at the risk of losing protection. Many may also be unprepared to pay an agent or attorney to make such efforts for them, especially if they are not sure whether a sufficient degree of exploitation will take place in the relevant countries. This situation exists in particular regarding works (such as artworks and sculptures), that are rarely published or otherwise exploited by businesses. Even where local publishers could take over the task of fulfilling formality requirements in foreign countries, they (especially the smaller publishers) might also be unaware of the problem or unprepared to make the necessary efforts. Moreover, these problems would be compounded when an author or publisher sought to exploit a work in multiple foreign countries, each of which could maintain different formality requirements. **5.59**

The requirement to fulfil formalities for the enjoyment and exercise of authors' rights has indeed proved to be a major stumbling block for an adequate and effect-ive international protection. In particular, when the USA was not yet in the Berne Union but only a party to the Universal Copyright Convention which allowed for formality requirements, most non-American works did not in fact obtain protection in the USA due to the failure to fulfil the formalities.[108] **5.60**

---

[108] On the formalities under US copyright law preceding the Berne Implementation Act, see Patry (n 73 above) 6–61 ff.

(d) Voluntary registration

5.61 Some countries provide for voluntary registration of all or certain kinds of work or of transfers of rights.[109] The legal effects of registration may be a rebuttable presumption that the person who registers the work is the author or other owner of copyright; or prima facie evidence that the work subsisted on the day of registration, or that copyright subsists in the work, or that the person registering the work is its right owner.[110] Thereby, voluntary registration may facilitate the exercise of copyright and for this reason alone does not contravene the 'no formalities' principle. Because of certain positive effects of voluntary registration, it has reappeared in recent policy debates, especially regarding 'orphan works' and digital rights management. In particular, WIPO envisaged this topic for its future agenda and submitted a survey on existing systems of voluntary registration on the basis of a questionnaire to its Member States.[111] At the same time, registration systems may have potential negative effects; for example, registration is often misunderstood as a guarantee for the subsistence of copyright protection in favour of the designated author; it might be abused by those who are not the real authors; and it may be costly for the author.

B. Substantive standards of protection

(1) Works protected under the Convention

(a) General remarks

5.62 **(i) Overview**   The notion of 'work' is essential for the application of the Berne Convention because it determines the very subject matter of protection under the Convention.[112] National treatment, minimum rights, and the absence of formalities need to be guaranteed only in respect of the protected works.

5.63 The provisions dealing with protected works[113] are not systematically arranged. Article 2(1) of the Berne Convention offers a basic definition of 'literary and artistic works', followed by a list of examples. Articles 2(3), (5) and 14bis(1) phrase 1 of the Berne Convention add specific works, namely translations, alterations, and collections of works, as well as cinematographic works. Article 2(7) of the Berne Convention leaves Union countries a certain leeway in respect of works of

---

[109] For examples, see WIPO Doc SCCR/13/2, in particular at 9–10 and Annex III.

[110] For more examples, see WIPO Doc SCCR/13/2, in particular at 11–12 and Annex III.

[111] WIPO Doc SCCR/13/2, November 2005; twelve Member States responded; the document mainly refers to the positive effects, at 4 ff. See also para 22.13 below.

[112] Art 2(6) phr 1 of the Berne Convention.

[113] Arts 2, 2bis, and 14bis ibid.

applied art and industrial designs and models; they may be protected either by a special design law, by copyright, or by both. Article 2(6) of the Berne Convention clarifies that works under Article 2 must be protected in the Union countries. Article 2(2) of the Berne Convention allows Union countries to condition protection upon the fixation of a work in some material form. Finally, Articles 2(4) and 2[bis](1) of the Berne Convention allow Union countries to exempt from protection certain kinds of works, namely official works and certain speeches; Article 2(8) of the Berne Convention clarifies that news of the day and certain facts are not covered by the Convention at all.

(ii) **The defined term**   The Convention defines the term 'literary and artistic   **5.64**
works'.[114] The choice of this term, instead of the more general term 'work', may be explained against the historical background: in many instances, protection was initially limited to literary works and only later extended to artistic works. For example, the International Literary and Artistic Association (ALAI), which exercised a crucial influence on the genesis of the Berne Convention,[115] was first founded as the International Literary Association and only later enlarged to the International Literary and Artistic Association.[116] Also, Germany initially had separate laws for the protection of literary works and for the protection of artistic works.[117] In addition, many bilateral treaties immediately preceding the Berne Convention used the term 'literary and artistic works' so as to include also musical, dramatic, scientific, and other works.[118] This historical background confirms what is clear from the definition: the term 'literary and artistic works', wherever used in the Convention, is not limited to works of literature and art proper, but must be understood in the meaning of the broader definition under Article 2(1) of the Berne Convention.

(iii) **Domain**   The first part of the definition, 'every production in the literary,   **5.65**
scientific and artistic domain' was already part of the original definition in the Berne Convention 1886[119] and not subject to discussion, since it was known

---

114   Art 2(1) ibid.

115   cf paras 2.35 ff above.

116   cf paras 2.31–2.32 above, also on the two separate congresses preceding the Berne Convention on literary and artistic works.

117   The law of 11 June 1870 of the Northern German Federation, taken over by the German Empire, covered literary works as well as musical and dramatic works, while the law of 9 January 1876 and a separate law of 10 January 1876 dealt with the authors' rights in works of art and photography, respectively. The same basic split continued in the laws of 19 June 1901 covering authors' rights in literary and musical works and of 9 January 1907 covering authors' rights in artistic works and photography.

118   Ricketson/Ginsburg (n 3 above) 1.34.

119   Art 4 of the Berne Convention 1886 where, unlike in the Paris Act 1971, the list of examples preceded the definition. Also, it specified that the works had to be able to be published in print or in other forms of reproduction.

from earlier bilateral treaties.[120] Regarding the scientific domain,[121] it has always been clear that the Berne Convention does not protect scientific inventions, especially since they were already covered by the earlier Paris Convention of 1883. The words 'literary' and 'artistic' must be interpreted in the light of the long list of examples following the definition and therefore in a broad sense; in particular, the word 'artistic' cannot be restricted to refer to the visual arts only. Otherwise, works such as dramatico-musical, choreographic, and musical works that are explicitly listed in Article 2(1) of the Berne Convention would not be covered. A very wide interpretation of 'artistic domain' might even cover the olfactory and gustatory domains so as to cover culinary creations and perfumes.[122]

5.66 **(iv) Production** 'Every production' in that domain is protected. The ordinary meaning of 'production' is very broad and could possibly even cover any mechanical production by machines or the manufacture of material products. However, this term has to be interpreted in its context and in line with the purpose of the Convention, namely, the protection of rights of authors in their literary and artistic works.[123] These are works of the mind.[124] Accordingly, 'production' refers only to the production of the mind, as also reflected in the term 'intellectual creation' as used in Article 2(5) of the Berne Convention. The historical interpretation confirms that 'production' was understood as complementary to 'literary and artistic works' and, hence, as an intellectual creation.[125] The term 'production' therefore only indicates that the protected object must have emerged from the mind of a person, left the sphere of the mind and become realized. This coincides with the term 'expression' also contained in the definition.[126]

5.67 Since the 'production' is understood as something originating from the mind of a person, it is also understood as implying originality or creativity, as reflected in

---

[120] Ricketson/Ginsburg (n 3 above) 8.02.

[121] The explicit mentioning of the scientific domain that is not contained in the defined term might not have been necessary since scientific works are usually expressed in writing and therefore could represent literary works in the broad sense, or in the form of graphs, illustrations, etc that could be considered as artistic productions in the broad sense, Ricketson/Ginsburg (n 3 above) 8.06.

[122] On the recent, well-known decision of the Dutch Supreme Court protecting parfums (Hoge Raad of 16 June 2006, <http://www.rechtspraak.nl> case no LJN AU98940 (in Dutch), and [2006] 37 IIC 997); see H Cohen Jehoram, 'The Dutch Supreme Court Recognizes Copyright in the Scent of a Perfume. The Flying Dutchman: All Sails, No Anchor' (2006) EIPR 629. See, however, an opposite decision by the French Supreme Court of 13 June 2006, [2006] 37 IIC 988.

[123] Art 31(1) of the Vienna Convention on the Law of Treaties; for a more detailed discussion on the interpretation of the definition on the basis of specific examples, see paras 7.13–7.21 below.

[124] This does not exclude the possibility of using technical tools for expressing the works.

[125] Ricketson/Ginsburg (n 3 above) 8.03; also ibid 8.87: an intellectual creation is implicitly required for all kinds of works, even if explictly mentioned only in Art 2(5) of the Berne Convention.

[126] Ricketson/Ginsburg (n 3 above) 8.03; D Gervais, *La Notion d'œuvre dans la Convention de Berne et en droit comparé* (1998) 44–5; and paras 5.69–5.70 below.

the national laws of Berne Union countries, even if not explicitly required by the Berne Convention.[127] In the absence of a definition, the required minimum degree of originality or creativity will have to be determined by the national law of the country for which protection is claimed. Yet, the requirement must not be so high as to exclude from protection most works of a particular category.[128]

The term 'literary and artistic works' shall 'include' the specified productions. **5.68** This wording might suggest that further productions not mentioned in the definition are covered. However, given the already broad definition and the need to delineate the subject matter of protection under the Convention in a reasonable way, the definition should be understood as being comprehensive.

(v) Expression Productions are protected in whatever mode or form of 'expression'. **5.69** sion'. Expression means manifestation of the work to the outside world. It is also interpreted as requiring concrete forms of expression of thoughts and feelings in contrast to, for example, simple ideas, concepts, facts, theories, methods, or the pure findings of scientific research.[129] One may assume that this expression/idea dichotomy was underlying the national laws and bilateral treaties preceding the Berne Convention so that no explicit mentioning seemed to be necessary.[130]

The broad definition that includes any mode or form of expression makes it **5.70** technology neutral and thereby dynamic; for example, expression in digital form is covered. Expression does not require any material form or mode but covers oral expression, for example, through improvisation of music or speech. This is confirmed by the inclusion of certain oral works (such as lectures) in the list of works, and by the fact that fixation is not a requirement for protection under the Berne Convention.[131]

(vi) Fixation and other requirements Since the Berne Convention does not **5.71** specify any other requirements for works in general,[132] works in principle must be protected in the Union countries irrespective of any additional requirement possibly established under national law.[133] In particular, artistic merit or quality, cultural value, or any particular purpose (or lack of purpose) of the work must not

---

127 C Masouyé, *Guide to the Berne Convention for the Protection of Literary and Artistic Works* (1978) 2.8; Gervais (n 126 above) 49, 213–14.
128 Ricketson/Ginsburg (n 3 above) 8.05, also for more detail.
129 Masouyé (n 127 above) 2.3; Ricketson/Ginsburg (n 3 above) 8.07.
130 This dichotomy was explicitly laid down only later in Art 9(2) of the TRIPS Agreement and Art 2 of the WCT, where it was understood as a simple clarification of the Berne Convention; cf paras 10.58 and 17.103 below.
131 Art 2(1) and (2) of the Berne Convention; paras 5.71–5.73 below.
132 For a specific requirement regarding collections, cf Art 2(5) of the Berne Convention.
133 The requirement of originality or creativity is already implied in the term 'production', cf paras 5.66–5.67 above.

be required for protection under the Convention.[134] The only exception to this principle is fixation, which is not a condition for protection under the Berne Convention, but permitted as a condition under national law that then has to be respected in the Berne Union context.[135]

5.72 Originally, the Berne Convention required fixation, though only in respect of choreographic works and pantomime, with a view to avoiding problems of evidence.[136] Proposals made at the Brussels Revision Conference to entirely delete the fixation requirement were rejected on grounds that fixation remained important as a means of proof.[137] A similar proposal made at the Stockholm Conference was met with similar opposition; this resulted, as a compromise, in the deletion of the mandatory fixation for choreographic works and pantomimes, combined with the permission of the fixation requirement for all kinds of works under national law.[138] Since, as a consequence, any Union country thereafter could also require foreign works to be fixed in order to obtain protection, this was a clear step back from the earlier situation. Yet, this step may have been useful not least to accommodate the needs of those Union countries, like the UK, which in general provided for a fixation requirement,[139] and to facilitate the then possible accession of the USA to the Berne Convention.[140]

5.73 The question of fixation is relevant for any kind of work before fixation, such as musical improvisations, or improvised speeches, simultaneous translations, dance, and pantomimes. It may also matter for the protection of folklore that is orally transmitted from generation to generation; yet, folklore meets additional obstacles to copyright protection, even where the law does not require fixation.[141] Where fixation is not required, improvised works are protected from the moment of their oral, physical, or other expression perceptible to human senses; any unauthorized fixation would be an infringement of copyright. Countries that require fixation may protect these works not under copyright, but arguably as unpublished works

---

[134] Ricketson/Ginsburg (n 3 above) 8.04.

[135] Art 2(2) of the Berne Convention.

[136] At the Berlin Revision 1908, the requirement that these works (in their 'acting form' only) be fixed 'in writing or otherwise' was introduced and kept in Art 2(1) of the Berne Convention up to the Brussels version. Ricketson/Ginsburg (n 3 above) 8.18 and 8.25.

[137] ibid 8.26.

[138] Art 2(2) of the Berne Convention.

[139] cf paras 3.30–3.31 above on the fact that mainly countries of the copyright system require fixation; for the UK, see Ricketson/Ginsburg (n 3 above) 8.18.

[140] ibid; D Reimer and E Ulmer, 'Die Reform der materiellrechtlichen Bestimmungen der Berner Übereinkunft' (1967) GRUR Int 431, 432; Nordemann/Vinck/Hertin/Meyer (n 20 above) Arts 2/2bis BC n 11.

[141] paras 20.07–20.09 below.

under common law, so that protection via national treatment is then, in principle, safeguarded.[142]

(b) Particular categories of works

(i) Historical background The Berne Convention of 1886 already included at   **5.74**
least half of the current list of works, namely 'books, pamphlets and other writings', 'dramatic or dramatico-musical works', 'musical compositions with or without words', 'works of drawing, painting, sculpture, engraving and lithography', and 'illustrations, plans, sketches relative to geography, topography, architecture or science'; as well as translations.[143] Most of these terms were taken over from earlier bilateral treaties and were not subject to discussion. The 1908 Berlin Act (later amended) then inserted most of the other categories of works (choreographic works and pantomime, works of architecture, photographic works, and works of applied art); the 1928 Rome Act added lectures and other oral works, and the 1948 Brussels Act included cinematographic works.

(ii) Article 2(1) of the Berne Convention The list of works in the current   **5.75**
Article 2(1) of the Berne Convention contains the most commonly protected works. In addition to specific examples, it includes broader terms, such as 'writings', and 'other works of the same nature' (referring to certain oral works); it is technology neutral in respect of cinematographic and photographic works, to which are assimilated 'works expressed by a process analogous to' cinematography and photography. In addition, translations, adaptations, and other alterations of works, as well as collections of works must be protected; indeed, for a long time they have been a standard element of most copyright laws in the world.[144] The list is so broad that little space is left for Union countries to protect additional categories of works. The exact meaning of the specified categories is not determined in the Berne Convention, and therefore must be established by the Union countries for which protection is sought. Most of the terms are largely self-explanatory.[145]

---

[142] Nordemann/Vinck/Hertin/Meyer (n 20 above) Arts 2/2bis BC n 11; for US law, see M Leaffer, *Understanding Copyright Law* (4th edn, 2005) § 2.06; see, however, for British law, W Cornish and D Llewelyn, *Intellectual Property: Patents, Copyright, Trademarks, and Allied Rights* (5th edn, 2003) 10-34.

[143] Arts 4 and 6 of the Berne Convention 1886.

[144] cf Ricketson/Ginsburg (n 3 above) 8.75 ff; Gervais (n 126 above) 112–14; in certain jurisdictions, they are called 'derivative works', cf paras 5.123, 5.125 below.

[145] The scope of this book does not allow for detailed explanations; for the individual categories of works, see Ricketson/Ginsburg (n 3 above) 8.15–8.73; Gervais (n 126 above) 107–206; Masouyé (n 127 above) 2.6(a)–2.6(j); on works of applied art, cf also above in the context of material reciprocity, paras 5.45–5.47 above.

5.76   (iii) **Listed and unlisted works**   Article 2(6) of the Berne Convention only makes the 'works mentioned in this article'[146] subject to mandatory protection in the Union countries. Accordingly, only the works explicitly mentioned in Article 2(1), (3), and (5) of the Berne Convention must be protected by Union countries in the Berne context, whether or not their national laws protect them. They constitute the minimum standard of protection under the Convention. At the same time, the list of works is only illustrative of the broader term 'literary and artistic works' in Article 2(1) of the Berne Convention. All works not explicitly mentioned but covered by this broader term are works for which authors are protected under the Berne Convention and, hence, enjoy national treatment, minimum rights, and the absence of formalities.[147]

5.77   Accordingly, a listed work must be protected in the Berne context even if it is not protected under the national law of a Union country. An unlisted work covered by the definition of 'literary and artistic works' is covered by the scope of protection of the Convention, so that a Union country that protects such work must grant national treatment and minimum rights in respect of this work; however, if the country does not protect such work, it is not obliged to do so in the Berne context. It is only when the national law of a Union country protects a 'work' that is neither listed in the Convention nor covered by the definition ('literary and artistic works'),[148] that no obligation whatsoever arises for such objects from the Berne Convention.

5.78   For example, a Union country that does not protect perfumes as copyright works is not under an obligation to do so, since perfumes are not listed in the Convention and therefore do not constitute a minimum standard. However, a Union country that provides for such protection has to grant the protection of the Convention[149] if perfumes fall under the general definition of a Berne work. In particular, a perfume would have to be an intellectual creation, possibly in the artistic domain, expressed through a combination of fragrances that are perceptible to the human senses. A more thorough analysis of this example is beyond the scope of this book.

---

[146]   The lack of a reference to Art 14bis of the Berne Convention is irrelevant here, since also Art 2(1) of the Berne Convention lists cinematographic works.

[147]   Art 5(1) of the Berne Convention: 'in respect of works for which they are protected under this Convention'; Nordemann/Vinck/Hertin/Meyer (n 20 above) Arts 2/2bis BC n 2, 3 seem to suggest that only national treatment, but not minimum rights apply to unspecified works; Ricketson/ Ginsburg (n 3 above) 8.11 only speak of national treatment in this case, but do not explicitly exclude minimum rights; they might mean national treatment only as regards the work rather than rights.

[148]   These might be, eg, objects from nature which are only presented as art; mere facts; ideas; phonograms; etc.

[149]   Based on national treatment, minimum rights and 'no formalities', Art 5 of the Berne Convention.

An unlisted work might obtain the character of a 'mentioned' one and, conse- **5.79**
quently, constitute an obligatory minimum standard, if a 'subsequent practice'[150]
has been established to this effect and has shown an agreement of all Union countries on the corresponding interpretation. This, however, may be difficult to
ascertain.[151]

(c) Exemptions from protection

(i) Official texts and public speeches[152]   The possibility of excluding from **5.80**
copyright protection official texts and their official translations, as well as certain
public speeches,[153] reflects not only the national laws prevailing at the time of its
introduction, but also the public interest in freedom of information.[154] In particular, citizens should know the laws and regulations governing their lives without
being impeded by copyright protection in such official texts. The term 'official
text' under Article 2(4) of the Berne Convention certainly includes any law, regulation, administrative order, and judicial decision. Its interpretation in detail is
left to the national laws of the Union countries.[155] While most countries exclude
copyright protection for legal texts, court decisions, and similar official documents, the 'crown copyright' in official texts has been a tradition in the UK and
other Commonwealth countries such as Australia and Canada, allowing the
governments to control their own legislative acts and other texts. Usually,
governments do not use crown copyright to hinder distribution of such texts, but
may license it for particular commercial uses, for example, where material that is
created by state employees and therefore represents official texts is used for
commercial training courses.[156]

Political speeches and speeches delivered in the course of legal proceedings **5.81**
can be excluded from protection, wholly or in part.[157] The underlying policy
reason—access to information—is reflected in Article 2^bis(3) of the Berne

---

[150] Art 31(3)(b) of the Vienna Convention on the Law of Treaties; cf also paras 7.02 ff below on
the interpretation rules for treaties.

[151] Ricketson/Ginsburg (n 3 above) 8.11 in n 31.

[152] Works of applied art may not be fully excluded from protection, but protected simply as
designs and models instead of copyright works, see in the context of reciprocity paras 5.45–5.47
above.

[153] Arts 2(4) and 2^bis(1) of the Berne Convention.

[154] This interest similarly serves as a justification for exceptions and limitations regarding exclusive rights.

[155] cf for more detail on the interpretation of Art 2(4) of the Berne Convention; Ricketson/
Ginsburg (n 3 above) 8.108.

[156] eg for Australia, S Ricketson and C Creswell, *The Law of Intellectual Property:
Copyright, Designs and Confidential Information* (2002) 14.170 ff: for Canada, eg D Vaver, *Copyright
Law* (2000) 92–4 and, regarding the possibility to freely use legislative acts and their
consolidations and decisions and reasons of Federal courts, L Harris, *Canadian Copyright Law*
(3rd edn, 2001) 207.

[157] Art 2^bis(1) of the Berne Convention.

Convention,[158] according to which the author keeps the right to make subsequent collections of such speeches. This safeguard shows that the possible exclusion of protection is exclusively to serve the immediate interest of the public in news reporting or information about the current political life and legal proceedings, so that citizens are not precluded from participation in public life. This purpose and policy reason is not at stake where the author later reassembles such speeches in a collection, such as a collection of the most important speeches of a politician during his career.[159]

5.82 Both of the above cases are exclusions from mandatory protection of the Convention, but not from its protection at all.[160] Accordingly, countries do not need to protect these kinds of works, but where they do so, the protection of the Convention applies. In addition, such exclusions are facultative: Union countries may decide to protect the specified kinds of works, or not to protect them at all, or only some of them, or only to a certain extent.

5.83 (ii) **News of the day** To the contrary, the exclusion from protection of 'news of the day and miscellaneous facts having the character of mere items of press information' is mandatory.[161] Accordingly, if a Union country protects such news and facts under copyright or a similar kind of right, it may do so under national law—even in favour of foreign works—but no one could claim protection for such items on the basis of the Berne Convention. This mandatory exclusion should primarily be considered as a clarification of what is protected under the Convention, namely, only intellectual creations in the form of concrete expressions such as commentaries or articles dealing with news, rather than mere news, facts, or information as such.[162]

(2) **Authors**

(a) Author as natural person

5.84 The Berne Convention does not define the term 'author'. It only specifies the criteria of eligibility and states that the protection for works under Article 2 shall operate for the benefit of the 'author and his successors in title'.[163] Specific questions such as the determination of the conditions for co-authorship are left to national law.

---

[158] It was inserted at the Brussels Revision Conference 1948, see also Masouyé (n 127 above) 2bis.5 for its background.

[159] On Art 2bis(1), (3) of the Berne Convention, cf Ricketson/Ginsburg (n 3 above) 8.16–8.17, 8.20–8.21.

[160] On mandatory protection of works, cf para 5.77 above.

[161] Art 2(8) of the Berne Convention.

[162] For the history and interpretation of this provision which was first linked to the right of reproduction and exceptions thereto, see Ricketson/Ginsburg (n 3 above) 8.104–8.106.

[163] Arts 3 and 4, and 2(6) phr 2 of the Berne Convention respectively.

Yet, one of the main questions to be solved by interpretation of the Convention is whether only natural persons who create works or (as under laws adhering to the Anglo-American system) also corporate entities or legal persons must be recognized as authors under the Berne Convention. All means of interpretation result in the first mentioned alternative—only natural persons are authors in the meaning of the Berne Convention.

Among the many arguments for this result are: the ordinary meaning of the word **5.85** 'author', which implies a natural person, and the use of this term instead of, for example, 'producer'; the protection of authors in respect of intellectual creations, which by their nature can only come from physical persons having a mind or intellect to create works; Article 6[bis] of the Berne Convention on the protection of an author's intellectual and personal interests through moral rights, which can possibly be vested in a natural person only; the calculation of the duration upon the death of the author (except for specific kinds of works such as anonymous and pseudonymous works), an event only occurring to natural persons; Article 15(3) of the Berne Convention under which the publisher is a mere representative of the author of an anonymous or pseudonymous work, and this only as long as the author does not reveal his identity; and Article 14[bis](2)(a) of the Berne Convention—the only explicit exception from the principle of authorship of natural persons, which leaves to national law the determination of ownership of copyright in a cinematographic work and, consequently, the distinction between 'habitual residence' for natural persons and 'headquarters' or habitual residence for the (exception of) authors of cinematographic works.[164] These arguments are reinforced by historical arguments, in particular the adoption of the Rome Convention that protects, among others, phonogram producers, which are mostly companies (and, accordingly, do not make intellectual creations).[165]

If one accepts this result, then the term 'author' under the Berne Convention **5.86** means the natural person from whose mind emanates an intellectual creation. Consequently, any such person must be granted protection under the Berne Convention *iure conventionis*, even if the Union country of protection instead provides for first ownership of a legal person (other than for cinematographic works)[166] or of any person that simply organizes but

---

[164] Arts 3(2) and 4(a) of the Berne Convention on the criteria of eligibility.

[165] cf more detailed arguments stated on the occasion of a WIPO proposal during the 'guided development' period in a committee of experts of 1990 to cover by the term 'author' also any 'person other than the author' where this person is 'the original owner of the rights in the work', A Dietz, 'The Concept of Author under the Berne Convention' (1993) 155 RIDA 2–56; cf also Nordemann/ Vinck/Hertin/Meyer (n 20 above) Art 2/2[bis] BC n 7; Ricketson/Ginsburg (n 3 above) 7.02–7.04.

[166] For the exception in Art 14[bis](2) of the Berne Convention, see Ricketson/Ginsburg (n 3 above) 7.24–7.41.

does not create the work.[167] The Union country of protection may apply corporate ownership under domestic law, but not in cases to which the Berne Convention applies. At the same time, a legal person, even if domestically protected as the first owner of copyright, cannot claim protection under the Berne Convention in other Union countries. Yet, contractual questions are unaffected by the rules of the Convention, so that transfers of rights under employment and other contracts remain possible.

(b) Film authorship

5.87 Film authorship has always been one of the most diversely regulated areas of copyright. In particular, under the copyright system, only the producer of the film is its first copyright owner; the film director, cameraman, or any other creative contributor is not a recognized author in the cinematographic work.[168] The authors of works used for the making of the film, such as the scenario, script, and music, only enjoy a copyright in these works as such rather than in the cinematographic work itself. Under the authors' rights system by contrast, only the natural persons who make creative contributions to the film are recognized as (joint) authors of cinematographic works; differences exist here in respect of the individual contributions that result in joint authorship. Authors of works used for the making of the film are recognized as joint authors of the cinematographic work in some countries and as authors of pre-existing works in others. In addition, different solutions are provided regarding presumptions of transfer of authors' rights to the producer, if they are provided at all.[169]

5.88 Against this background, Articles 14 and 14bis of the Berne Convention offer a compromise. Article 14(1) deals with authors of pre-existing works which are adapted for cinematographic use (such as a novel which is adapted to become a film script), while Article 14bis(2), (3) deals with authorship and copyright ownership in the cinematographic work itself. Article 14bis(2)(a) leaves the determination of the ownership of film copyright to the law of the country for which protection is claimed. It thereby takes account of the situation in copyright system countries by allowing them to provide for the first ownership in favour of the producer; at the same time, it is a compromise in the Berne system since it deviates from the general rule on authorship.[170]

---

167 Some national laws provide for the organizer of a collective work to be protected as an author; where this person is not an author as described in the above text, he may not claim protection under the Convention, but only the individual contributors who are authors may do so, if any.

168 The UK had to acknowledge authorship of the principal director of a film when implementing the EC Rental and Duration Dirs, see Vol II ch 6.

169 See also on authorship under both systems paras 3.37–3.43 above.

170 See paras 5.84 ff above.

Another element of compromise is the presumption of 'legitimation',[171] which is **5.89** relevant in countries where authors of creative contributions to the cinematographic work are protected as authors of the cinematographic work (rather than only of pre-existing works). Where these authors have contractually agreed to make contributions to the cinematographic work, they can no longer object to the specified ways of exploitation. This only applies unless the contract specifies otherwise, for example, by allowing the author to object to all or some of these ways of exploitation by the producer.[172] This presumption only refers to the right to object to the specified uses and in no way hinders national legislation from providing for the author's right to share in the income from exploitation or otherwise obtain an equitable remuneration for the use.[173]

The above presumption applies only where the contract was made in the form **5.90** prescribed by national law, if any. As a rule, it is the law of the country where the maker of the cinematographic work has his headquarters or habitual residence that governs the requirement of a particular form of the contract. However, any country for which protection is claimed may require written form for such contract as a condition for the presumption to apply; such provision must be notified to the Director General of WIPO so that he can inform the other Union countries.[174]

Notably, the above presumption does not cover authors of scenarios, dialogues, **5.91** and musical works created for the making of the cinematographic work, or the principal director thereof, unless the country for which protection is claimed provides to the contrary; if a country does not apply the presumption, it has to notify the Director General, though only in respect of the principal director.[175]

Article 14bis(3) of the Berne Convention shows that the Convention considers **5.92** the authors of scenarios, dialogues, and musical works created for the making of the cinematographic work and the principal director thereof as joint authors of the cinematographic work, thereby delineating authors of pre-existing works who are covered by Article 14 of the Berne Convention. Overall, Article 14bis(2), (3) is of reduced importance in practice because it only applies in countries where natural persons who make creative contributions to the film are recognized as joint authors, and because most of the modern contracts exactly specify the rights that are, or are not, assigned, so that there is little room for a presumption.

---

171 Art 14bis(2)(b) of the Berne Convention; Masouyé (n 127 above) n 14bis.6; Nordemann/ Vinck/Hertin/Meyer (n 20 above) Art 14/14bis BC n 10 consider this provision as a procedural minimum right of the film producer.
172 For the words 'contrary or special stipulation', see Art 14bis(2)(d) of the Berne Convention.
173 Masouyé (n 127 above) 14bis.16.
174 Art 14bis(2)(c); Masouyé (n 127 above) 14bis.10, 14bis.11.
175 Art 14bis(3) of the Berne Convention.

(c) Successors in title

5.93 The protection of successors in title logically follows from the mere duration of protection beyond the author's life. Not only are the author's heirs his successors, but also any others (including legal persons) who follow the author in all or some of his rights such as to become entitled to the rights, for example by assignment.[176] This provision is self-evident and therefore was first deleted from the original Berne Act at the Berlin Revision, but was then reintroduced at the Brussels Revision on insistence by the United Kingdom.[177] It is also self-evident that the successor in title follows the author in the eligibility for protection: where the author but not the successor in title fulfils the criteria under Articles 3 and 4 of the Berne Convention, the successor in title is qualified under the Convention, even if he himself does not fulfil them. At the same time, where the author is not eligible, the successor cannot become eligible if only he fulfils the criteria.

(3) Minimum rights

(a) General remarks

5.94 **(i) Minimum, not maximum**   The individual minimum rights set out in the Berne Convention only need to be granted under the conditions of its Article 5(1),[178] which refers to them as 'the rights specially granted by this Convention'. While the Convention does not use the term 'minimum rights', they were always understood as such, in accordance with the tradition of the preceding bilateral treaties. In addition, granting minimum rights also as maximum rights would not have been consistent with the separate provision of national treatment, which then would not have had any independent meaning.[179] Nevertheless, some misunderstandings persisted after 1886, so that the 1908 Berlin Revision adopted Article 19 of the Berne Convention as a clarification that greater protection is permitted in national law. Due to partly unclear language, the article was revised at the 1948 Brussels Conference. Accordingly, not only can Union countries provide for greater protection under domestic law, but foreign authors can also claim such greater protection on the basis of national treatment under the Convention.

5.95 **(ii) Relation between moral rights and economic rights**   Under the influence of the Continental European system, the Berne Convention protects the author both in her personal and intellectual as well as economic interests in her work through moral and economic rights. Continental European countries have

---

[176] Nordemann/Vinck/Hertin/Meyer (n 20 above) Art 2/2bis BC n 8; Masouyé (n 127 above) 2.22.

[177] Ricketson/Ginsburg (n 3 above) 7.23; 6.18.

[178] cf paras 5.08 ff above.

[179] Ricketson/Ginsburg (n 3 above) 6.80–6.82; Nordemann/Vinck/Hertin/Meyer (n 20 above) Art 19 BC n 1, 2.

differently solved the theoretical problem of whether moral rights are, together with economic rights, a part of one inseparable right of authors or whether they are self-standing rights in addition to the economic rights.[180] The Convention does not take any position on this issue.

(b) Moral rights

(i) **Overview and historical development**   Article 6[bis] of the Berne Convention   **5.96** only stipulates two of several moral rights that exist under many national laws.[181] It is supplemented by Articles 10(3), 10[bis](1) phrase 2, and 11[bis](2) phrase 2 of the Berne Convention that safeguard moral rights in the context of limitations. Moral rights were not introduced as a minimum standard until the 1928 Rome Conference, since they were not protected or considered to be protected in a sufficient number of Union countries until the mid-1920s. Already at that stage, the provision was a compromise that took into account the concerns of common law countries where moral rights were not protected as such, but only to a limited extent under other kinds of provisions. Further compromises were necessary when amendments were made at the 1948 and 1967 Revision Conferences.[182]

(ii) **Independence from economic rights and transferability**   Article 6[bis](1) of   **5.97** the Berne Convention stresses that the covered moral rights—the right to claim authorship (paternity right) and the right of integrity of the work—are independent from the author's economic rights and, as a logical consequence thereof, are not affected by any transfer of the economic rights. Accordingly, even if the author transfers her economic rights, the moral rights are not automatically covered by the transfer. The decision whether the assignment, any kind of transfer, the renouncement, or the waivability of moral rights shall be possible at all has been left to the Union countries, as a part of a compromise in favour of countries of the copyright system. While moral rights are inalienable and cannot be waived or assigned in any way in countries of the author's rights system,[183] they are not inherent in the copyright system, so that the relevant countries usually provide for the possibility to assign or otherwise alienate moral rights.[184]

---

180 Such theoretical questions may have repercussions on the way in which moral rights are realized under national law; the first mentioned theory is called monism and is realized, for example, under German law, while the second one is called dualism and realized under French law, see E Adeney, *The Moral Rights of Authors and Performers* (2006), 8.24 and 9.12 for a short explanation for France and Germany in the context of moral rights.

181 cf on the rights of disclosure ('droit de divulgation'), as well as withdrawal for change of conviction and for lack of exploitation, para 3.51 above.

182 For the historical development of moral rights under the Berne Convention, cf Ricketson/Ginsburg (n 3 above) 10.07–10.14; Nordemann/Vinck/Hertin/Meyer (n 20 above) Art 6[bis] BC n 1.

183 In practice, some flexibility is possible, see para 3.53 above.

184 Nordemann/Vinck/Hertin/Meyer (n 20 above) Art 6[bis] BC n 3; Ricketson/Ginsburg (n 3 above) 10.18.

5.98   (iii) **Right to claim authorship**   The right to claim authorship is the right to be recognized as the author of a particular work so that the public is capable of identifying the author as the creator of the work. The Berne Convention does not prescribe the way in which such identification must take place; yet, the purpose of the right requires that the public be able to identify the author without major effort.[185] In practice, this requirement is most commonly fulfilled by mentioning the author's name on the original and copies of a work or in context therewith, for example by indicating her name on the cover and title-page of her book. The author can exercise this right in three ways: by claiming that her name is indicated on or in connection with the work, by choosing a pseudonym, or by staying anonymous.[186] The right includes the right to be named as the only author where no co-author is involved, and as a co-author in the case of joint authorship. While the authorship right protects the personal interest of the author to be connected to her work, it may also have positive economic consequences through publicity.

5.99   Since moral rights only protect the relation of the author to her own work, cases of false attribution are not covered by the right to claim authorship. For example, if an unknown person creates a painting and signs with the name of Gerhard Richter or another famous painter, the latter is not affected in the relationship to his work, but only in respect of the use of his name. Therefore, Richter could not rely on his right to claim authorship but only, if national law so allows, on protection by other rights, such as a personality right or a right in one's name.

5.100   (iv) **Right of integrity**   The right to protect the integrity of the work[187] is spelled out as the author's right 'to object to any distortion, mutilation or other modification of, or other derogatory action in relation to, the said work, which would be prejudicial to his honour or reputation'. The aim of the integrity right is to protect the work in its integrity as created by the author. This right requires respect for the artistic choices of the author, irrespective of whether they please the public or promise economic success on the market. Therefore, the question whether something is 'distortion', 'mutilation', or 'derogatory action' must be judged exclusively from the subjective point of view of the author rather than from the point of view of consumers, the entertainment industry, or from any other, even 'objective' point of view. Even if, for example, average consumers in a certain country might prefer the colourized version of an original black and white movie, it is up to the author (in Continental countries the film director in particular) himself to determine his choice of artistic expression. If he decides that his intentions, thoughts, or feelings may be better expressed in black and

---

[185] Similarly: Ricketson/Ginsburg (n 3 above) 10.19.

[186] Masouyé (n 127 above) 6bis.3.

[187] In France, it is called *droit au respect de l'œuvre*, which illustrates well the underlying idea, ie, to pay respect to the work.

white, his choice must be respected under the right of integrity.[188] Otherwise, the purpose of the provision to protect the author's interest in integrity of the work could not be reached. The author may even object to any 'modifications', whether they distort the work or not.

Examples of modifications under Article 6[bis](1) of the Berne Convention are the just-mentioned colourization of a black and white movie as in the famous case of John Huston's *Asphalt Jungle*, whose broadcast in a colourized version was prohibited by courts in France;[189] the (partial) over-painting of a picture;[190] the change of a serious end into a happy end in the framework of the cinematographic adaptation of a novel;[191] abbreviations or cuts from a literary, dramatic, cinematographic, or other work; and the insertion of a logo of a TV station to the broadcast version of a cinema movie.[192]   **5.101**

The right of integrity can be violated not only through modification of the work, but also by 'derogatory action in relation to' the work, for example, by bringing the work into a context which changes the overall impression of the work against the author's intentions. In this case, the work or its copy remains unaffected, but the integrity right is indirectly violated. For example, placing an artwork of non-socialist art in the close context of socialist artworks in a public exhibition may change the impression of the character of the work. Other examples of such violations of the integrity right are the playing of spiritual music in an inadequate, profane context, and the recording of music on a sample CD together with neo-Nazi music against the author's wish, even if the author has generally consented to the reproduction of his music on a phonogram.[193]   **5.102**

Article 6[bis](1) of the Berne Convention does not mention the entire destruction of a work as a case of violation of the integrity right. The term 'modification' (including 'distortion' and 'mutilation') cannot cover 'destruction' because it means that the work remains in existence and is only changed to some extent. Also, the word 'derogatory' (action) only implies a damaging treatment rather than the entire destruction. The purpose of the integrity right supports this interpretation: the author must not be associated with a work which he did not create in the way it appears after modification or derogatory action, and   **5.103**

---

188 Under Art 6bis of the Berne Convention, this is also subject to the potential prejudice to his honour or reputation.

189 *Consorts Huston et al v Sté Turner Entertainment et al*, Cour de Cassation of 28 May 1991. On the different stages of legal proceedings, see E Adeney (n 180 above) 19.158; also eg J Ginsburg, 'Colors in Conflicts: Moral Rights and the Foreign Exploitation of Colorized US Motion Pictures' (1988) 36/1 J Copyright Soc USA 81 ff.

190 German Reichsgericht, RGZ 79, 397 ('Felseneiland mit Sirenen').

191 OLG München (1986) GRUR 460 ('Die unendliche Geschichte').

192 *Marchand v La Cinq*, TGI Paris of 29 June 1988 ('Logo la Cinque'), (1989) JCP I 3376.

193 For the latter case, see E Adeney (n 180 above) 9.89.

shall not suffer prejudice to his honour or reputation therefrom. However, if nothing of his work is left, there is nothing which could be associated with him in a way he would dislike or that would affect his honour or reputation. Indeed, the 1948 Brussels Conference discussed but rejected a proposal to include destruction. At the same time, Union countries were encouraged in a *vœu* to provide protection also against destruction of works.[194]

5.104   The condition of a potential prejudice to the honour or reputation was introduced as a condition in order to accommodate the needs of common law countries.[195] Indeed, many Continental countries, such as France, do not provide for such a condition. This is permitted since the Convention allows for greater protection. The Convention does not further specify how to understand 'honour or reputation', so the Union countries have some leeway in this regard. However, delegates at the 1948 Brussels Conference agreed that the author's honour and reputation related to authorship as well as to personality.[196] It is not entirely clear whether an actual prejudice must be established or whether the threat of a prejudice would be sufficient. There are better reasons for the second option—in particular the wording 'would be prejudicial'.[197] It is also established today that the potential prejudice refers both to any modification and to any derogatory action.[198]

5.105   **(v) Duration and remedies**   Article 6bis(2) of the Berne Convention on the duration of moral rights is also a compromise that takes into account the needs of common law countries.[199] The duration is at least as long as that of economic rights, so that both the countries that provide this limited duration and those that provide for a perpetual moral right can each continue their traditions. The Convention leaves it entirely to the Union countries to determine the persons to exercise moral rights after the author's death; mostly, these persons will be the heirs or, in some countries, others such as public authorities.

5.106   Article 6bis(3) of the Berne Convention confirms the general principle that the available remedies are governed by the law of the country for which protection is claimed, as already stated in Article 5(2) phrase 2 of the Berne Convention.[200]

---

[194] Ricketson/Ginsburg (n 3 above) 10.26; on this issue, para 3.50 above.
[195] ibid 10.27.
[196] ibid.
[197] Nordemann/Vinck/Hertin/Meyer (n 20 above) Art 6bis BC n 4.
[198] This had been controversial; some had argued that it only applies to 'other modifications', cf Ricketson/Ginsburg (n 3 above) 10.32; Nordemann/Vinck/Hertin/Meyer (n 20 above) Art 6bis BC n 4.
[199] In particular, phr 2. On its background and questions of interpretation, cf Ricketson/Ginsburg (n 3 above) 10.34.
[200] Nordemann/Vinck/Hertin/Meyer (n 20 above) Art 6bis BC n 5.

(vi) Provisions in context with limitations   Moral rights are also confirmed in   **5.107**
the framework of Articles 10(3), 10bis(1) phrase 2, and 11bis(2) phrase 2 of the
Berne Convention. These provisions limit certain economic rights of the author.
Since moral rights are independent from economic rights, it follows logically that
the limitations of economic rights leave unaffected the author's moral rights.
Accordingly, the above-mentioned provisions should be understood as cases of
explicit confirmation of the fact that moral rights apply even where economic
rights are limited. Article 10(3) of the Berne Convention makes it obligatory to
mention the source and the author's name, if it appears thereon, when permitted
quotations and uses for teaching are made. The fact that only the paternity right
but not also the integrity right is explicitly safeguarded must not be interpreted
e contrario to the effect that the integrity right could be affected by these uses.
This is confirmed by historical interpretation, which reveals the general agreement that moral rights are unaffected by the limitations of economic rights under
the Berne Convention.[201]

The same reasoning with regard to the integrity right applies to Article 10bis(1)   **5.108**
phrase 2 of the Berne Convention, which requires the source to be clearly indicated where permitted uses are made in context with news reporting. The legal
consequences of a breach of this obligation shall be determined, in conformity
with the general principle regarding remedies,[202] by the legislation of the country
for which protection is claimed.[203]

Article 11bis(2) phrase 2 of the Berne Convention explicitly confirms that the   **5.109**
moral rights must be unaffected by any compulsory licence allowed under its first
phrase in respect of broadcasting and communication to the public. Although
the term 'the moral rights of the author' seems unlimited, it must be interpreted
as only referring to the moral rights under Article 6bis of the Berne Convention,
which is the relevant context. Any additional moral rights, such as the right of
disclosure, are not dealt with in the Convention and therefore not envisaged in
this provision.[204] Yet, countries that provide such additional rights will usually
follow the principle of independence from economic rights and their
limitations.

(b) Economic rights

(i) Introduction   The economic rights under the Berne Convention are in   **5.110**
principle exclusive rights (ie rights of the author to exclude any third party from

---

201   Records of the Paris Conference 1967, 1165; Ricketson/Ginsburg (n 3 above) 13.46, pointing at the contrary opinion in the first edition (n 154).
202   This principle is also laid down in Art 6bis(3) of the Berne Convention.
203   Art 10bis(1) phr 2 ibid, second half-phrase.
204   On a controversy in this regard, cf Ricketson/Ginsburg (n 3 above) 13.71.

the relevant use). The Berne Convention uses the term 'the exclusive right of authorising'. This term has the same meaning as in the TRIPS Agreement and corresponds to the 'right to authorise or prohibit' used in the Rome Convention. It comprises the rights to grant licences and to prevent third parties from using the work in the relevant manner. These two aspects of the right, the positive and negative ones, reflect the characteristics of property rights in general. Like material property rights, authors' rights can be limited in favour of the general public or specific groups of the public. Accordingly, the exclusive minimum rights always have to be considered in context with their limitations. In a Union country for which protection is sought, the minimum rights of the Convention can be claimed only subject to the limitations and exceptions provided under national law, to the extent permitted by the Berne Convention.

5.111 Exceptionally, the Berne Convention provides for statutory remuneration rights instead of exclusive rights where it permits compulsory licences to take away the exclusive character of the right and requires provision at least of a statutory right to obtain an equitable remuneration for the relevant use.[205] In addition, it provides for the *droit de suite*,[206] which however does not constitute a minimum right.[207]

(ii) The reproduction right

5.112 *Importance and historical development* Reproduction constitutes the earliest form of use of works that had the potential for great economic benefit. The potential of another early form of use, public performance of musical works, was very limited until mechanical recording became available. Indeed, Johannes Gutenberg's invention of the printing press enabled much faster and more efficient reproduction than the earlier practice of hand-made reproduction by monks, and triggered the emergence of the predecessor of modern copyright law—the system of privileges. The reproduction right was the first one provided under a national law of the modern copyright system.[208]

5.113 Most uses of works are based on reproductions. In particular, distribution by sale or rental,[209] broadcasting, and different forms of communication to the public regularly necessitate reproductions as a basis. Only few uses do not rely on reproductions, such as the exhibition of the original of an artwork or live broadcasting or communication to the public.

---

[205] Arts 11bis(2) phr 2 and 13(1) of the Berne Convention.
[206] Art 14ter ibid.
[207] cf para 5.48 above.
[208] Statute of Anne (8 Anne, c 19 (1710)).
[209] The term 'publication right' is commonly used in practice for the combination of the reproduction and distribution rights.

Accordingly, it may seem astonishing that the reproduction right was explicitly **5.114** included in the Berne Convention as a general minimum right only at the 1967 Stockholm Conference. This late point in time may be explained by the lack of an explicit minimum right of reproduction in many pre-Berne bilateral treaties, under which the application of national treatment in this respect must have been considered sufficient. Indeed, the reproduction right was among the most frequently provided rights under early national laws.[210] Before 1967, the reproduction right appeared in the Berne Convention only regarding specific aspects, namely, for limitations regarding reproduction of certain newspaper articles,[211] regarding the rights of mechanical reproduction and reproduction in the context of broadcasting, as well as for the reproduction right for works adapted for cinematographic purposes.[212]

While the guarantee of the reproduction right on the basis of national treatment **5.115** seemed satisfactory for a long time, its absence as a minimum right appeared as a gap after several minimum rights had been explicitly provided in the Convention. Yet, the more immediate reason for the explicit recognition of the reproduction right in 1967 was the need to tackle the problem of private reproduction. Delegations felt that the right had to be included in the Convention before its limitations could be provided. The close context between the introduction of a reproduction right and the provision of its possible limitations already became evident at the 1948 Brussels Conference, when the proposal for the introduction of a reproduction right was not adopted due to problems in finding appropriate language for its limitations.[213] Also at the 1967 Stockholm Conference, problems arose not regarding the reproduction right itself, but regarding the determination of permitted limitations and exceptions. No need was seen for a further specification of the term 'reproduction'.

Reproduction and fixation 'Reproduction' is generally understood as any **5.116** incorporation of the work in material form, resulting in a duplication or separate copy of the work. Article 9(1) of the Berne Convention refers to the reproduction of 'works', irrespective of whether they are already fixed. Therefore, the reproduction also covers the fixation of a yet unfixed work, such as the recording of a live broadcast or performance of a work, as clarified in Article 9(3) of the Berne Convention.[214] The clarification was considered appropriate because the

---

210 J Cavalli, *La Genèse de la Convention de Berne pour la protection des œuvres littéraires et artistiques du 9 septembre 1886* (1986) 80.
211 Art 7 of the Berne Convention 1886; it is at the roots of the broader Art 10bis(1) of the 1971 Paris Act.
212 Arts 13, 11bis(3) and 14(1) respectively of the Berne Convention.
213 E Ulmer, 'Die Stockholmer Konferenz für geistiges Eigentum 1967: Das Vervielfältigungsrecht' (1967) GRUR Int 425, 443.
214 Accordingly, sound or visual recording shall be considered as a reproduction.

Rome Convention, adopted only six years earlier, distinguished between the terms 'fixation' of yet unfixed performances and broadcasts and 'reproduction' of already fixed performances or broadcasts. This example shows that a single term, such as 'reproduction', can have different meanings under different conventions.[215] In addition, the clarification was useful because the provision on the author's exclusive right of recording musical works[216] was deleted upon introduction of the general reproduction right in Article 9 of the Berne Convention; without such clarification, the consequences of the deletion might have been unclear.[217]

5.117 *Reproduction in any manner or form* The notion of 'reproduction . . . in any manner or form' is technically neutral and very broad, so that it does not exclude any technique by which the reproduction is effected, such as lithography, traditional printing, handwriting, typewriting, electronic storage, microfiche, and musical and audiovisual recording by mechanical, optical, magnetic, or other techniques. Logically, it also should be understood as including reproduction in a different dimension (making a photograph of a three-dimensional work such as a sculpture, or realizing an architectural design into a three-dimensional building) and in a different size, since the creation in such cases is still reproduced albeit in a different form or size. In contrast, 'reproduction' in a transformed manner, namely adaptation and translation, is not considered reproduction but covered by separate rights under the system of the Berne Convention.[218]

5.118 The essential characteristic of a 'reproduction' is the work's incorporation in some material form, as opposed to any kind of exploitation in non-material, intangible form such as public performance or broadcasting.[219] For transient digital reproductions that may occur on cache servers, the condition of 'material form' has been questioned in the context of the WCT, and the Berne Convention is not completely clear in this regard.[220]

5.119 *Partial reproduction* The Berne Convention does not specify whether the reproduction right is affected if only a part of the work is reproduced. Under the Anglo-American system, an act of reproduction (or other utilization) usually occurs only if the entire work or any substantial part thereof is reproduced or otherwise used.[221] Under Continental law, which has largely influenced the

---

215 On these terms in the Rome Convention cf paras 6.39–6.40 below.

216 Art 13(1) of the Berne Convention (up to the Brussels version), specifying 'by instruments capable of reproducing them mechanically'.

217 Ulmer (n 213 above), 443.

218 Arts 12 and 8 of the Berne Convention.

219 Masouyé (n 127 above) 9.3; Ricketson/Ginsburg (n 3 above) 11.27.

220 For a discussion, cf paras 17.52 ff below.

221 cf eg s 16(3)(a) UK CDPA; where this is not specified in the Act, it may be part of case law.

Berne Convention, this question does not regard the definition of the right but relates to the general issue of the scope of protection of a 'work'. Accordingly, protection by any right only exists to the extent that the work (or a part thereof) is protected, and this depends on the general conditions of originality or creativity. If the reproduced part of the work is not original or if it otherwise belongs to the public domain, it is not protected and, as a consequence, the author has no right of reproduction (or any other right) in that part.[222] As far as the Berne Convention relies on this logic, it does not need to define any substantiality criteria. In any case, since it has not defined any criteria of originality either, the concrete conditions for the protection of a part of a work are left to be determined by the Union country for which protection is claimed.

Cinematographic works   The reproduction right is separately provided for pre-existing works used for inclusion in a cinematographic work,[223] because it was already adopted in 1908, long before the introduction of the general reproduction right in the Berne Convention. Where a pre-existing work such as a novel is adapted for cinematographic purposes and then recorded in an audiovisual fixation, Article 14(1)(i) of the Berne Convention guarantees the author's rights to authorize not only the adaptation but also the related reproduction. The same rights apply to the cinematographic work itself.[224]   **5.120**

(iii) Translation right   Already in the bilateral treaties preceding the Berne Convention, the translation right was one of the standard elements, even if often limited in many ways. For example, it was granted only if the author had expressly reserved his translation right on the copies of the work in the original language, and only for a short period during which he had to use this right; the duration of the protection once acquired was often limited to five years and he had to fulfil complicated formalities. Only when the national laws became more generous did the bilateral treaties also begin to protect the translation right to the same extent as the reproduction right.[225] Accordingly, it is no surprise that the translation right was then also explicitly recognized in the Berne Convention 1886,[226] but subject to similar restrictions up to the 1908 Berlin Revision: it was limited to ten years from publication and, from the 1896 Paris Conference, it was granted for the entire term of copyright protection but made subject to publication of an authorized translation within ten years of the publication of the original work,   **5.121**

---

[222] eg for the German law, U Loewenheim, '§ 16' in G Schricker (ed), *Urheberrecht* (3rd edn, 2006) n 14; other countries may apply similar arguments.
[223] Art 14(1)(i) of the Berne Convention.
[224] Art 14bis (1) ibid.
[225] Cavalli (n 210 above) 80–1.
[226] Art 5 of the Berne Convention.

and this only in respect of translations into such languages in which an authorized translation had been published within the first ten years.[227]

5.122 The exclusive translation right under Article 8 of the Berne Convention covers the right of the author to make a translation herself and to authorize others to translate her work from one language into another language. Article 8 also specifies that this right lasts throughout the term of protection of the author's rights in the original work—a necessary addition given the initially shorter term that later was prolonged. Under modern national laws, this is no longer mentioned because they now usually provide the same duration for all economic rights; distinctions as to the duration of protection are only made, if at all, regarding specific categories of works rather than rights.

5.123 The Berne Convention establishes the translation right (just like the adaptation right under its Article 12) as a self-standing right which is juxtaposed with the other minimum rights. This approach does not, however, compel the Union countries to make the same systematic choice. Indeed, several Union countries have always considered both the translation and adaptation rights as simple corollaries of the basic rights of reproduction and communication to the public. Other countries, such as the United Kingdom and the USA, cover the translation right as part of the broader adaptation right (called under US law the 'right to prepare derivate works').[228]

5.124 The right to authorize translations must be distinguished from the protection of the translation as an original work.[229] Where a translation is exploited, both the author of the work in its original language and the translator enjoy separate exploitation rights in the translated work and both have to give their authorizations before exploitation takes place.

5.125 **(iv) Adaptation right** Unlike translation, adaptation was conceived in the early versions of the Berne Convention as a specific kind of reproduction: under Article 10 of the Berne Act 1886, so-called 'indirect appropriations' were 'especially included among the unlawful reproductions to which the present Convention applies'.[230] It was only at the 1948 Brussels Conference that the adaptation

---

[227] For more details on the history of the translation right under the Berne Convention, cf Ricketson/Ginsburg (n 3 above) 11.15–11.18.

[228] cf in particular the French law that provides as the two basic rights the right of reproduction and the right of representation/communication ('représentation'), Art L122-1 CPI; A Lucas and H-J Lucas, *Traité de la propriété littéraire et artistique* (3rd edn, 2006) n 236. For the UK, see s 21(1), (3)(a)(i) of the CDPA; for the USA, see s 106 n 2 and definition of 'derivative work' in s 101 of the Coypright Act (Title 17 USC).

[229] Art 2(3) of the Berne Convention.

[230] The term 'indirect appropriations' had already been used in several bilateral treaties preceding the Berne Convention, cf Ricketson/Ginsburg (n 3 above) 11.29.

right was formulated as a self-standing, independent exclusive right (Article 12 of the Berne Convention).[231] As in the case of the translation right, this approach does not require Union countries to make the same systematic choice.[232]

The author has the right to authorize any kind of 'alteration', including adapta-   **5.126**
tions and arrangements. 'Adaptation' is usually understood as the transformation of a work into another form of expression, mainly in the literary and cinemato-graphic domains where, for example, a novel is transformed into a theatre play, radiophonic work, or film script.[233] For the cinematographic adaptation of literary or artistic works, the adaptation right is specifically provided and, in addi-tion, extends to what could be called readaptation, namely adaptation of the cinematographic production which itself is based on an adaptation of the ori-ginal work.[234] Accordingly, if a theatre play is adapted into a cinematographic work which is then adapted into a novel, the author of the original theatre play (in addition to the authors of the cinematographic work) still must authorize this second adaptation.

The word 'arrangements' has usually been employed in the context of musical   **5.127**
works; previous texts of the Berne Convention even included the language 'musi-cal arrangements'.[235] Examples are transformations of a piece for orchestra into one for piano and violin, such as the well-known *Danse macabre* for orchestra by Saint-Saëns, who also wrote the adaptation, and vice versa, such as the *Pictures at an Exhibition* by Modest Mussorgsky composed for piano, and later orchestrated by many others, including Ravel. Since the restriction to 'musical' arrangements is no longer contained in the text of Article 12 of the Berne Convention, arrange-ments could include other transformations.

In any case, all such transformations are covered under the general term 'altera-   **5.128**
tions', which includes any change of a work where the original work can still be recognized in the alteration but, at the same time, is not simply reproduced, be it in the same or different size or format.[236] Accordingly, if the original work has only served as a source of inspiration for the second one such that the original is virtually imperceptible, then the second one is not an alteration of the original and authorization of the author of the original work is not needed. An example is

---

[231] For more details on the historical development of the adaptation right under the Berne Convention, cf Ricketson/Ginsburg (n 3 above) 11.30–11.33.
[232] cf para 5.123 above, eg for the broader concept of 'derivative works' under US law.
[233] Ricketson/Ginsburg (n 3 above) 11.34.
[234] Art 14(1)(i) and (2) of the Berne Convention.
[235] Art 12 of the Berlin Act.
[236] Changes by way of translations are, however, not covered by 'alterations' in the meaning of Art 12 of the Berne Convention on the basis of the systematic argument that the translation right is covered by Art 8.

Mussorgsky's musical composition *Pictures at an Exhibition*, created upon inspiration from an art exhibition. An example for a simple reproduction as opposed to an adaptation is the digitization of an analogue recording, since it is not the work itself but only the technical quality of the recording that is changed. Another example is the audiovisual recording of a theatre play which itself is not changed thereby. It is left to the law of the Union country for which protection is claimed to determine the exact delineations between an alteration and a mere reproduction on the one hand and between an adaptation and the creation of an independent work inspired by the original work on the other hand.

5.129   Authorization by the author of the original work remains necessary for the exploitation of the work in its altered form. Even if this is not explicitly stated in the Berne Convention,[237] it follows from the mere fact that authors are protected in respect of their 'works', including works in translated or otherwise altered form. Accordingly, both the author of the original work and the author of the alteration must authorize any exploitation of the work in altered form. The right to authorize alteration must be distinguished from the protection of the alteration as an original work.[238]

5.130   The adaptation right is independent of the author's right of integrity under Article $6^{bis}(1)$ of the Berne Convention: while the first is an economic right, and is usually assignable or subject to other forms of transfer or licensing under national law, the integrity right is a moral right protecting the personal and intellectual interests of the author in the work and is inalienable under many national laws. Accordingly, even if the author has authorized another person to make a musical arrangement of her work, she can still rely on the integrity right if the result of the arrangement is such that it takes away the specific character or expression of the original work and would be prejudicial to her honour or reputation.

5.131   **(v) Distribution right**   The Berne Convention does not provide for a general right of distribution as a minimum right; only Articles 14 and 14bis contain a distribution right for literary or artistic works adapted or reproduced for cinematographic purposes, and for cinematographic works. The resale right in Article 14ter of the Berne Convention, which might be considered as a residue of an exclusive distribution right is not a minimum right and was only introduced in order to allow an exception from national treatment.[239] A distribution right is considered to be

---

[237] It is only stated in Art 14(1) of the Berne Convention for works adapted for cinematographic purposes; however, one cannot draw an *e contrario* conclusion from this article with a view to the other minimum rights of the Convention.

[238] Art 12 *versus* Art 2(3) of the Berne Convention.

[239] cf para 5.48 above, and Ricketson/Ginsburg (n 3 above) 11.53–11.67.

implied in Article 16(2) of the Berne Convention on seizure of reproductions coming from a country where the work is not protected or has ceased to be so.[240]

The introduction of a general distribution right as a minimum right was discussed at the Brussels and Stockholm Conferences following proposals by different Union countries. However, the proposals were rejected.[241] One commentator stresses that the proposals at the Stockholm Conference were rejected not for substantive reasons but for lack of time to discuss them;[242] nevertheless, one cannot conclude that Union countries agreed in substance on a minimum right of distribution. Also, one cannot interpret Article 9(1) of the Berne Convention on the reproduction right as implicitly covering a right of first distribution. This is confirmed, among others, by historical interpretation: the French proposal at the Stockholm Conference to define the reproduction right as referring to reproduction in any manner or form 'and for any purpose' was rejected; against the background of the French law, under which the author's reproduction right includes the right to authorize the distribution of the copies,[243] this proposal could have meant the inclusion of a distribution right. The French delegation denied such inclusion, but the proposal was rejected anyway.[244] In addition, many delegations of a WIPO Committee of Experts in 1993 rejected the view of the WIPO Secretariat that the Berne Convention already implied (as a corollary of the reproduction right under Article 9) a general right of first distribution and even a right of importation for distribution.[245] Consequently, discussions continued on the assumption that the right needs to be introduced into international law. Only in the WIPO Copyright Treaty of 1996 (and for the first time in a broad multilateral treaty) was the distribution right established as a minimum right for all kinds of works.[246]

5.132

Article 14(1)(i) of the Berne Convention[247] does not further explain what is meant by 'distribution'; also, it does not contain any provision on the exhaustion

5.133

---

240 Nordemann/Vinck/Hertin/Meyer (n 20 above) Art 16 BC n 2; Ricketson/Ginsburg (n 3 above) 11.45; more cautious: M Ficsor, *The Law of Copyright and the Internet: The 1996 WIPO Treaties, their Interpretation and Implementation* (2002) n 4.09.

241 For the reasons, cf Ricketson/Ginsburg (n 3 above) 11.51; Ficsor (n 240 above) 4.05–4.07.

242 ibid 4.08.

243 On this so-called *droit de destination*, cf Lucas/Lucas (n 228 above) nn 246–62; for the distribution right under the WCT, see para 17.61 below.

244 Ricketson/Ginsburg (n 3 above) 11.52.

245 WIPO Memorandum for the Third Session of the Committee of Experts on a Possible Protocol to the Berne Convention (1993) Copyright 84, para 14 ff, in particular 17, 18 ff, and Report on the Third Session (1993) Copyright 179, 188 ff, in particular paras 63, 91, and J Reinbothe and S von Lewinski, *The WIPO Treaties 1996* (2002) Art 6 WCT nn 1–2.

246 cf paras 17.59 ff below; otherwise, it was established earlier in NAFTA, cf para 11.11 below.

247 Art 14bis(1) of the Berne Convention only refers to its Art 14 and does not even set out the individual rights.

of that right.[248] While the English wording is somewhat ambiguous regarding the contents of the right, recourse to the prevailing French wording[249] brings more clarity: the words *'la mise en circulation'* literally means 'the putting into circulation'. In other words, once a copy of a work has been put into circulation, it is in circulation and therefore cannot be put into circulation a second time. Accordingly, the distribution right is limited to the first distribution.[250] This result coincides with the national laws of most Union countries, which do provide for a right of putting into circulation or for a broader distribution right with its exhaustion after first sale. At the same time, this meaning does not prevent Union countries from providing further-reaching protection, given the character of the right as a minimum right.[251]

(vi) Rights of public performance and recitation, communication to the public, and broadcasting

5.134 *General remarks and systematic overview* Articles 11–11[ter], supplemented by Article 14(1)(ii) of the Berne Convention, are commonly dealt with here since they all refer to kinds of immaterial exploitation—exploitation of works in intangible form rather than as incorporated in a tangible copy—and since they have to be understood in relation to each other. In addition, the general rule that terms must in principle be interpreted separately for each treaty is particularly relevant for these Articles: terms such as 'communication to the public' and 'broadcasting' may well have different meanings in different conventions such as the Berne and Rome Conventions, and may be different from terms under national laws of the Contracting States. Diversity in this area is particularly high. For example, 'broadcasting' may have to be exclusively understood as wireless diffusion, such as under Article 11[bis](1)(i) of the Berne Convention, or can also include diffusion by cable, such as under § 20 German Copyright Act. 'Communication' may have different meanings even within one national law; for example, it may be used as a generic term for all kinds of exploitation in immaterial form and, at the same time, as a specific term only for the playing and showing of works in the presence of a public, including broadcast works.[252]

5.135 The main distinctions between Articles 11, 11[bis], and 11[ter] of the Berne Convention are as follows. Articles 11 and 11[ter] include the same rights, though for different kinds of works: Article 11 is limited to dramatic, dramatico-musical,

---

[248] On the different concepts of distribution rights with their exhaustion existing under national laws, cf para 17.61 below.

[249] Art 37(1)(c) of the Berne Convention: French prevails in case of differences of opinion on the interpretation.

[250] Ricketson/Ginsburg (n 3 above) 11.50.

[251] cf the similar discussion para 17.61 below.

[252] eg Arts 15(2), 21, 22 German Copyright Act.

and musical works, while Article 11ter is limited to literary works, as reflected also by the word 'recitation' (for literary works) instead of 'performance'. Both Articles deal with certain forms of exploitation in immaterial form other than broadcasting (namely public performance/recitation and communication), while Article 11bis of the Berne Convention covers broadcasting, rebroadcasting, and retransmission rights, as well as communication rights in respect of broadcasts of works; also, unlike the other two Articles, it covers all kinds of works ('literary and artistic works').

The arrangement of Articles 11–11ter of the Berne Convention reflects their historical development: the right of public performance of dramatic, dramatico-musical, and musical works was the first one incorporated into the Berne Convention,[253] followed by the right of broadcasting at the 1928 Rome Conference,[254] and the right of recitation only at the 1948 Brussels Conference.[255] The protection of cinematographic works and of works in respect of cinematographic adaptation was always dealt with separately, beginning with a right of 'public presentation' of pre-existing works 'by cinematography' in Article 14 of the 1908 Berlin Act and later amended so as to include the rights of public performance and communication to the public by wire in the 1948 Brussels Act.[256] By reference, cinematographic works also enjoy this right under Article 14bis(1) of the Berne Convention. **5.136**

Public performance and recitation under Articles 11, 11ter, and 14 of the Berne Convention One characteristic feature of public performance and recitation (as opposed to communication to the public and broadcasting) is its occurrence in the presence of a public or at a place open to the public, without the need of any transmission. As clarified by the 1967 Stockholm Revision, 'public performance' and 'public recitation' including, first, the performance by a physical person (such as the performance by a musician in concert, by an opera singer or a theatre actor on stage, or the public reading of literary works by the author or an actor) and, secondly, the **5.137**

---

[253] Art 9(1) ('representation') and (3) ('performance') in connection with Art 2 of the Berne Convention 1886, however, only made applicable the principle of national treatment to these rights; its Art 9(2) laid down a minimum right of public representation only in respect of the translations of dramatic and dramatico-musical works; cf for more detail on the history of the provision Ricketson/Ginsburg (n 3 above) 12.07, 12.09–12.11. For musical works, the 1908 Berlin Conference introduced a minimum right of public performance by means of instruments for mechanical reproduction, see Ricketson/Ginsburg (n 3 above) 12.08.

[254] Art 11bis of the Berne Convention; further amendments were made at the 1948 Brussels Conference; cf for the history of this Article Ricketson/Ginsburg (n 3 above) 12.22–12.23.

[255] Art 11ter of the Berne Convention. Probably by error, only the public performance right was provided in the 1948 Brussels text; the communication right was then added at the 1967 Stockholm Revision, cf Masouyé (n 127 above) 11ter.4; Nodemann/Vinck/Hertin/Meyer (n 20 above) note to Art 11ter BC; Ricketson/Ginsburg (n 3 above) 12.12.

[256] ibid 12.08, 12.11.

performance 'by any means or process'. Such means or processes may include devices from which the works can be made audible or visible at a place open to the public or in its presence, such as the playing of musical records in a discotheque, bar, or at a choreographic performance in a theatre, or the showing of an audiovisual recording of a theatre play, opera, or concert to the public at an educational establishment. The words 'by any means or process' are technically neutral so that any modern devices are covered.[257]

5.138 *Communication to the public under Articles 11, 11ter, and 14 of the Berne Convention* 'Any communication to the public' under the above Articles requires, unlike public performance and recitation, a transmission to a remote place. The meaning of 'communication' must also be delineated, by way of systematic interpretation, from the separate rights of communication to the public in relation to broadcasts and of broadcasting under Article 11bis of the Berne Convention.[258] Accordingly, the latter acts are not included in the term 'communication' under the above Articles. This term, however, includes the rights not contained in Article 11bis(1) of the Berne Convention, namely and in particular, wire transmission of a performance or recitation of the work or of a cinematographic work to a remote place, where otherwise the performance, recitation, or cinematographic work could not be seen or heard. Examples are the transmission of an opera performance to the place in front of the opera house, assisted by loudspeaker and screen; video transmission to hotel rooms and 'music on hold' played over the telephone (as far as these are to the 'public' under the law of the Union country of protection); and, more importantly, original cable transmission[259] of a concert or public lecture of a work, of a recorded work, or a cinematographic work to the public. While cable-originated transmissions were still of marginal economic importance when this right was added at the 1948 Brussels Conference,[260] exploitation by cable radio and television became highly important much later. Its importance may only grow with further technical developments, such as the transmission over digital networks as in the case of originated webcasting.[261] One might even interpret the communication

---

[257] ibid 12.13, 12.14; for public performance of cinematographic (and pre-existing) works, see Arts 14(1)(ii) and 14bis of the Berne Convention and ibid 12.15.

[258] For Art 11bis, cf paras 5.141 ff below.

[259] In contrast, cable retransmission of a broadcast of a work is covered by Art 11bis(1)(ii) of the Berne Convention.

[260] In particular, the documents of the Conference referred to original transmission by telephone distribution, cf Documents of the Conference of Brussels 1948 (1951), 255–6; Nordemann/Vinck/Hertin/Meyer (n 20 above) Art 11 BC n 3; such telephone distribution occurred in particular via the 'theatre phone' where customers could listen to a performance at home via a telephone line, see Ricketson/Ginsburg (n 3 above) 12.31 in n 109.

[261] On communication under the above articles, see ibid 12.31, 12.32.

right under the Berne Convention as applying to on-demand communications via the internet.[262]

This analysis shows an important gap of protection: the Berne Convention pro- **5.139** vides for the right of original cable transmission (in particular in the form of 'cable distribution', 'cable broadcasting', and webcasting) only in respect of the performance of musical, dramatic, and dramatico-musical works, the recitation of literary works, works adapted or reproduced for cinematographic purposes, and cinematographic works. This gap in respect of the remaining works has only been filled in the WIPO Copyright Treaty.[263]

Paragraph (2) of Articles 11 and 11[ter] of the Berne Convention each states the **5.140** obvious in confirming that the author of a work enjoys these minimum rights not only in respect of the work in its original form, but also when translated.[264]

Broadcasting under Article 11[bis] of the Berne Convention Article 11[bis](1) of the **5.141** Berne Convention lays down several rights in relation to broadcasting for any kind of work. Article 11[bis](1)(i) provides for the exclusive broadcasting right, which covers only wireless diffusion, as shown by the supplementary words 'communication . . . by any *other* means of *wireless* diffusion . . .'.[265] These words also show that 'broadcasting' in this Article is considered as a form of 'communication to the public'. Accordingly, 'communication' has a different meaning in different Articles;[266] in general, the systematic context in which a particular term is used in the Berne Convention may matter for its concrete meaning. Article 11[bis](1)(i) of the Berne Convention is technically neutral within the category of 'wireless' diffusion. It covers terrestrial radio and television broadcasting and—as largely accepted nowadays—satellite broadcasting or communication to the public by satellite. When the latter became a reality, the question of whether this new form of broadcasting would constitute a form of broadcasting in the meaning of copyright law was controversial for some time, in particular in respect of communication to the public via point-to-point satellites and distribution satellites.

---

262 For a discussion of this suggestion, see paras 7.24–7.26 below; Ricketson/Ginsburg (n 3 above) 12.48–12.51.

263 cf para 17.107 below.

264 Nordemann/Vinck/Hertin/Meyer (n 20 above) Art 11 BC n 7, Masouyé (n 127 above) 11.7; according to the same logic, this also applies to works when adapted, even if not spelled out in these provisions.

265 Emphasis added.

266 As developed above (para 5.138), the word 'communication to the public' in Arts 11, 11ter, and 14 of the Berne Convention is limited to forms of communication by wire.

5.142 For direct-broadcasting satellites, which transmit the signals directly to receiver stations of individual members of the public (satellite dishes), this question was hardly controversial.[267] In the cases of point-to-point and distribution satellites, doubts were expressed whether the communication would be 'to the public'. Indeed, in these cases, the signals are not directly received by the public, but rather intercepted by terrestrial stations which then further distribute the signals by wire to individual members of the public.[268] According to the prevailing opinion today, it suffices that the public is reached indirectly, namely after intermediate steps by an earth station. It is considered as more important that the satellite broadcaster has the intention to finally transmit the broadcast to the public. This is in accordance with the broad wording of Article 11bis(1)(i) of the Berne Convention which does not limit the 'communication' to any 'direct' communication, and also with the general tendency of the Berne Convention to be technically neutral.

5.143 *Rebroadcasting and retransmission under Article 11bis of the Berne Convention*   Article 11bis(1)(ii) of the Berne Convention covers the exclusive rights of rebroadcasting and retransmission by wire of a broadcast of a work. These acts must be done by an organization other than the original broadcasting organization. If the original broadcaster itself further retransmits or relays its broadcast, the Berne Convention does not grant any additional right to the author. In this case, the author must secure protection on the basis of his contract with the broadcaster. The object of rebroadcasting and retransmission is a (wireless) broadcast only.

5.144 'Communication to the public by re-broadcasting' means any wireless (re)diffusion of the broadcast, including by satellite.[269] 'Communication to the public by wire' of the broadcast is its rediffusion by any physical facilities which enable the conduct of signals of the broadcast. The most common form thereof is cable retransmission. Yet, given the broad wording ('any communication . . . by wire'), any new technical development which involves the transmission of signals by any physical conductor, such as retransmission of broadcasts by webcasting or by fibre-optic cable, are covered by this right.

5.145 The Berne Convention does not provide any specific criteria to distinguish between communication (an act covered by the author's right) and reception (an act not covered thereby). Therefore, one will have to acknowledge a certain leeway of interpretation in favour of the Union countries in this respect.

---

[267] E Ulmer, 'Protection of Authors in Relation to the Transmission via Satellite of Broadcast Programs' (1977) 93 RIDA 4, 14.

[268] For this early controversy, cf Ulmer (n 213 above) 14 ff, in particular 22–4.

[269] On the related term 'broadcasting', cf paras 5.141–5.142 above.

Such distinction particularly matters in the case of community antennas which receive broadcasts and further distribute them to apartments in a house, to several blocks of apartments, or even to homes in a broader area. This case is quite controversial.[270]

Public communication of a broadcast under Article 11bis of the Berne   **5.146**
Convention   Article 11^bis(1)(iii) of the Berne Convention covers a different act in relation to the broadcast of a work, namely its direct public communication by loudspeaker or any other analogous instrument. In particular, where bars, subway stations, supermarkets, or any other places open to the public play music from a radio broadcast or play and show TV programmes so that the public can listen to the programmes or watch them, the author of the broadcast work must authorize such uses. Logically, where only unprotected news reports or sports programmes rather than protected works are communicated, no authorization is needed under copyright. Unlike in Articles 11, 11ter, and 14 of the Berne Convention, under which the communication relates to certain works or their performance, the communication under Article 11^bis(1)(iii) of the Berne Convention relates to the broadcast of works.

'Public'   The Berne Convention does not define or further specify the term   **5.147**
'public' used in Articles 11–11ter and 14 of the Berne Convention. The word 'public' in its ordinary meaning is regularly opposed to 'private' so that performances in the closest family certainly fall outside the meaning of 'public'. However, not any family circle can be considered to be private: in certain areas of the world, family circles are understood so broadly that they might cover entire villages. The purpose of the Berne Convention requires that the core potential of these rights must be safeguarded and not undermined by an extremely narrow interpretation of the word 'public'. Within such limits, Berne Union countries are free to define the meaning of 'public' and thereby determine the very contents of the rights under Articles 11 to 11ter and 14 of the Berne Convention.[271]

(4) Exceptions and limitations

(a) General remarks

(i) Historical development   The Berne Convention 1886 contained only two   **5.148**
very narrow limitations, which were later amended: a mandatory one regarding articles published in newspapers and periodicals, and a voluntary one for

---

270 For a leeway of Union countries, cf Nordemann/Vinck/Hertin/Meyer (n 20 above) Art 11bis BC n 4; cf, however, Ricketson/Ginsburg (n 3 above) 12.38 against coverage where redistribution is made for a block of apartments.
271 ibid 12.02.

educational purposes.[272] The system of limitations under the Berne Convention then developed continuously. For example, limitations regarding mechanical recording were first introduced in 1908 and amended in 1967; the compulsory licence for broadcasting under Article 11[bis] was inserted at the 1928 Rome Conference, as was Article 2[bis](2); the limitations regarding quotation and incidental uses when reporting on current events were first introduced at the 1948 Brussels Conference; and those of the reproduction right were provided together with the right itself at the 1967 Stockholm Conference.[273]

5.149 (ii) **Different ways of restricting protection**   In general, authors' rights are not, and never have been, granted in an absolutely unrestricted way. First, restrictions of protection in the broad sense apply with regard to the protected object, the work. Works in general are only protected if they fulfil the conditions of protection, such as originality; ideas, facts, etc are not protected as confirmed in Article 2(8) of the Berne Convention for mere items of information. Even where works are in principle protected because they fulfil such conditions, certain kinds of works, such as official texts, may be entirely exempted from protection for the same public policy reasons that may also justify certain limitations of rights.[274] Secondly, the rights of the author are usually limited in time. Both kinds of restrictions are not dealt with here, but should be kept in mind when dealing with the extent of copyright protection in general.[275]

5.150 A third way of restricting copyright protection is to exempt particular kinds of uses from the author's exclusive rights. These restrictions are dealt with here. They may be further distinguished as follows. First, the author may be left with neither an exclusive right nor a statutory right of remuneration, such as in the case of quotations: such restrictions may be called exceptions. Secondly, the author may be deprived of his exclusive right, but instead may be guaranteed a right of remuneration under the law; such restrictions may be called limitations. Two subcategories can be identified here: a statutory licence where the law itself permits certain kinds of uses in combination with a statutory remuneration right; and a compulsory licence where the author has the exclusive right but is compelled by law to conclude a contract on the utilization of the work according to equitable terms. Statutory and compulsory licences are often designated as nonvoluntary licences. In this chapter, 'limitations' will be used as a general term to

---

[272] Arts 7, 8 of the Berne Convention 1886.

[273] For the details of the historical development of Arts 2[bis](2), 9(2), 10(1), 10(2), 10[bis](1), 10[bis] (2), 11[bis] and 13, cf Ricketson/Ginsburg (n 3 above) in this order: 13.56, 13.03 ff, 13.39–13.40, 13.44, 13.48–13.53, 13.54–13.55, 13.59–13.62, and 13.67–13.70.

[274] Arts 2(4) and 2[bis](1) of the Berne Convention regarding certain official texts and specified speeches, cf paras 5.80–5.82 above.

[275] On the limited duration, cf para 5.212 below.

cover all of the above restrictions to rights. However, the reader should be aware of the fact that there is no worldwide uniform terminology in this respect.[276]

For the sake of completeness, another kind of restriction to the scope of authors' **5.151** rights should be mentioned, even if it is not a limitation of the rights but a preceding restriction of the scope of rights by their definition. In particular, the author's communication rights (in the broad sense) regularly cover, by definition, only acts of communication 'to the public' rather than also, for example, private performances. Furthermore, the distribution right is limited to the first act of putting objects into circulation.

A different kind of restriction regarding the full enjoyment of author's rights **5.152** originates outside of copyright law, such as national provisions on censorship or competition law. These are not limitations of authors' rights in the narrow sense and are therefore not dealt with in this context.[277]

(iii) Interests protected by limitations of rights Limitations of rights in uses **5.153** may be further distinguished according to the interests to be protected. Most limitations are provided in favour of interests of the general public, such as education and research,[278] news reporting and access to information on current events,[279] the functioning of the judicial, administrative, or parliamentary system,[280] and specific interests such as in quotation, criticism, and review.[281] Other provisions promote interests of specific groups of the society rather than the general public, namely interests of broadcasting organizations[282] and phonogram producers.[283] These latter limitations have been drafted so as to allow the provision of compulsory licences.

(iv) Concept of limitations under the Berne Convention Against the back- **5.154** ground of the current new wave of claims expressed by user groups, specific developing countries, and a number of academics, to introduce minimum standards of free uses in favour of the general public,[284] it may be surprising to learn that the idea is far from being innovative: the complementary idea of maximum protection where the Convention provided for limitations had already been raised at the 1928 Rome Conference by the Austrian delegate; however, it was not further

---

276 Similarly Ficsor (n 240 above) 5.04.
277 For such provisions covered by Art 17 of the Berne Convention, cf paras 5.205–5.211 below.
278 Arts 10(2), 9(2) of the Berne Convention.
279 Arts 2bis(2), 10bis ibid.
280 Art 9(2) ibid.
281 Art 10(1) ibid.
282 Art 11bis(2) and (3) phr 2 ibid.
283 Art 13(1) ibid.
284 eg WIPO Doc SCCR/13/5 (proposal by Chile on limitations) Annex p 1.

pursued but later only discussed in literature.[285] Under its 1971 Act, the Convention even clearly expresses that the permitted limitations are not mandatory, so national laws may decide not to provide them at all or not to their full extent.[286] Accordingly, the limitations under the Berne Convention[287] present the outer limits of what is permitted under the Convention. Any provision under national law that restricts the protection further or, in other words, broadens the limitations as compared to those of the Berne Convention would not comply with the Convention.

5.155 Of course, such broader limitations can be provided under domestic law, though only for domestic situations to which the Berne Convention does not apply. However, Union countries do not intend to discriminate against domestic works in favour of foreign ones and are therefore likely to refrain from adopting such provisions. This concept of limitations corresponds to the fundamental aim of the Berne Convention to protect the 'rights of authors', as manifested in Article 1 and the Preamble, as well as in Article 19, which confirms the principle of minimum rights by explicitly allowing for greater protection (namely, through greater rights or through not fully or not at all providing for limitations).

(b) The individual limitations in favour of the public interest

(i) **Access to information, news reporting**

5.156 *Article 2bis(2) of the Berne Convention* Articles 2bis (2) and 10bis of the Berne Convention serve the purpose of access to information and news reporting. Article 2bis(2) concerns lectures, addresses, and other works of the same nature (such as orally expressed works of literature), when delivered in public. It allows Union countries 'to determine the conditions' under which specified uses thereof may be made, such as the payment of an equitable remuneration. The uses specified under the provision must be 'justified by the informatory purpose': this does not require the lectures and other works to deal specifically with news; they must only have the purpose of informing the public about their contents.[288]

---

[285] Nordemann/Vinck/Hertin/Meyer (n 20 above) Art 19 BC nn 1–2; Ricketson/Ginsburg (n 3 above) 6.110; A Baum, 'Droit international public, Convention de Berne et lois nationales' (1946) Droit d'auteur 85, 114 (third part), 116–17, with presentation of the Austrian question regarding maximum protection and the scholarly discussion; yet, the discussion was mainly based on legal-technical arguments, given the unclear 1908 version of Art 19 of the Berne Convention rather than on considerations of public interest.

[286] The relevant Articles use the expression 'it shall be a matter for legislation . . . to permit . . .'. Only for quotation, the words 'it shall be permissible' seem to indicate an obligatory character; cf, however, para 5.163 below.

[287] They also cover the so-called 'implied exceptions', cf paras 5.199–5.204 below.

[288] Ricketson/Ginsburg (n 3 above) 13.57; Masouyé (n 127 above) n 2bis.3.

Article 10 ᵇⁱˢ(1) of the Berne Convention   Article 10ᵇⁱˢ(1) of the Berne   **5.157**
Convention allows Union countries 'to permit' similar, specified uses regarding
articles and broadcast works. The possibility 'to permit' seems less flexible than
the possibility to 'determine the conditions'; yet, both expressions have the same
meaning in substance: where a country may permit specified uses, it may also
decide not to permit them at all, and this implies that it may permit the specified
uses under additional conditions.

The permissible uses are broadcasting, communication to the public by wire, and   **5.158**
'reproduction by the press'. Although the word 'press' ('la presse') originally only
referred to the printing press (and, hence, to the technique of printing), the word
is used today also in the online context where the word 'electronic press' has
become common. Reproduction by the electronic press should therefore be considered as covered by Article 10ᵇⁱˢ(1) of the Berne Convention. Where articles are
made available online by electronic press services, the limitation only applies if
one considers the right of making works available online to be covered by the
communication right of the Berne Convention.[289] All permissible uses, however,
remain subject to authorization by the author if he expressly reserves his rights. In
addition, the source must be clearly indicated; otherwise, the use is not automatically illegal, but the legal consequences of a breach of this obligation must be
determined by the national law of the country for which protection is
claimed.[290]

The uses must refer to articles published in newspapers or periodicals and to   **5.159**
broadcast works. The explicit mentioning of 'newspapers' seems to exclude any
electronic publication which does not occur in a 'paper'; however, the governing
French version ('journeaux') is technically neutral, so that electronic newspapers
are covered.[291]

The articles and broadcast works must deal with current economic, political, or   **5.160**
religious topics. Since these topics are explicitly mentioned without any opening
clause such as 'and similar topics', articles on other current events, such as reviews
of concerts or movies and articles on scientific news or sports must not be covered
by a limitation or exception.[292] This condition may reflect that the Berne
Convention only considers the mentioned topics as important enough to justify
restrictions of protection on the grounds of access to information. The condition

---

[289] On this question, see paras 5.139 above and 7.24–7.26 below.

[290] Art 10ᵇⁱˢ(1) phr 2 of the Berne Convention; this obligation follows from Art 6ᵇⁱˢ of the Berne
Convention and is a confirmation here only.

[291] Doubts might only arise in respect of whether articles available in online newspapers or periodicals have been 'published' in the meaning of Article 3(3) of the Berne Convention; see on this
problem paras 7.31–7.33 below.

[292] Ricketson/Ginsburg (n 3 above) 13.53.

that the events must be 'current' further illustrates the concept of access to information as incorporated in the Berne Convention as one that is essentially news related.

5.161 *Article 10 ^{bis}(2) of the Berne Convention*   The reporting on current events is privileged under Article 10bis(2) of the Berne Convention where works are incidentally included in the reporting by photography, cinematography, broadcasting, or communication to the public by wire. When reporting on current events, it is often inevitable that protected works may be seen or heard in the course of the event, such as an architectural building in the background, a sculpture standing at the place of the event, or a musical work played at a state ceremony. In such cases, it is mostly impossible to obtain an authorization from the author in due time. In order to enable licit news reporting in such cases, the limitation of Article 10bis(2) of the Berne Convention had to be provided.

5.162 The reporting must relate to 'current' events, namely events which take place in a close time context of the reporting. Unlike under Article 10bis(1) of the Berne Convention, there is no restriction to certain topics to which the event must relate. Yet, the exception must be justified in each case by the informatory purpose, and the limitation applies only 'to the extent' needed in order to fulfil the informatory purpose. Accordingly, works must not be reproduced or made accessible more extensively than needed for the reporting. For example, in the case of a state ceremony, it may not be necessary for the information of the public to broadcast the entire piece of music played in the course of the event.

5.163 **(ii) Quotations**   Quotations are privileged under Article 10(1) of the Berne Convention. This provision is the only one that does not explicitly leave the determination of limitations to the Union countries, but states that 'it shall be permissible' to make quotations. Therefore, one might conclude that Union countries must provide for a limitation for quotations; this seems all the more evident under the governing French wording *sont licites* ('are permitted').[293] However, one may also argue on the basis of Articles 19, 20, and even 5(1) of the Berne Convention that Union countries are allowed to grant greater protection in any respect, be it by additional rights or less limitations, and that it is therefore not obligatory to provide for a limitation for quotations.[294]

5.164 Making 'quotations' is usually understood as using parts of another person's work in order to illustrate or prove a statement or to otherwise refer to such work. While the wording 'from a work' suggests that only parts of a work may be quoted, it should also cover quotation of entire works, where this is the only way to reach

---

[293] In this sense ibid 13.42.
[294] Ficsor (n 240 above) 5.11.

the purpose of quotation, as in the case of a photograph, drawing, or other art-work.[295] Quotations may be made from any kind of work, be it a literary, musical, artistic, or other work. The work must have been lawfully made available to the public before quotation is allowed. This condition reflects the respect of the Convention towards the author who alone should have the decision on whether her work, or parts of it, becomes known to the public.[296] The Berne Convention intentionally has chosen the broader term 'lawfully made available to the public' instead of 'lawfully published'[297] in order to leave the author the decision on any kind of rendering the work or parts of it to the public. Quotation will mostly occur in the form of reproductions, and less often through broadcasting, per-forming, and other uses.

The making of the quotation must be compatible with 'fair practice'. This term **5.165** was not illuminated at the Stockholm Conference 1967 and must be further determined by the national laws of the Union countries. It has been suggested that the three conditions under Article 9(2) of the Berne Convention also apply in the context of 'fair practice'.[298]

Finally, the extent of quotation must not exceed that justified by the purpose. **5.166** The purpose of quotations is usually to make one's own statement, analyses, or comment on another person's work, to illustrate a thought, or to otherwise establish a literary, artistic, or musical link to another person's work. Such pur-pose must justify the extent of quotation.[299] For example, an article by a feminist writer on Helmut Newton's photographs published in a monthly magazine in November 1993 aimed at showing that his nudes were sexist, racist, and fascistic photographs. The article was published together with nineteen photographs without authorization from Newton's publisher. The defence of a quotation was not admitted since fewer photographs would have sufficed to fulfil the purpose of demonstrating the writer's proposition.[300]

The example of 'quotations from newspaper articles and periodicals in the form **5.167** of press summaries' is misleading because summaries of texts do not constitute

---

[295] Nordemann/Vinck/Hertin/Meyer (n 20 above) Art 10 BC n 1.

[296] This aspect has been explicitly regulated in many national laws by the moral right of disclo-sure or divulgation, cf para 3.47 above.

[297] For the narrower term 'published works', cf Art 3(3) of the Berne Convention and paras 5.32–5.34 above.

[298] Ficsor (n 240 above) 5.14; Ricketson/Ginsburg (n 3 above) 13.41; Nordemann/Vinck/ Hertin/Meyer (n 20 above) Art 10 BC n 1; on the three conditions, see paras 5.179–5.186 below.

[299] Ficsor (n 240 above) 5.15; at the 1967 Stockholm Conference and during earlier preparatory work, only indirect purposes of quotation such as educational or entertainment purposes were men-tioned, but not adopted as part of the text; they should not be taken into account (ibid).

[300] District Court (LG) München of 27 July 1994, *Schirmer/Mosel vs Emma*, (1994) Archiv für Presserecht 326, 328; see also <http://www.aliceschwarzer.de/235.html>.

quotations. What is meant is revealed in the governing French version which allows quotations in the form of *revues de presse*, ie collections of excerpts from articles from different papers on the same topic.[301]

5.168 In the context of a quotation, the source and the author's name must be mentioned.[302]

5.169 **(iii) Education (Article 10(2) of the Berne Convention)** Limitations for the purpose of teaching—another classical purpose—may be allowed under national law and special agreements between Union countries. They may cover any kind of works and permit uses by way of illustration in publications, broadcasts, or sound or visual recordings for teaching. Accordingly, the rights of reproduction and broadcasting (and, arguably, public performance) may be limited. Publications for teaching include, in particular, school books and course materials; it is questionable whether 'publications' include 'online publications'.[303] Broadcasts for teaching are programmes conceived especially for teaching purposes, such as so-called 'school broadcasts', even if they can be received by the general public while being intended only for schoolteaching. Despite the specific wording, it has been suggested that the public performance of such broadcasts in classrooms or other places where the students gather can also be permitted.[304] This suggestion corresponds to the purpose of the provision: the possibility of freely including works in broadcasts for teaching would not serve the purpose to facilitate teaching if the broadcast cannot be shown without the authors' consent to the pupils when they are gathered in a classroom rather than one by one in their homes. Sound or visual recordings for teaching may be any educational recordings made especially for school or other teaching; their use would normally occur by public performance.

5.170 The utilization of such works must be 'by way of illustration', 'justified by the purpose' and 'compatible with fair practice'.[305] The 'utilisation . . . by way of illustration' and the 'compatibility with fair practice' have replaced the earlier text which allowed 'excerpts' from works. The new wording allows more flexibility including, in particular, the utilization of entire works such as photographs or poems, subject to the other conditions. Yet, the condition to use the work 'by way of illustration' is limitative in principle; often, it will be sufficient to use a part of a work in order to illustrate the subject matter taught.

---

[301] Ricketson/Ginsburg (n 3 above) 13.41.

[302] Art 10(3) of the Berne Convention; paras 5.107–5.108, 5.128, and 5.158 above.

[303] On the related problem in the context of Art 3(3) of the Berne Convention (the definition of 'published works'), cf paras 7.31–7.33 below; in addition, online teaching is not covered by 'broadcasts', Ricketson/Ginsburg (n 3 above) 13.45.

[304] Masouyé (n 127 above) n 10.9.

[305] For the two last-mentioned conditions, see paras 5.165–5.166 above.

'Teaching' is not limited to any particular kind of teaching. Indeed, the Report of   **5.171**
Main Committee I at the 1967 Stockholm Conference clarified that 'teaching'
was to refer to all levels—schools for children, universities, or other educational
institutions—irrespective of their operators, but considered that 'education outside these institutions, for instance general teaching available to the public but
not included in the above categories' should be excluded.[306] Accordingly, it seems
that a broad range of teaching, including courses for adults, are covered by the
exception as long as they take place at universities, private or public schools, or
other educational institutions.[307] In respect of commercial teaching, a limitation
for teaching would, however, hardly be compatible with fair practice; where students pay course fees, and the teaching institution thereby earns money, it would
seem unfair to exclude authors from benefiting from the use of their works.

The word 'teaching' is technically neutral and therefore, in principle, is broad   **5.172**
enough also to cover distant teaching on the basis of correspondence courses in
the traditional world or online courses via the internet. Although teaching regularly involves face-to-face instruction, it can also be realized from a distance,
through particular ways of arranging and selecting written teaching materials,
written questions and answers, pedagogical ways of submitting questions to the
students, etc.[308] Yet, doubts about online teaching may arise regarding other
conditions.[309]

Finally, also in this context, the source and name of the author must be indi-   **5.173**
cated.[310] There is no specific exemption for research purposes; as regards reproduction, they are covered by the general provision of Article 9(2) of the Berne
Convention.

(iv) General limitation of the reproduction right (Article 9(2) of the Berne Convention)

General remarks   In addition to the specific limitations of the reproduction   **5.174**
right in Articles 2[bis](2), 10, 10[bis], 11[bis](3) phrases 2, 3, as well as 13 of the Berne
Convention, the Convention provides for general conditions to limit this right in
Article 9(2). The specific limitations must be considered as *lex specialis*; accordingly, where their more specific conditions are not fulfilled, the limitations cannot be justified on the basis of Article 9(2) of the Berne Convention.[311] As another

---

306 Records of the 1967 Stockholm Conference, 1148.
307 Similarly Ricketson/Ginsburg (n 3 above) 13.45.
308 Similarly ibid 13.45/793.
309 cf para 5.139 above, on 'publications'; also, the particular intensity of use may not be compatible with fair practice.
310 Art 10(3) of the Berne Convention. See hereon paras 5.107–5.108, 5.128, and 5.158 above.
311 For the same result, see Ricketson/Ginsburg (n 3 above) 13.10.

consequence, Article 9(2) will not apply in addition to the specific limitations, where their conditions are fulfilled. This is different from the relation between Article 13 of the TRIPS Agreement and the specific Berne limitations.[312]

5.175 Article 9(2) of the Berne Convention was introduced following a proposal by the United Kingdom.[313] Its conditions set limits for permitted limitations, while leaving the necessary flexibility of legislatures to take into account a large diversity of factual situations to be regulated, and of traditions in Union countries. Accordingly, different Union countries may easily arrive at different interpretations of this provision.

5.176 The three conditions to be fulfilled are (1) the provision of certain special cases, (2) no conflict with a normal exploitation, and (3) no unreasonable prejudice to the legitimate interests of the author. They constitute an order to national legislators to draft limitations accordingly. It is undisputed that they must be cumulatively fulfilled if a national provision on limitations of the reproduction right is to comply with Article 9(2) of the Berne Convention. In addition, the order of the conditions matters: in particular, the balancing of interests under the third condition must occur only where there is no conflict with a normal exploitation under the second condition.[314]

5.177 The conditions were later taken over into the TRIPS Agreement, the WCT, and the WPPT as general clauses for permitted limitations rather than merely in respect of the reproduction right. It was only in the context of the TRIPS negotiations that the catchword 'three-step test' was coined for these three conditions;[315] only afterwards was this word also used in respect of Article 9(2) of the Berne Convention. Indeed, the 'career' of the latter provision began not before its inclusion into the TRIPS Agreement and the WIPO Treaties of 1996, as reflected in abundant literature on the three-step test published primarily in the context of these treaties[316] and in the quite detailed decision of the WTO Panel on Section

---

[312] See para 10.84 below; similarly for the WCT: paras 17.84–17.85 below.

[313] The clause is much closer to the Anglo-American system than to Continental law; cf eg criticism of the concept of 'unreasonable prejudice' as 'too typically British' at the Stockholm Conference (Ricketson/Ginsburg (n 3 above) 13.25), and a comparison with the US fair use doctrine in M Senftleben, *Copyright, Limitations and the Three-Step Test* (2004) 112–13. Indeed, Continental countries had proposed specific limitations in addition to this clause, Ricketson/Ginsburg (n 3 above) 13.08, 13.09.

[314] Senftleben (n 313 above) 130–3. Ficsor (n 240 above) 5.54, referring to the Records of the Stockholm Conference.

[315] On the relevant provisions, see paras 10.83 ff, 17.83 ff.

[316] Apart from the existing commentaries on these treaties, see as a few examples J Ginsburg, 'Towards Supranational Copyright Law? The WTO Panel Decision and the "Three-Step-Test" for Copyright Exceptions' (2001) 187 RIDA 3; Senftleben (n 313 above); S Ricketson, *WIPO Study on Limitations and Exceptions of Copyright and Related Rights in the Digital Environment*, WIPO Doc SCCR/9/7; M Ficsor, 'Too much of what? The "Three-Step Test" and its Application in Two Recent

110 of the US Copyright Act 1976 (Title 17) on the basis of Article 13 of the TRIPS Agreement.[317] When interpreting the Berne Convention, however, one has to note that the interpretation by the WTO Panel is based on Article 13 of the TRIPS Agreement, which refers not only to the reproduction right but to all exclusive rights, and is made by reference to the law of GATT and GATS as interpreted by the Appellate Body in a non-intellectual property context. Since the WTO Panel only interprets WTO law, its interpretation is not binding within the Berne Union; it may have only a de facto influence.

The presentation of the individual conditions of Article 9(2) of the Berne Convention outlines some basic remarks; more detailed analysis is beyond the scope of this book.   **5.178**

Certain special cases   The condition of 'certain' special cases is an order to the legislator to precisely define limitations rather than formulating them vaguely.[318] Accordingly, it has been argued that, for example, the fair use provisions of the US Copyright Act (Title 17) do not comply with this condition and, hence, with Article 9(2) of the Berne Convention.[319] This condition aims at achieving legal certainty.   **5.179**

In addition, the cases must be 'special'. This element may be interpreted as requiring a narrow scope, based on the ordinary meaning of the word and in line with the purpose of the Convention, namely the protection of rights of authors in their works[320] rather than the protection of users of works.[321]   **5.180**

Some commentators argue that the word 'special' also implies that limitations must have a special purpose, namely one that is 'justified by some clear reason of public policy or some other exceptional circumstance'.[322] Indeed, specific public   **5.181**

WTO Dispute Settlement Cases' (2002) 192 RIDA 111; S Ricketson, *The Three-Step Test, Deemed Quantities, Libraries and Closed Exceptions* (Centre for Copyright Studies, 2002).

[317] cf para 10.87 below.

[318] This interpretation is based on the ordinary meaning of the word 'certain' in the context of the Berne Convention in line with its purpose, Ricketson/Ginsburg (n 3 above) 13.11; WTO Panel Decision WT/DS/160/R of 15 June 2000 para 6.108 (though without authority for the Berne Convention); by contrast, Senftleben (n 313 above) 133–7, understands 'certain' as 'some' and only requires cases to be distinguishable from each other, without requiring a precise and narrow definition.

[319] eg Ricketson (n 316 above, WIPO Doc.) at 68; H Cohen Jehoram, 'Restrictions on Copyright and their Abuse' [2005] EIPR 359, 360.

[320] Art 1 of the Berne Convention.

[321] Ricketson/Ginsburg (n 3 above) 13.11, following the WTO Panel Report (n 318 above); Senftleben (n 313 above) 140–4 rejects such quantitative aspect of 'special' by referring to the analysis of the WTO Panel.

[322] Ricketson (n 36 above) 9.6. This has been endorsed by commentators on the WCT which itself includes the three-step test, cf Ficsor (n 240 above) 5.55; Reinbothe and von Lewinski (n 245 above) Art 10 WCT n 15; other commentators do not develop the meaning of 'certain special cases'.

policy reasons underlie all other limitations of the Berne Convention and were also envisaged for the limitations of the reproduction right, thereby following the national laws of Union countries. They were not explicitly listed simply due to the diversity of public policy reasons that may justify the limitation of the reproduction right.[323] By contrast, some commentators follow the above-mentioned WTO Panel in considering sufficient 'a special purpose whose underlying legitimacy in a normative sense cannot be discerned'.[324]

5.182   *No conflict with normal exploitation*   The reproduction permitted by law must not conflict with a normal exploitation of the work. This condition raises several questions regarding its interpretation. While 'exploitation' of the reproduction right is generally understood as making use of this right in order to extract its value,[325] the word 'normal' leaves more room for different interpretations. In particular, it could be understood as referring to the de facto situation, or as implying a normative element. The first way of interpretation obviously could lead to largely undermining the author's protection, especially where the author cannot reasonably expect to gain revenues from the exploitation of his work, because a limitation has already been provided, or because he cannot control the use, or because a kind of exploitation has not yet been developed.[326]

5.183   In addition, the first way of interpretation would contravene the purpose of the Berne Convention to secure, in the first place, the protection of the rights of authors without taking away the main substance of these rights. Indeed, it has been stated that 'all forms of exploiting a work which had, or were likely to acquire, considerable economic or practical importance must in principle be reserved to the authors'.[327] The second, normative interpretation may better meet the purpose of the Convention: it would lead to a conflict with a normal exploitation, where such important forms of exploitation are undermined by uses covered by a limitation. This may be the case especially where the permitted uses under national law enter into economic competition with the ways in which authors normally extract economic value from a right.[328]

---

[323]   Ricketson/Ginsburg (n 3 above) 13.08.

[324]   WTO Panel (n 318 above) para 6.112. Ginsburg (n 316 above) 3, follows the interpretation of the WTO Panel, which is now also accepted by her co-author, in Ricketson/Ginsburg (n 3 above) 13.14.

[325]   Similarly: Ficsor (n 240 above) 5.56; WTO Panel Report (n 318 above) para 6.165; Ricketson/Ginsburg (n 3 above) 13.16.

[326]   For more detailed analyses of this interpretation, see Senftleben (n 313 above) 171–6; Ricketson/Ginsburg (n 3 above) 13.17; Ficsor (n 240 above) 5.56.

[327]   Records of the 1967 Stockholm Conference, 111; Ficsor (n 240 above) 5.56.

[328]   Records of the 1967 Stockholm Conference, 112; Ficsor (n 240 above) 5.56; WTO Panel Report (n 318 above), para 6.183. Ricketson/Ginsburg (n 3 above) 13.20–13.22 suggest that non-economic

No unreasonable prejudice to the legitimate interests of the author Finally, **5.184**
where the first and second conditions are fulfilled, the use must not, according to
the third condition, unreasonably prejudice the legitimate interests of the author.
This formulation gives leeway to balancing the author's interests against those of
the general public and to taking into account different factual situations in different countries. For example, the application of this condition to a particular use
may lead to different results depending on the intensity of use, which can be different in an industrialized country and a developing country—in particular, the
prejudice may be unreasonable in one country while it is, for the same kind of
use, reasonable in another country,. The 'legitimate' interests of the author certainly include all interests protected by the law through the recognition of rights.
However, 'legitimate' may be considered as different from 'lawful' so as to also
include a normative element that indicates the need to balance the author's interests with those of the general public; it may be viewed as implying the need that
his interests are also justified from a normative point of view.[329]

Strictly speaking, any restriction of the reproduction right automatically constitutes **5.185**
a prejudice.[330] Accordingly, the element 'unreasonable' has been introduced, in order
to allow a proper balancing of interests.[331] The prejudice resulting from the limitation
must be proportionate and within the limits of reason, which implies an element of
intensity and magnitude of the prejudice. Again, the wording leaves legislatures some
leeway for interpretation. An unreasonable prejudice may be made reasonable by
providing a statutory right of remuneration as it exists in many countries, for example, in context with limitations for private reproduction.[332] Accordingly, a national
law that limits the reproduction right for private reproduction without granting a
statutory remuneration right may not comply with the third condition under Article
9(2) of the Berne Convention, if the extent and intensity of private reproduction in
the relevant country leads to an unreasonable prejudice. Such a country would have
to introduce a statutory remuneration right for the private reproduction in order to
make the limitation compatible with Article 9(2) of the Berne Convention.

At the same time, not any limitation may be made compatible with the third **5.186**
condition through the provision of a remuneration right; one always has to take

---

aspects should also be considered when interpreting 'normal'. For a detailed elaboration of a (similar)
normative interpretation, see Senftleben (n 313 above) 177 ff, 195–6.

[329] Ricketson/Ginsburg (n 3 above) 13.24; for a different view, though with the overall same
result (meaning of 'legal interests', but normative element in the not unreasonable prejudice),
see Ficsor (n 240 above) 5.57.

[330] Masouyé (n 127 above) 9.8.

[331] Records of the 1967 Stockholm Conference Vol I, 883.

[332] This example was also mentioned in the discussions at the 1967 Stockholm Revision
Conference, Records of the 1967 Conference, Vol II, 1145–6; Ficsor (n 240 above) 5.58.

into account that a remuneration right is usually less strong, because the authors cannot prohibit the ongoing (legal) use and therefore do not have any comparable standing.

5.187 *Examples* Classic examples for the application of Article 9(2) of the Berne Convention include those already mentioned at the 1967 Stockholm Conference, namely, reproduction for judicial, administrative, and private purposes;[333] for purposes of research and private study;[334] for internal use in companies, law firms, and other businesses;[335] for preservation purposes in libraries and archives; and of non-commercial photography of buildings visible from the street or other public places, for example by tourists.[336] Another example which more recently has been introduced in many laws is the limitation in favour of disabled persons.[337]

5.188 All of these limitations are neither automatically nor unconditionally in compliance with Article 9(2) of the Berne Convention. It is, rather, necessary that in each individual case under the circumstances prevailing in the relevant country, all three conditions of this Article are fulfilled. This will usually require national laws quite specifically to formulate the conditions under which such uses are exempted from protection. In some cases, it may also require the provision of a statutory right to equitable remuneration, such as for private reproduction, as well as for reproduction in scientific and research institutes, companies, and businesses.

(c) Individual limitations in favour of interests of specific groups

5.189 (i) **Ephemeral recordings** Article 11^bis(3) of the Berne Convention contains another classic limitation that may be found in most national laws, namely, for so-called 'ephemeral recordings' by broadcasting organizations. This limitation is rooted in the following argument made at the time of its introduction: for technical reasons, broadcasting organizations had to reproduce works before they could be broadcast, in particular where a performance had to be broadcast live or where deferred broadcasts were made (such as in countries covering several time zones).[338] Accordingly, such reproduction was considered not to have an independent economic importance but

---

[333] Records of the 1967 Stockholm Conference Vol I, 113. On private reproduction, see Ricketson/Ginsburg (n 3 above) 13.33.

[334] This example was not explicitly included in the proposal at the Stockholm Conference, but mentioned in the discussions, Records 1967 (n 331 above) 885.

[335] This example also was not included in the proposal but mentioned at the Stockholm Conference, Records 1967 (nn 331 and 332 above) 883; 1146.

[336] For the two last-mentioned cases see, eg the UK CDPA 1988, ss 37 ff, and German Copyright Act of 1965, Art 59.

[337] See eg Art 5(3)(b) of the EC Information Society Dir 2001, OJ EC L167/10, which has been integrated in the laws of most Member States, even if it is a facultative exception under the Dir; on this Dir, see also Vol II ch 10.

[338] See Ricketson/Ginsburg (n 3 above) 13.72, 13.73 for further details on the historical background.

simply to enable the broadcast to be made. Therefore, broadcasters claimed that the reproduction right should not need to be acquired separately once the broadcasting right had been acquired.

These claims are partly taken into account in the following compromise: Article 11bis(3) phrase 1 of the Berne Convention recognizes the reproduction right as an independent one from the broadcasting right which both require separate authorizations. However, phrase 2 empowers national legislators to regulate ephemeral reproduction in particular by limitations of the reproduction right. Yet, they may do so only under specified conditions. First, the recording must be 'ephemeral'. Although no concrete time limit is indicated, the word implies some limitation in time. National laws have implemented this provision within a range from one month to one year.[339] If broadcasting organizations want to keep the recordings for a longer time, they need to get the authorization of the authors[340] or must destroy the recordings. **5.190**

Secondly, the recording must be made by the privileged broadcasting organization by means of its own facilities; this excludes the possibility of the organization putting someone else in charge of this task. Finally, the recording must be used for the organization's own broadcasts only and cannot in any way be made available to other broadcasting organizations. The use is not specified otherwise so that even repetitive uses are permissible, subject to the above-mentioned conditions. **5.191**

Article 11bis(3) phrase 3 is an exception from the conditions in phrase 2: if the recordings made under the limitation of phrase 2 have an exceptional documentary character, national laws may provide that these recordings do not need to be destroyed or authorized but may be preserved in official archives. This provision does not allow broadcasting organizations to regularly keep in their own archives the recordings made for the purpose of broadcasting. Rather, the documentary character must be 'exceptional', so that most recordings will have to be destroyed or authorized; in addition, the archives of the broadcasting organizations normally are not 'official archives' such as state archives or national libraries.[341] **5.192**

(ii) **Compulsory licences**[342] Articles 11bis(2) and 13(1) of the Berne Convention allow for compulsory licences. Accordingly, any limitation of the relevant rights must be accompanied by rights to equitable remuneration; without such **5.193**

---

[339] Ricketson/Ginsburg (n 3 above) 13.76 in n 338.

[340] This is subject to the special case of Article 11bis(3) phr 3 of the Berne Convention, see para 5.192 below.

[341] Ficsor (n 240 above) 5.44; Ricketson/Ginsburg (n 3 above) 13.77.

[342] For compulsory licences in favour of developing countries under the Appendix, see paras 5.232–5.233 below.

remuneration rights, limitations would not be compatible with these Articles. Both provisions are made for the benefit of particular groups of the society (broadcasting organizations and phonogram producers) rather than the general public. This may be explained historically: since the rights of broadcasting and mechanical recording were administered by collecting societies and by music publishers that usually exercised monopolistic practices, broadcasting organizations and phonogram producers raised concerns about an abuse of dominant positions and, therefore, about major impediments to their activities.[343] The different pre-existing approaches of Union countries to these claims are reflected in the compromises laid down in the Berne Convention.

5.194   *Article 11bis(2) of the Berne Convention*   In respect of broadcasting and related rights under Article 11bis(1) of the Berne Convention, national legislators may determine the conditions of exercise, though, subject only to the following conditions.[344] First, they must provide a statutory right of equitable remuneration for the respective uses; accordingly, this provision is usually understood as allowing compulsory licences. Secondly, compulsory licences or similar conditions of exercise only apply in the country which has established them, and only to acts of use taking place in that country; for satellite broadcasting, it may be difficult to determine where this act takes place.[345] Thirdly, it is clarified that the moral rights must be preserved and unaffected by the conditions of exercise.[346]

5.195   Notably, there is no obligation to provide for a compulsory licence, and experience in many countries that kept the exclusive right has shown that collective management organizations, which are commonly monopolies, have not abused their dominant positions, but have concluded licensing agreements with the broadcasting organizations and other users.

5.196   *Article 13 of the Berne Convention*   The other permitted compulsory licence concerns the recording of musical works.[347] It was first provided in the Berlin Act of 1908, when authors' rights in respect of mechanical reproduction started to be recognized in national laws. Phonogram producers felt impeded in their activities that so far were unimpeded by authors' rights, and objected to the introduction of such a right of authors, partly in view of the risk that music publishers could abuse their dominant positions. At that time, the phonogram industry had

---

[343] Ricketson/Ginsburg (n 3 above) 13.67 for broadcasting and 13.59 for mechanical recording.

[344] Art 11bis(2) of the Berne Convention.

[345] For the European Community, a solution has been found in Dir 93/83/EEC (OJ L 248/15), Art 2(b) by determining the place where satellite broadcasting is deemed to take place.

[346] Ricketson/Ginsburg (n 3 above) 13.71 argue that not only the rights under Art 6bis of the Berne Convention but also a right of divulgation would be meant.

[347] Art 13(1) of the Berne Convention.

grown powerful enough to obtain the following compromise:[348] an exclusive right of mechanical recording[349] was combined with the possibility to provide for broad reservations and conditions.[350]

After controversial discussion of this provision at several revision conferences, the **5.197** Paris Act shapes the compulsory licence as follows. First, unlike under Article 11[bis](2) of the Berne Convention, the possibility of providing for a compulsory licence only arises after the first authorization by the author(s) of the musical work and of any accompanying words. Accordingly, the first act of recording music with or without words on a phonogram must remain covered by the exclusive right and unaffected by any compulsory licence. Article 13(1) of the Berne Convention only works in favour of phonogram producers that subsequently would like to record the same music in a different interpretation. Secondly, where a country makes use of Article 13(1) of the Berne Convention, it must provide for a right of the authors to equitable remuneration. Thirdly, the compulsory licence shall only apply in the country where it has been provided. Article 13(3) of the Berne Convention reflects the latter condition: it allows Union countries to provide for the seizure of recordings imported without authorization, even where the recordings were legally made under a compulsory licence under Article 13(1) and (2) of the Berne Convention in the exporting country. Finally, moral rights remain applicable, even if Article 13(1) of the Berne Convention (unlike Article 11[bis](2)) does not explicitly safeguard them; no *e contrario* conclusion from Article 11[bis](2) of the Berne Convention is possible in this respect.[351]

In many countries, compulsory licences have not been considered necessary **5.198** because in practice, collective management organizations have usually licensed mechanical recording rights to the industry without problems. This practice is reflected, for example, by an intermediate way of implementation of Article 13(1) of the Berne Convention, namely, by a compulsory licence that only applies where the exclusive rights are not lawfully exercised by a collective management organization.[352]

---

[348] For the background of Art 13(1) of the Berne Convention, see Ricketson/Ginsburg (n 3 above) 13.59.

[349] A general reproduction right did not yet exist in the Berne Convention at that time.

[350] See Art 13(2) of the Berne Convention (Berlin Act); on the further historical development, see Ricketson/Ginsburg (n 3 above) 13.59–13.62.

[351] Masouyé (n 127 above) 13.9; indeed, the safeguard in Art 11[bis](2) is only a clarification (see para 5.194 above). On the transitional provision of Art 13(2) of the Berne Convention, which bears little importance today, see Masouyé (n 127 above) 13.10–13.15; Ricketson/Ginsburg (n 3 above) 13.64.

[352] See Art 42a of the German Copyright Act.

(d) Implied exceptions

5.199　Apart from these explicitly provided limitations, two kinds of 'implied exceptions' have been recognized as permitted under the Berne Convention: the so-called 'minor exceptions' or 'minor reservations', and the exceptions to the translation right. At first sight, it may seem astonishing that rules can be validly implied in an international treaty without being explicitly expressed in its text. Yet, under Article 31(3)(a) of the Vienna Convention on the Law of Treaties,[353] 'any subsequent agreement between the parties regarding the interpretation of the treaty or the application of its provisions' shall be taken into account as a means of interpretation together with the context. The implied exceptions under the Berne Convention were discussed at the Brussels and Stockholm Conferences, which resulted in an agreement on the compliance of certain kinds of exceptions with the Convention; this agreement was noted in the reports to the Revision Conferences.[354] The reason why this agreement was not being expressed in a concrete text of the Convention lies, for minor exceptions, in the impossibility of finding appropriate wording, and for the exceptions to the translation right, in a conceived lack of need for a written manifestation of the countries' interpretation.[355]

5.200　**(i) Minor exceptions**　The difficulty in finding a concrete wording for the minor exceptions becomes evident against the background of the problem at stake: when public performing rights were introduced in Article 11(1) of the Berne Convention, Union countries had already provided in their national laws for a number of often quite specific and also economically unimportant limitations, which they wanted to continue to apply in the context of the Berne Convention. The same was true for the right of recitation under Article 11[ter], and the rights under Articles 11[bis], 13,[356] and 14 of the Berne Convention. Examples of such limitations existing under the national laws of Union countries were 'musical performances made in the course of religious worship, concerts given by military bands, charitable performances, public concerts organized on the occasion of particular festivals or holidays'.[357] The inclusion of such concrete wording in the text of the Convention would have been inappropriate, given the high diversity of provisions under national laws.

5.201　At the same time, it seemed difficult to find a general, yet not too broad wording. First, the delegates at the Brussels and Stockholm Conferences agreed to simply

---

[353] For more details on this treaty, see paras 7.02 ff below.
[354] para 5.201 below; on the nature as agreed statement, see Ficsor (n 240 above) 5.63.
[355] Ricketson/Ginsburg (n 3 above) 13.79 and 13.85.
[356] In 1948, Art 13 still included an exclusive right of 'adaptation . . . to instruments' for mechanical reproduction and public performance by such instruments.
[357] (1933) Droit d'auteur 112, 114.

mention in the reports that certain exceptions provided by national laws to the rights under Articles 11, 11bis, 11ter, 13, and 14 of the Berne Convention would be considered compatible with the Berne Convention, if they had a restricted or *de minimis* character, which meant that they had no or little economic importance for the author. The examples indicated by the reports, such as exceptions for religious, cultural, or patriotic purposes[358] and for religious ceremonies; performances by military bands; and the requirement of education and popularization,[359] only remain examples for the kind of limitations that are permitted. For those and similar limitations, the condition of a minor economic importance is essential and may have to be considered at the time when the limitation is applied.

Although delegations initially wished to be able to continuously apply the then existing *de minimis* limitations, one should acknowledge that similar, new limitations are also covered as long as they fulfil the condition of minor economic importance. This is evident when considering that countries that accede to the Berne Convention may already provide and want to continuously apply similar limitations that may differ from those previously existing under the laws of the Union countries.[360]   **5.202**

(ii) **Translation right**   The Berne Convention does not provide for any explicit limitation of the translation right, thereby creating an inconsistency with most of the limitations explicitly provided under the Berne Convention: for example, where the reproduction for educational purposes or quotation is permitted by Article 10 of the Berne Convention, it would be inconsistent not to permit translating a work from a foreign language for these purposes; the same public policy reasons behind the explicit limitations of the Berne Convention in principle also apply to translations that are necessary in order to make the permitted use in a meaningful way. It seems that the explicit limitations were already considered to imply corresponding limitations of the right of translation and that the Convention was already applied in this way before the implied exceptions were agreed.[361] At the 1967 Stockholm Conference, delegations then agreed that Articles 2bis(2), 9(2), 10(1), (2), and 10bis(1), (2) of the Berne Convention implied the possibility of using the work in translated form, if the conditions of these article are also fulfilled in respect of the translation.[362] They also agreed that this should be mentioned in the Records of the Conference rather than explicitly inserted into the Convention.   **5.203**

---

358 Documents of the Brussels Conference 1948 (1951) 263–4.
359 Records of the 1967 Stockholm Conference (n 331 above) 1166.
360 The WTO Panel Report (n 318 above) in para 6.59 took a similar approach when considering minor exceptions in the framework of the TRIPS Agreement.
361 Records of the Stockholm Conference 1967 (n 331 above) 1164.
362 ibid 1165.

5.204   By contrast, the application of Articles 11bis and 13 of the Berne Convention to the translation of works was controversial,[363] so that, for lack of agreement, these Articles cannot be considered applicable to the translation right. This might reflect the fact that these two Articles allow the restriction of authors' rights not for purposes of the general public, but only for those of certain industries (ie broadcasting organizations and phonogram producers).

(e)   Article 17 of the Berne Convention

5.205   **(i) Censorship**   Article 17 of the Berne Convention addresses legislative and regulatory measures taken outside the field of authors' rights protection, yet with restrictive effects on the full enjoyment of authors' rights. The first of the two main situations covered by this Article is censorship, which has been a concern of most governments from the beginning of copyright protection. The bilateral treaties preceding the Berne Convention already included provisions safeguarding the countries' power to control the circulation of authors' works.[364] Since 1886, the Berne Convention has followed this idea in its Article 17, and this without any substantial amendment.

5.206   The relationship between authors' rights protection and censorship rules under the Berne Convention is no longer the same as it had been in the Middle Ages in Europe under the system of privileges. Such privileges were granted by sovereigns who had the power to choose as beneficiaries of the privileges publishers and authors who were well disposed towards them. Even more recently, in certain countries not yet members of the Berne Convention, authors' rights were strongly connected to censorship; authorities had to permit the circulation of works.[365] Article 17 of the Berne Convention does not allow for a linkage which would hinder the genesis of authors' rights if the work is censored; under the Berne Convention, the protection must be recognized upon creation, if the general requirements for a work to be protected are fulfilled.

5.207   Instead, censorship rules envisaged under Article 17 of the Berne Convention may only prohibit the circulation and similar uses of a work; their effect is that the author cannot make actual use of his author's rights because of reasons beyond the logics of protecting works, namely for public order reasons, such as state

---

[363] On the discussion at the Stockholm Conference, see Ricketson/Ginsburg (n 3 above) 13.84, 13.85.

[364] For examples, see ibid 13.88/n 380.

[365] eg Art 36 of the Copyright Law no 40 of 28 September 1992 of the United Arab Emirates, now replaced by Federal Law no 7 of 2002; it seems to have been understood in practice as a condition of protection. Under Art 4(1) of the Chinese Copyright Act, so-called 'forbidden works' (for which publication and dissemination is prohibited) are excluded from protection—a rule not in compliance with the Berne Convention or other international copyright treaties, see P Ganea, 'Copyright' in C Heath (ed), *Intellectual Property Law in China* (2005) 205, 226 f.

security and public morals. The governmental right 'to permit, to control, or to prohibit' certain acts reflects the ordinary activity of censorship authorities, which is to decide whether the relevant public order reasons require the prohibition or other control of the work's circulation.

This right is alien in nature to the author's right to authorize or prohibit. In particu- **5.208**
lar, even if a government grants the permission under Article 17 of the Berne Convention, the author still enjoys his author's rights, including the right to prohibit distribution if provided under national law. Article 17 does not allow any censorship body to exercise the author's rights in the place of the author.[366] The words 'circulation, presentation, or exhibition', which are not otherwise used in the context of minimum rights of the Berne Convention, show that this Article does not aim at directly interfering with authors' rights, but only at controlling public dissemination for public order reasons. Accordingly, Article 17 may indirectly affect authors' rights in respect of the public dissemination. For example, a national law complies with the Convention if it prohibits the sale of pornographic cinematographic works in places other than those reserved for adults, or if its application results in the prohibition to exploit a particular book that is considered a danger for state security.

(ii) **Competition law** The second main situation covered by Article 17 of the **5.209**
Berne Convention is the restriction of authors' rights on the basis of competition or antitrust law in the case of an abuse of a monopoly. Although this situation has been controversial to some extent at different revision conferences,[367] delegates generally understood that, in principle, the Berne Convention did not hinder national legislators from providing for measures against abuses of monopolies.[368] Of course, the relation between competition law and authors' rights protection is, and always has been, delicate; under Article 17 of the Berne Convention, it is clear that the application of competition law must not affect the very principle of authors' rights protection by exclusive rights, which *ipso iure* include the power of the authors to prohibit uses. Accordingly, competition law must not put into question the decision of the author to exercise his right by prohibition, unless specific circumstances of abuse of a monopoly can be ascertained.[369]

Unlike public order reasons, general public interest reasons must not be taken **5.210**
into account in the scope of Article 17 of the Berne Convention; they are

---

[366] Art 17 of the Berne Convention has been so interpreted by the overwhelming majority of Union countries; on the relevant discussions at the Stockholm Conference 1967, see Ricketson/Ginsburg (n 3 above) 13.89.

[367] On the relevant discussions, see ibid 13.91–13.92.

[368] For the understanding as set out in the Brussels Report, see Report of Main Committee I para 263, Documents of the Brussels Conference 1948 (1951) 1175.

[369] Such very specific circumstances were recognized, eg by the European Court of Justice in the cases *Magill* and *IMS Health*, cf Vol II ch 2.

comprehensively taken into account in the explicit and implied exceptions and limitations discussed above.[370]

5.211 In all cases, the permitted restrictive measures can be 'legislation or regulation'. These include laws as adopted by the legislative process under a country's national law and any acts based thereon, such as regulations issued by the competent authorities and, as a consequence, all individual administrative acts based on such normative acts.[371]

(5) Duration of protection

(a) General remarks

5.212 Another kind of restriction of authors' rights is the limitation of their duration. As for protection in general, the Berne Convention only provides for minimum standards; accordingly, Union countries may provide domestically for longer durations.[372]

(b) Moral rights

5.213 In respect of moral rights, many countries indeed provide for an eternal protection, while others provide for the same duration as for economic rights. This second solution has been adopted as the minimum standard in Article 6bis(2) of the Berne Convention (subject to the exception in phrase 2).[373] This Article does not specify whether the relevant 'expiry of the economic rights' refers to domestic law or the Berne Convention. For example, where a Union country provides economic rights for a longer duration than the Berne minimum of fifty years *pma*, the question for moral rights is whether it must provide for this longer duration or only for the Berne minimum of fifty years *pma*. Although Article 6bis(2) phrase 1 of the Berne Convention reflects a common pattern under national laws, namely the same duration for moral rights and economic rights, there is no reason why the Convention should force a Union country to follow this pattern rather than merely apply the Berne minimum to moral rights. Accordingly, a country may provide for the minimum of Article 7 (fifty years after the author's death) for moral rights while providing a longer duration for economic rights.

---

[370] Ricketson/Ginsburg (n 3 above) 13.89.

[371] ibid 13.90, on discussions of this issue at the Stockholm Conference.

[372] On the possibility of not providing national treatment where the national duration is higher than the minimum of the Berne Convention, see paras 5.41–5.44 above.

[373] Phr 2 was inserted at the Stockholm Conference when the rights were prolonged from the author's lifetime to the expiry of the economic rights. Since countries of the Anglo-Saxon system had protected moral rights only by common law which would not permit protection after the author's death, phr 2 allowed such countries to continue this system at least in respect of one of the two moral rights under Art 6bis(1) of the Berne Convention; see Masouyé (n 127 above) n 6bis.10, 6bis.11.

Another question arises where the duration for economic rights expires before the **5.214** author's death, as possible for cinematographic and photographic works and works of applied art.[374] It is suggested that Article 6bis(2) should be interpreted in this case so that the expiry of economic rights becomes relevant only after the author's death.[375]

(c) Economic rights

(i) **Historical background** In respect of economic rights, Articles 7 and 7bis of **5.215** the Berne Convention specify the minimum duration for works in general and for specific kinds of works. Different reasons have been indicated for different terms of protection, such as the wish to secure an income for two generations following that of the author, or the need of publishing companies or the like businesses to benefit from works of deceased authors for a certain time in order to be able to invest in new, as yet unknown authors.[376] In addition, there are basic differences between the Anglo-Saxon and the Continental European systems.[377] In fact, the choice of any particular duration in the Berne Convention has been determined largely by the pre-existing terms under the relevant national laws or the willingness of Union countries to prolong their duration.

National laws before the adoption of the Berne Convention provided for quite **5.216** diverse terms of protection, such as life plus twenty years and life plus eighty years.[378] In this situation, no agreement on a particular minimum term was possible in 1886; instead, even national treatment was made subject to the comparison of terms with the law of the country of origin, in order to prevent unwanted imbalances in the relation between Union countries.[379] Yet, very soon after the Berne Act, more and more countries domestically adopted a duration of fifty years *pma*; already in 1908, nine out of fifteen Union countries provided for this term that was then stipulated as the desirable (though not obligatory) term at the Berlin Revision. Not least as a consequence of this stipulation, the number of countries providing for this duration continuously grew, so as to reach more than

---

374 Ricketson/Ginsburg (n 3 above) 10.35.

375 For arguments see, in relation to the similar problem of Art 5 of the WPPT, Reinbothe and von Lewinski (n 245 above) Art 5 WPPT n 28.

376 A general elaboration on the justification of particular terms of protection is beyond the scope of this book; see eg Ricketson/Ginsburg (n 3 above) 9.07–9.12 on this issue.

377 See paras 3.64–3.67 above.

378 Law of Haiti of 8 October 1885, Arts 5 and 6 even distinguished between twenty years *pma* for the spouse and descendants, and ten years *pma* for other heirs if no spouse or descendant survived the author, see (1925) Droit d'Auteur 124; Spanish law of 1879, Art 6; see S Ladas, *The International Protection of Literary and Artistic Property* (1938) Vol II, 1089, 1091.

379 Art II(2) of the Berne Act of 1886; on comparison of terms under Art 7(8) of the Berne Convention, see paras 5.42–5.44 above. For a very detailed presentation of the historical development of the provision on the general term of protection under the Berne Convention, see Ricketson/Ginsburg (n 3 above) 9.14–9.26.

two-thirds of the Union countries at the time of the 1928 Rome Conference. Yet, only the 1948 Brussels Conference made this duration an obligatory minimum. Around the time of the Stockholm Conference (as well as later in the context of the WCT), ideas to prolong this duration even more did not attain support sufficient enough to result in amendment proposals.[380]

5.217 **(ii) General duration and joint works**   Under Article 7(1) of the Berne Convention, the duration of the author's life plus fifty years *pma* applies to all rights and kinds of works,[381] subject to the explicit exceptions in Articles 7 and 7[bis] of the Berne Convention and, regarding the translation right, in Article 30(2)(b) and the Appendix.

5.218   The nature of certain kinds of works may hinder the application of the general duration, or require at least further specification. For example, works of joint authorship[382] are created by several authors who usually die at different points in time. One cannot apply the durations for the respective contributions of each co-author, when the duration in respect of the entire work is at stake. At the 1928 Rome Conference, the Union countries adopted their favoured option, namely, to calculate the general duration after the death of the last surviving author rather than after the death of the author who died first.[383]

5.219   This rule does not apply to composite works, where several separately created works are combined (such as a book that includes text and photography), since here, the general duration may be separately applied to each contribution. The same is true for collections of works for which the collector has his own author's rights in the selection or arrangement of the material, irrespective of the separate authors' rights in the individual works collected. For example, for anthologies, separate general durations apply to the collection and to the individual works collected. So-called 'collective works', for which certain laws recognize an initial copyright of the person or entity organizing a common production are, in their essence, products protected for the organizational or other investment rather

---

[380] Records of the 1967 Stockholm Conference, Vol I, 105; Ricketson/Ginsburg (n 3 above) 9.25, 9.26; Memorandum for the WIPO Committee of Experts on a Possible Protocol to the Berne Convention (preparation leading to the WIPO Copyright Treaty) (1992) Copyright 66 ff, 80/paras 159–161 (proposal for general duration of 70 years *pma*) and Report (1992) Copyright 93 ff, 107/ paras 147– 60.

[381] While it was not uncommon in the early twentieth century to provide different terms of protection for different rights, in particular a shorter one for translation rights, such differentiation can hardly, if at all, be observed today, although it would in principle be possible under the Berne Convention, subject to compliance with its minimum durations; on the historical situation, see Ricketson/Ginsburg (n 3 above) 9.43.

[382] Art 7[bis] of the Berne Convention; since the Convention does not define the conditions for joint authorship, Union countries provide for different concepts.

[383] The latter rule had been provided in the UK Copyright Act 1911, s 16(1); for the historical development of this provision, see Ricketson/Ginsburg (n 3 above) 9.34–9.36.

than intellectual creations; therefore, they are not covered by the Berne Convention.[384]

(iii) Anonymous and pseudonymous works The general term also cannot be **5.220** applied to anonymous and pseudonymous works, since the author whose death triggers the term of protection is unknown. Accordingly, Article 7(3) phrase 1 of the Berne Convention instead has chosen the lawful making available to the public of the work—an act normally known even if the author is unknown. Since this act can be known even if it does not constitute 'publication' in the narrower meaning of Article 3(3) of the Berne Convention, it must be understood as encompassing any acts that make the work accessible to the public, such as public performance.

In accordance with the rationale of this provision, phrases 2 and 3 make the gen- **5.221** eral rule applicable where the author is known, be it because he discloses his identity during fifty years after the lawful making available, or because the pseudonym leaves no doubt as to his identity. Even if the author remains unknown, Union countries may terminate protection where there is reasonable ground to presume that the author has been dead for fifty years, irrespective of the lawful making available of the work to the public.[385]

(iv) Cinematographic works It is for a different reason that a special term of **5.222** protection is provided for cinematographic works,[386] namely different national laws of Berne Union countries. Countries following the Continental European system in principle only recognize natural persons as co-authors of a cinematographic work, so that the general rule on joint authorship applies. In contrast, countries following the Anglo-Saxon system recognize producers of films as first owners of copyright; since these are often companies, the general rule based on the life of a natural person cannot be applied. Article 7(2) of the Berne Convention offers the latter countries the possibility of continuing their system of protection by deviating from the rule on joint authorship, through calculation of the fifty years' duration after the work has been made available to the public with the consent of the authors or, failing such an event within fifty years from the making of the work, fifty years after the making. Nothing in the Convention prohibits countries that recognize only natural persons as co-authors of the cinematographic work from nevertheless applying Article 7(2) of the Berne Convention.[387]

---

[384] See, for example, the French and Spanish copyright acts, Arts L-113 and 78; and para 3.37 above.

[385] Art 7(3) phr 3 of the Berne Convention. For the historical development of this provision, see Ricketson/Ginsburg (n 3 above) 9.33 and 9.50.

[386] Art 7(2) of the Berne Convention.

[387] Indeed, countries of the Continental European system may do so, not least for better practicability, as did Luxembourg and Portugal before EC harmonization, see S von Lewinski, 'EC Proposal for a Council Directive Harmonizing the Term of Protection of Copyright and Certain Related Rights' [1992] IIC 785, 797.

5.223   As with Article 7(3) of the Berne Convention, the expression 'has been made available to the public' must be understood in a broader meaning than 'published works' (Article 3(3) of the Berne Convention), given the different context in which both expressions are used. Accordingly, even forms of communication to the public in the broad sense of a cinematographic work constitute 'making available to the public'.[388]

5.224   **(v) Photographic works**   Yet another reason exists for the special duration for photographic works under Article 7(4) of the Berne Convention. In the early years of the Berne Convention, a high degree of diversity characterized the national law approaches to the protection of photographic works including their duration, which was often shorter than the general one. Many countries considered photographic works as a less valuable category, because the pushing of the button of the camera did not seem to involve as much creativity as the painting of a picture.[389] Consequently, it was only at the 1967 Stockholm Conference that a minimum duration for photographic works could be adopted at all, and this only at the level of twenty-five years from the making available of the work; this shorter duration as compared to the general one reflected the national laws of a significant number of Union countries at the time.[390] Only in the 1996 WIPO Copyright Treaty was the general duration extended to photographic works.[391] Of course, national laws of Union countries can provide for any duration for photographic works as long as it exceeds that under Article 7(4) of the Berne Convention.

5.225   **(vi) Works of applied art**   The special duration for works of applied art has a similar background. For a long time, their status as works protected by copyright (rather than by a design right) was differently regulated in Union countries, as was their duration of protection, if protected as works. As with photographic works, they were often considered as meriting only a lower standard of protection than the main categories of works. Consequently, even as late as at the Stockholm Conference when a minimum duration was finally adopted, delegations could not agree on a longer duration than twenty-five years from the making available of the work.[392]

5.226   Article 7(4) of the Berne Convention does not deal at all with works of applied art that are domestically protected only as designs or models or otherwise outside

---

[388] For a (though rather theoretical) case where a publication in the meaning of Art 3(3) of the Berne Convention, but not the making available in the meaning of Art 7(2), occurs, see Ricketson/Ginsburg (n 3 above) 9.48.

[389] ibid 8.48.

[390] On the historical development, see ibid 9.28–9.29.

[391] paras 17.111–17.114 below.

[392] For the historical background, see Ricketson/Ginsburg (n 3 above) 9.32.

copyright protection; consequently, the duration of such other protection is not subject to the minimum standard of this provision.[393] Whether a work of applied art is protected as an artistic work is determined under the law of the country for which protection is sought.[394]

(vii) Article 7(5)–(7) of the Berne Convention   Article 7(5) of the Berne   **5.227**
Convention on the calculation of duration is self-explanatory. It establishes the general rule that the term is deemed to begin on January the first of the year following the relevant event (such as the death of the author). It serves to facilitate the determination of the duration. Thereby, it takes into account frequent difficulties in ascertaining the exact date of the relevant event.[395]

Article 7(6) of the Berne Convention reflects the general principle under Article   **5.228**
19, according to which Union countries may provide for greater protection, including a longer duration.[396] Article 7(7) of the Berne Convention historically aimed at facilitating accession of a few countries to the Stockholm Act and was accepted as a compromise.[397] As of today (2007), it is irrelevant since the few remaining countries bound only by the Rome Act do not have shorter terms of protection than under Article 7 of the Berne Convention.

(viii) Posthumous works   In many countries, posthumous works (works first   **5.229**
published after the author's death) have enjoyed a longer duration than the general one, be it in order to allow the author's heirs to receive some benefit from the exploitation of the work, or in order to encourage publishers to take the risk of publishing such a work.[398] This issue was also dealt with in the Berne Union history. At the Brussels Conference, a proposal for the fifty years' duration with a ten-year extension was adopted with respect to the fifty years but not regarding the extension so that the duration corresponded to the general one; accordingly, it was suppressed as superfluous at the Stockholm Conference.[399]

---

[393] On the related issue of material reciprocity, see paras 5.45–5.47 above.

[394] On the category of works of applied art, see Ricketson/Ginsburg (n 3 above) 8.59–8.69.

[395] ibid 9.56.

[396] For its background, see ibid 9.54.

[397] For more background, see ibid 9.53; Reinbothe/von Lewinski (n 245 above) Art 9 WCT n 6.

[398] For the solution in the EC Duration Directive, which clearly distinguishes between copyright protection that ends after the life of the author plus seventy years, and protection by related rights for those who first publish a work or communicate it to the public after the expiry of the authors' rights protection, see Vol II ch 7.

[399] Ricketson/Ginsburg (n 3 above) 9.38.

(6) Special provisions on developing countries

(a) Historical background

5.230 Most developing countries became independent and, consequently, pursued their own interests between the 1948 Brussels and 1967 Stockholm Conferences. During the same period, ideas were developed with a view to better take account of the special needs of developing countries; this resulted in the adoption of the Stockholm Protocol at the Stockholm Conference—a protocol supposed to become an integral part of the Berne Convention.[400] However, already in the year of adoption, it became clear that industrialized countries were not ready to commit themselves to the Protocol. They were supported in this attitude by representatives of authors and other right owners on many grounds.

5.231 The main reasons were the understanding that the concessions to developing countries were too far-reaching, and that authors in industrialized countries who must often live under difficult conditions in their societies should not 'pay' for the discrepancy between the richer industrialized countries and the poorer developing countries. Since it seemed unlikely that the necessary number of ratifications for the entry into force of the Stockholm Act would be achieved, informal consultations soon started aiming at a new solution that could both satisfy the industrialized countries and offer sufficient privileges to developing countries so as to prevent them from withdrawing from the Berne Convention. These discussions finally resulted in the adoption of the Paris Act and its Appendix at the 1971 Paris Revision Conference, the sole purpose of which was to find a suitable compromise on the provisions for developing countries.[401] Achieving this compromise was very difficult, especially since revisions of the Berne Convention require unanimity. Yet, the compromise this time resulted in enough ratifications and accessions to bring the entry into force of the Paris Act with the Appendix, which thereby replaced the Stockholm Protocol.[402]

---

[400] For a detailed description of the historical development leading to the Stockholm Protocol, cf Ricketson/Ginsburg (n 3 above) 14.03–14.15; on the discussion at the Stockholm Conference and on the Protocol: ibid 14.16–14.33.

[401] On the historical development between the Stockholm and Paris Conferences, see ibid 14.34–14.47; see also paras 4.17–4.22 and 4.27–4.28 above.

[402] Art 34(2) of the Berne Convention; five ratifications of all provisions of the Paris Act by Union countries and acceptance of the UCC 1971 by France, Spain, the UK, and the USA (Art 28(2) of the Berne Convention) were necessary for the entry into force of the Paris Act; see also para 4.22 above.

(b) Overview of the contents of the Appendix

Although the scope of this book does not allow for a detailed elaboration on the **5.232** Appendix to the Berne Convention,[403] some important points are made: the Appendix is an integral part of the Paris Act;[404] while countries may limit their ratifications to the administrative provisions of the Berne Convention, no country can ratify just the substantive provisions of Articles 1–21 without the Appendix (or vice versa). In essence, the Appendix confers upon developing countries the right to provide, only in respect of the rights of translation and reproduction and subject to just compensation, non-exclusive and non-assignable compulsory licences for the purposes of teaching, scholarship, research, or systematic instructional activities.[405] In detail, the Appendix includes many more substantive and procedural conditions for the introduction and application of such compulsory licences, reflecting diverging interests that had to be balanced at every stage. Among those conditions are specific time periods to be respected before a compulsory licence can be applied, a restriction of such licence to the relevant country, a prohibition to export copies made under the licence, qualification of the languages into which translations may be made, and specified payment of a just compensation.

The high complexity of procedural and substantive conditions under the **5.233** Appendix may explain why only a few developing countries have made use of the privileges under the Appendix: in August 2007, more than half of those 153 Berne Union countries that have ratified the entire Paris Act and the Appendix were developing countries, from which only eleven countries have declared under Article I of the Appendix that they will avail themselves of the faculties to provide compulsory licences under Article II and/or III of the Appendix.[406] Another reason may be a potential deterrent effect of the Appendix: right owners in industrialized countries may have preferred to voluntarily offer licences under privileged conditions for the exploitation in developing countries rather than being faced with compulsory licences. At the same time, users in developing countries may in fact 'rely' on the high level of piracy and low level of enforcement that may reduce the actual need to seek for compulsory licences. Even if the Appendix with its possibilities for developing countries seems to have been used to a limited extent only, its adoption was of major importance particularly for the

---

[403] For detailed commentaries on its contents see, as two major examples, Ricketson/Ginsburg (n 3 above) 14.50–14.102; A Dietz, *Urheberrecht und Entwicklungsländer* (1981).

[404] Art 21(2) of the Berne Convention.

[405] The Stockholm Protocol had provided, in addition, for restrictions of the broadcasting and public communication rights.

[406] See for the declarations <http://www.wipo.int/export/sites/www/treaties/en/documents/pdf/berne.pdf>; it seems that only a few of them have indeed applied compulsory licences, Ricketson/Ginsburg (n 3 above) 14.106.

survival of the Berne Convention as the convention with the largest membership in the field of international copyright law, comprising both industrialized and developing countries.

C. Enforcement

5.234 The Berne Convention contains very few provisions related to the enforcement of copyright. A reason may be that provisions on civil, criminal, or administrative sanctions, as well as civil and criminal procedure and other enforcement provisions traditionally have been considered as general rules that did not need to be included in copyright legislation or treaties. In addition, countries which adhered to the Berne Convention were generally ready to provide for efficient enforcement. This has changed with the rise of piracy, particularly in developing countries.[407]

5.235 The Berne Convention contains provisions on seizure and on presumptions in respect of the entitlement of authors and other persons to institute infringement proceedings or to represent the author for the purpose of protecting and enforcing his rights.[408]

(1) Seizure

5.236 Article 13(3) of the Berne Convention makes liable to seizure those recordings that have been legally made in a Union country under a compulsory licence or under the transitional provision,[409] if they are imported into another Union country where these provisions are not applied. It basically confirms that the compulsory licence applies only in the country where it is provided. As a logical consequence, these recordings are infringing and therefore liable to seizure once imported into another Union country where the author's consent for reproduction is required.[410]

5.237 Article 16 of the Berne Convention, which was already a part of the 1886 version,[411] obliges Union countries to provide for the possibility of seizure of infringing copies, ie copies made without the author's authorization that is necessary under the law of the country for which protection is claimed. Article 16(2) of the

---

[407] See more on this phenomenon paras 10.103–10.104 and 10.107 below, also for the concession made to developing countries in this context.

[408] Arts 13(3), 16 and 15 of the Berne Convention.

[409] Art 13(1) and (2) ibid.

[410] See above on Art 13, para 5.197.

[411] For the historical background, see Ricketson/Ginsburg (n 3 above) 11.46; para 2 was inserted at the 1908 Berlin Conference, otherwise the Article remained substantially unchanged.

Berne Convention clarifies that this obligation also applies to copies that have been lawfully made in another country, yet without the author's authorization because, for example, the rights there are validly limited or the work is already in the public domain; where these copies are imported into a Union country where the author's authorization would be necessary for such reproduction, they are infringing the importing country's law and therefore must be liable to seizure.[412] Where the work has been lawfully made in the other country in which it is still protected and then imported to the Union country, Article 16 does not apply.[413] Unlike confiscation, seizure only relates to a preliminary measure on the basis of a temporary injunction or similar provisional remedy, which thus also has to be provided under national law.[414] Article 16(3) of the Berne Convention leaves the regulation of the procedure (eg the determination of the competent body) in respect of the seizure to national legislation.

(2) Article 15 of the Berne Convention

In order to enforce one's copyright, one must demonstrate sufficient entitlement either as the author or as his representative—sometimes a difficult task. Article 15 of the Berne Convention facilitates this task by requiring a number of evidentiary rules to be provided in the international context, even if they are not contained in national law regarding domestic situations. They may therefore be considered as procedural minimum rights.[415] They do not deal with the substantive law question of authorship but establish a legal presumption of authorship or other entitlement under certain conditions, as a prima facie proof, which will stand unless successfully rebutted. Except for paragraphs (2) and (4), this Article has been part of the Convention since 1886.[416] **5.238**

Article 15 (1) of the Berne Convention presumes that the author is the person whose name appears as such on the work; accordingly, any publisher who has acquired the rights from the author can rely on this presumption only as to the authorship of the author, but has to separately prove his entitlement on the basis of the contract with the author.[417] The presumption extends to authorship and, consequently, to the entitlement to institute proceedings for the infringement of any author's rights. The only condition for this presumption is that the author's name appears on the work in the 'usual manner'. An author may use her initials **5.239**

---

412 On the suggestion that para (2) implies the provision of a distribution right, see para 5.131 above.
413 Nordemann/Vinck/Hertin/Meyer (n 20 above) Art 16 BC n 3.
414 ibid, n 2.
415 ibid, Art 15 BC n 1.
416 Those were inserted at the 1967 Stockholm Revision; Masouyé (n 127 above) 15.1.
417 Nordemann/Vinck/Hertin/Meyer (n 20 above) Art 15 BC n 5.

only (as often in the field of art), the given name, the family name, or both; it only matters that no doubts as to her identity arise. Even if she uses a pseudonym which leaves no doubt as to her identity, the presumption applies.[418] Whether there is a doubt as to her identity, and whether the name appears 'in the usual manner' has to be determined under national law.[419]

5.240 A similar presumption applies under Article 15(2) of the Berne Convention in favour of the maker of a cinematographic work whose name appears on that work in the usual manner. The maker can be a natural person or a corporate body. This provision is of importance in countries where the maker (producer) of a cinematographic work is its first right owner, such as in the United Kingdom, and where otherwise the quality as a maker/producer of a work matters.[420] Since the Convention is limited to authors' rights and only allows for legal persons to be recognized as first owners of cinematographic works, this provision does not require Union countries to provide for such a presumption for film producers where they are protected under neighbouring rights.

5.241 For anonymous or pseudonymous works (except where the pseudonym leaves no doubt as to the identity of the author), it is not possible to establish a presumption as to the authorship. In these cases, the publisher whose name appears on the work shall be deemed to represent the author and, consequently, to be entitled to protect and enforce the author's rights.[421] This presumption consistently differentiates between the author and the publisher as his mere representative. Indeed, where the author reveals her identity and establishes her claim to authorship, the presumption in favour of the publisher no longer applies.

5.242 Article 15(4) of the Berne Convention has a different background: it serves at establishing protection of folklore in the form of a procedural rule on the entitlement of a competent authority to enforce such protection.[422]

---

[418] Art 15(1) phr 2 of the Berne Convention.

[419] On the controversy whether the 'usual manner' is determined under the law of the country of origin or of the country of protection, see Nordemann/Vinck/Hertin/Meyer (n 20 above) Art 15 BC n 2; see ibid n 3 on different editions with different indications of names.

[420] It matters for Art 14^bis(2)(a) in respect of ownership and for Arts 4(a), 5(4)(c)(i) of the Berne Convention (points of attachment, country of origin).

[421] Art 15(3) of the Berne Convention.

[422] For the protection of folklore, cf paras 20.27–20.29 below.

D. Framework and institutional provisions

(1) Application in time (Article 18 of the Berne Convention)

(a) Overview

At the time of entry into force of a convention and of the accession of a country **5.243** to a convention, it must be clear whether existing subject matter is covered by its rules. Article 18 of the Berne Convention[423] addresses this issue in the following way: the Berne Convention applies to all works that, at the time of entry into force of the Convention or of accession thereto,[424] have not yet fallen into the public domain in the country of origin through expiry of the term of protection; the works must also not yet have fallen into the public domain (through the expiry of the term of protection) in the country for which protection is claimed.[425] The application of this principle may be modified by conditions such as transitional measures, contained in special agreements between Union countries or under their domestic laws.[426]

Today, after entry into force of the Berne Convention, the application of this **5.244** principle still plays a role when countries accede to the Union or reservations are abandoned.[427] The principle has been called the 'retroactive application' of the Berne Convention.[428] Yet, it is important to clarify that the Convention is not retroactive in respect of past acts and, hence, does not apply to any acts that occurred before the entry into force or an accession. Instead, retroactivity in the context of Article 18 of the Berne Convention simply means that pre-existing works (rather than only those created after entry into force or accession) are covered by the Convention.

(b) Article 18(1) and (2) of the Berne Convention

Works to which the Convention applies must not yet have fallen into the public **5.245** domain in the country of origin 'through the expiry of the term of protection'. Accordingly, the Convention applies to a work which is in the public domain in the country of origin due to other reasons, for example because the entire category of work (eg works of architecture) was never protected in the country of origin before accession. In this case, the Convention applies to existing works of

---

[423] It has been included in the Berne Convention since 1886 and slightly amended in 1896 and 1908; for the historical development, see Ricketson/Ginsburg (n 3 above) 6.113–6.116.
[424] See Art 18(4) of the Berne Convention on accession and application to other cases.
[425] Art 18(1), (2) ibid.
[426] Art 18(3) ibid.
[427] Art 18(4) ibid.
[428] eg Masouyé (n 127 above) 18.1, who speaks of the 'Rule of Retroactivity'.

such a category upon accession of the country to the Union, although these works have been in the public domain beforehand. Similarly, the Convention applies where the work has fallen into the public domain in the country of origin due to failure to comply with formalities required under domestic law before accession.[429]

5.246 The 'country of origin' must be understood in the meaning of Article 5(4) of the Berne Convention. Against the background of Article 19 of the Berne Convention, Union countries may provide stronger protection by applying the Berne Convention even to works that have already fallen into the public domain in the country of origin due to the expiry of the term of protection.[430]

(c) Article 18(3) of the Berne Convention

5.247 Article 18(3) of the Berne Convention allows Union countries to provide for conditions of application of this principle, for example, in the form of transitional provisions. Such provisions may serve to protect those in particular who have already invested in the exploitation of works that are in the public domain but that become protected again through Berne accession. Transitional provisions are most often laid down in the national laws of the countries acceding to the Convention or also in bilateral agreements. They only apply in countries that have adopted them.

5.248 Berne Union countries have some leeway in determining the conditions of application. However, they must not go so far as entirely to deny the application of the principle laid down in Article 18(1) and (2) of the Berne Convention. For example, any transitional period should be of an appropriately limited duration.

(d) Article 18(4) of the Berne Convention

5.249 Today, the rules on application in time are relevant for new accessions to the Berne Union and for the abandonment of reservations that lead to an extended protection.[431] Such reservations are those under Article 30(2)(b) of the Berne Convention, Articles II and III of the Appendix, and miscellaneous reservations maintained by countries from earlier Acts.[432] If a country that has made such a

---

[429] For the US restoration of protection, see Schwartz/Nimmer (n 71 above) § 6[4].

[430] Nordemann/Vinck/Hertin/Meyer (n 20 above) Art 18 BC n 5; the same is true for a work already fallen into the public domain through expiry of the term in the country where protection is claimed (para 2).

[431] Art 18(4) of the Berne Convention. Cases in which protection is extended by the application of Art 7 of the Berne Convention are no longer relevant today because they refer to the versions of the Berlin and Rome Acts, under which the duration of fifty years *pma* remained optional and Union countries could extend their terms of protection at any time, Ricketson/Ginsburg (n 3 above) 6.125. For the moment of application of the Convention to a newly acceding country, see Art 29(2)(a) of the Berne Convention.

[432] Ricketson/Ginsburg (n 3 above) 6.125.

reservation later withdraws it, then the Berne Convention applies to the resulting increase of protection, subject to the conditions of Article 18(1)–(3) of the Convention.

(2) Special agreements under Article 20 of the Berne Convention

Article 20 of the Berne Convention can be traced back to the time of adoption of **5.250** the Convention in 1886,[433] when a number of existing bilateral agreements were to be maintained between countries of the Berne Convention after its adoption, as far as these agreements provided for stronger protection than the 1886 Berne Convention.[434] In line with the principle of minimum protection, delegations from the outset agreed that these special agreements should neither affect the minimum standards of the Berne Convention nor otherwise be in conflict with it. Consequently, any 'special agreement' under Article 20 of the Berne Convention must grant to authors 'more extensive rights' than those granted by the Convention, according to the aim to maintain the minimum level of protection and to prevent its erosion by subsequent agreements between Union countries.[435] In light of this aim, also provisions that simply clarify existing norms or otherwise only provide for the same level of protection are permitted, as far as they do not provide for less protection.[436] Additionally, such agreement must not be contrary to the Berne Convention. This condition in particular refers to provisions on matters not covered by the Convention, such as the protection of performers, copyright contract law, or provisions on collective management organizations.[437] They are usually not contrary to the Convention, unless they would require a restriction of copyright protection.[438]

The importance of Article 20 of the Berne Convention has gone far beyond the **5.251** approval of more protective bilateral agreements existing in the early years of the Berne Convention. New generations of bilateral and regional agreements have emerged since the late 1980s,[439] and the TRIPS Agreement is understood as a special agreement.[440] In addition, Article 20 of the Berne Convention has been

---

[433] Only minor drafting amendments occurred until 1967/1971; for the historical development, see Ricketson/Ginsburg (n 3 above) 6.126–6.127.

[434] para 4.01 above.

[435] Ricketson/Ginsburg (n 3 above) 6.130. More extensive 'rights' should be understood in the meaning of 'protection', so as to include, eg a longer duration (or as to prohibit agreements with a shorter one), based on the context with Art 19 ('protection') and the purpose of Art 20 to hinder a lowering of protection.

[436] Reinbothe and von Lewinski (n 245 above) Art 1 WCT n 8.

[437] Ricketson/Ginsburg (n 3 above) 6.128; Ficsor (n 240 above) C1.11.

[438] Ricketson/Ginsburg (n 3 above) 6.128 for an example.

[439] See chs 12 and 11 below.

[440] eg Ficsor (n 240 above) C1.11; on its consistency with Art 20 of the Berne Convention, see paras 24.10–24.11 below.

the 'magic formula' to escape the deadlock in which the Berne Convention was felt to be after the 1971 Revision when the necessary unanimity for a revision was no longer considered a realistic option.[441] Since it allows agreements among two or more (and even possibly, but not necessarily, all) Union countries and therefore avoids the unanimity requirement of a revision, it was the approach chosen for the discussions on a possible protocol to the Berne Convention, which later led to the WIPO Copyright Treaty.[442]

(3) Institutional and other administrative and final clauses

(a) Administrative organs and financing

5.252 Due to the focus of this book, the administrative and final clauses will only be summarized. Articles 22–6 of the Berne Convention deal with the administrative organs of the Convention (ie Assembly, Executive Committee, and International Bureau) and with its financing. They were introduced at the 1967 Stockholm Conference and must be seen in context with the adoption of the Treaty on the World Intellectual Property Organization in the same year.[443] Issues such as the constitution and composition of the Assembly and the Executive Committee, their tasks and those of the International Bureau, as well as the budget of the Berne Union are dealt with in Articles 22–5 of the Berne Convention in a largely self-explanatory way. These four Articles may be amended by the Assembly alone rather than only by revision conferences; so far, this has happened only once, in 1979.[444]

(b) Revision

5.253 Article 27 of the Berne Convention, which has been part of it since 1886, reflects the perception of the founding members that the achieved level of protection under the Berne Convention 1886 was not the optimum many of them would have wished to adopt, and that the Convention should be revised with a view to improving the protection in the Union.[445] This is in line with Article 35(1) of the Berne Convention, which also dates back to the 1886 text and provides for the unlimited duration of the Convention.

5.254 The unanimity rule set out in Article 27(3) of the Berne Convention has been felt by some to be essential to safeguard the standard of copyright protection under the Convention. Others have pointed at its negative consequences, such as the need to accommodate a few or even one single outsider country with a compromise in

---

[441] cf paras 4.22 above and 9.05 below.

[442] See para 17.04 below.

[443] On this treaty and on WIPO, see paras 15.02 ff below.

[444] Art 26 of the Berne Convention. On more details regarding these administrative organs and the budget of the Berne Union, see Ricketson/Ginsburg (n 3 above) 16.08 and 16.48 and, regarding those of the WIPO, paras 15.06–15.09 below.

[445] See paras 2.45 and 4.05 above.

order to achieve any revision.[446] Indeed, after the difficult experience of 1971, the unanimity requirement seems to have discouraged WIPO from proposing a new revision conference.[447] Unanimity refers to the votes cast, so that abstentions or the lack of presence of countries belonging to the Union do not hinder unanimity. This was clarified at the Brussels Conference, which replaced the earlier wording that had required 'unanimous consensus of countries belonging to the Union' by the current wording.[448]

(c) Acceptance and entry into force of the Paris Act

Articles 28–29bis of the Berne Convention deal with the acceptance and entry into force of the 1971 Paris Act of the Berne Convention for both Union and non-Union countries. In particular, Article 28 allows Union countries to accept (by ratification or accession) only the administrative and final clauses of Articles 22–38 of the Paris Act rather than also the substantive provisions of Articles 1–21 and the Appendix for developing countries. This provision aimed at enabling an early and wide adoption of the structural reform, which was more easily acceptable for many Union countries than the substantive provisions with, in particular, the controversial Appendix.[449] Union countries may choose to only later accept these substantive provisions, by depositing a respective declaration with the Director General. In July 2007, there were only eleven Union countries left that were not yet bound to the Paris Act and for which this provision remains important. **5.255**

Countries outside the Union that want to accede to the Berne Convention do not have this option but must accede to the Convention in the version of its Paris Act including all its provisions.[450] Any country outside the Union can become a member of the Berne Convention without fulfilling any further conditions, such as being a member of the WIPO.[451] **5.256**

(d) Reservations

Reservations are permitted under the Convention only in the following cases: in context with the Appendix;[452] under Article 28(1)(b), which allows Union **5.257**

---

446 Masouyé (n 127 above) 27.4; Nordemann/Vinck/Hertin/Meyer (n 20 above) Art 28 BC n 2.

447 A Bogsch, 'The First Hundred Years of the Berne Convention for the Protection of Literary and Artistic Works' (1986) Copyright 291, 327; paras 9.05 and 17.01 below.

448 Nordemann/Vinck/Hertin/Meyer (n 20 above) Art 28 BC n 2; A Baum, 'Die Brüseeler Konferenz zur Revision der Revidierten Berner Übereinkunft' (1949) GRUR 1, 40–1, also regarding the proposal for a 5/6 majority.

449 Masouyé (n 127 above) 28.3. On the problems regarding the Appendix, cf paras 4.18–4.22 above.

450 Art 29 of the Berne Convention. Art 29bis regulates a specific problem in relation to Art 14(2) of the WIPO Convention, see Masouyé (n 127 above) 29bis.1–4.

451 ibid 29.2.

452 Art 30(2) of the Berne Convention on reservations made under earlier Acts than the Paris Act 1971, and on a reservation to the exclusive translation right under Article 8, to be substituted by the provisions of the 1886 text (as amended in 1896), under which the translation right ceased to exist

countries to accept only the administrative provisions and final clauses of the Paris Act; regarding dispute settlement;[453] and regarding the reproduction and translation rights under Articles II and III of the Appendix of the Berne Convention. Such reservations may be withdrawn at any time.[454]

(e) Application to territories

5.258   Article 31 of the Berne Convention was most important in the early days of the Convention when Union countries had colonies and were, under this Article, empowered to declare to which territories the Convention should apply; however, it is still important today after decolonization, because protected territories for the international relations of which a Union country is responsible continue to exist, such as Greenland, for which Denmark has declared the application of the Convention, and territories of Australia, France, the United Kingdom, the USA, New Zealand, Spain, and Portugal.[455]

(f) Applicability of different Acts

5.259   Article 32 of the Berne Convention regulates the relationship between Union countries bound to different Acts and is a consequence of the fact that not all Union countries have ratified all subsequent Revision Acts.[456] As of August 2007, five countries are still each members of the Rome and Brussels Acts, and four of these ten countries have ratified the Paris Act without its substantive provisions. In each case, the latest text accepted by two countries governs their relations.

5.260   Article 34 of the Berne Convention aims at avoiding further split membership of different Acts of the Convention, by not allowing countries to join earlier Acts after the entry into force of the substantive provisions of the Paris Act (or, in earlier versions, the relevant latest Act). Accordingly, after the entry into force of the Paris Act on 10 October 1974, a country bound by the Rome Act cannot accede to the Brussels Act, but only to the Paris Act, or simply continue to apply the Rome Act; also, a non-Union country only can adhere to the 1971 Act of the Convention. Article 34(2) of the Berne Convention clarifies that

---

ten years after the first publication, if within that time the author had not availed himself of it by a publication of a translation in the language in general use in that country; cf Masouyé (n 127 above) 30.4, 30.5.

[453]   Art 33(2) of the Berne Convention; see paras 8.23–8.26 below on dispute settlement under the Berne Convention.

[454]   Arts 30(2)(c), 28(1)(c), 33(3) of the Berne Convention. On reservations in the Berne Convention, see Ricketson/Ginsburg (n 3 above) 17.22–17.33; on the latest status of reservations, see <http://www.wipo.int/treaties/en/ShowResults.jsp?lang=en&treaty_id=15>.

[455]   Ricketson/Ginsburg (n 3 above) 17.48, in n 296, refer to the European Year Book 1985.

[456]   Newly acceding countries today cannot, however, choose any Act but have to adhere to the latest Act (Paris Act 1971); Art 34 of the Berne Convention, see on this phenomenon para 24.08 below.

countries can no longer make declarations under the Protocol to the Stockholm Act, which has been replaced by the Appendix to the Paris Act.

(g) Denunciation

Countries may not only accede to the Berne Convention, but also denounce it. **5.261** Denunciation under Article 35 of the Berne Convention can relate only to the entire Convention including all earlier Acts, so that, for example, the denunciation of the Paris Act and application of the earlier Brussels Act is not possible. This again corresponds to the logic inherent in Articles 32 and 34 of the Berne Convention. A denunciation remains limited to the country concerned and does not affect the relations among the remaining Union countries. Union countries must have been members for at least five years before they may denounce the Convention; this shall avoid any premature decision taken without sufficient experience as a member of the Convention.[457]

(h) Implementation

Article 36 of the Berne Convention obliges Union countries to adopt the meas- **5.262** ures necessary to ensure its application. It leaves the choice of the necessary measures to the countries' laws.[458] Article 36(2) clarifies that any country must be in a position to give effect to the provisions of the Berne Convention at the time when it becomes bound to it. Accordingly, from that moment, a Union author must be able to rely on the protection of the Berne Convention in the newly bound country. This provision does not indicate any specific way in which effect must be given. The Union author does not need to be able to rely directly on the Convention but may be referred to its implementation in domestic law.[459] Domestic law may also refer to the provisions of the Berne Convention if they are sufficiently clear to apply. In addition, a country only needs to be able to fulfil its obligations under the Berne Convention; these do not include the provision of the minimum protection for domestic authors.[460] The remaining important provisions will be mentioned in other places.[461]

---

[457] Masouyé (n 127 above) 35.2.

[458] On this standard element of international treaties, see para 8.11 below.

[459] On this aspect of internal applicability, cf paras 8.11–8.13 below; eg the US Berne Implementation Act has been determined not self-executing, 17 USC 104 (c) and HR 100-609, at 28.

[460] Art 5(1) of the Berne Convention and paras 5.08 ff above; Nordemann/Vinck/Hertin/Meyer (n 20 above) Art 36 BC n 2 seem to be of the opinion that the minimum rights must also be recognized for own nationals.

[461] See for Art 33 of the Berne Convention on dispute settlement below, paras 8.23–8.26, and on Art 37(1) on languages below, paras 7.11–7.12; the otherwise remaining provisions are largely self-explanatory.

6

THE ROME CONVENTION OF 1961[1]

A. Principles of protection

(1) National treatment and minimum rights

(a) Eligibility for protection

As compared to the Berne Convention, the Rome Convention provides for a **6.01** much easier system for the application of national treatment and minimum rights: it defines national treatment[2] and determines the criteria of eligibility for protection, supplemented by definitions,[3] but does not employ the concept of country of origin.[4] The criteria of eligibility are listed separately[5] for performers, phonogram producers, and broadcasting organizations. The indicated criteria apply alternatively; accordingly, it is sufficient for the application of the

---

[1] For an overview of the historical development towards the Rome Convention, see paras 4.49–4.59 above.

[2] Art 2(1) of the Rome Convention.

[3] Art 3 ibid.

[4] The Hague Draft, however, still used the term 'country of origin' and provided for protection in countries other than the country of origin (cf Art 3 and definition in Art 4), (1960) Droit d'auteur 161, 163.

[5] Arts 4, 5, and 6 of the Rome Convention.

Convention to a performer, for example, if one of the three conditions (a), (b), or (c) under Article 4 of the Rome Convention is fulfilled. All criteria of eligibility show that the intention of the drafters was to make the Rome Convention applicable only to international situations, as is the case of the Berne Convention.[6] At the same time, also as under the Berne Convention, Contracting States regularly have decided to grant the minimum standards of the Convention not only in international situations but also in domestic ones, in order to avoid any discrimination of their own right holders.

(i) Eligibility for protection of performers

6.02 *Overview* Unlike under the Berne Convention, nationality was not chosen as a criterion of eligibility, in particular because of the expected problems arising in cases of collective performances by orchestras or other ensembles whose members have different nationalities.[7] Instead, three alternative criteria apply. Under the first one, the performance takes place in another Contracting State.[8] The second and third criteria[9] aim to ensure that performers are protected in any case where the phonogram or broadcast incorporating or carrying the performance is eligible for protection under the Convention, even if the performance does not take place in another Contracting State but in the same one where protection is claimed, or even if it takes place outside any Rome country.

6.03 *Performance in another Contracting State* For example, where a violinist of any nationality (even from a non-Contracting State) gives a recital in France (a Contracting State) and a broadcast or recording thereof is then exploited in Belgium (also a Contracting State), the violinist is protected under Article 4(a) of the Rome Convention in Belgium but not in France where the performance took place (indeed, the performer in this case would be protected in any other Contracting State except France, where only domestic law applies).

6.04 *Performance incorporated in eligible phonogram* A performance is also protected if it is incorporated in a phonogram which itself is protected under the criteria of Article 5 of the Rome Convention. For example, where, in the above hypothetical case, the performer claims protection in France and the performance in France is recorded by a producer who is a national of Belgium, the performer is protected in France.[10] The same applies if the recording is first published

---

[6] A proposal made at the Rome Conference to extend the application of the Convention to domestic situations was rejected; cf E Ulmer, 'The Rome Convention for the Protection of Performers, Producers of Phonograms and Broadcasting Organizations—Part II' [1963] 10 Bulletin of the Copyright Society of the USA 165, 171.

[7] C Masouyé, *Guide to the Rome Convention and the Phonograms Convention* (1981) RC 4.7.

[8] Art 4(a) of the Rome Convention.

[9] Art 4(b) and (c) ibid.

[10] Art 4(b) in connection with 5(1) (a) ibid.

in Belgium.[11] In the two preceding cases (performance in France, Belgian nationality of producer, or first publication in Belgium), the performer may claim protection under Article 4(b) of the Rome Convention not only in France, but also in all other Contracting States except Belgium.[12]

The other criterion under Article 5 of the Rome Convention, fixation in another **6.05** Contracting State,[13] is not fulfilled in the above hypothetical case if the performer claims protection in France where the fixation took place.[14] The performer may rely on this criterion only in the same way as on Article 4(a) of the Rome Convention; namely, if he claims protection in a Contracting State other than France. Accordingly, this criterion regularly does not add any possibility of becoming eligible.

To conclude, the performer in the above case is protected under Article 4(b) in **6.06** connection with Article 5(1)(a) and (c) of the Rome Convention in all Contracting States except Belgium, where the producer of the phonogram is Belgian, or the phonogram was first published in Belgium. These criteria connected to the eligibility of the phonogram may be particularly relevant where Article 4(a) of the Rome Convention does not apply; namely where, for example, the performance takes place in a country which is not a Contracting State or which is a Contracting State but for which the performer claims protection.[15] In addition, and as under Article 4(a) of the Rome Convention (ie place of performance), he is protected in all Contracting States except France where the recording was made.[16]

Performance carried by eligible broadcast The performance is also protected if **6.07** it is carried by a broadcast which itself is protected under Article 6 of the Rome Convention. This criterion applies only where the broadcast is not based on a phonogram incorporating the performance, but only where it is based on an audiovisual fixation incorporating the performance[17] or where it is carried live. For example, where a live performance in the above case is broadcast from France into Belgium, the performance is protected in Belgium (and all other Contracting

---

[11] Art 4(b) in connection with 5(1)(c) ibid.

[12] Belgium does not qualify because it is the country of nationality/first publication rather than 'another' Contracting State, Art 5(1)(a), (c) ibid.

[13] Art 5(1)(b) ibid.

[14] Regularly, the fixation is made at the place of the performance (here: France); the possibility to fix the performance from a live broadcast or other communication will practically be without major importance to date, due to deficiencies in quality. If the fixation is however done in the same way in another Contracting State than France, the performer then can claim protection in France.

[15] The other criterion, first fixation (Art 4(b) in connection with Art 5(1)(b) of the Rome Convention), usually has no separate meaning in context with the eligibility of the performance, since it usually takes place in the same country as the performance, for which Art 4(a) already applies (cf n 14 above).

[16] Note however n 14 above.

[17] For the substantive protection, see, however, Art 19 of the Rome Convention and paras 6.45–6.49 below.

States except France) if the headquarters of the broadcasting organization are in France, or the broadcast is transmitted from a transmitter situated in France.

6.08 *Deficiency of the system* This system of criteria of eligibility may lead to a lack of protection where a national of Contracting State A makes a performance in Contracting State B if B only protects its national performers and those protected under the Rome Convention.[18] In particular, Article 4(a) of the Rome Convention is not fulfilled in this case. Accordingly, the national of A would not be protected in B (yet, he would be in all other Contracting States).[19]

6.09 **(ii) Eligibility for protection of phonogram producers** The three criteria for phonogram producers are nationality, as well as first fixation and first publication in another Contracting State. While the nationality is an obligatory criterion, Contracting States may choose to provide only the criterion of first publication or, alternatively, of first fixation.[20] This result was a necessary compromise between divergent positions. In particular, the Hague Draft[21] had proposed the criterion of first fixation in another Contracting State by a national of a Contracting State for unpublished phonograms. This cumulative requirement was considered too restrictive mainly because the place of fixation often is a matter of coincidence; for example, it may depend on the place where the artists give a concert. The proposed criterion of the country of first publication for published phonograms was considered too broad because it would allow producers from outside the Rome countries to easily gain protection in Rome countries through first publication (including publication within thirty days after the first publication[22]) in a Rome country, while producers from Rome countries would not be protected in the countries outside the Rome Convention. In particular, American producers could easily have gained protection in all Rome countries by simultaneously publishing in Canada or the United Kingdom, even if the USA remained outside the Rome Convention (as it actually did).[23] The situation was similar to

---

[18] It is quite common to only protect nationals or residents of the own country, cf para 1.11 above.

[19] A proposal by the German delegation to close this gap according to the model of Art 5(3) of the Berne Convention (ie at least equal treatment for non-nationals in the country of origin where the Convention does not apply, cf paras 5.35–5.36 above) was, however, rejected by other delegations, in particular the US delegation who did not consider this situation as an international one, see Ulmer (n 6 above) 172–3.

[20] Art 5(3) of the Rome Convention; cf, however, for the exception under Art 17 of the Rome Convention para 6.11 below.

[21] Art 4(b) in connection with Art 3 of the Hague Draft, (1960) Droit d'auteur 161, 163; cf para 4.59 above on the Hague Draft.

[22] ie 'simultaneous publication' as defined in Art 5(2) of the Rome Convention, cf para 6.12 below.

[23] For this example, cf Ulmer (n 6 above) 174.

that under the Berne Convention then addressed through the Additional Protocol of 1914 and later in Article 6 of the Berne Convention.[24]

The compromise finally adopted was rooted in a German proposal which pointed **6.10** at the aim of the Convention to protect the phonographic industry of the Contracting States. This aim, according to the proposal, could be best achieved when protecting producers for published and unpublished phonograms on the basis of nationality and allowing the Contracting States to choose between the additional criteria of first fixation and first publication (or even admit both of them alternatively).[25] Accordingly, if a state chooses to exclude the criterion of first fixation, it must protect unpublished phonograms on the basis of nationality and published ones on the basis of nationality and first publication. If it chooses to exclude the criterion of first publication, both published and unpublished phonograms must be protected on the basis of nationality and first fixation.[26]

One exception to the system of Article 5 of the Rome Convention was, however, **6.11** allowed in order to accommodate the needs of Denmark and Sweden, for whom it would have been difficult to adapt their laws which had been adopted only shortly before. Accordingly, where a state, on the date of signature of the Rome Convention (26 October 1971), granted protection to phonogram producers only on the basis of the criterion of fixation, it could make a reservation at the date of joining the Convention so as to apply only the criterion of fixation, instead of those of nationality and first publication.[27] The reservation can be withdrawn under Article 18 of the Rome Convention.

The nationality of a producer who is a company or legal entity is determined **6.12** according to the rules of private international law; ie on the basis of the location of the headquarters (Continental European concept) or the country under which laws the company was established and exists (Anglo-American concept).[28] 'Publication' is so defined that it clearly refers only to the offering of copies rather than to their production also[29] and requires the copies to be offered to the public in reasonable quantity. 'Reasonable quantity' may be interpreted as a quantity

---

[24] paras 4.11 and 5.49–5.52 above.

[25] Art 5(1) and (3) of the Rome Convention for the declaration of exclusion.

[26] As of August 2007, 12 out of 86 Contracting States have excluded fixation, and 19 publication; for Romania, no specification is indicated, <http://www.wipo.int/export/sites/www/treaties/en/documents/pdf/rome.pdf>; Canada has excluded both, although not provided in Art 5(3) of the Rome Convention.

[27] Art 17 of the Rome Convention; as of August 2007, two Contracting States have made this reservation; Masouyé (n 7 above) RC 17.3.

[28] W Nordemann, K Vinck, P Hertin, and G Meyer, *International Copyright* (1990) Art 5 RT n 3.

[29] Art 3(d) of the Rome Convention; Ulmer (n 6 above) 173 on the related discussion before adoption of the definition.

which is necessary to fulfil the reasonable demands of the public.[30] 'First publication' in a Contracting State is deemed to take place also in the case of simultaneous publication; ie publication in a Contracting State within thirty days of its first publication in a non-Contracting State.[31] This provision takes into account the fact that the exact date of publication is often beyond the control of the producer. It thereby also allows producers from non-Contracting States to easily gain protection of the Rome Convention in all Contracting States.[32] It follows the model of Article 3(4) of the Berne Convention.

6.13   **(iii) Eligibility for protection of broadcasting organizations**   For broadcasting organizations, two alternative criteria are provided:[33] the headquarters of the broadcasting organization being situated in another Contracting State, or the transmission of the broadcast from a transmitter situated in another Contracting State. The second criterion allows any organization whose headquarters are outside any Rome country to enjoy protection in Contracting States if its transmitter is situated in a Contracting State. Contracting States may choose to apply both criteria only cumulatively.[34] This possibility allowed the United Kingdom in 1961 to continue its newly adopted solution under its Copyright Act 1956.[35]

(b) Definitions of right owners and subject matter

6.14   **(i) Performers and performances**   Performers, producers of phonograms, and broadcasting organizations must not only fulfil the criteria of eligibility but also be covered by the definitions of Article 3 of the Rome Convention. The fact that a list of definitions has been included at all in the Rome Convention reflects the Anglo-American influence in the drafting; where laws under the Continental European system use definitions at all, they are inserted into the law in the immediate context of the appearance of the word.[36]

6.15   Although the definition of 'performers' is largely self-explanatory,[37] the following points are noteworthy. First, only performers of 'literary or artistic works' are

---

[30] Masouyé (n 7 above) RC 3.12 makes a link to the similar wording of Art 3(3) of the Berne Convention; Nordemann/Vinck/Hertin/Meyer (n 28 above) Art 5 RT n 5 and SM Stewart, *International Copyright and Neighbouring Rights* (2nd edn, 1989) n 8.13 even claim that the publication must be authorized by the producer, by referring to Art 3(3) of the Berne Convention which explicitly provides so; they argue that there is no need to give differing answers in both, closely related Conventions.

[31] Art 5(2) of the Rome Convention.

[32] On the related hesitations and the resulting compromise adopted in Art 5(3) of the Rome Convention, cf paras 6.09–6.10 above.

[33] Art 6 of the Rome Convention.

[34] Art 6(2) ibid; as of August 2007, 20 out of 86 Contracting States have made the relevant declaration.

[35] Ulmer (n 6 above) 176.

[36] ibid; see also para 3.23 above.

[37] Art 3(a) of the Rome Convention.

protected; the notion of works has to be understood as under the Berne and Universal Copyright Conventions.[38] It does not matter whether the works are still protected or not; the performance of a Shakespeare play is also covered by the definition. Yet, anything which is not a 'work', such as (usually) a circus or variety programme, the programme of an artistic ice skating competition, or folklore does not fall under the definition so that a 'performer' thereof is not recognized as such under the Rome Convention. Contracting States considered that otherwise, the term 'performers' would become too vague and too broad. Nevertheless, in order to acknowledge that protection of such other performers may be justified, it was explicitly clarified that Contracting States may also protect, under domestic law, those who do not perform works, such as circus or variety artists.[39] Performers of folklore were mandatorily protected for the first time in the WIPO Performances and Phonograms Treaty of 1996.[40]

Secondly, the French words *artiste-interprète ou exécutant* may indicate more **6.16** clearly than the English 'performer' that not only those who perform (*exécutent*) works but also those who interpret them are covered, as the definition itself shows by its examples. It is controversial how the distinction between 'interpretation' and 'performance/execution' should be made.[41] In any case, considered to be covered by the definition are, in particular: all those who perform themselves, be it individually or collectively, such as soloists and members of ensembles, and those who do not immediately perform but have a direct influence on the concrete performance, such as stage directors and conductors of orchestras or other ensembles.[42] On the contrary, those who perform any side activities such as technical or organizational assistance in context with the actual performance are not covered by the definition. The same is true for so-called 'extras' or 'supers'. In a number of cases, such as the lighting or sound engineering, the quality as a performance depends on the concrete influence on the actual performance on stage.

In the case of groups, such as orchestras and other ensembles, the individual **6.17** members are recognized as performers. In order to facilitate the joint exercise of

---

[38] Records of the Diplomatic Conference on the international protection of performers, producers of phonograms, and broadcasting organizations, Report of the Rapporteur-Général (referred to below as 'General Report') (1968) 39–40; Masouyé (n 7 above) RC 3.1.
[39] Art 9 of the Rome Convention. See General Report (n 38 above) 46; Masouyé (n 7 above) RC 9.4; Ulmer (n 6 above) 177.
[40] See para 17.133 below.
[41] cf J Reinbothe and S von Lewinski, *The WIPO Treaties 1996* (2002) Art 2 WPPT n 27 (with further refs); para 17.133 below.
[42] General Report (n 38 above) 40; cf also Masouyé (n 7 above) RC 3.3; Nordemann/Vinck/ Hertin/Meyer (n 28 above) Art 3 RT n 3.

their rights, Contracting States may specify under domestic law how they are represented in this context.[43]

6.18 Where a performer, as is often the case for singers, performs a work which she composed herself, at the same time she is a performer covered under Article 3(a) of the Rome Convention and an author whose protection is determined according to the copyright treaties such as the Berne Convention. In this case, one has to distinguish between the different subject matter for which she seeks protection, namely the performance on the one hand and the work (eg the song) on the other hand.

6.19 The subject matter of protection for performers (ie the performance) has not been defined. Yet, logically, the performance means the activities described in the Convention[44] of a performer as such.[45]

6.20 (ii) **Phonograms and phonogram producers** The term 'phonogram' is commonly used in countries of the Continental European system as a synonym for the word 'sound recording' which is common in Anglo-American countries. Indeed, the word 'phonogram' is rooted in the Greek language where *phonoi* means voice and *graphos* means to write. 'Phonograms' are defined as 'exclusively aural fixations of sounds'.[46] A 'sound' is understood as anything which may be perceived by the human ear and which, accordingly, is transmitted from a source to the human ear via sound waves.[47] The sound may stem from any source, for example from a performance of a work or a non-work, from nature such as birds singing,[48] or from street noise. While this definition thus includes sounds of any kind, it excludes by the term 'exclusively' any fixations of sounds when they are connected with images, such as in an audiovisual fixation. Accordingly, in particular soundtracks of films including television programmes are in principle not covered by the protection of the Rome Convention;[49] the film industry had strongly represented its interests at the Rome Conference.[50] Contracting States, however, are free under national law also to protect the sound parts of any audiovisual fixation as phonograms.[51] Soundtracks which are exploited separately from

---

[43] Art 8 of the Rome Convention.

[44] Art 3(a) ibid.

[45] A separate definition was considered superfluous, cf General Report (n 38 above) 40; Masouyé (n 7 above) RC 3.5.

[46] Art 3(b) of the Rome Convention.

[47] For the extension of the definition to 'representation of sounds' in Art 2(b) WPPT in order to cover new technical developments, see para 17.134 below.

[48] cf General Report (n 38 above) 40.

[49] Nordemann/Vinck/Hertin/Meyer (n 28 above) Art 3 RT n 11; Ulmer (n 6 above) 177.

[50] cf ibid Part III, 219, 242 in the context of Art 19 of the Rome Convention.

[51] eg French law seems to cover soundtracks as phonograms, cf A Lucas and HJ Lucas, *Traité de la propriété littéraire et artistique* (3rd edn, 2006) n 1002.

the audiovisual fixation should be treated as phonograms.[52] After 1961, the ways of combining sounds and images became so diverse that a clear distinction between phonograms and films was no longer possible, so that this definition has raised a number of questions and become subject to criticism.[53] Article 2(b) of the WPPT tries to improve on the demarcation between phonograms and films.[54]

The producer of a phonogram can be a natural person or a legal entity;[55] the latter includes any company or enterprise and does not need to be established in the exact form of what constitutes a 'legal person' under national law.[56] This inclusion of legal entities as right owners reflects the nature of the phonogram producer's right as a neighbouring right (under the Continental European system) which does not protect an intellectual creation but the organizational, technical, and financial investment in the production of a phonogram; therefore, unlike under authors' rights, right ownership is not limited to individual, natural persons.

6.21

Producers are defined as those who make the first fixation[57] of sounds—an activity which is undertaken by natural persons who are assisted by technical means. Nevertheless, following the above rationale for protection, the word 'producer' has always been understood as meaning the company or other enterprise which is responsible for the first fixation. Accordingly, the phonogram company rather than its employed sound engineer is regarded as the producer, even if the actual fixation of sounds is carried out by the engineer.[58] Where a broadcasting organization makes its own studio recordings, it has the quality of a phonogram producer, irrespective of its potential, additional quality as broadcasting organization once it broadcasts the sounds of the phonogram. Also a private person who makes recordings can be a phonogram producer under the Rome Convention.

6.22

Those who only effectuate the reproduction from the master tape are not phonogram producers; rather they need a licence to do so from the producer of the first fixation. The same is true for those who only market and distribute the phonograms for the actual producer who may be a private person or a company too

6.23

---

[52] It is, however, controversial as to what conditions this result may be obtained under, cf Nordemann/Vinck/Hertin/Meyer (n 28 above) Art 3 RT n 11 who state that the purpose of fixation must at least also have been a purely aural exploitation.

[53] ibid; in particular, the case of music videos raises such questions.

[54] See para 17.135 below with further references.

[55] Art 3(c) of the Rome Convention.

[56] For this clarification in reaction to concerns by the Austrian government, cf Ulmer (n 6 above) 178.

[57] The first fixation is not the (later) master tape used for the pressing of phonograms, but the actual, first fixation, cf ibid 177.

[58] On this result, cf General Report (n 38 above) 40.

small to carry out this work. Likewise, those who copy an analogue recording in digital form are not phonogram producers. Even if 'remastering' involves quality improvements through a sound engineer, this process does not constitute a 'first fixation' of sounds and therefore does not give rise to an additional protection in the new product. The person or company who digitally remasters existing phonograms instead has to acquire the rights in the existing phonograms in order to do so and may then be protected under this licence.

6.24 (iii) **Broadcasting organizations and broadcasts** Broadcasting organizations have not been defined. A proposal to do so was withdrawn, but its discussion showed the following understanding by delegates: a broadcaster is not the entity which owns the technical equipment. Rather, it is the organization which prepares or presents the material to be fed into the transmitter. In addition, independent producers of programmes made for the broadcasting organization and sponsors of a programme are not considered broadcasting organizations.[59] Irrespective of these hints from the debates of 1961, one may conclude from mere logic that broadcasting organizations must be understood as those entities which organize the activity of broadcasting which itself is defined in Article 3(f) of the Rome Convention. This definition includes both radio and television broadcasting since it refers to sounds, or images and sounds. It is limited to broadcasting as opposed to rebroadcasting, so that those who only rebroadcast the broadcasts of other organizations are not broadcasting organizations themselves.[60]

6.25 The definition clearly covers only traditional transmissions by Hertzian waves and, consequently, excludes any transmission by wire,[61] such as cable-casting, webcasting (as far as carried out by wire) and also cable retransmission, simulcasting, and any other retransmission by wire by another organization.[62] Satellite broadcasting is wireless; yet, its coverage by the above definition has been controversial mainly because the transmission must be 'for public reception'. This condition is not clearly fulfilled in the case of distribution satellites and point-to-point transmission: the transmission is first made to the satellite and only in a second step to the public or, in other cases, it is first made point-to-point and only thereafter retransmitted for reception by the public from ground receiving stations.[63]

---

[59] ibid 41.

[60] cf the definition in Art 3(g) of the Rome Convention; Art 6(2) of the EC Rental Dir incorporates an explicit solution to the same effect regarding retransmission organizations, cf Vol II ch 6.

[61] cf General Report (n 38 above) 40; the Austrian proposal to include wire transmission was rejected.

[62] The definition of 'rebroadcasting' in Art 3(g) of the Rome Convention relies on that of 'broadcasting'.

[63] cf also para 4.70 above; these views added to the perceived need to adopt the Brussels Satellite Convention in addition to the Rome Convention.

Today, however, it is largely recognized that broadcasting by distribution satellites is covered by the Rome Convention even if the public receives broadcasts only indirectly through a ground receiving station, because one has to consider the entire act from the uplink to the satellite and back to a receiver at the earth and from there to the final recipient, the public.[64] Point-to-point transmissions without further transmission to the public are, however, not covered.[65]

(c) Scope of national treatment and exceptions

(i) Scope If the right owners are covered by the relevant definition and fulfil **6.26**
the criteria of eligibility,[66] they enjoy the minimum protection under the Convention[67] as well as national treatment. National treatment has been defined in respect of the three groups of right owners.[68] For example, performers who are covered by the protection of the Rome Convention can claim in a Contracting State the same treatment as provided under its domestic law for national performers in respect of performances taking place, being broadcast, or first fixed in that state. Briefly, it is the treatment provided by domestic law for what that law considers as domestic performances, phonograms, and broadcasts.

National treatment is limited by specific exceptions.[69] It is less clear whether **6.27**
Article 2(2) of the Rome Convention also limits the scope of national treatment by making it 'subject to' the minimum protection. It may be argued that this wording, confirmed by further reasons, means not only that minimum rights must be granted if they are more extensive than under national law, but also that minimum rights govern even where national law provides for more extensive protection, so that national treatment would be confined to the minimum standards guaranteed under the Convention.[70] In other words, national treatment

---

[64] For a detailed discussion of the controversy with its arguments, see Nordemann/Vinck/Hertin/Meyer (n 28 above) Art 3 RT nn 22–31, in particular 26–9; Stewart (n 30 above) no 10.03; see also for the solution adopted in the European Cable and Satellite Directive Vol II ch 8.

[65] The General Report (n 38 above) 40, states as examples transmissions to ships at sea, planes in the air, and taxis circulating in a city.

[66] Also, the Convention must be applicable in time, cf Art 20 of the Rome Convention and para 6.76 below.

[67] The 'protection specifically guaranteed', cf Art 2(2) of the Rome Convention in connection with the minimum rights under Arts 7, 10, 12, and 13 as well as other minimum standards, such as Art 14 of the Rome Convention on the duration, cf para 6.37 ff below.

[68] Art 2(1) of the Rome Convention.

[69] Art 2(2) ibid grants national treatment 'subject to . . . the limitations specifically provided for in this Convention', cf paras 6.28–6.31 below.

[70] For this interpretation, see J Reinbothe, M Martin-Prat, and S von Lewinski, 'The New WIPO Treaties: A First Resume' [1997] EIPR 171; J Reinbothe and S von Lewinski, 'The EC Rental Directive One Year after its Adoption: Some Selected Issues' [1993] Ent LR 169, 177; J Reinbothe and S von Lewinski, *The EC Directive on Rental and Lending Rights and on Piracy* (1993) 203–4; A Sterling, *World Copyright Law* (1998) 508; B Knies, *Die Rechte der Tonträgerhersteller in internationaler und rechtsvergleichender Sicht* (1999) 7–8.

would not have its own importance but would be restricted to the same effects as minimum rights. According to a different interpretation, the scope of national treatment is not limited by that of minimum rights under the Rome Convention.[71] While subsequent treaties, namely the TRIPS Agreement and the WPPT, have explicitly limited the scope of national treatment to that of the minimum protection,[72] the situation under the Rome Convention remains unclear.[73]

6.28　(ii) **Exceptions to national treatment**　The Rome Convention provides for very few exceptions to national treatment, namely in cases where Contracting States may make reservations in order to limit the protection granted; in such cases, the other Contracting States may limit their protection towards the one making the reservation accordingly. Thereby, imbalances are to be avoided; for this reason, one may well argue that material reciprocity requires more than a comparison of mere legal provisions in different countries, but major practical differences in exercising a right should be taken into account. The two cases that allow material reciprocity concern the remuneration for performers and phonogram producers for secondary uses,[74] and the communication right of broadcasting organizations.[75]

6.29　The case of secondary uses is illustrated as follows: where a Contracting State A has made a reservation in order not, or not fully, to grant remuneration rights for secondary uses, Contracting State B which fully grants these remuneration rights may limit the protection for phonograms produced by a national of A to the extent to which, and to the duration for which A protects phonograms produced by nationals of B.[76] For example, assume that, from the Contracting States X, Y, and Z, X and Z fully apply the remuneration right, Y declares by a reservation under Article 16(1)(a)(i) of the Rome Convention that it does not apply that remuneration right, and Z declares under Article 16(1)(a)(iv) of the Rome Convention that it will apply material reciprocity. Where a commercial phonogram produced by a national of X is played in a discotheque (ie communicated to

---

[71] See P Katzenberger, 'Inländerbehandlung nach dem Rom-Abkommen' in C Heath and P Ganea (eds), *Urheberrecht: Gestern—Heute—Morgen, Festschrift für Adolf Dietz zum 65. Geburtstag* (2001) 481, 487–91; the early commentators often did not specifically elaborate on this problem but seemed to follow the concept of national treatment under the Berne Convention where national treatment is not limited by minimum rights.

[72] See para 10.34 below for TRIPS and paras 17.45–17.46 for the WPPT.

[73] See for a more detailed discussion of this problem paras 7.34–7.40 below.

[74] Art 12 in connection with Art 16(1)(a)(i)–(iii) (reservations), (iv) (reciprocity) of the Rome Convention. On the individual reservations, cf paras 6.57 and 6.65 below.

[75] Art 13(d) in connection with Art 16(1)(b) of the Rome Convention.

[76] Art 16(1)(a)(iv) ibid; B must, however, declare in a notification that it will apply reciprocity. As of August 2007, 30 out of 86 Contracting States have declared that they will apply reciprocity; in this context, one has to take into account that 10 do not even apply Art 12 at all, see n 146 below.

the public) in Z, the remuneration provided in Z must be paid. Yet, where the phonogram is produced by a national of Y, no payment is due in Z.

Material reciprocity cannot be applied, however, where one Contracting State **6.30** grants the remuneration right to both performers and phonogram producers and another Contracting State grants it only to performers or only to producers, or where otherwise the remuneration right is not granted to the same group of beneficiaries in the two countries, as allowed under Article 12 of the Rome Convention without reservation.[77] It was considered that in practice, mostly both groups would benefit anyhow, for example on the basis of contracts, so that reciprocity would not be justified in this case.[78]

In the case of material reciprocity, a Contracting State which grants the right of **6.31** communication to the public under Article 13(d) of the Rome Convention to broadcasting organizations is not obliged to grant this right to broadcasting organizations whose headquarters are in another Contracting State which has declared by a reservation under Article 16(1)(b) of the Rome Convention that it will not apply this communication right under Article 13 of the Rome Convention.[79]

(2) Limited formalities (Article 11 of the Rome Convention)

While the Berne Convention includes the principle that no formalities can be **6.32** required by a member country as a precondition for the genesis of copyright protection in respect of foreign works, Article 11 of the Rome Convention does not altogether rule out formalities. At the same time, it does not permit any conceivable kind of formality as a requirement for protection. It adopts an intermediate approach: if a Contracting State requires formalities, they are considered to be fully satisfied if the formalities specified in Article 11 of the Rome Convention are fulfilled. This approach facilitates the task of a phonogram producer who would otherwise have to ensure the fulfilment of the different formalities required in Contracting States where he wants protection for the phonogram. Under Article 11 of the Rome Convention, the producer who fulfils the formalities of this provision is deemed to have fulfilled all requirements of formalities in the Contracting States. The fact that any formalities at all were accepted as a condition of protection under the Rome Convention was a concession towards the countries with the Anglo-American tradition; the provision was modelled on Article III(1) of the Universal Copyright Convention.[80]

---

[77] Art 16(1)(a)(iv) second half-phr of the Rome Convention.
[78] Ulmer (n 6 above) Part III, 219, 231–2.
[79] Art 16(1)(b) second half-phr of the Rome Convention.
[80] Nordemann/Vinck/Hertin/Meyer (n 28 above) Art 11 RT n 1.

6.33 Contracting States of course are not obliged to introduce any requirement for formalities; accordingly, phonograms which do not bear the symbol (P) and the other indications listed in Article 11 of the Rome Convention are protected under the Convention in countries which do not require formalities.[81] Article 11 of the Rome Convention is limited to conditions for the protection of rights of producers and performers in relation to phonograms and, in addition, to international situations; thus, domestic phonograms can be made subject to any further-reaching formalities for the exploitation on the domestic market.[82]

B. Substantive standards of protection

6.34 In general, when the Rome Convention was adopted in 1961, related rights protection was not yet widespread and, where it existed at all, the level of protection differed considerably. Therefore, the minimum standards of protection under the Rome Convention had to be fixed at a relatively low level—low already at that time but even more so from today's perspective.[83] At the same time, given the absent or very low level of protection in many countries at that time, even a relatively low minimum standard offered better protection in many cases than simply national treatment. The 'protection specifically guaranteed'[84] is laid down in the form of minimum rights for performers in Article 7, for phonogram producers in Article 10, and—regarding the remuneration right for secondary uses—for both of them in Article 12, as well as for broadcasting organizations in Article 13. Article 14 of the Rome Convention guarantees a minimum duration. The limitations of all these rights are laid down in Article 15.

(1) Minimum 'rights' of performing artists

(a) The nature of 'rights' under Article 7 of the Rome Convention

6.35 Performers' protection is specified by the words 'the possibility of preventing' certain acts.[85] In contrast, Articles 10 and 13 of the Rome Convention grant to phonogram producers and broadcasting organizations the rights 'to authorise or prohibit' certain acts; the Berne Convention uses the words 'the exclusive right to authorise' certain acts. Both do so with a view to provide for exclusive rights by which the right owner can exclude others from performing certain acts. Indeed, the words 'possibility of preventing' do not mean 'exclusive rights'. They were chosen

---

[81] General Report (n 38 above) 48.
[82] Masouyé (n 7 above) RC 11.4.
[83] ibid RC 2.3.
[84] Art 2(2) of the Rome Convention.
[85] Art 7(1) ibid; cf on the separate issue of the remuneration right for secondary uses paras 6.49–6.58 below.

in order to accommodate different positions of delegations, in particular those from countries which were not ready to grant performers exclusive private rights in the nature of a property right.[86] In particular, the United Kingdom and other countries of the Commonwealth protected performers only by criminal sanctions, and considered that this protection was sufficiently strong and should not be changed. Also the delegations of France and Italy where strong authors' associations opposed the introduction of exclusive rights for performers preferred a softer version which would not oblige Contracting States to introduce exclusive rights as a minimum. Indeed, authors in countries with a strong authors' rights protection have succeeded in preventing the introduction of exclusive rights for performers at a national level for a long time.[87] They feared that performers' exclusive rights could have a negative impact on or even hinder the exercise of their own rights in their works.[88]

Accordingly, Article 7 of the Rome Convention allows Contracting States to pro-   **6.36**
tect performers by criminal law sanctions if performances are used without the performers' consent, by unfair competition, by personality rights, or by any other rights which have the effect of preventing unauthorized use. While such means are not as strong as exclusive rights which allow an injunction or another prohibition of the act of use before it occurs, the Rome Convention does not allow Contracting States to provide for mere remuneration rights or compulsory licences by which the uses cannot be prevented. Rather, it is required—but also sufficient—that the protection grants a legal position secured by sanctions and that it results in a deterrent or otherwise preventive effect.[89] Since Article 7 of the Rome Convention lays down a minimum standard, Contracting States are free to provide for exclusive rights, as they regularly do today.

(b) The acts which the performer must be able to prevent

(i) Live broadcasting and communication to the public   Both 'rights' are con-   **6.37**
siderably limited in their scope: only the broadcasting and communication of live performances is covered. The word 'live' (in French: *directe*) was, however, not used in Article 7(1)(a) of the Rome Convention, since it had different connotations in different languages and countries, and since it was not possible to find an appropriate definition. Instead, it was decided to explicitly describe those performances which are not covered by the broadcasting and communication 'rights'

---

[86] General Report (n 38 above) 43; Ulmer (n 6 above) Part III, 219, 220; Masouyé (n 7 above) RC 7.5; Nordemann/Vinck/Hertin/Meyer (n 28 above) Art 7 RT n 2.
[87] eg France introduced performers' exclusive rights only in 1985 and Belgium only in 1994.
[88] Masouyé (n 7 above) RC 7.8; these fears resulted in the adoption of Art 1 of the Rome Convention, see paras 6.73–6.75 below.
[89] General Report (n 38 above) 43; Masouyé (n 7 above) RC 7.4, 7.2; Nordemann/Vinck/Hertin/Meyer (n 28 above) Art 7 RT nn 4–6; Ulmer (n 6 above) Part III, 219, 220.

under Article 7 of the Convention.[90] Accordingly, the performer does not enjoy these 'rights' if the performance used for broadcasting or communication has already been broadcast or fixed beforehand. First, the performer cannot prevent the broadcasting where the performance has already been broadcast. In other words, he cannot prevent the rebroadcast of his broadcast performance. Secondly, the performer cannot prevent the broadcast from a fixed performance, for example where a broadcasting station uses a commercial phonogram, a recording made in its own studio or an ephemeral recording[91] for broadcasting. The performer may benefit in this case only from a remuneration right, and this only if a commercial phonogram is used.[92] Thirdly, the performer cannot prevent the communication to the public of a performance which has been broadcast. In other words, the performer cannot prevent the playing of a radio or television programme, which includes the performance, in hotels, bars, and other places open to the public. Fourthly, he cannot prevent the communication which is made from a fixation. For example, the performer cannot prevent the playing of a movie in a cinema[93] or of a phonogram which includes the performance in discotheques, hotels, bars, etc; in this fourth case, however, he may benefit from a remuneration right but only if a commercial phonogram is used for communication to the public.[94]

6.38   The live broadcasting and communication rights include the use of audio and audiovisual performances, as follows from the definitions in Article 3(a) and (f) of the Rome Convention. 'Broadcasting' as defined in the Rome Convention covers only wireless transmissions rather than also cable, internet, or other wire transmissions.[95] 'Communication to the public' is not defined in the Rome Convention but is usually understood, as regards live performances, as the transmission (by wire, loudspeaker/screen, or similar devices) to a public which is not present in the room of the performance. Since, therefore, such transmission of live performances at the time was usually limited to domestic rather than international situations, it was argued that it should not be covered by the Convention.[96] Nevertheless, the communication was included in the protection because communication could still, even if rarely,

---

[90] See the 'except'-clause of Art 7(1)(a) of the Rome Convention; General Report (n 38 above) 43–4; Masouyé (n 7 above) RC 7.10; Ulmer (n 6 above) Part III, 219, 221.

[91] Art 15(1)(c) of the Rome Convention.

[92] Art 12 ibid, subject to reservations under its Art 16, cf paras 6.57–6.58 below.

[93] Protection regarding audiovisual performances is in any case limited, cf paras 6.45–6.48 below.

[94] Art 12 of the Rome Convention, subject to reservations under its Art 16, cf paras 6.57–6.58 below.

[95] Art 3(f) ibid and para 6.25 above.

[96] This argument was submitted by the delegation of the United Kingdom, which at the time did not provide for such a right domestically. General Report (n 38 above) 44; Ulmer (n 6 above) Part III, 219, 221.

occur between two countries, and because the Rome Convention was considered to serve as a model for national laws, showing the importance of the communication right.[97] Today, where communication by cable between states is common, this provision has gained considerable importance.[98] Accordingly, while the performer cannot prevent live cable casts and the like transmissions of his performance under the broadcasting 'right', he can do so under the communication 'right'.

(ii) Fixation The performer must be able to prevent the fixation or recording **6.39** of his unfixed performance.[99] 'Fixation' is not defined in the Rome Convention but is usually understood as the embodiment of sounds or images of a performance in a tangible form, such as the recording on a phonogram of any kind or in an audiovisual medium. In particular, the provision protects against 'bootlegging',[100] which is, in this context, understood to mean the unauthorized fixation of a live performance at a concert. It also protects against the fixation of a performance from a live broadcast or communication to the public.[101] Where a fixation of a fixation of the performance is made, it constitutes a reproduction which is covered by Article 7(1)(c) of the Rome Convention. The terminology of reproduction versus fixation is different from that under authors' rights where the reproduction right covers also the fixation of a work from a live performance;[102] accordingly, under authors' rights, no distinction regarding rights is made between the fixation of an unfixed work and its reproduction from a fixation.[103] Yet, both under performers' rights and authors' rights, the fixation of an unfixed work or performance is covered by protection.

---

97 Ulmer (n 6 above) Part III, 219, 221.

98 Masouyé (n 7 above) RC 7.12; T Dreier, 'Kabelrundfunk, Satelliten und das Rom-Abkommen zum Schutz der ausübenden Künstler, der Hersteller von Tonträgern und der Sendeunternehmen' (1988) GRUR International 753, 756–8.

99 Art 7(1)(b) of the Rome Convention. The United Kingdom had, however, argued that the fixation of live performances does not involve the crossing of borders and should therefore not be provided, cf n 96 above.

100 This term has been borrowed from times of prohibition in the USA when bottles of alcohol were hidden in the leggings of the boots of those who engaged in illicit trafficking; it was later used again when high boots were fashionable and allowed young pop fans to hide small recording machines in their boots for the purpose of illicit recording, Stewart (n 30 above) no 8.18; it seems that the term 'bootlegging' then was used even for the subsequent production of the recording, ibid.

101 General Report (n 38 above) 44.

102 cf eg the clarification in Art 9(3) of the Berne Convention regarding the sound and visual recording of a work.

103 The only distinction may occur in the case of a fixation of an improvisation, where a country requires, in accordance with Art 2(2) of the Berne Convention, fixation in material form for the recognition of copyright. In this case, the mere fixation of an improvised work does not constitute an infringement of the reproduction right (see also para 5.116 above).

6.40   **(iii) Reproduction**[104]   'Reproduction' is defined as the making of a copy or copies of a fixation,[105] and thereby describes an act resulting in a tangible or material object. Obviously, it does not elaborate on the question of digital reproduction which only arose more than thirty years later. Yet, the wording and purpose is broad enough to cover digital reproduction, at least as far as it results in tangible copies, as is usually the case. The only doubts in this respect may arise regarding transient reproduction.[106] Performers must be able to prevent the reproduction only in three specified cases.[107] The performer can prevent reproduction only (1) if the fixation was made without her required consent,[108] such as in the case of bootlegging;[109] (2) when the reproduction is made for purposes other than those for which she gave her consent—eg where the performer gave her consent only for the production of a commercial CD but not for the use in context with the advertising of a product or with the inclusion as a soundtrack into a cinematographic work,[110] or where she gave her consent to a broadcasting station for a studio recording for broadcasting purposes but not for the production of a commercial CD;[111] and (3) where the fixation was made in accordance with an exception or limitation under Article 15 of the Rome Convention (and therefore usually without the performer's consent) but is then reproduced for other purposes—eg where the fixation was made for research purposes but is then reproduced for commercial purposes.[112]

6.41   With this restricted scope of the reproduction right, concerns of many delegations prevailed over the preference of some delegations for an unrestricted reproduction right.[113] These concerns related to the accumulation of necessary authorizations to be obtained not only from authors but also from phonogram producers and performers. The relevant delegations considered it sufficient that the phonogram producer enjoyed a reproduction right, since he would regularly enforce this right.[114] They expected that performers' interests could be taken into account on the basis of contracts.[115] Also, broadcasting organizations pointed at difficulties

---

[104] An additional distribution right was proposed by Austria but rejected, cf General Report (n 38 above) 45 and the text of the proposal (no CDR/63), ibid 217.

[105] Art 3(e) of the Rome Convention.

[106] On this problem as dealt with in the WPPT, see below, paras 17.52–17.57.

[107] Art 7(1)(c) of the Rome Convention.

[108] Where the consent is not required due to an exception or limitation, for example for private use under Article 15 of the Rome Convention, Article 7(1)(c)(iii) of the Rome Convention applies exclusively; cf also General Report (n 38 above) 44.

[109] Art 7(1)(c)(i) of the Rome Convention.

[110] General Report (n 38 above) 45.

[111] Art 7(1)(c)(ii) of the Rome Convention.

[112] Art 7(1)(c)(iii) ibid.

[113] In particular the USA, cf General Report (n 38 above) 44.

[114] ibid.

[115] Ulmer (n 6 above) Part III, 219, 222.

in obtaining the authorization also from performers rather than only from phonogram producers.[116] It follows from the principle of minimum protection that Contracting States are free to provide for any further-reaching protection of performers. Indeed, most current laws go well beyond this minimum.

(c) Relations between performers and broadcasting organizations regarding the rights under Article 7 of the Rome Convention

Broadcasting organizations had an interest in keeping the number of rights of other groups of right owners low, so as to avoid the need for additional negotiation. Article 7(2) of the Rome Convention takes this interest into account by a far-reaching exclusion of performers' minimum protection. This approach was favoured by many delegations, although broadcasters' interests could instead have been taken into account otherwise; in particular, broadcasting organizations could have secured performers' rights on the basis of contracts, as also proposed.[117] Nevertheless, the majority of delegations favoured and thus adopted the exclusion of protection. **6.42**

Accordingly, where performers have consented to broadcasting, Contracting States where protection is claimed may determine the protection against rebroadcasting[118] as well as fixation and reproduction of fixations for broadcasting purposes. In addition, where fixations were made for broadcasting purposes, the terms and conditions for their use by broadcasting organizations may be determined by Contracting States. In other words, in the context of broadcasting, the Convention guarantees the performers only the possibility of preventing the broadcast of the (live) performance; the protection against any later use, (such as rebroadcasting, fixation, and reproduction) of the broadcast performance for broadcasting purposes can be entirely denied. Contracting States may also lay down a legal presumption that the consent to broadcasting implies the consent to the other three acts; this would mean, in principle, even a higher level of performers' protection than required. Today, national laws mostly refrain from so restricting performers' rights. **6.43**

Yet, as a certain minimum guarantee, performers at least must be able to control their relations with broadcasting organizations on the basis of contracts,[119] including collective agreements between their trade unions and broadcasting **6.44**

---

[116] ibid.

[117] This was the argument of the American delegation which objected to the restrictions of the proposed Art 7(2) subparas (1) and (2), see General Report (n 38 above) 45; Ulmer (n 6 above) Part III, 219, 223.

[118] Since the Rome Convention does not cover any performers' minimum rights against rebroadcasting, it seems that this reference is superfluous.

[119] Art 7(2) subpara (3) of the Rome Convention, proposed by the UK delegation, General Report (n 38 above) 45 and the proposal (no CDR/77) ibid 218.

organizations. In particular, agreements may stipulate special remunerations for certain uses by the broadcasting organizations occurring after the first broadcast. Accordingly, national laws must not restrict the freedom to contract in disfavour of performers.[120]

(d) Performers' protection in films

6.45　A similar restriction of performers' protection has been chosen for relations with film producers. In principle, performers are protected under the Rome Convention regarding their audiovisual and visual fixations, such as the fixations of their acting, playing, or other performance on moving images with or without sound. This follows from the definition of the performer in Article 3(a) of the Rome Convention, which explicitly includes actors and is in no other way restricted to audio performers; it may also be seen from the protection in Article 7 of the Rome Convention, which does not distinguish between the audio and the audiovisual fields. In addition, the definition of 'broadcasting' explicitly refers to 'sounds or . . . images and sounds', and the definition of 'reproduction' is not in any way restricted to the audio field.

6.46　Yet, the protection of audiovisual performers has been considerably restricted. Similar to broadcasting organizations, the film industry did not want to be faced with any problems arising out of the recognition of protection for performers.[121] Finally, the following compromise was reached after long discussions on the basis of different proposals:[122] once a performer has consented to the incorporation of his performance in a visual or audiovisual fixation, the minimum protection under Article 7 of the Rome Convention no longer applies. In other words, the minimum protection provided for performers in the visual and audiovisual fields is limited to the possibility of preventing clandestine or otherwise unauthorized visual or audiovisual recordings. Where, for example, a concert or a theatre play is recorded by audiovisual means from the floor without authorization of the performer, and then further exploited, the performer keeps the full minimum protection of Article 7 of the Rome Convention. Beyond this case, the Rome Convention does not grant protection, and performers are left with the mere possibility of concluding contracts with film producers, such as for remuneration for subsequent uses of the film.[123]

---

[120] Ulmer (n 6 above) Part III, 219, 223; Masouyé (n 7 above) RC 7.24, 7.25; Nordemann/ Vinck/Hertin/Meyer (n 28 above) Art 7 RT n 11.

[121] At first, they also objected to any effects of the protection for broadcasting organizations, for whom the protection then was however not restricted, General Report (n 38 above) 53; Ulmer (n 6 above), Part III, 219, 242.

[122] Art 19 of the Rome Convention.

[123] General Report (n 38 above) 53; Masouyé (n 7 above) RC 19.7.

Yet, in the typical case where an actor participates in a movie (which implies his **6.47**
agreement to the incorporation of his performance into the movie), he is not
protected under the Convention. He may not, for example, prohibit reproduction of the recorded performance for other purposes than agreed (Article
7(1)(c)(ii) of the Rome Convention). This result has been widely criticized as an
inappropriate restriction of performers' protection in visual and audiovisual fixations because the merit of the performers' achievement is principally the same in
all media. There is no justification from a performers' point of view for protecting
a musician's performance when it is recorded on a phonogram but not doing so
when the same performance is recorded on an audiovisual fixation. The inappropriateness of this distinction becomes even more visible in the case of music videos which are audiovisual fixations where the music plays the dominant role.[124]
Indeed, most national laws do not discriminate between performers in the audio
and in the audiovisual fields, but provide the same level of protection for any kind
of performer. At the same time, the interests of the film industry are often taken
into account by way of legal presumptions of transfer of certain or all rights to the
producer under specific conditions.[125] Article 19 of the Rome Convention was
inserted mainly because the American film industry had insisted thereon;[126] ironically, the USA did not even become a Contracting State of the Rome
Convention.[127]

Article 19 of the Rome Convention applies not only where the performance is **6.48**
incorporated in a cinematographic work, but also where it is incorporated simply
in moving images which do not reach the required originality level in order to
constitute a 'work' in the meaning of copyright;[128] Article 19 of the Rome
Convention simply speaks of a 'visual or audiovisual fixation'. Accordingly, even
the static filming from one angle of a musical or other performance is an audiovisual recording to which this provision applies.

---

[124] For these and further reasons of criticism, see Ulmer (n 6 above) Part III, 219, 243; Masouyé
(n 7 above) RC 19.9, 19.10.

[125] cf S von Lewinski, 'The Protection of Performers in the Audiovisual Field in Europe and the
United States' in ALAI (ed), *Creators' Rights in the Information Society* (2004), 875, 882 for European
laws.

[126] Art 19 of the Rome Convention was based on a proposal by the USA, General Report (n 38
above) 53 and the proposal (no CDR/105) ibid 232.

[127] For the further development of the international protection of audiovisual performers see
below, paras 10.91–10.93 (TRIPS Agreement), paras 17.118, 17.125, and 17.133, and ch 18 with
further references.

[128] The qualification as mere moving images is more important in countries of the Continental
European than of the Anglo-American system, cf on the originality differences paras 3.32–3.34
above.

(e) Remuneration for secondary uses under Article 12 of the Rome Convention

6.49 **(i) General background**   Article 7(1)(a) of the Rome Convention only covers broadcasting and communication in respect of unfixed performances. Article 12 of the Rome Convention covers broadcasting and communication in respect of fixed performances, but only if incorporated in commercial phonograms or reproductions thereof. Unlike Article 7 of the Rome Convention, it lays down a right to remuneration rather than any legal position secured by sanctions. In addition, it is subject to many conditions, restrictions, and reservations. In fact, authors opposed the introduction of such a remuneration right because they feared a negative impact on their income from broadcasting and communication as a result of the additional claims by performers and the also covered phonogram producers. Broadcasting organizations also rejected these claims which would not only make them liable for payment but also put an additional administrative burden on them.[129] At the same time, the use of phonograms for purposes of broadcasting and public communication, for example in discotheques, is among the economically most important uses from the point of view of performers and phonogram producers who therefore expressed a strong interest in benefiting from this kind of use. Accordingly, this provision has been among the most controversial ones.[130]

6.50 **(ii) Phonograms published for commercial purposes**   The following elements limit the scope of the remuneration right for performers and phonogram producers. To begin with, only phonograms give raise to the remuneration right but not audiovisual fixations. This is in line with the general approach taken under Article 19 of the Rome Convention[131] to exclude as far as possible the protection of performers in the audiovisual field. Many countries, however, go beyond this minimum and provide a corresponding remuneration right also for performers who appear in films, be it as actors, musicians, dancers, or otherwise, when these films are shown on television and in cinemas in other public places.[132] Indeed, there is no reason to discriminate between performers in the audio and audiovisual fields.

6.51 In addition, these phonograms must be 'published for commercial purposes'. This qualification envisages phonograms which are put on the market for sale or

---

[129] Ulmer (n 6 above) Part III, 219, 226.

[130] The degree of controversy is reflected not only in the restrictions and permitted reservations of the provision, but also in the vote which had to be taken: twenty delegations were in favour of the adopted solution, eight were against, and nine abstained which was sufficient to reach the necessary two-thirds majority, see General Report (n 38 above) 48–9; Ulmer (n 6 above) Part III, 219, 226–7.

[131] See paras 6.45–6.48 above.

[132] eg Art 78(2) of the German Copyright Act; Art 35(1) of the Swiss Copyright Act.

rental to the general public. It excludes studio recordings made by broadcasting organizations (in this case, the performer can rely for protection only on her contract with the broadcasting organization) and private recordings which are not put on the market. The fact that phonograms must be 'published' also excludes phonograms which are made available to the public exclusively online, because the definition of 'publication'[133] is limited to the offering of 'copies' which have always been understood as tangible objects.[134] Phonograms are 'commercial' in particular if they are sold on the market, but can be so even if they are distributed for free, provided such distribution serves an indirect commercial purpose, such as advertising for a business. It is irrelevant whether the commercial phonogram itself or a reproduction thereof is used; in fact, broadcasting organizations very often make their own, ephemeral reproductions of commercial phonograms which they use for broadcasting.[135] Contracting States are free to go beyond the above conditions and provide the remuneration right even for non-commercial and unpublished phonograms.[136]

(iii) Direct uses Thirdly, remuneration is only due if the phonogram is used 'directly' for broadcasting or communication to the public. This means that only the uses for the broadcast or communication made directly on the basis of the phonogram are covered. Important direct uses include the broadcasting on the basis of a commercial phonogram and also of a copy thereof,[137] as well as the playing of commercial phonograms to the public (eg in discotheques, bars, restaurants, supermarkets, and any other place open to the public where the sounds from the recording can be heard without the need of any intermediate transmission, and the transmission by an original cable programme, including internet radio).[138] Yet, where another use occurs as an intermediate step, the broadcasting or communication to the public is indirect and therefore not covered. In particular, indirect uses occur where a broadcast or cable-cast made on the basis of a phonogram is rebroadcast or communicated to the public, for example, where it is played from a radio in a bar, train station, etc and where it is retransmitted from a transmitted cable programme. The limitation to direct uses reflects a cautious approach in the area of neighbouring rights. Negotiating parties did not want to

6.52

---

[133] Art 3(d) of the Rome Convention.

[134] See also for Art 15(4) of the WPPT which fills this gap para 17.127 below; for a similar discussion on 'online publication' in the context of Art 3(3) of the Berne Convention, see paras 7.31–7.33 and paras 17.139 and 17.151–17.152 below.

[135] For the need to make ephemeral recordings, see paras 5.189 above and 6.68 below on Art 15(1)(c) of the Rome Convention.

[136] eg Art 78(2) of the German Copyright Act. Yet, the question whether the Rome Convention established only a minimum protection or also a maximum protection was raised in literature, given the aim of balancing the different interests, cf Ulmer (n 6 above) Part III, 219, 228–9.

[137] General Report (n 38 above) 49.

[138] cf on the contents of the live communication right paras 6.37–6.38 above.

simply copy the broader protection from the Berne Convention for authors.[139] Again, many national laws have gone beyond this minimum and include indirect uses for broadcasting and communication to the public.[140]

6.53 Whether making available on demand is covered as a form of communication to the public is likely to be controversial. The fact alone that this kind of use did not exist in 1961 and was therefore not envisaged does not suffice to reject this proposition. The wording seems broad enough to cover this act. A dynamic interpretation may well lead to its coverage. Yet, the importance of this question is likely to be limited, given the explicit provision of an exclusive making available right in the WPPT and in a significant number of national laws worldwide.[141]

6.54 **(iv) Beneficiaries of single equitable remuneration** As beneficiaries of the right, Contracting States may choose either performers or producers of phonograms or both. Accordingly, it is not even obligatory to grant the remuneration right to performers (or phonogram producers) at all. National laws were so different at the time that such flexibility was necessary. In particular, the UK Copyright Act granted an exclusive right to phonogram producers while performers only in practice participated in the licensing fees. Yet, the UK delegation did not want to put at risk the achieved balance by a legal obligation to make performers participate.[142]

6.55 If a Contracting State grants the right to both groups, it must ensure that the users must pay only a single equitable remuneration. This condition was included in order to accommodate the needs of broadcasting organizations and other users who were interested in minimizing their administrative efforts and in being faced only with one (common) claim rather than two or more separate ones. This result can be achieved by a common exercise of the rights of performers and phonogram producers through a common collective management organization or the recognition of the remuneration right only to performers, combined with a right of phonogram producers against the performers in participating in the obtained remuneration, or vice versa.[143] Domestic law may determine the conditions as to the sharing of the remuneration between the two groups, unless they have agreed between themselves. The practice of common collective management organizations mostly shows an equal sharing between both groups.[144]

---

[139] Ulmer (n 6 above) Part III, 219, 228.
[140] For the European Community, see Dir 92/100, Art 8(2) and Vol II ch 6; for the question of a potential maximum protection, cf also Ulmer (n 6 above) Part III, 219, 228–9.
[141] On the WPPT, see paras 17.72–17.78 below.
[142] Ulmer (n 6 above) Part III, 219, 229.
[143] ibid.
[144] Masouyé (n 7 above) RC 12.14, 12.15.

In any case, the 'single equitable remuneration' does not mean that users would **6.56** have to pay the remuneration only once forever. This simply follows from the condition 'equitable'. An 'equitable' remuneration must take account of the frequency of use during the entire term of protection, and of the value of use, which may be measured against the background that such uses make studio recordings unnecessary.[145]

(v) Reservations Different kinds of reservations had to be conceded to those **6.57** countries which were opposed to the remuneration right. In particular, a Contracting State may declare that it will not apply the remuneration right at all,[146] or only in respect of certain uses;[147] for example, it may grant the remuneration right only for broadcasting or only for communication to the public or only for certain kinds of broadcasting or communication to the public, such as commercial broadcasting or communication to the public in bars as opposed to hotels.[148] A Contracting State may also exclude protection for phonograms when the producer of the phonogram is not a national of another Contracting State;[149] in other words, it may reject protection for phonograms which would otherwise be eligible for protection under Article 5(1)(b), (c) of the Rome Convention on the basis of first fixation or publication in another Contracting State. Such an exclusion is then automatically also valid for the performer's claim to remuneration, even if the performer would otherwise be eligible for protection, for instance because the performance took place in another Contracting State. For example, where a producer from the USA (not a Rome member) makes a recording or first publishes it in the United Kingdom (Rome member), Austria (Rome member) which provides for the remuneration right but has declared a reservation so as to exclude phonograms produced by a national from outside the Rome Convention does not need to pay the remuneration for the producer or the performer in respect of this phonogram.

Finally, any Contracting State may apply material reciprocity towards those Con- **6.58** tracting States which have limited the protection on the basis of a reservation.[150]

---

145 For more criteria, see Masouyé (n 7 above) RC 12.9–12.11.
146 Art 16(1)(a)(i) of the Rome Convention; as of August 2007, 10 out of 86 Contracting States have declared this reservation.
147 Art 16(1)(a)(ii) ibid; as of August 2007, 11 out of 86 Contracting States have declared this reservation.
148 eg Masouyé (n 7 above) RC 16.6.
149 Art 16(1)(a)(iii) of the Rome Convention; as of August 2007, 27 out of 86 Contracting States have declared this reservation. This possibility is superfluous for those countries which have made use of Art 17 of the Rome Convention which accommodated the interests of Scandinavian countries and which allowed the criterion of fixation to be applied instead of nationality, cf para 6.11 above, in the context of Art 5(3) of the Rome Convention.
150 See paras 6.28–6.30 above.

(f) Unregulated issues

6.59 **(i) The possibility to transfer rights** Austria had proposed to provide that performers should be entitled to transfer their rights, for example, to an exploiting business such as a phonogram producer or broadcasting organization even after having transferred the same rights to an individual or an entity such as a collective management organization or a labour union.[151] However, this proposal was rejected as a restriction of freedom of contract; it was, though, considered that such rules would be allowed under national law.[152] Anyway, the possibility to transfer rights would have applied only to those national laws which provided for exclusive rights rather than only criminal law or other protection. Article 8 of the Rome Convention does not concern the question of transfer or transferability of rights but only of the representation of performers who are members of a group by other performers in connection with the exercise of their rights.[153]

6.60 **(ii) Moral rights** The Rome Convention does not provide for moral rights. A proposal to include them had been made in the draft of Samaden, but was then not reintroduced in the drafts preceding the Rome Convention.[154] The last part of Article 11 of the Rome Convention cannot be seen as a right of the performer to be mentioned as the performer. The lack of an obligation has not prevented many Contracting States from providing for moral rights of performers under national law.[155] At the international level, the WPPT of 1996 is the first treaty to provide for moral rights of performers.

(2) Minimum rights of phonogram producers

6.61 Apart from the remuneration right for secondary uses, which is subject to reservations,[156] phonogram producers enjoy only the exclusive right of direct or indirect reproduction.[157] The 'direct' reproduction is understood as the reproduction from a fixation without any intermediate act. The 'indirect' reproduction refers

---

[151] General Report (n 38 above) 45; Ulmer (n 6 above) Part III, 219, 224.

[152] ibid.

[153] See para 6.17 above.

[154] Resolution no 2(b) pt 3 adopted at the Permanent Committee of the Literary and Artistic Union in reaction to *vœu* VIII at the Brussels Revision Conference of the Berne Convention 1948, with a view to communicating the draft of Samaden to governments, yet subject to certain changes, such as the suppression of moral rights, cf Anon, 'La Première Session du Comité permanent de l'Union littéraire et artistique' (1949) Droit d'auteur 130, 132; cf also paras 4.55–4.57 above.

[155] Most European, many Latin American, and other countries have introduced moral rights of performers, cf S von Lewinski, 'Neighbouring Rights: Comparison of Laws' in G Schricker (ed), *International Encyclopedia of Comparative Law: Copyright and Industrial Property* (2006) nos 13–20.

[156] See paras 6.49–6.58 above.

[157] Art 10 of the Rome Convention. For the definitions of 'phonogram' and 'producers of phonograms', see paras 6.20–6.23 above, and Art 3(b), (c) of the Rome Convention.

in particular to the fixation of a broadcast which was itself made on the basis of a phonogram.[158] In 1961, digital reproduction was not yet possible; yet, the definition of 'reproduction' which refers to the making of a copy of a fixation is broad enough also to cover digital reproduction.[159] The question of whether parts of a phonogram are also protected against reproduction was discussed but not explicitly dealt with in the text, because it was considered as self-evident that the protection of related rights in general (also regarding performers' and broadcasters' rights, and concerning rights other than only reproduction) covered the use of performances, phonograms, and broadcasts also in parts, as far as such parts are eligible for protection as such.[160] Indeed, this question refers to the subject matter of protection rather than to rights.

A proposal not to recognize the reproduction right where reproductions needed **6.62** to be made by broadcasting organizations 'for technical reasons' was rejected as being too vague.[161] Indeed, the limitation for ephemeral reproductions is more precise and takes account of related interests.[162] Additional proposals to provide for a minimum right of distribution or at least of seizure of imported infringing phonograms based upon the model of Article 16 of the Berne Convention were rejected, inter alia, because the distribution right at the time was not yet recognized in many countries even in the field of copyright,[163] and because the provision on seizure in the Berne Convention raised many doubts in respect of its interpretation.[164]

(3) Minimum rights of broadcasting organizations

Like phonogram producers, broadcasting organizations are granted exclusive **6.63** rights (the 'right to authorise or prohibit').[165] As for other neighbouring rights, the protection extends not only to the entire object of protection but also to parts thereof.[166] Yet, upon the proposal that still pictures of broadcasts should also be protected, it was decided that such detail should be left to the determination by

---

158 General Report (n 38 above) 46; Ulmer (n 6 above) Part III, 219, 224; Masouyé (n 7 above) RC 10.2.

159 cf the definition in Art 3(e) of the Rome Convention. For the more delicate question of transient reproductions, see the discussion in the context of the WPPT paras 17.52–17.58 below; cf also para 6.40 above for performers.

160 General Report (n 38 above) 47; Masouyé (n 7 above) RC 10.3; Ulmer (n 6 above) Part III, 219, 224.

161 General Report (n 38 above) 47.

162 Art 15(1)(c) of the Rome Convention and para 6.68 below (with reference to para 5.189).

163 General Report (n 38 above) 47; cf also above for a similar proposal for performers' rights, para 6.40/n 104; in particular, France did not recognize this concept.

164 Ulmer (n 6 above) Part III, 219, 225; Masouyé (n 7 above) RC 10.5.

165 Art 13 of the Rome Convention.

166 For the parallel discussion in the context of the rights of phonogram producers, cf para 6.61 above.

Contracting States.[167] The rights of broadcasting organizations cover, first, the rebroadcasting of their broadcasts, namely the simultaneous broadcasting of their broadcast by another broadcasting organization.[168] Secondly, they cover the fixation of their broadcasts;[169] this enables broadcasters also to control deferred rebroadcasting which necessitates the previous fixation. The recording of a broadcast by a private person also constitutes fixation but will usually be exempted from protection under national law on the basis of Article 15(1)(a) of the Rome Convention (limitation for private use). Thirdly, the exclusive right of reproduction of such a fixation is granted; however, it applies only where the fixation was made without the broadcaster's consent or where it was made under a permitted limitation (such as private use) but reproduced for other purposes (such as commercial purposes).[170]

6.64 Fourthly, broadcasting organizations enjoy the exclusive right of communication to the public of their broadcasts. This right is, however, limited as follows: it applies only to television broadcasts, and only to communications made in places accessible to the public against the payment of an entrance fee. The background of this very specific provision is the factual situation at the time of the adoption of the Rome Convention: many households did not yet possess television sets and it was quite common that cinemas, hotels, restaurants, and other places offered the showing of broadcast programmes to the public against an entrance fee—often regarding sport events, but also theatre or other programmes. Organizers in particular of sport events were afraid that this practice would result in a decrease in spectators coming to the events and considered refusing their permission to broadcast these events by television. Accordingly, both the event organizers and the broadcasting organizations had an interest in being able to control the public communication in this way. Article 13(d) of the Rome Convention takes into account these interests. Of course, this argument is no longer convincing in industrialized countries today where most households have television sets. Yet, the situation may be different in developing countries, and other cases may arise anew.[171]

6.65 This historical situation is reflected in the condition that an entrance fee be charged for the possibility to enter (in order to view) the broadcast; the mere increase

---

[167] General Report (n 38 above) 50; Ulmer (n 6 above) Part III, 219, 234–5.

[168] See the definition of 'rebroadcasting' in Art 3(g) of the Rome Convention.

[169] On the notion of fixation, see para 6.39 above.

[170] These two restrictions in Art 13(c) correspond to those of the performers' reproduction right under Art 7(a)(c)(i), (iii) of the Rome Convention; see paras 6.40–6.41 above.

[171] One may wonder whether, eg, the possibility to view broadcast programmes at airports upon payment at coin-box screens would fall under Art 13(d) of the Rome Convention; cf also the current discussion on the communication right for broadcasting organizations in the framework of a discussed new treaty below, para 19.30.

of the regular prices for meals, drinks, etc does not fulfil this condition.[172] Contracting States may determine the conditions under which the right may be exercised; this includes the possibility of providing for compulsory licences.[173] In addition, Contracting States may declare in a reservation not to apply the communication right at all; for purposes of clarity, the reservation cannot be limited to certain kinds of communication.[174]

Initially, the overall protection for broadcasting organizations was made subject to **6.66** major reservations in the Monaco and Hague Drafts for the Rome Convention, because at the time, the USA was not ready to grant such protection;[175] unfair competition[176] and public law[177] were considered sufficient. Yet, the US broadcasters then changed their position, recognizing the value of private rights in international relations, and thereby cleared the way for the deletion of most reservations.[178]

(4) Limitations of rights

The permitted exceptions and limitations are laid down in a common provision **6.67** for the rights of performers, phonogram producers, and broadcasting organizations.[179] They include four specific cases,[180] supplemented by a general reference to those exceptions and limitations that are provided under national law in respect of authors' rights.[181] Initially, only the four cases had been proposed, but many governments claimed that additional exceptions and limitations would be needed. The problem to comprehensively formulate a large number of limitations or general conditions for permitted limitations under international law became evident and confirmed the experience so far made under the Berne Convention;[182]

---

172 Masouyé (n 7 above) RC 13.6.
173 Art 13(d) 2nd half phr of the Rome Convention. For the parallel term, see Art 11bis(2) and Art 13 of the Berne Convention and paras 5.193–5.198 above; cf also Ulmer (n 6 above) Part III, 219, 236.
174 Art 16(1)(b) of the Rome Convention. Masouyé (n 7 above) RC 16.12. As of August 2007, 8 out of 86 Contracting States have declared this reservation. The possibility of a reservation was adopted in particular in favour of the USA (which finally did not adhere to the Convention) where such communication had already been established without problems being indicated by the broadcasting organizations, Ulmer (n 6 above) Part III, 219, 236. On the possibility of the other Contracting States applying material reciprocity in this context, see para 6.31 above.
175 Ulmer (n 6 above) Part III, 219, 234; Art 15(1)(b) of the Hague Draft, (1960) Droit d'Auteur 161, 166.
176 cf in particular the case *Metropolitan Opera Ass, et al v Wagner-Nichols Recorder Corp et al*, 101 NYS 2nd 483 (Sup Ct 1950).
177 Protection against rebroadcasting under the Federal Communications Act, 47 USC § 325.
178 Ulmer (n 6 above) Part III, 219, 234. The initial scepticism later however reappeared in the context of TRIPS (cf paras 10.96–10.97 below) and also, at first, of the WIPO initiatives for a Treaty on the protection of broadcasting organizations, cf para 19.05 below.
179 Art 15 of the Rome Convention.
180 Art 15(1) ibid.
181 Art 15(2) ibid.
182 Ulmer (n 6 above) Part III, 219, 240, also on the historical background.

the 'magic formula' of the three-step test which prevails today had not yet been conceived.[183] In this situation, the German proposal to include a reference to provisions on authors' rights was adopted as a welcome solution to the difficult problem. This solution also avoids owners of related rights being treated better than authors.[184]

6.68 The four exceptions are classical. First, in respect of private use, which is relevant mainly in respect of fixation and reproduction, exceptions and limitations can be provided unconditionally, unlike in the field of authors' rights[185] and under Article 16 of the WPPT.[186] When the Rome Convention was adopted, private copying was not yet as widespread and intensive as it is today. Secondly, the use of short excerpts in connection with the reporting of current events aims to facilitate news reporting, for example, where performances at a state ceremony are incidentally covered by the reporting; this exception has been modelled on Article 10bis of the Berne Convention.[187] Thirdly, the possible exception of ephemeral fixations by a broadcasting organization by means of its own facilities and for its own broadcasts is modelled upon Article 11bis(3) of the Berne Convention and justified by the same need of broadcasting organizations.[188] Fourthly, as under copyright,[189] teaching and scientific research are likewise classical justifications for exceptions.

6.69 The reference to limitations and exceptions to authors' rights as laid down in the Rome Convention is applied in many countries.[190] Compulsory licences which are permitted under copyright may, however, be applied to the relevant neighbouring rights only if they are compatible with the Rome Convention. Consequently, those permitted under Articles 11bis(2) and 13 of the Berne Convention may not be applied in the field of the relevant neighbouring rights.[191] The Rome Convention allows compulsory licences in respect of performers' rights regarding

---

[183] Art 9(2) of the Berne Convention was introduced only at the 1967 Stockholm Conference, see paras 5.148 and 5.175 above; it was later introduced in Art 13 of the TRIPS Agreement and into the WCT and WPPT, cf paras 10.83–10.88 and paras 17.83–17.87 and 17.90 below.

[184] On this aspect, see para 3.68 above.

[185] Art 9(2) of the Berne Convention, Art 13 of the TRIPS Agreement, and Art 10 of the WCT require the fulfilment of the three-step test, see paras 5.174 ff above, esp. 5.185, 5.187; 10.83 ff and 17.83–17.87 below.

[186] This Article also contains the three-step test, cf para 17.90 below.

[187] Masouyé (n 7 above) RC 15.3.

[188] See for more detail para 5.189 above

[189] Art 10(2) of the Berne Convention in respect of teaching is, however, more restrictive, as is Art 9(2) of the Berne Convention regarding reproduction for different purposes including research; on these exceptions, see paras 5.169–5.173 above for Art 10(2) of the Berne Convention.

[190] von Lewinski (n 155 above) no 38; eg Arts 83, 85(4), and 87(4) German Copyright Act for performers, phonogram producers, and broadcasting organizations.

[191] The specific *ratio legis* for these compulsory licences under the Berne Convention does not apply in the field of related rights, cf Ulmer (n 6 above) Part III, 219, 241; on the compulsory licences under the Berne Convention, cf paras 5.193–5.198 above.

uses of fixations made for broadcasting purposes and in respect of the television broadcasters' right of public communication.[192]

(5) Duration of protection

The minimum duration of twenty years was a compromise between proposals for **6.70** longer and shorter durations.[193] As the starting point for the duration, the fixation was chosen regarding phonograms and performances incorporated therein, irrespective of whether the phonograms are published or not. A proposal to choose the first publication as a starting point for published phonograms was not adopted, since there was a wish to accommodate the needs of Scandinavian countries which had just adopted the fixation for all kinds of phonograms under national law.[194] Regarding performances not incorporated in phonograms and regarding broadcasts, the duration starts after the performance and broadcast respectively take place.[195] These points in time seem superfluous at first glance because a broadcast and a performance not incorporated in a phonogram exist only in the moment of the broadcast and performance. Yet, they have their own meaning: where a performance is incorporated in a film without the performer's consent, it continues to exist and protection is granted under the Convention. Also, broadcasts which are fixed continue to exist thereafter.[196]

Unlike the Berne Convention, the Rome Convention does not provide for a **6.71** general rule of material reciprocity regarding the duration of protection. Such a rule was considered unnecessary for the following reasons: first, the duration is important only where fixations are used. In this respect, only the reproduction rights of phonogram producers and broadcasting organizations were considered important. For these rights, it was argued that the great differences between the protection in different countries (eg between twenty and fifty years) did not necessarily lead to imbalances, because in many countries the right owners would be protected against reproduction under unfair competition rules even after the expiry of the terms of related rights. The reproduction right for performing artists

---

[192] Art 7(2) subpara (2) and 13(d) of the Rome Convention; Masouyé (n 7 above) RC 15.11 and Nordemann/Vinck/Hertin/Meyer (n 28 above) Art 13 RT n 7. The remuneration right under Art 12 of the Rome Convention might be considered as a fictitious exclusive right which is restricted by a compulsory licence, cf Ulmer (n 6 above) Part III, 219, 241, although it would be more accurate to acknowledge that it is a simple statutory remuneration right rather than a 'reduced' exclusive right.

[193] Art 14 of the Rome Convention. Others proposed, eg 10, 20, 25 (with a possible renewal for another 25 years) and 30 years, General Report (n 38 above) 51.

[194] Ulmer (n 6 above) Part III, 219, 237.

[195] Art 14(b), (c) of the Rome Convention.

[196] cf the related discussion, General Report (n 38 above) 51; Ulmer (n 6 above) Part III, 219, 237.

applied anyway only under narrow conditions[197] so that the differences in duration did not have a major impact, given the limited level of protection.[198]

6.72 Secondly, the only case where material reciprocity was considered important was the remuneration right for secondary uses of commercial phonograms. In respect of this right, material reciprocity was already provided in general as also, specifically, in respect of the duration.[199]

C. Framework provisions

(1) Relation to author's rights protection

6.73 From the beginning, authors objected to the introduction of neighbouring rights at the national and international levels. Although there is no overlap of the protected subject matter, since author's rights protect works (ie intellectual creations) and neighbouring rights protect different achievements (ie performances, phonograms, and broadcasts), the full enjoyment of author's rights can be impeded by neighbouring rights. For example, a phonogram may incorporate a protected work, a performance, and a recording, in respect of which the author, performer, and phonogram producer each have their separate rights. Where all of them enjoy exclusive reproduction rights, each of them must separately authorize the reproduction if it is to be legal. Accordingly, the protection of neighbouring rights does not affect the protection of author's rights. This is self-evident and laid down in Article 1 of the Rome Convention as a clarification.

6.74 In addition, authors aimed at excluding any prejudice to the exercise (as opposed to the protection) of their rights caused by neighbouring rights. The proposing delegations stated that this proposal was meant to be applied only in extreme cases.[200] Authors argued that the creation of works was a necessary precondition for performances, recordings, and broadcasts thereof, showing the primacy of author's rights which should be recognized by the rule that even the exercise of author's rights should remain unaffected by neighbouring rights. For example, in a situation where an author wanted to authorize the reproduction and performers and phonogram producers exercised their right by prohibiting reproduction, the proposed rule envisaged the primacy of the author's decision, so that the performers and phonogram producers could not exercise their rights by prohibition. Most delegations, when identifying the potential impact of the proposal,

---

[197] See Art 7(1)(c) of the Rome Convention.
[198] General Report (n 38 above) 50; Ulmer (n 6 above) Part III, 219, 238–9.
[199] General Report (n 38 above) 50; Ulmer (n 6 above) Part III, 219, 238–9; Arts 12 and 16(1)(a)(iv) of the Rome Convention.
[200] cf proposals by France and Italy, General Report (n 38 above) 38.

rejected such a far-reaching restriction of the neighbouring rights with the possibility of rendering them ineffective.[201] The British delegation announced that it would not ratify the Convention if such a provision were included. Consequently, Article 1 of the Rome Convention remains restricted to the clarification that author's rights protection remains unaffected by the neighbouring rights.[202]

The primacy of author's rights was, however, to some extent recognized in the **6.75** provisions on membership: the Rome Convention is open for signature and accession only by states which are a party of the Universal Copyright Convention or of the Berne Convention; when a Contracting State is no longer bound by either the Universal Copyright or the Berne Conventions, it automatically ceases to be a party to the Rome Convention. The same applies to any territory of a Contracting State to which the Convention applies.[203] This link with the copyright treaties was justified by the proponents of the proposal by the above-mentioned primacy of author's rights on which the other rights would only be 'neighbouring'.[204]

(2) Application in time

Unlike the Berne Convention which applies 'retroactively',[205] the Rome Convention has chosen a more restrictive, 'non-retroactive' approach: it applies only to performances and broadcasts which take place after its coming into force for the relevant Contracting State and to phonograms which are fixed thereafter.[206] Of course, countries can provide for greater protection and also protect pre-existing performances, phonograms, and broadcasts. Indeed, this more generous solution has been adopted later in the TRIPS Agreement and the WPPT.[207] Rights which have been acquired before the entry into force of the Convention in the relevant Contracting State are safeguarded;[208] this corresponds to a usual pattern in many areas.

---

[201] General Report (n 38 above) 38.

[202] Ulmer (n 6 above) 165–7. Interestingly, Art 211-1 of the French Intellectual Property Code states that the neighbouring rights must not be interpreted so as to limit the *exercise* of authors' rights. Yet, it seems that this clause is often understood as symbolic and has not yet resulted in any practical problems; cf Lucas/Lucas (n 51 above) n 991.

[203] Arts 23, 24(2), 28(4), as well as 28(5), 27 of the Rome Convention. On the historical background, cf Ulmer (n 6 above) 167–9.

[204] cf in particular the French and Italian views, General Report (n 38 above) 55.

[205] cf Art 18 of the Berne Convention and, for details and the term 'retroactive' in this context, para 5.244 above.

[206] Art 20(2) of the Rome Convention.

[207] cf Art 14(6) of the TRIPS Agreement, Art 22 of the WPPT; paras 10.101–10.102 and 17.164 below.

[208] Art 20(1) of the Rome Convention.

(3) Further protection of neighbouring rights owners

6.77 Article 21 of the Rome Convention clarifies that its rules do not prejudice any other sources of protection of performers, phonogram producers, and broadcasting organizations, such as unfair competition, and personality rights.

6.78 Article 22 of the Rome Convention enables Contracting States to enter into special agreements among themselves, provided that their provisions grant greater protection or at least are not contrary to the Rome Convention.[209] It should be sufficient that only one of the three groups is covered by a special agreement.[210] It is controversial whether 'special agreements' require that their members are limited to Contracting States of the Rome Convention.[211] If not, the TRIPS Agreement and the WPPT notably may be considered special agreements to the Rome Convention for those parties that are Contracting States of the Rome Convention.[212]

(4) Administrative and Final clauses

6.79 Articles 23–8 of the Rome Convention deal with signature, ratification, and accession, entry into force, necessary domestic measures, extension to territories related to Contracting States, and financing of the Convention.[213] Contracting States cannot make any reservations except those explicitly provided for in the Convention.[214] The settlement of disputes concerning the interpretation or application of the Convention between two or more Contracting States is referred to the International Court of Justice, subject to an agreement on another way of settlement. Unlike under the similar Article 33(2) of the Berne Convention, no reservation to this submission to the International Court of Justice is possible; accordingly, subject to another agreement, the recourse to the International Court is obligatory for Contracting States. As in the field of copyright, no case has ever been referred to the Court under the Rome Convention.[215]

---

[209] The provision is modelled on Art 20 of the Berne Convention (and Art 19 of the Paris Convention 1883), cf on its background paras 5.250–5.251 above.

[210] Masouyè (n 7 above) RC 22.4; his argument is based on the word 'or' between the three groups of right owners.

[211] For this condition, cf T Ilosvay, 'Article 22 of the Rome Convention on Neighbouring Rights (Special Agreements)', (1962) Droit d'auteur 211, 213; Masouyé (n 7 above) RC 21.1; opposite view: A Namurois, ' "Special Agreements" under the Rome Convention, 1961' (1960) 80 EBU Review 52, 55–8.

[212] cf para 24.14 below.

[213] On the link between the membership of the copyright conventions and the Rome Convention in this context, see para 6.75 above.

[214] Art 31 of the Rome Convention which refers to Arts 5(3), 6(2), 16(1), and 17 of the Rome Convention.

[215] Art 30 of the Rome Convention. On dispute settlement under the Berne and Rome Conventions, see also, paras 8.23–8.26 below; on the relevant languages of the Convention (Art 33), see also, paras 7.11–7.12 below.

Article 32 of the Rome Convention deals with the establishment and tasks of the **6.80** Intergovernmental Committee. It has to prepare, among others, any revision of the Convention that is possible under Article 29. Unlike the Berne Convention which requires unanimity for a revision, the Rome Convention requires only an affirmative vote by two-thirds of the Contracting States attending the revision conference. Nevertheless, the Rome Convention has never been revised. This may be due to the facts that it is administered by three different UN organizations, namely the International Labour Office, UNESCO, and the WIPO,[216] and that it covers three different groups of right owners whose interests are often conflicting.[217]

---

[216] The Rome Convention still mentions the predecessor of WIPO, the Bureau of the International Union for the Protection of Literary and Artistic Works; see also para 15.01 below and paras 4.60 ff above.

[217] Indeed, the further development of the international protection of neighbouring rights has brought about a split between the rights of performers and phonogram producers in the WPPT and broadcasting organizations, dealt with in a separate project of WIPO, cf below, paras 17.05–17.06 (WPPT) and 19.01 (broadcasting organizations).

7

NEW PHENOMENA AS A CHALLENGE TO THE INTERPRETATION OF THE BERNE AND ROME CONVENTIONS

A. Rules of interpretation

(1) General remarks

All legal norms, whether in a national law, an international treaty, or other legal **7.01** instrument, were drafted at a particular point in time against the factual background prevailing at that time. In order to continue to be useful, the norms have to be adapted to new phenomena such as new technical, economic, and legal developments. Such adaptations may occur through amendments to legislation, revisions of treaties, or the conclusion of new treaties; where these are not realistic options (as in the case of the Rome and (after 1971) Berne Conventions), interpretation may help to a certain degree. Regarding the Berne and Rome Conventions, many new developments took place after 1961 and 1971, when the Rome Convention and the last revision of the Berne Convention were respectively adopted. They constituted challenges for the interpretation of these Conventions. This chapter illustrates these challenges on the basis of selected examples in order to show the need for new international provisions that indeed were later adopted as part of the TRIPS Agreement, the WCT, and the WPPT.

Before presenting selected examples, the general rules of interpretation of inter- **7.02** national treaties are summarized, especially since the rules set out in Articles 31 and 32 of the Vienna Convention on the Law of Treaties[1] differ to some extent from rules of statutory interpretation under national law. In particular, unlike under national law, historical interpretation must not play more than a supplementary role in treaty interpretation; also, subsequent agreements between, and a subsequent practice by Contracting Parties constitute separate means of interpretation under international law only.

7.03　In the context of treaty interpretation, the basic distinction between three different kinds of interpretation must be recalled:

> (i)　the interpretation by individual parties to a treaty, be it by means of national legislation that implements the treaty; statements by governments; decisions by their courts; or otherwise—an interpretation not binding on the other parties to the treaty (unless it corresponds to the interpretation of all other Contracting Parties and constitutes a subsequent agreement or practice under Article 31(3) of the Vienna Convention);
>
> (ii)　the judicial interpretation by international courts or arbitration courts—an interpretation which is usually binding only *inter partes*; and
>
> (iii)　the authentic interpretation—the only interpretation to bind all contracting parties to the same extent as the interpreted treaty.

7.04　An authentic interpretation can only be made by an agreement of all parties to the relevant treaty—be it by an explicit addition in a protocol or other written agreement, or by a subsequent agreement laid down only in the records of a diplomatic conference, or by a subsequent practice of all parties to the treaty.[2] Since the parties are sovereign states, they may collectively attribute any meaning to a treaty text which then prevails over a judicial interpretation and over a merely unilateral, national interpretation.[3]

(2) Methods of interpretation

7.05　In the absence of an authentic interpretation, recourse must be had to the above-mentioned interpretation by individual parties and the judicial interpretation, for which international courts and arbitration courts in their practice have developed a number of rules. These rules constitute customary international law, most of which were later codified in the Vienna Convention. Therefore, they are a source of law even where the Vienna Convention does not apply, such as in

---

[1] UN Doc A/CONF 39/27 (1969); (1969) 8 ILM 679. The Convention was adopted on 22 May 1969 and signed one day later by thirty-two countries. It came into force, according to its Article 84(1), upon deposit of thirty-five documents of ratification or adherence, on 27 January 1980.

[2] Art 31(3)(a), (b) of the Vienna Convention.

[3] On the notion of 'authentic interpretation', cf R Bernhardt, 'Interpretation in International Law' in R Bernhardt (ed), *Encyclopaedia of Public International Law* (1995) Vol II, 1416, 1423.

relation to a Berne Union country that is not a Contracting Party to the Vienna Convention, and for countries in respect of treaties that they concluded before the Vienna Convention entered into force.[4] In addition, while panels of the GATT 1947 for a long time did not apply these rules,[5] they are obligatory under the WTO dispute settlement system.[6]

One of the main achievements of the Vienna Convention was to decide on the ranking of the different rules of interpretation: the methods of objective interpretation (literal, systematic, and teleological interpretation as well as subsequent practice and agreements of all Contracting Parties) are primary means of interpretation and therefore represent the general rule, whereas the subjective, historical method only constitutes a supplementary means of interpretation.[7] **7.06**

(a) Objective methods of interpretation

Any treaty interpretation starts from the wording, ie the ordinary meaning given to the terms of the treaty (literal interpretation).[8] Often, it may be difficult and even inappropriate to ascertain the ordinary meaning of a term in an abstract way; indeed, the meaning of a particular word can change according to its context and the purpose of the legal text. Therefore, Article 31(1) of the Vienna Convention requires that the terms are interpreted in their context and in the light of the object and purpose of the treaty. **7.07**

The context in which the terms occur (systematic interpretation) are all other provisions of the treaty, including its preamble and annexes, as well as 'any agreement relating to the treaty which was made between all parties in connection with the conclusion of the treaty' and 'any instrument which was made by one or more parties in connection with the conclusion of the treaty and accepted by the other parties as an instrument related to the treaty'.[9] Equally, the object and purpose of the treaty must be taken into account (teleological interpretation).[10] **7.08**

---

[4] Art 4 of the Vienna Convention.
[5] C Tietje, 'Grundlagen und Perspektiven der WTO-Rechtsordnung' in H-J Prieß and G Berrisch (eds), *WTO-Handbuch* (2003) 17, 33.
[6] Art 3(2) phr 2 of the Dispute Settlement Understanding (DSU) refers to the 'customary rules of interpretation of public international law' instead of the Vienna Convention, since several WTO Members, including the USA, are not parties to the Vienna Convention; see P-T Stoll and F Schorkopf, *WTO: Welthandelsordnung und Welthandelsrecht* (2002) n 476.
[7] On the objective (Art 31 of the Vienna Convention) and subjective (Art 32 ibid) methods of interpretation in international law, cf Bernhardt (n 3 above) 1419; A Aust, *Modern Treaty Law and Practice* (2000) 187 ff.
[8] Art 31(1) of the Vienna Convention.
[9] Art 31(2) ibid; examples for a systematic interpretation will be shown in paras 7.13 ff below.
[10] Art 31(1) ibid; examples will be shown in paras 7.13 ff below.

7.09 On the same level as the context, the following also has to be taken into account: '(a) any subsequent agreement between the parties regarding the interpretation of the treaty or the application of its provisions; (b) any subsequent practice in the application of the treaty which establishes the agreement of the parties regarding its interpretation; and (c) any relevant rules of international law applicable in the relations between the parties.'[11] The subsequent agreement does not need to be in written form but, like the subsequent practice, must cover all parties to the treaty and therefore sometimes may be difficult to establish, especially in the multilateral context.

(b) Subjective method of interpretation

7.10 In addition to the primary means of interpretation—the literal, systematic, and teleological interpretation as well as subsequent agreements and practice—the historical interpretation has to be taken into account. Yet, it is only a subsidiary means of interpretation: it may only be relied upon 'in order to confirm the meaning resulting from the application of Article 31, or to determine the meaning when the interpretation according to Article 31: (a) leaves the meaning ambiguous or obscure; or (b) leads to a result which is manifestly absurd or unreasonable'.[12] Under these conditions, recourse may be had, in particular, to the preparatory work of a treaty and the circumstances of its conclusion; however, the preparatory work may be relied on only if all contracting parties participated in the drafting of the text or the documents, or the preparatory work was made accessible to adhering parties before their adherence.[13] The circumstances of the treaty's conclusion may include the historical background against which the treaty was negotiated, and the individual characteristics and attitudes of the Contracting Parties, such as reflected in governmental records or decisions of national courts. They are still, however, of limited weight only.[14]

(c) Languages

7.11 (i) **Authentic and official texts** A specific feature of many treaties is that they are drafted in several languages. As a rule, only those languages in which a treaty is authenticated can be considered as 'authentic' and therefore can be a basis for

---

[11] Art 31(3) of the Vienna Convention; an example for a subsequent agreement are the implied exceptions under the Berne Convention, see paras 5.199 ff above; subsequent practice is dealt with in more detail below, para 7.30.

[12] Art 32 of the Vienna Convention.

[13] Permanent Court of International Justice, Series A, no 23, p 42 ('Territorial Jurisdiction of the International Commission of the River Oder', 1929) and Series B, no 14, p 32 (in the legal opinion on the 'Jurisdiction of the European Commission of the Danube', 1927).

[14] I Sinclair, *The Vienna Convention on the Law of Treaties* (2nd edn, 1984) 141 ff.

interpretation.[15] Official texts usually are not authentic or binding texts, but they may have a higher authoritative value than unofficial translations. This is true in particular where official texts have been agreed on by all contracting parties. Official texts mainly serve to harmonize the language versions for all Contracting Parties using the same language; as a result, Contracting Parties cannot reproach each other for having applied the treaty in the version of an official text rather than in the authentic version, where no doubts arise.[16] However, the later such official texts are adopted and the smaller the number of Contracting Parties participating in the translation, the less is the possibility in case of doubt that such texts can be relied on for the purpose of interpretation.[17]

(ii) Several authentic texts   Where a treaty has been authenticated in two or   **7.12** more languages, its text is equally authoritative in each authentic language, subject to a treaty provision or an agreement of the parties on a particular text to prevail in case of divergence.[18] Such a treaty provision is contained in the Berne Convention, which determines that the French text shall prevail in case of differences of opinion on the interpretation of the authentic texts (ie in French and English).[19] Where several language versions are considered equally authentic without any priority for a particular language,[20] the terms of the treaty are presumed to have the same meaning in each of those languages and, 'when a comparison of the authentic texts discloses a difference of meaning which the application of Articles 31 and 32 does not remove, the meaning which best reconciles the texts, having regard to the object and purpose of the treaty, shall be adopted.'[21]

---

[15] Art 33(1), (2) of the Vienna Convention; this is, however, subject to treaty provisions and agreements of the parties to the contrary.

[16] Where doubts arise, the authentic text remains the only binding one.

[17] M Hilf, *Die Auslegung mehrsprachiger Verträge* (1973) 222 ff.

[18] Art 33 of the Vienna Convention.

[19] Art 37(1)(a) of the Berne Convention determines the French and English texts to be authentic; before the 1948 Brussels Act, the French text was the only authentic one. Art 37(1)(c) provides for the primacy of the French text.

[20] Such as under Art 33(1) of the Rome Convention (English, French, Spanish), Art 26(1) of the WCT, and Art 32(1) of the WPPT (the six UN languages Arabic, Chinese, English, French, Russian, and Spanish), as well as under the TRIPS Agreement (that is a WTO Agreement, which itself was 'done in the English, French and Spanish languages, each text being authentic' (text concluding the WTO Agreement, following its Art XVI)).

[21] Art 33(3), (4) of the Vienna Convention. For more details on the interpretation of copyright and neighbouring rights treaties, see S Ricketson and J Ginsburg, *International Copyright and Neighbouring Rights: The Berne Convention and Beyond* (2006) 5.08 ff.

B. Examples[22]

(1) Subject matter

(a) Computer programs

7.13 The question of whether computer programs are covered as 'works' under the Berne Convention[23] and, consequently, benefit from national treatment and minimum rights,[24] is not easy to answer;[25] indeed, for some time after the emergence of computer programs, views were quite divergent and no authentic interpretation could be ascertained. To start with the literal interpretation, Article 2(1) of the Berne Convention on the covered works obviously does not contain computer programs in the list of explicitly mentioned works.[26] This does not, however, prevent them from being covered by the Convention since the list only contains examples, as indicated by the words 'such as' at its beginning. Accordingly, a computer program may be covered under the general clause of Article 2(1) of the Berne Convention if it is a 'production in the literary, scientific and artistic domain, whatever may be the mode or form of its expression'. The word 'production' has a very broad meaning and includes any result of a productive activity; the context of the Convention,[27] however, limits its meaning to the result of an intellectual activity, ie a creation by an author (rather than, for example, a production by printing a book).[28] Such intellectual creation must occur in the literary, scientific, or artistic domains which themselves must be interpreted in the context of the explicit examples listed in Article 2(1) of the Berne Convention.

7.14 In order to consider whether a computer program is a production in one of the domains under Article 2(1) of the Berne Convention, one has to look at the particular features of a computer program. Its source code may be described as a series of instructions, which are then transformed into a machine code that may

---

[22] Due to the scope of this book, the discussion of the following examples is restricted to the most important arguments.

[23] Subsequent developments under the TRIPS Agreement and the WCT are not taken into account in this context, see paras 10.56–10.59 and 17.103–17.104 below

[24] These principles, as well as the principle of 'no formalities', only apply in respect of 'works for which they are protected under this Convention', Art 5(1), (2) of the Berne Convention.

[25] For analyses, see M Ficsor, *The Law of Copyright and the Internet: The 1996 WIPO Treaties, their Interpretation and Implementation* (2002) C4.08 ff; Ricketson and Ginsburg (n 21 above) 8.92–8.103.

[26] A different result is reached if one considers computer programs as 'writings', according to today's qualification as 'literary works'; yet, the lack of protection in laws of Berne countries initially did not reflect such an interpretation. On the difference between listed and unlisted works, see paras 5.76–5.78 above.

[27] In particular its Art 2(5); more arguments from the context could be made in favour of the coverage of only intellectual creations, see paras 5.66–5.67 above.

[28] On the interpretation of 'author' as a human person who 'produces' the work by his or her mind, see paras 5.84–5.86 above.

interact with the computer's central processing unit in order to achieve a certain result. The machine code is represented by a corresponding object code that is understandable to programmers. The code is an expression of thoughts, namely, the instructions to the machine, by a human author and therefore a 'production' in the meaning of Article 2(1) of the Berne Convention.[29] It uses alphanumeric, binary, or other notations, that is, signs with a specific meaning when they are combined. This tool of expression can therefore be understood as a language in the broad sense. Indeed, the word 'programming language' is commonly used for the different forms of notation. Literary works are those expressed by a language of any kind, whether or not understood by everyone. Therefore, the fact that programming languages are only understood by programmers does not prevent them from being works in the literary domain. In addition, a work must be 'expressed' in a way perceptible for human beings. While the source and object codes are perceptible for them (though only understandable to programmers), this is less certain for the machine code, which is not perceptible to humans.

The lack of aesthetic appeal to the human eye and the utilitarian character of **7.15** computer programs do not prevent them from being covered, since the Berne Convention does not establish any such requirements. This is confirmed by the systematic interpretation, in particular the list of examples in Article 2(1), which includes works without aesthetic appeal (such as, regularly, technical drawings, letters, geographical maps) and works with a utilitarian character as opposed to *l'art pour l'art*-works, such as works of architecture, applied art, or maps. The teleological interpretation also results in the coverage of computer programs, since the purpose of the Convention—the protection of authors in their works[30]— justifies covering computer programs that are created by human authors.

Accordingly, the literal, systematic, and teleological interpretations carried out **7.16** above lead to the *interim* result that computer programs are covered by the Berne Convention. However, together with the context, one also has to take into account the subsequent state practice as an equally important means of interpretation.[31] After the last revision of the Berne Convention in 1971, most member countries did not immediately consider computer programs as works protected under copyright in general, and as being covered by the Berne Convention in particular. Many rather looked upon them as industrial products the nature of which was quite different from the works of the mind protected until then under copyright. Several features of copyright protection, such as the long duration of

---

[29] On the fact that the Berne Convention protects human authors, see paras 5.84–5.86 above; on the necessary expression of thoughts or feelings, see paras 5.69–5.70 above.

[30] Preamble and Art 1 of the Berne Convention.

[31] Art 31(3)(b) of the Vienna Convention, see para 7.09 above.

at least fifty years after the author's death, were considered inappropriate for computer programs.[32] Often, a special related rights protection was regarded as more appropriate than copyright protection.[33] In particular, Switzerland envisaged not only a related right for computer programs, but also material reciprocity in respect of foreign programs.[34] Since the Berne Convention does not allow material reciprocity in respect of works except works of applied art, this draft reflected the opinion that computer programs were not works under copyright and, in particular, under the Berne Convention.

7.17 Major doubts whether computer programs would be covered by the Berne Convention were also reflected in work of member countries in the framework of WIPO. WIPO's Model Provisions on the Protection of Computer Software[35] of 1977 did not provide for protection by copyright law but for a *sui generis* protection; on the one hand, it provided for originality as a result of the authors' own intellectual creation, but on the other only suggested a duration of twenty years from first use, sale, lease, or licensing but not beyond twenty-five years from creation. This approach reflected the view that no existing regime of legal protection would be entirely adapted to the particularities of computer programs[36]—certainly not a strong argument for coverage by the Berne Convention. Likewise, the suggestion of the WIPO Expert Group on the Legal Protection of Computer Software in the early 1980s to protect computer programs by a special treaty because protection was not fully covered by the existing international Conventions, such as the Paris and Berne Conventions[37] reflected the opinion

---

[32] Ricketson and Ginsburg (n 21 above) 8.99; even after the worldwide introduction of copyright protection for computer programs, doubts are expressed in literature, eg P Samuelson et al, 'A Manifesto Concerning the Legal Protection of Computer Programs' (1994) Columbia Law Review 2308; G Dworkin, 'Copyright, Patents, and/or *sui generis*: What Regime Best Suits Computer Programs?' in H Hansen (ed), *International Intellectual Property Law & Policy* Vol I (1996) 165 ff, presents the controversies; P Samuelson, 'Comments on Gerald Dworkin's Article on Copyright, Patents, and/or *sui generis*: What Regime Best Suits Computer Programs' in Hansen, ibid 183 ff, and 'Session IIIA Panel Discussion', ibid 195.

[33] eg a Swiss Draft for a new copyright act in 1987 included a provision on a kind of related or *sui generis* right upon the model of the protection of integrated circuits, see Arts 81 ff of the Draft Act Concerning Copyright and Neighbouring Rights, prepared by the III. Expert Commission, 18 December 1987; cf T Dreier, 'National Treatment, Reciprocity and Retorsion: The Case of Computer Programs and Integrated Circuits' in FK Beier and G Schricker (eds), *GATT or WIPO? New Ways in the International Protection of Intellectual Property* (1989) 64, 69. Also the French Copyright Act of 3 July 1985 regulated computer programs under a separate Title V, with a duration of twenty-five years from creation, so that they were considered protected by a neighbouring right, see A Lucas and H-J Lucas, *Traité de la propriété littéraire et artistique* (3rd edn, 2006) 111, in particular n 331.

[34] Art 81(1), (2) of the Swiss Draft (n 33 above).

[35] (1978) Copyright 6 ff.

[36] Dworkin (n 32 above) 166; Dreier (n 33 above) 66.

[37] First Session November 1979, (1980) Copyright 36. See also the subsequent discussion on quite specific rules for software protection in the Second Session, (1983) Copyright 271, 276 ff.

that computer programs were not covered by the Berne Convention. It was only from around 1985 that opinions started to change on a large scale.[38]

Accordingly, in the initial phase after the emergence of computer programs, this **7.18** early practice where member countries differently interpreted the Berne Convention had to be taken into account so that the interpretation of the Berne Convention did not then lead to a clear coverage of computer programs.

After the mid-1980s, however, most member countries adopted copyright pro- **7.19** tection for computer programs under national law, not least due to strong lobbying by the software industry and high, unilateral economic pressure by the USA.[39] While only around fifteen countries explicitly included computer programs as works under their copyright acts in 1988,[40] all Berne Union countries protect computer programs under copyright today; so, the subsequent practice now clearly shows their current, new interpretation that computer programs are covered by the Berne Convention.

(b) Phonograms

Whereas phonograms at first sight might be considered as 'productions' in the **7.20** musical domain, which is covered as an artistic domain under Article 2(1) of the Berne Convention, doubts arise on the basis of the context and purpose of the Convention, which is to protect authors in their works, ie intellectual creations. A phonogram is a fixation of sounds that is mostly aimed at the technically best possible reproduction of the recorded sounds of a work or of other sounds rather than a separate creation. Even if the contribution of a sound engineer might be creative in cases of particular kinds of recordings, this will be the exception. Also, protection for phonograms usually vests in companies that are responsible for the fixation of sounds or the production of phonograms and that are protected for the overall investment in such production; accordingly, protection vests in 'phonogram producers', while the Berne Convention grants protection to 'authors'.

Without elaborating on other possible arguments against the coverage of phono- **7.21** grams, this case can be solved on the basis of an interpretation by the Berne member countries as reflected in the Reports of the 1928 Rome and 1948 Brussels Revision Conferences of the Berne Convention. During these conferences, the inclusion of phonograms as works was discussed but rejected on the argument that they were not produced by human intelligence and did not engage creative

---

[38] Ficsor (n 25 above) 4.09 attributes this 'landslide change' to WIPO's 'guided development' work; yet, influence by interested parties is likely to have played a major role too.

[39] Dreier (n 33 above) 67–9; on US unilateral measures in general, see paras 13.01–13.10 below.

[40] ibid 67 and n 9.

activity as required by the Berne Convention.[41] Accordingly, even where countries of the copyright system provide copyright protection for phonograms under national law, they are not obliged to grant national treatment or minimum rights under the Berne Convention since phonograms do not fall under the general definition of 'literary and artistic works'. The adoption of several separate treaties that cover the protection of phonograms and the rejection by most countries in 1991 to include phonograms in a protocol to the Berne Convention[42] confirm this result.

(2) New uses

7.22 As regards newly emerging kinds of uses, a distinction must be made between (a) their coverage by particular minimum rights of the Berne Convention, and (b) their coverage by the national treatment obligation.

(a) Making available works on demand[43]

7.23 Works are made available on demand where users individually gain access to them over the internet or similar networks, which regularly occurs by wire but increasingly also by wireless means. When this use became possible, its legal qualification under the existing copyright law—national and other—was controversial; proposals were made to apply the existing rights of distribution, rental, broadcasting, communication, or any newly created right.[44] The most widespread approach today is to qualify it as a form of communication to the public.[45]

7.24 'Communication to the public' under Articles 11, 11[bis], 11[ter], 14, and 14[bis] of the Berne Convention has been understood as an act of transmission to the public at a remote place.[46] The particular feature of on-demand transmissions is the possibility of individual users choosing the time at which, and the place from which, they want to access a particular work. Accordingly, unlike for traditional forms of communication to the public, such as original cable radio, on-demand transmissions of a particular work are not made at the same time to the public, but at different times to individual members of the public. Although the Berne Convention does not explicitly require the communication

---

[41] For more detail regarding the Revision Conferences, see paras 4.52–4.57 above; Ricketson and Ginsburg (n 21 above) 8.112 with further references also to similar discussions at the 1908 Berlin Conference.

[42] paras 17.05–17.06 below.

[43] On another important new use, digital reproduction, see paras 5.117–5.118 above, and for the clarification in the WCT, paras 17.52–17.58 below. For a separate analysis, see also Ricketson/Ginsburg (n 21 above) 12.48–12.51.

[44] See para 17.72 below in the context of the WCT and WPPT.

[45] eg Art 8 of the WCT and Arts 10, 14 of the WPPT, usually followed by national laws, even if implementation is also permitted in the form of a different right, see paras 17.72 and 17.80 below.

[46] For more details, see paras 5.134, 5.138–5.140 above.

to be simultaneous, it does so implicitly because one and the same act of communication must be made to 'the public', ie more than one person and beyond family or similar groups. Accordingly, if 'communication' is read in the meaning of 'transmission', then on-demand use would not be a communication because it would not take place 'to the public' but only to individual members of the public.

If one interprets the word 'communication' in a broader way than as transmission **7.25** only, so as to also cover the prior making available of works on a server for access by members of the public, the communication (in that case, offering of works for access) would be simultaneously made to the public and therefore be covered by the Berne Convention.[47]

Like the wording, the systematic and teleological methods of interpretation do **7.26** not give much more assistance for the correct interpretation. Any subsequent agreement or practice by the Berne Union countries under the conditions of Article 31(3) of the Vienna Convention would need to clearly show whether the making available right is considered a minimum right under the Berne Convention. The agreement by Berne Union countries at the 1996 Diplomatic Conference to cover on-demand transmission by a communication right under the WCT cannot be anything more than an indication of how they would interpret the Berne Convention, considering that it is a self-standing treaty.[48] So long as no such subsequent agreement or practice is specifically ascertained in respect of the Berne Convention, the coverage of the making available right as a minimum right under Articles 11–11[ter], 14, and 14[bis] of the Berne Convention remains subject to doubt. Obviously, historical interpretation also cannot remove doubt, given the emergence of the on-demand uses after the last revision of the Berne Convention in 1971.

(b) Public lending right and national treatment

The public lending right (PLR) is a statutory remuneration right for the lending **7.27** of books (and, in some countries, also other media) by public and other non-commercial libraries. It was initially conceived as a means to promote local literature and other culture particularly in places with small language areas such as Scandinavia.[49] Therefore, many countries integrated the remuneration right for

---

[47] The fact that on-demand transmissions are initiated by the user rather than by a sender or other communicator is irrelevant for the term 'communication', which simply requires that a work is 'transported' from one place to another one, ie, the public; see also Ricketson/Ginsburg (n 21 above) 12.49.

[48] Also, the requirement of an agreement by all Berne countries must be fulfilled.

[49] The first scheme was introduced 1946 in Denmark, other Scandinavian countries followed; see for the historical development S von Lewinski, 'Public Lending Right: General and Comparative Survey of Existing Systems in Law and Practise' (1992) 154 RIDA 3 ff.

public lending into their library acts or other specific acts outside copyright. Also, many schemes deviated in substance from traditional copyright rules, for example by restrictions to particular kinds of works (such as fiction literature) or media (such as books), or to specified kinds of authors (such as authors of fiction only) or lending institutions, or by limiting the duration of the right to the author's lifetime. Some systems also included or consisted of fund systems, ie systems where the money is not distributed according to the extent of use but according to social need or cultural merit.[50]

7.28   The question whether the PLR is subject to national treatment depends on its qualification as a right that the Berne Union countries' 'respective laws' grant to their nationals.[51] 'Respective laws' are not further defined; in the context of the Convention and in the light of its purpose as set out in its Preamble and Article 1, they have to be understood as all laws that protect the rights of authors in their works. Above all, this means that the substance of national laws rather than their label matters; a formal classification such as the position of PLR rules inside or outside a copyright act (eg in a library act) must not be taken into account for the interpretation of the Berne Convention. In essence, the question is whether PLR constitutes a matter of copyright—namely, a right of authors in their works.

7.29   Doubts have been raised whether a simple remuneration right would be a right 'in' a work—an expression that may be understood as only covering exclusive rights. These doubts may be refuted on grounds of systematic interpretation: the resale right under Article 14[ter] of the Berne Convention shows that remuneration rights are considered authors' rights in their works. Other doubts may be less easily refuted: the limited groups of beneficiaries, works, and groups of libraries covered by the schemes are each quite uncommon features under copyright laws and, in respect of the duration, even inconsistent with the Berne Convention. Moreover, major doubts may be raised where fund systems apply and the remuneration is not paid according to the frequency of use. The words 'rights of authors in their . . . works' imply the possibility of benefiting from payment for the use of the work, to be made by the user in accordance with the extent of use. Where the payment is mainly or exclusively made according to other criteria such as social

---

[50] For a detailed analysis of the different systems existing in the early 1990s, see ibid, and S von Lewinski, *Die urheberrechtliche Vergütung für das Vermieten und Verleihen von Werkstücken (§ 27 UrhG)* (1990) 1 ff; for an overview of systems after EC harmonization, see S von Lewinski, 'European Harmonization in a Controversial Field: The Case of Public Lending Right' in L Gorton, J Herre, E Nerep, J-P Nordell, and J Rosén (eds), *Festskrift till Gunnar Karnell* (1999) 439 ff.
[51] Art 5(1) of the Berne Convention.

need or cultural merit, one can no longer speak of a connection with the use of works or of 'rights of authors in their . . . works'.

In this situation of ambiguity, recourse to the subsequent state practice shows **7.30** that Berne Union countries do not generally consider that national treatment under the Berne Convention would apply to PLR;[52] this fact could be interpreted as their understanding that PLR is not in the nature of copyright and therefore does not fall under national treatment, or that an unwritten, agreed exception to national treatment applies for PLR. The latter option was indeed suggested by the WIPO Secretariat, when it proposed explicitly to provide for the possibility of denying national treatment but applying reciprocity instead.[53] Most delegations did not support the inclusion of PLR into the then planned protocol to the Berne Convention.[54] Only few delegations opposed the proposal on an exception to national treatment, while some considered PLR clearly covered thereby. Most of the delegations that opposed WIPO's proposal on an exception argued for different reasons that PLR was not even covered by national treatment, so that no exception could apply.[55] The WIPO Director General concluded that 'what was needed was a clear answer to the question whether PLR was a copyright matter or not'.[56] Today, given this continuously ambiguous situation, it cannot be clearly ascertained that PLR would fall under national treatment.

(3) 'Publication' on the internet

Article 3(3) of the Berne Convention defines 'published works' in a way that **7.31** raises many doubts regarding the question whether the act of making available a work to the public on the internet constitutes a publication under this definition. Only the important arguments are summarized here.[57] To start with a literal interpretation, the wording alone may result in a self-contradictory statement: on

---

[52] For a detailed analysis of state practice, legal relevance of silence, and the states' understanding that PLR does not fall under national treatment of the Berne Convention, see S von Lewinski, 'National Treatment, Reciprocity and Retorsion: The Case of Public Lending Right' in Beier/ Schricker (n 33 above) 54, 60–2; see also with inclusion of more recent developments, S von Lewinski, 'Status of the Writer and Intellectual Property: Legislation and the Effect of International Laws on PLR' in Anon (ed), *Third International Public Lending Right Conference: The Right to Culture and a Culture of Rights. Conference Papers* (1999) 95, 97 ff.

[53] 'Committee of Experts on a Possible Protocol to the Berne Convention for the Protection of Literary and Artistic Works, Third Session' (1993) Copyright 72, 98 ff (paras 88 ff, 94 ff, 129 ff, and on reciprocity para 131).

[54] For the reasons, see Report of the Third Session of the Committee (n 53 above), (1993) Copyright 179, 189 (paras 73 f).

[55] For delegations' statements, see Report, ibid, paras 102–5.

[56] ibid, para 113.

[57] For a much more detailed presentation, see Reinbothe and von Lewinski, *The WIPO Treaties 1996* (2002) Art 3 WCT nn 18–21; for a different way of analysis, see Ricketson/Ginsburg (n 21 above) 6.52, 6.59–6.64.

the one hand, the requirement that works are published by any 'means of manufacture of the copies, provided that the availability of such copies has been such as to satisfy the reasonable requirements of the public, having regard to the nature of the work'[58] may be considered fulfilled for copies that are uploaded on a server from which they are made available to the public via the internet. On the other hand, making available could constitute a 'communication by wire' under phrase 2 of the same provision and therefore be excluded from the definition. This ambiguous situation thus requires recourse to the context where the term is used;[59] yet, the systematic interpretation also does not lead to a clear result.[60]

7.32 Consequently, one has to consider which of the two possible ways of interpretation would best serve the purpose of the provision and the Convention itself. Covering internet publication as a 'publication' would lead to further problems. In particular, it would be difficult to determine the country of origin that is in most cases defined as the country of first publication. If one acknowledges that internet publication means immediate, simultaneous, and therefore first publication in all countries of the world where the internet is accessible, all of these countries with the same, shortest term of protection would constitute countries of origin, so that the Berne Convention would largely be inapplicable.[61] This result would certainly run counter to the purpose of the Berne Convention. At the same time, the Berne Convention does not allow the determination of any particular country among all those countries as the country of 'first' publication; this remedy to the problem would need to be specified in a revision.

7.33 Accordingly, it better corresponds to the purpose of the Berne Convention to consider internet 'publication' not to be covered as publication under the Berne Convention. Consequently, the Berne rules for unpublished works would apply to works exclusively 'published' online: only nationals of another Berne Union country and authors residing there would be eligible for protection, and the country of origin would be that of the author's nationality.[62] Moreover, the comparison of terms under Article 7(8) of the Berne Convention would apply by comparing the terms in the country for which protection is claimed and in the

---

[58] Art 3(3) phr 1 of the Berne Convention.

[59] The term 'publication' is important as a criterion of eligibility under Art 3(1) of the Berne Convention, for the term 'country of origin' under Art 5(4) of the Berne Convention and, consequently, the way in which the Convention as such applies (it does not apply in the country of origin), as well as for the comparison of terms under Art 7(8) of the Berne Convention.

[60] Reinbothe/von Lewinski (n 57 above) Art 3 WCT n 20.

[61] Art 5(4)(a) of the Berne Convention defines the Union country of first publication with the shortest term of protection as country of origin; most countries provide for the same, shortest term of fifty years *pma*. Under Article 5(3) of the Berne Convention, domestic law applies in the country of origin, except for a specific non-discrimination rule of the same provision.

[62] Art 5(4)(c) of the Berne Convention on unpublished works with further details; for the assimilation of habitual residents, see Art 3(2) of the Berne Convention.

country of which the author is a national or habitual resident. Accordingly, this interpretation on the basis of Article 3(3) phrase 2 of the Berne Convention leads to acceptable results and is much clearer than the coverage of internet 'publication' under Article 3(3) phrase 1 of the Berne Convention—an interpretation that would raise too many new questions that cannot be answered under the Berne Convention.[63]

(4) The scope of national treatment under the Rome Convention

Under Article 2(2) of the Rome Convention, national treatment is 'subject to'[64] the minimum rights. This wording may be interpreted as covering situations where the level of protection in a Contracting State is both higher than and lower than the minimum rights under the Rome Convention. Where the national law level is lower than the minimum rights, national treatment must be granted but is subject to the higher Rome standards; accordingly, the minimum rights must be granted even if they are not provided under national law. This situation is not controversial. Yet, where the national law grants a higher level of protection than the minimum under the Rome Convention, the way in which national treatment applies is controversial.[65] **7.34**

The words 'subject to' could mean that national treatment (the full assimilation to nationals) only needs to be granted to the extent required by the minimum standards of the Rome Convention. Accordingly, national treatment would not have a separate meaning, apart from assimilating foreign beneficiaries to nationals as regards the concrete way in which the Rome minimum rights are implemented in national law. Although it may seem at first sight that such a limited meaning of a treaty provision would in itself be an argument against this way of interpretation, the subsequent examples of the TRIPS Agreement and the WPPT, where the same result is reached by very clear provisions, shows that this counter-argument is not very weighty. Also, the Rome Convention has not followed the wording of Berne national treatment, which clearly prevails over lower minimum standards by juxtaposing the obligations of national treatment 'as well as' minimum rights.[66] **7.35**

In the systematic context of national treatment, provisions on reciprocity as a form of exceptions from national treatment must be considered. The Rome Convention only allows for reciprocity where reservations to minimum rights **7.36**

---

[63] For unsuccessful essays at the WIPO Diplomatic Conference 1996 to include internet publication as publication and to determine the country of first publication, see paras 17.151–17.152 below.

[64] In French: *compte tenu*; in Spanish: *sujeto a*.

[65] See refs in para 6.27 nn 70, 71 above.

[66] Art 5(1) of the Berne Convention.

can be made, namely, regarding the remuneration rights for secondary uses and the broadcasters' communication right.[67] Accordingly, these are cases where different levels of protection exist, due to declared reservations. Reciprocity here has the function to prevent an imbalanced situation where, without a reciprocity clause, countries that provide for full protection would unilaterally have to grant protection to those that made a reservation. Given the low minimum level of the Rome Convention and thus the possibility that general levels of protection under national laws strongly differ, and (unlike in the Berne Convention) the absence of further exceptions from national treatment, full national treatment would seem inconsistent with the rationale of the permitted cases of reciprocity; rather, the interpretation of a limited scope of national treatment would seem in harmony with this rationale; unilaterally granted advantages always have been considered unfair and remedied accordingly where major differences of protection existed in national law.[68]

7.37 While the purpose of the Convention is simply 'to protect' neighbouring rights,[69] broad membership is a general aim of treaties in intellectual property. A situation of a full national treatment obligation in combination with low minimum rights and possibly large differences in national standards would probably deter countries with higher protection standards from joining the Convention, in contradiction to this aim.

7.38 Notable arguments can be drawn from a possible subsequent practice of Contracting States, once fully established. To date, only indications of such practice and views of states can be observed. First, the negotiating parties of the TRIPS Agreement obviously started from the assumption that the earlier national treatment under the Rome Convention was limited in the same way as the explicit provision in the TRIPS Agreement.[70] Similarly, most negotiating parties to the WPPT objected to full national treatment and specifically did not object to the explanatory notes in the Basic Proposal for negotiations. The Basic Proposal combined a paragraph on a limited scope of national treatment according to the TRIPS model with a paragraph following Article 2(2) of the Rome Convention; the

---

[67] Art 16(1)(a)(iv) for secondary uses of performers and phonogram producers and Art 16(1)(b) of the Rome Convention for the communication right of broadcasting organizations, see paras 6.57 and 6.65 above.

[68] For the Berne Convention, see paras 5.40 and examples in 5.41 ff above; for the secondary uses under the Rome Convention, see E Ulmer, 'The Rome Convention for the Protection of Performers, Producers of Phonograms and Broadcasting Organisations—Part III' [1963] 10 Bulletin of the Copyright Society of the USA 219, 230.

[69] Preamble to the Rome Convention.

[70] This is implied in J Reinbothe (who was involved in the negotiations on the part of the EC), 'Der Schutz des Urheberrechts und der Leistungsschutzrechte im Abkommensentwurf GATT/ TRIPS' (1992) GRUR Int 707, 713.

notes stated that the interpretation of the second paragraph was intended to fol-low the interpretation of that Rome provision.[71] In addition, the view that a lim-ited scope of national treatment corresponded to the approach of the Rome Convention was expressed by the Chair of Main Committee I at the Diplomatic Conference and by the EC in particular, but not opposed by other delegations.[72]

If delegations had seen a contradiction between the Rome Convention and this   **7.39** proposal, they would have needed to oppose the proposal of a limited scope of national treatment in this context, as well as in the context of both the TRIPS Agreement and the WPPT, because these are special agreements of the Rome Convention under its Article 22, which does not allow for lesser protection in the new agreement.[73] The silence of delegations in this regard may have to be viewed as their agreement to the interpretation of the Rome national treatment as being limited in scope. A similar situation arose in the framework of the discussions on the draft treaty for the protection of broadcasting organizations, where the Chair's notes to the draft basic proposal on limited national treatment following the WPPT model stated: 'This proposal continues the tradition of a limited, non-global national treatment, which, in the area of related rights takes its origin from Article 2.2 of the Rome Convention.'[74] No delegation opposed this view. Even if not all Rome Convention parties were negotiating parties of the TRIPS Agreement and the WPPT or delegations at the SCCR regarding the broadcasters' treaty, these facts are at least strong indications for a widespread interpretation by Rome parties in favour of limited national treatment.

Given these strong indications of an authentic interpretation of the Contracting   **7.40** States of the Rome Convention in favour of limited national treatment, it seems worthwhile to more clearly ascertain their interpretation before having recourse to historical interpretation, which is only a supplementary means of interpreta-tion in case of ambiguity. In addition, this would correspond to the trend in international law towards a dynamic, evolutionary form of interpretation rather than the orientation to the original intentions of the parties.[75]

---

[71] WIPO Doc CRNR/DC/5 n 4.03; on discussions at the Committee of Experts and the Diplomatic Conference, see Reinbothe/von Lewinski (n 57 above) Art 4 WPPT n 1 ff.

[72] WIPO (ed), *Records of the Diplomatic Conference on Certain Copyright and Neighbouring Rights Questions* (1996) paras 594 (p 726) and 609 (p 729).

[73] On the quality of the WPPT as a special agreement, see Reinbothe/von Lewinski (n 57 above) Art 1 WPPT n 12; for TRIPS, see para 6.78 above, and paras 10.90, and 24.14 below. The main and largely isolated country in favour of unlimited national treatment in the WPPT was the USA, which is not a Contracting State of the Rome Convention.

[74] WIPO Doc SCCR/15/2 rev n 8.03.

[75] Bernhardt (n 3 above) 1416, 1419. Also Ficsor ((n 25 above) PP4.15) vaguely admits that, after further study, 'some new forms of restrictive interpretation will be developed' in compliance with the Vienna Convention.

(5) Résumé

7.41 These examples show that the emergence of new factual situations often constitutes a challenge for interpretation of treaties; while mostly technology-neutral provisions and dynamic interpretation allow treaties to remain relevant, a clear understanding of an authentic interpretation often is only gained after a certain period of time following the emergence of new situations.

8

CONSEQUENCES OF A VIOLATION OF A TREATY AND OF DIVERGENCES OF INTERPRETATION AMONG ITS MEMBER COUNTRIES

A. Introduction

As Chapter 7 has shown, it is not always easy to unequivocally ascertain the meaning behind a particular provision of a treaty when applied to a specific scenario. In case of ambiguity, there is a need for clarification; where the provision leaves no doubt as to its correct interpretation but a country does not comply with it, enforcement is needed. Both clarification and enforcement may be sought by a private party through a lawsuit in the country for which protection is claimed. Where this is not helpful,[1] recourse to dispute settlement at the state level remains an option.[2] In both cases, where a treaty provision is invoked,

8.01

---

[1] See para 8.15 below.
[2] See paras 8.16–8.26 below.

a number of conditions must be fulfilled in respect of the treaty itself.[3] In the case of a private lawsuit, the treaty must also be internally applicable.[4]

B. General public international law conditions regarding treaties

(1) Full powers for the conclusion of treaties

8.02 In order to be successfully invoked as a basis for a claim, a treaty must have been concluded, be valid, have entered into force, and bind the specific country for which protection is claimed. Treaties are concluded between states,[5] which are represented by persons who have 'full powers' for the adoption or authentication of a treaty or for expressing the consent of the state to being bound by the treaty.[6] Where a person who acts for a state does not enjoy 'full powers' of that state in the context of the conclusion of a treaty, his acts are without legal effect and therefore do not bind the state, subject to later confirmation by the state.[7] If the person has full powers under Article 7 of the Vienna Convention but if this empowerment violates domestic law regarding the competence to conclude treaties, the state concerned can invoke such violation of domestic law to make the consent invalid only under conditions that are rarely fulfilled; through this safeguard, the other states' confidence is protected.[8]

(2) Majority and unanimity

8.03 As a rule, the adoption of a treaty text at an international conference, such as a WIPO Diplomatic Conference, only requires a majority vote of two-thirds of states present and voting, unless otherwise agreed by the same majority; other treaties are adopted by unanimity.[9] In practice, though, the consensus procedure without formal votes is increasingly applied in negotiations; only where no consensus can be reached, votes may take place, as demonstrated for example regarding individual

---

[3] See paras 8.02–8.10 below.

[4] See paras 8.11–8.15 below. Conditions of international civil procedure law and private international law are not considered here.

[5] Under Art 6 of the Vienna Convention on the Law of Treaties, any state has the capacity to conclude treaties. Art 2(1)(a) ibid defines a treaty as 'an international agreement concluded between States'.

[6] Art 7 ibid identifies the conditions under which a person is considered to represent a state; its Art 2(1)(c) defines 'full powers'. On full powers, see in detail eg A Aust, *Modern Treaty Law and Practice* (2000) 57 ff. In the context of the WCT and WPPT, see para 17–18 below,

[7] Art 8 Vienna Convention.

[8] Art 46 ibid.

[9] Art 9 ibid; Art 27(3) of the Berne Convention requires unanimity for the adoption of any revision, while Art 29(2) of the Rome Convention requires only two-thirds of the states attending the revision conference if they are Contracting States to the Rome Convention.

provisions adopted at the 1996 WIPO Diplomatic Conference.[10] The preference for consensus aims at protecting minority interests; it may well lead to the failure of a treaty, where parties do not proceed to a vote.[11] Together with the treaty, the so-called Final Act is often adopted at the end of a diplomatic conference; it describes the procedure at the conference and summarizes its results.

(3) Authentication

After the adoption of a treaty, the concrete text must be authenticated. There- **8.04** after, the contents of the treaty can no longer be modified except by a revision or other subsequent agreement of the parties, or by individual parties' reservations that are expressly permitted or accepted by all other parties. A treaty may be authenticated in one or several languages.[12] Authentication may occur by way of signature or as otherwise agreed.[13]

(4) Signature, ratification, accession

The signature alone can, but usually does not, constitute the consent of the state **8.05** to be bound by the treaty. In general, a wide variety of means to express consent to be bound by a treaty are available.[14] Mostly, the treaties themselves specify the required means. In practice, it is mostly the deposit of instruments of ratification or accession rather than the signature.[15] Where a state has signed a treaty but under the rules only becomes bound upon ratification or accession, the signature itself does not oblige it to proceed to the ratification; for example, Cambodia, Holy See, and India each signed the Rome Convention on 21 October 1961 but to date have not ratified it. The rationale for this procedure becomes evident where, under domestic law, the ratification is subject to an act of parliament and where the parliament does not approve the treaty. Yet, even where the parliament does so, the signature does not constitute any obligation of the state to indeed ratify the treaty. However, a signatory state in this case has certain minimum

---

[10] M Shaw, *International Law* (5th edn, 2003) 817; Aust (n 6 above) 67–8. At the 1996 Conference, only very few votes on individual provisions were needed, see paras 17.22 and 17.25 below.

[11] This was experienced at the 2000 WIPO Audiovisual Conference, see para 18.21 below. See Aust (n 6 above) 68 on the reason for the new preference.

[12] eg Art 37(1)(a) of the Berne Convention; Art 31(1) of the Rome Convention; on the effects, see paras 7.11–7.12 above.

[13] For more detail, see Art 10 of the Vienna Convention, and Aust (n 6 above) 71 f.

[14] Art 11 Vienna Convention lists the possible means, while its Arts 12–15 determine under which conditions the signature, exchange of instruments constituting the treaty, ratification, accept-ance, approval, or adhesion constitute consent to be bound by a treaty. See also on these means, Aust (n 6 above) 75 ff.

[15] eg Arts 28(1)(a), 29 of the Berne Convention; Art 24 of the Rome Convention, which also restricts membership to certain states, in particular those that are also members of the UCC or the Berne Union. On ratification and accession in the context of the Berne Convention, see S Ricketson and J Ginsburg, *International Copyright and Neighbouring Rights: The Berne Convention and Beyond* (2006) 17.03 ff.

obligations to abstain from acts that would go against the purpose of the treaty.[16] Often, it is provided that signatory states can become a party by ratification, while other states that have not signed the treaty while it was open for signature[17] can become a member by accession. This distinction makes no difference once membership is achieved.

(5) Entry into force

8.06 Usually, treaties determine the conditions under which they enter into force. Such conditions are mostly a minimum number of countries to join the treaty; sometimes, additional conditions apply.[18] Usually, treaties determine that they enter into force three months after instruments of ratification or accession in the required number have been deposited.[19] Only 'failing any such provision' in a treaty or agreement by the negotiating parties, the treaty enters into force when all negotiating states express their consent to be bound by the treaty through ratification or otherwise.[20]

8.07 Before the necessary number of ratifications or accessions is achieved and the treaty has entered into force, it does not bind any state—not even those which have already ratified the treaty. For example, the WCT and the WPPT which were concluded in December 1996 entered into force only in March and May of 2002, respectively; consequently, they did not bind any states that had ratified them beforehand. States that accede to or ratify a treaty after its entry into force become bound by it on the date when their consent to be bound is established, or as provided in the treaty[21]—usually three months after the deposit of the relevant instrument.[22]

(6) Reservations

8.08 Even where a state is bound by a treaty, it may have excluded the application of particular provisions by means of a reservation. Reservations are only permitted

---

[16] Art 18 of the Vienna Convention.

[17] eg under Art 23 of the Rome Convention, the Convention was open for signature until 30 June 1961; see also Art 19 of the WCT and Art 28 of the WPPT.

[18] eg Art 28(2)(a) of the Berne Convention regarding Arts 1–21 and the Appendix of the Berne Convention under the Paris Act; it requires ratification or accession by at least five countries which have not declared a reservation with a view to not applying Arts 1–21 and the Appendix, and it requires that France, Spain, the United Kingdom and Northern Ireland as well as the USA have become bound by the Universal Copyright Convention in the version of 1971; for further conditions, see also Art 28(2)(b)–(d) of the Berne Convention.

[19] eg Art 25(1) of the Rome Convention; Art 20 of the WCT and Art 29 of the WPPT.

[20] Art 24(2) of the Vienna Convention.

[21] Art 24(3) ibid; such consent would be established, in this case, by accession or ratification.

[22] eg Art 25(2) of the Rome Convention; Art 21(ii), (iii), and (iv) of the WCT and Art 30(ii)–(iv) of the WPPT.

under certain conditions; in particular, they must not be prohibited by the treaty itself. Mostly, treaties determine whether—and if so, which—reservations are permitted.[23] Where reservations are explicitly permitted, they usually do not require acceptance by other Contracting States.[24] Where a state has made a valid reservation, it is not bound by the treaty provisions that it has excluded from application. As a rule, any state can withdraw its reservation at any point in time and then be fully bound by the relevant treaty provision.[25]

(7) Invalidity, termination, denunciation, and other issues

The invoked treaty must also be valid; the permitted reasons for invalidity are limited to rare cases.[26] Cases of termination, denunciation, and suspension of operation of a treaty by individual Contracting States are similarly rare.[27] Additional issues may have to be examined where treaty application matters, such as transitional provisions and the relation between different treaties.[28] Among such additional issues is also the important one of succession of states with related questions, such as the validity of a treaty for successor states. State succession has been especially relevant to the Berne Convention, which throughout its long history has experienced many instances of extinction, occupation, annexation, separation, re-establishment, creation of states, and particularly cases of independence of formerly dependent territories, such as colonies or the British dominions.[29]

8.09

Legal issues may be quite complex in such cases. For example, Estonia was considered as never having ceased to exist but having been occupied throughout the Soviet period (1940–91), so that the application of treaties to which it had

8.10

---

[23] eg Art 16 of the Rome Convention permits specific reservations; Art 22 of the WCT excludes any reservations; and Art 21 of the WPPT only permits reservations under its Art 15(3). On reservations throughout the different Acts of the Berne Convention, see Ricketson/Ginsburg (n 15 above) 17.22–17.33.

[24] Reservations are unilateral statements, cf the definition in Art 2(1)(d) of the Vienna Convention; for the condition of an acceptance by the other Contracting States, see Art 20 ibid.

[25] Art 22 ibid; Art 18 of the Rome Convention also explicitly allows the scope of the reservation to be reduced. On reservations in detail, see also Aust (n 6 above) 100–30.

[26] Art 42(1) of the Vienna Convention; Arts 46–53 include, eg the reasons of error, fraud, corruption, coercion, and conflict with *ius cogens*. On invalidity, see Aust (n 6 above) 252 ff.

[27] See Arts 54–64 of the Vienna Convention; for the fear, in the context of the adoption of the UCC, that developing countries would denunciate the Berne Convention in order to only become members of the UCC, see also paras 4.20, 4.38, as well as paras 5.231 and 4.16 above and Art 35(2)–(4) of the Berne Convention. For denunciation in respect of the Berne Convention, see Ricketson/Ginsburg (n 15 above) 17.34. For the procedures to be followed in order to assert the invalidity, extinction, denunciation, or suspension, see Arts 65–8 of the Vienna Convention, and for the consequences of invalidity, extinction, or suspension of the application of a treaty, see Arts 69–72 of the Vienna Convention. For suspension, see the example in para 8.10 below.

[28] On the relation between treaties, see ch 24, in particular paras 24.02–24.19 below; also, for the UCC and the Berne Convention, see para 4.38 above.

[29] For a detailed presentation of such instances, see Ricketson/Ginsburg (n 15 above) 17.35–17.68; for the Baltic countries, see para 8.10 below.

acceded during independence (1918–40), including the Berne Convention,[30] was simply suspended during the Soviet period.[31] Accordingly, after independence from the Soviet Union in 1991, Estonia could have been considered bound by all treaties to which it had acceded during earlier independence.[32] Logically, a new accession to the Berne Convention would not have been necessary, but a Declaration of Continuity would have sufficed. Yet, Estonia deposited its instruments of accession to the Berne Convention (Paris Act) on 26 July 1994 to WIPO, and the Berne Convention is considered as having entered into force on 26 October 1994. This contradiction might be solved by considering the re-accession in 1994 as declaratory. Yet, the situation before re-accession remains somewhat unclear, since the Berne Convention was not applied between 20 August 1991 and 26 October 1994 in Estonia, and the Estonian foreign ministry declared in a note to WIPO that Estonia did not recognize its obligations from the 1927 accession; also, the re-accession Act stated that Estonia will apply the Berne Convention (only) from the date of re-accession.[33] This contradiction remains to be resolved.

C. Internal applicability of treaties

(1) Transformation into national law

8.11   The fact that a state is bound by a particular treaty does not automatically mean that a foreign right owner who invokes the treaty in a lawsuit in that state could rely on the application of the treaty; this is only possible if the treaty also applies internally. While treaties generally oblige Contracting States to ensure their

---

[30] Estonia became a Member of the Berne Union (Berlin Act of 1908) in 1927, see <http://www.wipo.int/treaties/en/Remarks.jsp?cnty_id=949C>; the situation of Latvia is similar to that of Estonia. Lithuania's efforts to join the Berne Convention were however not accomplished before Soviet occupation, but the general issues of state succession are similar here.

[31] In Estonia, this is legally less clear than politically; all information on this issue for Estonia was received by Prof H Pisuke (e-mail correspondence of 26/27 September 2007); for the situation in Estonia and a declaration of the Estonian Parliament on the identity of the Republic of Estonia before and after independence, see H Pisuke, 'Building a National Intellectual Property Protection System: Some Issues Concerning Copyright and Related Rights in Estonia' in P Wahlgren (ed), *Scandinavian Studies in Law* Vol XLII: *Intellectual Property* (2002) 127, 141–2. On the clearer international legal status of Lithuania, see S Jakštonytė and M Cvelich, 'Constitutional and International Documents Concerning the International Legal Status of Lithuania' in I Ziemele (ed), *Baltic Yearbook of International Law* (2002) 301 ff. For all Baltic countries in general, see also Aust (n 6 above) 314 f.

[32] In Estonia, this is again legally less clear than politically. For Lithuania, which considered itself bound by treaties joined before 1940, see Letter from Lithuanian President A Brazauskas to the UN Secretary Genera, B Ghali of 4 March 1993; excerpt repr in Jakštonytė/Cvelich (n 31 above) 301, 306. Restoration of Independence was proclaimed by Act of 11 March 1990, ibid 301.

[33] On the date of re-accession, see in the text above; Pisuke (n 31 above) 141–2 and e-mail correspondence.

application in domestic law, they mostly leave the implementation measures to the individual Contracting States.[34] In general, two systems exist for the incorporation of treaties into domestic law; the applicable system is usually determined by national constitutions or similar legal frameworks. First, the so-called 'individual' or 'specific' transformation requires the adoption of specific national norms for all treaty provisions, as in the United Kingdom; in this system, claims in context with a treaty can only be based on the national law that transforms the treaty. Secondly and in contrast, the so-called 'general' transformation only requires legislation to globally express approval of a treaty and to make it part of the domestic law; in this case, the provisions of the treaty are regularly annexed to the parliamentary act or other norm.[35] For this system, it is controversial whether the basis for claims would be the national law which globally transforms the international law, or whether the transformation must only be considered as an order to execute the treaty, so that the treaty would remain the basis of the claim. The approach taken has consequences for the interpretation and application of the law.[36]

As a result of transformation, a treaty is internally applicable. Internal or domestic application can be ascertained not only by a specific national norm, but also by means of its interpretation by a court in light of the underlying treaty. For example, a particular Austrian provision required the relevant collecting society to allocate the 'greater part' of the income from a particular kind of use to its social funds that were usually accessible only to domestic authors.[37] The question was whether the greater part related to the overall income (including from the use of foreign works) or the income from the use of domestic works only. The court interpreted the provision on the basis of domestic law and, in an *obiter dictum*, in

8.12

---

[34] eg Art 36(1) of the Berne Convention; Art 26(1) of the Rome Convention; Art 14(1) of the WCT; and Art 23(1) of the WPPT; Art 1(1) phr 3 of the TRIPS Agreement is even more explicit. However, recent bilateral treaties concluded by the USA do not admit this flexibility, see para 12.40 below. For a short description of relevant national rules in the USA and several European countries, see Aust (n 6 above) 146 ff.

[35] This is the practice, eg in Germany, Austria, and Switzerland, and other civil law countries; B Simma, *Universelles Völkerrecht* (1984) paras 856–8; Shaw (n 10 above) 129; on the related doctrines of dualism (international and national law as two separate legal orders) and monism (unity of international and national law), see ibid 121–4; K Partsch, 'International Law and Municipal Law' in R Bernhardt (ed), *Encyclopaedia of Public International Law* (1995) Vol II, 1183, 1184 ff.

[36] In particular, the legal basis and therefore the methods of interpretation would be different; these consequences are, however, theoretical rather than practical today; eg Partsch (n 35 above) 1191; A Bleckmann, *Völkerrecht* (2001) nn 428–9.

[37] More precisely, they were open to authors who had a direct contract with the collecting society; according to the prevailing international system, these were mainly domestic authors.

the light of the obligation of national treatment so as to allow deduction only from the income for domestic works.[38]

8.13 A treaty norm is self-executing, if it is specific enough to be directly applied by the courts; often, also the establishment of subjective rights or duties for individual persons is considered a condition. The term 'self-executing' was developed under US constitutional law; in Europe, the term 'direct applicability of treaties' is used instead; both terms presuppose internal applicability of treaties, but concepts may vary. Usually, a judge decides by treaty interpretation whether a provision is self-executing, unless the treaty or implementing law itself clearly and explicitly excludes provisions from being self-executing.[39]

(2) Rank in the national hierarchy of norms

8.14 Even where international law has been transformed into national law, its applicability may be affected by other conflicting national norms. Therefore, the rank in the hierarchy of different national law sources is relevant. States are free to determine the rank of transformed international law within the national legal order; usually, they do so under constitutional law. For example, laws transforming treaties in France and Lithuania have a higher rank than other national laws, so that they cannot be derogated by subsequent national law.[40] In the Netherlands, courts cannot review the constitutionality of laws transforming treaties (though not customary international law), but they can test the validity of such laws against treaties that are directly applicable (Articles 120 and 94 of the Dutch Constitution). By contrast, the Lithuanian Constitutional Court has specified that no international agreement may contradict the constitution; in some European countries, only 'general rules of public international law' prevail over national law.[41]

---

[38] Austrian Supreme Court (OGH of 14 July 1987, (1987) Medien und Recht 212 ff, with comment by M Walter, 216–18).

[39] At the origin of the term under US constitutional law was the case *Foster and Elam v Neilson*, 27 US (2Pet) 253 (1829), see AD McNair, *The Law of Treaties* (1961) 79 ff. Where a treaty is self-executing in the USA, it is directly applicable in domestic proceedings as part of the 'Law of the Land'. The US Berne Implementation Act (PubL 100-568, s 2) has explicitly excluded direct applicability, not least with a view to moral rights under the Berne Convention, but also according to general US practice, see P Geller, 'International Copyright: An Introduction' in P Geller (ed), *International Copyright Law and Practice*, Vol I (looseleaf release 17) § 3[2] (a), 3 [2] (d); W Patry, *Patry on Copyright* (2007) 23–4. On self-executing treaties in the USA, see also Aust (n 6 above) 158–9. On direct applicability mainly in Europe, see A Bleckmann, 'Self-executing Treaty Provisions' in R Bernhardt (ed), *Encyclopaedia of Public International Law* Vol IV (2000) 374.

[40] For Lithuania, see Jakštonytė/Cvelich (n 31 above) 309; Art 55 of the French Constitution.

[41] Jakštonytė/Cvelich (n 31 above) 308, regarding Art 138 of the Lithuanian Constitution under which ratified treaties are a constituent part of the Lithuanian legal system. For prevailing 'general rules', eg Art 25 of the German Constitution; for an overview of some European countries (in context with implementation of treaties) and the USA, see Aust (n 6 above) 146 ff, 159–60.

In most countries of the Continental European system and in the United States, **8.15**
and in particular where a constitution does not explicitly provide for any particular rank, transformed treaties are equal to other national laws. Within the national
hierarchy of norms, it is therefore possible for a subsequent national law to derogate the earlier law that transforms a treaty (ie the rule of *lex posterior derogat legi
priori*).[42] Accordingly, if subsequent or higher-ranked national law of a given
country has derogated the law transforming the treaty, a foreign right owner who
invokes the treaty can no longer be successful in a private law suit because the
judges are bound to the national rules valid in that country, even if these rules are
not in compliance with the international treaties to which the country is bound.
For example, in context with the above-mentioned Austrian court decision,[43] the
national legislator introduced a norm according to which the 'greater part' of the
relevant income of the collecting society had to refer to the 'entire' relevant
income (ie including that earned from the exploitation of foreign works).[44] This
amendment was meant to clarify the previous norm. Even if a right owner
considered this amendment to violate the national treatment obligation under
the Berne Convention,[45] he could not pursue his rights in a private lawsuit and
not even obtain a clarification on the basis of the Berne Convention. In such a
case, the only possibility of obtaining clarification and, possibly, ensuring the
application of a treaty is then to proceed to the governmental level at which it may
be decided to seek dispute settlement between or among states.

D. Dispute settlement under international law

(1) Overview

In general, public international law provides for the following means for the **8.16**
peaceful settlement[46] of disputes between sovereign states: (a) political or diplomatic means, which leave the parties in control of the dispute and enable them to
accept or dismiss proposals for settlement, and (b) legal forms of settling disputes,

---

[42] Partsch (n 35 above) 1194; for the USA in particular, see eg D Bederman, *International Law
Frameworks* (2001) 164–5.
[43] n 38 above; already in context with the initial phase of legal proceedings, the law was
amended.
[44] Art II(6) phr 3 of Federal Law of 1980 amending the Copyright Act, as amended by Federal
Law of 29 November 1989 Amending the Copyright Act and the Copyright Amendment Law
1980.
[45] Upon an in-depth analysis, different views may be held on this issue, see Walter (n 38 above)
217 with further refs; M Walter, 'Le Principe du traitement national et le récent développement du
droit d'auteur: rapport supplémentaire' in P Brügger (ed), *Congress for the Centennial of the Berne
Convention* (1987) 170, 172 f.
[46] Art 2(3) of the Charter of the United Nations obliges Member States to settle their international disputes by peaceful means (rather than military or similar means).

which result in binding decisions by international courts or arbitration bodies on the basis of public international law.

(2) Political means

8.17 The political means include direct diplomatic negotiations and various procedures involving disinterested third parties. A third party can perform 'Good Offices' by persuading the disputing parties to negotiate with each other without itself becoming involved in the negotiations.[47] Instead, it can mediate by participating in the negotiations and submitting non-binding proposals for a solution.[48] Good Offices and mediation can result from an initiative by the third party or from the request of the disputing parties. In conciliation procedures, third party committees or individuals submit to the disputing parties proposals for solutions based on political or equitable considerations rather than, as in arbitration and court procedures, legal regulations.[49]

(3) Legal forms

8.18 The legal forms of dispute settlement are performed by international arbitration bodies and judicial authorities.[50] Both fora are similar in the following regards: their competence initially derives from the will of the parties; arbitrators and judges, once appointed, are independent of the parties and their governments; decisions are reached on the basis of legal rules and a strictly regulated procedure; and judgments or arbitration awards are binding on the parties. At the same time, both types of proceeding differ in particular by the greater degree of institutionalization of the international courts, and the greater influence of the disputing parties on the composition of the arbitration bodies and the procedures to be applied in arbitration.

8.19 Many treaties lay down obligations to peacefully settle disputes.[51] They include treaties that exclusively deal with dispute settlement[52] or that deal with other matters but also include specific dispute settlement provisions,[53] or that refer to

---

[47] On Good Offices, eg R Bindschedler, 'Good Offices' in Bernhardt (n 35 above) 601 ff.
[48] On mediation, eg R Bindschedler, 'Conciliation and Mediation' ibid Vol I (1992) 721 ff.
[49] ibid.
[50] On arbitration proceedings, eg H-J Schlochauer, 'Arbitration' in Bernhardt (n 48 above) 215 ff; on international law courts, see H Steinberger, 'Judicial Settlement of International Disputes' ibid Vol III (1997) 42 ff; on both, see Aust (n 6 above) 291 ff and 294 ff.
[51] In particular, the Charter of the United Nations, Art 33(1), Art 36(3).
[52] eg the WTO's Dispute Settlement Understanding, see paras 10.116 ff below.
[53] Many bilateral and regional trade agreements do so, see paras 12.38, 12.40 and 11.22–11.23, 11.26, and 11.66 below.

the relevant provisions of the United Nations' Charter or directly to the procedures before the International Court of Justice (ICJ).[54]

(4) The ICJ

The ICJ was created as the principal judicial organ of the United Nations and is **8.20**
an integral part of this organization.[55] The Statute of the ICJ requires the parties
in dispute to accept the Court's jurisdiction. Even for the parties to the Statute of
the ICJ, such acceptance is optional. It can be declared at any time *ad hoc, post
hoc*, or even *ante hoc*. A prior, binding recognition of the jurisdiction of the ICJ
occurs through declaration to recognize the compulsory jurisdiction of the ICJ,
or through ratification of agreements that contain a reference to the ICJ.[56] Absent
such prior, binding recognition, the ICJ only hears a dispute between state parties
if they specifically agree to present it there.[57]

Where a dispute is successfully brought, the ICJ has to render its judgment in **8.21**
accordance with international law; this does not exclude a decision *ex aequo et
bono* if the parties so agree.[58] Disputes are then resolved in a number of ways.
Where, during the proceedings, the parties inform the ICJ that they have reached
a settlement, the Court issues an order for the removal of the case from its list.
Where an applicant state withdraws the case, the ICJ issues the same kind of
order. Otherwise, the Court delivers a judgment which only has binding force
between the parties (*inter partes*) and in respect of the particular case.[59]
Accordingly, the interpretation of a particular provision of a treaty does not bind
those member countries that have not been parties to the dispute.[60]

The ICJ judgment throughout its long history is final and without appeal.[61] It **8.22**
only clarifies the contents of the international provision at issue, but does not

---

[54] For the Berne, Universal Copyright, and Rome Conventions, see paras 8.23–8.26 below.

[55] Art 92 of the Charter of the United Nations to which its Statute is annexed. It succeeded the
Permanent Court of International Justice also as regards the Rules of Court and the Statute. On Arts
92–6 ibid and on the ICJ in general, see B Simma, *The Charter of the United Nations: A Commentary*
(1994) 973 ff. On the Court and its work, see S Rosenne, *The World Court* (6th edn, 2003).

[56] Art 36 (2) of the ICJ Statute for the compulsory jurisdiction and Art 36(1) ibid for the general
recognition; on the jurisdiction of the ICJ, see H-J Schlochauer, 'International Court of Justice' in
Bernhardt (n 35 above) 1084 ff, 1089 ff, and on the procedure 1093 ff.

[57] Art 36(1) of the ICJ Statute.

[58] Art 38(1) ibid, which further specifies what law the Court applies, such as international conventions, customary international law, and general principles of law; as well as Art 38(2) ibid. On
these sources of international law and their hierarchical order, as well as judgments *ex aequo et bono*,
see Schlochauer (n 56 above) 1092–3.

[59] Art 59 of the ICJ Statute.

[60] Art 33(1) phr 2 of the Berne Convention obliges a country bringing the dispute before the ICJ
to inform the International Bureau which then informs the other member countries so that they
may decide whether to enter the dispute.

[61] Art 60 of the ICJ Statute.

convict a party or order any sanctions.[62] Also, national laws or final court decisions at the national level that do not comply with the ICJ's statement of the law continue to be valid, unless they are voluntarily amended or overruled by the national authorities. The relevant party simply undertakes to comply with the ICJ's decision; failure to comply means a violation of the UN Charter, but a suit to appeal non-compliance may only be made to the UN Security Council, which may make recommendations and decide on measures.[63] Although the virtual lack of sanctions in case of continuous violations seems to make ICJ dispute settlement a weak mechanism, general experience has shown that parties have complied with most of the ICJ's judgments.[64]

(5) Copyright and neighbouring rights conventions

8.23 The Berne, Universal Copyright, and Rome Conventions contain practically identical references to proceedings before the ICJ.[65] While recourse to the ICJ is generally possible without such references, they have a self-standing meaning in that they constitute binding *ante hoc* declarations to recognize the jurisdiction of the ICJ.[66] The WCT and the WPPT do not contain such references; accordingly, no party is bound to accept the jurisdiction of the ICJ where a dispute about the WCT or WPPT is brought before the ICJ; yet, if both parties agree, recourse is possible under the conditions of the ICJ Statute.

8.24 The obligatory nature of recourse to the ICJ was already controversial under the Rome Convention. While the references to the ICJ under the Rome Convention and the Brussels Act of the Berne Convention were obligatory, a later tendency towards optional recourse emerged, since many countries found the recognition of the ICJ's obligatory jurisdiction and the resulting loss of sovereignty difficult to accept.[67] Accordingly, the Stockholm Act of the Berne Convention introduced the possibility of declaring a reservation by which the obligatory jurisdiction of the Court may be excluded.[68]

---

[62] W Nordemann, K Vinck, P Hertin, and G Meyer, *International Copyright* (1990) Introduction n 40.

[63] Art 94 of the UN Charter.

[64] R Wallace, *International Law* (5th edn, 2005) 337; in intellectual property though, no cases have been brought before the ICJ to date.

[65] Arts 33, XV, and 30, respectively; see para 24.21 below. The same is true in industrial property for the Paris Convention (Art 20) and the Patent Cooperation Treaty (Art 59/Art 64(5)). For an overview of dispute settlement provisions in intellectual property treaties, see WIPO Doc WO/GA/XXI/3 at 3 ff.

[66] See para 8.20 above; they are not declarations of recognition of compulsory jurisdiction under Art 36(2) of the ICJ Statute, see Steinberger (n 50 above) 49–50.

[67] C Masouyé, *Guide to the Rome Convention and to the Phonograms Convention* (1981) n 30.3 RC; for the Berne Convention: Ricketson/Ginsburg (n 15 above) 17.85–17.86.

[68] Art 33(2) of the Berne Convention; similar reservations are contained in Art 28(2) of the Paris Convention and Art 64(5) of the Patent Cooperation Treaty. The following Berne Union countries

Where no reservation is made or permitted, the *ante hoc* recognition of juris- **8.25**
diction only applies where the disputing parties do not agree on some other
method of settlement[69] and where negotiations have failed. It also only applies to
'disputes' between two or more parties; in individual instances, the delineation of
disputes in international law from mere differences of opinion may be difficult.
For a dispute, parties must disagree on a specific point of law or fact and the resolution of the dispute must have practical effects on the relations of the parties.[70]
The disputes must concern the interpretation or application of the Convention;
regarding any other disputes, the general rules apply.[71]

In the field of copyright and related rights, countries have not yet made use of the **8.26**
possibility of having recourse to the ICJ, although the texts of the relevant conventions have given rise to a number of issues needing clarification. One may
only presume that it would seem politically risky to possibly affect generally good
international relations by bringing an intellectual property dispute before the
ICJ;[72] by contrast, panel procedures applied in international trade law seem to
have been accepted as less 'weighty' procedures in view of political relations.
Reactions to this situation are described in the following chapter.[73]

---

have declared a reservation: Algeria, the Bahamas, Cuba, Democratic People's Republic of Korea,
Egypt, Guatemala, India, Indonesia, Israel, Jordan, Lesotho, Liberia, Libya, Lithuania, Malta,
Mauritius, Mongolia, Nepal, Oman, Saint Lucia, South Africa, Tanzania, Thailand, Tunisia, Turkey,
Venezuela, and Vietnam.

[69] On other methods of settlement, see paras 8.16 ff above.

[70] L Henkin, RC Pugh, O Schachter, and H Smit, *International Law* (1993) 776 ff.

[71] For the means of dispute settlement under public international law, see paras 8.18–8.19, and
for the ICJ, paras 8.20–8.22 above.

[72] Similarly, U Joos and R Moufang, 'Report on the Second Ringberg Symposium' in FK Beier
and G Schricker (eds), *GATT or WIPO? New Ways in the International Protection of Intellectual
Property* (1989) 1, 19 ('the sued state would interpret the action as an unfriendly act').

[73] paras 9.05 and 9.07 ff below; see also ch 16 below on WIPO's initiative in the early 1990s.

Part II

THE INCLUSION OF COPYRIGHT AND NEIGHBOURING RIGHTS IN TRADE TREATIES AND TRADE MEASURES

9

REASONS FOR THE SHIFT TOWARDS
THE TRADE CONTEXT

A. Factual developments after the last revision of the Berne Convention and the adoption of the Rome Convention

(1) Technical and social developments

From the very beginning of copyright protection, when the emergence of print- **9.01**
ing techniques triggered the system of privileges,[1] technical developments have
resulted in the emergence of new kinds of works and new kinds of uses which
have provoked the adaptation of existing laws in the field. The extent of the technical progress that has taken place since the last revision of the Berne Convention
and the adoption of the Rome Convention has inevitably had repercussions on
copyright and neighbouring rights laws. Examples have included: the emergence
of cable (re)transmission and satellite broadcasting; the improvement of reproduction techniques available even to consumers (offering better quality, greater
speed, and more options such as colour reproduction and private audio and
audiovisual copying); the emergence of computer programs; and the growing
importance of databases.[2]

---

[1] See J Cavalli, *La Genèse de la Convention de Berne pour la protection des œuvres littéraires et artistiques du 9 Septembre 1886* (1986) 12–15, and paras 1.07 and 2.03 above.
[2] Digital technology and challenges by the internet were perceived as important for copyright
only after the adoption of the TRIPS Agreement, see eg paras 17.07–17.09 below.

9.02   This increase in new modes of exploitation and emergence of new types of work has been accompanied by increased possibilities for the population in industrialized countries, in particular in Europe, for making use of protected works and the subject matter of neighbouring rights. Importantly, trade unions had attained greater amounts of leisure time and also increasing wages for their employees. As a result, more time and money than before became available for enjoying music, films, theatre plays, watching TV, playing computer games, etc—an opportunity greatly enhanced by a diversification of exploitation, for example the exploitation of cinema films also on television, by video sales, rental or lending, and private reproduction. Indeed, the nature of these social developments was reflected in notions such as 'mass markets' (or specifically 'mass uses' in other languages), 'consumers' and 'cultural *industries*' or 'copyright *industries*' that emerged in the 1980s. In developing countries, the more easily accessible reproduction techniques and the resulting piracy were perceived as a quite attractive means to escape from poverty.[3]

(2) Economic developments

9.03   Due to these technical and social developments, as well as to the globalization of markets, the economic importance of copyright and neighbouring rights grew tremendously. Yet, rather than this fact alone, it was the awareness of it in industry and government that was perhaps the most significant reason for the shift of intellectual property toward the trade context. Such awareness was brought about by economic studies, carried out in several countries since the 1970s.[4] The unexpectedly high percentages of gross national product generated by the copyright industries, and the ranking of the copyright industries ahead of other national industries which, until then, had been considered as the leading ones drew industrial and governmental attention to the fact that copyright had become an important element of the national and worldwide economy, in particular for those countries which exported large quantities of copyright-relevant products. Therefore, it became a greater focus of interest for trade politicians, even in countries which had until then looked upon copyright and neighbouring rights as an essentially cultural matter. This was all the more true in view of the phenomenon of piracy, which became increasingly threatening during the 1980s. 'Piracy' as used by the affected industries referred to the exploitation of works or other protected subject matter without the consent of the authors or other right holders and,

---

³ S von Lewinski, 'The Role of Copyright in Modern International Trade Law' (1994) 161 RIDA 5, 37–41.

⁴ On the economic studies with respect to copyright industries conducted and published between 1959 and 1984 in the USA, Sweden, Germany, etc, cf H Cohen Jehoram, 'Critical Reflections on the Economic Importance of Copyright' in ALAI (ed), *Journées d'études, Munich 1988* (1989) 19 ff.

hence, without paying any licence fees; the reasons for the lack of consent or payment were either that the relevant countries did not provide for any protection at all, or that they did not provide for the protection of foreign works or other subject matter (so that such 'piracy' uses were actually legal), or that such protection was granted but not adequately enforced. The losses of potential profits suffered by the copyright industries were particularly great in the 'newly industrialized countries' (eg at the time, India, Brazil, and South Korea), where so-called 'piracy industries' developed. The desire of copyright-exporting countries to secure the potential profits from such exploitation[5] thus became a matter of priority.[6]

B. The potential of the existing conventions

The potential of the Berne and Rome Conventions to meet the needs that had **9.04** arisen from the above-mentioned factual developments was limited. Their provisions either did not, or did not clearly, cover new kinds of uses, such as original cable transmission,[7] or were unclear as to their coverage of new kinds of products, in particular computer programs, as protected works.[8] In addition, these Conventions contained no (or extremely limited) minimum standards on enforcement provisions.[9] Yet, appropriate enforcement provisions are essential for the proper operation of copyright and neighbouring rights protection; even the highest standards of protection under substantive law have no or very little effect if they cannot be enforced by police, customs authorities, courts, etc.[10]

These deficiencies of the Conventions could have been remedied, in principle, **9.05** through the available dispute settlement mechanisms in respect of unclear provisions or by revision in respect of lacking or unclear provisions. However, as previously illustrated, available dispute settlement mechanisms, in particular recourse to the International Court of Justice, have not been used, presumably because Member Countries were discouraged by their shortcomings;[11] the idea of a revision of the Berne Convention was not pursued by WIPO within the usual rhythm of twenty years, presumably because Member Countries in WIPO were

---

⁵ Similar reasons apply to other fields of intellectual property, see paras 9.07 ff and n 19 below.

⁶ von Lewinski (n 3 above) 41–3; for the economic importance of all intellectual property, see P Katzenberger and A Kur, 'TRIPS and Intellectual Property' in FK Beier and G Schricker (eds), *From GATT to TRIPS: The Agreement on Trade-Related Aspects of Intellectual Property Rights* (1996) 1, 8–9.

⁷ Under the Berne Convention, a minimum right for this use is provided only for specific kinds of works as specified in its Arts 11, 11ᵗᵉʳ.

⁸ See paras 7.13–7.19 above on the respective problems of interpretation.

⁹ For the Berne Convention, see paras 5.234–5.242 above; the Rome Convention does not contain any enforcement provision.

¹⁰ For an example, see para 10.103 below.

¹¹ See for more detail para 8.26 above.

discouraged by the difficulties in achieving the required unanimity[12] that was experienced at the last Revision of 1971.[13] Unanimity seemed all the more difficult to achieve since the economic importance of copyright and, consequently, the conflicts of interests between developing and industrialized countries, but also among industrialized countries, had grown after 1971.[14] The WIPO instead chose to encourage a harmonious, parallel development of national laws by the so-called 'guided development';[15] although this strategy was certainly useful,[16] it could not completely satisfy the needs of, in particular, industrialized countries for the introduction or clarification of certain minimum standards of protection.

9.06 A revision of the Rome Convention, although requiring only a two-thirds majority,[17] would have been difficult too, because it would have involved the three different international organizations which administer the Convention (WIPO, UNESCO, and ILO), and also the often conflicting interests of the three different groups of rights owners (performers, phonogram producers, and broadcasting organizations). Also, these Conventions themselves did not provide for any means to gain new Member Countries, in particular those whose 'piracy industries' benefited from the fact that their countries were not yet members of these Conventions. Finally, those governments which were being urged by their copyright industries to work intensively on improving international protection standards perceived certain obstacles in the WIPO framework: the important role of developing countries in WIPO (as a UN specialized agency) tended to promote the typical north–south confrontation, and it would be copyright experts rather than pragmatically thinking trade representatives who would be representing Member Countries in WIPO.[18]

---

[12] Art 27(3) of the Berne Convention; see also para 5.254 above.

[13] See paras 4.22 above and 17.01 below.

[14] For the pessimistic view in respect of a possible future revision of the Berne Convention, see the General Director of WIPO, A Bogsch, 'The First Hundred Years of the Berne Convention for the Protection of Literary and Artistic Works' (1986) Copyright 327 and A Bogsch, 'Brief History of the First 25 Years of the World Intellectual Property Organisation' (1992) Copyright 247, 262.

[15] M Ficsor, *The Law of Copyright and the Internet: The 1996 WIPO Treaties, their Interpretation and Implementation* (2002) nn 1.03 ff; paras 17.01–17.02 below.

[16] Among others, it brought to the attention of governments new challenges to copyright law and promoted exchange of information and concurrent developments.

[17] See para 6.80 above; Art 29(2) of the Rome Convention.

[18] J Reinbothe and A Howard, 'The State of Play in the Negotiations on TRIPS (GATT/Uruguay Round)' (1991) 5 EIPR 157; for the deficiencies mentioned under paras 9.04–9.06, see also von Lewinski (n 3 above) 43–5; Katzenberger/Kur (n 6 above) 10–16, in particular of the issue of limited membership.

C. The choice of GATT as a new forum

Given this situation of stagnation in the development of international copyright **9.07** and neighbouring rights protection,[19] and the growing need in particular of industrialized countries to improve international protection, the search for new and more efficient ways to achieve better international protection led to the realm of trade law. The USA was one of the main promoters of this new approach; in its Trade Act of 1988, it treated intellectual property as an important focus of trade law not only at the multilateral level but also in the context of bilateral treaties and unilateral measures.[20] Early attempts to include certain aspects of intellectual property into the General Agreement on Tariffs and Trade (GATT) had already been made at the Tokyo Round which preceded the Uruguay Round, but were not finally successful until the Uruguay Round.[21] The perspective of including intellectual property in the GATT framework promised the copyright industries and the governments of their countries several advantages over the fora of the existing Conventions, in particular WIPO.

First, new provisions could be adopted more easily in the GATT than in the **9.08** framework of specialized treaties that had a very limited scope. Although decisions in the GATT similarly had to be taken under the principle of consensus,[22] consensus was easier to achieve because, at the end of a negotiation round, decisions had to be made on the entire package of quite diverse matters which had been negotiated in parallel and which could touch upon, for example, the free movement of specified goods of different categories or particular kinds of services. In such a situation, a country would have to weigh its respective interests in the different areas of negotiation and might be ready to compromise, for example in the field of intellectual property, in order to secure advantages in agriculture or other areas which might seem more important for the economy of that country. In other words, the overall economic importance of the entire package would lead countries to make concessions in a field such as intellectual property that they would otherwise not have been ready to make.

---

[19] The same stagnation occurred, for similar reasons, in the other areas of intellectual property, see eg Katzenberger/Kur (n 6 above) 15; Reinbothe/Howard (n 18 above) 157.

[20] For the Trade Act and the bilateral treaties and unilateral measures, see paras 12.02 ff and 13.01–13.10 below.

[21] It concerned counterfeit goods; see the Draft Agreement negotiated by the European Community and the USA during the Tokyo Round on measures against the importation of counterfeit goods, and a detailed analysis of the negotiation results in (1980) GRUR Int 656 (in German); Katzenberger/Kur (n 6 above) 1, 4.

[22] See para 10.14 below.

9.09 Secondly, the negotiations in the GATT framework were perceived as more dynamic and less institutionalized, which may have been an advantage for industrialized, but possibly a disadvantage for developing countries.[23] Thirdly, the more pragmatic attitude of negotiators who were mainly trade experts rather than intellectual property experts was seen as an advantage by industry.[24] Fourthly, extended coverage of international protection was perceived as one of the advantages: the GATT already covered, if not more countries than the traditional Conventions, then at least many countries that were not members of the traditional Conventions.[25] In addition, trade liberalization in the broad areas covered by the GATT was perceived as bringing about overall economic advantages and a resulting increase in prosperity for all countries[26]—including developing countries—and thus seemed so attractive that the prospects of including many more countries in the international protection system than those already members of the traditional copyright and related rights conventions appeared very positive. The strategy of the package deal here again made it possible to include even those countries for which the particular area of intellectual property was of less interest. Finally, the GATT had already established a very successful mechanism for the settlement of disputes between countries, including sanctions in cases of ongoing non-compliance. Industrialized countries saw the potential application of this mechanism to intellectual property disputes as another advantage, all the more so as it turned out that the Uruguay Round would even strengthen the dispute settlement procedure.[27]

---

[23] On this aspect, see J Watal, *Intellectual Property Rights in the WTO and Developing Countries* (2001) 43 ff.

[24] Reinbothe/Howard (n 18 above) 157. However, in particular academics were rather hesitant towards this aspect, since they feared lack of expert knowledge within GATT, see U Joos and R Moufang, 'Report on the Second Ringberg Symposium' in FK Beier and G Schricker (eds), *GATT or WIPO? New Ways in the International Protection of Intellectual Property* (1989) 1, 32. Indeed, 'between 1986 and almost 1990, virtually no government sent intellectual property experts to GATT negotiations in Geneva', E Simon, 'Intellectual Property Issues in the General Agreements on Tariffs and the North American Free Trade Agreement' in H Hansen (ed), *International Intellectual Property Law & Policy* Vol I (1996) 153, 154.

[25] See for the situation at the end of 1994 Katzenberger/Kur (n 6 above) 11–12.

[26] On these advantages and the goal of GATT in general, see para 10.01 below.

[27] On the more critical attitude of developing countries towards the inclusion of intellectual property into the TRIPS Agreement and towards the WTO in general, see paras 10.19–10.22 below. On the critical attitude of experts, see eg Joos and Moufang (n 24 above) 32–4, 40–1, and Simon (n 24 above) 153, referring to scepticism about integration of trade and intellectual property as expressed at the Ringberg Symposium of the Max Planck Institute. On the dispute settlement under GATT and WTO, see paras 10.15–10.16 and 10.114–10.132 below.

10

THE INCLUSION OF COPYRIGHT
AND NEIGHBOURING RIGHTS IN
THE GATT/WTO

A. Short presentation of GATT/WTO in general

(1) The General Agreement on Tariffs and Trade (GATT)

(a) The genesis of GATT

(i) Historical background   The GATT is one of several international instru- **10.01** ments aimed at avoiding the mistakes that led to the world economic crisis in the 1930s. In 1930, the USA, followed by another twenty-five countries, increased their tariffs by about 60 per cent on the basis of the Smoot-Hawley Tariff Act. As a consequence, world trade decreased by two-thirds. The resulting world economic crisis, which was worse than any before, was also considered one of several reasons for the emergence of totalitarian systems in Europe and for the Second World War.[1] Against the background of these experiences, the founders of the

---

[1] HG Krenzler, 'Die Nachkriegsentwicklung des Welthandelssystems: Von der Havanna-Charta zur WTO' in HJ Prieß and GM Berrisch (eds), *WTO-Handbuch* (2003) 1, 2.

GATT sought to prevent any protectionism and closed national economies; instead, the liberalization of trade, in particular by abolishing or reducing tariffs and by unhampered competition on the world markets, was viewed as crucial means for worldwide prosperity, full employment, and healthy economies—and, as a consequence, as a guarantee for peace.[2]

10.02 With these aspirations in mind, the Bretton Woods Conference led to the founding of the International Monetary Fund and the International Bank for Reconstruction and Development (World Bank) as early as 1944. As a third pillar of a new world economic order, an International Trade Organization (ITO) was to be established as a specialized agency of the United Nations Organization (UNO) founded in 1945, under the auspices of the Economic and Social Council, one of the principal organs of the UNO.[3] Since the negotiations on the establishment of the ITO took more time than the simultaneous ones on tariffs, and since tariff reductions were considered to be very urgently needed, states decided to first and provisionally regulate the reduction of tariffs and non-tariff trade barriers.[4] Accordingly, on 31 October 1947 twenty-three states signed the GATT 1947, a multilateral trade agreement made provisionally applicable from 1 January 1948.[5]

10.03 (ii) **The ITO failure** This provisional Agreement was to be integrated into the planned ITO at a later time. In the meantime, an Interim Commission provisionally administered the GATT. The plan for the ITO was further pursued at the UN Conference on Trade and Employment[6] in Havana, when fifty-four of sixty-three participating countries adopted the Havana Charter on 24 March 1948. This Charter provided not only for the establishment of the ITO, but also for a dispute settlement mechanism, the abolition of trade barriers, competition rules, and other economic issues, such as employment and economic policy. Still, its adoption seemed unacceptable to several countries, in particular the USA, where resistance had built up in the legislative branch. Liberals were afraid of a strong regulatory character of the ITO, while protectionists opposed the restriction of the USA's sovereignty to take protectionist measures. The fact that the USA had initially proposed the establishment of the ITO but then was no longer willing to

---

[2] This is also reflected in the Preamble of the GATT 1947, which mentions as its goals the raising of living standards, realization of full employment, an increasing level of real income, and an effective demand. See also A Lowenfeld, *International Economic Law* (2002) 21–2.

[3] Conference on Trade and United Nation Employment (1947–8) UNYB 522–3, 972 ff.

[4] This procedure was followed also because the US President at that time was only empowered to decide on the conclusion of trade agreements, but not on the accession to an international organization for which only the legislative branch was competent.

[5] Protocol of Provisional Application of the General Agreement on Tariffs and Trade, UNTS 55, 308. On the development up to this time, see Lowenfeld (n 2 above) 22–5.

[6] cf n 3 above.

ratify the Havana Charter finally hindered its entry into force.[7] Accordingly, the plan to establish the ITO was never realized. A second attempt by the parties of the GATT in 1954/5 to establish an international trade organization, the then so-called 'Organization for Trade Cooperation', failed due to the US legislature.[8]

(b) GATT as a de facto organization

Thereafter, the GATT functioned as a simple agreement; the Interim Commission that had provisionally administered the agreement later became its Secretariat. The Contracting Parties' needs to coordinate, cooperate, and settle disputes resulted in a de facto machinery that included permanent organizational bodies, structures, and procedures. As a result, the GATT was recognized as a de facto international organization.[9] In particular, the GATT worked as a forum for regular negotiations on the reduction or abolition of tariffs and non-tariff trade barriers; Contracting Parties negotiated in so-called Rounds, which lasted for relatively longer periods[10] and concerned predetermined issues.[11]

10.04

(c) Crisis of GATT before the Uruguay Round

After the conclusion of the Tokyo Round in 1979, the GATT entered into a crisis. In the preceding Rounds, many self-standing agreements had been adopted in a way that not all Contracting Parties of the GATT were bound. Also, some of the agreements adopted in GATT Rounds provided for separate administrative bodies and special provisions, such as those regarding dispute settlement. Individual Contracting Parties often modified the scope of application of particular agreements between one another by separate, implicit or explicit agreements. The dispute settlement mechanism, which required the consensus of all parties including the 'defendant', became ever less successful due to this requirement. In addition, the role of the GATT became subject to doubts as a consequence of unilateral trade sanctions.[12] Indeed, major trade powers succeeded in concluding so-called 'voluntary' agreements on the self-restriction of exports to benefit the

10.05

---

7 Krenzler (n 1 above) n 11.

8 ibid n 12.

9 J Jackson, *The World Trading System* (1997) 42.

10 The overall eight concluded negotiation rounds took place in 1947 in Geneva, in 1949 in Annecy, in 1950–1 in Torquay, as well as—each in Geneva—in 1955–6 and 1961–2 (so-called Dillon Round), in 1964–7 (so-called Kennedy Round), in 1973–9 (Tokyo Round), and in 1986–94 (Uruguay Round).

11 The first five Rounds only dealt with the reduction of tariffs for industrial goods; thereafter, negotiations also covered the reduction of non-tariff trade barriers in many areas, including, in the Uruguay Round, intellectual property.

12 PT Stoll and F Schorkopf, *WTO-Welthandelsordnung und Welthandelsrecht* (2002) n 17.

domestic industries while violating GATT obligations—which themselves could not be sufficiently enforced.[13]

10.06 The subsequent Uruguay Round (1986–94) therefore had the important task of making the GATT coherent and enforceable again. In addition, after the GATT 1947 up to the Tokyo Round had successfully reduced or abolished tariffs and non-tariff barriers in the very large area of the trade in goods, it had to increase its importance by extending its rules to new areas of international trade, such as services and intellectual property that were then included in the new General Agreement on Trade in Services (GATS) and the Agreement on Trade-Related Aspects of Intellectual Property Rights (TRIPS) as adopted at the end of the Uruguay Round.

(2) The World Trade Organization

(a) The success of the Uruguay Round

10.07 (i) '**Single undertaking approach**' The Uruguay Round succeeded in accomplishing these tasks. Besides extending its rules to services and intellectual property, it adopted the 'single undertaking approach', under which all Contracting Parties either had to adopt all multilateral agreements concluded under the preceding GATT and at the Uruguay Round as one package, or to refuse the entire package. This approach replaced the preceding 'à la carte approach' and successfully re-established the coherence of the world trade system. Accordingly, the Final Act of the Uruguay Round contains forty-six agreements and twenty-five resolutions.

10.08 One of them, the Agreement Establishing the World Trade Organization (WTO Agreement) itself includes the following annexes: Annex 1A comprises the so-called 'GATT 1994',[14] which is essentially the so-called 'GATT 1947' (all agreements adopted under the GATT before the entry into force of the WTO Agreement, namely around thirty agreements adopted at the Uruguay Round and around 200 previous GATT agreements with six Understandings, and twelve further separate agreements on the trade in goods). Annex 1B contains the GATS with its annexes, and Annex 1C includes the TRIPS Agreement. Annex 2 includes the Dispute Settlement Understanding, Annex 3 contains rules on the Trade

---

[13] Krenzler (n 1 above) nos 18, 19.

[14] The GATT 1994 is legally independent of the GATT 1947, see Art II(4) of the WTO Agreement. Accordingly, Members of the GATT 1947 that do not adhere to the WTO (including the GATT 1994) remain such Members; the GATT 1994 does not replace the GATT 1947; accordingly, different membership is possible. Annex 1A notably contains adaptations of the GATT 1994 in order to allow its integration into the new organizational framework. Nevertheless, the previous practice of GATT is supposed to continue in the framework of the WTO, Art XVI(1) of the WTO Agreement.

Policy Review Mechanism, and Annex 4 concerns Public Procurement and other issues. Annexes 1–3 are multilateral trade agreements, which are binding on all Members of the WTO; only Annex 4 contains so-called 'plurilateral trade agreements', which are optional.

(ii) The establishment, tasks, and structure of the WTO Another success of the Uruguay Round was the establishment of an international organization that was initially planned as the ITO and is now called the World Trade Organization (WTO). Remarkably, establishing the WTO was not part of the initial mandate of the Uruguay Round. Canada was the first to submit a related proposal in May 1990, followed by the European Community. The USA abandoned its long-lasting scepticism to this idea only in the final phase of negotiations against the background that this organization could constitute a common institutional framework for the multitude of agreements. As a result, the WTO was established on the basis of the WTO Agreement on 1 January 1995.[15] Unlike the GATT, the WTO is an international organization that has international legal personality, which makes it a subject of international law, ie a personality that can exercise rights and observe duties under international law. **10.09**

The sixteen Articles of the WTO Agreement deal with the institutional and procedural framework. The WTO's tasks and functions include the administration and enforcement of the covered agreements and related legal acts, in particular by means of the dispute settlement mechanism and the periodical review of its Members' trade policy. It is also to serve as a forum for negotiations among Members on trade issues, even if not covered by the existing Agreements; the dynamic character of the WTO is also referred to as 'built-in-agenda'.[16] **10.10**

The WTO's main administrative body is the Ministerial Conference, which meets at least once every two years and is composed of all Members. Among others, it appoints the Director General of the WTO, exercises important tasks in respect of the interpretation and modification of the multilateral agreements, and decides on the negotiation and regulation of new issues as well as on the acceptance of new Members.[17] Members are represented by high-ranking politicians. **10.11**

The General Council is the permanent executive body of the WTO and, like the Ministerial Conference, also consists of all its Members; it meets in between the meetings of the Ministerial Conference, whose tasks it fulfils in addition to its own competences. It is responsible for the Trade Policy Review Body and the **10.12**

---

[15] On this day, the WTO Agreement also entered into force, Art XXX of the WTO Agreement.
[16] On the tasks and functions, see Art III of the WTO Agreement; Stoll/Schorkopf (n 12 above) n 23.
[17] Arts VI(2), IX(2), X(1), III(2), and XII(2) of the WTO Agreement; for further tasks of the Ministerial Conference, see Arts IV(1), VI(3), IV(7) IX(3), and X(9) of the WTO Agreement.

Dispute Settlement Body, and it directs the three special councils: the Council for Trade in Goods, the Council for Trade in Services, and the Council for Trade-Related Aspects of Intellectual Property Rights.[18] Members are represented by the persons accredited at the headquarters of the WTO Secretariat.

10.13 The Secretariat[19] works under the direction of the Director General as a technical and professional assistant to, for example, the different councils, committees, and developing countries, and for communication with the press. In the framework of dispute settlement, it offers its legal expert opinion. Also, it gives advice to countries that are candidates for membership.[20]

10.14 Decisions are regularly taken by consensus, which is established if no Member explicitly expresses its opposition.[21] Under special conditions, decisions can also be taken by majority votes, in particular when an authentic interpretation is established.[22]

10.15 (iii) **Amendments of the dispute settlement mechanism**[23]   As yet another success, the Uruguay Round improved the GATT dispute settlement mechanism, in particular by a streamlined procedure, the legalistic rather than political approach, and the binding nature not only of the Dispute Settlement Understanding (DSU) but also of the final rulings of panels and the Appellate Body. In addition, the DSU applies to all of the covered agreements[24] and is no longer split into eight different dispute settlement procedures.[25]

10.16 The dispute settlement procedure is streamlined in particular by clear time limits for each of the procedural stages and an overall maximum time of nine months without an appeal and twelve months where the Panel Report is appealed.[26] The legalistic approach is also reflected in the establishment of the Dispute Settlement Body (DSB). Although the Body is composed of all WTO Members and, hence, has the same Members as the WTO's administrative body, the General Council, the separate establishment of the DSB at least stresses its different functions.

---

[18] On the TRIPS Council, see Art IV(5) of the WTO Agreement and paras 10.136–10.137 below; on the General Council, see in particular Arts IV(2)–(4), V, and IX (1), (2) of the WTO Agreement.

[19] Art VI ibid; it is based in Geneva.

[20] Stoll/Schorkopf (n 12 above) n 30.

[21] Art IX(1) of the WTO Agreement, which thereby continues the preceding GATT practice.

[22] Art IX(2) ibid; see also eg Art IX(1) ibid in case of lack of consensus, as well as Arts IX(3), VII(3), XII(2), and X(1), (3)–(5) ibid.

[23] For more details, see paras 10.114 ff below.

[24] Appendix I of the DSU lists the Agreements.

[25] On the prior diversity of procedures under the GATT and the Tokyo Round Agreements, which allowed 'forum shopping', see E-U Petersmann, 'The Dispute Settlement System of the World Trade Organization and the Evolution of the GATT Dispute Settlement System since 1948' (1994) 31 CML Rev 1157, 1203; see also para 10.05 above.

[26] Art 20 of the DSU.

The legalistic approach is furthermore reflected in the new 'negative consensus' procedure, according to which the DSB must adopt a panel or appellate report unless it decides by consensus not to adopt it.[27] Accordingly, the defending (or any other) party to a dispute can no longer individually block the adoption of a report or the establishment of a panel. Another reflection of the legalistic approach is the newly introduced possibility of appellate review of the panel report as well as the establishment of the standing Appellate Body.[28]

(b) Dynamic character of the WTO

The WTO is open to new members. Yet, unlike for most other treaties, WTO **10.17** accession is dependent on more conditions than the mere implementation of WTO law, namely, on terms to be agreed between the WTO Members and the country which desires to accede to the WTO.[29] Such terms may be any further-reaching, negotiable concessions, such as the reduction of any trade restrictions or the provision of measures for further liberalization. Such concessions are negotiated between the candidate country and the WTO Members in a committee called the Working Party on Accession; it is open to all Members. Usually, major trading partners such as the USA and the EC assert their interests through simultaneous and separate bilateral negotiations with a candidate country.[30] Any commitments made within such bilateral negotiations[31] in principle apply to all other WTO Members on the basis of the most-favoured-nation clause. Given these circumstances, any candidate country is obviously in a rather weak bargaining position. As a consequence, candidate countries to date often must provide for TRIPS-plus protection, such as the implementation and ratification of the WCT and WPPT, in order to become a WTO Member. It is up to the Ministerial Conference to decide by a two-thirds majority vote on the acceptance of a new Member.[32]

The status of the European Communities is that of a Member in addition to its **10.18** Member States.[33]

---

[27] Arts 16 and 17(14) of the DSU regarding panel reports and appellate reports, respectively.

[28] Art 16(1)–(3), (8) of the DSU on the Appellate Body and Art 17(9)–(13) of the DSU on the procedures for appellate review.

[29] Art XII(1) of the WTO Agreement.

[30] Stoll and Schorkopf (n 12 above) n 35.

[31] They may lead to separate bilateral agreements outside the WTO or in so-called 'Schedules' in the WTO framework.

[32] Art XII(2) of the WTO Agreement and WTO Document WT/ACC/7/Rev2 of 1 November 2000.

[33] Art IX(1) of the WTO Agreement; it also states that the EC has the same number of votes as it has Member States that are WTO Members.

B. The TRIPS Agreement

(1) The negotiations leading to the TRIPS Agreement

10.19 As early as during the GATT Tokyo Round, the US and EC attempts to negotiate a limited set of intellectual property provisions against counterfeiting were unsuccessful.[34] Also during the Uruguay Round, industrialized country *demandeurs*, such as the USA, Japan, and the EC, met with strong opposition to including the entire area of intellectual property into the mandate of negotiations.[35] Opposition mostly came from developing countries, some of which denied the competence of GATT for intellectual property in any respect and advocated for the exclusion of all new areas from negotiations.[36] Others agreed to a compromise text for negotiation on 'trade-related aspects of intellectual property rights, including trade in counterfeit goods' so that developing countries were confident that they could limit the mandate to negotiations on trade in counterfeit goods and similar issues.[37]

10.20 From the beginning of formal negotiations in February 1987 until the midterm review in 1988/9,[38] little progress was made in part because most of the time was needed to gather information on this highly technical area—an area much more complex than other areas that trade negotiators had been faced with in earlier GATT rounds.[39] Also, the opposition of developing countries to negotiate on substantive issues other than counterfeit goods continued to be strong; they argued that only the WIPO was competent for intellectual property and, as stated in the 1986 Ministerial Declaration, that they had to be granted differential and more favourable treatment and would need to make concessions only if consistent with their status of development.[40] At the midterm review in April 1989, Ministers issued a statement according to which, in particular, future discussions should cover the applicability of principles of GATT and of intellectual property treaties, adequate protection standards and effective enforcement measures, dispute settlement between governments, and transitional arrangements. The midterm review statement was interpreted as a victory for industrialized countries

---

[34] J Watal, *Intellectual Property Rights in the WTO and Developing Countries* (2001) 15.

[35] ibid 19.

[36] ibid 19, 24.

[37] The text was adopted by the Ministerial Conference, which launched the Uruguay Round, GATT Doc MIN DEC of 20 September 1986, pp 7-8; Watal (n 34 above) 21 (in respect of the last-mentioned perception by developing countries); D Gervais, *The TRIPS Agreement: Drafting History and Analysis* (2nd edn, 2003) nn 1.11–1.12.

[38] Mid-term meetings were held on 5–8 December 1988 and 5–8 April 1989.

[39] Gervais (n 37 above) n 1.14.

[40] Watal (n 34 above) 24–5.

which clearly obtained the agreement from developing countries to include negotiations on substantive law provisions.[41] This victory has been attributed not only to the concession of transitional periods to developing countries and the acknowledgement that disputes should be resolved through multilateral procedures (an implicit rejection of unilateral trade measures), but also to the pressure exercised by the USA on the basis of unilateral measures under its Trade Act.[42] Yet, developing countries still left open whether the future treaty would be lodged in the GATT or the WIPO.[43]

On the basis of the midterm review statement, the negotiations on intellectual **10.21** property accelerated and focused on the basic principles of protection, substantive standards, enforcement provisions, and dispute settlement. In respect of substantive copyright standards, negotiators soon decided to follow the so-called 'Berne plus approach', under which the standards of the Berne Convention in its latest version (Paris Act 1971) serve as a basis for protection and are supplemented by additional elements of protection.[44]

Developing countries continued to stress that only the 'traditional' GATT issues, **10.22** such as trade in counterfeit or pirated goods, should be included in the GATT framework and that any negotiated text on other substantive standards should be implemented in the 'relevant international organization', which supposedly meant the WIPO.[45] Notwithstanding such opposition, negotiations were provisionally concluded as early as in December 1991 on the basis of the so-called 'Dunkel Draft',[46] not least due to several negotiation techniques, such as the early submission of treaty language proposals by the EC and later the USA, and discussion in informal groups.[47] Despite several attempts, this draft was hardly

---

[41] Gervais (n 37 above) n 1.16, also for the statement; Watal (n 34 above) 27 and, for the statement, App 2 (at 444).

[42] Watal (n 34 above) 25–7; on unilateral measures under Special 301, see paras 13.01–13.10 below; Gervais (n 37 above) 1.16.

[43] Watal (n 34 above) 28.

[44] This approach was proposed for the first time by Australia and was also applied to the Paris Convention, which has, however, standards comparatively lower than those of the Berne Convention, Gervais (n 37 above) 1.17; see also on the advantages of this choice against the establishment of a new system, ibid 1.96–1.98.

[45] This option was explicitly incorporated in the report of the chairman of the TRIPS Negotiating Group of 23 July 1990 (Document MTN.GNG/NG11/W/76); see Gervais (n 37 above) 1.21, 1.22.

[46] This draft final GATT Agreement ('Dunkel Draft') included a draft of the TRIPS Agreement, which was cleared of any prior alternative options, endorsed by the then Director General Arthur Dunkel, and included in the 'Draft Final Act Embodying the Results of the Uruguay Round of Multilateral Trade Negotiations', Doc MTN.TNC/W/FA of 20 December 1991, see Gervais (n 37 above) 1.30; Watal (n 34 above) 37.

[47] On the negotiations, see in detail Gervais (n 37 above) 1.16–1.32.

modified during the reopened negotiations between the end of 1992 and the end of 1993.[48]

10.23 The TRIPS Agreement (together with all other agreements negotiated in the Uruguay Round of the GATT) was thereafter adopted on 15 April 1994 at Marrakesh. The WTO Agreement entered into force on 1 January 1995. Industrialized country Members had to apply the TRIPS Agreement from 1 January 1996 only; on the same date, developing countries, transition countries, and least developed countries only had to apply Articles 3–5 of the TRIPS Agreement (in particular national treatment and the most-favoured-nation clause) while they enjoyed transitional periods for the main thrust of the TRIPS Agreement.[49]

(2) Principles of protection of copyright and neighbouring rights

10.24 The basic approach during the TRIPS negotiations was, as stated in the midterm review of 1989 and restated in the Preamble to the TRIPS Agreement,[50] to apply the basic principles of both the GATT 1994 and the relevant intellectual property treaties—namely, in the field to copyright and neighbouring rights, the Berne Convention (Paris Act 1971) and the Rome Convention of 1961. Accordingly, the TRIPS Agreement was to integrate not only the principle of national treatment (an element of the GATT regarding goods and of the Berne and Rome Conventions) and the principles of minimum standards and no or limited formalities (elements of the Berne and Rome Conventions) but also the most-favoured-nation clause (a GATT-only element).

(a) National treatment

10.25 (i) **General** Article 3 of the TRIPS Agreement is part of the 'General Provisions and Basic Principles' and therefore restates the principle of national treatment in respect of all covered intellectual property rights.[51] Accordingly, this principle had to be worded broadly enough to cover all rights of intellectual property regulated in the TRIPS Agreement,[52] yet without unintentionally deviating from the different ways in which national treatment was stipulated in the pre-existing Conventions; the underlying idea had always been to follow and build upon the

---

[48] Gervais (n 37 above) 1.32; on the reasons for which developing countries were less successful in the negotiations than they might have been, see Watal (n 34 above), in particular 43–7.

[49] Arts 65, 66 of the TRIPS Agreement; on transitional periods, see further paras 10.133–10.134 below.

[50] Second recital, (a).

[51] On the need to restate this principle, which is already part of the GATT and the pre-existing intellectual property conventions, see J Reinbothe and A Howard, 'The State of Play in the Negotiations on TRIPS (GATT/Uruguay Round)' (1991) 5 EIPR 157, 159.

[52] Art 1(2) of the TRIPS Agreement defines 'intellectual property' as all categories under Ss 1–7 of its Part II, ie copyright and related rights, trade marks, geographical indications, industrial designs, patents, layout designs, and undisclosed information.

existing conventions rather than to reinvent a satisfactorily working system. Against this background, the general term 'nationals'[53] was chosen to designate the beneficiaries of national treatment in accordance with the different criteria of eligibility under the existing conventions. In other words, the term 'nationals' simply was to serve as a generic term, which was then exclusively defined by reference to the criteria of eligibility under each specified convention (in particular Berne and Rome).[54]

10.26 The reference to the criteria of eligibility under the pre-existing intellectual property conventions has independent meaning where those conventions (such as the Rome Convention) have provisions not integrated into the TRIPS Agreement by a compliance clause; it was also needed to safeguard the existing system, which deviates from national treatment under the GATT in that it relates to works and other intangible subject matter of protection rather than to material goods.[55]

10.27 National treatment under Article 3(1) phrase 1 of the TRIPS Agreement explicitly applies to the 'protection' of intellectual property, which includes not only the rights granted but also the important matter of enforcement of rights.[56]

10.28 (ii) **Copyright** Under the reference to the criteria of eligibility of the Berne Convention, an author who wants to enjoy protection under the TRIPS Agreement must either be a national of another WTO Member, or have a habitual residence there, or have first published a work in such a country or simultaneously in a country outside and inside the WTO,[57] or must fulfil the criteria under Article 4 of the Berne Convention by analogy. The application of national treatment in the field of copyright further follows the conditions under Article 5(1) of the Berne Convention, which applies in the framework of the TRIPS Agreement on the basis of its Article 9(1) phrase 1. Accordingly, protection is granted only in a WTO Member that is not the country of origin under Article 5(4) of the Berne Convention as applied by analogy. Article 9(1) phrase 1 of the TRIPS Agreement is *lex specialis* to the general Article 3, which covers several rights of intellectual

---

[53] Art 3(1) phr 1 of the TRIPS Agreement; a footnote (which is, like all other footnotes to the TRIPS Agreement, a part of its text) to Art 1(3) phr 1 clarifies who shall be considered a 'national' of a separate customs territory. Such territory can be, unlike under the previous intellectual property conventions, a party to the treaty (ie a party to the WTO Agreement including the TRIPS Agreement); the drafters particularly envisaged the EC.

[54] Art 1(3) phr 2 of the TRIPS Agreement.

[55] P Katzenberger, 'TRIPS and Copyright Law' in FK Beier and G Schricker (eds), *From GATT to TRIPS: The Agreement on Trade-Related Aspect of Intellectual Property Rights* (1986) 59, 70.

[56] Footnote to Arts 3 and 4 of the TRIPS Agreement. On this issue, see Katzenberger (n 55 above) 73.

[57] Art 3 of the Berne Convention with further specifications.

property and therefore cannot be as specific. Indeed, Article 3 has been viewed, in respect of copyright, as a simple clarification.[58]

10.29 The hypothetical case presented in the context of the Berne Convention[59] therefore follows exactly the same solution as in the Berne context, *mutatis mutandis*: the author enjoys protection in the WTO Member USA according to the same provisions, as applied by analogy on the basis of Articles 3 and 1(3) of the TRIPS Agreement.

10.30 As for the principle of national treatment, the TRIPS Agreement also remains consistent with the pre-existing conventions in respect of exceptions. Therefore, national treatment is subject to the exceptions under the existing treaties, notably Article 7(8) of the Berne Convention.[60] Accordingly, where WTO Member A provides for a term of fifty years *pma* and Member B seventy years *pma*, Member B may decide to grant only fifty years of protection to a work for which the country of origin (determined by an analogous application of Article 5(4) of the Berne Convention) is Member A. Where a WTO Member makes use of the exception under Article 6 of the Berne Convention (retorsion), it also has to make a notification to the TRIPS Council as foreseen in this Article.[61]

(iii) Neighbouring rights

10.31 *Eligibility of performers*   Under the TRIPS reference to the criteria of eligibility of the Rome Convention, a performer is protected under the TRIPS Agreement if her performance takes place in another WTO Member, if it is incorporated in a phonogram protected under the criteria of Article 5 of the Rome Convention, or if it is unfixed and carried by a broadcast that fulfils the criteria of Article 6 of the Rome Convention.[62] Only the Rome criteria apply; thus, a performer's nationality is irrelevant. The term 'national' under the TRIPS Agreement does not refer to nationality, since it is exclusively defined by the above reference. Accordingly, where a violinist is a national of a WTO Member but the

---

[58] J Reinbothe (who was involved in the negotiations on the part of the EC), 'Der Schutz des Urheberrechts und der Leistungsschutzrechte im Abkommensentwurf GATT/TRIPS' (1992) GRUR Int 707, 713.

[59] It is repeated here, as adapted to the TRIPS context: Author A, a national and habitual resident of Laos (not a WTO Member) published a novel on 8 March 2004 in Laos and, in addition, on 28 March 2004 in Mexico (a WTO Member). The novel is then exploited without the author's consent in the USA (a WTO Member). Can the author claim protection for his novel in the USA on the basis of national treatment under the WTO/TRIPS Agreement? For the solution under the Berne Convention, see paras 5.09 ff above.

[60] Art 3(1) phr 1 of the TRIPS Agreement. For all exceptions to national treatment (under Arts 2(7) phr 2, 6, 7(8), 14ter(2), and 30(2)(b) in connection with the Appendix of the Berne Convention), see paras 5.40–5.53 above.

[61] Art 3(1) phr 3 of the TRIPS Agreement.

[62] Art 1(3) phr 2 ibid in connection with Art 4 of the Rome Convention, to be applied by analogy.

performance does not take place in a WTO Member, nor do the other criteria of eligibility apply, the violinist is not protected under the TRIPS Agreement in any of the WTO countries. However, where this performer has any nationality (even from a non-WTO Member) and gives a recital in France (a WTO Member) and a broadcast or recording thereof is then exploited in Belgium (also a WTO Member), the violinist is protected in Belgium but not in France where the performance took place (indeed, the performer in this case would be protected in any other WTO Member except France, where only domestic law applies).[63]

Eligibility of phonogram producers A phonogram producer is protected if he is **10.32** a national of another WTO Member, or if the first fixation of sounds is made in another WTO Member, or if the phonogram is first published in such a country or simultaneously (within thirty days) published in a non-WTO Member and in a WTO Member.[64] Article 1(3) phrase 3 of the TRIPS Agreement allows WTO Members to make use of the notification provided under Article 5(3) of the Rome Convention, which allows parties not to apply the criteria of either first publication or first fixation for the purposes of the TRIPS Agreement.

Eligibility of broadcasting organizations A broadcasting organization is pro- **10.33** tected if its headquarters is situated in another WTO Member or the broadcast was transmitted from a transmitter situated in such a country.[65] Article 1(3) phrase 3 of the TRIPS Agreement allows WTO Members to make the same kind of notification as permitted under Article 6(2) of the Rome Convention in the framework of the TRIPS Agreement.[66]

Scope of national treatment The scope of national treatment for performers, **10.34** phonogram producers, and broadcasting organizations is explicitly limited to the 'rights provided under this agreement'.[67] This corresponds to the economic interests of most countries in the world to limit their financial obligations.[68] Under the Rome Convention, such limitation is less clear and controversial,[69] although the negotiating parties of the TRIPS Agreement obviously assumed that national

---

[63] Art 1(3) phr 2 of the TRIPS Agreement in connection with Art 4(a) of the Rome Convention, to be applied by analogy; see for the same solution directly under the Rome Convention, and for further examples of application, para 6.03 above.

[64] Art 1(3) phr 2 of the TRIPS Agreement in connection with Art 5(1), (2) of the Rome Convention, to be applied by analogy. See for the Rome criteria paras 6.09–6.12 (and, for examples of application, paras 6.04–6.06) above. For Art 17 of the Rome Convention, see n 210 below.

[65] Art 1(3) phr 2 of the TRIPS Agreement in connection with Art 6(1) of the Rome Convention, to be applied by analogy. See for the Rome criteria para 6.13 (and, for examples of application, para 6.07) above.

[66] On this notification, see above, para 6.13 with n 34.

[67] Art 3(1) phr 2 of the TRIPS Agreement.

[68] For the similar situation and background, see para 17.44 below on national treatment under Art 4 of the WPPT.

[69] On this controversy under Art 2(2) of the Rome Convention, see para 6.27 above.

treatment under the Rome Convention was already limited in the same way.[70] Accordingly, where a WTO Member provides for a higher standard of protection than that guaranteed under Article 14 of the TRIPS Agreement, such as an exclusive distribution right for performers, or arguably also a remuneration right for private reproduction,[71] it is not obliged to grant such higher standards to 'nationals'[72] of other WTO Members but may limit national treatment to the standards under Article 14 of the TRIPS Agreement. Accordingly, national treatment does not have any effect separate from that of the minimum rights.

10.35   In respect of broadcasting organizations, one may doubt whether rights are at all 'provided under this Agreement' and, hence, whether national treatment applies at all. The broad exception from the apparent obligation to provide such rights[73] might justify an answer in the negative.[74]

10.36   *Exceptions to national treatment*   Exceptions to national treatment are taken over from the Rome Convention.[75] Where a WTO Member makes use of the exception regarding the communication right of broadcasting organizations under Article 16(1)(b) of the Rome Convention in the framework of the TRIPS Agreement, it has to make a notification (as foreseen in this Article) to the TRIPS Council.[76]

(b) Minimum rights

10.37   The principle of minimum rights is reflected in Article 1(3) phrase 1 of the TRIPS Agreement, which obliges Members to grant the treatment under the TRIPS Agreement to the nationals of other Members, and in Article 1(1) phrase 2, which explicitly allows Members to grant more extensive protection. As under most of the pre-existing conventions, such as the Berne and Rome Conventions, minimum rights only need to be granted in international rather than purely domestic

---

[70] This is implied in Reinbothe (who was involved in the negotiations on the part of the EC) (n 58 above) 713.

[71] Gervais (1st edn, 1998) 2.25 (n 25) on such statutory remuneration rights, in some countries called 'levies', referring to the US General Accounting Office's Report to Congress on the Uruguay Round results, which complains that the US interest in participating in these revenues for related rights owners has not been satisfied by the TRIPS Agreement.

[72] Term as defined in Art 1(3) phr 2 of the TRIPS Agreement.

[73] Art 14(3) phr 2 ibid; para 10.79 below.

[74] M Ficsor, 'WIPO-WTO' in H Cohen Jehoram, P Keuchenius, and L Brownlee (eds), *Trade-Related Aspects of Copyright* (1996) 79, 89, suggests that it was 'clear' that these rights were 'intended to be covered by the notion of being "provided"', so that national treatment would apply.

[75] Art 3(1) phr 1 of the TRIPS Agreement. For the exceptions under Art 16 of the Rome Convention, see paras 6.29–6.31 above.

[76] Art 3(1) phr 3 of the TRIPS Agreement; in the framework of the Rome Convention, a separate notification must be deposited with the Secretary General of the UN.

situations.[77] As for national treatment, the beneficiaries are 'nationals' of other WTO Members, defined by reference to the criteria of eligibility under the Berne and Rome Conventions;[78] for copyright, the conditions of Article 5(1) of the Berne Convention also apply.[79]

The minimum standards themselves are contained in Articles 9–13 and Article 14 of the TRIPS Agreement for copyright and for neighbouring rights, respectively.   **10.38**

(c) The principles regarding no or limited formalities

These principles are peculiar to copyright and neighbouring rights and therefore   **10.39**
are not contained in Part I of the TRIPS Agreement, which deals with common aspects of all covered intellectual property rights. For copyright, the principle of 'no formalities' applies on the basis of the compliance clause, which refers to the relevant Article 5(2) of the Berne Convention.[80] For neighbouring rights, Article 14(6) phrase 1 of the TRIPS Agreement allows WTO Members to provide the same 'conditions' as permitted by the Rome Convention. Article 11 of the Rome Convention itself considers formalities as a condition of protection, so that the Rome principle has been indirectly integrated into the TRIPS Agreement. Accordingly, those formalities that are permitted under Article 11 of the Rome Convention are also permitted under the TRIPS Agreement.[81]

(d) Most-favoured-nation clause

(i) Background and contents of the clause   The only principle of protection   **10.40**
that does not exist under the intellectual property conventions but that always has been an important principle in the GATT framework is the principle of most-favoured-nation (MFN) treatment.[82] While the principle of national treatment prohibits discrimination between 'foreign' works or other subject matter of protection and domestic ones where exploitation takes place on the domestic market, the MFN clause prohibits discrimination by one country in relation to several other countries. Where, for example, a country provides a particular privilege (such as a tariff exemption) to one of its trading partners, the MFN clause obliges it to grant the same privilege to all other trading partners. In the case of the TRIPS Agreement, a WTO Member that grants any privilege (such as a

---

[77] This may be clearly concluded from Art 1(3) phr 2, 3 of the TRIPS Agreement. See also Katzenberger (n 55 above) 70.

[78] Art 1(3) phr 2, 3 of the TRIPS Agreement.

[79] They apply by analogy on the basis of Art 9(1) phr 1 ibid.

[80] Art 9(1) phr 1 ibid; on the contents of this principle, see paras 5.55 ff above.

[81] On Art 11 of the Rome Convention, see paras 6.32–6.33 above.

[82] Art I of the GATT; this principle has also been a traditional element of any kind of trade agreements, see on the history of international copyright, paras 2.16–2.22 above.

specific standard of protection) to the nationals[83] of any other country (not necessarily another WTO Member) must grant the same privilege to the 'nationals' of all other WTO Member Countries.

10.41   The incorporation of this principle into the TRIPS Agreement was controversial. In particular, the EC considered the MFN clause as largely unnecessary, given the similar effect obtained by national treatment;[84] it also pointed at a possible, unwanted free-rider effect of future bilateral or multilateral treaties with a higher level of protection.[85] In contrast, smaller countries welcomed the MFN clause as improving their situation in an environment dominated by countries or groups of countries which could use their overwhelming economic power to gain bilateral concessions,[86] as demonstrated by the US–Korea bilateral agreement concluded immediately before the TRIPS negotiations began.[87] Moreover, the MFN clause was a fundamental element of the GATT and for this reason alone was a strong candidate for inclusion. Finally, as a compromise, the MFN clause was included as a principle, but by GATT standards its effects were quite strongly reduced.

10.42   **(ii) Effects of the clause in the intellectual property context**   The possible scope of application of the MFN clause is practically limited, because its effects are in most cases obtained through the mere application of national treatment. For example, if the national law of a WTO Member vests in authors of musical works an exclusive distribution right that is not part of the TRIPS minimum, the Member in any case must extend this protection, subject to applicable exceptions, to the 'nationals' of all other WTO Members on the mere basis of national treatment.[88]

10.43   Consequently, the MFN clause possibly has independent effects only in two cases: first, where a right is granted not on the basis of national treatment, but on a voluntary basis; and secondly, where protection under a bilateral agreement is granted exclusively to the nationals of the other country (rather than also the own nationals). The second situation is probably rare, since countries that conclude bilateral agreements in the field of intellectual property usually grant the

---

[83] Since the definition of 'nationals' in Art 1(3) phr 2 of the TRIPS Agreement only refers to nationals of other Members, it seems that 'nationals' where it is mentioned for the first time in Art 4 phr 1 (namely, as 'nationals of any other country' rather than of 'all other Members') must be understood in its ordinary meaning.

[84] This effect is illustrated in the subsequent text.

[85] Reinbothe (n 58 above) 159.

[86] ibid.

[87] Watal (n 34 above) 18–19.

[88] Art 3 of the TRIPS Agreement.

minimum protection stipulated therein also to their domestic right owners, so that national treatment applies.

(iii) Exceptions from the clause   The TRIPS Agreement exempts precisely   **10.44**
most of the situations where the MFN clause has possible independent effects, such as the voluntary grant of rights where national treatment does not apply.[89] Where for example WTO Member A, which provides a copyright duration of seventy years *pma*, grants full national treatment to a work from WTO Member B but applies reciprocity to a work from WTO Member C,[90] and where both B and C provide for a duration of fifty years *pma*, an unrestricted MFN clause would oblige A to grant its duration of seventy years *pma* also to C. However, Article 4 phrase 2(b) of the TRIPS Agreement exempts this precise situation from the application of the MFN clause, and thereby perpetuates the pre-existing situation under the Berne and Rome Conventions. Accordingly, discrimination by one WTO Member among several other WTO Members remains possible in all cases of exceptions to national treatment under the Berne and Rome Conventions.[91]

Similarly, regarding the limited scope of national treatment for performers,   **10.45**
phonogram producers, and broadcasting organizations,[92] Article 4 phrase 2(c) of the TRIPS Agreement ensures that the MFN clause does not reintroduce through the back door an unlimited scope of national treatment. For example, where the national law of a WTO Member grants a higher level than the TRIPS minimum, the Member does not need to grant this higher level of protection to other WTO Members, either under national treatment or under the MFN clause. Likewise, where a WTO Member grants stronger protection to another WTO Member on the basis of a bilateral agreement, or to several WTO Members under any subsequent multilateral agreement, such additional, stronger protection does not need to be granted under the MFN clause.[93] For instance, even where a WTO Member grants, on the basis of the WPPT, a performer's distribution right to another country, it is not obliged to grant this right to an eligible performer under WTO law. Thereby, the unwanted free-rider effect is avoided.

In addition, Article 4 phrase 2(a) of the TRIPS Agreement exempts from the   **10.46**
MFN clause any advantages, etc, deriving from treaties that generally cover judicial assistance or law enforcement (rather than being particularly confined to

---

[89] Art 4 phr 2(b) and (c) of the TRIPS Agreement.
[90] The application of material reciprocity in this case is permitted (but not obligatory) under Art 3(1) phr 1 of the TRIPS Agreement in connection with Art 7(8) of the Berne Convention.
[91] For these exceptions, see paras 10.30 and 10.36 above.
[92] Art 3(1) phr 2 of the TRIPS Agreement.
[93] Katzenberger (n 55 above) 76.

intellectual property protection)—areas that could indirectly cover intellectual property rights.[94]

10.47 Finally, another important exemption from the MFN clause applies to any advantage, etc, deriving from pre-existing[95] international agreements related to intellectual property protection. Yet, such agreements must be notified to the TRIPS Council and not constitute an arbitrary or unjustifiable discrimination against nationals of other WTO Members.[96] This exemption has an impact, for example, on former bilateral treaties.[97]

10.48 This last exception also applies to any advantages granted among Member States of the EC, be they granted on the basis of primary EC law (such as the non-discrimination rule under Article 12 of the EC Treaty which prohibits EC Member States from discriminating on the basis of nationality, as was clarified in respect of the duration of protection)[98] or on the basis of secondary EC law, such as harmonization directives.[99] In order to assure that advantages granted among EC Member States on the basis of supranational (EC) law do not fall under the MFN clause of the TRIPS Agreement, the EC and its Member States notified the EC Treaty as well as the Agreement on the European Economic Area[100] to the TRIPS Council, specifying therein that the notification covered not only the treaties themselves as interpreted by the relevant jurisprudence, but also any (existing and future) secondary law adopted on their basis.[101]

10.49 **(iv) Assessment** Accordingly, the MFN clause usually will have minimal independent effects in the fields of copyright and related rights, given the usual practice of implementing standards under bilateral agreements into national law, so that national treatment results in protection of other WTO Members, and given the wide exclusions from its limited applicability—a probably appropriate result, considering the traditional function in the area of goods to decrease tariffs, which is

---

[94] Gervais (n 37 above) 2.52 points to the bilateral nature of judicial assistance agreements as a rationale for this exemption. For a few examples, see C Correa, *Trade Related Aspects of Intellectual Property Rights: A Commentary on the TRIPS Agreement* (2007) 67.

[95] Agreements that entered into force before the WTO Agreement, ie before 1 January 1995.

[96] Art 4 phr 2(d) of the TRIPS Agreement. The second condition stems from Art XX of the GATT, see Gervais (n 37 above) 2.50. On agreements under phr 2(d), see Correa (n 94 above) 68–72.

[97] For the example of the bilateral German–American Agreement on Copyright of 1892, which excluded material reciprocity in respect of the copyright duration, see Katzenberger (n 55 above) 77; despite this treaty, material reciprocity can still be applied towards other WTO Members (note also that the situation has changed with the prolongation of duration under US law). For the bilateral treaties concluded by the USA before 1 January 1995, see paras 12.09–12.15 below.

[98] On the relevant Phil Collins case, see Vol II ch 2.

[99] For a detailed discussion of the related problems, see Katzenberger (n 55 above) 77–9.

[100] On this Agreement, see para 11.67 below and Vol II ch 15.

[101] <http://www.wto.org/english/tratop_e/trips_e/intel7_e.htm>; also repr in part in Katzenberger (n 55 above) 79, in n 163.

different from its possible effects in the area of intellectual property where standards would be raised.[102] Negotiating parties thereby also took account of their concern that the unwanted free-rider effect would have discouraged countries from negotiating and adopting treaties with stronger protection.[103]

(3) Substantive standards of protection of copyright and neighbouring rights

(a) Copyright

(i) The Berne-plus approach

The compliance clause According to the 'Berne-plus' approach that was followed during the TRIPS negotiations,[104] Article 9(1) phrase 1 of the TRIPS Agreement—'the compliance clause'—obliges WTO Members to comply with the substantive law provisions of the Berne Convention, namely, Articles 1–21 and the Appendix regarding developing countries in its latest version (ie the Paris Act of 1971).[105] It does not, however, oblige WTO Members to become members of the Berne Union.[106] Its basic effect is simply the integration of the specified Berne provisions into the TRIPS Agreement as TRIPS obligations; thereby, this clause avoided lengthy negotiations on the specifics of these standards, and at the same time made these standards subject to the WTO dispute settlement mechanism.   **10.50**

These effects alone constitute considerable progress as compared to the previous situation for the following reasons. First, many countries that wanted to become WTO Members were not previously bound by the Berne Convention, or at least not by its latest version of 1971; they then had to introduce these standards upon WTO accession. Secondly, the Berne Convention suffered from an ineffective dispute settlement mechanism.[107] Although any interpretation of Berne provisions by a WTO dispute settlement panel would only bind the WTO Members   **10.51**

---

102 S Frankel, 'WTO Application of "the Customary Rules of Interpertation of Public International Law" to Intellectual Property' (2006) 46/2 Virginia J'l of International Law 365, 419. P Drahos, 'BITs and BIPs: Bilateralism in Intellectual Property' (2001) J'l of World Intellectual Property 791, 802, who attributes to the MFN clause 'major effects in spreading new minimum standards', seems to overlook the reasons for the limited effect of this clause.

103 Reinbothe and Howard (n 51 above) 159, and Reinbothe (n 58 above) 713.

104 Above, para 10.21.

105 This option of explicitly mentioning the relevant provisions instead of generally referring to the 'substantive provisions' was finally chosen in order to exclude any doubts about which provisions would be subject to the TRIPS dispute settlement through their integration into the TRIPS Agreement, see Reinbothe (n 58 above) 709; Gervais (n 37 above) 2.89 mentions Arts 20, 21 and the Appendix of the Berne Convention as potential candidates for doubts.

106 This is also reflected in the fact that the institutional and administrative provisions of Arts 22–38 of the Berne Convention do not need to be complied with.

107 para 9.05 above.

and only refer to the Berne provisions as integrated in the TRIPS Agreement, rather than constituting a direct interpretation of the Berne Convention, strong repercussions on the interpretation of the Berne Convention would seem obvious at least in theory—though with probably little practical effect within the Berne Convention due to the lack of an effective dispute settlement mechanism.[108] At the same time, due to the WTO dispute settlement mechanism and possible sanctions, the integration of Berne provisions into the TRIPS Agreement allows a more efficient and uniform implementation of these provisions under national law.

10.52 *Exception to the compliance clause: moral rights*   As an exception to the compliance clause, Article 9(1) phrase 2 of the TRIPS Agreement contains what could be called a 'Berne-minus' element, namely, moral rights under the Berne Convention. The *demandeurs* of this exception made sure they excluded not only Article 6[bis] of the Berne Convention itself, but also any other rights derived therefrom, such as the provisions on moral rights in Articles 10(3), 11[bis](2) of the Berne Convention and IV(3) of its Appendix.[109] The *demandeurs* of this provision were the USA, whose implementation of moral rights was already widely criticized as insufficient when it adhered to the Berne Convention.[110]

10.53 At first sight, it may seem self-contradictory that a country which is already subject to a particular obligation under one treaty (here the Berne Convention) fiercely opposes the inclusion of the same obligation into another treaty (here the TRIPS Agreement). This apparent self-contradiction is, however, easily explained by the lack of an efficient dispute settlement mechanism under the Berne Convention versus the existence of such mechanism under the TRIPS Agreement. Obviously, the USA considered it realistic that a WTO panel decision would state a violation of the moral rights obligations by the USA; otherwise, it would not have needed to continuously insist on explicitly excluding moral rights.

10.54 The argument initially submitted for moral rights' exclusion was that moral rights were not 'trade related'; however, as was demonstrated in the famous John Huston case, this was not convincing, because exercising the integrity right and other moral rights may well have the effect of hampering the exploitation

---

[108] For a discussion of the possible impact of TRIPS dispute settlement on the Berne Convention, see P Geller, 'Intellectual Property in the Global Market Place: Impact of TRIPS Dispute Settlements' (1995) 29/1 The International Lawyer 99, 107 ff. The self-standing nature of the Berne Convention is also reflected in the non-derogation clause of Art 2(2) of the TRIPS Agreement; on the relation between the Berne Convention and the TRIPS Agreement, see paras 24.09–24.11 below.

[109] On moral rights, see also paras 5.96–5.97 above.

[110] eg cf J Ginsburg and J Kernochan, 'One Hundred and Two Years Later: The US Joins the Berne Convention' [1988] 13/1 Columbia-VLA Journal of Law & the Arts 1, 31.

of a work.[111] Still, it seems that the exclusion of moral rights was so crucial for the USA that it exercised 'considerable pressure' on the rest of the world to accept the exclusion.[112] Nevertheless, Article 2(2) of the TRIPS Agreement confirms that its Article 9(1) phrase 2 does not derogate from Article 6[bis] of the Berne Convention and related obligations, but has the mere effect of excluding moral rights from the TRIPS Agreement and in particular from the WTO dispute settlement.[113]

(ii) Works   For works, computer programs and databases are the plus elements provided by the TRIPS Agreement within the Berne-plus approach.   **10.55**

Computer programs   For a long time after the emergence of computer pro-   **10.56** grams, it was controversial whether they qualified as works (and if so, as what kind of work), or whether they should be protected by a *sui generis* right or were otherwise outside copyright law.[114] Since copyright had the advantages of a high level of protection, no formality requirements, and existing international treaties in the field, industrialized countries and their industries strongly advocated for a clarification of the Berne Convention or, depending on its interpretation, the introduction of a new kind of work. In parallel to the TRIPS negotiations, they obtained recognition of computer programs as copyright works in a number of national laws.[115] The USA opted for the strongest possible protection in the TRIPS Agreement.[116]

Yet, at the beginning of TRIPS negotiations, many features of the protection of   **10.57** computer programs under copyright remained quite controversial. In particular, developing countries wanted to restrict protection as far as possible. Consequently, they opposed the qualification of computer programs as literary works, preferring instead to qualify them as another type of work (eg applied art), where a shorter duration and otherwise lower level of protection applied; alternatively, they considered introducing a *sui generis* protection.[117] In an early submission,

---

[111] The colourized version of *Asphalt Jungle* produced in the USA violated moral rights in France and therefore could not be exploited as such in France; on the John Huston case, see para 5.101 above; see also Gervais (n 37 above) 2.90.

[112] Reinbothe (n 58 above) 709 where he labels the topic of moral rights as an 'emotionalised' one; see also Reinbothe/Howard (n 51 above) 161.

[113] Gervais (n 37 above) 2.90 n 12; S Ricketson and J Ginsburg, *International Copyright and Neighbouring Rights: The Berne Convention and Beyond* (2006) 6.136, 6.137, both also on the relation to Art 20 of the Berne Convention; Reinbothe (n 58 above) 709.

[114] See paras 7.13 ff, in particular 7.16–7.18 above.

[115] Gervais (n 37 above) 2.104 and, in particular, n 50; the relevant industry had played a strong role in this development, see para 7.19 above.

[116] Reinbothe (n 58 above) 709.

[117] Watal (n 34 above) 216; Reinbothe/Howard (n 51 above) 161; Reinbothe (n 58 above) 709; Gervais (n 37 above) 2.106. Arts 2(7) and 7(4) of the Berne Convention would have allowed considerable flexibility. On similar ideas and earlier discussions in the WIPO framework, see paras 7.16–7.17 above.

the EC had proposed lesser protection as works of applied art with their duration of twenty-five years from creation, and only later joined the USA's proposal.[118]

10.58   Japan wanted specific exceptions to protection but did not fully succeed; at least, it obtained the statement that copyright shall extend to expressions and not to ideas, procedures, methods of operation, or mathematical concepts as such. This statement of the expression/idea dichotomy was first discussed in the mere context of computer programs,[119] and only later recognized as a principle underlying copyright protection in general. Consequently, it was then worded so as to apply to all kinds of works, and transferred to the preceding general Article 9 of the TRIPS Agreement as a new paragraph (2).[120] Although explicitly stated for the first time in an international agreement, this principle has always been implicitly included in the Berne Convention,[121] and implicitly or explicitly included in national copyright laws worldwide.[122] Article 9(2) of the TRIPS Agreement therefore can only be understood as clarifying the law under the pre-existing copyright conventions.[123]

10.59   Thus, computer programs are covered as literary works. The source and object code of computer programs were explicitly mentioned in order to clearly reject an earlier opinion that only the source code could be a literary work.[124]

10.60   *Databases*   As for computer programs, the status of collections of mere data—databases—as works was unclear under the Berne Convention; a clear international rule was thus needed. Article 2(5) of the Berne Convention protects collections of works, but does not explicitly cover collections of mere data (that are not works by definition). If one considers Article 2(5) of the Berne Convention as *lex specialis* to Article 2(1) of the Berne Convention, databases are excluded from protection.[125] Otherwise, recourse is possible to Article 2(1) of the Berne

---

[118]   MTN.GNG/NG1/W/26 of 7 July 1988; see also Watal (n 34 above) 216.

[119]   Gervais (n 37 above) 2.98.

[120]   Reinbothe (n 58 above) 709 who also justifies this move with the risk that otherwise one could conclude *e contrario* that the expression/idea dichotomy would only apply to computer programs but not to other works.

[121]   eg Ricketson/Ginsburg (n 113 above) 8.07.

[122]   The wording of Art 9(2) of the TRIPS Agreement is said to have been inspired by s 102(b) of the US Copyright Act, (Title 17 USC).

[123]   If this provision were a new exception, it would violate Art 9(1) of the TRIPS Agreement in context with Art 20 of the Berne Convention and be inconsistent with Art 2(2) of the TRIPS Agreement, see Gervais (n 37 above) 2.99. Art 9(2) of the TRIPS Agreement also corresponds to Art 1(2) of the EC Computer Program Dir, which was discussed in the EC in parallel with the TRIPS negotiations and adopted in 1991, see Vol II ch 5.

[124]   Gervais (n 37 above) 2.106.

[125]   S Ricketson, *The Berne Convention 1886–1986* (1987) 6.71 on Art 2(5); he did not elaborate on Art 2(1) in this context.

Convention, which is drafted broadly enough to cover collections of data.[126] In contrast to this ambiguity, Article 10(2) of the TRIPS Agreement clearly states that not only compilations of works, but also of data and other material are covered by the Agreement, and are even subject to mandatory protection. This provision was considered important given the increasing trade in databases, especially in electronic form.[127]

Apart from the additional coverage of collected material other than works, Article **10.61** 10(2) of the TRIPS Agreement does not in substance deviate from Article 2(5) of the Berne Convention. In particular, the qualification 'whether in machine readable or other form' simply stresses the importance of electronic versus non-electronic databases but does not add to the Berne Convention, which covers expressions in any form (as specifically stated in its Article 2(1)). Also, the TRIPS Agreement applies the same conditions for protection: either the selection or the arrangement of the material must constitute an intellectual creation.[128]

Like the Berne Convention, the TRIPS Agreement clarifies that the protection in **10.62** the collection is without prejudice to any copyright in the collected material. While the Berne Convention is precise in leaving without prejudice 'the copyright in each of the works forming part of such collections', Article 10(2) of the TRIPS Agreement needed to take account of data within the contents of collections. Its 'without prejudice' clause therefore covers 'any copyright subsisting in the data'. Since copyright cannot subsist in mere data, this provision is imprecise and has to be read as also leaving without prejudice any right (if any exists) subsisting in the data or other material.

Moreover, the protection of the collection does not extend to the data or material **10.63** itself, as explicitly stated in the TRIPS Agreement; in the Berne Convention, this self-evident rule is only implied, namely in the positive description of what is protected (that is, the selection or arrangement only). Although the TRIPS Agreement uses the word 'compilations' rather than 'collections' (Article 2(5) of

---

[126] WIPO, *Implications of the TRIPS Agreement on the Treaties Administered by WIPO* (1996) n 36; Gervais (n 37 above) 2.107 with further references; yet, collections of data would anyway not be subject to mandatory protection, see paras 5.76–5.77 above; Ricketson/Ginsburg (n 113 above) 8.89–8.90. On the reasons for need for clarification, see Reinbothe and von Lewinski, *The WIPO Treaties 1996* (2002) Art 5 WCT n 13.

[127] Katzenberger (n 55 above) 83, also stressing the lead of the USA in this matter; the USA was one of the *demandeurs* of this provision, see Reinbothe/von Lewinski Art 5 WCT n 6. Also in the EC, database protection was a topic in respect of possible harmonization from 1988 onwards, see Vol II ch 9 in the context of the EC Database Dir that was adopted in 1996.

[128] The alternative application of 'selection' and 'arrangement' corresponds to the prevailing French version of the Berne Convention; only its English version uses them cumulatively.

the Berne Convention), it does not result in a different meaning—the words should be considered synonymous terms.[129]

(iii) Rights

10.64 *Background* The only minimum right provided as a 'Berne-plus' element is the exclusive rental right under Article 11 of the TRIPS Agreement and, possibly, under its Article 14(4).[130] Rental had emerged, after the last revision of the Berne Convention in 1971, as a new form of exploitation mainly of computer programs, musical recordings, and video cassettes. Rental in combination with (often permitted) private reproduction primarily threatened the phonogram and computer software industries, whose income was mainly calculated on the basis of sales that suffered from the combined rental and private copying activities.[131] Consequently, these industries started a major worldwide campaign in favour of exclusive rental rights to be introduced at the national level and later also at the international level.[132] Interested parties sought to prohibit rental in order to considerably reduce the possibilities of private reproduction and, hence, to regain their sales. The *demandeur* of this provision was the USA, whose national law provisions of 1984 finally served as a model for the TRIPS provisions.[133] As for protection of computer programs, the EC and Japan initially were not *demandeurs* but only followed later after coordination with the USA.[134]

10.65 *Compromise character* Articles 11 and 14(4) of the TRIPS Agreement reflect the influence of the interested parties, the pragmatic approach of regulating problems on a case-by-case basis rather than systematically,[135] as well as a compromise character. They were a compromise between countries that wanted full coverage for all kinds of works (mainly the EC),[136] those that rejected the

---

[129] Ricketson/Ginsburg (n 113 above) 8.86 explain that in the context of Art 2(5) of the Berne Convention (upon which Art 10(2) of the TRIPS Agreement is based) both notions are synonymous because 'compilations' is just another translation of the original French *recueil*, so that slight differences between 'compilation' and 'collection' in the English language (the first implying an element of skill in the activity of compiling, the second being more neutral) does not matter.

[130] On a rental right for authors of works incorporated in phonograms, see paras 10.72–10.79 below.

[131] Gervais (n 37 above) 2.113 in respect of computer programs and 1.29 in respect of phonograms, quoting US industry; Watal (n 34 above) 221.

[132] For the USA, which accordingly amended its copyright law in 1984, see ibid.

[133] ibid.

[134] ibid.

[135] The EC Rental Rights Dir, which was negotiated in parallel and adopted in November 1992, chose the systematic approach in accordance with the Continental European system: the rental right is granted to all kinds of authors of all kinds of works (except for works of applied art and architecture only, for specific reasons), see Vol II ch 6 on that Dir. See also para 3.22 above on the principle-based Continental European system.

[136] See Reinbothe (n 58 above) 710.

rental right (most of the developing countries),[137] those that wanted to exclude cinematographic works in particular (the USA),[138] and those that wanted a remuneration right instead of an exclusives right (particularly Japan).[139]

Rental right for selected categories of works only   First, the rental right does not   **10.66**
apply to all kinds of works, but only to computer programs and, at first sight, cinematographic works (as well as possibly, under Article 14 of the TRIPS Agreement, to authors of works embodied in phonograms[140]). It applies 'at least' to these kinds of works—a wording that reflects the opinion of those countries which preferred to extend this minimum right to additional kinds of works.[141] Yet, this wording does not have any independent legal meaning because the TRIPS Agreement in any case provides for minimum standards beyond which countries may provide further protection.

Cinematographic works   Secondly, regarding cinematographic works, the   **10.67**
exception from the rental right has been formulated as the rule:[142] a rental right only needs to be granted where rental of cinematographic works has led to their widespread copying which materially impairs the exclusive reproduction right (ie the so-called 'material impairment test'). This highly complicated language is the result of a compromise between negotiating parties for and against a rental right for cinematographic works. Its aim was seen 'to impose a rental right on as many countries as possible, while leaving the United States out'.[143] Indeed, the US film industry previously had failed to obtain an exclusive rental right at the domestic level due to the strong lobby of video rental outlets. The same situation was likely to reappear, and the USA did not want to risk endangering ratification of the Uruguay Round Agreements.[144]

According to the compromise, a rental right must only be provided if the video   **10.68**
sales or other uses based on the exclusive reproduction right suffer from widespread private copying that results from rental. This wording mirrors arguments of the US phonogram industry expressed to justify a rental right for phonograms.[145] These conditions at the time of TRIPS negotiations were mostly unfulfilled, given the then low quality of private audiovisual copies, the low number of

---

137   ibid, and Watal (n 34 above) 222.
138   Reinbothe (n 58 above) 710; Gervais (n 37 above) 2.114.
139   See Reinbothe (n 58 above) 711.
140   On the rental right for works embodied in phonograms, see Art 14(4) of the TRIPS Agreement and paras 10.72–10.79 below.
141   Art 11 of the TRIPS Agreement; mainly the EC preferred a broad coverage, see Reinbothe (n 58 above) 710.
142   Under Art 11 phr 2, 'a Member shall be excepted from this obligation . . . unless . . .'.
143   Gervais (n 37 above) 2.113.
144   ibid 2.114; Reinbothe (n 58 above) 711.
145   Gervais (n 38 above) 1.29.

households with video copying devices, and the rentals-based rather than sales-based market. Accordingly, many countries have not seen the need to introduce an exclusive rental right for videos.[146] Today, the digital quality of rented videos, together with the availability of copying devices and the installation of technical copy protection, may require a new assessment. At the same time, where video exploitation suffers from digital downloads, a new assessment will not be required because this is not a result of rental.

10.69   The impairment test may be difficult to apply. So far in TRIPS practice, its conditions are presumed to be unfulfilled (so that a rental right need not be granted) where the film industry of the relevant country takes no issue with ongoing, uncontrolled rental activities.[147]

10.70   *Exception regarding computer programs*   Thirdly, Article 11 phrase 3 of the TRIPS Agreement excludes computer programs that are not the essential object of the rental. It thereby aims at avoiding interference of a rental right based on copyright with the rental of cars or similar objects incorporating computer programs; a right holder in a computer program should not be able, for example, to prohibit car rentals only because cars include computer programs.[148]

10.71   *'Rental' and 'public'*   'Rental' is not defined but qualified by its 'commercial' nature, which includes any direct or indirect profit-making purposes.[149] The WTO Members may further specify the commercial nature, as well as the 'public' to which rental is directed.[150]

10.72   *Article 14(4) on phonograms*   Article 14(4) of the TRIPS Agreement also contains a rental right; it is provided in favour of phonogram producers and 'any other right holders in phonograms as determined in a Members' law'. This qualification of other right holders is somewhat ambiguous and reflects different positions of negotiating parties. Some wanted to grant the rental right only to phonogram producers. Others, in particular those of the author's rights system, sought to grant it to authors in the first place (and also performers) rather than to related rights owners only; as a matter of principle, they would not grant a right to a neighbouring right owner, such as a phonogram producer, where an author's work is equally concerned by exploitation.[151]

---

[146] For a criticism of this argumentation, see Reinbothe (n 58 above) 710–11.

[147] When the TRIPS Council reviewed the US provisions implementing the TRIPS Agreement, it was satisfied with the answer that the Hollywood film industry did not see a need to introduce a rental right, Watal (n 34 above) 223 n 56.

[148] Gervais (n 37 above) 2.113; Reinbothe (n 58 above) 710.

[149] For the definition of 'rental' in Art 1(2) of the EC Rental Right Dir 1992, which was developed in parallel to Art 11 of the TRIPS Agreement, see Vol II ch 6.

[150] Reinbothe (n 58 above) 710.

[151] This approach is also reflected in Katzenberger (n 55 above) 87.

In such a situation, where diverging opinions in substance could not be recon- **10.73** ciled, negotiating parties during the Uruguay Round often had recourse to a negotiating technique called 'constructive ambiguity'.[152] The intention behind this technique was to leave the text sufficiently ambiguous, so as to justify both, though opposite, opinions. In other words, the parties agreed not to agree in substance. This ambiguity was considered 'constructive' because it would help in constructing the overall consensus for the Uruguay Round agreements and avoid the risk that the entire package to be negotiated as a single deal at the Uruguay Round would fail because of relatively minor issues (seen in the broad context of all agreements of the entire Round).

While legal drafters usually strive to achieve the utmost clarity in their texts, the **10.74** drafters of Article 14(4) of the TRIPS Agreement had to master the art of drafting an intentionally ambiguous provision that would equally well justify diverging interpretations. The words 'any other right holders in phonograms' indeed leave room for different interpretations. The question is who might be covered by such 'other right holders'. Successors in title are certainly not meant, since the TRIPS Agreement, like previous treaties, only deals with the grant of rights to the first right owners, which automatically includes successors in title without the need for special mention.[153] Therefore, it is obvious that any successor in title also can enjoy the rights granted by these treaties. If one interpreted 'any other right holder' as the successors in title of the phonogram producer, one would even risk an unintended conclusion *e contrario* to the effect that other rights contained in the TRIPS Agreement could not be enjoyed by successors in title.

Rather, this expression could mean the authors of the music and texts recorded **10.75** on a phonogram as well as the performers of the music and texts. Negotiating parties that do not want to be obliged to grant rental rights also to authors and performers could argue as follows: strictly speaking, authors hold rights in their works, ie the musical composition or the text, but not in a phonogram which is a recording of their work; similarly, performers are protected in their performances rather than in the phonogram. In respect of authors, parties could also put forward a systematic argument, namely, that Article 14 of the TRIPS Agreement only covers performers, phonogram producers, and broadcasting organizations (related rights) but not composers of music and other authors in the meaning of the Berne Convention whose rights are only covered in Articles 9–13 of the TRIPS Agreement.

---

[152] Watal (n 34 above) 7 (in a different context).
[153] This is clarified eg in Art 2(6) of the Berne Convention.

10.76 The opposite view would be based on the argument that authors and performers indirectly hold rights in phonograms, because they can prohibit the use of the phonogram in which their work or performance is incorporated.[154] In addition, the reference to 'other right holders' would be void of any meaning under the first interpretation—a result unlikely to stand under treaty interpretation, since treaty provisions may be presumed to convey a meaning.[155] Moreover, right owners in phonograms 'as determined in a Member's law' would be, under this opposite view, authors and performers if they enjoy any kind of right (such as the reproduction right) at all in their works and performances when incorporated in phonograms.[156] This is usually the case, since the protection of works and performances does not disappear with their incorporation in phonograms.

10.77 Against the background of negotiations, it has been argued that countries, such as the USA, that grant phonogram producers a copyright (rather than a related right) in the phonogram would not need to grant a separate rental right to the authors of the music and text incorporated therein.[157] However, this is hardly convincing since the way in which rights in phonograms are granted to their producers—be it as a copyright or a related right—cannot matter for the supplementary obligation to provide for rental rights in favour of other right holders.[158]

10.78 Under Article 14(4) of the TRIPS Agreement, Article 11 shall be applied *mutatis mutandis* (ie by analogy) in respect of computer programs only. Consequently, the exception under Article 11 phrase 3 of the TRIPS Agreement also applies, but the exception for cinematographic works in Article 11 phrase 2 must not be applied. This choice reflects the (then) higher intensity of private copying of music as compared to films in the context of rental, so that an exception was not justified.[159]

10.79 Article 14(4) phrase 2 of the TRIPS Agreement was a concession to Japan in particular, which wanted to continue its existing remuneration rights for rental instead of introducing an exclusive right. This concession was only granted subject to the same 'material impairment test' as applied to the exception regarding films, and

---

[154] Gervais (n 37 above) 2.147.

[155] Similarly: ibid.

[156] This would correspond to the intention behind the provision, see Reinbothe/von Lewinski (n 126 above) Art 7 WCT n 12 (and, for further analysis, nn 13, 14); similarly: Katzenberger (n 55 above) 87.

[157] Reinbothe (n 58 above) 711.

[158] Similarly: Katzenberger (n 55 above) 87–8. WIPO (n 126 above) n 70 is of the view that the 'Members are free to extend or not to extend that right' to authors and performers.

[159] Katzenberger (n 55 above) 88–9; in addition, one of the major reasons for the introduction of the exception regarding films, ie the domestic situation in the USA (see above in the text), did not apply here since record rental outlets had not organized themselves early enough to successfully fight an exclusive rental right, as reflected in the corresponding 1984 amendment of the US Copyright Act.

is limited to remuneration rights existing on 15 April 1994; consequently, it does not allow for the introduction of a remuneration right for rental.[160]

(iv) Special term of protection The Berne Convention quite comprehensively   **10.80**
regulates the duration of protection of authors' rights. Yet, since it is based on the authors' rights concept under which an author can only be a natural person,[161] it does not determine any duration where legal persons are recognized as initial owners of copyright.[162] During the TRIPS negotiations, the US film industry in particular aimed at the recognition of 'corporate authorship' at the international level.[163] Article 12 of the TRIPS Agreement does not go so far, but is limited to providing for a minimum duration in cases where a national law provides for a calculation other than on the basis of the life of the author; it does not in any way recognize, or even oblige Members to introduce, initial corporate ownership.[164]

The Berne Convention already provides for a minimum duration in specific   **10.81**
cases, where the duration is calculated on a basis other than the life of a natural person, namely for photographic works and works of applied art, as well as for anonymous, pseudonymous, and cinematographic works.[165] The former cases are explicitly excepted from Article 12 of the TRIPS Agreement and continue to be regulated under Article 7(4) of the Berne Convention as applied through Article 9(1) phrase 1 of the TRIPS Agreement.[166] For the latter cases, the Berne provisions largely correspond to the criteria of Article 12 of the TRIPS Agreement.[167] Yet, should a conflict between the Berne provisions and Article 12 of the TRIPS Agreement arise, then Article 12 of the TRIPS Agreement must not

---

160 See above on Art 11 phr 2 of the TRIPS Agreement regarding films; see also Reinbothe (n 58 above) 711; Katzenberger (n 55 above) 89; Gervais (n 37 above) 2.147; 15 April 1994 was the date of signature of the Uruguay Round Agreements.

161 See para 5.84 above.

162 Only in respect of cinematographic works, it arguably also allows initial corporate ownership under Art 14^bis(2)(a) and Art 7(2) of the Berne Convention, see paras 5.87–5.88 above.

163 Gervais (n 37 above) 2.68 n 22 with reference to TP Stuart, *The GATT Uruguay Round: A Negotiating History (1986–1992)* 2286.

164 On the US strategy to instead obtain a similar recognition in bilateral and regional agreements, namely recognition of free transferability and the concept of work made for hire, see paras 11.18, 11.42, and 12.35 below.

165 Art 7(4), (3), and (2) of the Berne Convention.

166 As an exception from the general rule, Art 7(4) ibid provides for a minimum term of twenty-five years after the making of the work, see paras 5.224–5.226 above; for photographic works see, however, Art 9 WCT and paras 17.111–17.114 below.

167 Art 7(2) of the Berne Convention: 50 years after making a work available to the public with the author's consent; Art 7(3) phr 1 ibid: 50 years after the lawful making available of the work to the public; Art 12 TRIPS Agreement: 50 years after authorized publication. Failing such event within 50 years from the making, both Arts 7(2) of the Berne Convention and 12 of the TRIPS Agreement set the duration at 50 years from the making of the work. For the slight difference between 'making available to the public' and 'publication' see H Wager, 'Substantive Copyright Law in TRIPS' in H Cohen Jehoram, P Keuchenius, and L Brownlee (eds), *Trade-Related Aspects of Copyright* (1996) 31, 34.

be interpreted in a way that would lead to less protection than under the Berne Convention.[168]

10.82 In countries of the author's rights system, where corporate ownership of authors' rights is usually not recognized except for so-called 'collective works' if protected at all under national law,[169] Article 12 of the TRIPS Agreement will hardly find application. In countries of the copyright system, corporate ownership is particularly recognized for employers. Application of Article 12 to collective and corporate works seems self-contradictory in view of lack of their coverage by Berne (and, thus, TRIPS).[170] Cinematographic works, whose producers are usually recognized as 'authors' in these countries, are already covered by Article 7(2) of the Berne Convention, as integrated into the TRIPS Agreement. Yet, producers of phonograms that enjoy copyright protection under the copyright system are exclusively covered by Article 14 of the TRIPS Agreement; thus, Article 12 does not apply.[171]

10.83 **(v) Limitations and exceptions**   The Berne Convention provides a set of limitations of, and exceptions to, the minimum rights contained therein.[172] These limitations and exceptions also apply as part of the TRIPS Agreement on the basis of the compliance clause.[173] The role of Article 13 of the TRIPS Agreement is, first, to provide conditions for permitted limitations and exceptions regarding the TRIPS minimum right not covered by the Berne Convention (ie the rental right). Secondly, it provides what could be called a 'safety net' against too broad an interpretation of the Berne limitations when applied in the framework of the TRIPS Agreement. For example, where a national provision limits the broadcasting right in respect of news reporting, it only complies with the TRIPS Agreement if both the conditions of Article 10bis of the Berne Convention (as referred to in Article 9(1) phrase 1 of the TRIPS Agreement) and also the three conditions of Article 13 of the TRIPS Agreement are fulfilled.

10.84 Where limitations and exceptions under the Berne Convention cumulatively apply with Article 13 of the TRIPS Agreement, the latter functions as an interpretation rule with respect to the former. It does not, however, allow WTO Members to create new limitations and exceptions that are not covered by the

---

[168] Art 9(1) phr 1 of the TRIPS Agreement in context with Art 20 of the Berne Convention.

[169] On this deviation from the principle of authorship by natural persons only, see para 3.37 above. Notably, they are not covered by the Berne Convention (and, hence, TRIPS), para 5.219 above.

[170] eg the work-made-for-hire rule under s 201(b) Title 17 USC; para 3.41 above.

[171] For the duration, see para (5) and para 10.99 below.

[172] Arts 2bis(2), 9(2), 10, 10bis, 11bis(2), (3) phr 2 and 13 of the Berne Convention and the so-called 'implied exceptions', see paras 5.156ff, 5.199ff above.

[173] Art 9(1) phr 1 of the TRIPS Agreement in connection with the relevant Articles of the Berne Convention.

Berne provisions, because this would be inconsistent with the compliance clause in connection with Article 20 of the Berne Convention.[174]

The three conditions of Article 13 of the TRIPS Agreement are copied from **10.85** Article 9(2) of the Berne Convention on the reproduction right.[175] Hence, they have existed in an international copyright instrument since 1971, but it was only during the TRIPS negotiations that they were labelled by the catchword 'three-step test'—obviously, trade negotiators liked to save time by using such labels.[176] Article 13 of the TRIPS Agreement extends the application of the three-step test to any exclusive rights covered—all exclusive rights under the Berne Convention and the rental right;[177] moral rights are not 'exclusive rights' and are anyway not covered by the TRIPS Agreement.[178]

The obligation to 'confine' the limitations and exceptions under Article 13 of the **10.86** TRIPS Agreement indicates that, if a country restricts minimum rights in a specific case, then it has no choice but to fulfil the three conditions (as the case may be in addition to the Berne conditions) in order to comply with the TRIPS Agreement. The three-step test, in accordance with the system of the Berne Convention, restricts the possibilities for national legislators to provide limitations and exceptions. It represents the necessary counterpart of minimum rights, which could otherwise be rendered completely meaningless. At the same time, the word 'confine' does not compel WTO Members to provide for any limitations or exceptions at all.

The three conditions—certain special cases, no conflict with a normal exploita- **10.87** tion, and no unreasonable prejudice to the legitimate interests of the author—are analysed above in connection with the Berne limitations.[179] They have been subject to a detailed WTO Panel Report and a vast amount of literature, an analysis of which would go beyond the scope of this book.[180] This Panel Report so far has been the only one adopted in the field of copyright and related rights on the basis of the TRIPS Agreement in a WTO dispute settlement procedure.

---

[174] Art 9(1) phr 1 of the TRIPS Agreement; the TRIPS Agreement itself is also a special agreement in the meaning of Art 20 of the Berne Convention. In addition, Art 2(2) of the TRIPS Agreement confirms that it does not derogate from the Berne Convention, see also Gervais (n 37 above) 2.124.

[175] For an analysis, see paras 5.178–5.186 above.

[176] Other catchwords employed were, eg, 'impairment test' and 'compliance clause'.

[177] Art 9(1) phr 1 of the TRIPS Agreement in connection with the Berne Convention's rights and Art 11 (and possibly 14(4)) of the TRIPS Agreement.

[178] See paras 10.52–10.55 above.

[179] paras 5.178–5.186 above.

[180] See the Panel Report WT/DS/160 of more than 70 pages, <http://www.wto.org>; references in ch 5 n 316 above.

10.88   Article 13 of the TRIPS Agreement only applies in the field of copyright as reflected in its wording, which refers to 'the work' (rather than to a phonogram, performance, or broadcast), and in its systematic context: it is the last provision in a series of copyright provisions that appear before Article 14, which is the first and only one dealing with performers, phonogram producers, and broadcasting organizations. In respect of the latter right holders, limitations and exceptions are separately regulated in Article 14(6) of the TRIPS Agreement.

(b) Related rights

10.89   (i) **General remarks**   Article 14 of the TRIPS Agreement deals with the same three related rights as covered by the Rome Convention, namely, the rights of performers in their performances, of phonogram producers in their phonograms, and of broadcasting organizations in their broadcasts. At an earlier stage of negotiations, the supposedly more neutral term 'related rights'—rather than 'neighbouring rights'—was chosen in the text in order to express the neutrality of the TRIPS Agreement towards the copyright system versus the author's rights system;[181] the copyright system protects these right holders, if at all, under copyright, while the author's rights system protects them under the concept of neighbouring rights.[182] In its final version, the Article even avoids the term 'related rights' and only designates the right holders and subject matter as such and thereby is even more neutral. Accordingly, countries of the copyright system may, for example, continue to provide protection for phonogram producers under copyright, while countries of the author's rights system may continue to protect them under neighbouring rights. The neutrality towards both systems is also reflected by the synonymous use of 'phonograms' and 'sound recordings' in the title of this Article.[183]

10.90   Unlike Article 9(1) of the TRIPS Agreement for copyright, Article 14 does not contain a compliance clause in respect of the substantive provisions of a neighbouring rights convention, such as the Rome Convention. At the time of the TRIPS negotiations, the Rome Convention enjoyed a far lower degree of acceptance than the Berne Convention, so that this approach initially seemed unrealistic.[184] Only its criteria of eligibility are explicitly referred to in Article 1(3)

---

[181] On the initial choice of 'related rights', see Reinbothe/Howard (n 51 above) 161. Also in the framework of EC harmonization, 'related rights' was chosen as more neutral, see eg J Reinbothe and S von Lewinski, *The EC Directive on Rental and Lending Rights and on Piracy* (1993) 84.

[182] See paras 3.39 and 3.66–3.69 above on these differences.

[183] 'Sound recording' is usually employed in countries of the copyright system, and 'phonogram' is used under the author's rights system with its neighbouring rights concept, as reflected in the Rome Convention.

[184] The Rome Convention had thirty-two members on 1 January 1988, (1988) Copyright 9, as compared to the Berne Convention (seventy-seven members, (1988) Copyright 6. For an appreciation, see Reinbothe/Howard (n 51 above) 161.

phrase 2 of the TRIPS Agreement.[185] Nevertheless, Article 14 of the TRIPS Agreement largely follows the standards established under the Rome Convention. In addition, Article 2(2) of the TRIPS Agreement clarifies that TRIPS does not derogate from the obligations under the Rome Convention for the Contracting States thereof. For Contracting States to the Rome Convention, one may consider the TRIPS Agreement as a 'special agreement' in the meaning of Article 22 of the Rome Convention.[186]

(ii) Minimum rights of performers and phonogram producers   Article 14(1)   **10.91** of the TRIPS Agreement lays down the minimum rights of performers in their performances. Like the Rome Convention, it confers on performers the mere 'possibility of preventing' specified acts rather than full exclusive rights.[187] The substance of protection largely corresponds to the Rome minimum standards. The possibility of preventing the fixation and reproduction under the TRIPS Agreement is slightly more restricted than under the Rome Convention, since it is limited to fixations on phonograms. Musicians, actors, and others whose performances are to be recorded on an audiovisual fixation therefore cannot prevent such fixation or any reproduction thereof.[188] The reproduction right under TRIPS at first sight seems slightly broader than under the Rome Convention, since it is not subject to the three conditions.[189] Yet, Article 14(6) of the TRIPS Agreement permits the provision of any conditions provided by the Rome Convention, such as those regarding the reproduction right.[190]

Regarding the possibility of preventing live broadcasting (by wireless means) and   **10.92** live communication to the public, the TRIPS Agreement is substantially similar to the Rome Convention, though differently worded. Article 7(1)(a) of the Rome Convention does not use the term 'live', but excludes the broadcasting and communication where performances are already fixed or broadcast.[191] The term 'live' in Article 14(1) phrase 2 of the TRIPS Agreement is less clear; where it is only understood as 'unfixed', the TRIPS Agreement would grant performers the possibility of preventing the rebroadcasting of a broadcast performance and, hence, would be broader than the Rome Convention. Yet, Article 14(6) of the TRIPS

---

185 See paras 10.25–10.26 and 10.31–10.33 above.

186 See paras 6.78 above and 24.14 below.

187 This term has to be interpreted as under the Rome Convention, see Gervais (n 37 above) 2.142, 1.44; on this term in the Rome Convention, see paras 6.35–6.36 above.

188 Under the Rome Convention, performers can prevent fixation and reproduction in respect of audiovisual fixations as long as they have not consented to the incorporation of their performance in a visual or audiovisual fixation, see Art 19 of the Rome Convention; see also paras 6.45–6.48 above. On the limitation of the reproduction right to audio fixations, see Gervais (n 37 above) 2.143.

189 Art 7(1)(c)(i)–(iii) of the Rome Convention.

190 On the fixation and reproduction rights under Art 7(1)(a), (c) of the Rome Convention, see paras 6.39–6.41 above.

191 See paras 6.37–6.38 above.

Agreement in connection with Article 7(1)(a) of the Rome Convention may be interpreted as permitting the exclusion of such a live rebroadcasting right.[192]

10.93   Musicians whose concerts and actors whose stage performances are broadcast live or communicated by loudspeaker and screen to an outside audience can prevent these uses. Both rights refer to any performances, including audio and audio-visual performances.

10.94   Article 14(2) of the TRIPS Agreement on phonogram producers' rights entirely corresponds to Article 10 of the Rome Convention; it only provides for an exclusive reproduction right.[193] Phonogram producers and arguably performers also enjoy an exclusive rental right under Article 14(4) of the TRIPS Agreement.[194]

10.95   Unlike the Rome Convention,[195] the TRIPS Agreement does not provide for any remuneration right in secondary uses. Yet, this apparent difference largely amounts to the same result, since the Rome Convention offers the possibility of excluding such protection by way of declaration of a reservation.[196]

10.96   **(iii) Minimum rights of broadcasting organizations**   Article 14(3) of the TRIPS Agreement reflects its nature as a compromise between countries that favoured and opposed protection for broadcasts. In particular, the USA did not (and was not ready to) protect broadcasts, while most other countries usually protected them either by related rights (countries of the author's rights system) or by copyright.[197] Similarly to the Rome Convention, Article 14(3) phrase 1 of the TRIPS Agreement lays down the obligation to grant the exclusive rights of fixation, reproduction, wireless rebroadcasting, and communication to the public of television broadcasts[198] in favour of broadcasting organizations for their broadcasts.

10.97   Phrase 2 however completely eliminates this obligation, to the extent that a WTO Member provides copyright protection in the contents of the broadcast. This condition is mostly fulfilled, since WTO Members regularly protect works contained in the broadcast, as they are anyway obliged to do under the

---

[192] See Gervais (n 37 above) 2.144; on Art 14(6) of the TRIPS Agreement, see para 10.100 below.

[193] On Art 10 of the Rome Convention, see paras 6.61–6.62 above.

[194] See paras 10.72–10.77 above.

[195] Art 12 of the Rome Convention and paras 6.49–6.58 above.

[196] Art 16(1)(a) of the Rome Convention.

[197] See a later overview (of 1998) in WIPO Doc SCCR/1/3 paras 34–8. In respect of the USA, see Reinbothe (n 58 above) 712.

[198] In respect of the communication right, this provision seems to go further than Art 13(d) of the Rome Convention, which makes this right subject to the communication being accessible to the public against payment of an entrance fee, see paras 6.64–6.65 above. Yet, this condition may also be applied in the TRIPS context, see Art 14(6) of the TRIPS Agreement.

compliance clause.[199] Especially in countries of the copyright system, where the originality level is quite low, the contents of broadcasts will usually be protected.[200] Indeed, it is these very countries (as far as they do not provide for copyright in broadcasts), in particular the USA, that were envisaged by phrase 2.[201] Accordingly, in most situations the TRIPS Agreement does not oblige Members to provide specific rights to broadcasting organizations in their broadcasts. Similarly to the rental right for cinematographic works, the apparent principle that protection must be granted applies only under exceptional circumstances. Thereby, mainly US interests were taken into account, while other parties obtained language on the principle of protection for broadcasters in their broadcasts at least as a signal for the importance of the issue.

(iv) Duration of protection Article 14(5) phrase 1 of the TRIPS Agreement   **10.98** lays down the minimum term of fifty years for performers and phonogram producers and thereby clearly goes beyond the duration of twenty years under Article 14 of the Rome Convention. The term is calculated after the fixation or making of the performance. As under the Rome Convention,[202] the criterion of the making of the performance will have to be understood as only applying where the performance is unfixed.[203] In respect of broadcasting organizations, the TRIPS Agreement follows the Rome Convention with its minimum term of twenty years after the broadcast. This approach (as the weak protection under Article 14(3) of the TRIPS Agreement[204]) reflects the different positions and, in particular, the lower level of interest by a number of parties towards protecting broadcasting organizations.

Where a country only provides copyright protection to the authors of the content   **10.99** of the broadcasts under Article 14(3) phrase 2 of the TRIPS Agreement, the longer minimum duration of the Berne Convention[205] applies to that content. However, where a country protects broadcasts as such under copyright, the minimum duration is not governed by the Berne Convention, which does not cover broadcasts as subject matter,[206] but only by Article 14(5) phrase 2 of the TRIPS Agreement.

---

199 Art 9(1) of the TRIPS Agreement in connection with the relevant provisions of the Berne Convention.

200 For the originality level, see paras 3.33–3.34 above; for the USA regarding broadcast works in particular, see WIPO Doc SCCR/1/3 para 36.

201 Reinbothe (n 58 above) 712, Katzenberger (n 55 above) 92.

202 Art 14(a) and (b) of the Rome Convention.

203 On the relevant provisions of the Rome Convention, see para 6.70 above.

204 See para 10.97 above.

205 Art 9(1) phr 1 of the TRIPS Agreement in connection with Arts 7, 7[bis] of the Berne Convention.

206 It only covers 'intellectual creations', para 5.66 above; Gervais (n 37 above) 2.148 seems to be of a different opinion.

10.100 **(v) Restrictions of protection** Article 14(6) phrase 1 of the TRIPS Agreement simply refers to the relevant provisions of the Rome Convention as regards its 'conditions, limitations, exceptions and reservations', which are thereby also permitted under the TRIPS Agreement. Accordingly, the rights of performers, phonogram producers, and broadcasting organizations under the TRIPS Agreement may be limited according to Article 15 of the Rome Convention.[207] In addition, performers' rights may be limited according to Articles 7(1)(c) (conditions for the application of the reproduction right) and 7(2) (uses in context with broadcasting) of the Rome Convention.[208] In respect of performers and phonogram producers, Article 11 of the Rome Convention on permitted formalities has to be taken into account.[209] The relevant restrictions in respect of broadcasting organizations (as far as they are protected at all) are the additional condition for the communication right and the related possibility of a reservation.[210]

10.101 **(vi) Application in time** Article 14(6) phrase 2 of the TRIPS Agreement contains one of the few plus elements as compared to the Rome Convention: it obliges WTO Members to apply Article 18 of the Berne Convention by analogy to (only) the rights of performers and phonogram producers. This is a deviation from Article 20(2) of the Rome Convention.[211] As a consequence, the TRIPS Agreement must also be applied to performances and phonograms existing before the entry into force of the TRIPS Agreement or the accession of a country thereto, if they are then still protected in the country of origin, unless they are no longer protected in the country for which protection is claimed.[212] This principle is subject to provisions in special conventions.[213] In this respect, Article 70(5) of the TRIPS Agreement has to be taken into account: the rental right does not need to be applied to phonograms purchased before the date of application of the TRIPS Agreement for a Member.[214]

10.102 This provision has a high economic importance; it was subject to complaints by the USA and the EC against Japan that were resolved by mutual agreement.[215]

---

[207] On Art 15 of the Rome Convention, see paras 6.67–6.69 above.

[208] Another restriction, Art 19 of the Rome Convention, does not need to be applied here, since Art 14(1) of the TRIPS Agreement does not even grant protection in respect of the consent to an audiovisual fixation.

[209] See hereon paras 10.24 and 10.39 above.

[210] Art 13(d) (condition of an entrance fee, see para 6.65 above); and Art16(1)(b) of the Rome Convention (reservation). The reservation of Art 17 ibid is unlikely to apply (Art 1(3) phr 3 of TRIPS *e contrano*), cf para 10.32 above

[211] On this provision, see para 6.76 above.

[212] For the details of Art 18 of the Berne Convention, see paras 5.243 ff above.

[213] Art 18(3) phr 1 of the Berne Convention.

[214] See also para 10.138 below; Art 70(5) also applies to rental rights under copyright.

[215] See Docs WT/DS28/1 and 42/1, and notification of mutually agreed solutions in Docs WT/ DS28/4 and 42/4. For the previous situation in Japan, see Watal (n 34 above) 237; C Heath, 'All her

Specifically, the phonogram or performance must not have fallen into the public domain in the country of origin 'through the expiry of the term of protection'. This term is understood to be the minimum term under the TRIPS Agreement. Accordingly, where a country (such as Japan did at the time) provides, before accession, a term of twenty years, it cannot rely on the argument that phonograms and performances older than twenty years are in the public domain through expiry of the term of protection, but have to directly apply the fifty-years term of the TRIPS Agreement. Consequently, they must restore protection retroactively, so that all phonograms and performances fixed up to fifty years earlier are covered by the TRIPS Agreement.[216]

(4) Enforcement provisions under Part III of the TRIPS Agreement

(a) Background

The lack or poor availability of enforcement standards under the pre-existing conventions was perceived as a major deficiency when piracy industries emerged, in particular in developing countries. Where, for example, national laws did not allow a plaintiff to be represented by an attorney but required him to appear in person, most foreign artists or other right owners would obviously be unable to pursue their rights in the local courts of many different countries worldwide. Also, where national laws permitted the police to perform raids only during the day, piracy activities in the reproduction plants blossomed during the night, while enforcement against individual street vendors during the day was much less effective.[217] In order to guarantee not only substantive standards but also their effective implementation in practice, it was clear to negotiating partners that minimum standards to enforce the rights were needed—in the fields of copyright and neighbouring rights as well as in the other areas of intellectual property. Therefore, Part III of the TRIPS Agreement applies to all covered intellectual property rights.[218]

10.103

The *demandeurs* of this Part were the (exporting) industrialized countries, as they were most affected by piracy. Accordingly, the EC and the USA took the lead in

10.104

---

troubles seemed so far away: EU vs Japan before the WTO' (1996) EIPR 677; T Doi, 'The TRIPS Agreement and the Copyright Law of Japan: A Comparative Analysis (1996) Journal of the Japanese Group of AIPPI 3, 14; M Kennedy and H Wager, 'WTO Dispute Settlement and Copyright: The First Seven Years' in P Brügger (ed), *Copyright-Internet World: ALAI Study Days Neuchâtel 2002* (2003) 223, 242–3.

[216] Japan, after bilateral consultations with the USA, introduced retroactive protection from 1946 (instead of 1971), see Watal (n 34 above) 237.

[217] For these examples, see E Simon, (1993) 4/1 Fordham Intellectual Property, Media & Entertainment Law 171, 276.

[218] Art 41(1) in connection with Art 1(2) of the TRIPS Agreement, which refers to Part II ss 1–7, ie copyright and related rights, trade marks, geographical indications, industrial designs, patents, layout designs of integrated circuits, and the protection of undisclosed information.

preparing and coordinating detailed and, eventually, almost identical draft proposals[219] that were largely incorporated into the chairman's text,[220] which was then influenced by a number of other proposals from industrialized and developing countries.[221] Unlike for the substantive provisions, developing countries did not question the mandate of GATT in respect of enforcement provisions, which are arguably trade-related especially considering trade in pirated goods and border measures.[222]

(b) General remarks

10.105 Presenting the enforcement provisions of Articles 41–61 of the TRIPS Agreement in detail goes well beyond the scope of this book. Therefore, this presentation is limited to an overview and general remarks.

10.106 First, all of the enforcement provisions reflect the differences between the civil law and common law systems—differences that are particularly pertinent in the area of enforcement. In this respect, the European Community could play a leading role because it already had considerable experience in bridging the gap between the laws of its own Member States, which adhere to the different systems,[223] and because it could rely on existing Community instruments.[224]

10.107 Secondly, another major controversial issue during the TRIPS negotiations was the concern of developing countries that did not have sufficient resources to establish a working system of judicial and other enforcement means specifically for the area of intellectual property rights. Developing countries did not want to be obliged to allocate their already scarce public resources to intellectual property enforcement over anything else. Under the achieved compromise,[225] no country is obliged to provide a better enforcement system for intellectual property rights than for the law in general, or to allocate resources primarily to the enforcement of intellectual property law in lieu of other fields of law. Also, the TRIPS Agreement does not affect the capacity of a WTO Member to enforce its laws in general; accordingly, a developing country might argue that it is not able

---

[219] J Reinbothe, 'Trade-Related Aspects of Copyright: The Enforcement Rules in TRIPS' in H Cohen Jehoram, P Keuchenius, and LM Brownlee (eds), *Trade-Related Aspect of Copyright* (1996) 41, 43.

[220] Reinbothe/Howard (n 51 above) 163.

[221] See the list of documents presented by Australia, Austria, Canada, Switzerland, Scandinavian countries, Japan, India, Hong Kong, and Korea in T Dreier, 'TRIPS and the Enforcement of Intellectual Property Rights' in FK Beier and G Schricker (eds), *From GATT to TRIPS: The Agreement on Trade-Related Aspects of Intellectual Property Rights* (1996) 248, 257, in n 46.

[222] Reinbothe (n 219 above), 43.

[223] Reinbothe, ibid, mentions the different role of the courts as an example for the differences.

[224] Dreier (n 221 above) 256, 251, referring in particular to the Council Reg EC 3842/86 regarding the release for free circulation of counterfeit goods.

[225] Art 41(5) of the TRIPS Agreement.

to enforce its laws in general and that it is therefore not under an obligation to enforce intellectual property rights. Hence, the effects of enforcement obligations under the TRIPS Agreement in developing countries may be marginal in certain countries and limited in others.[226]

Thirdly, the overall trade liberalization aim of the GATT and the Uruguay Round **10.108** negotiations had to be duly taken into account, especially by ensuring that enforcement rules would not create new barriers to trade. As a compromise, Article 41(1) phrase 2 of the TRIPS Agreement requires application of the enforcement procedures in ways that create no new barriers to legitimate trade and that safeguard against abuse of these provisions.

(c) Different enforcement measures

While Part III Section 1 (Article 41 of the TRIPS Agreement) contains general **10.109** obligations in respect of enforcement, Section 2 more specifically deals with obligations regarding civil and administrative procedures and remedies, such as a due process clause; rules on evidence; and remedies[227] (in particular: injunctions,[228] damages, as well as the destruction of infringing goods and of production devices); the right to claim information from the infringer about the channels of distribution and the identity of other involved persons[229]—an important means to fight piracy; and the right of the defendant to be indemnified for any abuse of the enforcement procedure by the plaintiff.[230]

Section 3 on provisional measures is particularly important in an environment of **10.110** high-speed piracy activities. Article 50 of the TRIPS Agreement determines the purposes of provisional measures, namely, to prevent imminent infringements and to preserve relevant evidence. Moreover, it specifies the conditions for the adoption of provisional measures (such as a risk of irreparable harm to the right holder or of destruction of evidence) and the requirements to be fulfilled by the right holder (sufficient evidence as to his right ownership, (imminent) infringement, and provision of a security). It covers the follow-up of provisional measures and concerns the interests of the defendant.[231] This provision was subject to

---

[226] Similarly, Reinbothe (n 219 above) 45; see also the annual reports by US industry (IIPA) to the USTR regarding intellectual property and its enforcement in other countries, <http://www.iipa.com>.

[227] Arts 42, 43, and 44–6 of the TRIPS Agreement respectively.

[228] The importance of injunctions is highlighted by Gervais (n 37 above) 2.375, in particular regarding South East Asian countries which did not provide for such remedies.

[229] Art 47 of the TRIPS Agreement.

[230] Art 48 ibid.

[231] Art 50(4) and the following paras ibid.

requests for consultation under the WTO dispute settlement mechanism, followed by mutual agreements.[232]

10.111 Border measures are particularly important in the fight against international piracy. Section 4 (Articles 51–60 of the TRIPS Agreement) must be applied to the importation of counterfeit trade marks and pirated copyright goods,[233] and allows WTO Members also to apply the provisions to goods that involve other infringements of any intellectual property rights and to the exportation of infringing goods.[234] Border measures are of a primarily provisional nature and envisage the suspension of goods rather than their destruction or disposal, which is also possible. Article 51 of the TRIPS Agreement and the related footnotes contain general provisions in this regard, while Articles 52–60 deal with more specific conditions for applications with a view to border measures, issues related to the suspension, and special procedural requirements.

10.112 Lastly, Section 5 (Article 61 of the TRIPS Agreement) obliges Members to provide for criminal procedures and penalties in respect of trade mark counterfeiting and copyright piracy[235] on a commercial scale; it also specifies the remedies to be provided. The inclusion of criminal procedures has been considered a 'big success', not least against the background that there was little awareness of criminal enforcement of intellectual property rights even in many industrialized countries.[236]

10.113 In sum, Part III on enforcement constitutes a major step forward in the international protection of copyright and neighbouring rights, as well as intellectual property rights in general.[237]

(5) Dispute settlement mechanism

(a) Basic choices made during the TRIPS negotiations

10.114 **(i) Three options for a dispute settlement mechanism for TRIPS** One of the main deficiencies of the existing conventions in intellectual property is the lack of an effective dispute settlement mechanism; the International Court of Justice

---

[232] USA versus Denmark and Sweden, see the requests in Docs WT/DS86/1 and 83/1, and notification of agreed solutions in Docs WT/DS/86/2 and 83/2.

[233] Art 51 phr 1 of the TRIPS Agreement; the related footnote 14 defines under (b) 'pirated copyright goods' also by reference to related rights.

[234] Art 51 phr 2 and 3 ibid.

[235] Related rights are also covered, see n 14 to Art 51 ibid.

[236] Reinbothe (n 219 above) 50.

[237] For a more detailed analysis of the individual provisions, see eg Correa (n 94 above) 409–66; Gervais (n 37 above) 2.372–2.474; Dreier (n 221 above) 259–67; Reinbothe (n 219 above) 44–50; Watal (n 34 above) 333–62.

has never been invoked to decide on an intellectual property case.[238] In contrast, the dispute settlement mechanism of the GATT 1947 had, at least for a long time, proved to be successful in its goal-oriented and pragmatic rather than judicial focus.[239] Yet, through the years it showed several setbacks. Consequently, the Uruguay Round negotiations envisaged its transformation from a political to a more legalistic instrument, not least to the benefit of weaker Members in their relations with economically powerful Members.[240]

During the TRIPS negotiations, one of the main controversies related to the so-called 'GATTability'[241]—the way in which a dispute settlement mechanism should be integrated into the TRIPS Agreement. Unlike industrialized countries, developing countries favoured a completely separate dispute settlement mechanism for the TRIPS Agreement, in order to avoid cross-retaliation as known under the GATT (ie retaliation for a TRIPS violation in other trade areas covered by the GATT/WTO). While retaliation in the field of intellectual property against developing countries would mostly lack any considerable economic effect, if any at all, given the generally limited exportation of intellectual property-related goods and services by developing countries, they feared that retaliation in other trade areas could be a strong weapon for other countries to enforce intellectual property obligations.[242] Therefore, while developing countries preferred the first option of a separate dispute settlement mechanism for TRIPS, they could also live with the second option of a dispute settlement mechanism within the (future) WTO but without the possibility of cross-retaliation. **10.115**

Finally, however, a third option was adopted: the full application of the WTO dispute settlement mechanism to the TRIPS Agreement, including cross-retaliation.[243] Accordingly, the relevant provisions of the GATT and the Dispute Settlement Understanding, which was adopted as one of the Uruguay Round agreements to improve the prior mechanism, apply to the TRIPS Agreement.[244] **10.116**

---

238 paras 8.26 and 9.05 above.

239 F Weiss, 'International Public Law Aspects of TRIPS' in H Cohen Jehoram, P Keuchenius, and LM Brownlee (eds), *Trade-Related Aspects of Copyright* (1996) 7, 18, differentiates between the aims of the International Court of Justice to reach legal consistency, predictability, and certainty, and the aims of the GATT dispute settlement mechanism to accommodate the different interests by showing flexibility in order to reach the overall aim of settlement.

240 Weiss, ibid 18; paras 10.15–10.16 above.

241 Watal (n 34 above) 27; Gervais (n 37 above) 1.26.

242 Watal (n 34 above) 63.

243 On the negotiations, see Gervais (n 37 above) 1.26.

244 Art 64(1) of the TRIPS Agreement; it refers to the relevant GATT provisions, ie Arts XXII and XXIII of the GATT 1994 as elaborated and applied by the Understanding on Rules and Procedures Governing the Settlement of Disputes (DSU), which was adopted in 1994 as Annex 2 of the WTO Agreement. Arts XXII and XXIII of the GATT 1994 are the main dispute settlement provisions in respect of goods and largely correspond to the relevant provisions of the GATT 1947.

To date, only one panel report has been issued in the field of copyright and related rights; in several cases, mutual agreement terminated the procedure before the stage of a panel report was reached.[245]

10.117   (ii) **Three different complaints**   The GATT 1994 distinguishes between three main kinds of complaints: the violation complaint in the case of a direct violation of a provision of a covered agreement; the non-violation complaint where the expected benefits from an agreement are nullified or impaired without a concrete violation of a provision;[246] and the situation complaint.[247] In the entire history of the GATT dispute settlement, both the non-violation complaint and the situation complaint were rarely used.[248]

10.118   Developing countries in particular were opposed to the inclusion of non-violation and situation complaints, since they feared that their legitimate measures could become an object of a non-violation complaint on the argument that they would take away benefits from patents.[249] As a compromise, the application of non-violation and situation complaints was excluded for a period of five years after entry into force of the WTO Agreement; in addition, the TRIPS Council had to examine the scope and modalities for such complaints and make a recommendation to the Ministerial Conference for approval by consensus.[250] To date, the TRIPS Council has not made such recommendations. After the failure of the Seattle Ministerial Conference at the end of 1999, the two complaints became applicable under Article 64(2) of the TRIPS Agreement but their application was suspended and the moratorium renewed in 2001 and again in 2004 and in 2005.[251]

---

[245] For the s 110 case, see paras 10.129–10.132 below; for an overview of mutually agreed solutions until 2002, see Kennedy/Wager (n 215 above) 223, 242–6. The most recent requests for consultations were brought by the USA against China on 10 April 2007, Docs WT/DS362 and 363, followed by the establishment of a panel on request of the USA (Doc WT/DS362/7) on 25 September 2007, <http://www.wto.org>.

[246] Art XXIII (1)(b) of the GATT 1994; E-U Petersmann, *The GATT/WTO Dispute Settlement System* (1997) 135 ff; S Ohlhoff, 'Die Streitbeilegung in der WTO' in HJ Prieß and GM Berrisch (eds), *WTO-Handbuch* (2003) 739; Watal (n 34 above) 81.

[247] Art XXIII(1)(c) of the GATT 1994, according to which any benefit accruing to a WTO Member under the WTO Agreement is nullified or impaired, or the attainment of one of its objectives is impeded as a result of an existing situation that is neither a violation nor a non-violation under Art XXIII(1)(a) or (b) of GATT 1994.

[248] E-U Petersmann, 'International Trade Law and the GATT/WTO Dispute Settlement System 1948–1996: An Introduction' in E-U Petersmann (ed), *International Trade Law and the GATT/WTO Dispute Settlement System* (1997) 3, 37; the situation complaint had even less importance than the non-violation complaint.

[249] Watal (n 34 above) 41.

[250] Art 64(2), (3) of the TRIPS Agreement.

[251] Decision on Implementation-Related Issues and Concerns, WTO Doc WT/MIN(01)/W/10 of 14 November 2001, n 11.1., adopted at a meeting of Ministers. In a preceding TRIPS Council in 1999, the US was strongly opposed to the extension of the five-year period under Art 64(2) of the TRIPS Agreement, while many other countries, including developing countries, Canada, and the EC, were in favour of (at least) a limited extension—in the case of Canada and the EC possibly

To date, Members have not brought any non-violation or situation complaints under the TRIPS Agreement.[252]

The way in which the non-violation and situation complaints would apply to the TRIPS Agreement remains uncertain; for example, it could be difficult to determine a nullified 'benefit' that is ensured under the TRIPS Agreement.[253] The necessary nullification or impairment of a benefit under the TRIPS Agreement has been considered to exist prima facie in the case of a violation of its obligations.[254]

10.119

(b) Dispute settlement procedure

(i) Procedure leading to panel or appellate body report   Only the main elements of the dispute settlement procedure can be summarized here.[255] First, before a party may request the establishment of a panel, bilateral or multilateral consultations between the relevant parties must have taken place without success within sixty days.[256] In parallel, other non-judicial procedures for dispute settlement (good offices, conciliation, and mediation) may take place at any time if the parties so agree.[257] Once a party has properly requested the establishment of a panel,[258] a panel must in principle be established.[259] The Secretariat assists the

10.120

---

because of their concerns about cultural exceptions to copyright and related rights, see Watal (n 34 above) 79, 80 n 56. The General Council on 1 August 2004 extended the moratorium to the Hong Kong Ministerial; at that 6th Ministerial Conference, Ministers instructed the Council to continue examination and make recommendations to the next Ministerial Conference, and agreed not to initiate non-violation and situation complaints under the TRIPS Agreement in the meantime (para 45 of the Hong Kong Ministerial Declaration of December 2005). In a TRIPS Council in May 2003, most Members preferred to ban non-violation complaints or at least to extend the moratorium, see <http://www.wto.int/english/tratop_e/trips_e/nonviolation_background_e.htm>; Members' positions have largely stayed the same since then.

252 <http://www.wto.org/english/tratop_e/dispu_e/disp_settlement_cbt_e/c4s5p1_e.htm>; see also for the corresponding agreement at the Hong Kong Ministerial Conference n 251 above.

253 Watal (n 34 above) 81–3; JH Jackson, *The World Trade Organization: Constitution and Jurisprudence* (1998) 92–3 stresses the ambiguity of the conditions for non-violation complaints even in general and criticizes that they are not precise enough for new matters; also Petersmann (n 246 above) 149–50 has doubts about the appropriateness of these complaints.

254 Art 3(8) of the DSU.

255 For an analysis and assessment of the procedure, see eg Jackson (n 253 above) 72 ff; Petersmann (n 246 above) 177 ff; E Olsen et al, *WTO Law from a European Perspective* (2006) 57 ff; for a very detailed presentation, see D Palmeter and P Mavroidis, *Dispute Settlement in the World Trade Organization* (2nd edn, 2004); and K Lee and S von Lewinski, 'The Settlement of International Disputes in the Field of Intellectual Property' in F-K Beier and G Schricker (eds), *From GATT to TRIPS: The Agreement on Trade-Related Aspects of Intellectual Property* (1996) 278 ff.

256 On consultations, see Art 4 of the DSU, in particular Art 4(5), (7) ibid; for more details, see the entire Art 4 ibid.

257 Art 5 ibid.

258 For conditions and terms of reference, see Arts 6, 7 ibid.

259 The Dispute Settlement Body (DSB), see hereon para 10.16 above, can reject the establishment of a panel, though only by consensus, Art 6(1) of the DSU.

parties by proposing well-qualified governmental and/or non-governmental individuals as Members who shall not be opposed by the parties except for compelling reasons.[260] Within six to nine months, the panel must objectively assess the facts of the case and the applicability of and conformity with the relevant covered agreements, and then make findings that will assist the DSB in making its recommendations or rulings.[261] For this purpose, the panel may make investigations.[262]

10.121   After discussion of arguments made at the interim review stage,[263] the panel lays down its findings in a final report. The final report is then circulated to the WTO Members and considered for adoption by the DSB no earlier than twenty days thereafter. The DSB has to adopt the report within sixty days, unless one of the parties notifies the DSB of its decision to appeal or the DSB decides by consensus not to adopt the report; this latter requirement of 'negative consensus' usually results in the adoption of the report.[264]

10.122   If a party to the dispute appeals a panel report, a standing Appellate Body established by the DSB must submit its report within sixty to ninety days thereafter.[265] The establishment of a standing Appellate Body is a novel element of the dispute settlement procedure, and one that rendered the procedure more legalistic.[266] The appeal is limited to issues of law covered in the panel report and to the panel's legal interpretations.[267] The Appellate Body report shall be adopted by the DSB and unconditionally accepted by the parties to the dispute unless the DSB decides by consensus not to adopt it within thirty days of its circulation to its Members.[268] The condition of a negative consensus again will usually lead to an automatic adoption of reports.

10.123   (ii) **Implementation of reports**   The adoption of the panel or Appellate Body reports is followed by the implementation of their recommendations.[269] The recommendations will usually require the Member to achieve consistency with the

---

[260] Usually, three (or, as an exception, five) panellists are nominated; for details on the composition of panels, see Art 8 of the DSU.

[261] Art 11 ibid.

[262] Art 13 ibid; for procedural questions, see in particular Arts 12, 14, and 15 ibid.

[263] This stage of interim discussion and interim report by the panel was introduced in 1994 and enables the parties to make comments, Art 15 ibid.

[264] Art 16 ibid; Kennedy/Wager (n 215 above) 227.

[265] Art 17(1), (5) of the DSU.

[266] For the composition of seven independent experts appointed for four years, three of which serve on each case, see Art 17(1)–(3) ibid.

[267] Art 17(6) ibid; for further procedural questions, see the entire Art 17 ibid.

[268] Art 17(14) ibid.

[269] On the implementation phase, see eg Gleason and Walther, 'The Dispute Settlement Implementation Procedures: A System in Need of Reform' (2000) Law & Policy in International Business 709.

TRIPS Agreement; this corresponds to the main aim of dispute settlement, namely, the implementation of the ruling so as to achieve compliance with WTO law.[270] Within thirty days after the adoption of the panel or Appellate Body reports, the Member concerned must indicate to the DSB its intentions regarding the implementation.[271] Where it cannot promptly comply, it is conceded a 'reasonable period of time' for doing so.[272] Most Members comply within this period of time.[273]

(iii) Compensation and suspension of concessions   Only where and as long as   **10.124** the prevailing aim of compliance is not reached within a reasonable period of time can the complaining party of the dispute seek voluntary compensation from the Member concerned or, as a last resort, suspend concessions.[274] Accordingly, these measures are only considered temporary. They were already basic elements of the traditional dispute settlement mechanism and have been specified in the DSU.[275]

The compensation must be agreed between the parties of the dispute and also be   **10.125** compatible with the covered agreements.[276] Consequently, the compensation must be granted in accordance with the most-favoured-nation clause, which may make it much more unattractive for the Member concerned than suspension of concessions.[277]

If no agreement on the compensation is achieved within twenty days after the   **10.126** reasonable period of time,[278] the complaining party may request authorization from the DSB to suspend the application of concessions or other obligations under the covered agreements to the Member concerned, for example by raising import duties for specific goods.[279] Accordingly, a party cannot unilaterally decide on the object of suspension. However, the complaining party can choose the object of suspension that it proposes to the DSB as long as certain principles

---

[270] Arts 21(1) and 3(7) of the DSU.

[271] Art 21(3) phr 1 ibid; its phrases 2 and 3 allow a 'reasonable period' if this is impracticable.

[272] This period is approved by the DSB or agreed by the parties or determined through arbitration, see Art 21(3) ibid. It is generally between 6 and 12 months (for the repeal of a regulation and an act of legislation, respectively), see Kennedy/Wager (n 215 above) 227.

[273] ibid; any dispute on whether the Member has complied may be resolved by another panel proceeding, ibid. The DSB continuously supervises implementation; Members must regularly submit status reports, Art 21(6) of the DSU.

[274] Arts 22(1) and 3(7) phr 4–6 ibid.

[275] Art XXIII(2) of the GATT 1994 and Art 22 of the DSU.

[276] Art 22(1) phr 3 ibid; the Member concerned shall upon request negotiate with the complaining party in order to agree on a mutually acceptable compensation, Art 22(2) phr 1 ibid.

[277] Ohlhoff (n 246 above) 733.

[278] ie the period within which compliance should have been reached, see para 10.124 above.

[279] Art 22(2) phr 2 and the following paras.

are followed; in particular, retaliation must first take place in the same sector as that of the complaint, and only if this is not practicable or effective may cross-retaliation be deployed (in other sectors under the same Agreement or, if not practicable or effective, under another covered Agreement).[280] Also, the DSB can only reject the authorization if a covered Agreement prohibits the suspension of concessions, or if the DSB decides by consensus to reject the request.[281] The suspension must not go beyond what is equivalent to the level of the nullification or impairment[282] as retaliation must not have a punitive character. The determination of such an equivalent level may pose major problems of economic evaluation.[283]

10.127 If the Member concerned objects to the level of suspension proposed, or if it claims that the other party did not follow the principles or procedures in Article 22(3) of the DSU, the matter is then subject to an arbitration procedure.[284] Such arbitration must be completed within sixty days after the expiry of the reasonable period of time.[285]

10.128 Cross-retaliation has only been authorized once under the TRIPS Agreement. In the *EC—Bananas* case on a violation of provisions of GATT 1994 and GATS in May 2000,[286] Ecuador was authorized to deny protection for related rights owners under Article 14 of the TRIPS Agreement.[287] Yet, while understandings on the amendment of the Banana regime in the EC were signed, Ecuador has never exercised such retaliation.[288] Indeed, it may be difficult to imagine how such denial of protection could be practised, especially as regards the level of losses that is not to be surpassed.

10.129 **(iv) The copyright case under TRIPS**   In the only copyright case so far submitted to a WTO Panel, the USA was requested to bring Section 110(5)B of its Copyright Act into conformity with the TRIPS Agreement.[289] After the agreed reasonable time of twelve months and an agreed prolongation until December 2001, the USA had not implemented the ruling. Already in July 2001 and before

---

[280] Art 22(3) of the DSU.
[281] Art 22(5), (6) ibid; the DSB must grant authorization or reject the request within 30 days of the expiry of the above reasonable period of time (n 271 above).
[282] Art 22(4) of the DSU.
[283] See paras 10.130–10.131 below.
[284] Art 22(6) phr 2 of the DSU; for the principles under Art 22(3), see para 10.126 and n 280 above.
[285] Art 22(6) phr 3 of the DSU; for the period of time, see para 10.124 and n 278 above.
[286] WT/DS27.
[287] WT/DS27/ARB/ECU; such denial was also granted for geographical indications and industrial designs.
[288] Kennedy/Wager (n 215 above) 242.
[289] WT/DS160/R on the basis of Art 13 of the TRIPS Agreement, see para 10.87 above.

proceeding to negotiations on compensation or to a subsequent request for retaliation, the parties agreed to arbitrate the level of nullification or impairment of benefits—the amount to be paid by the USA to the complainant, the EC.[290] Such direct and voluntary recourse to arbitration was unique in the WTO practice.[291]

The Arbitrators' Award, which was final, showed the problems of evaluating the economic losses due to a violation of a copyright provision. While the EC estimated the amount of nullification and impairment to be US$25,486,974, the USA proposed an amount between US$446,000 and US$733,000.[292] This discrepancy was rooted in different calculation methods that were based either on the potential licensing income that could be realized from exercising the public performance right, or the factual income, calculated on the basis of the three past years before the violation occurred.[293] The Award, issued in November 2001, largely followed the US views and determined the amount to be €1,219,900 per year, or US$1.1 million at the time.   **10.130**

The USA and the EC agreed that this amount be paid into a fund for unspecified 'projects and activities for the benefit of EC music creators'.[294] In order to fully safeguard their rights, in January 2002 the EC requested the DSB to authorize retaliation in form of a fee to be collected from US nationals in connection with border measures concerning copyright goods within the amount determined by the Award.[295] After the USA objected to the level of retaliation and the principles applied, the matter was referred to arbitration[296] but the procedure was soon suspended upon request by both parties in order to facilitate an overall positive outcome of continued discussions.[297] To date, the USA has not complied with the law, and it has been suggested that this situation will not change until a particular senator leaves his functions.[298]   **10.131**

This case shows the limits and deficiencies of the WTO dispute settlement mechanism: first, no country can be forced to adopt the necessary laws in order to bring its rules into compliance with the international agreement; the democratic   **10.132**

---

290 Notification of both parties to the DSB on 23 July 2001; WT/DS160/ARB25/1 n 1.1

291 Kennedy/Wager (n 215 above) 236. Agreed arbitration under Art 25 of the DSU is available for any clearly defined issues; yet, mostly it is used where it is compulsory (as for the determination of a reasonable period of time under Art 21(3)(c) of the DSU) or where retaliation has already been requested (Art 22(6) of the DSU).

292 nn 4.2 and 4.3 of the Arbitrators' Award, WT/DS160/ARB25/1.

293 For an analysis of these methods and other criteria, see the Arbitrators' Award, III and IV; R Owens, 'TRIPs and the Fairness in Music Arbitration: The Repercussions' [2003] EIPR 49, 50–2.

294 ibid 54.

295 WT/DS160/19.

296 Art 22(6) of the DSU.

297 WT/DS160/22.

298 M Peters, Statement in Talk at the 10th Fordham International Intellectual Property Law & Policy Conference, April 2002.

(or even other) procedures of domestic law-making by sovereign states remain respected and unaffected. Where, as in the case of the USA, eventually an important senator may successfully block the necessary amendment of the law, and where, in addition, the financial sanctions are at such a low level that it seems more profitable for the infringing country to make payments than to amend the law,[299] the credibility of the system is at stake.[300]

(6) Other provisions

(a) Developing countries

10.133 **(i) Transitional provisions** One of the elements of compromise between industrialized and developing countries during the TRIPS negotiations was the concession of transitional periods. Accordingly, developing countries were permitted to delay the application of the TRIPS Agreement (except its Articles 3–5 on national treatment, most-favoured-nation treatment, and acquisition or maintenance of protection) for four years after industrialized countries had to implement it, namely, up to 1 January 2000.[301] The same transitional period was conceded to former socialist countries, which were in the process of transforming their centrally planned economies into market economies (so-called 'transition countries' or 'transformation countries').[302] Least-developed countries (LDCs) were conceded a transitional period of ten years until 1 January 2006, which was later extended until 1 July 2013;[303] yet, they also immediately had to apply Articles 3–5 of the TRIPS Agreement from the general application date.[304] Regardless of development status, however, these transitional periods usually had to be given

---

[299] The proper application of Art 13 of the TRIPS Agreement would most likely lead to much higher benefits of right owners in the EC than the amount awarded.

[300] See also the criticism in Owens (n 293 above) 52–4. For a critical appreciation of the WTO dispute settlement system, see also S von Lewinski, 'The Role of the TRIPS Dispute Settlement Mechanism and its Perspective for the Future' in P Brügger (ed), *Copyright Internet World: ALAI Study Days Neuchâtel 2002* (2003) 329, 335–7.

[301] Art 64(2) of the TRIPS Agreement; see also the specific period in its para 4 regarding patent protection.

[302] Art 65(3) ibid, which also contains conditions for the application of the delay.

[303] Art 66(1) ibid; it was first extended for the Maldives only, upon its request following the tsunami disaster, and only until 20 December 2007, when it would cease to be an LDC, see TRIPS Council Doc IP/C/35 of 17 June 2005. Soon thereafter, the transition period was extended for all LDCs until 1 July 2013, though in combination with the obligation to provide information on the priority needs for technical assistance to be provided by developed country Members in order to effectively assist implementation of the TRIPS Agreement—a clause that reflects higher pressure to make best use of the transitional period; also, LDCs are obliged to ensure that their law and practice during this practice do not result in lesser consistency with TRIPS provisions, TRIPS Council Doc IP/C/40. The possibility of a further extension thereafter under Art 66(1) is maintained, ibid.

[304] On the 'circumvention' of these transitional periods through, in particular, the USA by means of commitments upon WTO accession and bilateral treaties see para 12.39 below.

up (sometimes indirectly or in part) by non-WTO countries as a condition for WTO accession.[305]

The determination of a 'developing country' is made by the General Council **10.134** rather than on the basis of the system of the United Nations or another body.[306] The recognition as a 'transition country' and the fulfilment of its conditions are determined by the TRIPS Council or, in general, the General Council.[307] To the contrary, the determination of LDCs follows the relevant list established by the United Nations.[308]

(ii) Technology transfer Another element of compromise was the obligation **10.135** of industrialized countries to provide incentives within their own territories in order to promote and encourage technology transfer to LDC Members.[309] In favour of least-developed and developing countries, industrialized country Members shall also provide technical and financial cooperation, including assistance in the preparation of norms on intellectual property and in respect of domestic offices, such as intellectual property offices, including the training of their personnel.[310] Industrialized country Members have agreed to submit to the TRIPS Council and annually to update reports on their technical and financial cooperation activities.[311]

(b) Institutional provisions

The TRIPS Council is one of three special councils within the WTO structure.[312] **10.136** Its task is to monitor the operation of the TRIPS Agreement.[313] In particular, all Members scrutinize each other's national implementing legislation for compliance with the TRIPS Agreement.[314] In this context, the Members' obligation to publish and notify to the TRIPS Council their laws and regulations implementing the TRIPS Agreement[315] is an important precondition. The WIPO, which traditionally collected and translated relevant laws, agreed to make these laws

---

305 For examples, see Watal (n 34 above) 53 (in n 7).
306 Gervais (n 37 above) 2.508, with a reference to the GATT analytical index.
307 ibid.
308 ibid.
309 Art 66 (2) of the TRIPS Agreement.
310 Art 67 ibid.
311 The reports are available in the IP/C/W series under <http://www.wto.int/english/ tratop_e/trips_e/intel9_e.htm>.
312 Art IV(5) of the WTO Agreement; in addition, Councils for Trade in Goods and for Trade in Services have been established. On the General Council, see para 10.12 above.
313 Art 68 of the TRIPS Agreement contains further details.
314 On the review process, see Watal (n 34 above) 53–7. For a report on the first review in 1997, see <http://www.wto.org/english/news_e/pres97_e/pr_nov97.htm>.
315 Art 63 of the TRIPS Agreement provides for more detail.

accessible to the WTO,[316] which itself has only a small Secretariat. In the context of such monitoring, different views on the interpretation of a provision may emerge. Where a Member prefers to avoid dispute settlement, it may discuss and resolve problems bilaterally or within the TRIPS Council; otherwise, it may request the WTO Ministerial Conference or General Council for an authoritative interpretation;[317] they have to adopt such interpretation on the basis of a recommendation of the TRIPS Council. If that Council does not reach the required consensus, the matter will be dealt with by the General Council, which may, for lack of consensus, decide by a three-fourths majority.[318] Where a dispute settlement procedure is chosen, the TRIPS Council shall provide assistance, such as through information on specific intellectual property issues.[319]

10.137 The TRIPS Council is also responsible for a number of notifications under the TRIPS Agreement.[320] Among its important tasks are the decision on the possible extension of the transitional period for LDC Members,[321] the preparation and submission of recommendations to the Ministerial Conference regarding non-violation complaints,[322] and its function as a forum for discussions with a view to reviewing and possibly amending the TRIPS Agreement.[323]

(c) Final provisions

10.138 **(i) Application in time** Article 70 of the TRIPS Agreement regulates its application in time in respect of all intellectual property rights. Paragraph (1) is a standard in that it does not cover any acts that occurred before the date of application in the relevant Member. Accordingly, the TRIPS Agreement is not retroactive. In respect of the covered subject matter under copyright and neighbouring rights, the application in time is exclusively determined according to Article 18

---

[316] In particular, Art 2 of the Agreement between the World Intellectual Property Organization and the World Trade Organization of 22 December 1995 (<http://www.wto.int/english/tratop_e/trips_e/wtowip_e.htm>). It entered into force on 1 January 1996; on cooperation in the field of legal-technical assistance and technical cooperation, see Art 4.

[317] Under Art IX (2) of the WTO Agreement, they have the exclusive authority to adopt such interpretations.

[318] M Geuze, 'The TRIPS Council and the Implementation of the TRIPS Agreement' in H Cohen Jehoram, P Keuchenius, and LM Brownlee (eds), *Trade-Related Aspects of Copyright* (1996) 69, 76.

[319] Geuze (n 318 above) 77.

[320] They were mainly due in its initial period, eg notifications concerning the beneficiaries of protection under Art 1(3), national treatment under Art 3(1), MFN treatment under Art 4(d), copyright (Art 9(1) in connection with the provisions of the Berne Convention), neighbouring rights (Art 14(6) in connection with provisions of the Rome Convention), notification of laws (Art 63(2)), and the establishment of contact points under Art 69 of the TRIPS Agreement.

[321] Art 66 ibid, see para 10.133 above.

[322] Art 64(3) ibid; see paras 10.117–10.119 above.

[323] See paras 10.139–10.140 below.

of the Berne Convention.[324] Article 70(5) of the TRIPS Agreement exempts Members from the obligation to apply the rental right in respect of already purchased originals or copies.[325]

(ii) Review and amendment, reservations   Upon the adoption of the TRIPS   **10.139**
Agreement, it was certain that technology and further globalization would bring about new challenges that would have to be addressed in a review process in order to secure the long-term success of the TRIPS Agreement. Moreover, a number of questions were left open for future work.[326] Therefore, the first review was planned to take place after 1 January 2000, when the Agreement would be in force for industrialized and developing country Members.[327] In line with the recent general, political problems in the WTO and other international frameworks, the review has not led to any new proposals regarding copyright and related rights.

Article 71(2) of the TRIPS Agreement offers a peculiar route: any intellectual   **10.140**
property standards can be incorporated en bloc into the TRIPS Agreement as amendments thereto simply by the Ministerial Conference without a further formal acceptance process as long as those standards are higher than those of the TRIPS Agreement and, in the meantime, have been adopted and are in force as part of other multilateral agreements, and are accepted under those agreements by all WTO Members.[328] The TRIPS Council would have to propose such incorporation by consensus. Indeed, when the WCT and the WPPT were adopted in December 1996, the idea was expressed to later incorporate their standards en bloc into the TRIPS Agreement.[329] Given the radical change of atmosphere after 1996 in international fora towards criticism of high standards of protection and, in general, of globalization as promoted through the WTO,[330] such a development seems unrealistic today.

Article 72 of the TRIPS Agreement does not allow any reservations without the   **10.141**
consent of all the other Members; the reservations permitted under the Berne and

---

[324] It applies to copyright on the basis of Art 9(1) of the TRIPS Agreement and to neighbouring rights by analogy on the basis of Art 14(6) phr 2 ibid; see on its exclusive application Art 70(2) phr 3 ibid.

[325] See para 10.101 above in the context of application in time for related rights.

[326] They concerned geographical indications, certain exclusions from patentability and the applicability of the non-violation complaints (Arts 23(4), 27(3)(b) and 64(3) of the TRIPS Agreement).

[327] Art 71(1) ibid, which also provides for further periodical reviews.

[328] Art 71(2) ibid in connection with Art X(6) of the WTO Agreement.

[329] The topic of 'incorporating new trade-related intellectual property treaties adopted outside the WTO' was on the agenda for the Seattle Ministerial Conference in 2000, see <http://www.wto.org/english/thewto_e/minist_e/min99_e/english/about_e/10trips_e.htm>; see also the allusion in Gervais (n 37 above) 2.547.

[330] See hereon in particular paras 26.01–26.05 below.

Rome Conventions are consented to by the adoption of Articles 9(1) and 14(6) of the TRIPS Agreement.

C. Assessment of the inclusion of copyright and neighbouring rights in the TRIPS Agreement as compared to the Berne and Rome Conventions

(1) Principles of protection

10.142 As regards the principles of protection, the progress of the TRIPS Agreement as compared to the Berne and Rome Conventions is quite limited. In both fields, the most-favoured-nation clause has been added, though with limited effects.[331] While in the field of copyright, the main three principles of protection remain unchanged, the scope of national treatment in the field of neighbouring rights has been clarified (or, according to a different opinion, reduced)[332] so as only to extend to the minimum rights under the TRIPS Agreement.

(2) Substantive standards

10.143 Progress is also limited for the substantive standards. Regarding copyright, protection for computer programs and compilations of data was clarified or, according to a different opinion, introduced. An exclusive rental right was introduced for authors of computer programs and, under specific conditions only, for authors of cinematographic works, and arguably for authors of works fixed on phonograms. Further 'plus elements' are the term of protection for a very specific case (in particular, corporate ownership) and the three-step test as a 'safety net' with respect to the application of limitations and exceptions. At the same time, moral rights are a 'minus' element.

10.144 In the field of neighbouring rights, the only plus elements are the exclusive rental right for phonogram producers and, arguably, performers; the duration of fifty years for performers and phonogram producers; and the application of the Agreement to existing performances and phonograms under Article 18 of the Berne Convention applied by analogy.[333] Otherwise, the minimum standards are in part even lower than under the Rome Convention: a fixation right in respect of audiovisual performances and a strict obligation to protect broadcasts in favour

---

[331] para 10.49 above.

[332] See on the controversial scope of national treatment under the Rome Convention paras 7.34–7.40 above.

[333] Other differences are only apparent: eg the unconditional reproduction right for performers in Art 14(1) of the TRIPS Agreement can be made subject to the conditions of Art 7(1)(c) of the Rome Convention, according to Art 14(6) of the TRIPS Agreement.

of broadcasting organizations are lacking.[334] The lack of a remuneration right for secondary uses for performers and phonogram producers is not a real minus element, because this right is not a strict obligation under the Rome Convention as it can be excluded by reservations.[335]

(3) Other aspects

This limited development regarding minimum standards can be explained by the already relatively high level of protection of the Berne Convention (as compared in particular to the Paris Convention in the field of industrial property, where hardly any minimum standards were contained and the TRIPS Agreement could make a considerable difference).[336] Instead, one of the main successes of the TRIPS Agreement (as seen by industrialized countries) was its inclusion of an increased number of countries into the system of international protection; many countries that might not have wished to become subject to international copyright or neighbouring rights obligations were attracted by the potential benefits from WTO accession in other fields and, as a consequence, accepted obligations under the TRIPS Agreement. For many of them, even compliance with the standards of the latest version of the Berne Convention meant a big step, as did the adoption of Rome-like neighbouring rights standards. **10.145**

As another notable effect, many TRIPS Members voluntarily adhered to the Berne and Rome Conventions, although the TRIPS Agreement only obliges them to largely adopt their substantive standards rather than to oblige them to adhere to these Conventions. Indeed, eleven years after the general entry into force of the TRIPS Agreement and irrespective of the still applicable transitional periods for LDCs, the number of Berne Union countries has grown in general by forty-seven up to 163—thus by around 40 per cent—and, in respect of ratifications of its Paris Act 1971 through Members of earlier Acts, by five countries; membership of the Rome Convention has grown by thirty-seven up to 86 countries—thus by around 75 per cent. **10.146**

Other major achievements are the detailed enforcement provisions under Part III of the TRIPS Agreement and the availability of a working dispute settlement mechanism, even with its potential setbacks. **10.147**

---

[334] For details on audiovisual performances and broadcasters' rights, see paras 10.91–10.93 and 10.97 above.

[335] See Arts 12 and 16(1)(a) of the Rome Convention.

[336] On the then comparatively limited needs to improve the substantive standards in international copyright, see also Reinbothe (n 219 above) 708.

11

COPYRIGHT AND NEIGHBOURING RIGHTS UNDER THE NAFTA AND OTHER REGIONAL AGREEMENTS

A. NAFTA

(1) General remarks

One of the avenues taken by the USA since the mid-1980s to include intellectual **11.01** property in international trade law, besides the GATT/TRIPS approach and unilateral trade measures, has been the conclusion of bilateral and regional trade agreements on the basis of its Trade Act 1988.[1] The Canada–United States Free Trade Agreement of 1988[2] was the second bilateral agreement in a series of many to follow. Only some months after the USA and Mexico had decided to pursue a free trade agreement (FTA), Canada showed interest in participating in negotiations with a view towards a trilateral agreement. Within fourteen months between 1991 and 1992, the North American Free Trade Agreement (NAFTA) was

---

[1] paras 12.04 ff, in particular 12.07 below.
[2] 27 ILM 281 (1988); the Agreement was signed on 2 January 1988 and entered into force on 1 January 1989.

successfully negotiated among the three countries; it entered into force on 1 January 1994. It was based on the Canada–US FTA but went beyond it in many areas, in particular in intellectual property where the bilateral agreement had only included a provision on cable retransmission. NAFTA was concluded not least to build a counterpart to the perceived emergence of trade blocs in Europe and Asia.[3] It created a free trade area of around 370 million inhabitants and aimed at enhanced trade liberalization and better access to the respective markets.[4] Major parts of the NAFTA deal with the reduction or abolition of tariffs and other trade barriers.

(2) Provisions with regard to copyright and neighbouring rights

11.02 The first version of a consolidated draft text for NAFTA was prepared in early January 1992, shortly after the TRIPS negotiations had been provisionally concluded in December 1991 on the basis of the so-called Dunkel Draft.[5] It is no surprise that NAFTA negotiations closely followed this Draft and added further elements. Some of these new elements had already been suggested by the USA in the large framework of GATT-TRIPS negotiations, though without success; it was only in the trilateral negotiations that the USA were able to carry them through. Indeed, US negotiators were not satisfied with many TRIPS provisions, and successfully obtained in the NAFTA what they could not obtain in TRIPS, which they only considered a 'starting point'.[6] Accordingly, one may consider NAFTA in its copyright and neighbouring rights provisions as a TRIPS-plus agreement, even though it entered into force before the TRIPS Agreement.

(a) Basic principles of protection

11.03 (i) **General remark** Similarly to the TRIPS Agreement, the NAFTA contains an entire chapter on different intellectual property rights, including industrial property.[7] Therefore, it regulates certain issues in common provisions, such as the principles of protection.[8] Unlike the TRIPS Agreement, it does not contain an MFN clause.

---

[3] In particular, the achievement of the 'internal market' within the European Community, planned for 1992, was perceived from the outside as the creation of a 'trade fortress' to which a response had to be found; on the aim to achieve the internal market, see Vol II ch 1.

[4] While access of the two other countries to the Canadian market was already developed, the NAFTA brought about in particular the enhanced access of the Canadian and US industries to the Mexican market—see External Affairs and International Trade Canada, *NAFTA: What's it all about?* (1993) 8.

[5] See para 10.22 above.

[6] C Levy and S Weiser, 'Intellectual Property' in J Bello, A Holmer, and J Norton (eds), *The North American Free Trade Agreement: A New Frontier in International Trade and Investment in the Americas* (1994) 269, 270, 289.

[7] See Part 6 ch 17 of the NAFTA.

[8] Arts 1701–4 ibid.

A notable, general provision in favour of Canada (only) is the cultural exemption, **11.04** which has been integrated into the NAFTA from the earlier Canada–US FTA.[9] As a consequence, the defined cultural industries are excluded from basically all provisions of NAFTA. Cultural industries are 'persons engaged in . . . the publication, distribution, or sale' of music and books and similar products in print and machine readable form, and, for music recordings and video recordings, also those engaged in exhibition thereof, as well as those engaged in broadcasting and cable communication. The cultural exemption particularly permits 'Canadian content' requirements in the field of broadcasting or restrictions regarding US investment in Canada, but it may also be relevant for national treatment restrictions regarding the phonogram industry. As a counterpart to this exemption, the USA can undertake measures of equivalent commercial effect against Canadian acts that would have been inconsistent with NAFTA but for the cultural exemption.[10] Usually, both countries strive at avoiding potential conflicts through negotiation.[11]

(ii) National treatment   First, the principle of national treatment largely fol- **11.05** lows the TRIPS approach as regards the beneficiaries of protection by integrating the criteria of eligibility of the pre-existing conventions. Accordingly, the word 'nationals'[12] must not be understood in its ordinary meaning, but by reference to the relevant criteria of the Berne, Geneva Phonograms, and Rome Conventions.[13] Given the compliance clause in Article 1701(2)(b) of the NAFTA, one may assume that the entire system of national treatment under Article 5 of the Berne Convention would also apply in the framework of the NAFTA.[14] Unlike in the TRIPS Agreement, the scope of national treatment in respect of performers and phonogram producers is not limited to the minimum rights.[15]

Exceptions to national treatment provided in the existing conventions are not **11.06** explicitly mentioned in the NAFTA. Yet, those of the Berne Convention apply through the compliance clause in Article 1701(2)(b) of the NAFTA.[16] For performers' and phonogram producers' rights, only one exception regarding

---

9 Art 2106, Annex 2106, and definition of 'cultural industries' in Art 2107.

10 Art 2005.2 Canada–US FTA as integrated into the NAFTA; see also para 13.02 in n 10 below.

11 R Folsom, *NAFTA and Free Trade in the Americas* (2nd edn, 2004) 37.

12 Art 1703(1) of the NAFTA.

13 Definition of 'nationals' in Art 1721 ibid. For the criteria of eligibility, see Arts 3, 4 of the Berne Convention (1971), Arts 2 and 7(4) of the Geneva Phonograms Convention 1971, and Arts 4–6 of the Rome Convention.

14 This would include, in particular, protection in a country other than the country of origin, see paras 5.08 ff, in particular 5.19 ff above. For the similar assumption for the TRIPS Agreement, see para 10.28 above.

15 Art 3(1) phr 2 of the TRIPS Agreement includes such a limitation, see para 10.34 above.

16 Levy/Weiser (n 6 above) 175 do not mention this possibility and seem to assume that such exceptions do not apply.

performers' rights for secondary uses is provided.[17] The USA viewed the unrestricted scope of national treatment and the lack of further exceptions to it as progress from TRIPS, especially regarding remuneration rights for private reproduction provided in other countries, in which they wanted to participate.[18]

11.07 **(iii) Minimum rights** Secondly, the principle of minimum rights is reflected in the obligation to give effect to the substantive provisions of the Berne and Geneva Phonograms Conventions 'at a minimum',[19] as well as in Article 1702 of the NAFTA on the possibility to grant more extensive protection than the minimum standards under NAFTA.[20] Like the TRIPS Agreement and the classical conventions, the NAFTA only lays down obligations in respect of international rather than also domestic situations, as is reflected in the obligation to provide adequate and effective protection only 'to the nationals of another party'. As for national treatment, 'nationals' must be understood as a reference to the criteria of eligibility of the Berne, Geneva, and Rome Conventions.[21]

11.08 **(iv) 'No formalities'** Thirdly, the principle that formalities must not be required as a condition for granting national treatment is specifically provided for copyright and the rights of performers and phonogram producers.[22] This principle presents a 'plus element' as compared to the Geneva and Rome Conventions.[23]

(b) Substantive standards of protection

11.09 **(i) Principal approaches** Regarding copyright, the NAFTA follows the TRIPS Agreement in its 'Berne-plus' approach by requiring compliance with the substantive Berne provisions[24] and introducing additional elements of protection. Likewise, it carries over from TRIPS a 'minus element'; namely, the exclusion of moral rights,[25] though much less visibly: Article 1701(3) of the NAFTA refers to Annex 1701.3, under which a clause similar to Article 9(1) phrase 2 of the TRIPS

---

[17] Art 1703(1) phr 2 of the NAFTA; in addition, an exception relates to judicial and administrative procedures, similar to the TRIPS Agreement, Art 1703(3) of the NAFTA.

[18] Levy/Weiser (n 6 above) 275.

[19] Art 1701(2)(a), (b) of the NAFTA; the lack of a reference to the substantive provisions of the Rome Convention reflects the situation of the USA that was not, and did not envisage becoming, a Contracting State of the Rome Convention. See also para 11.10 below on performers.

[20] In addition to giving effect to the Berne and Geneva substantive provisions, parties must make every effort to accede to these Conventions if they have not yet done so.

[21] Art 1721 of the NAFTA; para 11.05 above.

[22] Art 1703(2) of the NAFTA. For copyright, this principle is also part of the obligation to comply with the substantive provisions of the Berne Convention under Art 1701(2)(b) of the NAFTA.

[23] On permitted formalities under the Rome Convention, see its Art 11 and paras 6.32–6.33 above; see also Art 5 of the Geneva Phonograms Convention.

[24] So-called 'compliance clause', Art 1701(2)(b) of the NAFTA.

[25] Art 9(1) phr 2 of the TRIPS Agreement; see paras 10.52–10.54 above.

Agreement exempts (here, only) the United States from moral rights obligations.[26]

For related rights, only a 'Geneva-plus' approach for phonograms was adopted, reflecting the situation and interests of the USA.[27] For the same reasons, the NAFTA covers minimum rights only for phonogram producers, rather than also for performers and broadcasting organizations.[28] Phonograms are treated separately rather than as another type of copyright work, thereby honouring the Continental European system to which Mexico adheres.[29]   **11.10**

(ii) **Copyright**   The 'Berne-plus' elements in respect of copyright largely follow, and in some cases even go beyond, Articles 10–13 of the TRIPS Agreement.[30] In particular and similarly as under TRIPS, protection must be provided for computer programs as literary works, and for compilations of data or other material (rather than of works only) under the conditions derived from the Berne Convention.[31] A minimum right beyond Berne and similar to TRIPS is a rental right in respect of computer programs (only).[32] Beyond Berne and even TRIPS, the NAFTA provides for the exclusive rights of importation (where the copies are made without the right holder's authorization); first public distribution by sale, rental, or otherwise; and communication to the public for all kinds of works.[33] The communication right is further defined—for the first time in a multilateral treaty—to include on-demand uses and similar interactive communications over the internet: the definition of 'public' includes 'any aggregation of individuals intended to be the object of, and capable of perceiving, communications or   **11.11**

---

[26] Annex 1701.3(2) of the NAFTA; accordingly, NAFTA 'confers no rights and imposes no obligations on the United States with respect to Article 6bis of the Berne Convention, or the rights derived from that Article'.

[27] Above, n 19. On the low level of protection under the 1971 Geneva Convention, see paras 4.66–4.68 above.

[28] See also para 11.15 below; only national treatment is extended to performers, see Art 1703(1) phr 2 of the NAFTA.

[29] Canadian law also treats them separately, together with performers and broadcasting organizations, even if it protects them by a copyright.

[30] Art 1705 of the NAFTA.

[31] For these conditions under Art 2(5) of the Berne Convention, see S Ricketson and J Ginsburg, *International Copyright and Neighbouring Rights: The Berne Convention and Beyond* (2006) 8.86–8.87. For the similar, differently worded provisions in Art 10 of the TRIPS Agreement, see paras 10.60–10.63 above.

[32] The TRIPS Agreement additionally provides for a rental right in respect of cinematographic works (though only under certain conditions) and, arguably, authors' works fixed on phonograms (Arts 11 phr 1 and 14(4) phr 1). This additional protection was a compromise necessary in view of major negotiating parties against which the USA, unlike for NAFTA, did not succeed in excluding such protection, see paras 10.65, 10.67 ff above.

[33] The Berne Convention (and, through the compliance clause, the TRIPS Agreement) only include a distribution right regarding cinematographic adaptations and works, and a communication right regarding specific kinds of works, see paras 5.131–5.133 and 5.138–5.139 above.

performances of works, *regardless of whether they can do so at the same or different times or in the same or different places . . .'.*[34]

11.12 The mandatory application of the three-step test to any limitations of or exceptions to the rights provided under the Berne Convention[35] and the NAFTA, as well as the minimum duration regarding works for which the duration is calculated otherwise than on the basis of the life of a natural person, correspond to the relevant provisions of the TRIPS Agreement.[36]

11.13 Another provision that goes beyond Berne and TRIPS envisages Mexico as the only developing country under the NAFTA.[37] It prohibits Mexico from granting a compulsory licence, otherwise permitted under the Appendix to the Berne Convention (as integrated in the NAFTA by its compliance clause), where Mexico's legitimate needs could be fulfilled by voluntary action, such as a licence of the right holder, but for obstacles created by Mexico.

11.14 Finally, another 'plus element' in the field of copyright was to benefit Canadian and Mexican films, which had been published in the USA between 1 January 1978[38] and 1 March 1989[39] without a copyright notice and therefore had not been protected in the USA.[40] The NAFTA obliges the USA to restore protection for such cinematographic works, though only to the extent that is consistent with the US Constitution and subject to budgetary considerations. The restoration rule was criticized for its restrictive approach and for not applying to the renewal of registration after twenty-eight years under the former US system.[41]

---

[34] Art 1721 of the NAFTA with emphasis added. A similar definition of 'public' had already been envisaged in the TRIPS Agreement but was eventually not adopted, see the Draft of the TRIPS Agreement of 23 July 1990, repr in D Gervais, *The TRIPS Agreement: Drafting History and Analysis* (2nd edn, 2003) n 2.153. It is curious that this definition is limited to 'at least' the rights of communication and performance of works under Arts 11, 11[bis](1), and 14(1)(ii) of the Berne Convention rather than also extended to those under Art 11[ter] of the Berne Convention and Art 1705(2)(c) of the NAFTA itself. For a similar wording in bilateral agreements, see paras 12.10, 12.31 above, and in the WCT and the WPPT ('right of making available'), see paras 17.72–17.82 below.

[35] Art 1705(5) of the NAFTA refers to the rights 'in this Article', which makes applicable the Berne rights in its para (2). Where Berne rights are limited, the Berne limitations have to be examined on the basis of Art 1701(2)(b) of the NAFTA, before the three-step test additionally applies (for the corresponding situation under the TRIPS Agreement, see paras 10.83–10.84 above).

[36] Art 1705(5), (4) of the NAFTA and Arts 13, 12 of the TRIPS Agreement; on TRIPS, see paras 10.83–10.88 and 10.80–10.82 above.

[37] Art 1705(6) of the NAFTA.

[38] Entry into force of the 1976 Copyright Act.

[39] US accession to the Berne Convention, which prohibits formalities.

[40] On the formalities required in the USA during this time, see paras 3.26–3.27 above with further references.

[41] Art 1705(7) in connection with Annex 1705.7 of the NAFTA. The US provisions implementing these Articles in 1993 were soon thereafter superseded and entirely revised by s 104A of the US Coypright Act (Title 17 USC), implementing the TRIPS Agreement in 1994, see E Schwartz

(iii) Neighbouring rights In the field of neighbouring rights, no provisions for **11.15** performers[42] and broadcasting organizations were adopted. This again reflects the stronger bargaining position of the USA in the trilateral context as opposed to the GATT negotiations, where countries of the Continental European system insisted on the inclusion of the other two groups of neighbouring rights owners. Also, NAFTA (like the US and Canadian laws) exclusively uses the expression 'sound recordings', while the TRIPS text refers to phonograms.[43]

The minimum rights to be provided for phonogram producers are, beyond the **11.16** reproduction and rental rights contained also in the TRIPS Agreement, the exclusive rights of importation and first public distribution corresponding to those for authors.[44] The minimum duration is fifty years after fixation, as under the TRIPS Agreement.[45]

Limitations of and exceptions to these rights are permitted under the conditions **11.17** of the three-step test to the rights of phonogram producers;[46] it is the first multilateral agreement to make this test applicable to a related right, followed only in 1996 by the WPPT regarding the rights of performers and phonogram producers.

(iv) Common provisions Another additional element as compared to the **11.18** TRIPS Agreement is the obligation to provide, in respect of copyright and neighbouring rights, for the free and separate transferability of economic rights by contract and for the possibility of persons acquiring or holding such rights on the basis of a contract, including an employment contract, to fully exercise them in their own names, and to fully benefit from them.[47] This clause was especially directed against mandatory provisions under copyright contract law, usually employed under the Continental European system in order to protect the typically weaker parties of a contract. It also aimed at protecting employers through the concept of work-made-for-hire.[48] The USA had already tried to insert such a

---

and D Nimmer, 'United States' in P Geller (ed), *International Copyright Law and Practice*, Vol II (looseleaf release 17) § 6[4] (nn 70–1).

[42] Except national treatment for performers, Art 1703(1) phr 2 of the NAFTA.

[43] The title only also mentions 'sound recordings'.

[44] Art 1706(1) as compared to Art 1705(2) on copyright; para 11.11 above; yet, the rental right is subject to an explicit stipulation to the contrary by contract between the author and producer.

[45] Art 1706(2) of the NAFTA.

[46] Art 1706(3) ibid; on the three-step test, see, in the context of copyright, paras 5.179 ff and 10.83–10.87 above.

[47] Art 1705(3) of the NAFTA.

[48] See on these differences between the copyright and author's rights system paras 3.70–3.72 above; Levy/Weiser (n 6 above) 274 deplore European rules on transferability as harmful to the US movie industry and the 'failure' of TRIPS not to oblige Members to fully protect works-made-for-hire as in the USA.

clause in the TRIPS Agreement, though not successfully.[49] This is another example showing that a certain demand may be carried through much more easily in trilateral negotiations than in those with more than 100 negotiating parties.

11.19 An interesting provision is Article 1707 of the NAFTA, which may be called the first multilateral provision on technical protection measures and related legal sanctions, albeit limited to encrypted programme-carrying satellite signals. Parties are obliged to legally sanction, by criminal law remedies, the manufacturing of relevant decoders and additional related acts without the authorization of their lawful distributor. They must also make a civil offence both the reception in a commercial context and the further distribution of a relevant decoded signal. Legal sanctions in connection with technical protection measures in general appeared in a multilateral treaty for the first time only in the WCT and the WPPT of 1996.[50]

11.20 The application in time of the NAFTA is also regulated upon the model of the TRIPS Agreement. Accordingly, the NAFTA in principle does not apply to past acts, and it is exclusively Article 18 of the Berne Convention that is made applicable, by analogy, to existing works and (unlike in TRIPS) phonograms.[51]

(c) Enforcement provisions

11.21 The intellectual property chapter of the NAFTA also includes quite detailed provisions on the enforcement of all covered intellectual property rights, in large part but with some deviations following the provisions of Articles 41–61 of the TRIPS Agreement. As in the TRIPS Agreement, Articles 1714–18 of the NAFTA specifically address general provisions, administrative procedures and remedies, provisional measures, border measures, as well as criminal procedures and penalties.

(3) Dispute settlement

11.22 The NAFTA has its own dispute settlement provisions, which build upon those of the GATT and the Canada–US Free Trade Agreement.[52] They aim at dispute

---

[49] See the Draft of 23 July 1990 of the TRIPS Agreement in Gervais (n 34 above) 2.156; J Reinbothe, 'Der Schutz des Urheberrechts und der Leistungsschutzrechte im Abkommensentwurf GATT/TRIPS' (1992) GRUR Int 707, 714–15, highlighting the context between US claims for recognition of full right ownership of employers as 'authors' and their claims to participate in foreign remuneration rights granted to authors (in the Continental European meaning only). On this latter aspect, see also Gervais (n 34 above) 1.31.

[50] See Arts 11, 12 of the WCT and 18, 19 of the WPPT; paras 17.91–17.101 below.

[51] For the details, see Art 1720(1), (2) of the NAFTA and, for more specific provisions, para (3) ff. In comparison, see Art 70 of the TRIPS Agreement and paras 10.138 and, specifically for neighbouring rights owners, 10.101–10.102 above.

[52] See Part 7, ch 20 of the NAFTA and ch 19 of the Canada–US Agreement; on the GATT/WTO provisions, see paras 10.114 ff above. For an assessment under the NAFTA, see A de Mestral, 'NAFTA

avoidance and fast and effective settlement of disputes, primarily by amicable means such as consultations. If consultations fail, the Free Trade Commission[53] can be called to organize a meeting with all parties in order to resolve the conflict by using alternative means, such as good offices, mediation, or conciliation.[54] Only if this effort also fails can any consulting Party request the establishment of an arbitration panel.[55] A panel shall determine whether any measure by the defending country is consistent with NAFTA obligations or causes nullification or impairment, and shall make recommendations for settlement.[56] The main aim is to reach conformity of the national measure with the NAFTA; only if no agreement on a resolution is reached may the winning complainant impose retaliation. For example, it may temporarily suspend the application of benefits, preferably in the same trade sector, subject to the extent authorized by the panel.[57]

Where the dispute can be brought under either the WTO or the NAFTA, the complainant Party may choose the forum. Where another NAFTA Party wants to bring the same case in the other forum, the complainant must consult in order to agree on a single forum; failing agreement, the case will be heard under the NAFTA. After selection of one forum, the other may no longer be addressed with the same case.[58] **11.23**

(3) Other provisions

Similarly to Articles 67 and 69 of the TRIPS Agreement, NAFTA provides for the obligation to provide technical assistance and promote cooperation, for example by the training of personnel and the establishment of contact points for the exchange of information on trade and infringing goods.[59] **11.24**

B. Other regional trade agreements (RTAs)

(4) General remarks

The NAFTA is highlighted in this chapter because it is one of the first, most important, and well-known RTAs with a chapter on intellectual property, and because it was developed in a close context with the TRIPS Agreement in respect **11.25**

Dispute Settlement: Creative Experiment of Confusion?' in L Bartels and F Ortino (eds), *Regional Trade Agreements and the WTO Legal System* (2006) 359 ff.

[53] On the NAFTA Free Trade Commission, see Art 2001 of the NAFTA.
[54] Art 2007 ibid.
[55] Art 2008 ibid; for the panel composition and procedures, see Art 2009 ff ibid.
[56] Art 2016 (and, for the final report, Art 2017) ibid.
[57] Arts 2018, 2019 ibid.
[58] Art 2005 ibid, para 24.22 below.
[59] Art 1719 of the NAFTA.

of time and contents. Yet, regional agreements worldwide are not a new phenomenon, and more recently, many of them have included intellectual property provisions.[60] One may even discern a recent trend towards regionalization,[61] which has triggered debate on the desirability and purpose of RTAs in the face of the WTO.[62] In the framework of the WTO, while Members at the Fourth Ministerial Conference in Doha acknowledged the principally positive role of RTAs in promoting trade liberalization, they also saw the need to avoid negative consequences for global free trade. They decided to negotiate better procedures to determine whether any particular regional trade agreement complies with WTO law.[63] On 14 December 2006, the WTO General Council established a transparency mechanism for these agreements to be provisionally applied until the conclusion of the Doha Round.[64]

11.26 RTAs differ in many respects. According to the level of integration, they may constitute free trade areas or customs unions; or more far-reaching, common markets, currency unions, or even political unions. RTAs envisage, for example, trade liberalization, technical and other cooperation, peacekeeping, or political stabilization. To reach these aims, the RTAs usually establish institutions, that may be intergovernmental[65] or even supranational.[66] Most RTAs provide for their own dispute settlement systems, which are similar to the WTO system.[67] Often, broader RTAs include sub-RTAs. Here, only the most important agreements will be briefly presented in respect of their copyright provisions.[68]

---

[60] 'Regional agreements' in this book are understood as multilateral agreements in one region and between regions; for bilateral agreements, see ch 12 below.

[61] The so-called 'new regionalization' started as a second wave of regional agreements from the 1980s, following the 'old regionalization' in the 1950s and later, see C Damro, 'The Political Economy of Regional Trade Agreements' in L Bartels and F Ortino (eds), *Regional Trade Agreements and the WTO Legal System* (2006) 23, 26–9.

[62] eg on the potential roles as building or stumbling blocks for world trade, Damro (n 61 above) 24, 25 ff, and 39 ff; J Mathis, *Regional Trade Agreements in the GATT/WTO* (2002) 1 ff; R Then de Lammerskötter, *WTO und Regional Trade Agreements (RTAs)* (2004), in particular 130 ff.

[63] Under Art XXIV of the GATT 1947 as amended, the GATT 1994 (Understanding on Art XXIV) and Art V of the GATS, RTAs must be notified to the WTO and are subject to certain requirements; in February 1996, the WTO General Council established the Committee on Regional Trade Agreements, which has to examine such agreements. Its work was largely hampered by differences of opinion among Members on compliance of individual trade agreements with WTO law.

[64] <http://www.wto.int/english/news_e/news06_e/rta_15dec06_e.htm>.

[65] eg NAFTA and MERCOSUR.

[66] eg Andean Community, para 11.46 below.

[67] For a comparison, see W Davey, 'Dispute Settlement in the WTO and RTAs: A Comment' in L Bartels and F Ortino (eds), *Regional Trade Agreements and the WTO Legal System* (2006) 343 ff; he suggests that the WTO system is more frequently used, at 349. On the relation between the RTA and WTO systems, see also paras 24.16–24.18 and 24.22–24.23 below.

[68] With the FTAA, one draft agreement is also included under paras 11.28–11.36 below. For the complete list of more than 350 RTAs notified to the WTO up to December 2006 (including those without

(2) The Americas

(a) General remarks

Following different periods of RTAs in Latin America from the 1960s to the **11.27**
1980s,[69] a new attitude arose in the 1990s. It was characterized by the aims of
better market access, attractiveness of the economic system for foreign investors,
and broad liberalization of trade instead of earlier protectionist strategies. The
NAFTA reflected this new attitude, which also revived existing RTAs such as the
Andean Pact (from 1996: Andean Community or CAN), MERCOSUR, and for
the Caribbean, CARICOM.[70] In addition, the elaboration of North–South
agreements continued with more intensity. As a first step, the USA sought to
broaden the NAFTA by encouraging the accession of additional Latin American
countries. Indeed, the NAFTA is conceived with a view to enlargement: additional members can accede to it under conditions similar to those within
the WTO.[71]

(b) Draft FTAA

(i) **Overview and background**   The USA invited thirty-three democratically   **11.28**
elected leaders of the 'Western Hemisphere' to the first Summit of the Americas
in December 1994 in Miami, where the participants committed to democracy
and economic integration. Joined by Canada and Mexico, it first invited Chile to
apply for NAFTA membership. Yet, without the 'fast-track' authority of the
US President at the time, this plan did not seem realistic.[72] Instead, the USA
replaced this idea with the plan of creating a free trade area of the Americas. At
the subsequent Summit in Santiago in April 1998, government leaders directed
their trade ministers to begin negotiations for the Free Trade Area of the Americas
(FTAA), to be concluded by 2005. Due to well-known general political problems, their plan was unsuccessful.[73]

A working group on intellectual property elaborated several drafts of highly   **11.29**
detailed provisions, with many alternative proposals and square brackets in the
latest draft of 2003.[74] The USA tabled the first proposal, which aimed at the
highest level of protection and incorporated references to the WTO/TRIPS

---

intellectual property provisions), see <http://www.wto.int/english/tratop_e/region_e/region_
e.htm>.

[69] On these early years, see de Lammerskötter (n 62 above), 46–9.

[70] On these, see paras 11.45 ff, 11.51, and 11.52 ff below.

[71] Art 2204 of the NAFTA; cf Art 12 of the WTO Agreement.

[72] Folsom (n 11 above) 241.

[73] On the current status, see para 11.36 below.

[74] The Third Draft of 21 November 2003 contains intellectual property in Chapter XX,
and copyright and related rights under its subsection B.2.c. (Arts 1–24), <http://www.ftaa-alca.
org/FTAADraft03/TOCWord_e.asp>.

Agreement.[75] The high degree of detail in the 2003 Draft largely corresponds to that of national laws rather than international agreements. The 2003 Draft in many respects follows existing international law; yet, many alternatives are strongly influenced by elements of the copyright system, although thirty-two of thirty-four countries belong to the author's rights system. The following presentation of the Draft FTAA focuses on its basic features, and for most Articles, to notable, selected alternatives.

11.30 (ii) **General provisions**   Under a key obligation, parties must give effect to the substantive provisions of the Berne Convention, the TRIPS Agreement, the WCT, and the WPPT; even draft international instruments for the protection of audiovisual performers and non-copyrightable databases (whose adoption is unlikely for the foreseeable future)[76] are included under the compliance clause, as is the planned treaty for the protection of broadcasting organizations.[77] Moreover, parties must make best efforts to ratify or accede to these international treaties, rather than simply comply with them.[78] In respect of national treatment and the most-favoured-nation clause, the Draft largely follows the TRIPS Agreement.[79]

11.31 (iii) **Specific copyright and related rights provisions**   The copyright subsection starts with a very long list of definitions; excludes certain subject matter from protection; contains moral rights as under the Berne Convention; and lays down the following exclusive rights: reproduction (including temporary reproduction), distribution, and importation of copies made without the right holder's authorization, as well as communication to the public (including the traditional ways of communication, making available on demand, and even public display), public access to computer databases, and 'dissemination of signs, words, sounds or images by any known or future process'.[80] Also, rights of translation and adaptation as well as a resale right are provided.[81] Limitations are subject to the three-step test, as under TRIPS, NAFTA, and the WCT.

11.32 The term of protection can be based on the Berne Convention, or (under an alternative) it shall be at least seventy years after the author's death,[82] or it shall be

---

[75] Anon, 'Free Trade Area of the Americas' (1997) WIPR 314, 315.

[76] See paras 18.21, 18.25 and 22.01 ff, in particular 22.04 below.

[77] On this plan, which has meanwhile also lost momentum, see ch 19 and particularly paras 19.11 and 19.37 below.

[78] Arts 5.3 and 5.4 of subsect A of the Draft FTAA.

[79] Arts 1 and 2 under subsect B.1 ibid; yet, the exception from national treatment for neighbouring rights regarding TRIPS-plus rights would only apply to countries not Parties to the FTAA and of the Rome Convention, see Art 3.1 ibid.

[80] Art 8.1 first alternative under subsect B.2.c. of the Draft FTAA.

[81] Arts 4.1e. and 7 under subsect B.2.c. ibid.

[82] For calculations other than on the basis of the author's life, it is 50 years after authorized publication or making (second alternative, b)).

the same term for works, performances, and phonograms. The latter is seventy years after 'the author's' death or, if calculated on a basis other than the life of a natural person, it shall be at least ninety-five years from authorized publication or, failing such publication within twenty-five years from creation, it shall be at least 120 years from 'creation of the work, performance, or phonogram'.[83]

The proposals for substantive protection of the rights of performers, phonogram **11.33** producers, and broadcasting organizations go slightly beyond the level of the WPPT and the TRIPS Agreement; the proposed duration for all three groups is fifty years. Limitations may be the same as under national copyright law, subject to the three-step test.[84]

For both copyright and related rights, an Article similar to the one under NAFTA **11.34** provides for the free and separate transferability of rights and for other contractual provisions favourable to entrepreneurs, such as for employers of authors; yet, as an alternative, there are clauses limiting the scope of transfer.[85] Very detailed provisions on technological measures and rights management information supplement an Article on encrypted programme-carrying satellite signals modelled upon the corresponding NAFTA provision.[86] Enforcement measures are proposed along the lines of those of the TRIPS Agreement.[87] For application in time, the Draft follows pre-existing law by requiring the analogous application of Article 18 of the Berne Convention.[88]

As a *novum* in international copyright (draft) law, the Draft FTAA includes an **11.35** Article on collective administration of rights; it calls on the parties to encourage collective administration, transparency, due participation of members, inspection and supervision by the state, and other principles.[89] Another *novum* is the obligation of parties to mandate that all government agencies use only authorized computer programs.[90] A likewise novel proposal to protect expressions of folklore likely stems from Latin American countries.[91]

(iv) Outlook   Since around 2003, the FTAA negotiations have become more **11.36** difficult, especially after protests by critics of globalization as well as criticism

---

[83] Last alternative of Art 9.1 under subsect B.2.c. of the Draft FTAA.
[84] Arts 15–19 under subsect B.2.c. ibid.
[85] Art 12.1 under subsect B.2.c. ibid.
[86] Arts 22, 23 as well as 21 under subsect B.2.c. ibid; Art 1707 of the NAFTA.
[87] Subsect B.3. of the Draft FTAA.
[88] Art 11 under subsect B.2.c. ibid.
[89] Art 24 under subsect B.2.c. ibid.
[90] Art 25 under subsect B.2.c. ibid. Similar provisions are included in bilateral treaties of the second generation concluded by the USA, see para 12.37 below.
[91] Art 1 under subsect B.2.d. of the Draft FTAA. Some bilateral treaties involving Latin American countries also include similar clauses, para 12.64 below. On folklore, see ch 20 below.

by negotiating parties (including Canada) regarding agricultural subsidies and the need of developing countries for more time to adapt to world standards and competition. Furthermore, in line with general political changes in Latin America, Venezuela and Bolivia in particular have openly opposed and effectively stymied the FTAA on grounds that it is merely a tool of US imperialism. As a consequence, current prospects for success of the FTAA are low. Even if this stagnation will clear in the future, any agreement (at least on intellectual property) will likely need much more negotiation, as reflected by the alternative versions that represent highly divergent positions[92] and by the square brackets that appear in nearly every Article of Chapter XX on intellectual property.

(c) CAFTA-DR

11.37 **(i) Historical development** In January 2002, the US President announced negotiations on a free trade agreement with Central American countries. Negotiations took place in 2003 and resulted in an agreement between the USA, El Salvador, Guatemala, Honduras, and Nicaragua, which were joined in 2004 by Costa Rica and Dominican Republic. They all signed the Agreement in 2004 and, except Costa Rica, ratified it. The Central American Free Trade Agreement—Dominican Republic (CAFTA-DR) entered into force on a rolling basis, because the USA needed to determine that each country had taken sufficient steps to implement their commitments.[93] It entered into force on 1 March 2006 for El Salvador and the USA, and subsequently for Honduras, Nicaragua (1 April 2006), and Guatemala (1 July 2006).

11.38 **(ii) General provisions** One of the explicitly mentioned objectives of the CAFTA-DR, in addition to general expansion and diversification of trade and elimination of trade barriers, is to 'provide adequate and effective protection and enforcement of intellectual property rights in each Party's territory'.[94] The presence of intellectual property in the objectives highlights its special importance considering that many other areas covered by the agreement are not separately mentioned in the objectives.

11.39 Chapter 15 on intellectual property rights includes the general obligations of the Parties to ratify or accede by different dates to the Brussels Satellite Convention, the WCT, and the WPPT (rather than only to comply with their substantive law), and to provide for the entire protection under Chapter 15 as minimum protection.

---

[92] As seen in the examples above, they reflect the copyright versus the author's rights system and industrialized versus developing countries.

[93] On this procedure, see different press declarations, eg that of 30 December 2005, under <http://www.ustr.gov/Trade_Agreements/Bilateral/CAFTA/CAFTA_Press_Releases/Section_Index.html>.

[94] Art 1.2(1)(e) of the CAFTA-DR.

Parties must affirm their existing rights and obligations under TRIPS and treaties administered by WIPO to which they are a party.[95] Parties must grant national treatment along the lines of the TRIPS model; yet, exceptions from national treatment as under Article 3(1) phrases 1 and 2 of the TRIPS Agreement regarding exceptions under the Berne and Rome Conventions and related rights are not explicitly provided.[96] One should conclude from the non-derogation and affirmation clauses regarding existing rights and obligations under the TRIPS and other agreements that these exceptions also apply in the framework of the CAFTA-DR.[97] In principle, the agreement applies to all existing subject matter that is protected in the country where protection is claimed or that meets the criteria of protection under the CAFTA-DR.[98]

(iii) Specific copyright and related rights provisions Many of the specific **11.40** obligations with respect to copyright and related rights recite in more detail the provisions of the WCT and the WPPT to which the Parties must anyway adhere under the above-mentioned general obligation of the CAFTA-DR. Such specific obligations particularly relate to the exclusive rights of reproduction and distribution, limitations and exceptions according to the three-step test, the extensive provisions on technological measures (including permitted exceptions) and rights management information, and the relation between authors' rights and related rights.[99] Like these, also the minimum duration is commonly regulated for works, performances, and phonograms; namely for each, at seventy years after the author's death, or where the term is not calculated on the basis of the life of a natural person, at seventy years after the first authorized publication, or failing such publication within fifty years from the creation, seventy years after creation[100]—a self-contradictory provision in the author's rights system that is followed by all parties except the USA.[101]

Article 8 of the WCT on the communication right of authors is basically copied **11.41** into the text,[102] as are the WPPT definitions and provisions on performers' protection in unfixed performances.[103] For performers and phonogram producers, the CAFTA-DR provides an exclusive right of broadcasting and communication

---

95 Art 15.1(1), (2), (4)(a), (7) ibid.

96 Art 15.1(8) ibid.

97 Art 1.3 and 15.1(7) ibid. For a similar question in bilateral agreements, see para 12.30 below.

98 Art 15.1 (11), (12) ibid.

99 Art 15.5(1), (2), (10)(a), (7), (8), and (3) ibid. On the last issue, the prohibition of a 'hierarchy' between authors' rights and related rights, see also para 12.34 below.

100 Art 15.5(4) of the CAFTA-DR.

101 In particular, laws of the authors' rights system would, in principle, not provide for the same duration of protection for authors and related right owners, and not use the word 'creation' regarding phonograms and performances.

102 Art 15.6 of the CAFTA-DR.

103 Art 15.7(2)(a) and (5) ibid.

to the public (including making-available) of performances and phonograms subject to the possibility of introducing a compulsory licence for traditional and other non-interactive transmissions.[104] Yet, the retransmission of television signals on the internet must remain subject to authorization by the right holder(s) of the contents of the signal and, if any, of the signal itself.[105]

11.42 Additional obligations refer to encrypted programme-carrying satellite signals,[106] require the active regulation of the acquisition and management of only authorized software by governmental agencies at the central level,[107] and provide for the free and separate transferability of rights and full enjoyment of rights and benefits by any person acquiring or holding derived economic rights.[108]

11.43 The intellectual property chapter also includes detailed provisions on enforcement and, as does the US Digital Millennium Copyright Act (DMCA), detailed provisions on limitations of the liability of internet service providers regarding copyright and related rights infringements.[109]

11.44 In sum, the basic strategy was to extend the obligations of the WCT and WPPT to the participating Central American countries by specifying some of their provisions to a detail otherwise seen in the US DMCA, and to add even further-reaching obligations, such as the seventy years' duration, the exclusive broadcasting and communication rights for performers and phonogram producers, and the entrepreneurial-friendly provision on contracts. The USA also applies this strategy to other regional agreements, such as the Draft FTAA,[110] as well as to its bilateral second-generation trade agreements.[111]

(d) Andean Community and MERCOSUR

11.45 (i) **Andean Community/CAN** The Andean Community (Comunidad Andina, CAN) was originally founded as the Andean Pact (Pacto Andino) in 1969 with the aim of sub-regional integration.[112] It includes Bolivia, Colombia, Ecuador, and Peru; Chile left in 1976, and Venezuela, which had acceded in 1973, left in April 2006. Instead, Chile was accepted as Associated Member in

---

[104] Art 15.7(3) ibid. Similarly the second-generation bilateral treaties of the USA, paras 12.31–12.32 below.

[105] Art 15.5(10)(b) of the CAFTA-DR.

[106] Art 15.8 ibid, modelled on Art 1706 of NAFTA.

[107] Art 15.5(9) of the CAFTA-DR.

[108] Art 15.5(6) ibid; cf also for specific NAFTA provision paras 11.02–11.20 above and for the unsuccessful trial to introduce such provisions in the TRIPS Agreement, para 11.18 above.

[109] Art 15.11(1)–(26) (enforcement) and (27) (liability) of the CAFTA-DR.

[110] paras 11.30 ff above.

[111] paras 12.26 ff below.

[112] The original agreement of Cartagena was modified several times and CAN was founded on the basis of the Protocol of Trujillo of 10 March 1996.

September 2006. Also, Mexico, Panama, and the Members of MERCOSUR[113] are associated since July 2005.

In general, the CAN aims at an advanced level of integration beyond a mere free **11.46** trade area. After having achieved the status of a customs union, it seeks to achieve an internal market that would include the harmonization of currency, financial, and tax policies. It plans to reach the goal of a harmonious development through integration of the Member States and their economic and social cooperation through, among other actions, an approximation of national laws. The Commission of the CAN, which consists of governmental representatives of the Member States, has the mandate to adopt decisions that, in principle, directly apply after the entry into force in each Member State.

On 17 December 1993, the Commission adopted Decision 351 on a 'common **11.47** regulation on authors' rights and related rights'.[114] In short, this Decision largely follows the Berne and Rome Conventions and, in part, the then Spanish Copyright Act. In respect of copyright, noteworthy features are the coverage of computer programs and databases,[115] three moral rights (right of divulgation, authorship, and integrity) with an unlimited duration, and a long list of economic rights, including a very broad communication right (which could cover on-demand uses), an importation right for copies made without the authorization of the right owner, and a resale right. Both moral rights and economic rights are minimum rights.[116] The minimum duration is fifty years after the author's death.[117] Eleven specified, permitted exceptions and limitations are supplemented by the three-step test.[118] Transfer or assignment of economic rights is basically governed by domestic legislation, except that Decision 351 requires that any transfer and authorization or licence for use is understood to be limited to forms of exploitation expressly agreed upon in the contract.[119]

In respect of related rights, performers are granted the classical exclusive rights of **11.48** fixation, reproduction, and communication to the public of live performances, as well as the moral rights of performership and integrity.[120] Phonogram producers enjoy exclusive rights of reproduction, importation (where the copy is made

---

[113] See para 11.51 below.

[114] For a short description, see <http://www.comunidadandina.org/ingles/propriedad/copyright.htm>; also S von Lewinski, 'Urheberrechtsharmonisierung im Andenpakt: Interessant auch für Europa?' (1994) GRUR Int 470 ff. The Decision 351 is available under <http://www.comunidadandina.org/ingles/normativa/D351e.htm>.

[115] Arts 23–8 of Decision 351.

[116] The minimum rights are specified in Arts 11–17 ibid.

[117] For details, see Arts 18–20 ibid.

[118] Arts 21, 22 ibid.

[119] Art 31 ibid; for all transfer rules, see Arts 29–32.

[120] Arts 34, 35 ibid.

without authorization), and distribution, as well as a remuneration right for 'every use for commercial purposes' that may be shared with performers.[121] The rights of broadcasting organizations are similar to those under the Rome Convention (except the lacking communication right), and explicitly include satellite broadcasts.[122] The duration is fifty years for all three groups of related rights owners.[123]

11.49 Unlike in most other multilateral agreements, collective administration is addressed in quite some detail. Decision 351 requires a permit to collectively administer rights, makes the collective administration organizations subject to supervision, and sets out obligations, for example, regarding transparency and the establishment of tariffs and of plans for just and fair distribution.[124]

11.50 While Decision 351 with its 61 Articles is quite comprehensive, it leaves many issues to the decision of Member States, such as when it refers to the laws of Member States or explicitly permits further-reaching provisions under national law. Accordingly, it corresponds more to regular RTAs than to advanced, supra-national copyright harmonization according to the European model.[125] A comparison between Decision 351—an agreement among countries of the author's rights system and in line with it—and CAFTA-DR—an agreement by the like countries but with participation of one major country of the copyright system—shows the strong influence of that country and the resulting impact of the copyright system on the law of the Central American countries.

11.51 (ii) **MERCOSUR**   The generally more important Latin American regional community (though less important for copyright) is MERCOSUR (in Spanish: the Mercado Común del Sur). It was created in 1991 and includes member countries Argentina, Brazil, Paraguay, Uruguay, Venezuela, and associated countries Chile, Bolivia, Peru, Colombia, and Ecuador. In addition, Mexico is connected with MERCOSUR through an FTA. Similarly to the CAN, its aims go beyond a customs union to include a common market as well as economic coordination even in monetary and currency politics. Harmonization of laws is one means for the integration process. So far, only industrial property matters have been harmonized in MERCOSUR.[126]

---

[121] Art 37 ibid. One may presume that the last-mentioned right refers to secondary uses (broadcasting and communication to the public) of commercial phonograms, as regulated in Art 12 of the Rome Convention.

[122] Arts 39, 40 of Decision 351.

[123] Arts 36, 38, 41 ibid.

[124] Arts 43–50 ibid.

[125] On European copyright harmonization, see Vol II Part II; briefly para 11.64 below.

[126] Decision No 8/25 of 5 August 1995—Harmonization Protocol on Intellectual Property in MERCOSUR in the Fields of Trademarks, Geographical Indications and Appellations of Origin; on industrial designs, see Decision no 16/98, Harmonization Protocol in the Field of Industrial

(e) CARICOM

The Caribbean Community (CARICOM) was founded on the basis of the Treaty   **11.52**
of Chaguaramas on 4 July 1973, and entered into force on 1 August 1973. Its
roots are in the Caribbean Free Trade Association of 1965 (later replaced by
CARICOM) and the East Caribbean Common Market of 1968, which respectively aimed at a free trade zone and a common market. Upon a decision of the
Conference of Heads of Government in 1989 to transform the common market
into a single market and economy, the Treaty of Chaguaramas was revised in
2001. Also, the Conference adopted the document 'Single Market and Economy'
at its thirteenth conference in 1992.

Today, CARICOM has fifteen members: Antigua and Barbuda; the Bahamas;   **11.53**
Barbados; Belize; Dominica; Grenada; Guyana; Haiti; Jamaica; Montserrat;
Saint Lucia; St Kitts and Nevis; St Vincent and the Grenadines; Suriname; and
Trinidad and Tobago. Associated members are Anguilla, Bermuda, British Virgin
Islands, Cayman Islands, and Turks and Caicos Islands. Twelve CARICOM
members participate in the CARICOM 'Single Market and Economy', which
aims at establishing a customs union and, beyond, at achieving free movement of
goods, skilled nationals, services, and capital, as well as harmonization of laws,
including in the field of intellectual property.[127] As of August 2007, no action has
been taken to harmonize intellectual property rights; yet, at some point in time
one may expect such initiatives, which might follow the model of European harmonization.[128] In addition, the Council for Trade and Economic Development
shall promote the protection of intellectual property rights within CARICOM
by different measures, including the legal protection of expressions of folklore;
the establishment of a regional administration is only foreseen for industrial
property rights, due to their nature; this does not, however, discourage regional
cooperation between collecting societies.[129]

Designs, of 10 December 1998; <http://www.mercosur.int/msweb/portal%20intermediario/es/
index.htm>; S O'Connor, *Harmonization of Industrial Property in MERCOSUR* (1996).

[127] Art 74(2)(b) of the Revised Treaty of Chaguaramas (<http://www.caricom.org/jsp/commun-
ity/revised_treaty-text.pdf>) according to which Member States shall harmonize their laws and
administrative practices in respect of intellectual property rights.

[128] Harmonization of intellectual property rights is already listed as a key element of the
establishment of the CARICOM 'Single Market and Economy', see the document 'Summary of
Status of Key Elements', no 10.9, <http://www. caricom.org/jsp/single_market/csme_summary_
key_elements_may_07.pdf>.

[129] Art 66 of the Revised Treaty of Chaguaramas. For collecting societies, note that on 22 June
2007, the decision was taken to form the Eastern Caribbean Reproduction Right Association for
reprographic rights.

(3) Asia and the Pacific

(a) ASEAN and AFTA

11.54　One of the major sub-regional organizations in Asia is the Association of South East Asian Nations (ASEAN). It was established on 8 August 1967 in Bangkok by Indonesia, Malaysia, the Philippines, Singapore, and Thailand. Today, ASEAN has five more members: Brunei Darussalam, Cambodia, Laos, Myanmar, and Vietnam. Like many other regional integration organizations, ASEAN aims at accelerating economic growth, social progress, cultural development, political stability, and adherence to the principles of the UN Charter. In addition, ASEAN countries decided in 2003 to establish an ASEAN Community on the basis of security, economic, and socio-cultural communities. The ASEAN Economic Community seeks a single market and free movement of goods, services, investment, and capital. It plans to reach these goals by 2020 through new mechanisms, such as the ASEAN Free Trade Area (AFTA), which was launched in 1992 and created by 2003.[130]

11.55　Intellectual property is mainly addressed in the 1995 ASEAN Framework Agreement on Intellectual Property Cooperation. It was initiated at the Senior Economic Officials Meeting in 1994 following the request of the ASEAN Music Association for the protection of phonograms across the ASEAN countries.[131] The Framework Agreement is largely limited to cooperation in intellectual property enforcement and protection, including cooperative activities in relation to the implementation of the TRIPS Agreement and other treaties in the field. In practice, it initially focused on industrial property. More recently, it was extended to copyright and related rights. While the main focus of the ASEAN 'Intellectual Property Action Plan 2004–2010' is still on industrial property, the Action Plan includes the review and aligning of the intellectual property laws of WTO Members for TRIPS compliance, and the consideration of the accession to and compliance with the WCT, WPPT, as well as the Berne and Rome Conventions.[132]

11.56　ASEAN itself has concluded and is negotiating free trade or similar agreements with other countries, in particular China, India,[133] Korea,[134] Australia and

---

[130] On AFTA, see <http://www.aseansec.org/12025.htm>.

[131] On the elaboration of the Framework Agreement, see W Weeraworawit, 'The Harmonisation of Intellectual Property Rights in ASEAN' in C Antons, M Blakeney, and C Heath (eds), *Intellectual Property Harmonisation within ASEAN and APEC* (2004) 205, in particular 207 ff; the Framework Agreement on Intellectual Property Cooperation is reprinted there as an annex, and available under <http://www.aseansec.org/6414.htm> and at (1996) 35 ILM 1072.

[132] See the Action Plan under <http://www.aseansec.org/7980.htm>.

[133] They entered into force on 1 January 2005 and 1 April 2005, respectively.

[134] The FTA between ASEAN (minus Thailand) and South Korea entered into force on 1 June 2007.

New Zealand (through AFTA and CER),[135] and Japan.[136] As far as these include provisions on intellectual property, such provisions usually contain no more than a broad and general commitment to protect and enforce intellectual property and to cooperate.[137]

(b) APEC

The Asia-Pacific Economic Cooperation Forum (APEC) is rooted in informal **11.57** consultations that took place in 1989 between Asia-Pacific heads of state. It works mainly through regular meetings of heads of state, and on the basis of non-binding agreements and decisions adopted by consensus. The current members are Australia, Brunei Darussalam, Canada, Chile, People's Republic of China, Hong Kong, China, Indonesia, Japan, Republic of Korea, Malaysia, Mexico, New Zealand, Papua New Guinea, Peru, The Republic of the Philippines, the Russian Federation, Singapore, Chinese Taipei, Thailand, the United States, and Vietnam. At the 1994 meeting in Bogor, APEC industrialized and developing country members committed to free trade and investment by 2010 and 2020, respectively. In 1995, intellectual property issues were included in the programme of regional economic cooperation.[138] One year later, the Intellectual Property Expert Group was established. Its work has mainly been limited to information exchange, consultations, and policy harmonization, rather than extended to legislative or other regulatory activities.[139] At the 2006 meeting in Hanoi, the USA did not achieve its plan to transform the APEC into a free trade zone.

---

135 Closer Economic Relations; on the plan to establish a Closer Economic Partnership between AFTA and CER, see <http://www.dfat.gov.au/cer_afta/index.html#freetrade>.

136 Negotiations have started; see a list of the regional and bilateral free trade agreements involving ASEAN or ASEAN countries in Appendix 1 of R Sen, '"New Regionalism" in Asia: A Comparative Analysis of Emerging Regional and Bilateral Trading Agreements Involving ASEAN, China and India' (2006) 40/4 Journal of World Trade 553, 587 ff.

137 eg Arts 3(8)(h) and 7(2) of the ASEAN–China Framework Agreement on comprehensive economic cooperation of 4 November 2002 (intellectual property as object of future trade negotiations; cooperation in this area); similarly, see Arts 3(3), 3(8)(h), and 6(1)(b)(viii) of the ASEAN–India Framework Agreement on Comprehensive Economic Cooperation of 8 October 2003.

138 Osaka Action Agenda, aiming at the realization of the free trade and investment objective in different sectors. See also in more detail M Blakeney, 'The Role of Intellectual Property Law in Regional Commercial Unions' (1998) 1/4 Journal of World Intellectual Property 691, 703–4.

139 On the work of the IP Expert Group, see critically A Taubman, 'Collective Management of TRIPS: APEC, New Regionalism and Intellectual Property' in Antons/Blakeney/Heath (n 131 above) 161, 192–9.

(4) Africa

(a) OAPI

11.58 **(i) General remarks** The African Intellectual Property Organization, an inter-governmental organization of French-speaking African states,[140] was founded on the basis of the Agreement of Bangui on 2 March 1977. This Agreement was a revision of the preceding Agreement of Libreville of 1962, which was adopted after independence of most French-speaking countries (in most of which French industrial property law governed until 1962) in order to create common structures and adopt uniform legislation in the field of industrial property.

11.59 Unlike the earlier Libreville Agreement, the Bangui Agreement extends to copyright ('literary and artistic property'). It entered into force in 1982 and was revised in 1999 mainly in order to make it compliant with the TRIPS Agreement.[141] The Bangui Agreement contains general obligations in the field of intellectual property and regulates the structure and other aspects of the organization. Ten Annexes comprise detailed provisions on intellectual property rights, including Annex VII on literary and artistic property.[142]

11.60 **(ii) General provisions** The general aim of this Agreement is to 'promote the effective contribution of intellectual property to the development of their States . . . and . . . to protect intellectual property rights on their territories in as effective and uniform a manner as possible'.[143] The Agreement is motivated, in the field of copyright, by the 'advantages of establishing a uniform system of protection of literary and artistic property'.[144] In respect of copyright and related rights, the Agreement is explicitly designated as a special agreement in the meaning of Articles 20 of the Berne Convention and 22 of the Rome Convention.[145] The Member States undertake to accede to the Berne and Rome Conventions as well

---

[140] Currently, the following states are members of the Organization, which is usually abbreviated OAPI (Organisation Africaine de la Propriété Intellectuelle): Benin, Burkina Faso, Cameroon, Central African Republic, Congo, Ivory Coast, Gabon, Guinea, Guinea-Bissau, Equatorial Guinea, Mali, Mauritania, Niger, Senegal, Chad, and Togo.

[141] Agreement Revising the Bangui Agreement of 2 March 1977, on the Creation of an African Intellectual Property Organization (Bangui (Central African Republic), 24 February 1999), <http://www.oapi.wipo.net/doc/en/bangui_agreement.pdf>; also published in WIPO (ed), *Copyright and Related Rights Laws and Treaties* Vol VI, *Multilateral Treaties*, Text 13-01.

[142] The other Annexes deal with patents, utility models, trademarks and service marks, industrial designs, trade names, geographical indications, unfair competition, layout designs, and plant variety protection; in autumn 2007 rules on the protection of traditional knowledge and folklore have been elaborated, and adopted as another annex to the Bangui Agreement.

[143] Preamble to the Revised Bangui Agreement, First Recital.

[144] ibid, Recital 14.

[145] On these Articles, which prohibit the protection of lower-level protection, see paras 5.250–5.251 and 6.78 above. See also Recitals 5, 6 of the Revised Bangui Agreement.

as to the TRIPS Agreement and the Convention establishing the WIPO.[146] The intellectual property rights covered by the Agreement remain independent national rights subject to the legislation of the Member States.[147] Where protection under an Annex is less favourable than under the Berne and Universal Copyright Conventions and the TRIPS Agreement, the latter international Agreements are to prevail.[148]

(iii) Specific provisions   Annex VII on literary and artistic property includes   **11.61** detailed provisions on the protection of authors' works and, under related rights, performances, phonograms, and broadcasts. It is comparable to a complete national copyright act that follows the author's rights system.[149] In general, the level of protection corresponds to that of the TRIPS Agreement and, in part, goes beyond. Notably, the duration of authors' economic rights is seventy years *pma*; the duration of moral rights is unlimited. It also provides, in accordance with the author's rights system, provisions on copyright contracts and on collective administration—provisions rarely covered under international treaties.

(b) ARIPO

The English-speaking African countries founded a corresponding organization   **11.62** in the field of industrial property in order to pool their resources. Assisted by the UN Economic Commission for Africa and the WIPO, the Lusaka Agreement establishing the African Regional Intellectual Property Organization (ARIPO) was adopted in December 1976. Among other goals, it is to promote the harmonization and development of industrial property laws. It was only in 2002 that the Council of Ministers decided to extend its mandate to copyright and related rights. The subsequent and current strategic plan does not include any legislative measures, but provides for formulation of policy matters, sensitization of stakeholders and explanation of the practical implementation of the new mandate on copyright and related rights, as well as extensive training of members of staff of the ARIPO Secretariat and officials from Member States.[150]

---

[146] ibid, Recitals 5, 6, and 2; the obligation to accede to treaties also extends to specified industrial property treaties.

[147] Art 3(1) ibid.

[148] Art 3(2) ibid.

[149] For characteristics of the author's rights system, see ch 3 above, in particular paras 3.77–3.78; eg an author shall enjoy, under Art 9, 'the exclusive right to exploit his work in any form whatsoever and to obtain monetary advantage therefrom'; this general clause is followed by specific examples of exclusive rights.

[150] <http://www.aripo.org/articles.php?Ing=ng&pg=62>.

(c) AU

11.63 The African Union (AU), founded in 2000 as a successor organization of the Organization of African Unity (OAU),[151] in many respects seems to be modelled on the European Union; for example, the AU has planned to establish institutions, including a court of justice and in the long run a central bank. Besides broader political aims, the AU aims at an African common market, trade liberalization, and economic integration;[152] yet, it is unlikely that intellectual property will be made part of any obligations within the AU, given the work of the specialized organizations OAPI and ARIPO.

(5) Europe

(a) EC

11.64 One of the main aims of the European Community (EC; initially: European Economic Community) is the achievement of the internal market—an area where free movement of goods, services, persons, and capital is guaranteed.[153] Copyright and related rights first were considered by the European Court of Justice in relation to their capacity as trade barriers, and from 1991 were harmonized in many respects by legislative measures, which in principle determine the exact level of protection to be achieved at a minimum and maximum.[154] Although the EC started out as an economic community with a focus on the common market,[155] it is a supranational organization with a much higher level of integration than a mere regional trade agreement. Volume II covers a detailed analysis of copyright law in the EC.[156]

(b) EFTA

11.65 Volume II also covers the European Free Trade Association (EFTA). Briefly, it was founded in 1960 as a response to the establishment of the three European Communities in 1957. Today, after several members left to become EC Members, it consists of Iceland, Liechtenstein, Norway, and Switzerland.[157] The EFTA was

---

[151] Constitutive Act of the African Union, 11 July 2000, http://www.africa-union.org/root/au/index/index.htm (go to Documents, then Treaties, Conventions and Protocols); it entered into force on 26 May 2001.

[152] For a general presentation of the AU, see C Packer and D Ukare, 'The New African Union and its Constitutive Act' (2002) 96 The American Journal of International Law 365 ff.

[153] Art 14(2) of the EC Treaty.

[154] In this respect, EC harmonization is different from the (minimum) standards in RTAs covered by this chapter, cf eg para 11.50 above.

[155] Later, the Single European Act of 1986 set the more ambitious aim of creating the 'internal market', see Vol II ch 1.

[156] Vol II chs 2, 4 ff.

[157] On the history of EFTA and its provisions regarding copyright and related rights, see Vol II chs 1.B., 15.

revised in 2001.[158] It provides for general provisions on the free movement of goods and services similar to those of the EC Treaty.

Unlike the previous version, the revised EFTA includes a general Article on intel- **11.66**
lectual property and a related Annex.[159] The Article is limited to the Member States' obligation to grant and ensure adequate and effective protection of intellectual property rights, and to provide for enforcement, national treatment, and most-favoured-nation treatment. In the Annex, EFTA states reaffirm their international obligations, in particular regarding the Berne and Rome Conventions and the TRIPS Agreement; they also undertake to adhere to the WCT and WPPT, if they are not yet parties thereof. Other provisions relate to industrial property and reaffirm the obligations on enforcement under the TRIPS Agreement.[160] In addition, a separate dispute settlement mechanism is provided.[161]

(c) EEA

The Agreement on the European Economic Area (EEA) was concluded between **11.67**
the EC, its Member States, and the EFTA States, and came into force on 1 January 1994.[162] Upon the accession to the EC of ten new Member States in May 2004, the EEA was enlarged by the EEA Enlargement Agreement, which came into force on 1 May 2004 to cover the new members. Its principal approach is to extend the EC primary and secondary law (*acquis communautaire*) in certain areas, including the internal market (and, hence, intellectual property), to the entire EEA. Accordingly, even EEA countries that are not members of the EC but only of the EFTA must observe the relevant case law of the European Court of Justice and the specified harmonization directives in the field of copyright and related rights. Today, after most of the original EFTA countries have adhered to the EC, remaining EEA countries that must implement the *acquis communautaire* (although they are not EC Members) are only Norway, Iceland, and Liechtenstein. Switzerland remains outside the EC, and although it is an EFTA member, it has not ratified the EEA Agreement; also, the bilateral agreements it has concluded with the EC do not cover intellectual property; yet, it has adopted a policy to voluntarily follow the EC *acquis communautaire*.

---

158 The so-called Vaduz Convention ('Convention of 21 June 2001 to Consolidate the Convention Establishing the European Free Trade Association (EFTA) of 4 January 1960') is available on <http://secretariat.efta.int/Web/legaldocuments>. It entered into force on 1 January 2002.

159 Art 19 of the Vaduz Convention 2001; Annex J.

160 For the bilateral agreements concluded by EFTA with outside countries, see para 12.62 below.

161 Art 47 ff of the Vaduz Convention; see A Ziegler, 'Dispute Settlement in Bilateral Trade Agreements: The EFTA Experience' in L Bartels and F Ortino (eds), *Regional Trade Agreements and the WTO Legal System* (2006) 407, 408–12.

162 The texts of the agreement and related documents are available on <http://secretariat.efta.int/Web/legaldocuments>.

(d) CEFTA

11.68 The Central European Free Trade Agreement (CEFTA) was concluded on 21 December 1992 by the initial parties Poland, Hungary, and the then Czechoslovakia. These and the soon thereafter joining Slovenia left CEFTA when they adhered to the European Union in 2004; Romania and Bulgaria left CEFTA upon their accession in 2007. In 2007, CEFTA has the following eight members: Croatia, Macedonia, Albania, Bosnia and Herzegovina, UNMIK on behalf of Kosovo, Moldavia, Montenegro, and Serbia. In general, CEFTA aims at a free trade area, not least in order to guarantee political stability. In its consolidated version of 2006, the CEFTA obliges parties to grant adequate and effective intellectual property protection and enforcement 'in accordance with international standards, in particular with TRIPS'; parties reaffirm their existing international obligations and, where applicable, undertake to accede to and implement specified agreements (in particular: the Berne, Rome, Universal Copyright, Geneva Phonograms, and Brussels Satellite Conventions, the TRIPS Agreement, the WCT, and the WPPT) by 1 May 2014.[163]

(e) Cotonou Agreement

11.69 Apart from these agreements, which are limited to European countries, a broader regional agreement is noteworthy: the EC and its Member States concluded a Partnership Agreement with seventy-seven African, Caribbean, and Pacific (ACP) countries in June 2000, which came into force on 1 April 2003 and succeeds to the former Lomé Conventions with these countries. It is called Cotonou Agreement.[164] On the basis of twenty-five years of cooperation between the EC and the ACP countries, it seeks improvements in order to reach the development goal and to reduce poverty, not least by new economic and trade partnerships.

11.70 On intellectual property, it contains one general Article[165] under which the parties 'recognise the need to ensure an adequate and effective level of protection in intellectual, industrial, and commercial property rights, and other rights covered by TRIPS . . . in line with international standards with a view to reducing

---

[163] Arts 38, 39 of the CEFTA in the consolidated version of 2006, to enter into force in 2007, and its Annex 7 with a list of the agreements that may be supplemented by the Parties (Art 39(2)), see <http://www.stabilitypact.org/wt2/TradeCEFTA2006.asp>. In the original version of the Agreement ((1995) 34 ILM 3), Art 25, as one of 42 Articles, provided merely general obligations on intellectual property; namely, to grant protection on a non-discriminatory basis, and to improve protection within 5 years to 'a level corresponding to the substantive standards of the multilateral agreements which are specified in Annex VI' (in particular the Berne and Rome Conventions).

[164] OJ EC L/317 of 15 December 2000; also: <http://ec.europa.eu/development/index_en.cfm> (go to Geographical Partnerships, then Cotonou Agreement).

[165] Art 46 of the Cotonou Agreement.

distortions and impediments to bilateral trade' and underlines the importance of adhering to the TRIPS Agreement. Similarly, the Article includes an agreement on the need to accede to 'all relevant international conventions on intellectual, industrial, and commercial property as referred to in Part I of the TRIPS Agreement, in line with their level of development'. The parties also agree to strengthen their cooperation in the field; for example, by preparing laws and regulations for the protection and enforcement of intellectual property rights upon request and on mutually agreed terms and conditions. The parties shall negotiate Economic Partnership Agreements (EPAs) that shall enter into force on 1 January 2008 at the latest.[166] If these negotiations succeed, it is not excluded that more detailed provisions on intellectual property will be included.[167]

(6) Résumé

'New regionalism' since the 1980s has brought about a multitude of regional **11.71** agreements worldwide. These agreements show a high degree of diversity, for example, in their aims, economic or political focus, and level of integration. In respect of copyright and related rights, many do not—or not yet—include these matters or are limited to cooperation clauses. Among those RTAs that do include substantive provisions on copyright and related rights, some have harmonized their national laws to different degrees of detail and according to their own traditions and with the purpose of integration, such as the CAN, EC, and OAPI. Others are limited to rather soft and general provisions on the need for an adequate and effective level of protection, such as the inter-regional Cotonou Agreement; or they provide somewhat more concrete and still not unreasonably demanding provisions, such as under the CEFTA.[168]

The RTAs with US participation stand out from all others by their high standards **11.72** of protection that go beyond TRIPS in the early case of NAFTA, and even beyond the WCT and WPPT in the later cases of CAFTA-DR and the planned FTAA. They also stand out by their high degree of detail and because they are often largely modelled upon domestic US law. They follow the patterns generally also used by the USA for bilateral agreements, and they serve the same aim: to enhance benefits for the US industry.

---

[166] Art 37(1) ibid.

[167] See however a report on diverse obstacles to smooth negotiations on the EPAs, M Julian, 'EPA Negotiations Update' (2006) 5/6 Trade Negotiations Inside 6–7 (<http://www.ictsd.org/tni>).

[168] Especially, the accession to specified agreements is required only within 8 years.

12

BILATERAL TREATIES

The fundamentally new development since the mid-1980s to include intellectual **12.01** property into international trade law was not limited to the multilateral framework.[1] It extended to bilateral and regional treaties as well as unilateral trade measures.[2] In all cases, the driving forces behind this new development were industrialized countries. The USA and the EC concluded most of the bilateral trade agreements covering intellectual property.[3] Less known are similar treaties in other parts of the world.[4] The agreements reveal major differences in content, scope, and policy.

---

[1] On the GATT approach resulting in the TRIPS Agreement, see paras 9.07–9.09 and 10.19–10.23 above; on regional trade agreements, see ch 11 above.

[2] On the unilateral trade measures, see ch 13 below.

[3] A (paras 12.02 ff), B (paras 12.43 ff) below.

[4] C (paras 12.61 ff) below.

A. Treaties between the USA and other countries

(1) Reasons for including intellectual property in modern-era bilateral trade agreements (TAs)

12.02 At first sight, one may wonder why the USA began, in the mid-1980s, to systematically and on a large scale include copyright and other intellectual property in bilateral TAs—after all, modern international intellectual property agreements were available. In fact, around 100 years ago, the unsatisfactory situation of a complicated and unstable network of bilateral trade agreements that covered copyright provisions was largely replaced by the Berne Convention, which was hailed as a progress from this earlier situation.[5] Could the recent recourse to bilateral TAs be seen as a step backwards to a pre-Berne situation?

12.03 On closer inspection, certainly not. First, these recent bilateral treaties are not concluded for lack of multilateral treaties; rather, they integrate and often increase the minimum standards of protection previously laid down in a multilateral context. Secondly, they have mainly been pushed by a few, major, industrialized players who shaped the contents of such agreements with many other countries upon the same models. In particular, the USA with its strong negotiating power, succeeded in establishing similar standards of protection in national laws throughout the world according to its own desires. Thereby, it has also exercised a strong influence on the standards available in international relations on the basis of national treatment and the MFN clause.[6] Unlike the complex pre-Berne network of bilateral agreements between many nations and with quite different standards of protection,[7] the new network would rather look like a sun, representing the powerful player(s) who transmit certain legal standards to other countries like a sun radiates light.

12.04 The domestic background for the wave of bilateral TAs initiated by the USA is the same as for the GATT initiative: the economic strength of the USA had declined since the 1960s, and the US trade deficit reached a peak in the mid-1980s. The threat of losing hegemony over the global economy was countered by an increasingly activist trade policy that resulted in ever more and stronger protectionist measures, through the Trade Expansion Act of 1962 and the Trade Act

---

[5] On this situation, see paras 2.24–2.25 above.

[6] On the limited effects of the MFN clause where national treatment applies, see paras 10.42–10.49 above.

[7] See the picture of this rather decentralized network existing before the Berne Convention in S Ricketson and J Ginsburg, *International Copyright and Neighbouring Rights: The Berne Convention and Beyond* (2006) 40.

of 1974, to the substantially stronger Omnibus Trade and Competitiveness Act of 1988.[8]

The 'findings and purposes' of the Trade Act 1988 (Title I)[9] illustrates the back-   **12.05**
ground against which the trade activities of the USA can be explained. They deplore, for example, the 'fundamental disequilibrium in its trade and current account balances and a rapid increase in its net external debt',[10] as a result of, among others, 'the large United States budget deficit' and 'serious shortcomings in United States trade policy'.[11] They consider that 'it is essential, and should be the highest priority of the United States Government, to pursue a broad array of domestic and international policies—(A) to prevent future declines in the United States economy and standards of living . . .'.[12] A missionary tone is added in the following statement: 'While the United States is not in a position to dictate economic policy to the rest of the world, the United States is in a position to lead the world and it is in the national interest for the United States to do so'[13]—a statement that may reflect their own endeavours or pretensions and, at the same time, may seem somewhat presumptuous to other sovereign states and leave them stupefied.

One area in which the US economy of the mid-1980s could easily be strength-   **12.06**
ened and its trade imbalance could be improved was that of intellectual property. The new importance of all intellectual property rights within the entire field of trade is reflected, for example, in the explicit mention of intellectual property next to investment, finances, and services, as an object of future trade agreements,[14] and in the separate highlighting of negotiation objectives regarding intellectual property.[15] Unlike other industries, copyright industries were particularly successful because movies, computer programs, and other copyright products were intensively used worldwide.[16] Yet, the US right owners could not benefit from such uses where countries either provided for no protection at all, for no

---

[8] Omnibus Trade and Competitiveness Act of 1988, PL 100-418 of 23 August 1988, 102 Stat 1107. On this development since the 1960s, see Dhar, 'The Decline of Free Trade and US Trade Policy Today' (1992) 26/6 J'l World Trade 133, 137 ff.
[9] Section 1001 of the Trade Act 1988 (n 8 above), under the Title I 'Trade, Customs, and Tariff Laws' (19 USC § 2901).
[10] Section 1001(a)(3) ibid.
[11] Section 1001 (a)(3)(B), (G) ibid.
[12] Section 1001(a)(4) ibid.
[13] Section 1001(a)(6) ibid.
[14] Section 1001(a)(5) ibid.
[15] Section 1101(b)(10) ibid; similarly, s 2102 (b) (4) of the Trade Act of 2002 (19 USC 3802), PL 107–210, 116 Stat 995–6.
[16] On the strength of copyright in US trade at that time, see E Schwartz, 'Recent Developments in the Copyright Regimes in the Soviet Union and Eastern Europe' (1991) J Copyright Soc USA 123, 125.

protection for foreigners, or for inadequate and inefficient enforcement rules or measures. This lack of protection may have existed because countries disregarded applicable international treaties or because they remained outside the relevant international treaties, and therefore were not even obliged to grant protection in respect of foreign works.

12.07 Given this situation, it is no surprise that the USA developed an overall trade strategy designed to create, open, and strengthen foreign markets for the US copyright industries by establishing legal rules and enforcement measures in foreign countries so as to help guarantee that the continuous use of US works would yield profits. This aim was to be reached by three different, parallel means: the inclusion of the relevant rules into the multilateral framework,[17] bilateral and regional trade agreements,[18] and unilateral measures on the basis of the 'Special 301' provisions.[19] The 'teeth' of all three means were the possibility of retaliation not only in the same trade area, but also in different ones where the relevant countries were more vulnerable.[20]

12.08 For the USA, the added value of bilateral agreements as opposed to the multilateral framework is the fact that their negotiating power is much stronger towards a single country than in a framework of far more than 100 countries, as can be seen from a comparison of the texts of the TRIPS Agreement and bilateral treaties of the same time.[21] In addition, the USA could target different countries according to its own priorities, taking into account the respective degrees of piracy and losses for the US industry, or even aspects outside intellectual property.[22] Bilateral trade agreements may also have separate functions in the context of multilateral negotiations, such as during the Uruguay Round and regarding the accession of a country to the WTO, or in the context of the 'Special 301' procedure.[23]

---

[17] Section 1101(b)(10)(B) of the Trade Act 1988 regarding the inclusion of intellectual property into the GATT, and (C) regarding the possibility of 'other complementary initiatives undertaken in other international organisations' such as the WIPO.

[18] On regional agreements, see paras 11.01–11.24 and 11.28–11.44 above. For the power of the President of the USA to enter into bilateral trade agreements under the 'fast-track' procedure (this procedure under certain conditions facilitates the adoption of such trade agreements, because it limits the role of Congress to approving or rejecting (rather than amending) the agreement within specific times frames), see s 1102(c)(3), in particular (A), of the Trade Act 1988; this power is limited in time but renewable. After more than 8 years without that procedure, the Trade Act of 2002, under its title XXI ('Trade Promotion Authority') to be cited 'Bipartisan Trade Promotion Authority Act of 2002', reintroduced it under certain conditions until 1 July 2007 at the latest, when it expired, as the so-called 'Trade Promotion Authority' of the President (in particular s 2103(b), ie 19 USC § 3803 (b)).

[19] Hereon, see paras 13.01–13.10.

[20] On these dynamics, see paras 10.115–10.116 and 10.126–10.128 above, also on the advantage of simultaneously negotiating on different trade areas.

[21] See paras 12.09–12.15 below; similarly for NAFTA: paras 11.02 ff, esp. 11.18 above.

[22] For such aspects, see in particular paras 12.21–12.22 and 12.24 below.

[23] See para 14.05 below.

(2) The first generation of TAs

(a) General provisions

As an example for the first generation of bilateral agreements which were **12.09** concluded on the basis of the 1988 Trade Act, the trade agreement between the USA and Romania of 3 April 1992 is presented in respect of its copyright and neighbouring rights provisions.[24] Like the TRIPS Agreement, it covers several areas of intellectual property rights. In respect of obligations regarding existing international agreements, it goes beyond the TRIPS Agreement: it not only obliges the parties to comply with the substantive provisions of, in particular, the Berne Convention,[25] but reaffirms the commitments already made with respect to the Berne (and Paris) Conventions and even obliges the parties to adhere to the Berne Convention and the Geneva Phonograms Convention.[26] Thereby, the principles of protection under the Berne and Geneva Phonograms Conventions are integrated into the Agreement. In addition, it specifically sets out the principle of national treatment in partially similar words as in the TRIPS Agreement and the NAFTA.[27]

(b) Minimum standards for copyright

The minimum substantive standards for copyright are as follows: beyond the **12.10** Berne works, computer programs and collections of data and other material must also be protected, as under the TRIPS Agreement and the NAFTA; the relevant wording is slightly more detailed.[28] The following rights beyond the Berne standard have to be provided: a rental right for computer programs (only), similar to the TRIPS Agreement and NAFTA;[29] as well as (beyond the TRIPS level but as

---

[24] Agreement on Trade Relations between the Government of the USA and the Government of Romania; the intellectual property provisions thereof are contained in Art VIII and in a Side Letter and repr in (1992) World Intellectual Property Report 198 ff; see also <http://tcc.export.gov/ Trade_Agreements/All_Trade_Agreements/exp_005369.asp>, also for all other agreements of the early 1990s based on the same pattern, with Albania, Armenia, Azerbaijan, Bulgaria, Georgia, Hungary and Jamaica (in these two cases, specific intellectual property agreements), Kazakhstan, Kyrgyzstan, Latvia, Moldova, Mongolia, China, Philippines (IPR Understanding), Poland, Sri Lanka, Taiwan, Tajikistan, Ukraine, and Uzbekistan.

[25] On the so-called compliance clause in the TRIPS Agreement, see paras 10.50–10.54 above.

[26] This obligation only envisaged Romania, since the USA was already a member of these Conventions; the obligation is laid down in para 2 of the Side Letter. It is obvious that the USA, not being a Contracting State to the Rome Convention, had no interest in adding the Rome Convention.

[27] para 1 of the Side Letter; the beneficiaries are supposed to be the 'right holders of the other party'; para 3 defines this term as including exclusive licensees and 'other authorised persons', but does not refer to the criteria of eligibility under the Berne and Geneva Phonograms Conventions (cf explicit references to these criteria in Art 3(1) phr 2 of the TRIPS Agreement and Art 1721 of the NAFTA). Yet, as far as these Conventions apply, their criteria have to be applied too.

[28] para 2(a)(i) of the Side Letter as compared to Art 10 of the TRIPS Agreement and Art 1705(1) of the NAFTA.

[29] Art 11 of the TRIPS Agreement, Art 1705(2)(d) of the NAFTA.

under NAFTA) the exclusive rights of importation where copies of the work were made without the authorization of the right holder; first public distribution by sale, rental, or otherwise; and communication to the public,[30] including communications via the internet. [31] A plus element even as compared to the NAFTA is the additional exclusive importation right regarding lawfully made copies of a work.[32]

12.11 Like the NAFTA, the US–Romania TA contains provisions on the free and separate transferability of exclusive rights and the unrestricted principle of freedom of contract.[33] In addition to what the USA could achieve in the TRIPS Agreement and the NAFTA, it ensures that the protection is afforded to 'authors of the other Party, whether they are natural persons or, where the domestic law of the Party seeking protection so provides, juridical entities . . .'.[34] Such clauses were to secure protection to US legal entities even where the other country, such as Romania, did not recognize corporate ownership because its laws were drafted in accordance with the author's rights system.[35] Accordingly, the USA has achieved that its own legal system, which recognizes the 'authorship' of legal persons, must be recognized in favour of US right owners also in countries whose legal system otherwise would not allow for such protection—an action often labelled as 'export' of US law.

12.12 Quite similar to the terms of the TRIPS Agreement and the NAFTA, the US–Romania Agreement provides for the duration of protection when calculated on a basis other than the life of a natural person, and the three-step test for permitted limitations of rights.[36] A plus element as compared to the TRIPS Agreement and the NAFTA is the obligation to limit resort to compulsory licences that are permitted under the Berne Convention, and to ensure, where they are applied, that means to enforce the right of remuneration are available.[37]

---

[30] For these rights, see para 2(a)(ii)(2), (3) and (5) of the Side Letter as compared to Art 1705(2)(a)–(c) of the NAFTA.

[31] On the definition of 'public' in the context of the communication right and its relevance for internet uses, see para 11.11 above. The essential element is the reception by members of the public in the same place or separate places and at the same time or at different times.

[32] para 2(a)(ii)(1) of the Side Letter.

[33] para 2(a)(iv) ibid and Art 1705(3) of the NAFTA; hereon, see para 11.18 above.

[34] para 2(a)(iii) of the Side Letter.

[35] paras 3.37–3.40 above.

[36] para 2(a)(v), (vi) of the Side Letter; Arts 12, 13 of the TRIPS Agreement and Art 1705(4), (5) of the NAFTA; for explanations hereon, see paras 10.80–10.88 and 11.12 above.

[37] para 2(a)(vii) of the Side Letter; Art 1705(6) of the NAFTA on compulsory licences is different.

(c) Minimum standards for neighbouring rights

In the field of neighbouring rights, the US–Romania TA, like NAFTA, limits **12.13** protection to phonogram producers. It sets out the exclusive rights of reproduction, importation, distribution, and rental under the same conditions as for authors; accordingly, as compared to the NAFTA, the importation right regarding lawfully made copies is a plus element also for phonogram producers.[38] A plus element as compared to both TRIPS and NAFTA is the analogous application of the provisions on free transferability to phonogram producers.[39] As under NAFTA, the three-step test applies also to phonogram producers' rights. The minimum term of fifty years goes beyond that of NAFTA, because it is calculated upon publication rather than fixation.[40] As in NAFTA, but beyond the TRIPS Agreement, the 'no formality' principle is laid down also in respect of the protection of phonogram producers.[41]

(d) Enforcement

The Side Letter also contains a number of intellectual property enforcement provisions, though in much less detail than under the NAFTA and the TRIPS **12.14** Agreement.[42]

(e) Conclusion

As this analysis has shown, this bilateral agreement is very similar in its structure **12.15** and contents of copyright provisions to the TRIPS Agreement and the NAFTA, while even going beyond their levels of protection. This is true for all other bilateral agreements initiated by the USA during the same period.[43]

(3) Second (and current) generation of TAs

(a) General remarks

Following the conclusion of the WIPO Copyright Treaty and the WIPO **12.16** Performances and Phonograms Treaty in December 1996,[44] the USA initiated a second generation of bilateral TAs. While the first generation TAs largely incorporated the level of protection of the TRIPS Agreement and the NAFTA,

---

[38] para 2(a)(viii) of the Side Letter. The rights of importation and distribution are plus elements as compared to the TRIPS Agreement.

[39] para 2(a)(ix) of the Side Letter makes applicable by analogy para 2(a) (iv) to phonogram producers.

[40] para 2(a)(x)(2) of the Side Letter as compared to Art 1706(2) of the NAFTA; for particular criteria of eligibility (first fixation or publication in the other country), see para 2(a)(c)(1) of the Side Letter.

[41] para 2(a)(xi) ibid and Art 1703(2) of the NAFTA.

[42] para 2(f) of the Side Letter.

[43] For the agreements, see n 24 above.

[44] On these treaties, see below, ch 17.

the second generation FTAs basically incorporate the WCT and WPPT standards and, in part, even go beyond them. The copyright and related rights provisions of the second generation TAs greatly differ in their extent and detail.[45] Yet, they all follow models that are presented below. The first FATs were concluded with Singapore, Chile, the Kingdom of Jordan, and Australia.[46]

(b) Different agreements

12.17 **(i) TIFAs** The USA chooses different kinds of agreements, according to the circumstances. With countries that should, in the view of the USA, generally open up their economies or improve their economic situation so as to attract foreign investment,[47] the USA first concludes Trade and Investment Framework Agreements (TIFAs) in order to initiate trade liberalization and, among others, improve intellectual property protection.[48] Such agreements are usually very general; for example, they may simply establish a joint council for exploring expanded trade and investment cooperation and for similar tasks,[49] sometimes stressing the importance of intellectual property protection in the preamble.[50] They are non-binding, consultative mechanisms that are considered helpful in leading a country into the global economy and, finally, to the conclusion of a free trade agreement, where appropriate.[51]

12.18 **(ii) BITs** As a second step, or as a first one for other countries, the USA concludes Bilateral Investment Treaties (BITs), which aim at ensuring national or most-favoured-nation treatment and further protection of US investments in the other country. 'Investment' is defined so broadly as to include intellectual property, including copyright and related rights.[52] Accordingly, BITs usually provide for national treatment and most-favoured-nation treatment in respect of intellectual property and protect against any conditions by the other country relating

---

[45] The FTAs with Australia and Singapore are examples for extensively detailed provisions; eg ch 17 of the US–Australia FTA on intellectual property has 29 single-spaced pages, of which about 8.5 pages concern copyright and related rights, nearly 4 pages service provider liability, 7 pages enforcement, and 2.5 pages general provisions; by contrast, the US–Jordan FTA includes 5 pages on intellectual property, including one on copyright and related rights; for TIFAs and BITs, see paras 12.17–12.19 below.

[46] All FTAs are accessible on <http://www.ustr.gov>; the US–Jordan FTA was the earliest to be concluded in 2001.

[47] <http://www.state.gov/e/eeb/tpp/c10333.htm>.

[48] For a list of current TIFAs, see <http://www.ustr.gov/Trade_Agreements/TIFA/Section_Index.html>

[49] eg Arts 2 and 3 of the TIFA with Saudi Arabia of 31 July 2003, <http://www.ustr.gov/assets/Trade_Agreements/TIFA/asset_upload_file304_7740.pdf>.

[50] eg US-ASEAN TIFA of 25 August 2006, <http://www.ustr.gov/assets/Trade_Agreements/TIFA/asset_upload_file932_9760.pdf>.

[51] <http://www.state.gov/e/eeb/tpp/c10333.htm>.

[52] Art 1 (definitions) of the 2004 Model BIT, <http://www.state.gov/documents/organization/38710.pdf>.

to expropriation, transfers of any proceeds from the investment into and out of the host state, performance requirements such as mandatory local content or technology transfer requirements for investments, and conditions on dispute settlement (so that the parties' investors can submit a dispute with the treaty partner's government for binding international arbitration without depending on the country's domestic courts).

The BITs are usually based on the 2004 US Model BIT.[53] The USA presents BITs **12.19** as tools for other countries to develop their economies by creating more favourable conditions for US investors and thereby strengthening the local private sector.[54] Others see BITs as a tool to establish 'a secure, predictable, and unduly favourable legal framework for US investors' in the other country.[55]

(iii) FTAs FTAs have been concluded either as a subsequent step after TIFAs **12.20** or BITs, or directly without such initial agreements. They usually provide both for investment chapters (including intellectual property) similar to the contents of BITs[56] and for more comprehensive provisions on intellectual property. These provisions regularly aim at enabling US intellectual property rights' industries to dynamically ensure their required and sought-after standards of protection.[57]

(c) Different strategies

When concluding FTAs, the USA carefully considers which country of a region **12.21** to target first. The strategy is often to choose a country that either may be more dependent than the others on the access to the US market, or otherwise has general economic or political advantages, such as, for Jordan, its role in the Middle East process combined with the fact that Jordanian imports into the USA would not have any measurable impact on US industries.[58] Alternatively, an ideal target country of a region may be a country that has more important goals in other fields

---

[53] See the link to the Model BIT at <http://www.state.gov/e/eb/rls/othr/38602.htm> and <http://www.ustr.gov/Trade_Agreements/Bilateral/Section_Index.html>; summary of its substantive obligations: G Fischer, 'Reviving the US Bilateral Investment Treaty Program' (announced for publication in The International Lawyer 2005, though not yet published (see (2005) ILM 265, n 9)). The Model BIT was revised to integrate the negotiating objectives of the Trade Act of 2002. For a link to lists of BITs (currently in force or recently concluded), see <http://www.ustr.gov/Trade_Agreements/BIT/Section_Index.html>.

[54] Secretary of State Albright, letter of submittal to the US Congress regarding the US–Bahrain BIT, 23 March 2000, 1, as quoted in D Price, 'The US-Bahrain Free Trade Agreement and Intellectual Property Protection' (2004) 7/6 Journal of World Intellectual Property 829, in n 25.

[55] ibid 834.

[56] <http://www.state.gov/e/eeb/rls/othr/38602.htm>.

[57] USTR Industry Trade Advisory Committee on Intellectual Property Rights (ITAC-15) report, 4, <http://www.ustr.gov/assets/Trade_Agreements/Bilateral/Bahrain_FTA/Reports/asset_upload_file822_5528.pdf>.

[58] For Jordan, see W Malkawi, 'The Intellectual Property Provisions of the United States–Jordan Free Trade Agreement: Template or not Template' (2006) 9/2 Journal of World Intellectual Property 213.

than intellectual property, such as Bahrain, which aims at establishing itself as a major gateway for US trade in the Gulf Region with US support;[59] negotiations in such a case will allow the introduction of highest possible standards of protection.

12.22 Even if such a country were not very important from an intellectual property point of view, this strategy of choosing a target country in a region is particularly attractive for the USA because it puts pressure on the other countries of the region: under this 'building-block' approach, the first agreement with a country of a region serves as a model for negotiations with the other countries for whom it will hardly be possible successfully to argue for more favourable conditions than those agreed in this precedent.[60] Accordingly, the US–Bahrain FTA serves as a precedent for the region of the Gulf and, in combination with the US–Jordan FTA as a precedent for other Arab countries, it is finally supposed to lead to the higher step of a US–Middle East Free Trade Area.[61] The 'building-block' countries in Asia and Latin America are, respectively, Singapore and Chile.[62] Yet, even the best strategy is no guarantee for negotiations to directly result in the conclusion of bilateral agreements; in several cases, negotiations may well become stalled or even be suspended; for example, the high American intellectual property demands seem to have been a major stumbling block for the US–SACU negotiations.[63]

12.23 To date (August 2007), the USA has concluded bilateral FTAs with Jordan (2001) as a precedent for other Arab countries, planned to be followed by an FTA with Egypt;[64] Bahrain (2004/entry into force 2006) as a precedent for the Gulf region, to be followed by an FTA with Oman;[65] Morocco (2004/entry into force 2006)

---

[59] Price (n 54 above) 849, 850.

[60] On the building-block approach, see Malkawi (n 58 above) 214 (with further references in n 8); similarly: Price (n 54 above) 849.

[61] For Jordan as a model for other Arab countries, see Malkawi (n 58 above) 214; for the US–Middle East Free Trade Area which is planned to be achieved in 2013, see <http://www.ustr.gov/Trade_Agreements/Regional/MEFTA/Section_Index.html>.

[62] US FTAs with both countries were concluded in 2003, see the link to both FTAs at <http://www.ustr.gov/Trade_Agreements/Bilateral/Section_Index.html>.

[63] SACU is the Southern African Customs Union (South Africa, Botswana, Namibia, Lesotho, and Swaziland), <http://www.bilaterals.org/rubrique.php3?id_rubrique=15>.

[64] On the US–Jordan FTA, see Malkawi (n 58 above) and M el Said, 'The Evolution of the Jordanian TRIPS-Plus Model: Multilateralism Versus Bilateralism and the Implications for the Jordanian IPRs Regime' (2006) IIC 501; on the Jordanian FTA, see also <http://www.ustr.gov/Trade_Agreements/Bilateral/Jordan/Section_Index.html>; on current negotiations with Egypt, see <http://www.bilaterals.org/rubrique.php3?id_rubrique=123>.

[65] On the US–Bahrain FTA, see Price (n 54 above) 830; negotiations with Oman have already been concluded in 2005; for negotiations with other Gulf countries, see <http://www.ustr.gov/Trade_Agreements/Regional/MEFTA/Section_Index.html>; <http://www.bilaterals.org/rubrique.php3?id_rubrique=55>; and, in particular the UAE, <http://www.bilaterals.org/rubrique.php3?id_rubrique=145>.

as a possible precedent for other North African countries;[66] Singapore (2003) as a precedent for other Asian countries, to be followed by Thailand and others;[67] Chile (2003) as a precedent for other Latin American countries, to be followed by Colombia, Panama, and Peru;[68] and Australia (2004).[69] Negotiations for an FTA with Korea were concluded in March 2007.

Another strategy pursued by the conclusion of bilateral agreements, namely, their use in the context of the accession of countries to the WTO, is further analysed in the overall assessment of including intellectual property into the trade framework.[70]   **12.24**

(d) Principal negotiation objectives

Before presenting the standard elements of the second generation FTAs, the underlying principal negotiation objectives under the US Trade Act of 2002 are recalled in order to illustrate the background of the FTAs. They include the aim 'to further promote adequate and effective protection of intellectual property rights, including through (i)(I) . . . accelerated and full implementation' of the TRIPS Agreement and through '(II) ensuring that the provisions of any multilateral or bilateral trade agreement governing intellectual property rights that is entered into by the USA reflect a standard of protection similar to that found in US law; (ii) providing strong protection for new and emerging technologies and new methods of transmitting and distributing products embodying intellectual property; . . . (iv) ensuring that standards of protection and enforcement keep   **12.25**

---

[66] Price (n 54 above) 830; on this FTA, see also <http://www.moroccousafta.com/index_ang. htm#>; on Tunisia and Algeria: <http://www.bilaterals.org/rubrique.php3?id_rubrique=55>.

[67] On the US–Singapore FTA, see C Kenneth, 'Harmonising Intellectual Property Law between the United States and Singapore: The United States-Singapore Free Trade Agreement's Impact on Singapore's Intellectual Property Law' (2005) 18/2 Transnational Lawyer 489–513; on negotiations with Thailand, Korea, Malaysia, and Taiwan, see <http://www.bilaterals.org/rubrique.php3?id_rubrique=2>.

[68] On the FTA with Chile, see P Roffe, *Bilateral Agreements and a TRIPS-Plus world: The Chile–USA Free Trade Agreement* (2004), also available on <http://www.qiap.ca> or <http://www.geneva. quno.info>; for Panama (negotiations concluded in December 2006), see <http://www.bilaterals. org/rubrique.php3?id_rubrique=139>; for Peru and Colombia (as part of the Andean Trade Promotion Act), see <http://www.ustr.gov/Trade_Agreements/Bilateral/Section_Index.html>; on plans for Ecuador, see <http://www.bilaterals.org/rubrique.php3?id_rubrique=55>; also on the similar regional agreement with Central American countries, CAFTA-DR, paras 11.37–11.44 above.

[69] On the US–Australian FTA (<http://www.ustr.gov/Trade_Agreements/Bilateral/Australia_FTA/Section_Index.html>) which has raised a lot of unease in Australia, not least due to the way in which concrete wordings of provisions were imposed, see L Weiss, E Thurbon, and J Mathews, *How to Kill a Country: Australia's Devastating Trade Deal with the United States* (2004) (in particular ch 5 on intellectual property); C Antons, 'Intellectual Property Chapters in Australia's Free Trade Agreements with Countries in the Asia-Pacific Region', conference paper given on 30 March 2005 at the New York Conference 'Recent Developments in and Enforcement of Asian Intellectual Property Law' (Fordham University School of Law and IP Academy Singapore), at 3–6.

[70] See para 14.05 below.

pace with technological developments, and in particular ensuring that right holders have the legal and technological means to control the use of their works through the Internet and other global communication media, and to prevent the unauthorised use of their works; and (v) providing strong enforcement of intellectual property rights . . .'. Also, fair, equitable, and non-discriminatory market access opportunities for US persons that rely upon intellectual property protection must be secured.[71]

(e) Contents of FTAs

12.26 **(i) General provisions** The general approach, as already in the NAFTA and bilateral treaties of the first generation, is to build upon existing international intellectual property law and to require additional protection. In the field of copyright and related rights, this approach leads to provisions that include higher standards of protection than not only those under the TRIPS Agreement (often referred to as 'TRIPS-plus provisions') but also those under the most recent multilateral treaties, the WCT and the WPPT. A 'TRIPS-plus' level seems to be a *sine qua non* for the USA.[72] Indeed, today the USA considers the existing multilateral treaties (including especially the WCT and WPPT) as the basis for protection under FTAs.[73]

12.27 Consequently, a standard element of the FTAs is the obligation to join the Brussels Satellite Convention 1974,[74] the WCT, and the WPPT.[75] Variations are the mere obligation to give effect to the substantive provisions of such treaties,[76] to accede to or ratify only some of these treaties,[77] or to affirm having acceded to or ratified such an agreement.[78] In the context of these obligations, many FTAs contain the general affirmation of rights and obligations of the parties under the TRIPS

---

[71] Section 2102 of the Trade Promotion Authority Act (Trade Act of 2002) (n 15 above).

[72] Roffe (n 68 above) 9: 'For the USA a trade agreement without higher standards of protection was not an option'; V Espinel, USTR, in a contribution at the 13th International Intellectual Property Law & Policy Conference, New York, 2005, stated that US FTAs are based on US law, so that problems might arise once US law is amended. See also the applause for the TRIPS-plus approach in most Advisory Committee Reports, such as that of ITAC 15 on the FTA with Bahrain (n 57 above) 5 f.

[73] V Espinel, Assistant US Trade Representative for Intellectual Property and Innovation, at a talk at the 15th Annual International Intellectual Property Law & Policy Conference at Fordham University, New York, 13 April 2007.

[74] On this Convention, see paras 4.70–4.74 above.

[75] eg Art 16.1(2)(a)(i), (iii), (iv) of the US–Singapore FTA; standard language is 'to ratify and accede to' these treaties.

[76] eg Art 4(1)(c), (d) of the US–Jordan FTA, only in respect of the WCT and WPPT.

[77] eg Art 17.1(3)(c) of the US–Chile FTA, referring only to the Brussels Satellite Convention rather than also the WCT and WPPT.

[78] eg Art 17.1(2)(b) and (h) of the US–Australia FTA in respect of the Brussels Satellite and Berne Conventions.

Agreement[79] and state that the FTA obligations on intellectual property rights are only minimum obligations.[80]

Other general clauses refer to non-derogation in respect of any or specified inter- **12.28** national legal obligations between the parties;[81] application in time (no application to acts occurred before the entry into force of the FTA,[82] but application to subject matter existing at the time of entry into force, if the subject matter is protected or meets the criteria for protection at that time in the country where protection is claimed[83]); transparency obligations in respect of the implementing laws, regulations, and procedures that have to be in writing and published;[84] and general national treatment clauses.

Usually, such national treatment clauses are similarly formulated as in the TRIPS **12.29** Agreement; in some cases, they even explicitly extend to 'any benefit derived from' intellectual property rights.[85] To the extent that such benefits include statutory remuneration rights for private reproduction, as explicitly specified in the US–Singapore FTA,[86] the USA has obtained on a bilateral basis what the world rejected at the multilateral level in the framework of the WPPT,[87] provided such provision prevails over national treatment under the WPPT.[88] Beneficiaries of national treatment are, as under TRIPS, designated as 'nationals'. While the TRIPS Agreement defines this term by reference to the criteria of eligibility of the Berne, Rome, and other pre-existing Conventions, only some FTAs include such a reference, and this—unlike TRIPS—as an additional criterion to the ordinary meaning of 'national'.[89]

---

[79] eg Art 17.1(3) of the US–Australia FTA; Art 1(2) of the US–Jordan FTA.

[80] eg Art 17.1(1) of the US–Australia FTA; Art 17.1(1) of the US–Chile FTA; Art 16.1(1) of the US–Singapore FTA; Art 4(1) of the US–Jordan FTA.

[81] These clauses are worded differently, eg Art 1(3) of the US–Singapore FTA as general obligations regarding national treatment and, eg, Art 17.1(5) of the US–Chile FTA specifically regarding non-derogation from TRIPS or any treaties concluded under the WIPO.

[82] eg Art 17.1(11) of the US–Australia FTA; Art 17.1(9) of the US–Chile FTA.

[83] eg Art 17.1(9), (10) (Art 17.1(10) is specified by Art 17.7(7) (which refers to Art 18 of the Berne Convention) of the US–Chile FTA; Art 16.1(6) of the US-Singapore FTA.

[84] eg Art 17.1(12) of the US–Australia FTA; transparency is also required, eg in the TRIPS Agreement (Art 84).

[85] eg Art 17.1(6) phr 1 of the US–Australia FTA; Art 16.1(3) of the US–Singapore FTA; Art 3 of the TRIPS Agreement.

[86] fn 16-4 to Art 16.1(3) of the US–Singapore FTA, explaining that such benefits include 'levies on blank tapes'.

[87] On the vote which mainly singled out the USA, see para 17.44 below.

[88] On the exclusion of statutory remuneration rights for private reproduction under Art 4 of the WPPT, see paras 17.45–17.46 below. On the relations between treaties, see paras 24.15, 24.18; also para 12.30 below.

[89] eg fn 17-1 to Art 17.1(6) of the US–Australia FTA; similarly fn 16-2 to Art 16.1(3) of the US–Singapore FTA.

12.30 Most FTAs provide for exceptions to national treatment only regarding judicial and administrative procedures (corresponding to Article 3(2) of the TRIPS Agreement) and, for some of them, regarding rights of performers and phonogram producers in secondary uses of phonograms.[90] The more recent tendency is to provide for full national treatment without exceptions, as in the FTAs with Bahrain and Singapore.[91] Again, it seems that the USA aims at achieving at the bilateral level what it could not obtain at the multilateral level, in particular regarding related rights.[92] Yet, one may wonder whether the pre-existing exceptions to national treatment under the Berne and Rome Conventions, the UCC, and the TRIPS Agreement would no longer apply between these countries. Depending on their actual wording, non-derogation clauses in FTAs especially with respect to the TRIPS Agreement may be a strong argument for the right of each FTA Party to apply the exceptions to national treatment under the TRIPS Agreement (and, hence, the Berne and Rome Conventions) also in the context of the relevant FTA.[93]

12.31 **(ii) Specific copyright and related rights obligations** Although FTA Parties regularly must adhere to the WCT and WPPT under a general clause, many FTAs still explicitly spell out the obligations under these treaties in wording similar to that of the WCT and the WPPT or in more detail, which is usually modelled upon US law. These specific provisions mostly do not differentiate between copyright and related rights but, be it for pragmatic or for principal reasons,[94] they cover these different rights in common Articles. In detail, standard elements of substantive protection are the exclusive rights of reproduction (including temporary storage in electronic form), making available on demand,[95] distribution,

---

[90] For the first exception only: Art 4(4) of the US–Jordan FTA and Art 16.1(4) of the US–Singapore FTA; also regarding secondary uses: Art 17.1(6) of the US–Chile FTA and Art 17.1(6) phr 2 of the US–Australia FTA.

[91] See the applauding comment by the ITAC in its report (n 57 above) 7.

[92] For the multilateral provisions restricting national treatment, see eg Art 3(1) phr 2 of the TRIPS Agreement and Art 4 of the WPPT, paras 10.34 above and paras 17.45–17.47 below. See also the ITAC report (n 57 above) 7: 'The US has always supported full national treatment without exception'.

[93] For the TRIPS exception to national treatment, see paras 10.30 and 10.36 above. Similarly on the exceptions to national treatment under the US–Chile FTA, see Roffe (n 68 above) 18; on the CAFTA-DR, see para 11.39 above.

[94] A principal objection to separating copyright and related rights, as under Arts 17.5 and 17.6 of the US–Chile FTA, has been expressed by the US industry which objects to record producers and performers being 'relegated to second-class citizenship under "related" or "neighbouring" right regimes' IFAC-3-CAFTA, 2004, 10, <http://www.ustr.gov/assets/Trade_Agreements/Regional/CAFTA/CAFTA_Reports/asset_upload_file571_5945.pdf>; the desired equal treatment is justified, though not convincingly, by the digitization, ibid; rather, this attitude reflects the copyright system versus the author's rights system, see para 3.68 above.

[95] eg Art 4(10) of the US–Jordan FTA (only for the reproduction right); Art 16.4(1), (2)(a) of the US–Singapore FTA; Arts 17.5(1), (2) and 17.6(1), (2) of the US–Chile FTA; and Art 17.4(1), (2) of the US–Australia FTA.

and, in part, importation of authorized copies for authors, performers, and phonogram producers.[96] For performers and phonogram producers, some FTAs additionally provide for an exclusive right of broadcasting and communication to the public, with the possibility of introducing exemptions for analogue transmissions and free over-the-air broadcasts as well as statutory licences for non-interactive services under further conditions.[97]

These exclusive communication and broadcasting rights for performers and **12.32** phonogram producers—even if subject to statutory licences—reflect the copyright system with its principally equal status of authors and related rights owners versus the author's rights system where performers' and producers' rights are more limited in principle, such as is often true with remuneration instead of exclusive rights for broadcasting and communication to the public.[98]

A similar attitude is visible from the FTA provisions on duration of protection. **12.33** These provisions distinguish on the basis of whether duration is calculated on the life of a natural person or otherwise. In the first case, which only applies to authors, the duration is usually stipulated at seventy years *pma*. In the second case, most provisions do not distinguish between authors on the one hand and related rights owners on the other hand. They provide for all of these groups of right owners for seventy years after first authorized publication or, failing such publication within fifty years from creation, seventy years from creation.[99] Although a difference between the duration for authors' and for related rights usually subsists in the first case, because the duration after the author's death is mostly longer than that after fixation or publication,[100] the wish to align the duration for performers and phonogram producers to that of authors is obvious. In contrast, countries of the

---

[96] eg Art 17.4(2) of the US–Australia FTA (for which Australia was successful in obtaining the possibility to apply international exhaustion, see fn 17-13); Arts 17.5(3) and 17.6(2) of the US–Chile FTA; Art 16.4(3) of the US–Singapore FTA and Art 4(11) of the US–Jordan FTA (only on an importation right).

[97] eg Art 4(12) of the US–Jordan FTA; Art 16.4(2)(a) of the US–Singapore FTA which, in its first part, repeats the wording of Art 8 of the WCT (which refers to Articles of the Berne Convention) while also applying it to performances and phonograms, thereby creating problems of interpretation of this communication right; lit (b) also provides for an exclusive right of retransmission of television signals on the internet; Art 17.6(5) of the US–Chile FTA.

[98] On this difference, see para 3.68 above.

[99] eg Art 17.4(4) of the US–Australia FTA; Art 16.4(4) of the US–Singapore FTA; as an exception, Arts 17.5(4) and 17.6(7) of the US–Chile FTA distinguish between authors and related right owners—though, not regarding the duration of 70 years, but only regarding the starting point: for related right owners, it is 'fixation' instead of 'creation'.

[100] An exception exists where a performance is published within 50 years from fixation but after the performer's death, in which case the duration (70 years after publication) may be longer than 70 years *pma*.

author's rights system usually provide for a longer duration for authors than for related right owners.[101]

12.34 The concern of the US industry about any potential privilege of authors over related rights owners is also expressed in a US–Chilean FTA article that explicitly requires the authorization of both the author and related right owner where these groups are involved.[102] This provision is directly aimed against a pre-existing Chilean copyright provision under which the author's interest always prevailed over those of performers and phonogram producers regarding the public performance of a phonogram. It seemed important for the US industry to '[make] clear that there is no hierarchy of rights between those of authors and those of record producers. This is a welcome clarification of dangerous provisions in some Latin American copyright laws . . .'.[103]

12.35 Other basic characteristics of the copyright system have been introduced in many FTAs, such as the free and separate transferability and the enjoyment of rights and their benefits by persons acquiring or holding any economic rights by contract, including employment contracts.[104] The USA had already unsuccessfully tried to introduce such provisions into the TRIPS Agreement;[105] it was only in the trilateral (NAFTA), bilateral, and regional agreements with developing countries, that the USA was able to introduce these provisions, and it did so irrespective of their effects of distorting the domestic legal systems in cases where the author's rights system was followed.[106]

12.36 Regarding limitations and exceptions, most FTAs repeat the three-step test from the TRIPS Agreement, the WCT, and the WPPT. Some FTAs even repeat the relevant agreed statements of the WCT and WPPT, and specify permitted exceptions and limitations with regard to transient and incidental copies.[107]

12.37 Many FTAs contain extremely extensive provisions on circumvention of technological measures and rights management information as well as on liability of

---

[101] Very often, 70 years are provided for authors' rights and 50 years for related rights; see also para 3.68 above, and Vol II ch 7 for the EC.

[102] Art 17.7(1) of the US–Chile FTA; similarly Art 15.5(3) of the CAFTA (para 11.40 above).

[103] IFAC-3-CAFTA, 2004, p 11, as quoted in Roffe (n 68 above) 31.

[104] eg Art 4(14) of the US–Jordan FTA; Art 16.4(6) of the US–Singapore FTA; Art 17.7(2) of the US–Chile FTA and Art 17.4(6) of the US–Australia FTA (which is the only one of the FTAs quoted here which provides this rule only 'for copyright' rather than also related rights, although the subsequent text of the provision refers to performances and phonograms).

[105] paras 11.18, 11.42 above.

[106] Critical on this development Roffe (n 68 above) 32; on the differences between the copyright and author's rights systems in this regard, see para 3.70 above.

[107] eg Art 4(16) of the US–Jordan FTA; Art 16.4(10) of the US–Singapore FTA; Art 17.7(3) of the US–Chile FTA (with footnote 17 on transient and incidental copies and exceptions in the digital environment); Art 17.4(10) of the US–Australia FTA.

internet service providers, all largely modelled upon the US Digital Millennium Copyright Act (DMCA) provisions.[108] Another frequent provision relates to protection against decryption of encrypted satellite signals, similar to that of NAFTA.[109] A novel provision protects mainly US software companies by obliging parties to take measures, including the adoption of laws, to ensure that all government agencies only use authorized computer programs.[110]

(iii) Enforcement and dispute settlement   An important element of FTAs, as already under the first generation, is a set of provisions on enforcement of intellectual property rights. Many FTA provisions largely follow the enforcement provisions of the TRIPS Agreement.[111] The FTAs also regularly include provisions on dispute settlement that are in principle similar to those of the WTO, subject to variations in detail. In general, where the parties to the FTA are also parties to the WTO, the complaining party has the right to choose the forum; thereafter, recourse to the other fora is no longer possible.[112]   **12.38**

(f) Implementation

While some of the FTAs provide for different transitional periods of several years to implement the required standards or adhere to specified treaties,[113] the more recently prevailing US tendency is to deny any transition period and to require full compliance and accession to the relevant treaties at the date of entry into   **12.39**

---

108 Art 4(13) of the US–Jordan FTA is an exception for its brevity, as opposed to Art 16.4(7), (8) of the US–Singapore FTA (covering nearly 4 single-spaced pages); Art 17.7(5), (6) of the US–Chile FTA and Art 17.4(7), (8) of the US–Australia FTA (each covering nearly 5 single-spaced pages), all exclusively on technological measures and rights management information; for liability of internet service providers, see eg Art 17.12(23) of the US–Chile FTA; Art 17.11(29) of the US–Australia FTA (3.5 single-spaced pages alone for ISP liability), supplemented by a side letter of 18 May 2004, specifying in detail the models of an effective notice of a right owner to a service provider, and of an effective counter-notification by a subscriber (also available at <http://www.ustr.gov>); Art 16.9(22) of the US–Singapore FTA (also with a side letter of 6 May 2003, with the like models). The US Digital Millennium Copyright Act (DMCA) implemented the WCT and WPPT and introduced provisions on liability of internet service providers.

109 Art 1707 of the NAFTA, para 11.19 above; for similar provisions, see Art 16.6 of the US–Singapore FTA; Art 17.8 of the US–Chile FTA; Art 17.7 of the US–Australia FTA.

110 eg Art 4(15) of the US–Jordan FTA; Art 16.4(9) of the US–Singapore FTA; Art 17.7(4) of the US–Chile FTA; Art 17.4(9) of the US–Australia FTA.

111 eg Art 17.11(1)–(28) of the US–Australia FTA; Art 17.11(1)–(22) of the US–Chile FTA; Art 16.9(1)–(21) of the US–Singapore FTA; in contrast, the US–Jordan FTA contains only 5 paragraphs: Art 4(24)–(28), and a related Memorandum of Understanding (available at <http://www. ustr.gov>) adds 2 short provisions in this respect; for the provisions of the US–Chile FTA, see Roffe (n 68 above) 42–5.

112 For dispute settlement provisions in the US–Chile FTA see Roffe (n 68 above) 46–8; the provisions are in ch 22 of the US–Chile FTA, (on the just mentioned right to choose the forum, see Art 22.3); ch 21 (in particular B) of the US–Australia FTA; Art 17 of the US–Jordan FTA; and ch 20 (in particular Art 20.2) of the US–Singapore FTA.

113 eg Art 17.1 and 17.12 of the US–Chile FTA (n 68 above), distinguishing between individual standards.

force, as under the US–Bahrain FTA.[114] This tendency corresponds to the negotiation objectives to ensure 'accelerated and full implementation' of the TRIPS Agreement[115] (irrespective of whether the transitional periods of the TRIPS Agreement have elapsed).[116]

12.40 The different bilateral agreements—TIFAs, BITs, and FTAs—usually provide for a Joint Committee or Council as a forum for continuous dialogue between the United States Trade Representative (USTR) and the relevant country or even as a tool to 'supervise the proper implementation' of the relevant agreement.[117] Such committees play an essential role in the concrete implementation of the agreements. They have been considered as factually creating laws of other nations, all the more since the Joint Committees usually also act as dispute settlement bodies in first instance.[118] In fact, the Committees' work and other measures may result in a guarantee for the US that the foreign 'laws will be written according to the US formula'.[119] This restriction of sovereignty in the implementation phase is also reflected in the lack of a standard clause of many multilateral intellectual property treaties, under which contracting parties may determine the method of implementation in accordance with their own legal system and practice.[120]

12.41 In the example of the US–Australia FTA, the US was not satisfied with the concrete wording of the sovereign Australian implementation of the WCT and WPPT in 2000 but insisted on a particular way of implementation of specific provisions according to the FTA.[121] Although the FTA had already been concluded and signed by the parties, approved by the US Congress and signed into law by the US President, as well as passed by the Australian Parliament and received Royal Assent, the US concerns on implementation had to be resolved before the FTA could enter into force. Under the US Trade Agreements Act of 1979, the President has the right to unilaterally determine whether a bilateral agreement, which has already been accepted by him and approved by

---

[114] The ITAC in its report (n 57 above), at 22, hails this principle (which is subject only to two exceptions) as a 'major advance' over preceding FTAs: 'All other treaty obligations, and, indeed, *all* other obligations in the IPR chapter, must be implemented upon entry into force, making this FTA the most positive of all others . . ., setting an excellent precedent for future FTA negotiations'; see also p 7 ibid.

[115] Section 2102 of the Trade Act of 2002 and para 12.25 above.

[116] On the possible conflict with the TRIPS Agreement, see paras 13.07–13.10 below.

[117] eg Art 15.1, Memorandum of Understanding of the US–Jordan FTA.

[118] For a criticism of these possibilities for far-reaching influence, see P Drahos, 'BITs and BIPs: Bilateralism in Intellectual Property' (2001) 4/6 Journal of World Intellectual Property 791, 798; on the Joint Committee under the US–Jordan FTA, see el Said (n 64 above) 517.

[119] Price (n 54 above) 847 in respect of the US–Bahrain FTA; similarly for Australia, Weiss/Thurbon/Mathews (n 69 above) 115, 125, 133.

[120] eg Art 1 of the TRIPS Agreement, Art 14(1) of the WCT and Art 23(1) of the WPPT.

[121] An allusion to this is made in Weiss/Thurbon/Mathews (n 69 above) 133; see also Ricketson/Ginsburg (n 7 above) 4.54, nn 108, 111.

Congress, has been properly implemented by the other party and, in the negative, may hinder its application.[122]

(4) Résumé

The recent bilateral FTAs initiated by the USA include minimum standards that **12.42** are usually not only higher than the TRIPS standards, but even higher than the level of the WCT and WPPT, mostly in a wording similar to US domestic law. Bilateral TAs are a part of a broader trade strategy stringently pursued by the USA; it therefore seems appropriate to make a separate assessment of TAs and similar strategies.[123]

B. Treaties between the European Communities and non-EC countries

(1) General remarks

(a) Early motivation for the inclusion of intellectual property in bilateral agreements

The early free trade and similar agreements concluded between the European **12.43** Communities and non-EC countries had covered intellectual property by mere safeguard clauses similar to those of the EC Treaty and of Article XX(d) of the GATT.[124] The European Communities started to envisage the inclusion of intellectual property into bilateral agreements with non-EC countries at around the same time as the USA. In 1988, when the USA adopted the relevant Trade Act,[125] the European Commission stated in its Green Paper of 1988 the need to complete the existing multilateral conventions and negotiations (in particular in the GATT framework) by provisions in bilateral treaties. Similarly to the USA, it criticized 'the absence of adequate substantive standards protecting intellectual property, [and] the lack of effective enforcement where such standards exist'.[126]

---

122 USTR press release of 17 November 2004 on the US–Australia FTA, <http://www.ustr.gov/assets/Document_Library/Press_Releases/2004/November/asset_upload_file236_6752.pdf>. Under 19 USC s 2503(b)(2)(A), the President may determine whether the other party 'has accepted the obligations under the agreement in respect of the United States'.

123 Ch 14 below; for a short comparison between bilateral agreements in different parts of the world, see also paras 12.76–12.89 below.

124 See Art 30 of the EC Treaty (ex-Art 36) and Vol II ch 2; as an example, see Art 20 of the agreement between the EEC and Switzerland OJ L 300, 189 of 31 December 1992; see also para 14.01 below in respect of the GATT.

125 paras 12.04–12.05 above.

126 Green Paper on Copyright and the Challenge of Technology: Copyright Issues Requiring Immediate Action, COM (88) 172 final, 7.3.1. See also the working programme of the Commission in this field, 'Follow-up to the Green Paper' COM (90) 584 final, 7.8.2. See also Vol II. Indeed,

12.44   An additional, very specific motivation arose three years later as a result of the collapse of socialism in Eastern and Central European countries and their opening up to the West. As a natural development, Eastern and Central European countries strove towards the EC; they were the main focus of bilateral activities by the EC at that time. Broad association agreements (including intellectual property obligations) were the tool to prepare their accession to the EC.[127]

(b) Kinds of agreements

12.45   Apart from association agreements aiming at EC accession, the EC concludes agreements aiming at two other kinds of association: free trade associations with the goal of establishing free trade zones, and development associations with the focus on aspects of development politics. All types of association agreements are international treaties[128] based on Article 310 of the EC Treaty; their primary goal is a particularly close and long-term relationships with non-EC countries. They must be realized by 'common action and special procedures'.[129] In other words, they must have their own institutions (with equal representation) that are empowered, in the framework of their tasks, to make binding decisions and thereby to promote the realization and further development of the association.

12.46   Standard elements of their contents include rules on free trade, rules of origin, free movement of persons, and even rules prohibiting discrimination of nationals of the other party in certain situations. Accordingly, association agreements are much further reaching than trade agreements based on the EC's general, common commercial policy competence under Article 133 of the EC Treaty.[130] The titles of agreements do not always reveal their legal nature; for example, 'cooperation and partnership' agreements may be association agreements or those based on Article 133 of the EC Treaty. These agreements may also contain intellectual property obligations. Yet other agreements, such as Framework Cooperation Agreements, usually do not contain any intellectual property provisions that would go beyond general rules on cooperation.[131]

---

certain existing bilateral agreements were renegotiated thereafter in order to include intellectual property.

[127] The legal basis for these agreements was Art 238 EC Treaty (Art 310 in the version of the Treaty of Nice); S von Lewinski, 'Copyright within the External Relations of the European Union and the EFTA Countries' (1994) 10 EIPR 429, 430. On agreements ultimately leading to accession, see paras 12.47–12.53 below.

[128] By referring to the reciprocal rights and obligations of the parties, Art 310 of the EC Treaty expresses a typical feature of treaties under public international law.

[129] Art 310 of the EC Treaty.

[130] They have more recently been used for non-preferential trade agreements.

[131] eg Agreement between the EEC and Argentina of 2 April 1990, [1990] OJ L295/67.

(2) Agreements aimed at preparing for accession to the EC

(a) First generation of agreements

Between 1989 and 1991, European Communities[132] concluded the first gener- **12.47**
ation of agreements[133] that covered obligations to provide intellectual property
protection. They focused on Central and Eastern European countries,[134] which
were able to independently conclude agreements directly with the EC only after
the signing of a Joint Declaration between the European Economic Community
and the Council for Mutual Economic Assistance (COMECON) on 25 June
1988.[135] Beforehand, the COMECON's claims of exclusive competence effectively prevented the individual countries from concluding international agreements, but the Community did not recognize this competence and was only
prepared to deal directly with the countries. After the Berlin wall collapsed in
November 1989, the relation with Central and Eastern European countries proceeded to a new dimension.

The intellectual property provisions in these agreements reflected the consider- **12.48**
ation of the specific political, social, and economic situation in these countries,
which needed time to restructure their economies after the collapse of socialism
in order to adapt their structures to the upcoming market economies. Also, the
provisions triggered a dialogue.[136] Accordingly, these provisions were limited to
the following obligations: (a) to ensure adequate protection and enforcement of
intellectual property rights, (b) to ensure the compliance with the countries' existing international commitments in the field, (c) to encourage appropriate arrangements between undertakings and institutions within the Community and the
non-EC country, and (d) to encourage cooperation and exchanges of views
between organizations and institutions responsible for intellectual property.[137]

---

132 In some cases, such agreements were concluded on the European side by the European
Economic Community and the European Atomic Energy Community (Euratom) or possibly by all
three European Communities.

133 They were called 'agreements on trade and commercial and economic cooperation', such as the
agreement between the EEC, Euratom, and the USSR of 18 December 1989, [1990] OJ L 68/1.

134 Similar agreements were also negotiated and in part concluded with other countries, such as
China, Vietnam, and certain Mediterranean countries, see von Lewinski (n 127 above) 430.

135 [1988] OJ L 157, 34. The COMECON included the Soviet Union, the former state-trading
countries of Eastern Europe, Mongolia, Vietnam, and Cuba.

136 D Franzone, 'Les Relations entre la Communauté et les pays d'Europe Central et Oriental: vers
une voie européenne des droits de propriété intellectuelle?' (1993) Diritto d'autore 245, 256 ff, 249 ff.

137 Art 19(4) of the Agreement between the European Economic Community and the People's
Republic of Bulgaria on Trade and Commercial and Economic Cooperation, OJ L 291/9 of 23
October 1990; similar provisions were contained in Art 15(3) of the Agreement with the Czech and
Slovak Federal Republics of the same date (ibid 28) and Art 18 of the Agreement with Romania of
26 March 1991, OJ L 79/13 of 26 March 1991. See also Art 19 of the Agreement between
the European Economic Community and the European Atomic Energy Community and the

(b) Second generation of agreements and Europe Agreements

12.49 The conclusion of a second generation of bilateral trade and cooperation agreements started in 1992 as an interim step with countries that were not immediately envisaged as future accession candidates, namely, the Baltic countries, Albania, and Slovenia.[138] They included slightly more demanding intellectual property obligations[139] and mentioned the further aim of concluding association agreements. These association agreements, called 'Europe Agreements', then replaced the previous bilateral agreements of both generations.[140] They were considered the last step before accession to the European Union. In order to facilitate accession for the candidate countries, it was necessary to provide some flexibility so that their laws could be smoothly brought into conformity with the *acquis communautaire*.[141] Such harmonization with the *acquis communautaire* was not an act of imposing any standards for the benefit of EC industries, but corresponded to the obligation of any EC Member State to respect and properly implement EC law.

12.50 Accordingly, the Europe Agreements covered many more areas, such as free movement of goods, services, capital, and persons, competition, harmonization of laws, as well as economic, financial, and cultural cooperation. Their intellectual property obligations were more concrete than under the earlier agreements. First, the obligation to provide 'effective and adequate protection' was qualified by the words 'at a level similar to that existing in the Community, including comparable means of enforcing such rights'. This qualification reflected the aim of approximating laws in order to enable future accession to the European Union (EU). An advantage of this method was the possibility to integrate, by mere reference to existing Community law, any future harmonization within the

---

Union of Soviet Socialist Republics on Trade and Commercial and Economic Cooperation, OJ L 68/3 of 15 March 1990; this agreement did not contain the last obligation mentioned above.

[138] Agreement between the EEC and Estonia, OJ L 403/2 of 31 December 1992; Agreement between the EEC and Latvia, OJ L 403/11 of 31 December 1992; Agreement between the EEC and the EAEC (European Atomic Energy Community) and Lithuania OJ 1992 L 403/19 of 31 December 1992; Agreement between the EEC and Albania, OJ L 343/2 of 25 November 1992; Agreement Between the EEC and Slovenia, OJ L 189/1 of 29 July 1993.

[139] In particular, the adequate protection had to be 'at a level similar to that which exists in the Community', and the parties had to adhere to (though, not specified) international treaties on intellectual property.

[140] For Poland and Hungary, see the agreements in OJ L 348 and L 347 of 31 December 1993; they came into force on 1 February 1994; for Bulgaria, Slovak Republic, Czech Republic, Romania, Lithuania, Latvia, Estonia, and Slovenia see, respectively, OJ L 358/2, 359/2, 360/3, 357/2 (all 1994), 51/3, 26/3, 68/3 (all 1998), and 51/3 (1999). So-called interim agreements that contained those provisions for which the European Community (as opposed to its Member States) was exclusively competent were concluded earlier, see von Lewinski (n 127 above) 430.

[141] The *acquis communautaire* is the EC law in the relevant fields, including primary and secondary law, a well as their interpretation by the EC courts, see Vol II.

Community as an automatic obligation under the bilateral agreements.[142] At the same time, this obligation left a certain degree of flexibility by only demanding a 'similar' level to that of the EC. Secondly, the agreements required adherence to specified international conventions. Both of these obligations were to be achieved by the end of the fifth year from the entry into force of the agreement. Thirdly, the compatibility of future legislation with EC legislation 'as far as possible'—again a flexible term—was required.[143]

Finally, after renegotiation of these agreements and further interim steps, the rele-   **12.51**
vant countries acceded to the EU.

(c) Stabilization and association agreements

After 2000, the EC proceeded with so-called 'stabilization and association agree-   **12.52**
ments' (SAAs) with countries of the Western Balkans, starting with Macedonia, Croatia, and later Albania.[144] Negotiations with Bosnia and Herzegovina, Montenegro, and Serbia started in 2006.[145] SAAs are considered as association agreements both for accession and for development. General political stabilization, economic prosperity, and peace for the entire region are among their main aims that distinguish SAAs from the Europe (and other accession) agreements. Fundamental obligations refer to the safeguard of principles of democracy, international law, human rights, the rule of law, and market economy.

At the same time, their Preambles explicitly mention the option of EU accession.   **12.53**
Both Croatia and Macedonia are already candidates for EU membership.[146] Given the principal option for accession,[147] it is no surprise that the structure and rules of the SAAs essentially correspond to those of the Europe Agreements. In respect of copyright and related rights, the parties typically confirm the importance of adequate and effective intellectual property protection and enforcement, including the importance of compliance with the Berne, Rome, and Geneva Phonograms Conventions as well as the WCT and WPPT. In addition, the non-EC country 'shall take the necessary measures' in order to guarantee a level of protection 'similar to' the EC level within three to five years after entry into force

---

142 Franzone (n 136 above) 256 ff.

143 eg Arts 67, 68 of the Hungarian Europe Agreement (n 140 above).

144 Stabilization and Association Agreements with the Former Yugoslav Republic of Macedonia and Croatia of 2001 (in force since 1 May 2004 and 1 February 2005 respectively), [2004] OJ L84/13 and [2005] OJ L26/3; with Albania of 2006 (interim Agreement, [2006] OJ L239/3, in force since 1 December 2006).

145 Negotiations with Serbia were interrupted in May 2006 and resumed in May 2007.

146 Croatia: June 2004; Macedonia: December 2005.

147 The European Council stated on several occasions, eg in 1993, 1995, and 2000, that all countries of the Western Balkans would in principle be considered for accession, see Press release no 200/1/00 no 67 of 19 June 2000.

of the SAA; and the parties agree that the Stabilization and Association Council may oblige the non-EC country to accede to specific conventions, and to refer to the Council problems of intellectual property regarding trading conditions. Also, an MFN clause in respect of intellectual property is included.[148]

(3) Partnership and cooperation agreements with former Soviet countries

12.54 From the mid-1990s, the EC initiated partnership and cooperation agreements with former Soviet countries.[149] In general, these agreements aim at political dialogue, extension of economic relations, and cooperation in many areas; yet, they do not envisage accession to the EU. Intellectual property obligations are very similar to those of SAAs.[150]

(4) Development association agreements

12.55 The EC has concluded development association agreements with countries from different regions of the world, in particular with Mediterranean countries (the so-called 'EuroMed Association Agreements'), African-Caribbean-Pacific countries (Agreement of Cotonou),[151] South Africa,[152] and Chile.[153] These agreements typically aim, in particular, at trade liberalization, enhanced cooperation, political stabilization, as well as respect for democratic principles and fundamental rights.

12.56 Regarding Mediterranean trading partners, the EU in November 1995 adopted the 'Barcelona Declaration', which sought to add a new dimension to the relations between the EU and certain Mediterranean countries: comprehensive cooperation and bilateral association agreements to ultimately create a Euro-Mediterranean Partnership and Free Trade Area in 2010. After Cyprus and Malta

---

[148] eg Art 71 and Annex VIII of the SAA with Croatia (n 144 above).

[149] Agreements with the Russian Federation of 24 June 1994, [1997] OJ L327/3; Moldova of 28 November 1994, [1998] OJ L181/3; Ukraine of 14 June 1994, [1998] OJ L49/3; Kyrgyzstan of 9 February 1995, [1999] OJ L196/48; Kazakhstan of 23 January 1995, [1999] OJ L196/3; Uzbekistan of 21 June 1996, [1999] OJ L229/3; Azerbaijan of 22 April 1996, [1999] OJ L246/3; Georgia of 22 April 1996, [1999] OJ L205/3; Armenia of 24 April 1996, [1999] OJ L239/3.

[150] eg Preamble and, for intellectual property, Art 54 and Annex 10 of the Agreement with Russia; similarly, Preamble and Art 50 and Annex III of the Agreement with Ukraine (n 149 above).

[151] The Cotonou Agreement is covered under regional agreements, see paras 11.69–11.70 above.

[152] Agreement with South Africa, [1999] OJ L311/3 (in force since 1 May 2004); see Art 46 on intellectual property.

[153] Agreement with Chile, [2002] OJ L352/3; similar association agreements with Latin American countries are planned. With other developing countries, other types of agreements exist and, in part, contain intellectual property obligations (eg Agreement with Korea of 28 October 1996, [2001] OJ L90/46, Art 9 and Annex, including very general intellectual property obligations); see also n 131 above on Argentina.

acceded to the European Union in 2004, the following ten Mediterranean partners are left in this context: Algeria, Egypt, Israel, Jordan, Lebanon, Morocco, Palestinian Authority, Syria, Tunisia, and Turkey.[154] To date, negotiations with all of them have been completed.[155] Since 1995, these agreements have replaced earlier ones of the 1970s.

These and other above-mentioned agreements are part of yet another policy that **12.57** covers not only Mediterranean countries, but also other neighbours of the EU: the European Neighbourhood Policy (ENP), which covers Algeria, Armenia, Azerbaijan, Belarus, Egypt, Georgia, Israel, Jordan, Lebanon, Libya, Moldova, Morocco, Palestinian Authority, Syria, Tunisia, and Ukraine; with Russia, the EU has instead developed a strategic partnership. This policy was developed in 2004 to offer the EU's neighbouring countries a privileged relationship so as to avoid a new dividing line between the EU (after its enlargement of 2004) and its new neighbours.[156] Like the Euro-Mediterranean Partnership, the ENP is based on bilateral agreements.

The intellectual property provisions of most of these agreements closely follow **12.58** the same pattern. They continue the tradition of earlier EC bilateral treaties in being brief and relatively general. For example, under a typical clause, parties shall 'grant and ensure adequate and effective protection of intellectual property rights in accordance with the highest international standards', or '. . . in accordance with the prevailing international standards, including effective means of enforcing intellectual property rights'.[157] Such broad wording may offer, on the one hand, a certain amount of flexibility, but on the other hand, reasons for potential disputes. In particular, it may not be clear in any instance what the 'highest international standards' are—these standards could be under multilateral treaties, bilateral treaties, or both, and they could include only those existing at the time of the conclusion of the agreement or at any later time.

---

154 See the Agreements with Tunisia, [1998] OJ L97/2; Algeria [2005] OJ L265/2; Morocco [2000] OJ L70/2; Egypt [2004] OJ L304/39; Jordan [2002] OJ L129/3; Lebanon [2002] OJ L262/2 (Interim Agreement), and Israel (the latter, though is not a development association agreement) in [2000] OJ L147/3.

155 For the current status (signature, entry into force), see <http://ec.europa.eu/trade/issues/bilateral/regions/euromedy/aa_en.htm>.

156 On the ENP, see <http://ec.europa.eu/world/enp/policy_en.htm> and Communication from the Commission of 12 May 2004 (COM 2004 373 final), 'European Neighbourhood Policy: Strategy Paper'.

157 eg Art 55(g) of the EC–Chile Association Agreement (n 153 above); Art 37 of the EC–Egypt Association Agreement (n 154 above); Art 46(1) of the EC–South Africa Association Agreement (n 152 above).

12.59 Under other obligations that are not particular to development association agreements, the parties must accede to specified conventions[158] and ensure their adequate and effective implementation, as well as 'confirm the importance they attach to' treaties to which they are already parties. The time allowed for the relevant accessions is usually four or five years after the entry into force of the agreement (which itself may well occur between three and five years after signature).[159] Any obligation to accede to the TRIPS Agreement respects the transitional periods granted for developing countries under Article 65 of the TRIPS Agreement.[160] In only some agreements, the parties also undertake to accede to the WCT and WPPT.[161] In most treaties, the accession obligations are supplemented by an opening clause under which the Association Council (ministers of the parties) may decide to add other multilateral conventions in the field to which the parties would have to accede.[162] By this clause, the agreements remain dynamic and, as to future decisions, subject to mutual agreement.

12.60 In some Agreements, the special situation of the contracting party as a developing country has been taken into account by additional elements. For example, South Africa is not obliged to adhere to specific treaties; instead, the Community confirms the importance it attaches to the obligations of such treaties, while South Africa 'could favourably consider accession' to these treaties.[163] Furthermore, 'the Community may provide, on request and on mutually agreed terms and conditions, technical assistance to South Africa' in the preparation of laws, but also in the prevention of abuse of intellectual property rights.[164]

C. Bilateral treaties of other countries

(1) General remarks

12.61 Although the USA and Europe have been most active in initiating bilateral free trade or similar agreements that include provisions on intellectual property rights,

---

[158] They vary for each country; often, they are limited to the Rome Convention, eg, Annex 6 of the EC–Egypt Association Agreement and Annex 7 of the EC–Morocco Association Agreement (n 154 above); Art 170(c)(i) of the EC–Chile Association Agreement also includes the Geneva Phonograms Convention.

[159] The above provisions (n 158 above) of the agreements with Egypt and Morocco provide for four years.

[160] eg Annex 6 of the EC–Algeria Association Agreement (n 154 above).

[161] eg ibid; Art 170(b)(ii), (iii) of the EC–Chile Association Agreement (n 153 above).

[162] eg Art 171 of the EC–Chile Association Agreement; Annex VI of the EC–Egypt Association Agreement (nn 153 and 154 above).

[163] Art 46(4) of the Agreement (n 152 above).

[164] Art 46(6) ibid.

other countries have, essentially since the mid-1990s, also practised bilateralism. In some cases, more than two countries of different regions have concluded such agreements,[165] or a group of countries already bound by a regional agreement, such as CAFTA or EFTA, have concluded agreements with individual countries.[166] Although they are not strictly speaking 'bilateral' agreements, they are closer to bilateral than to regional agreements, and are therefore covered in this chapter.[167] Instead of a detailed analysis of all agreements that cover intellectual property rights, this section focuses on the main patterns to be found in the existing treaties.

(2) EFTA

The European Free Trade Association (EFTA) has concluded fifteen FTAs to date **12.62** (November 2007); first with other European countries after 1990 and more recently with Mexico, Chile, Korea, Singapore, Egypt, Israel, Jordan, Lebanon, Morocco, Palestinian Authority, Tunisia, Turkey, and Southern African Customs Union (not yet in force).[168] These FTAs usually lay down the general obligations to provide adequate and effective protection and enforcement of intellectual property rights and to grant national treatment and most-favoured-nation treatment, subject to the exceptions under the TRIPS Agreement. They also list a number of treaties for which the parties reaffirm their commitments and others for which they undertake to become a party. The conditions vary between the countries; for example, the obligation to become a party to the WCT and WPPT on 1 January 2007 is contained in the Chile–EFTA FTA, while the Mexico–EFTA FTA only obliges Mexico 'to make every effort to complete the necessary procedures for accession [to the WCT and WPPT] at their earliest possible opportunity'.[169]

(3) Latin America

Many Latin American FTAs—just like bilateral investment treaties—cover **12.63** intellectual property rights in their investment chapters as investments that are subject to the obligations of national treatment and the most-favoured-nation

---

[165] eg the 'Trans-Pacific Strategic Economic Partnership' between Brunei Darussalam, Chile, New Zealand, and Singapore, signed in 2005 (not yet in force), see <http://www.mfat.govt.nz/Trade-and-Economic-Relations/Trade-Agreements/Trans-Pacific/index.php>.

[166] eg the agreements of EFTA, see <http://secretariat.efta.int/Web/legaldocuments/>; similarly, the Central America–Panama agreement (signed 2002) between Costa Rica, El Salvador, Guatemala, Honduras, and Nicaragua on the one hand and Panama on the other hand, see <http://www.sice.org/ctyindex/PAN/PANagreements_e.asp>.

[167] For regional agreements, such as EFTA, see ch 11 above.

[168] <http://secretariat.efta.int/Web/legaldocuments/>. Also seven Declarations on cooperation with other countries are available there.

[169] Annex XXI of the Mexico–EFTA Agreement, see <http://secretariat.efta.int/Web/External Relations/PartnerCountries/Mexico>.

clause.[170] In addition, they often contain general obligations to provide 'adequate and effective protection and enforcement of intellectual property rights', and reaffirmations of obligations under the TRIPS Agreement[171] or other treaties to which the countries are parties.[172] The agreements frequently state that parties may provide for more extensive protection of intellectual property rights.[173]

12.64 While some treaties' provisions on intellectual property are limited to such general obligations,[174] others include much more detailed rules that are often based on the model of the NAFTA. Notably, even those elements of the NAFTA that are characteristic for the copyright system are copied into these agreements, although Latin American countries follow the author's rights system.[175] Where national treatment and the most-favoured-nation clause are explicitly stated, the exceptions allowed under the Berne and Rome Conventions and the TRIPS Agreement are explicitly admitted.[176] Some agreements oblige the parties to apply the substantive provisions not only of the Berne and Geneva Phonograms Conventions, but also of the Rome Convention.[177] Other notable variations of the NAFTA model are additional provisions for performing artists based on the model of the Rome Convention,[178] and a general obligation to efficiently protect expressions of folklore and traditional knowledge.[179]

---

[170] eg Arts X.02(d) and X.05 of the FTA between CARICOM and Costa Rica (signed in 2004, in force with Barbados (2006), Guyana (2006), Trinidad and Tobago (2005)), as part of Chapter X on investment, see <http://www.sice.org/Trade/crcrcom_e/crcrcomind_e.asp>.

[171] eg Art 16.1 of the FTA between Chile and Korea (in force since 2004), <http://www.sice.org/Trade/Chi-SKorea_e/ChiKoreaind_e.asp>.

[172] eg FTA between Chile and EFTA (in force since 2004) Annex XII, <http://secretariat.efta.int/Web/ExternalRelations/PartnerCountries/Chile>; Trans-Pacific Strategic Economic Partnership (n 165 above) Art 10.3.

[173] eg Art 16.2 of the FTA between Chile and Korea (n 171 above), similarly to Art 1(1) phr 1 of the TRIPS Agreement.

[174] See also eg Art 19.7 of the Chile–Peru FTA of 22 August 2006, <http://www.sice.oas.org/ctyindex/CHL/CHLAgreements_e.asp>.

[175] In particular the provision on free transferability of rights and full enjoyment of acquired rights, including by employers.

[176] eg the Costa Rica–Mexico FTA (in force since 1995), <http://www.sice.org/trade/Mexcr_s/mcrind.asp> and the Chile–Mexico FTA (in force since 1999), <http://www.sice.org/trade/chmefta/indice.asp>.

[177] eg ibid; in contrast, the NAFTA does not include a Rome compliance clause.

[178] eg Arts 16-10–16-14 of the Mexico–Bolivia FTA (in force since 1995), see <http://www.sice.org/trade/mexbo_s/mbind.asp>; Arts 15-09–15-14 of the Chile–Mexico FTA (n 176 above); Arts 14-20 ff of the Costa Rica–Mexico FTA (n 176 above); similarly: the trilateral agreement between Columbia, Mexico, and Venezuela (in force since 1995), <http://www.sice.org/Trade/go3/G3INDICE.ASP.>

[179] eg Arts 15.04 and 15.03 of the Guatemala–Taiwan ('Repùblica de China (Taiwán)') FTA (in force since 2006), <http://www.sice.org/Trade/GTM_TW/Index_s.asp>; and Art 16.06 of the Panama–Taiwan FTA of 2004, <http://www.sice.org/Trade/PanRC/ PANRC_e.asp.

Agreements between Chile and EFTA as well as Mexico and EFTA follow the **12.65**
EFTA model, which is similar to the model applied by the EC.[180]

(4) Trans-Pacific Strategic Economic Partnership Agreement

A somewhat different, more 'balance-oriented' approach is reflected in the Trans- **12.66**
Pacific Strategic Economic Partnership Agreement between Brunei Darussalam,
Chile, New Zealand, and Singapore.[181] While its Article 1.1(4)(e) lists among the
general trade objectives the provision of adequate and effective protection and
enforcement of intellectual property rights, its Chapter 10 on intellectual property
includes general provisions according to which the parties recognize the importance of intellectual property in promoting economic and social development and
the need for a balance between the rights of rights owners and the legitimate
interests of users. Other provisions explicitly allow measures to prevent the abuse
of intellectual property rights and anti-competitive practices; others confirm that
the parties may provide for international exhaustion (subject to international
obligations) and may establish provisions to facilitate permitted acts where technical measures have been employed.[182]

In respect of copyright and related rights, the Agreement only obliges parties to **12.67**
introduce rights of reproduction and communication to the public by reference
to the WCT and WPPT, as well as a TRIPS-similar protection of performers. In
addition, it refers to permitted limitations and exceptions under the Berne Convention, the TRIPS Agreement, the WCT, and the WPPT, and provides for reciprocity in respect of related rights, subject to the TRIPS Agreement.[183] Much
more detail is devoted to geographical indications, as in some other agreements
involving Latin American countries.

(5) Australia and New Zealand

(a) Australia

While Australia's priority in trade negotiations remains with the WTO, the tem- **12.68**
porary stagnation of WTO talks has spurred Australia's new FTA agenda. Bilateral
as well as regional FTAs are favourably considered for allowing fast trade liberalization, especially with important foreign markets.[184] In addition to the FTA
with the USA of 2005,[185] Australia has concluded FTAs with Singapore (SAFTA,

---

180 For the EC, see paras 12.55, 12.58–12.60 above; for EFTA, see para 12.62 above.
181 n 165 above. Also, see para 12.61 above.
182 Art 10.3 (1)–(3) of the above agreement.
183 Art 10.3 (4)–(5) of the above agreement.
184 <http://www.dfat.gov.au/trade/fs_fta_essential_guide.html>. On Australia's FTA trade
policy in general, see C Dent, *New Free Trade Agreements in the Asia Pacific* (2006), 66 ff.
185 <http://www.ustr.gov/Trade_Agreements/Bilateral/Australia_FTA/Section_Index.html>.

2003) and Thailand (TAFTA, 2005)[186] and currently (in 2007) negotiates FTAs with China, Malaysia, New Zealand/ASEAN, Japan, and Chile. It also plans free trade negotiations with the Gulf Cooperation Council (GCC);[187] initially, it had started bilateral negotiations with the United Arab Emirates (UAE), but could not pursue them, after the UAE informed Australia about the decision of the GCC Supreme Council that member countries could negotiate FTAs only collectively. As a first step towards possible FTA negotiations, Australia and the Republic of Korea have also agreed to conduct a joint study on an FTA between them.[188]

12.69 The SAFTA and TAFTA include much less detail than the Australia–US FTA. Chapter 13 of the SAFTA on intellectual property only consists of seven articles. In respect of copyright and related rights, the parties reaffirm their commitments to the TRIPS Agreement and undertake to join the WCT and WPPT within four years of the entry into force of the SAFTA.[189] The only specific copyright provision explicitly extends the reproduction right to electronic copies of works, sound recordings, and cinematographic films, subject to limitations or exceptions permitted under the laws of the Parties.[190] The only other regulatory obligation is to take measures to prevent the export of infringing goods on receipt of information or complaints; this obligation is not covered by the border control measures under the TRIPS Agreement.[191] The other provisions relate to cooperation on enforcement, on education, and on exchange of information regarding intellectual property rights.[192]

12.70 The TAFTA contains even fewer obligations regarding copyright and related rights. While the parties to this agreement also 'fully respect' the TRIPS Agreement 'and any other multilateral agreements relating to intellectual property to which both are parties',[193] they do not undertake to accede to the WCT or the WPPT. Also, the TAFTA does not provide for the reproduction right covering electronic copies; only the same obligation as in SAFTA to take measures to prevent the export

---

[186] The SAFTA entered into force on 28 July 2003 and was the first one to include intellectual property, and also the first bilateral FTA since the 1983 Closer Economic Relations Trade Agreement with New Zealand; the TAFTA entered into force on 1 January 2005; for the text of both agreements and related information, see <http://www.fta.gov.au/default.aspx?FolderID=260&ArticleID=206>.

[187] The GCC consists of Bahrain, Kuwait, Oman, Qatar, Saudi Arabia, and the UAE. On the negotiations with the GCC and a study on the prospects and possible benefits of an FTA with the GCC, see <http://www.dfat.gov.au/trade/fta/gcc/index.html>.

[188] <http://www.trademinister.gov.au/releases/2006/wtt026_06.html>.

[189] Art 2(1), (2), (3) of ch 13 of the SAFTA.

[190] Art 3 of ch 13 ibid.

[191] Art 4 of ch 13 ibid.

[192] Arts 5, 6 of ch 13 ibid; its Art 7 deals with domain names and trademarks.

[193] Art 1302 of the TAFTA.

of infringing goods is provided.[194] It also focuses on cooperation in the enforcement and awareness of and education in intellectual property rights and related areas; it explicitly mentions the aim of 'stimulating the creation and development of intellectual property by persons of each Party, particularly individual inventors and creators as well as small to medium-sized enterprises (SMEs)'.[195]

(b) New Zealand

Like Australia, New Zealand has concluded bilateral agreements that cover intel- **12.71**
lectual property with Thailand[196] and Singapore.[197] They contain only very limited intellectual property provisions, such as the general reference to the governing TRIPS Agreement,[198] or similar clauses reaffirming obligations under the TRIPS and other intellectual property agreements as well as cooperation clauses.[199] New Zealand currently negotiates additional bilateral agreements that would typically include intellectual property.[200]

(6) Asia

(a) Developing countries[201]

Many of the bilateral FTAs between Asian developing countries do not provide **12.72**
for any intellectual property provisions. Most of those that do so provide, only include very basic provisions, such as the affirmation of commitments in connection with intellectual property under the WTO Agreement;[202] otherwise, they focus on cooperation in the field,[203] or include intellectual property only as

---

[194] Art 1303 ibid.
[195] Art 1305b.ii. ibid. On the SAFTA and TAFTA, see briefly also Antons (n 69 above) 6–7. On a comparison to other agreements, see paras 12.76–12.80, in particular 12.79 below.
[196] Agreement between New Zealand and Thailand on a closer economic partnership, <http://www.mfat.govt.nz/Trade-and-Economic-Relations/Trade-Agreements/Thailand/index.php>.
[197] Agreement between New Zealand and Singapore on a closer economic partnership, <http://www.mfat.govt.nz/Trade-and-Economic-Relations/Trade-Agreements/Singapore/index.php>.
[198] Art 57 ibid.
[199] Arts 12.1–12.5 of the New Zealand–Thailand Agreement (n 196 above).
[200] With the Gulf Cooperation Council, China, Malaysia, and Hong Kong, see <http://www.mfat.govt.nz/Trade-and-Economic-Relations/Trade-Agreements/index.php>. On New Zealand's FTA policy in general, see Dent (n 184 above) 87 ff.
[201] On the FTA policy in general of Singapore, South Korea, Taiwan, and Thailand, see Dent (n 184 above) 96 ff, 104 ff, 112 ff, and 120 ff.; on selected bilateral agreements with countries of the region in general, ibid 150 ff.
[202] Art 8.8 of the Singapore–Jordan FTA of 2004, <http://www.bilaterals.org/IMG/pdf/SJFTA-2004.pdf>.
[203] eg ch 17 of the Korea–Singapore FTA of 2005, which also reaffirms the Parties' TRIPS obligations and contains a general obligation to provide 'adequate and effective protection of intellectual property rights to the nationals of the other Party' as well as enforcement consistent with the TRIPS Agreement, and the clarification that more extensive protection than under the FTA may be provided, if it is consistent with the TRIPS Agreement; <http://www.bilaterals.org/IMG/pdf/KSFTA-2005.pdf>.

investment in their investment chapters.[204] They usually do not include detailed provisions on copyright and related rights; rather, they may include a certain degree of detail regarding trademarks and, even more so, geographical indications.[205]

(b) Japan

12.73 Japan has concluded a number of bilateral agreements[206] with different provisions on intellectual property. For example, the FTA with Mexico only includes a general non-derogation clause regarding multilateral intellectual property rights treaties to which Japan and Mexico are parties, an investment-related provision, and a general article on cooperation in intellectual property.[207]

12.74 In other FTAs of Japan, the general objectives include the enhancement of protection of intellectual property and strengthening of cooperation in the field as a means to promote trade and investment.[208] Also, such FTAs cover intellectual property in provisions on the exchange of information as well as in the context of investments.[209] Moreover, they include entire chapters on intellectual property rights.[210] Such chapters include, for example, the general obligation to ensure adequate and non-discriminatory protection and enforcement of intellectual property rights in accordance with the international agreements to which both countries are parties; provisions on strengthened cooperation in the field; provisions on promotion of transparency (for example, by forwarding easily available information on the intellectual property protection system); and provisions on promotion of public awareness.

12.75 In the field of copyright and related rights, such FTAs include the obligation to provide the right of making available (upon the model of Article 8 of the WCT)

---

[204] eg Art 10.1 (definition of 'investment' covering intellectual property rights: (g)); Art 10.9(5) (non-derogation of TRIPS and other relevant intellectual property treaties); Art 10.13(6) (expropriation rules do not apply to compulsory licences under TRIPS) of the Korea–Singapore FTA (n 203 above).

[205] eg Arts 16.3 and 16.4 of the Korea–Chile FTA of 2003, <http://www.bilaterals.org/IMG/pdf/korea-chile_FTA.pdf>. On intellectual property in bilateral and regional trade agreements in Asia, see also R Sen, ' "New Regionalism" in Asia: A Comparative Analysis of Emerging Regional and Bilateral Trading Agreements Involving ASEAN, China and India' (2006) 40/4 Journal of World Trade 553, 579.

[206] On Japan's FTA policy in general, see Dent (n 184 above) 76 ff.

[207] Arts 73 and 144 of the Japan–Mexico FTA of September 2004, <http://www.bilaterals.org/IMG/pdf/JAP-MEX_FTA_Sep_2004.pdf>.

[208] eg Art 1(d) Japan–Philippines FTA of 2006, <http://www.bilaterals.org/IMG/pdf/JPEPA_2006_.pdf>; Art 1(d) Japan–Malaysia EPA of 2005, <http://www.bilaterals.org/IMG/doc/JMEPA_2005_.doc>; Art 1(d) Japan–Chile FTA of 2007, <http://www.bilaterals.org/article.php3?id_article=7680>.

[209] eg Arts 53 and 88(b)(vi) of the Japan–Philippines FTA (n 208 above).

[210] eg ch 9 (Arts 112–30) of the Japan–Malaysia EPA (n 208 above).

for authors, performers, and producers of phonograms, and to provide adequate legal protection against the circumvention of effective technological measures as well as in respect of rights management information, both modelled on the WCT and WPPT.[211] They may also include limitations of internet providers' liability and obligations to take measures for the development of collective management organizations.[212] In addition, enforcement provisions in accordance with the TRIPS Agreement, but less detailed, are provided.[213] Furthermore, a subcommittee on intellectual property shall be established for the purposes of the effective implementation and operation of the intellectual property provisions.[214]

D. Comparison of approaches

As shown in this chapter, the FTAs concluded by the USA require the adoption of the highest level of protection, and this through provisions with the highest degree of detail that are, in addition, tailor-made to the US industry's wishes and irrespective of legal or other traditions of the other countries. The provisions usually build upon the highest standards available under multilateral agreements as implemented in US law, and extend to further provisions that reflect the market-driven and industry-friendly concept of the copyright system. **12.76**

In contrast, most FTAs between non-US countries provide, if any, very general and usually softer obligations regarding copyright and related rights. Among developing countries, FTAs are often limited to cooperation clauses, the affirmation of existing obligations under multilateral treaties, or to general rules (such as national treatment) in investment chapters. Other FTAs usually also contain general clauses that require 'adequate and effective protection and enforcement' of intellectual property, sometimes in accordance with (unspecified) 'highest international standards' or, for EC agreements, 'at a level of protection similar to that existing in the Community'.[215] Accordingly, FTAs between non-US countries do not provide any particular details, nor impose any concrete wording, so that the other parties may remain well within their (copyright or author's rights) **12.77**

---

[211] eg Arts 126, 127 of the Japan–Philippines FTA (n 208 above); Art 133 of the Japan–Thailand EPA of 2007, <http://www.bilaterals.org/article.php3?id_article=7748>.

[212] eg Art 122(2), (3) of the Japan–Malaysia EPA (n 208 above).

[213] eg Art 129 of the Japan–Philippines FTA (n 208 above); Art 164 of the Japan–Chile FTA (n 208 above).

[214] eg Art 130 of the Japan–Philippines FTA (n 208 above); Art 165 of the Japan–Chile FTA (n 208 above).

[215] For some countries, the obligation was softly worded so as to 'endeavour to ensure that its laws will be gradually compatible with the EU laws', eg Art 50 of the Partnership and Cooperation Agreement with Moldova, and Art 51 of the agreement with the Ukraine.

systems and legal traditions while complying with the obligations under the agreement.

12.78   The non-US FTAs usually also require the accession to specified agreements (which do not always include the WCT and WPPT as highest-level multilateral agreements), and this within less stringent time periods than under US FTAs.[216] Sometimes, the parties only need to make 'every effort' to accede, at their 'earliest possible opportunity'.[217] Another particularity, mainly of most European Agreements, is their focus on the overall aim of integration into a large European area and the aim of promoting democracy and human rights,[218] rather than only on free trade and access to markets.

12.79   Some FTAs between non-US industrialized and developing countries include provisions that are favourable to developing countries, such as the confirmation of the possibility to provide for international exhaustion of the distribution right or to prevent abuse of intellectual property.[219] In particular, Australia and New Zealand have conceded much more flexibility than the USA in its FTAs.[220] In addition, the negotiation principles for one of the upcoming FTAs, the ASEAN–Australia and New Zealand Free Trade Area, reveal Australia's readiness to take into account the differences in the level of development of the participating countries by providing for technical assistance and capacity-building programmes; the ten years' duration for full implementation of the FTA also reflects this attitude.[221] Accordingly, depending on the level of development of the other party, this and similar FTAs concluded by Australia and New Zealand with ASEAN and others will probably be somewhat similar to the TAFTA and focus on cooperation.[222]

12.80   In sum, bilateralism is practised by many countries worldwide, with different approaches and intensity. Where they provide for more far-reaching provisions

---

[216] eg in the Europe Agreements, the time limits were usually around 5 years, versus not much more than 1 year in US agreements of the same time, von Lewinski (n 127 above) 431 (n 28).

[217] See para 12.62 above.

[218] Under the second generation agreements, their application could even be suspended by the European Union if democratic principles and human rights as established by the Helsinki Final Act and the Charter of Paris for a New Europe were substantially affected, Franzone (n 136 above) 247.

[219] para 12.66 above.

[220] The obligations under the SAFTA for Singapore to accede to the WCT and WPPT and to cover electronic copies by the reproduction right must be seen against the background that Singapore in parallel was subject to FTA negotiations with the USA on the same (and more extensive) obligations.

[221] For the negotiation principles (<http://www.dfat.gov.au/trade/fta/asean/principles.html>), see in particular its lit (e) and, for the envisaged consistency with WTO provisions and the aim to 'build on members' commitments in the WTO', also (j), (c).

[222] See Antons (n 195 above) 8.

than mere cooperation clauses, their common tendency is to refer to multilateral treaties by confirmation of existing obligations, integration of their substance, or the obligation to adhere to them; in particular under FTAs with the USA, obligations usually even go beyond the highest levels of multilateral treaties and mirror US law.

13

UNILATERAL TRADE MEASURES

A. Measures applied by the USA

(1) Background

As one of the US responses to the economic decline that had started in the 1960s,[1] **13.01** Section 301 of the US Trade Act of 1974 introduced the new trade policy of promoting US exports by forcing foreign countries to provide fair access to their markets for US products and services. This provision allowed the President to impose trade sanctions against countries that were considered to harm US exports by unfair practices, whether or not such practices violated any international law. Due to the economic power of the USA, threats of retaliation were efficient. Although this provision also covered intellectual property rights, the US Congress and industry subsequently preferred a more stringent and aggressive application of these provisions to intellectual property rights by the Office of the US Trade Representative (USTR),[2] not least in order to use this provision during the negotiations of the GATT Uruguay Round.[3] As a result, the 1988 Omnibus Trade and Competitiveness Act introduced the so-called 'Special 301' provisions

---

[1] See para 12.04 above.

[2] The Office of the USTR is part of the Executive Office of the US President; its head, the US Trade Representative, is a Cabinet member and serves the President as its principal trade adviser, negotiator, and spokesperson on trade issues, 19 USC §2171.

[3] On this aspect, see para 10.20 above on GATT and para 14.04 below on TRIPS.

on intellectual property rights[4] as a part of the overall reform of Sections 301 ff of the Trade Act of 1974,[5] labelled as the 'Super 301' provisions on the enforcement of US trade rights. The Special 301 provisions aimed at securing an efficient intellectual property protection through legal provisions and enforcement measures in foreign countries in favour of US industry in order to allow the US industry to reap the benefits[6] from the ongoing utilization of their works on foreign markets.

(2) Contents and working of 'Special 301'[7]

13.02 The law obliges the USTR to identify '(1) those foreign countries that (A) deny adequate and effective protection of intellectual property rights,[8] or (B) deny fair and equitable market access to United States persons that rely upon intellectual property protection,[9] and (2) those foreign countries identified under paragraph (1) that are determined by the Trade Representative to be priority foreign countries.'[10] On this basis, the USTR has established the following practice: relying in particular on the information gathered by the relevant US industries[11] and on investigations in all countries that are US trading partners, it publishes an annual

---

[4] In particular, s 1303(b) of the Trade Act of 1988 (Omnibus Trade and Competitiveness Act 1988, PubL 100-418 of 23 August 1988) amended s 182 of the Trade Act of 1974 (19 USC § 2242, later amended by the Uruguay Round Agreements Act enacted in 1994) which is the statutory authority for 'Special 301'.

[5] PubL 93-618; 19 USC §§ 2411–16.

[6] This language has been used by the US Trade Representative, R Zoellick, in the context of the US–Australia FTA, see Press Release of 17 November 2004, <http://www.ustr.gov/assets/Document_Library/Press_Releases/2004/November/asset_upload_file236_6752.pdf>: 'US businesses are eager to begin reaping the benefits of this historic agreement'.

[7] On the s 301 requirements and procedures in general, see 19 USC §§ 2411–19 and eg M Getlan, 'TRIPs and the Future of Section 301: A Comparative Study in Trade Dispute Resolution' (1995) 34 Columbia J'l of Transnational Law 173, 179–82; C Schede, 'The Strengthening of the Multilateral System' (1997/8) 20/1 World Competition 109, 123–30.

[8] For the broad definition of this notion, see 19 USC § 2411(d)(3)(F)(i).

[9] For the definition, see ibid.

[10] 19 USC § 2242 (a); for another identification exclusively addressed to Canada see 19 USC § 2242 (f)(1); it relates to measures affecting US cultural industries, adopted after 17 December 1992 and actionable under Art 2106 of the NAFTA; see para 11.04 above; J McIlroy, 'American Enforcement of Intellectual Property Rights: A Canadian Perspective' (1998) 1/3 J'l of World Intellectual Property 445, 451 f.

[11] In the field of copyright, the International Intellectual Property Alliance (IIPA) annually makes recommendations to the USTR on the basis of its experiences in foreign countries, see eg for 2007 <http://www.iipa.com/2007_SPEC301_TOC.htm>; 19 USC § 2242 (b)(2)(B) obliges the USTR to take into account information from interested persons (definition: 19 USC § 2411(d)(9)) in identifying priority foreign countries; under 19 USC § 2242 (b)(2)(A) the USTR must also consult with the Register of Copyrights and other offices. The Industry Trade Advisory Committee (ITAC) 15 on intellectual property is one of 22 sectoral, and technical advisory committees in the system of the USTR's Advisory Committee System; for its composition, see <http://www.ustr.gov/assets/Who_We_Are/Advisory_Committee_Lists/asset_upload_file786_5754.pdf>.

'Special 301 Report'[12] which classifies foreign countries into several categories: on the lowest threat level, a foreign country may simply be 'under observation', or be subject to 'growing concern'.[13] On a higher level, the country may be placed on the 'watch list', leading to negotiations with the aim of improving certain elements of intellectual property protection in that country. Where concerns are stronger, a country may be placed on the so-called 'priority watch list', resulting in accelerated action plans, such as reviews after less than the regular period of one year. This status brings about increased pressure on the foreign country to act in accordance with the US wishes.

Finally, the most severe category is the designation as a 'priority foreign country'. **13.03** Such countries are defined as those '(A) that have the most onerous or egregious acts, policies, or practices that —

(i) deny adequate and effective intellectual property rights, or

(ii) deny fair and equitable market access to United States persons that rely upon intellectual property protection,

(B) whose acts, policies, or practices described in subparagraph (A) have the greatest adverse impact (actual or potential) on the relevant United States products, and

(C) that are not—

(i) entering into good faith negotiations, or

(ii) making significant progress in bilateral or multilateral negotiations, to provide adequate and effective protection of intellectual property rights.'[14]

While the placing of a foreign country on one of the above-mentioned lists may **13.04** burden its relationships and dealings with the US regarding other trade and diplomatic matters, the designation as a 'priority foreign country' regularly[15] requires the USTR to take retaliatory action.[16] For example, the USTR may impose duties or other restrictions on goods imported from that country, suspend trade benefits, or revoke tariff exemptions granted under the Generalized System of Preferences

---

[12] Under 19 USC § 2242 (a), the USTR must identify countries under 'Special 301' no later than 30 days after the National Trade Estimate report is published, which is annually due on 30 March, 19 USC § 2241 (b).

[13] M Young, *United States Trade Law and Policy* (2001) 108–9; 1998 Trade Policy Agenda and 1997 Annual Report of the President of the United States on Trade Agreements Program, March 1998, 244 (as quoted in McIlroy (n 10 above) n 27); the IIPA Report to the USTR 2007 also mentions countries earning 'special mention' as a lower category than the watch list.

[14] 19 USC §2242(b)(1).

[15] Exceptionally, the USTR is not required to do so in specified situations, eg when the country has taken measures to eliminate the offending practices, 19 USC § 2411(a)(2)(A), (B).

[16] 19 USC §2411(a)(1); on the preceding obligations to investigate against such country and to request consultations see 19 USC §§2412(b)(2)(A), 19 USC § 2413(a)(1); for more details and deadlines, see these and the following provisions.

(GSP); the USTR may also choose to conclude an agreement by which the country undertakes to stop the offending practices or provide compensatory trade benefits.[17] Since the negotiations with the priority foreign country are backed by the threat of possibly severe trade sanctions, they usually lead to agreements or measures by the foreign country as required by the United States, such as the closure of piracy production plants.[18]

13.05 As in the multilateral and bilateral trade framework, the teeth of such sanctions here lie in the possibility of cross-retaliation, that is, retaliation in a different trade sector, such as a sector where the foreign country is particularly vulnerable.[19] The only limit to be respected by the USTR is that any retaliatory action must 'be devised so as to affect goods and services from the foreign country in an amount that is equivalent in value to the burden or restriction imposed by that country on the United States commerce'.[20] Where the USTR has taken a measure, it must monitor the implementation and observe whether the foreign country removes offending practices; this process enables the USTR to take further, relevant action.[21]

13.06 While the 'Special 301' reports are regularly published by 30 April of each year,[22] the USTR also conducts so-called 'out-of-cycle' Special 301 reviews, in order to promptly react to new information submitted in complaints by the US industry or others;[23] such information could trigger retaliation or, if sufficient progress

---

[17] 19 USC §2411(c)(1); on the GSP, ie preferential treatment (unilateral duty-free trade privileges) for developing and least developed countries, see 19 USC § 2462, last renewed by Congress in December 2006; for similar special systems, see 19 USC §§ 2702, 3202 (Caribbean Basin, Andean countries); eg the USTR suspended duty-free treatment for Ukrainian imports under the GSP on 7 August 2001.

[18] eg China was close to trade sanctions in 1994/5 and signed intellectual property agreements with the USA in 1995 and 1996 under the threat of such sanctions, see the report in (1999) World Intellectual Property Report 193, 194; K Newby, 'The Effectiveness of Special 301 in Creating Long Term Copyright Protection for US Companies Overseas' (1995) 21 Syracuse J Int'l Law and Commerce 29, 42, in particular 44; P Yu, 'From Pirates to Partners: Protecting Intellectual Property in China in the Twenty-First Century' (2001) 50/1 American University Law Review 131, 144–51.

[19] eg the USTR announced on 20 December 2001 that it would retaliate against Ukraine for not having combated optical media piracy, by placing 100 per cent tariffs on $75 million worth of metals, footwear, and other imports (Anon, 'US hits Ukraine with Sanctions for Failure to Combat Optical Media Piracy', (2002) World E-commerce & IP Report 21).

[20] 19 USC § 2411(a)(3).

[21] 19 USC §§ 2416, 2417; eg in the 2007 Special 301 Report of the USTR, Paraguay is classified as a country to be monitored under Section 301, after having been a priority foreign country and, thereafter, having signed a Memorandum of Understanding on intellectual property protection.

[22] 19 USC §§ 2242(a) in connection with §2241(b).

[23] 'Out-of-cycle' reviews were introduced by the Clinton Administration in 1993 in order to ensure full and effective implementation of Special 301 and a 'strong, speedy response' to countries that do not fulfil their commitments, see Anon, 'US Trade Representative's Fact Sheet on Actions

was made in the meantime, removal from a list or revocation of the designation as a priority foreign country.

(3) Relation of 'Special 301' measures to the WTO and other agreements

Being subject to such systematic and threatening unilateralism is certainly not desirable.[24] Indeed, during the Uruguay Round of the GATT, many affected countries viewed the establishment of an improved dispute settlement procedure within the GATT as an opportunity to discipline US unilateralism.[25] Article 23 of the DSU,[26] which envisages the strengthening of the multilateral system vis-à-vis unilateralism, obliges Members to use the DSU in the context of disputes on violations of the 'covered agreements', including the TRIPS Agreement. Accordingly, unilateral measures are thereby implicitly excluded, as reaffirmed by the aim of this provision.[27] As a result, unilateral measures may no longer be used for the purpose of dispute settlement where the parties to the dispute are Members of the WTO and the question concerned is governed by the TRIPS Agreement.

13.07

Since the USA has expressed its wish to continue employing Special 301 to the greatest extent possible,[28] the crucial question in each individual case will be whether or

13.08

Taken under "Special 301" Provisions of Trade Act, Released April 30, 1993', (1993) World Intellectual Property Report 165.

[24] On reactions by foreign countries, see paras 14.20–14.23 below.

[25] J Bello and A Holmer, 'US Trade Law and Policy Series No 24: Dispute Resolution in the New World Trade Organisation: Concerns and Net-Benefits' (1994) 28/4 Int'l Lawyer 1095, 1101 ff; Schede (n 7 above) 138 on initial proposals of the EC and its trading partners for Art 23 of the DSU; S Chang, 'Taming Unilateralism under the Multilateral Trading System: Unfinished Job on the WTO Panel Ruling on US Sections 301–310 of the Trade Act of 1974' (2000) 31 Law & Policy Int Business 1151, 1154.

[26] On the WTO Dispute Settlement Understanding (DSU), see paras 10.116 ff above.

[27] K Lee and S von Lewinski, 'The Settlement of International Disputes in the Field of Intellectual Property' in F-K Beier and G Schricker (eds), *From GATT to TRIPS: The Agreement on Trade-Related Aspects of Intellectual Property Rights* (1996) 278, 325; LM Montén, 'The Inconsistency between Section 301 and TRIPS: Counterproductive with Respect to the Future of International Protection of Intellectual Property Rights?' (2005) 9/2 Marquette Intellectual Property Law Review 387, 404 ff with further reference; for an analysis also against the historical background see N Telecki, 'The Role of Special 301 in the Development of International Protection of Intellectual Property Rights after the Uruguay Round' (1996) 14 Boston International L J'l, 187, 213–18.

[28] During the implementation of the Uruguay Round Agreements in US law, one of the most controversial issues was how to adapt, if at all (or, rather, how to keep alive), the Section 301 provisions, see Schede (n 7 above) 110. This is reflected in different House Reports referred to in Getlan (n 7 above) 173 and Montén (n 27 above) 404; it is also reflected in 19 USC § 2242(d)(4) under which a foreign country may 'deny adequate and effective protection' under Section 301 even if it complies with the TRIPS Agreement; and in the Statement of Administrative Action (HR Doc no 103-316 (Vol I, 656 ff.) accompanying the Uruguay Round Agreements Act. V Espinel of the USTR at the 12th International Intellectual Property Law & Policy Conference of Fordham Law School 2004.

not the issue at stake is covered by the jurisdiction of the WTO.[29] This question may not always be easily answered. For example, the transitional periods for developing, so-called 'transformation',[30] and least developed countries in Articles 65 and 66 of the TRIPS Agreement seem to protect these countries against any claims to introduce TRIPS protection during these periods; at the same time, they could be interpreted as periods of time during which the TRIPS Agreement would not govern intellectual property law, so that unilateral measures could be applied.[31] Also, it has been argued that TRIPS-plus protection would not fall within the WTO jurisdiction, since TRIPS only provided for minimum protection, and its scope would exclusively cover the specific minimum standards.[32] As a consequence of such narrow interpretation of Article 23 of the DSU, any WTO Member could unilaterally require TRIPS-plus protection from other Members without violating that provision. Under a broader interpretation, Article 23 of the DSU would regulate the areas of intellectual property covered by the TRIPS Agreement already during the transitional periods or the TRIPS Agreement would imply the right of its Members only to implement the standards of protection required by TRIPS, so that such unilateral action would not be permitted.[33]

13.09 Where the matter of a dispute is covered by the WTO jurisdiction, the Special 301 provisions can only be deployed on the domestic level as a first step toward deciding whether to initiate dispute settlement procedures under the WTO.[34] Indeed, the USA has applied Special 301 in this way.[35] Given a number of remaining doubts on the consistency of Section 301 provisions with the WTO, the European Union in 1999 initiated a WTO panel procedure to suggest in a general context that specific Section 301 provisions were incompatible with WTO

---

[29] For an analysis of consistency of Section 301 with Art 23 of the DSU, see Schede (n 7 above) 130–5.

[30] Transformation countries are former socialist countries which had to transform their economies into free market economies, see Art 65(2) of the TRIPS Agreement.

[31] Getlan (n 7 above) 215; the Report of the (US) Advisory Committee for Trade Policy and Negotiations concerning the Uruguay Round of Negotiations on the General Agreement on Tariffs and Trade (1994) (ACTPN) suggested to the Congress that Special 301 should be used, among others, to obtain improved intellectual property protection in relevant countries before the 'long transition periods' expired, at 3, 11, 74, 79.

[32] Schede (n 7 above) 132 f. This is also the US position expressed in the Statement of Administrative Action (n 28 above) 1035, and described in Telecki (n 27 above) 218–20.

[33] eg European Commission, '1995 Report on US Barriers to Trade and Investment' (May 1995) 11; Telecki (n 27 above) 220 f.

[34] 19 USC § 2413(a)(2).

[35] eg its Special 301 Report of 1997 announced the initiation of WTO dispute settlement actions against Denmark, Sweden, Ireland, and Ecuador; such actions often become unnecessary after consultations that lead to the demanded measures. In the Special 301 Report 2000, the USTR announced the instigation of WTO dispute settlement procedures against Argentina and Brazil because of alleged violations of the TRIPS Agreement.

law, in particular the DSU.[36] Thirteen countries joined the EU in the panel procedure. The Panel, in its Report of 22 December 1999,[37] essentially decided that the most important Section 301 provisions at stake prima facie violated WTO obligations,[38] but that they were not inconsistent with WTO law and therefore did not violate WTO obligations since and as long as the USA applied these provisions as specified in the Statement of Administrative Action[39] and as declared by the US representatives during the panel procedure.[40] Since this panel procedure was limited to an abstract review of Section 301 provisions, the Panel could not decide on any specific case of application, and several times acknowledged that its conclusions might have been different in such cases.[41]

Accordingly, the use of unilateral measures is restricted by WTO law. Hence, **13.10** many—in particular industrialized—countries no longer seem to be impressed by the now less credible Special 301 Reports and threats of retaliation.[42] Yet, others continuously feel threatened. The appropriateness of unilateralism thus remains highly controversial.[43]

B. Measures applied by the European Community

The European Community (EC) has been much more hesitant than the USA in **13.11** adopting a specific legal instrument as a basis for measures against certain trade practices by non-EC countries. Initial considerations to this effect by the European Commission in 1964 and a resolution by the European Parliament in 1980 did not lead to any formal result. Also, in 1982, when the French government suggested that the Commission propose provisions similar to the Section 301 instrument of the USA,[44] the Commission considered such provisions

---

36 eg relating to different time frames, 19 USC §§2414(a)(2)(A) and 2416(b) to be incompatible with Art 23(2)(a) of the DSU; 19 USC §§2416(b), 2415(a) with Arts 23(2)(c), 21(5) and 22 of the DSU; 19 USC § 2416(b) with Arts I, II, III, VIII, and XI of the GATT 1994.

37 WT/DS152/R.

38 19 USC § 2414 (a)(2)(A); for the other provisions, legal problems were mostly left unresolved since the Panel was satisfied with their practical application by the USA on the basis of the Statement of Administrative Action, see also D Jakob, 'Die Zukunft US-amerikanischer unilateraler Section-301 Maßnahmen' (2000) GRUR Int 715, 720–2.

39 n 28 above; Panel Report (n 37 above) 350, 365 f, 330; the Panel considered this Statement, which was submitted by the President and adopted by Congress, as sufficiently obliging in the international context.

40 Panel Report (n 37 above) 333.

41 Jakob (n 38 above) 723.

42 For a similar appreciation, see J Gero and K Lannan, 'Trade and Innovation: Unilateralism versus Multilateralism' (1995) 21 Canada-US L J'l, 81, 94–5.

43 For this aspect, see paras 14.20–14.23 below.

44 H Beekmann, 'The 1994 Revised Commercial Policy Instrument of the European Union' (1995/6) 19/1 World Competition 53, 54.

unnecessary, given the existing general commercial policy powers[45] as well as the anti-dumping, anti-subsidy, and escape-clause actions. Subsequently, upon pressure from the European Council, the Commission presented a proposal for a new commercial policy instrument in 1983,[46] but this was met with opposition from Denmark, Germany, the Netherlands, and others who considered the instrument as unnecessary and potentially protectionist and who disliked the right of EC industry to lodge complaints.[47] Finally, in 1984, the EC adopted its 'New Commercial Policy Instrument' (NCPI),[48] which allowed unilateral measures towards non-EC countries to fight illicit commercial practices that cause injury to industry within the EC. The NCPI was a response to and inspired by the general Section 301 provisions of the US Trade Act;[49] however, the EC never went so far as the United States, which introduced special provisions regarding intellectual property only four years later.[50] Also, the EC never practised a comparably systematic or stringent approach.

13.12   The NCPI required certain conditions to be fulfilled before trade sanctions, such as the suspension of preferential treatment could be applied. Unlike the Special 301 provisions, the NCPI only applied to 'illicit' rather than simply 'unfair' or 'unjustifiable' trade practices, and therefore was based on international law rather than purely domestic demands. Furthermore, the NCPI was more difficult to apply than the Special 301 provisions, due to its stronger requirements regarding the possible complaints and the evidence of an injury caused by the trade practices made. In addition, retaliatory measures could be imposed only if international dispute settlement had been followed. Also, the NCPI did not intend 'to force trade partners into new concessions, but' was 'geared to the enforcement of the Community's rights existing under international trade rules'. [51] Finally, the NCPI, unlike 'Special 301', did not specifically envisage intellectual property. Accordingly, until its repeal in 1994, it was only used twice in the field of

---

[45] Art 113 of the EEC Treaty, today: Art 133 of the EC Treaty.

[46] Commission Proposal for a Council Regulation on the Strengthening of the Commercial Policy with Regard in Particular to Protection against Unfair Commercial Practices, [1983] OJ C 83/6.

[47] On the historical background of the trade practices instrument of the EC, see Beekmann (n 44 above) 54.

[48] Council Regulation (EEC) no 2641/84 of 17 September 1984 on the Strengthening of the Commercial Policy with Regard in Particular to Protection against Illicit Commercial Practices, OJ EC L 252/1 of 20 September 1984.

[49] J-C van Eeckhaute, 'Private Complaints against Foreign Unfair Trade Practices: The EC's Trade Barriers Regulation' (1999) 33/6 Journal of World Trade 199, 200.

[50] On the Special 301 provisions introduced by the 1988 Omnibus Trade and Competitiveness Act, see paras 13.02–13.06 above.

[51] Van Eeckhaute (n 49 above) 200 (in n 4); for a comparison of both instruments, see C Mavroidis, *Handelspolitische Abwehrmechanismen der EWG und der USA und ihre Vereinbarkeit mit den GATT-Regeln* (1993) 173; for a description of the NCPI, see Beekmann (n 44 above) 55–61.

copyright and neighbouring rights. The targeted countries satisfied the EC's demands before unilateral measures would become necessary.[52]

After the entry into force of the WTO-TRIPS Agreement, the NCPI could no **13.13** longer be applied in the same way as before since the WTO dispute settlement system prevails to the extent that disputes between its Members concern matters covered by WTO law. The NCPI was first amended in order to take account of the new WTO dispute settlement system. Shortly thereafter, the EC adopted a new instrument, the 'Trade Barriers Regulation' (TBR),[53] which repealed and partly incorporated the NCPI.[54]

Like its predecessor, the TBR is a general instrument not limited to intellectual **13.14** property. It aims at removing barriers to exports from Europe and thereby at opening markets in non-EC countries where such barriers are prohibited by international trade rules, namely those under WTO law and in bilateral agreements of the EC. It no longer refers to 'illicit practices' but, instead, to 'obstacles to trade', defined by reference to violations of international trade law[55]—be they direct violations or non-violations in the meaning of WTO law[56]—rather than to any standards established by the domestic industry, as under US law. The TBR is not a basis for imposing new trade concessions on non-EC countries, and does not grant any rights to the Community beyond those under international law. The TBR is broader than its predecessor in covering certain services, and in extending the range of potential complainants to include 'Community industry', a 'Community enterprise', and Member States.[57] A novelty is the possibility of one or several Community enterprises lodging a complaint if they have suffered adverse trade effects as a result of obstacles to trade that have an effect on the market of a non-EC country, provided that the obstacle to trade is the subject of a right of action under a multilateral or plurilateral trade agreement. Accordingly,

---

[52] S von Lewinski, 'Copyright within the External Relations of the European Union and the EFTA Countries' (1994) 10 EIPR 429, 432–3, with further references on the two cases; Beekmann (n 44 above) 59–60.

[53] Council Regulation (EC) 3286/94 of 22 December 1994 laying down Community procedures in the field of the common commercial policy in order to ensure the exercise of the Community's rights under international trade rules, in particular those established under the auspices of the World Trade Organization, [1994] OJ L349/71; amended by Council Regulation (EC) 356/95 of 20 February 1995 amending Regulation (EC) 3286/94 laying down Community procedures in the field of the common commercial policy in order to ensure the exercise of the Community's rights under international trade rules, in particular those established under the auspices of the World Trade Organization, [1995] OJ L041/3.

[54] Art 15(2) of the TBR (n 53 above).

[55] See the definition in Art 2(1) ibid.

[56] Art 2(1) phr 2, second part ibid; van Eeckhaute (n 49 above) 201.

[57] On the definitions of 'Community industry' and 'Community enterprise', see Art 2(5), (6), and on the three ways of complaints, see Arts 3, 4, and 6 of the TBR (n 53 above).

enterprises enjoy the possibility of triggering, among others, the WTO dispute settlement procedure, which is not possible directly under WTO law.

13.15 Complaints must be submitted with sufficient evidence of the obstacles to trade, injury, adverse trade effects, or other effects resulting therefrom.[58] The European Commission, to which the complaint must be submitted, must decide within forty-five days on the admissibility of a complaint; if the Commission admits the complaint, it initiates an examination procedure at the end of which several decisions can be taken.[59] Where the interests of the Community do not require any action, the Commission, in cooperation with the Council, shall terminate the procedure.[60] Where the non-EC country has taken satisfactory measures that make any Community action obsolete, the procedure may be suspended.[61] Another option is the suspension of the procedure in order to conclude an agreement with the non-EC country to resolve the problem.[62]

13.16 Where, however, an action by the Community is necessary in order to ensure the exercise of its rights under international trade rules, the Community may take appropriate measures, such as the 'suspension or withdrawal of any concession resulting from commercial policy negotiations, the raising of existing customs duties or the introduction of any other charge on imports, or the introduction of quantitative restrictions or any other measures modifying import or export conditions or otherwise affecting trade with the non-EC country concerned'.[63] Yet, where the international law obliges the Community to follow international consultation or dispute settlement procedures, the aforementioned measures can be decided on only after such international procedures, such as a WTO dispute settlement procedure, are terminated.[64] Accordingly, the TBR excludes any conflict with Article 23 of the DSU by giving explicit priority to this and other dispute settlement mechanisms which enjoy priority. At the same time, it tries to avoid any such procedure by informal bilateral consultations. The Commission is not limited to using the TBR procedure; it also remains empowered to initiate WTO dispute settlement procedures on its own initiative or at the request of Member States on the basis of Article 133 of the EC Treaty.[65]

---

[58] Ss 3(2), 4(2), and 6(2) ibid.

[59] For the procedure from the submission of the complaint, see Arts 7–10 ibid; van Eeckhaute (n 49 above) 204–6; E Turnbull and M Attew, 'Protecting International Trade Rights' (1995) 4 International Trade Law and Regulation 128, 131–2.

[60] Art 11(1) in connection with Art 14 of the TBR.

[61] Art 11(2) ibid.

[62] Art 11(3) ibid.

[63] Art 12(3) ibid.

[64] Art 12(2) ibid; van Eeckhaute (n 49 above) 208–9 on the different options.

[65] The so-called '133 Committee' consists of all the Member States. They have a stronger impact in this procedure than under the TBR; see also van Eeckhaute (n 49 above) 210–11.

Similar to its predecessor, the TBR has not been invoked frequently. Within its **13.17** first ten years of existence, twenty-four TBR examination procedures were initiated; in some cases, negotiations and actions by the non-EC countries resulted in solutions, while in other cases, WTO dispute settlement procedures were necessary.[66] Two of them concern copyright and related rights, namely the complaint by the Irish Music Rights Organization on section 110(5) of the US Copyright Act 1976, which led to the initiation of dispute settlement procedures under the WTO in June 1997,[67] and a complaint by the IFPI regarding piracy in Thailand[68] (this procedure was suspended more than four years later after Thailand had adopted a new copyright law and created a court specializing in intellectual property).[69] In subsequent years, the Commission continued to monitor the situation in Thailand and proposed to the Thai authorities that they should enter into a dialogue on suggestions of how to further reduce piracy of sound recordings; it recommended a number of actions, such as the targeting of criminal organizations acting behind the piracy business.[70]

As a reaction to the annual 'Special 301' lists of the USA, the European Commis-   **13.18** sion has established a practice of issuing annual reports on 'United States Barriers to Trade and Investment' where it lists and describes EU concerns about US trade barriers, whether or not those barriers violate international law.[71] Reports are currently issued in respect of the United States only, and they mainly serve as a tool for focusing dialogue and negotiations.

C. Résumé

This parallel presentation of unilateral trade measures of the USA and the EC   **13.19** shows major differences in the approaches taken. The USA has systematically and comprehensively used such measures in intellectual property from the mid-1980s and continues to do so as far as compatible with the TRIPS Agreement; it has used them as an efficient, aggressive tool in different contexts[72] but always with

---

66 <http://ec.europa.eu/trade/issues/respectrules/tbr/cases/index_en.htm.>

67 Notice of initiation of the examination procedure: (1997) OJ C77; investigation report available from <http://ec.europa.eu/trade/issues/respectrules/tbr/cases/usa_mus.htm>; decision of the Commission to initiate a WTO dispute settlement procedure: (1998) OJ L 346/60; on the relevant WTO Panel Report and further procedure, see paras 10.129–10.132 above.

68 For the Notice of Initiation of an examination procedure, see (1991) OJ C189.

69 Decision of Suspension of 20 December 1995, (1996) OJ L11.

70 On these activities, see <http://ec.europa.eu/trade/issues/respectrules/tbr/cases/tha_sou.htm>.

71 For the report on 2006, issued by the European Commission in February 2007, see <http://trade.ec.europa.eu/doclib/docs/2007/february/tradoc_133290.pdf>; for a summary of the twelfth annual report 1996, see an overview, Anon, 'European Commission Criticises US IPR Legislation in Annual Report' [1996] World Intellectual Property Report 281.

72 For these different contexts, see paras 14.04–14.07 below.

the same goal, namely to improve protection for US industry in foreign countries, irrespective of whether these countries are under a related international obligation. By contrast, the EC's initial instrument was not very efficient, and was general rather than intellectual property-specific; the current, improved trade instrument was only introduced after hesitations and is relatively rarely applied to intellectual property.

14

OVERALL ASSESSMENT OF THE INCLUSION OF COPYRIGHT AND NEIGHBOURING RIGHTS INTO THE TRADE FRAMEWORK

A. The role of copyright and neighbouring rights within trade agreements

(1) Before the mid-1980s

In the early history of international copyright law, bilateral trade agreements regulated international protection, before the Berne Convention largely replaced this insufficient and unsatisfactory system. Later, intellectual property (including copyright and neighbouring rights) only played a defensive role in trade agreements: it was considered a non-tariff barrier to trade and, hence, in principle contrary to the fundamental aim of a trade treaty, namely, to reduce or remove barriers to trade. Yet, safeguard provisions usually excluded intellectual property from trade agreements or free trade provisions therein, unless it was a means of arbitrary discrimination or disguised restriction of trade.[1]

14.01

---

[1] eg Art XX(d) of the GATT; for more examples and more detail, see S von Lewinski, 'Copyright in Modern International Trade Law' (1994) 171 RIDA 5, 9 ff.

(2) After the mid-1980s

14.02   In the second half of the 1980s, the role of intellectual property in trade agreements dramatically changed from a defensive, negative one to a positive one. Manifold reasons led to the inclusion of provisions on the protection of intellectual property into trade agreements, such as the need to adapt international law to new developments, the deficiencies of the existing conventions, and the specific possibilities in the trade framework to reach the goal of an updated protection.[2]

(a) The main players

14.03   The fundamental change towards the trade framework was primarily promoted by industrialized countries and among them most fervently by the USA. As exporters of copyright and neighbouring rights goods, they had an interest in improving international protection; yet, perspectives in the traditional forum for intellectual property rights, the WIPO, had proved unpromising. Alternatively, the trade framework seemed to be particularly advantageous for industrialized countries, because it offered them broader possibilities to make use of their strong bargaining power than the UN/WIPO framework with its rules on transparency and guarantees for developing countries.

(b) Tools for inclusion of copyright and neighbouring rights into the trade framework

14.04   Trade law offers different tools to improve international copyright and neighbouring rights protection: unilateral measures as well as bilateral, regional, and multilateral agreements. Not all of them have been fully used by all countries; the USA has applied these tools most systematically and intensively. In general, these trade tools may be used in different ways. First, unilateral measures can be differently used towards foreign countries: powerful countries may exercise economic pressure backed by trade sanctions in order to make foreign countries amend their laws or enforcement measures as desired, or in order to demand the conclusion of bilateral agreements that would then stipulate the desired protection to be provided in the foreign country. In addition, powerful countries can use unilateral measures during multilateral negotiations in order to gain a stronger influence on negotiations, as reported from the TRIPS negotiations.[3] Finally, they can use these measures as supplementary, parallel means of pressure during negotiations with candidate countries for the accession to the WTO. On the basis of the Special 301 provisions under the US Trade Act, the USA leads in the use of unilateral measures as an effective and varied tool.

---

[2] For these reasons, see von Lewinski (n 1 above) 35 ff, and ch 9 above.
[3] J Watal, *Intellectual Property Rights in the WTO and Developing Countries* (2001) 44.

Secondly, bilateral trade agreements are frequently used either as a self-standing **14.05**
tool in order to gain improved protection, or in parallel with negotiations with
candidate countries on their accession to the WTO; WTO accession is usually
made dependent on additional conditions (beyond compliance with WTO law)
negotiated between WTO Members and the candidate country, and, in some
cases, is accompanied by supplementary bilateral agreements between individual
WTO Members and the candidate country.[4] Unilateral measures and bilateral
agreements allow major players to use their bargaining power and own strategies
in the most efficient way.

Thirdly, regional agreements are another tool that is increasingly used—in part even **14.06**
among developing countries to gain strength by joining forces. Finally, the multilateral framework of the WTO with its TRIPS Agreement is probably the most important, since it is the most widespread tool—initially for the inclusion of most countries
of the world into the international intellectual property protection system, and then
for the enforcement of intellectual property protection through the dispute settlement mechanism and the review of Members' laws in the TRIPS Council.[5]

The major players tend to shift between the different tools according to the **14.07**
momentarily best chances for success. When multilateral negotiations do not
seem promising or are difficult, as experienced during the Doha Round and in
WIPO from around 2004, the major players tend to more aggressively use bilateral and regional or plurilateral agreements.[6] Accordingly, developing countries
that initially complained about the outcome of the TRIPS Agreement and blamed
WTO negotiations for being disadvantageous to them have experienced that the
WTO framework may still give them more strength when they jointly negotiate
than when they individually face an economically much more powerful country.

(c) Aims of trade agreements that include copyright and neighbouring rights

The overall aims of trade agreements that include copyright and neighbouring rights **14.08**
provisions differ according to the individual kinds of agreements and provisions;
they may be larger political aims, such as stabilization and peacekeeping in a certain

---

[4] See para 10.17 above; eg the Special 301 Report of 2007 mentions that Vietnam enacted a
comprehensive intellectual property law in order to create a 'modern legal framework' (p 3).

[5] See, in particular, the USTR's statement according to which 'the US aggressively has used the
TRIPS Council to press for full and timely implementation of the TRIPS Agreement by all Members.
This has included vigorous use of WTO dispute settlement procedures . . .' (quoted in J McIlroy,
'American Enforcement of Intellectual Property Rights: A Canadian Perspective' [1998] Journal of
World Intellectual Property 445, 460.

[6] eg V Zahrnt, 'How Regionalisation Can Be a Pillar of a More Effective World Trade Organisation'
[2005] Journal of World Trade 671, referring to the more aggressive regional integration approach
following the 'fiasco in Cancun in 2003'. See also B Mercurio, 'TRIPS-plus Provisions in FTAs:
Recent Trends' in L Bartels and F Ortino (eds), *Regional Trade Agreements and the WTO Legal System*
(2006) 215, 235–6. For the recent initiative of ACTA, see para 26.05/n5 below.

region, overall integration, such as in Europe, or trade liberalization.[7] Most of the intellectual property provisions in trade agreements aim at improving the level of protection and enforcement of these rights; as described by the US copyright industry, the most important global goal is to 'significantly reduce piracy levels in order to open foreign markets so as to create increased revenue and employment'.[8] In this respect, intellectual property provisions in trade agreements could be viewed as 'money-making machines' for major exporters of copyright-protected products.

(d) Contents of provisions or demands

14.09 In brief, the copyright and neighbouring rights provisions of most of the trade agreements that provide for more than cooperation clauses build upon the existing multilateral treaties; parties are obliged either to comply with or even ratify these treaties. Many trade agreements also include the non-specified requirement of adequate and effective protection and enforcement of intellectual property rights, sometimes specified by qualifications such as 'at the highest international level' or 'at a level similar to that of EC law'. By contrast, the USA usually does not rely on such general clauses but stands out in respect of the high level of detail in which concrete provisions must be implemented into the national law of the other party. Likewise, the US agreements stand out in requiring a very high level of protection, such as standards that go beyond the highest multilateral standards (currently: the WCT and WPPT, and before 1996, the TRIPS Agreement), and in reducing or eliminating transitional periods of the TRIPS Agreement.[9] It is easily visible from the agreements concluded by the USA that most wishes of the US industry that were not fulfilled in the broader multilateral context—the TRIPS Agreement, the WCT, and the WPPT—were and continue to be successfully fulfilled in bilateral or regional agreements, such as free transferability of rights, recognition of the work-made-for-hire rule, and lately payment of private copy remuneration.

B. Results of the inclusion of copyright and neighbouring rights into the trade framework

(1) Factual outcome

14.10 A clear result of the trade approach is the increased number of countries that are now part of the international protection system—as members of the

---

[7] For an analysis of the trade aims in the TRIPS Agreements, see S Frankel, 'WTO Application of "the Customary Rules of Interpretation of Public International Law" to Intellectual Property' (2006) 46 Virginia Journal of International Law 365, 390 ff.

[8] IIPA Special 301 Letter to the USTR of 12 February 2007, p 4; similarly: von Lewinski (n 1 above) 59.

[9] eg McIlroy (n 5 above) 459.

WTO/TRIPS Agreement or other trade agreements and, mostly as a consequence thereof, often also as members of the classical conventions, including in particular the Berne and Rome Conventions.[10] Accordingly, the traditional system of international protection has also been indirectly strengthened through the trade approach. This result was mainly possible through the link of intellectual property with other trade areas in the framework of the 'single undertaking' of the Uruguay Round and within other trade agreements. Accordingly, countries that otherwise would not have been interested in joining international intellectual property treaties were led into obligations in this field only because they were interested in trade liberalization and advantages in other fields.

As another result, unilateral measures and bilateral agreements in particular have led to the introduction of very high levels of protection in the laws of many countries of the world according to the same templates, and mostly irrespective of the general level of development of the other country. As stated by the IIPA, 'without these trade tools and their full implementation, the US copyright industries would still be facing a world of inadequate copyright laws—the world our industries faced in the early 1980s. In that world, most countries' laws did not protect US works at all, and ninety percent to hundred percent piracy levels prevailed in most developing countries'.[11]   **14.11**

Moreover, those agreements that specify the required copyright provisions in much detail—namely those concluded by the USA—follow the same templates and are irrespective of the system followed in the other country. As a result, even countries of the author's rights system have to introduce elements of the copyright system, such as the free transferability of rights. Accordingly, while the Berne and Rome Conventions are anchored in the author's rights system, unilateral US influence increasingly propagates elements of the copyright system into national laws worldwide. This usually occurs in very detailed language based on US law, so that one might describe bilateral or regional trade agreements as vehicles for the 'export' of US law.[12] Accordingly, another result of the trade approach is a widespread similarity—at least on the surface—of national laws worldwide.   **14.12**

---

[10] para 10.146 above.

[11] IIPA Special 301 Letter (n 8 above) 3.

[12] L Weiss, E Thurbon, and J Mathews, *How to Kill a Country: Australia's Devastating Trade Deal with the United States* (2004) allude to this idea by speaking of ' "transfusion" from the system of a foreign dominant power' (113), and of Australia being taken 'towards a US-style system' (115); similarly, regarding language of the law, ibid 125; and they refer to 'cutting and pasting strong pieces of the Digital Millennium Copyright Act 1998 without any means of changing or updating the law ourselves other than through changes introduced and implemented by the US Congress and the US courts', at 133.

14.13 Even where protection is introduced into national laws on the mere basis of uni-lateral measures or bilateral agreements, it must then also be granted in relation to other countries to the extent that national treatment obligations of the TRIPS Agreement or other agreements apply. Where the protection exceptionally has not been integrated into the national law for nationals so that national treatment does not apply to such protection, it usually must still be granted to any other WTO Member on the basis of the most-favoured-nation clause.[13]

14.14 In the trade framework, such protection can effectively be enforced in particular through the dispute settlement mechanisms of the WTO and other trade agreements, and through reviews of Members' laws performed by the TRIPS Council. As a side effect, the substantive standards of the classical conventions (except for moral rights under the Berne Convention) can also now be better enforced—though interpreted through 'trade glasses', since the provisions must be interpreted in their (trade) context and in view of the (trade) purpose of the relevant agreement.[14]

14.15 The economic results of the trade approach especially for exporting countries of copyright protected goods have been described by US industry as follows: 'Since the first marriage of intellectual property and trade . . ., US government initiatives have helped produce significant legal and enforcement improvements. This largely untold success story has produced billions of dollars of increased revenue and millions of new jobs to both US and local copyright industries.'[15] It seems that the 'triple-m-goal' of trade agreements as 'money-making machines'[16] is being reached—at least for those that are in a position to make use of them.

(2) Discussion of the de facto outcome

(a) Economic aspects

14.16 The assessment of the outcome of the trade approach differs according to the perspective. In general, making an overall economic assessment is difficult and depends on the individual agreement;[17] it may well be that right owners especially from industrialized countries yield more revenues than before, and that developing or other countries which concluded bilateral trade agreements benefit

---

[13] These cases are very rare, though.

[14] On the aspect of interpretation, see paras 7.07, 7.08 above and Frankel (n 7 above), in particular 402 ff.

[15] IIPA Special 301 Letter (n 8 above) 3.

[16] para 14.08 above.

[17] See C Fink and P Reichenmiller, 'Tightening TRIPS: Intellectual Property Provisions of US Free Trade Agreements', World Bank Trade Note no 20 (2005), <http://siteresources.worldbank.org/INTRANETTRADE/Resources/239054-1126812419270/24.TighteningTRIPS.pdf>, pp 298–300. For copyright industry in the USA, see, however, the quote in para 14.15 above.

in other trade areas than intellectual property; at the same time, it seems that strengthened intellectual property protection does not, or not immediately, enhance foreign investment.[18] It would also be necessary to make a detailed assessment of the economic consequences of international, high-level protection in particular for developing countries. Where, for example, a least developed country, which has not yet developed its own infrastructure for a proper protection of copyright and neighbouring rights since it faces more fundamental challenges of poverty such as supply of clean water, has to invest in such infrastructure to effectively administer these rights and make payments to foreign right owners, its own development would be hampered, and the understanding in such a country of the need for copyright protection might fade away. One may also doubt whether it is appropriate to use trade tools to force highest-level standards of protection upon least developed countries, even if the countries receive advantages in other trade areas as a counterpart; where not even the responsible governmental experts of such countries are in a position to appreciate the consequences of such provisions, nor to fully understand them, the appropriateness of this approach is questionable.[19]

(b) Legal and legal policy aspects

Furthermore, it seems questionable that countries are compelled by unilateral **14.17** measures and bilateral agreements concluded by the USA to legislate against their own traditions and cultures, namely, where they have to take over elements of the copyright system into the author's rights system. Legal traditions are also distorted by imposed detailed wording which may be inconsistent with legal drafting styles in the relevant countries. Similarly, the copyright system-related focus on businesses and industries versus the individual creators is a tendency promoted by the trade activities of the USA and may have a negative impact on individual creators and, consequently, cultural diversity in many countries.[20]

As another effect of the inclusion of copyright and related rights standards into **14.18** trade agreements, parties to these agreements will indirectly also feel bound by these standards as regards their domestic policy-making in copyright and neighbouring rights. Although such trade agreements only relate to international situations, most legislators will refrain from granting higher levels of protection in

---

[18] Fink/Reichenmiller (n 17 above) 299.

[19] Experience gained by the author of this book during technical assistance missions to least developed countries revealed a government expert who admitted not understanding provisions on eg technical measures and rights management information that had been inserted into the draft law.

[20] This industry-based approach is reflected eg in the IIPA Special 301 Letter (n 8 above) at 16 and other places where reference is only made to publishers, while writers or other creators do not seem to exist.

relation to foreign countries than to their own nationals. Accordingly, their own freedom for policy-making in the future may at least de facto be hindered. While this situation is normal also for multilateral treaties in the field, the difference with trade treaties is the link with other trade areas and the resulting readiness of countries to accept standards that they might otherwise not voluntarily accept. Where these standards are inappropriately high in relation to the general status of development, the effects of such de facto restrictions of domestic options are particularly burdensome.

14.19 From a point of view of domestic legislation in the USA, the inclusion of certain provisions in free trade agreements seems questionable where such provisions are domestically controversial or would have little chances for adoption as part of US law,[21] especially given the less democratic procedure of 'fast track' (or, more recently, 'Trade Promotion Authority') that only allows Congress to support or reject an entire agreement rather than to discuss the individual provisions; indeed, without this procedure, the trade agreements would most likely not be adopted.[22]

(c) General political aspects

14.20 From a political point of view, these trade strategies often yield negative reactions. Developing countries consider that already during the Uruguay Round, they have been taken advantage of without proper regard to their needs.[23] In addition, in particular the bilateral treaties initiated by the USA and their unilateral measures have been largely perceived in a rather negative way. The use of economic pressure towards sovereign countries in order to force them to modify their laws and practices in a specific way, often even against their own legal traditions or systems, cannot possibly be expected to meet with a friendly or joyful welcome.

14.21 In particular in China, constant 'threats and bullying'[24] by the US government mainly provoked strengthened resistance to American demands; national leaders were expected to try hard not to give in to pressure, since this would damage themselves.[25] In addition, these procedures created a loss of US credibility and hostility among the people, so that the Chinese government became even more

---

[21] P Yu, 'P2P and the Future of Private Copying' (2005) 76/3 University of Colorado Law Review 653, 690.

[22] 'Without extension of this authority, it will be virtually impossible to get those important FTAs . . .', IIPA Special 301 Letter (n 8 above) 17.

[23] eg Yu (n 21 above) 689.

[24] P Yu, 'From Pirates to Partners: Protecting Intellectual Property in China in the Twenty-First Century' (2001) 50/1 American University Law Review 131, 133–4.

[25] SK Sell, *Power and Ideas: North-South Politics of Intellectual Property and Antitrust* (1998) 215: 'if they succumb to U.S. pressure, they are subject to criticisms of selling out sovereignty to foreign interests'.

reluctant to give in to the demands.[26] The use of pressure in this case has been considered as 'ineffective, misguided, and self-deluding',[27] since it only led to different cycles of negotiating, followed by concluding agreements or understandings, and then the revival of piracy after the fading away of close foreign attention. At the same time, it has been argued that Chinese intellectual property protection has improved especially after the USA used less pressure than before.[28] Other reactions of countries that have been subject to US bullying (in addition to enforcement) are a loss of influence or appeal of American ideas and concepts or even the avoidance of benefits to the US industry by promoting, for example, open-source software.[29]

Such negative reactions may be explained by the exemplary situation of any eco- **14.22** nomically weak country that is in need of foreign investment or strives for economic progress and, at the same time, has a long-standing cultural and legal tradition, has been a member of the Berne Convention (unlike the USA) since the early twentieth century, and that may even have well-educated and knowledgeable copyright lawyers. The act of imposing on a representative of such a country the choice of renouncing economic benefits or renouncing parts of the legal culture and values adopted there will be considered as unethical in itself, all the more since it implies taking advantage of the country's weak economic situation. In certain cases it may be perceived like the option, or rather de facto obligation, to sell one's soul—losing the identification with local culture and values, as expressed in the law—for (often urgently needed) money. The so-called carrot or stick approach is felt as being aggressive,[30] arrogant, and disrespectful of state sovereignty;[31] it may violate national pride;[32] and it is likely to engender resentment[33] rather than anything else.

---

[26] Yu (n 24 above) 133–4.

[27] ibid 133.

[28] P Yu, 'The Second Coming of Intellectual Property Rights in China', Occasional Paper no 11 in Intellectual Property from Benjamin N Cardozo School of Law Yeshiva University 1, 26 ff.

[29] Yu (n 21 above) 691–2; Yu quotes the example of Vietnam regarding open-source software to be employed by all state-owned companies and government ministries; in this context, it is recalled that many US-initiated bilateral agreements oblige the parties to ensure that government agencies only use authorized software, see para 12.37 above.

[30] J Bhagwati and HT Patrick (eds), *Aggressive Unilateralism: America's 301 Trade Policy and the World Trading System* (1991).

[31] R Burrell, 'A Case Study in Cultural Imperialism: The Imposition of Copyright on China by the West' in L Bently and S Maniatis (eds), *Intellectual Property and Ethics* ('Perspectives on Intellectual Property' Vol 4) (1998) 195, in particular 198, 206, focusing in particular on American behaviour, see 197 n 2 and 205.

[32] eg SS Kim, *China and the World: Chinese Foreign Relations in the Post Cold War Era* (1994) 86.

[33] eg K Newby, 'The Effectiveness of Special 301 in Creating Long Term Copyright Protection for US Companies Overseas' (1995) 21 Syracuse J Int Law and Commerce 29.

14.23 Indeed, resentment has already led to a lack of enforcement, or 'a lack of willingness at the political level'.[34] Even if in particular the USA will focus its attention on better enforcement of intellectual property rights in foreign countries, the question remains whether the employed carrot or stick approach, or the exercise of economic power to yield certain benefits irrespective of sovereignty, pride, or their legal traditions in foreign countries will in the long term be successful. Already now, the USA is seen as an adversary by many other countries such that any US initiatives or proposals, even in a multilateral framework, are likely to meet with a general distrust and objections upfront, irrespective of the value of such initiatives or proposals.[35] These effects may already be observed in WIPO and other international organizations, where particularly Brazil started to enter into continuous power-plays with the USA that are not constructive for multilateral treaty-making.[36]

(3) Résumé

14.24 Beyond doubt, the trade approach has brought about major changes to the international intellectual property scene—today more than ever before, international protection is available in many more countries, is provided at higher levels, is better enforceable, and is largely responsible for the considerable degree of similarity seen in national laws (at least at their surface). These effects are positively considered by those who benefit therefrom, namely in particular copyright industries that export protected goods. In mainly importing countries, an isolated look at intellectual property may lead to the perception of enhanced international copyright obligations as an undue burden, while a broader look at the overall effects of the relevant trade agreement may result in the acknowledgement of a more balanced outcome for the country concerned.

14.25 The crucial question here remains whether the balancing of different sectors, a dynamic inherent in the trade approach, is appropriate for the delicate areas of copyright and neighbouring rights, which are so genuinely linked to culture that it is widely recognized that 'music [and other works] is not a commodity', as recently affirmed by the European Parliament.[37] The trade approach and thus the exchange of intellectual property concessions for benefits in other areas is also questionable where it brings with it inappropriate levels of protection. Maybe the

---

[34] IIPA Special 301 Letter (n 8 above) at 4; McIlroy (n 5 above) 446.

[35] eg Yu (n 21 above) 689; von Lewinski (n 1 above) 591.

[36] For the recent example of the planned treaty on the protection of broadcasting organizations, see paras 19.07 and 19.10 below; for a similar scenario, see also paras 20.38 and 20.41 below.

[37] European Parliament, Report on the Commission Recommendation of 18 October 2005 on collective cross-border management of copyright and related rights for legitimate online music services (2005/737/EC), (2006/2008(INI), <http://www.europarl.europa.eu/oeil/file.jsp?id=5303682> p 5 (lit H).

doubts about the trade approach initially prevailing in copyright expert circles at least in Europe were justified;[38] a final assessment is left to the future. Still, while the provision of strong protection required in trade agreements seems to be a necessary consequence of the trade approach and must be discussed in this broader context, other effects (such as the requirement of concrete wording practised by the USA)[39] are not necessary but go beyond what are logical consequences of the trade approach, as shown through the success of many trade agreements with broadly worded obligations.

---

[38] U Joos and R Moufang, 'Report on the Second Ringberg-Symposium', in FK Beier and G Schricker (eds), *GATT or WIPO? New Ways in the International Protection of Intellectual Property* (1989) 1, 18.

[39] On this aspect, see paras 12.31 and 12.76 above.

PART III

DEVELOPMENTS IN THE WORLD INTELLECTUAL PROPERTY ORGANIZATION (WIPO) AFTER THE ADOPTION OF THE TRIPS AGREEMENT

15

PRESENTATION OF THE WIPO

A. The development towards WIPO

Before the WIPO was established in 1970, the Paris and Berne Unions as well as **15.01** other intellectual property treaties were administered by the BIRPI (Bureaux Internationaux Réunis pour la Protection de la Propriété Intellectuelle).[1] The BIRPI itself had its roots in the International Bureau of the Paris Convention for the Protection of Industrial Property adopted in 1883 and the International Bureau of the Berne Convention of 1886, which were united in 1893 into one common bureau with the same staff and director. The word 'bureau' was commonly used at that time as a designation for the secretariat of an international organization. Since at that time the League of Nations and the United Nations (UN) did not exist, the BIRPI was placed under the 'high supervision' of the government of the Swiss Confederation.[2] The Swiss government appointed the Director and staff of the BIRPI and controlled its activities and finances, while the Member States of the Berne and Paris Unions and other related international

---

[1] In English: United International Bureaux for the Protection of Intellectual Property; cf also para 4.03 above.

[2] For more details on the development of the BIRPI, see A Bogsch, 'Brief History of the First 25 Years of the World Intellectual Property Organization' 1992, Copyright 247, 249–50; S Ricketson and J Ginsburg, *International Copyright and Neighbouring Rights: The Berne Convention and Beyond* (2006) 16.29–16.32; para 4.03 above.

treaties made decisions only when needed, namely at revision conferences rather than continuously within an established structure such as a governing body.

15.02 After the Second World War, many other Unions which had been established in the late nineteenth century modernized their structures and became Specialized Agencies of the newly established United Nations. In particular, the International Telecommunication Union and the Universal Postal Union of 1865 and 1874 did so in 1949 and 1948, respectively. BIRPI took somewhat longer to do the same. First, the WIPO was founded on the basis of the Convention Establishing the World Intellectual Property Organization of 14 July 1967.[3] When this Convention entered into force in 1970, WIPO was established.[4] It has its headquarters in Geneva.[5] As envisaged from the beginning, the WIPO then became a Specialized Agency of the United Nations system of organizations in 1974, after agreement with the United Nations.[6]

15.03 Specialized Agencies of the United Nations are, unlike their name seems to suggest, autonomous international organizations with an affiliation to the UN[7] rather than just organs of the UN. They are established by intergovernmental agreement.[8] 'Specialized' also does not mean that they would have exclusive competence in their special field of activity; for example, WIPO has its responsibilities 'subject to the competence and responsibilities of the United Nations and its organs'.[9] Specialized Agencies usually have a General Assembly, an Executive Committee, and a Secretariat. They are responsible for the conclusion of treaties in different areas, such as intellectual property; telecommunication; postal services; education, science, and culture; food and agriculture; and finances.[10] Although most specialized agencies aim at universal membership, not all UN members are also members of every specialized agency. These agencies, just like the representatives of their member countries and staff members, enjoy similar privileges and immunities as in the UN framework.[11]

---

[3] The Convention was signed at the Stockholm Conference, which also resulted in the revision of the Paris and Berne Conventions and further multilateral treaties in the field, see Bogsch (n 2 above) 250.

[4] See Art 1 of the WIPO Convention, and its Art 15 on entry into force.

[5] Art 10 ibid.

[6] For the agreement between the UN and WIPO, which entered into force on 17 December 1974, cf Bogsch (n 2 above) 254 and <http://www.wipo.int>, go to 'About WIPO', 'Treaties and Contracting Parties', and 'Related Documents'.

[7] Art 57 of the UN Charter describes such relationship.

[8] Art 63 ibid.

[9] Art 1 of the UN-WIPO Treaty of 1974 (n 6 above).

[10] The respective organizations are: International Telecommunications Union, Universal Postal Union, UNESCO, FAO, the World Bank, and the International Monetary Fund.

[11] B Simma, *Universelles Völkerrecht* (1984) § 286. On all aspects of Specialized Agencies, see also I Seidl-Hohenveldern, 'Specialized Agencies' in R Wolfrum (ed), *United Nations: Law, Policies and Practice* (1995) 1202 ff.

This step of joining the United Nations system seemed to open a perspective of **15.04** universal membership, given the impressive enlargement of the United Nations in the 1960s and 1970s as a consequence of the transformation of former colonies into independent states.[12] In particular, it was hoped that many developing countries which were not yet members of the BIRPI would become members of the WIPO. Another advantage of joining the UN system was the perspective that the Member States would no longer have to deal with the working conditions of the staff, since all questions related to the employment of staff members would be governed by the so-called 'common system' of the United Nations and its specialized agencies.[13] Hesitations by industrialized countries regarding the aim of making the WIPO a UN specialized agency were founded in the fear that developing countries would become the great majority of the WIPO and, on the basis of the one-by-one voting system, dominate its decision-making, possibly resulting in a weakening of the international intellectual property protection.[14]

The WIPO offers (but does not make obligatory) membership to any state which **15.05** is a Member of the Berne or Paris Unions or any other treaty administered by the WIPO. In addition, membership of WIPO is open to any state which is a Member of the United Nations, any of its specialized agencies, or the International Atomic Energy Agency, or which is a party to the statute of the International Court of Justice, as well as to any other state which is invited by the WIPO General Assembly to become a Member.[15] Accordingly, any state associated either with the preceding BIRPI, even if not belonging to the UN system, or associated with the UN system without necessarily being associated with the BIRPI, could become a Member of the WIPO. As of July 2007, 184 states are Members of the WIPO.

---

[12] MP Ryan, 'Adaptation and Change at the World Intellectual Property Organization' [1998] J'l World Intellectual Property 507, 509, also pointing at a critical attitude by parts of the intellectual property community.

[13] Bogsch (n 2 above) 253; Arts 14, 15 of the UN-WIPO Treaty (n 6 above). Additional advantages are the reciprocal representation in other bodies and meetings of the United Nations (Art 3 ibid) and exchange of information between WIPO and the UN, which also includes the obligation of WIPO to deliver information, if requested (Arts 6 and 8 ibid).

[14] Indeed, developing countries joined in 1974 in the 'Group 77' in the UN system, reflecting their potential power; Ryan (n 12 above) 509; Bogsch (n 2 above) 253–5, concluding also that the decision was worthwhile, in particular in view of the improved and wider international relations in the field of intellectual property.

[15] Art 5 of the WIPO Convention.

B. Structure and working mechanisms of the WIPO

15.06   The transformation of the BIRPI into a member-driven organization (the WIPO)[16] is reflected in the structure of the WIPO, which has three governing bodies:[17] the General Assembly as its supreme organ, the Conference, and the Coordination Committee. The General Assembly consists of all states that are both parties to the WIPO Convention and to any of the treaties administered by the WIPO.[18] The Conference consists of parties to the WIPO Convention whether or not they are also parties of any of the treaties administered by the WIPO.[19] The Coordination Committee consists of the states party to the WIPO Convention which are also members of the Executive Committee of the Paris or Berne Unions or of both.[20]

15.07   The General Assembly has the highest requirement for membership and also the most important tasks of the three governing bodies, in particular the appointment of the Director General and the adoption of the biennial budget. It meets every second year in ordinary sessions.[21] The Conference mainly has advisory tasks and ordinarily meets in the context of the General Assembly.[22] The Coordination Committee meets annually and has preparatory and advisory tasks; in particular, it has to prepare the draft agenda of the General Assembly, nominate a Director General to be appointed by the General Assembly, and prepare the draft agenda and the draft programme and budget of the Conference.[23]

15.08   The International Bureau is the Secretariat of the WIPO in respect of all the Unions and treaties administered by the WIPO. It is directed by the Director General who is the chief executive of the WIPO and represents it. He also has to report to, and conform to the instructions of, the General Assembly as well as prepare the draft programmes and budgets and periodical reports on activities.[24] In 2007, the Secretariat staff was from more than ninety countries.

---

[16] A first step in this direction was already made in 1948 when the 'Permanent Committee of the Berne Union' was established at the Brussels Revision Conference, see Bogsch (n 2 above) 249.

[17] For a short presentation of the governing bodies, cf Bogsch (n 2 above) 252–3.

[18] Art 6(1)(a) and Art 2(vii) of the WIPO Convention.

[19] Art 7(1)(a) ibid.

[20] Art 8(1)(a) ibid with further specifications.

[21] Art 6(2), (4) ibid, also for further tasks; in practice, it has also been meeting every second year in extraordinary sessions, alternating with the ordinary sessions.

[22] Art 7(2), (4) ibid.

[23] Art 8(3), (4) ibid.

[24] Art 9 ibid, with further details on the tasks of the Director General. Note that the budget of expenses common to the Unions is separate from that of the Conference, see Art 11 ibid.

In addition to the General Assembly of the WIPO, each of the Unions, such as **15.09** the Berne Union, has its own Assembly whose main function is the establishment of the biennial programme and budget of each of the Unions separately.[25]

C. Tasks of the WIPO

In general, the main objective of the WIPO is to promote the protection of intel- **15.10** lectual property worldwide through cooperation among states and, where appropriate, in collaboration with any other international organization.[26] In order to reach this objective, the WIPO undertakes a number of tasks, five of which are discussed below.[27]

(1) Administration and creation of treaties

The WIPO administers the existing treaties for which it is responsible, and where **15.11** appropriate, prepares and assists in their revisions.[28] As of 2007, the WIPO administers twenty-four treaties in addition to the WIPO Convention. In addition, it prepares and facilitates the adoption of new treaties, where requested by Member States; often, interested parties have played a role before such a request is made.

In the particular context of preparing revisions or adopting treaties in the field of **15.12** copyright and neighbouring rights, different Committees of Experts, followed by the Standing Committee on Copyright and Related Rights (SCCR) since 1998, have been convened by decisions of the General Assembly.[29] They consist of governmental experts who mostly hail from the competent ministries or the Permanent Missions in Geneva; possibly also observer states; intergovernmental organizations such as the UNCTAD, UNESCO, or the WTO; and the non-governmental organizations representing private interests, such as associations of authors' societies, performing artists, the phonogram industry, the film industry, or users such as library associations. As of 2007, sixty-six intergovernmental organizations and 201 international non-governmental organizations have an

---

[25] For the Berne Convention and its additional organs, see its Arts 22–6 and para 5.252 above; also Ricketson/Ginsburg (n 2 above) 16.08–16.14.

[26] Art 3(i) of the WIPO Convention.

[27] See Art 4 ibid specifying WIPO's most important functions; for its functions within the Berne Union, cf more specifically Art 24 of the Berne Convention.

[28] For the Berne Union, cf Art 24(1), (7) of the Berne Convention.

[29] In addition, Art 24(7)(a) of the Berne Convention requires cooperation with the Executive Committee.

observer status with the WIPO; thirty-one national non-governmental organizations have also been admitted.[30]

15.13 More recently, new treaties within the WIPO have usually been prepared according to the following pattern:[31] sessions of the Committees typically take place twice a year and last between three and five days each. In an initial phase, discussions are mostly based on detailed memoranda submitted by the International Bureau, which also drafts and, after adoption by the Member States, publishes the reports of the sessions.[32] At an advanced stage of discussion, usually after several years, it is often the Member States themselves which submit their own proposals, often in treaty language. When the Member States finally decide to convene a Diplomatic Conference for the purpose of revising or adopting a treaty, they usually also mandate the International Bureau and/or the Chairman of the Committee to draft, on the basis of preceding discussions, a so-called Basic Proposal, which is sent to the governments, intergovernmental organizations, and non-governmental organizations before the Diplomatic Conference. The Basic Proposal serves as a basis for negotiations at such a Conference.[33] During a Diplomatic Conference, the International Bureau of the WIPO assists the process in different ways.

(2) Model laws and legislative advice

15.14 In addition, the WIPO drafts model laws and submits them to interested Member States, mostly in order to assist them in drafting national laws in the field of intellectual property law. Such assistance is particularly important for developing countries or any other countries which may not have any (or not sufficient) experience in this area of law. Model laws have been drafted, for example, in respect of the protection of neighbouring rights in 1974 (an area which was then not yet as widespread and well known as today),[34] the protection of computer programs

---

[30] <http://www.wipo.int/members/en/organizations.jsp>; of the intergovernmental organizations, 17 belong to the UN System, 9 are in the field of intellectual property, 11 are other worldwide, and 29 other regional organizations. Particular organizations have been admitted ad hoc to specific bodies only, eg, in the field of indigenous heritage; for the IGC, see paras 20.36 ff below; cf also Art 24(7)(b) of the Berne Convention.

[31] These observations are based in particular on the practice in the cases of the WIPO Treaties of 1996, the proposed treaty on audiovisual performances 2000, and the planned treaty on broadcasting organizations, cf paras 17.05 ff, 18.01, and 19.02 ff below.

[32] Until December 1994, publication of memoranda and reports took place in WIPO's monthly review 'Copyright', and thereafter in 'Industrial Property and Copyright'; for Committee meetings after 1997, see the memoranda and reports of the SCCR under <http://www.wipo.int/meetings/en/topic.jsp?group_id=62>.

[33] For the example of the WIPO Copyright Treaty and the WIPO Performances and Phonograms Treaty, cf paras 17.10–17.12 below.

[34] 'Model Law concerning the protection of performers, producers of phonograms and broadcasting organizations' drafted by the Intergovernmental Committee of the Rome Convention in

in 1978 (hence, on a possible new object of protection under copyright, still controversially discussed at that time),[35] and developing countries in 1976 taking into account their specific needs (the so-called 'Tunis Model Law on Copyright'),[36] and model statutes for collecting societies in 1980 and 1983.[37] The 'Model Law on Copyright', which was completed but not published, and initial work on a 'Model Law on the Protection of Producers of Sound Recordings' at the beginning of the 1990s were surpassed by more important developments, namely the Committees of Experts whose work resulted in the WCT and WPPT.[38] More recent model laws, such as for the so-called 'transformation countries' (countries which transformed their centrally planned economies to market economies after the collapse of socialism in the former Soviet Union and in Central and Eastern Europe after 1989) and for developing countries have no longer been published but simply submitted to the relevant governments. Such model laws have no binding effect; they are only recommendations to national legislators. Nevertheless, their influence is often very strong, such that one might consider them as soft law.

Apart from the submission of model laws to national legislators, the WIPO **15.15** prepares draft laws, or gives concrete advice on legislative drafts submitted by governments of Member States with a view to the compliance of such drafts with the relevant international law, both on the Member States' request only.[39]

(3) Training and other technical assistance

The WIPO promotes intellectual property through the organization of seminars **15.16** of different kinds, mostly in developing countries or for their representatives in Geneva. It has granted scholarships to individual students for the participation in master programmes in intellectual property. Another more recent activity in the realm of education in intellectual property has been the establishment of the

---

1974, 1974 Copyright 163 ff. This model law was also to encourage Member countries to promote national legislation in the field of the newly adopted Rome Convention of 1961, cf para 4.60 above.

[35] Model Provisions on the Protection of Computer Software, (1978) Copyright 6 (Introduction), 12 (model provisions). In this context, cf also para 7.17 above.

[36] Model Law on Copyright for Developing Countries, (1976) Copyright 139 (report), 165 (Model law); cf also in the context of folklore paras 20.30 and, for 1982 Model provisions on folklore, 20.31 below.

[37] Model Statutes for Institutions Administering Authors' Rights in Developing Countries, (1983) Copyright 348, on the basis of drafts of 1980, (1980) Copyright 271, separately for public institutions and private societies.

[38] Model Provisions for Legislation in the Field of Copyright, (1989) Copyright 146, 362; (1990) Copyright 241 (session documents and reports); reports on the Committee of Experts on a model law for producers of sound recordings: (1992) Copyright 151, 188; M Ficsor, *The Law of Copyright and the Internet* (2002) 1.16, 1.17.

[39] Art 24(4) of the Berne Convention.

WIPO Worldwide Academy, which offers training through on-the-spot teaching and distance learning as well as research possibilities. Assistance by the WIPO may also include concrete advice and financial assistance regarding the setting-up of the necessary infrastructure, such as collective management organizations, and financial assistance to developing or transformation country Members in order to enable or facilitate their participation in WIPO meetings.[40]

(4) Studies, conferences, documentation

15.17 The WIPO has been organizing conferences with a view to exploring new issues which could become relevant in the future or which need more attention. Copyright and neighbouring rights-related topics in the 1990s were, for example, the possible protection of artificial intelligence (Stanford 1991), digitization and its consequences (Harvard 1993), audiovisual works and new technologies (Paris 1994), copyright in the global information infrastructure and in the information society (Mexico and Naples 1995), as well as collective management and digital technology (Seville 1997).[41] More recently, the topics of electronic commerce, liability of internet service providers, and applicable law have been addressed, among others.[42] In order to promote knowledge on specific areas of intellectual property or to make available relevant information to anyone interested, WIPO has continuously mandated studies on particular topics.[43] Also, it has published, for example, information regarding the Unions and national laws of member states, as well as articles on relevant legal questions in its monthly legal journals *Copyright*, *Industrial Property*, and, from 1995, *Industrial Property and Copyright*.[44] For example, country reports in these journals informed about the development of copyright in selected countries during certain time periods.[45] The journals were replaced in 1999 by the WIPO Magazine and, for documentation, the WIPO website.[46] In addition, the WIPO translates and publishes the laws of its Member States in the field of intellectual property in three UN languages: English, French, and Spanish.[47]

---

[40] Art 24(5) ibid.

[41] WIPO publications 698 (1991), 723 (1993), 731 (1994), 746 (1995), 751 (1996), and 756 (1998).

[42] cf paras 22.08 ff for more detail.

[43] Such studies were either published separately (cf for example studies in the context with audio-visual performances, paras 18.23–18.24 below), or in books eg by Masouyé on the Rome Convention, cf <http://www.wipo.int> (Resources, Electronic Bookshop and Guides/Studies and Handbooks) or in the journals indicated in the following text. cf also Art 24(5) of the Berne Convention.

[44] Until 1965, only French editions of the journals existed, cf para 4.03 above; cf also Art 24(3) of the Berne Convention.

[45] For a résumé of the regular contents of *Copyright*, cf Ricketson/Ginsburg (n 2 above) 16.35.

[46] cf <http://www.wipo.int>, go to resources.

[47] Art 24(2) of the Berne Convention; see the electronic database CLEA at <http://www.wipo.int/clea/en/index.jsp>.

(5) Arbitration and mediation

In 1994, WIPO started another important activity. Given the growth of the eco-   **15.18**
nomic importance of intellectual property and, consequently, the growth of the
need for Alternative Dispute Resolution, which is faster and less expensive than
regular court proceedings, the WIPO established an arbitration and mediation
centre for the settlement of intellectual property disputes between private parties.
The WIPO Arbitration and Mediation Centre administers the following four
procedures to settle disputes: mediation (non-binding assistance of parties with
the aim of a mutually agreed settlement), arbitration (binding decision by an
arbitrator or a tribunal of several arbitrators), expedited arbitration (particularly
rapid procedure of arbitration at reduced cost), and mediation followed, in the
absence of a settlement, by arbitration.[48] The arbitration and mediation services
have been used primarily in respect of internet domain names.[49]

D. Outlook

The WIPO has been challenged in more recent times by the work of the GATT   **15.19**
resulting in the WTO/TRIPS Agreement in 1994. Yet, it has largely met the challenges by, first, the conclusion of its cooperation agreement with WTO in 1995
on the basis of which the WIPO assists WTO Members in particular in implementing the TRIPS Agreement or otherwise by technical assistance.[50] Secondly,
in the field of copyright and neighbouring rights, it has largely met the challenge
by adopting the WCT and the WPPT in 1996 with their substantially higher
levels of protection.[51] Yet, both organizations have met new, political challenges
since around 2004, mainly consisting of a fundamental opposition by developing
countries and user groups to further development of international intellectual
property. These will be dealt with in a different context.[52]

---

[48] On the particular features of these procedures, cf F Gurry, 'The Dispute Resolution Services of
the World Intellectual Property Organization' (1999) J'l of International Economic Law 385–98; in
general on ADR and intellectual property: C Collar Fernandez and J Spolter, 'International
Intellectual Property Dispute Resolution' (1998) J'l of World Intellectual Property 555–69.
[49] On the Arbitration and Mediation Centre, see <http://www.wipo.int/amc/en/>.
[50] For the Agreement, cf <http://www.wipo.int>, go to 'About WIPO', 'Treaties and Contracting
Parties', and 'Related Documents'. Such cooperation is useful since only WIPO has the relevant staff
and fulfils most tasks under the Agreement anyway, such as the collection and translation of laws;
cf also ch para 10.136 above.
[51] On the WCT and WPPT, cf ch 17 below; cf also the comparative tables in ch 23 below.
[52] cf paras 25.24 and 25.27–25.32 below.

16

DISPUTE SETTLEMENT DRAFT TREATY

A. The emergence of the plan for a dispute settlement treaty

It is certainly not a mere coincidence that the WIPO General Assembly decided **16.01**
in September/October 1989 to establish a Committee of Experts on the Settlement of Intellectual Property Disputes between States with a view to working on
a possible draft treaty on dispute settlement.[1] Only a few months earlier in 1989,
the mid-term review of the GATT Uruguay Round had shown major progress by
considerably softening the resistance of developing countries against the inclusion of intellectual property into the GATT framework, thereby paving the way
for negotiations on intellectual property in that framework.[2] In other words, this
was the point in time when a success of the GATT approach seemed realistic and,
consequently, the emergence of a new forum dealing with intellectual property
left the WIPO with the perspective of possibly losing its impact as the leading
international intellectual property organization. It was also clear that the intellectual property conventions administered by the WIPO suffered not only from the
need to update the substantive standards and the lack of enforcement provisions,[3]
but also from the lack of efficient dispute settlement mechanisms.[4] A separate
WIPO treaty on dispute settlement may have been seen as a means to make the
conventions of the WIPO more attractive by offering a serious alternative to the

---

[1] Anon, 'WIPO: Overview of Activities and Developments in 1989' (1990) Copyright 18, 23.
[2] On the negotiations leading to the TRIPS Agreement, see paras 10.19 ff above.
[3] cf paras 9.04 ff above.
[4] For the Berne and Rome Conventions, cf paras 5.257 and 6.79 above; also paras 8.26,
9.05 above.

then developing WTO/TRIPS Agreement to which the well-working GATT dispute settlement mechanism would apply.[5]

B. Discussions and draft treaty

16.02 Yet the first session of the then established Committee of Experts in February 1990[6] already showed a split of views: developing countries were strongly in favour of mandating the International Bureau with the preparation of a draft treaty, while the USA and some other industrialized countries seemed to favour a solution in the GATT Uruguay Round which would allow more efficient sanctions, such as cross-retaliation in particular.[7] The industrialized countries at the same time wanted to keep the option for a WIPO dispute settlement treaty open as long as the WTO/TRIPS Agreement with the dispute settlement understanding had not been adopted. They could achieve a compromise by limiting the mandate of the International Bureau to the preparation of mere 'principles of a draft treaty'. Such principles were then drafted by the International Bureau for the Committee's second session.[8]

16.03 In the subsequent six sessions between 1991 and 1994, the governmental experts nevertheless discussed a draft treaty on dispute settlement.[9] The Draft Treaty[10] contained the following main elements. It was only to apply to disputes between states and certain intergovernmental organizations rather than

---

[5] On this aspect, cf paras 9.05 and 9.09 above; the other deficiencies were also tackled at the same time, namely in the decision to start discussions on a protocol to the Berne Convention at the Berne Union Assemblies 1989 and also 1991, Anon (n 1 above) 23; A Bogsch, 'Brief History of the First 25 Years of the World Intellectual Property Organisation' (1992) Copyright 247, 262.

[6] See in particular the memoranda prepared by the International Bureau for the session, WIPO Documents SD/CE/I/2 and 3.

[7] On this aspect, see paras 9.09, 10.115, 10.126, and 10.128 above.

[8] See in particular WIPO Docs SD/CE/II/2–4 of the second session of the Committee in October 1990.

[9] The third to eighth sessions were held in September 1991, July 1992, May 1993, February 1994, May/June 1995, and July 1996; the relevant documents have the numbers SD/CE/III–VIII, completed by Arabic numbers for the individual documents. For selected résumés, cf (1992) Copyright 217 (4th session); (1993) Copyright 121 (5th session and draft treaty and regulations) and 141 (note on preparatory meeting for diplomatic conference); (1994) Industrial Property 122 (6th session); (1995) Industrial Property and Copyright 168, 264 (document and report, 7th session); (1996) Industrial Property and Copyright 319 (8th session).

[10] The version discussed in the sixth session of the Committee is reprinted in (1994) Copyright 70, 71 ff; it was revised for the seventh session in WIPO Document SD/CE/VII/2 (1995) Industrial Property and Copyright 168, and regulations: 205), in particular regarding the relationship between the dispute settlement system under the Draft Treaty and other systems. The latest draft (WIPO Document WO/GA/XXI/2 of 30 April 1997) was prepared, together with revised explanations and new draft Regulations, by the International Bureau in 1997, following a decision by the WIPO General Assembly at its September/October 1996 session (WIPO Document WO/GA/XIX/4, paras 22, 23).

between private parties.[11] It was to apply to disputes on intellectual property treaties administered by the WIPO alone or with other intergovernmental organizations.[12] The settlement procedure resembled that of trade treaties such as GATT/WTO; however, it did not include the application of sanctions. In particular, it started with consultations between the parties and allowed for Good Offices as well as conciliation and mediation. If these measures were not successful, it offered a panel procedure resulting in a panel report that was to be followed by reports of the parties on the implementation of the panel's recommendations.[13] The fact that sanctions for non-compliance with these recommendations could not be imposed or authorized under the Draft[14] may reflect the expectation that the respective party would be sufficiently encouraged to take all measures for compliance simply by the mere public exposure of the report to all parties of the relevant treaty and the possibility of having an exchange of views among them.[15] At the same time, the lack of specific sanctions[16] was in the interest of all those industrialized countries that preferred the forum of the GATT/WTO because this would make it easier for them to argue against the weaker WIPO dispute settlement treaty.

The proposed treaty also offered a formal arbitration procedure as an alternative for the other, above-mentioned mechanisms. The arbitration award by the Arbitration Tribunal was to be final and binding, but again not enforceable by any sanctions.[17] **16.04**

C. The outcome of discussions

At the seventh session of the Committee of Experts in May/June 1995, chances **16.05** seemed good that the work could result in a treaty, given the strong support by the overall majority of countries. Only the USA denied any need for an additional international treaty on dispute settlement besides the WTO mechanism

---

11 Arts 1(i), 2 of the Draft Treaty (later called 'proposed treaty', see WIPO Doc WO/GA/XXI/2, 5 ff); for disputes between private parties, see para 15.18 above on the WIPO Arbitration and Mediation Centre.

12 For more details and alternatives reflecting the different positions of Member States, see Art 2 of the Draft Treaty.

13 See Arts 3–6 ibid for further details of these steps of the procedure.

14 The Assembly of the proposed dispute settlement union was not allowed to do so, Art 5(10)(d) ibid.

15 Art 5(10)(c), (d) ibid.

16 General international law regarding the consequences of a breach of an obligation was not precluded, paras 5.32 and 5.54 WIPO Doc WO/GA/XXI/2.

17 Art 7 of the Draft Treaty.

which had meanwhile been adopted.[18] At its eighth session in July 1996, the Committee was close to setting a date for the proposed diplomatic conference at which a dispute settlement treaty could have been adopted by late 1997 or early 1998. However, due to the opposition of Japan, Canada, and the USA, the decision on a diplomatic conference was referred to the General Assembly of WIPO in the autumn of 1996.[19] The General Assembly 1996 maintained the aim of a Diplomatic Conference to be organized in the first half of 1998; the International Bureau was to submit a revised draft, and the General Assembly 1997 was to decide on a Diplomatic Conference, particularly in the light of new WTO experiences.[20] The General Assembly 1997 then decided to continue consultations on whether to convene a diplomatic conference at a later time, but then no initiative in this regard followed.[21]

16.06   The opponents of the WIPO dispute settlement treaty mainly argued that there was no need for such a treaty within the WIPO because the TRIPS Agreement with its effective dispute settlement mechanism had already been adopted in the framework of the WTO. Again, their attitude may reflect a preference towards the WTO over the WIPO. Indeed, if only the WTO had an efficient dispute settlement mechanism, this advantage over the WIPO could have the effect of drawing even more countries into the WTO. Other countries argued correctly that different systems could coexist; indeed, concurring dispute settlement mechanisms exist, for example, under the NAFTA and the WTO.[22] One would only have to clarify the relationship between the different mechanisms. Also, countries such as China and Russia argued that they were not members of the WTO and would have liked a dispute settlement mechanism within the WIPO.[23]

16.07   After Member Countries refrained from further pursuing the aim of a WIPO dispute settlement treaty, the issue has not come up again within WIPO and,

---

[18] See Report on the Seventh Session, WIPO Doc SD/CE/VII/8, para 25 for the opinion of the USA, and Anon, 'WIPO to Press on with Treaty on Settlement of IP Disputes' (1995) World Intellectual Property Report 241, mentioning only that other countries stressed the need to avoid an overlap between the WIPO system and that of the WTO.

[19] Anon, 'Committee of Experts on the Settlement of Intellectual Property Disputes between States' (1996) Industrial Property and Copyright 319; Anon, 'Committee on Dispute Settlement May Call Diplomatic Conference in 1997' (1996) World Intellectual Property Report 292.

[20] WIPO Doc WO/GA/XIX/4 paras 20 and 22–3; Anon, 'Governing Bodies of WIPO and the Unions administered by WIPO' (1996) Industrial Property and Copyright 342, 344.

[21] WIPO Doc WO/GA/XXI/13 para 184 and, for the discussion, paras 165–83; the USA, Japan, and Australia considered such a treaty unnecessary, while Europe, Israel, and most developing countries were in principle in favour.

[22] On WTO, see paras 10.114–10.132 above; on NAFTA and the relation between both systems, cf paras 11.22–11.23 above.

[23] Anon, 'Committee on Dispute Settlement May Call Diplomatic Conference in 1997' (1996) World Intellectual Property Report 292.

accordingly, remains on ice. It seems that this initiative might have had a chance to succeed if it had been started earlier, well before the GATT approach became a realistic option. Even if the (already so far) inefficient mechanism of the ICJ referred to in the Berne and Rome Conventions remains available,[24] it may well be expected that countries will only have recourse to the WTO mechanism, all the more since the TRIPS Agreement contains most of the substantive standards of these Conventions as well as additional ones.

---

[24] cf paras 5.257 and 6.79 above; also para 8.26 above.

17

THE WIPO COPYRIGHT TREATY (WCT) AND THE WIPO PERFORMANCES AND PHONOGRAMS TREATY (WPPT) OF 1996

A. Background of and development towards the WIPO Treaties of 1996

(1) 1971–1991: between 'guided development' and the new approach of a 'protocol'

17.01   The Berne Convention of 1886 was revised about every twenty years up to 1971. In 1971, the unanimity required for a revision of the Convention was achieved only with major efforts, due to the North–South conflict between industrialized and developing countries which had arisen in the meantime.[1] Thereafter, the economic importance of copyright and, consequently, conflicts of interest among Member States increased—not only between industrialized and developing, but also among industrialized countries, so that it seemed even more difficult to reach unanimity in the future.[2] Nevertheless, copyright needed to be adapted to new technical and other developments that occurred after 1971. WIPO decided to meet this challenge by the so-called 'guided development' rather than by the preparation of a new revision conference. The strategy of 'guided development' aimed at discussing and promoting common and new standards of protection regarding new kinds of works and new forms of uses. The related work was accomplished mainly in common Committees of Experts of WIPO and UNESCO which resulted in recommendations, guiding principles, or model provisions, and were accompanied by studies mandated or carried out by WIPO and UNESCO. Although these results were not binding upon Member States, they had a considerable impact on the awareness of governments of particular problems and on the development of national copyright laws.[3]

17.02   This strategy of 'guided development' was, however, not considered as sufficient, in particular by industrialized countries whose right owners suffered from the deficiencies of the existing conventions.[4] When these countries consequently approached the forum of GATT in order to include intellectual property in the Uruguay Round negotiations, WIPO must have perceived the threat of potentially powerful competition by this other forum and of a loss or decrease of its own importance as the until then only international organization dealing with intellectual property law. This threat must have been felt even more strongly after

---

[1] See paras 4.22, 9.05 above.

[2] The Director General of WIPO himself, at the relevant time, expressed a pessimistic assessment in respect of a possible future revision: A Bogsch, 'The First Hundred Years of the Berne Convention for the Protection of Literary and Artistic Works' (1986) Copyright 291, 327.

[3] On the issues dealt with in the period of 'guided development', see in detail M Ficsor, *The Law of Copyright and the Internet: The 1996 WIPO Treaties, their Interpretation and Implementation* (2002) 1.03–1.17.

[4] See ch 9, in particular paras 9.04–9.06 above.

the mid-term review of the GATT Uruguay Round in April 1989, when developing countries gave up their fundamental opposition to the inclusion of intellectual property into the GATT, allowing negotiations on substantive provisions to begin.[5]

It is certainly not by coincidence that only a few months later, namely in September/October 1989, the WIPO Governing Bodies decided for the next biennium to convene a Committee of Governmental Experts in order to examine whether a protocol to the Berne Convention should be prepared with a view to submitting a draft for adoption at a Diplomatic Conference after 1991. Existing provisions of the Berne Convention were envisaged to be clarified or supplemented by new international norms. The new approach was justified because the existing norms were often interpreted differently by Berne Union Members.[6] The first such Committee on a Berne Protocol took place in November 1991, just one month before the negotiations on the substance of the TRIPS Agreement were provisionally concluded as part of the so-called 'Dunkel Draft'—hence, at a moment when it was very realistic that this Agreement would be adopted in the foreseeable future and the (then) GATT would take the lead over WIPO.[7]   **17.03**

With its approach of a 'protocol' to the Berne Convention, WIPO had successfully found a way to meet the need for new international copyright norms without taking the risk of a (unanimous) revision. The 'protocol' was envisaged as a multilateral treaty under Article 20 of the Berne Convention, a so-called 'special agreement'.[8] Such agreement can be adopted by a restricted number of Berne Union Members, thereby allowing WIPO to avoid the unanimity requirement—provided only that such agreement grants more extensive rights than those by the Berne Convention or includes provisions not contrary to it.[9] The expression 'protocol' was chosen irrespective of the title of the future instrument and of the question which countries could adhere to it.   **17.04**

(2) 1991–1993: initial discussions on the Berne Protocol and the establishment of a second Committee of Experts

The document for the first session of the Committee of Experts[10] discussed different kinds of objects of protection for inclusion in the Berne Protocol, namely   **17.05**

---

[5] See paras 10.20–10.21 above.

[6] On this item of the programme for 1990–1, see WIPO Doc AB/XX/2, Annex A, item PRG.02(2). On uncertainties in the interpretation of the Berne Convention, see ch 7, in particular paras 7.13 ff, and 7.22–7.33.

[7] On the Dunkel Draft, see para 10.22; see also the similar timely coincidence between the TRIPS negotiations and WIPO's proposal to work on a dispute settlement treaty, para 16.01 above.

[8] WIPO Doc BCP/CE/I/2, para 3; on Art 20 of the Berne Convention, see paras 5.250–5.251 above.

[9] Art 20 of the Berne Convention and paras 5.250–5.251 above.

[10] 'Questions concerning a Possible Protocol to the Berne Convention, Part I Memorandum', (1992) Copyright 30 ff; it was submitted by the Secretariat of WIPO.

computer programs, databases, expert systems and other artificial intelligence systems, computer-produced works, and phonograms. The Member States agreed that computer programs and databases should, in principle, be included,[11] and that it was premature to talk about expert systems and other artificial intelligence systems, and computer-produced works. Most of them, however,[12] objected to the inclusion of phonograms into the Berne Protocol because phonograms were not covered as works by the Berne Convention, as confirmed by the WIPO document itself,[13] and therefore were not to be regulated in the broader context of the Berne Convention.

17.06   At the same time, Member States did not object to an improvement in the international protection of phonograms. Therefore, the WIPO Governing Bodies, in September 1992, established a second Committee of Experts that was to prepare, in parallel to the Committee on a Berne Protocol, a possible new instrument on the protection of the rights of performers and producers of phonograms.[14] Performers were added to phonogram producers because their situation was closely connected to the exploitation of phonograms. Yet, no final decision was made on whether audiovisual performers would also be included.[15]

(3) 1993–1996: substantive discussions including the 'digital agenda'

17.07   Consequently, from 1993 both Committees held their sessions in parallel, and from September 1995, in common because some of the issues, such as the new right of making available, implied the same kinds of problems.[16] At an early stage

---

[11] Doubts, however, existed in the details, in particular in respect of computer programs, see the Report on the First Session (1992) Copyright 40, 48–50 (paras 75 ff); on databases: paras 89 ff.

[12] Except for the USA, United Kingdom, Egypt, and India, S von Lewinski, 'Erste Sitzung des Sachverständigenausschusses der WIPO über ein Protokoll zur Berner Konvention zum Schutz von Werken der Literatur und Kunst—III' (1992) GRUR Int 45, 49; Report (n 11 above) para 107 (without indicating countries).

[13] See the document of the First Session (n 10 above) paras 60–1.

[14] The Committee was officially called 'Committee of Experts on a Possible Instrument on the Protection of the Rights of Performers and Producers of Phonograms'; the Berne Committee was called 'Committee of Experts on a Possible Protocol to the Berne Convention'. The new terms adopted for both Committees specified the issues for the agenda, the status of members and observers in the Committees (including in particular the Commission of the European Communities as a member), et al, WIPO Doc B/A/XIII/2, para 22.

[15] The WIPO Memorandum for the First Session of that Committee of Experts deliberately left this question open, (1993) Copyright 142, 144 (paras 7–9); the issue remained controversial throughout the Committee meetings, J Reinbothe and S von Lewinski, *The WIPO Treaties 1996* (2002) 470–2 (nn 20–3).

[16] The Committee on a possible Berne Protocol held seven sessions before the Diplomatic Conference of 1996: in November 1991, February 1992, June 1993, December 1994, September 1995, February and May 1996; see the respective memoranda and reports in (1992) Copyright 30 ff, 66 ff, 93 ff; (1993) Copyright 84 ff, 179 ff; (1994) Copyright 214 ff; (1995) Industrial Property and Copyright 107 ff, 299 ff; (1996) Industrial Property and Copyright 118 f and 236 f. The Committee on a Possible New Instrument held six sessions, namely in June/July 1993, November 1993,

of the discussions, many proposed provisions were eliminated from the agenda, particularly because they were too detailed, such as those on limitations of the reproduction right for private use and for uses by libraries and archives. At a later stage, though, new items were put on the agenda, in particular those connected to the development of digital technology and the internet. Indeed, it was only after the adoption of the TRIPS Agreement in April 1994 that governmental awareness of the impact of such technologies on copyright and neighbouring rights became sufficiently concrete for consideration by legislators: the major industrialized countries published documents on the possible consequences of digital technology for their national laws only from mid-1994.[17]

These new issues had not been foreseen when the initiative for the Berne Protocol **17.08** was taken in 1989. When they emerged after the adoption of the TRIPS Agreement, they presented a unique chance for WIPO to take an advantage over WTO's TRIPS Agreement by including them into the envisaged treaty. Since the internet instantly allows global uses, global solutions were immediately needed, even before national laws could develop. Accordingly, the timing turned out to be perfect for WIPO. The solutions for the internet later adopted in the WIPO

December 1994, September 1995, February and May 1996; see the respective memoranda and reports in (1993) Copyright 142 ff, 196 ff; (1994) Copyright 44 ff, 241 ff; (1995) Industrial Property and Copyright 110 ff, 363 ff; (1996) Industrial Property and Copyright 118 f and 236 f.

[17] Green Paper of the USA, 'Intellectual Property and the National Information Infrastructure: Preliminary Draft of the Working Group on Intellectual Property Rights' (July 1994) and final version (White Paper, September 1995), see S von Lewinski, 'Das Weißbuch der USA zum geistigen Eigentum und zur National Information Infrastructure' (1995) GRUR Int 858. European Community: 'Green Paper: Copyright and Related Rights in the Information Society (Doc COM (95) final, July 1995), and version amended on the basis of consultations: 'Follow-up to the Green Paper on Copyright and Related Rights in the Information Society' (Doc COM (96) 568 final, November 1996); see S von Lewinski, 'Das europäische Grünbuch über Urheberrecht und neue Technologien' (1995) GRUR Int 831, and Vol II chs 4 and 10; France: 'Industries culturelles et nouvelles technologies' (report submitted by a commission chaired by P Sirinelli, September 1994), see T Dreier, 'Der französische 'Rapport Sirinelli' zum Urheberrecht und den neuen Technologien' (1995) GRUR Int 840 ff and, on a second Report, F Genton, 'Multimedia im französischen Urheberrecht: der zweite Sirinelli-Bericht' (1996) GRUR Int 693. Germany: 'Urheberrecht auf dem Weg zur Informationsgesellschaft' (mandated by the Ministry of Justice in July 1996, written by T Dreier, P Katzenberger, S von Lewinski, G Schricker, published 2007). Australia: 'Highways to change: Copyright in the New Communications Environment' (Copyright Convergence Group, mandated by the Ministry of Justice, August 1994), see T Dreier, ' "Highways to change": Der Bericht der australischen Copyright Convergence Group zum Urheberrecht im neuen Kommunikationsfeld' (1995) GRUR Int 837. Canada: 'Copyright and the Information Highway' (draft: December 1994; final report: March 1995), mandated by Ministry of Industry ('Industry Canada'); see S von Lewinski, 'Der kanadische Bericht des "Copyright Subcommittee" über Urheberrecht und die Datenautobahn' (1995) GRUR Int 851. Japan: 'A Report on Discussions by the Working Group of the Subcommittee on Multimedia, Copyright Council: Study of Institutional Issues Regarding Multimedia' (Ministry of Culture, February 1995, following a preliminary report of 1993); see C Heath, 'Multimedia und Urheberrecht in Japan' (1995) GRUR Int 843 ff . For aspects of the US, EC, and Japanese studies, see Ficsor (n 3 above) 4.57 ff .

Treaties are indeed among the distinctive features of the treaties, which therefore have also been labelled the 'internet treaties', even if they contain much more than solutions to problems provoked by the internet.

17.09 With the emergence of digital technology on the agenda, labelled as the 'digital agenda' from 1995,[18] discussions intensified and accelerated. Already at the session in December 1994, the idea of a Diplomatic Conference had been ventilated; at the session in September 1995, the USA then officially proposed to convene a Diplomatic Conference in the second half of 1996 in order to adopt the Berne Protocol and the new instrument.[19] Although many participants who were aware of the multitude of remaining divergences and doubts unofficially considered this proposal as premature and not very realistic,[20] they further intensified and streamlined their negotiations, which from that very session were based on proposals submitted by Member States rather than the WIPO Secretariat, and were drafted in treaty language. These participants certainly did so because they perceived the need for a rapid international reaction to the challenges of the internet before national laws developed independently and in different ways. This need was indeed later met by the WIPO Treaties 1996, which, probably for the first time in international copyright law, laid down certain rules at the international level prior to their development at the national level.

(4) 1996: preparations for a Diplomatic Conference

17.10 Immediately at the following session in February 1996, the Committees of Experts adopted all decisions and recommendations necessary to proceed to a Diplomatic Conference. In particular, they recommended that a preparatory committee and the Governing Bodies of WIPO should be convened for the purpose of preparing the Diplomatic Conference to be held from 2 to 20 December 1996.[21] They also recommended that the Chairman of the Committees should establish draft texts, called 'Basic Proposals', as a basis for negotiations at the Diplomatic Conference. Further, they adopted proposals for preparatory group consultations, in particular in favour of regional groups of developing countries to be organized by the International Bureau of WIPO.[22]

---

[18] The Memorandum for the joint sessions in September 1995, WIPO Doc BCP/CE/V-INR/CE/IV/INF.2 used this term for the first time.

[19] Report of the Session, WIPO Doc BCP/CE/V/9-INR/CE/IV/8, para 20.

[20] R Kreile, 'Bericht über die WIPO-Sitzungen zum möglichen Protokoll zur Berner Konvention und zum "Neuen Instrument" im September 1995' (1995) Zeitschrift für Urheber- und Medienrecht 815, 816; A Schäfers, 'Normsetzung zum geistigen Eigentum in internationalen Organisationen: WIPO und WTO—ein Vergleich' (1996) GRUR Int 763, 777.

[21] Report in (1996) Industrial Property and Copyright 118, 119 (WIPO Doc BCP/CE/VI/16-INR/CE/V/14, para 275, erroneously indicates the dates of 1 to 21 December).

[22] For details, see WIPO Doc BCP/CE/VI/16-INR/CE/V/14, para 277. The regional groups were supposed to meet in May, September, and November. In addition, a mixed group of each 12

During preparatory work and later during the Diplomatic Conference, the **17.11** regional meetings of developing countries replaced the former 'Group 77' or 'Group D', which so far had represented all developing countries in the UN framework.[23] The new three groups represented African countries, Asian countries with China, and Latin American and Caribbean countries ('GRULAC'). The decision to split the old 'Group 77' proved to be appropriate because the three groups in some respects expressed different views. For example, the basic proposals were, overall, positively considered by the African group and GRULAC while the Asian group was much more reserved. Coordination before the Diplomatic Conference also took place within the European Community, an ad hoc group of Central and Eastern European with Baltic countries, and in the framework of many bilateral and multilateral contacts among industrialized countries, rather than in the formal structure of the so-called 'B-Group' (industrialized countries).[24] Group coordination in any case facilitated the preparation of the negotiations and made them more efficient.

By 1 September 1996, WIPO submitted to the participants invited to the Diplo- **17.12** matic Conference the Basic Proposals for the substantive provisions of three envisaged treaties, namely of a treaty on copyright, a treaty on the rights of performers and phonogram producers, and a treaty on the *sui generis* protection of databases.[25] In addition, the Basic Proposal for the administrative and final clauses of the treaties as well as the Draft Agenda and Draft Rules of Procedure of the Diplomatic Conference were distributed.[26] The contents of the substantive provisions of the Basic Proposals and their Explanatory Memoranda reflected the results of the discussions in the Committees of Experts and contained alternative proposals where governments had expressed strongly diverging opinions.[27]

---

developing and industrialized countries was supposed to meet in October; that meeting was, however, enlarged later, see Fiscor (n 3 above) 3.55, also on the regional meetings.

[23] On 'Group 77', which was essentially a negotiating group within the framework of the UNCTAD and other UN Bodies, see A Fatouros, 'Developing States' in R Bernhardt (ed), *Encyclopedia of Public International Law* (1992) Vol I, 1019 ff.

[24] On the 'B-Group', see ibid 1019.

[25] 'Basic Proposal for the Substantive Provisions of the Treaty on Certain Questions Concerning the Protection of Literary and Artistic Works to be Considered by the Diplomatic Conference', WIPO Doc CRNR/DC/4; 'Basic Proposal for the Substantive Provisions of the Treaty for the Protection of the Rights of Performers and Producers of Phonograms to be Considered by the Diplomatic Conference', WIPO Doc CRNR/DC/5; 'Basic Proposal for the Substantive Provisions of the Treaty on Intellectual Property in Respect of Databases to be Considered by the Diplomatic Conference', WIPO Doc CRNR/DC/6.

[26] WIPO Docs CRNR/DC/3, 1 and 2.

[27] For a summary of the contents of the Basic Proposals, see Reinbothe/von Lewinski (n 15 above) 6–7.

B. Procedure at the Diplomatic Conference

17.13 The example of the WIPO Treaties of 1996 is to give an insight into the procedural issues at a diplomatic conference in order to illustrate how an international treaty of this kind may be adopted.

(1) Invited participants

17.14 WIPO had invited delegations of all Member States of WIPO, the so-called 'Special Delegation' (ie the European Community), and, as observers, delegations of states which were Members of the United Nations but not of the WIPO. In addition, representatives of intergovernmental and non-governmental organizations were invited as observers. At the Diplomatic Conference, 127 out of 161 WIPO Member States were represented[28]—many more states than at the Stockholm Conference of 1971, when seventy-four of 129 existing states were represented in order to establish the WIPO and revise the Berne and other Conventions. The increase in states was partly due to the emergence of new states after the collapse of the Soviet Union and the restructuring of states in Central and Eastern Europe. Also, the European Community was not yet represented at the 1971 Conference. In 1996, Ethiopia, Iran, and the Dominican Republic participated as observer states. Only seven intergovernmental organizations were represented[29] (as opposed to thirteen out of nineteen invited ones in 1971).

17.15 As compared to 1971, the number of non-governmental organizations was considerably larger: in 1996, seventy-six non-governmental organizations were represented—nearly three times as many as in 1971, when twenty-six out of twenty-seven invited organizations participated in the Conference. This difference is particularly notable since these twenty-six organizations included even those in the field of industrial property which was also negotiated at that time. In recent times, the non-governmental organizations have become highly diversified and include no longer just international associations but also regional and national ones, such as, at the 1996 Diplomatic Conference, the American Bar Association, the Asociación Argentina de Intérpretes, the American Film Marketing Association, the Japan Electronic Industry Development Association, the American National Association of Broadcasters, the National Music Publishers' Association, and the United States Telephone Association. Examples

---

[28] On 1 January 1997, the Berne Union had 121 and the Rome Convention 53 Member States.

[29] The Organization of African Unity, the UNESCO, the International Labour Organization (ILO), the International Maritime Organization, the World Meteorological Organization, the World Trade Organization, and the International Telecommunications Union.

of highly diversified non-governmental organizations were the European Project-Digital Video Broadcasting organization, and the Japan Compact Disk Rental Commerce Trade Association. User associations no longer only represented traditional areas such as education (eg the Educators' ad hoc Committee of Copyright Law and the Fédération Internationale des Écoles de Musique), but also online service providers and other representatives of the communication industries who mainly aimed at avoiding their liability for copyright infringements by preventing increased copyright protection.

The high number of non-governmental organizations like the high overall number of more than 750 delegates and observers accredited at the Diplomatic Conference[30] reflected the increase in the economic importance of copyright and neighbouring rights, as did the strong interest of the media.[31] **17.16**

(2) Committees at the Diplomatic Conference

The Plenary of the Diplomatic Conference was active only at its beginning and its end. A number of Committees accomplished the main work of formal discussions.[32] As at earlier WIPO Diplomatic Conferences, Main Committee I dealt with the substantive provisions of the proposed treaties, including any agreed statements, recommendations, or resolutions; Main Committee II dealt with the administrative and final clauses of the treaties. Only these Main Committees were open to all Member and observer delegations as well as to intergovernmental and non-governmental organizations. **17.17**

More limited membership and tasks had the Drafting, Credentials, and Steering Committees. The Drafting Committee had to review and coordinate all texts submitted to it by the Main Committees and to harmonize the six language versions,[33] without altering the substance of the texts.[34] The task of the Credentials Committee was to examine the credentials, full powers, letters of appointment, **17.18**

---

[30] At the Stockholm Conference 1971, more than 400 delegates and observers participated; yet, that Conference did not deal only with copyright and neighbouring rights, but also with the establishment of the WIPO and with industrial property.

[31] eg, reports on the developments at the Diplomatic Conference were published nearly daily in the *Financial Times*.

[32] On the importance of informal discussions at this Diplomatic Conference, however, see para 17.25 below.

[33] In accordance with UN rules, the six languages are Arabic, Chinese, English, French, Russian, and Spanish.

[34] On the latter obligation, see Rule 13(3) of the Rules of Procedure as adopted on 3 December 1996 and amended on 5 December 1996 by the Diplomatic Conference, WIPO Doc CRNR/DC/9 rev; on the obligation to translate any written proposals and reports of the Committees and of any working group from one into the other five official languages and to distribute them in the six languages, see Rule 43 of the Rules of Procedure (ibid).

and other similar documents.[35] This task is very important at any diplomatic conference because a state can be bound by a treaty only where its delegates are fully empowered to represent it for the purposes of adopting and authenticating the text of the treaty and expressing the consent of the state to be bound by it. Since an act relating to the conclusion of a treaty performed by a person without the necessary empowerment is without legal effect, unless afterwards confirmed by the state,[36] negotiators have an interest in seeing the full powers of their co-negotiators at an early stage of the negotiations.[37]

17.19   The Steering Committee has to manage a Diplomatic Conference and may be essential to further progress, where needed. At the Diplomatic Conference 1996, it rarely had to intervene, but when it did, the impact was strongly felt. It consisted of the President and all Vice-Presidents of the Conference and of the Chairpersons of both Main Committees, and the chairpersons of the Drafting and the Credentials Committees.[38]

(3) Particular procedural questions

(a) Posts

17.20   Among the most difficult tasks at the beginning of the Diplomatic Conference was the repartition of posts in a number of committees, and the allocation of membership in the Drafting and Credentials Committees. This task was mainly of a political nature; different groups of countries had to be taken into account in a balanced way so as to satisfy all participants. In order to reach an agreeable solution, the number of posts and members proposed in the Draft Rules of Procedure had to be increased.[39] For the Drafting Committee, the drafting capabilities of the candidates were essential in addition to political considerations. For the post of the Chair of Main Committee I dealing with the substance of the treaties, it seemed logical to envisage the person who so far had chaired both Committees of Experts leading to the WIPO treaties of 1996, Jukka Liedes.

---

[35] Rule 9 ibid.

[36] Art 8 of the Vienna Convention on the Law of Treaties.

[37] S Rosenne, 'Treaties, Conclusion and Entry into Force' in R Bernhardt (ed), *Encyclopaedia of Public International Law* (2000) Vol IV, 932, 934, also on full powers and their inclusion in credentials; see also Art 7 of the Vienna Convention, and para 8.02 above.

[38] Rule 14(2), (3) of the Rules of Procedure.

[39] It was decided that the Conference should have one President, eighteen Vice Presidents, as well as a Chairperson and three Vice Chairpersons each of the two Main Committees, the Drafting and Credentials Committees, and eighteen members of the Drafting Committee as well as seven members of the Credentials Committee, see Rule 15(1), (2) ibid.

(b) EC voting rights

Another important procedural issue was the exercise of voting rights of the EC **17.21** Member States by the Special Delegation[40] during the Diplomatic Conference. It was understood from the beginning that the EC should not have its own voting right but only be allowed to exercise those of the EC Member States, if empowered by them. In this context, however, other delegations had several claims to the EC. First, some claimed that the EC should submit a declaration on the allocation of jurisdiction between the EC and its Member States in respect of the different subject matter, in order to make it clear to outside parties whether the EC or the Member States were empowered according to the internal rules of the EC.[41] This claim was later withdrawn.

Secondly, the USA in particular claimed that the delegations of all (then) fifteen **17.22** EC Member States should be physically present during the exercise of their voting rights by the Special Delegation, so that a delegation which happened to be outside the room during a vote could not be counted as a vote. This rule was adopted,[42] as was the rule that the Special Delegation could not exercise the voting rights of the EC Member States when those voted themselves, and vice versa. These rules put an additional burden on the European Community and its Member States, all the more so since all state delegations were placed in an alphabetical order so that the EC Member States were scattered throughout the room. Coordination among the EC and its Member States accordingly had to be highly intensive. In the end, however, this rule had a small impact, since votes were necessary only in the case of three Articles and one Agreed Statement, while the aim of reaching decisions by consensus was achieved for most provisions.[43]

(4) The process at the Diplomatic Conference

The Diplomatic Conference was opened on 2 December 1996, by the Director **17.23** General of WIPO, Arpad Bogsch. Most of the draft rules of procedure were immediately adopted in Plenary. Yet, the allocation of posts and membership as well as the procedural questions in respect of the EC voting rights[44] needed to be dealt with in informal discussions. On 3 December, the problem of EC voting rights was solved by a vote, while the allocation of posts and membership in committees took until 6 December. Accordingly, the substantive provisions of the three envisaged treaties could be tackled only from the Friday of the first of three weeks.

---

40 The European Community (EC), see para 17.40 above.
41 On the allocation of competence between the EC and its Member States, see Vol II ch 3.
42 Rule 33 (in particular para (3)) of the Rules of Procedure.
43 Rule 34(1) ibid lays down the aim of making decisions 'as far as possible' by consensus.
44 See paras 17.20–17.22 above.

17.24 The work of the Plenary then started with opening statements, followed by a first screening of the texts of the Basic Proposals for the Copyright Treaty and the Neighbouring Rights Treaty in Main Committee I until December 12. Agreement was immediately reached on very few provisions only. Even proposals that did not seem to be candidates for major controversy, such as the draft provisions on the protection of computer programs and databases (which were similar to those already adopted as part of the TRIPS Agreement two years before) did not find consensus within a reasonably short time; controversy in these cases concerned the concrete wording of the drafts. In respect of other proposals, the nature and importance of the remaining problems became clear.

17.25 In the remaining time of eight days, it seemed impossible to achieve the adoption of even one treaty if discussions were to continue in the formal framework of Main Committee I. Accordingly, delegations decided to continue discussions, after the weekend of 13 and 14 December when group coordination and bilateral contacts took place, in an informal framework with all governmental delegations and the EC.[45] This decision proved to be the key for the final success of the Conference: between 15 and 19 December only, most provisions of the Copyright and the Neighbouring Rights Treaties were informally agreed upon and could then be formally adopted by consensus without any further discussion in Main Committee I on 19 and 20 December.[46] Only a few votes had to be taken in Main Committee I: votes on rental rights and the abolition of non-voluntary licences for broadcasting in the Copyright Treaty, on national treatment in the Neighbouring Rights Treaty, and on the agreed statements regarding the reproduction right in both treaties. The Draft Administrative and Final Clauses of both treaties were formally discussed in Main Committee II, and also informally on 17 and 18 December. The Drafting Committee revised all adopted provisions on 19 and 20 December.

17.26 During the last evening of the Conference on the agreed statements in context with the reproduction right in both treaties, a long procedural debate threatened the success so far obtained: if these last remaining problems were not resolved and the treaties not adopted before midnight, the possibility that no treaty would be adopted seemed realistic, although agreement had been reached on nearly all provisions. The only 'rescue' in such a situation, namely the decision to prolong the Diplomatic Conference, was not self-evident.[47] In the case of a failure, the

---

[45] On the particularity of informal discussions, see para 17.27 below.

[46] The third envisaged treaty dealing with the *sui generis* protection of databases was not even discussed at all; for the reasons, see paras 17.155–17.157 below.

[47] For the reasons, see S von Lewinski, 'Negotiation Methods and Role of Lobby Groups' in ALAI (ed), *Exploring the Sources of Copyright, ALAI Congress, 18–21 September 2005, Paris* (2007) 154, 157.

chances of regaining the momentum[48] for another attempt in the following year would have been fairly small, not least since the movement of users opposing copyright protection had already emerged and started to grow.[49] Accordingly, the pressure was high to adopt the remaining provisions and the treaties as such before midnight. Finally, after participants had lived through what might be called a thriller,[50] it was only some moments before midnight when the Agreed Statements on the reproduction right were adopted in Main Committee I, and the Treaties on Copyright and Neighbouring Rights, the related Agreed Statements, as well as the Resolution and the Recommendation concerning further work on audiovisual performances and databases, were adopted in Plenary.[51]

(5) Characteristics of the negotiations

This Diplomatic Conference was distinguished from former WIPO diplomatic conferences by a number of features that may have been inspired by negotiations in the GATT framework. In particular, WIPO negotiations traditionally have been very transparent, allowing the participation of all Member delegations, observer states, intergovernmental and non-governmental organizations. In contrast, the GATT framework did not allow intergovernmental and non-governmental organizations to attend the negotiations at governmental level, which mostly took place informally and in different groups.[52] Similarly, transparency at the 1996 WIPO Conference had to be reduced in particular by passing over to informal discussions, in order to obtain a realistic chance to adopt the treaties.[53] The exclusion of intergovernmental and non-governmental organizations, the lack of any official records, and the choice of a relatively small room where not even all members of all governmental delegations would have found a space, enabled compromises within a short time. Despite this lack of transparency, intergovernmental and non-governmental organizations had many possibilities to express their views and to be informed about the progress of deliberations.[54]

17.27

Another feature possibly inspired by the GATT practices was the coordination of positions in a number of formal and informal groups, such as in the ad hoc group of Central and Eastern European countries, joined by the Baltic countries.[55]

17.28

---

48 On this necessary element in international negotiations, see ibid at 156.
49 See on that movement paras 25.27–25.32 below.
50 That last night can indeed be appropriately described as a 'crazy' night only, as done by Ficsor (n 3 above) in the title of n 2.10; on the discussions in that night, see there, 2.11.
51 On such further work, see paras 18.08 ff and paras 22.01–22.04 below.
52 Little has changed in the WTO in this respect, see on the GATT/WTO practices von Lewinski (n 47 above) 158, 164–5.
53 See para 17.25 above.
54 Reinbothe/von Lewinski (n 15 above) 15.
55 On the different groups at the 1996 Conference, see paras 17.10–17.11 above.

This procedure speeded up the pace of discussions and thereby contributed to the success of the Conference. Another new phenomenon, as compared to earlier WIPO Diplomatic Conferences, but similar to experiences made during the GATT Uruguay Round, was the high diversity of Member States' interests and, consequently, of coalitions which varied according to the relevant issues in question. In the past, after decolonization, negotiations were dominated by 'a rather sterile North–South confrontation'.[56] In 1996, however, conflicts of interest also appeared among industrialized countries, or between individual industrialized and developing countries on the one hand and other industrialized countries on the other, depending on the particular provision at stake (as in the case of the exhaustion of the distribution right[57]). Also, the different groups of developing countries did not always take the same positions. This diversification of interests and coalitions regarding different issues rendered the negotiations particularly complex.

C. Principles of protection under the WCT and the WPPT as compared to the preceding international law

17.29 The principles of protection under the Berne and Rome Conventions are, though differently shaped, the principles of national treatment, minimum rights, and 'no formalities'. These three principles have been taken over from the Berne Convention to the WCT without any modification, and from the Rome Convention to the WPPT with the specification of a limited scope of national treatment[58] and the conversion of the principle of 'limited formalities'[59] into an unlimited scope of the principle of 'no formalities'. Yet, a fourth principle which is laid down in the TRIPS Agreement, the most-favoured-nation clause, has not been taken over into the WIPO treaties because it is an element inherent to trade treaties, but alien to pure intellectual property treaties.

(1) WCT

17.30 The WCT is a special agreement in the meaning of Article 20 of the Berne Convention, so that any restriction of the principles of the Berne Convention would not have been permitted; indeed, such restriction was not even discussed in substance.[60] In addition, such restriction would have been contradictory to the

---

[56] J Reinbothe and A Howard, 'The State of Play in the Negotiations on TRIPS (GATT/Uruguay Round)' (1991) 5 EIPR 157.

[57] paras 17.62–17.64, in particular 17.63 below.

[58] Even as compared to the TRIPS Agreement (para 10.34 above), it is more clearly limited.

[59] paras 6.32–6.33 above.

[60] Only the way in which the WCT should refer to the Berne principles was discussed, see Reinbothe/von Lewinski (n 15 above) Art 3 WCT nn 8 ff. On the nature as a special agreement within

inclusion of the compliance clause.[61] Article 3 of the WCT therefore simply clarifies[62] that the three Berne principles apply by analogy ('*mutatis mutandis*') to the WCT; the Agreed Statement concerning Article 3 of the WCT clarifies how to apply the Berne provisions by analogy.[63] Article 3 of the WCT refers not only to the entire Article 5 of the Berne Convention, which incorporates the principles and the definition of 'country of origin', but also to its Articles 2 and 2bis on works protected (clarifying that they are subject matter of the WCT), as well as to its Articles 3 and 4 on the criteria of eligibility. In the latter context, a new definition of 'published works' (Art 3(3) of the Berne Convention) was considered regarding works published exclusively online, but no text was adopted.[64]

Article 3 of the WCT also refers to two of the Berne exceptions to national treatment (Articles 6 and 2(7) phrase 2 of the Berne Convention); the other exceptions under the Berne Convention are covered by the compliance clause of Article 1(4) of the WCT, so that all exceptions to national treatment under the Berne Convention are applicable in the context of the WCT.[65] **17.31**

As an illustration for the way in which national treatment operates in the framework of the WCT, the hypothetical case examined in the Berne context[66] is presented as follows: Author A, a national of Laos (not a Party to the WCT) published a novel both on 8 March 2004 in Laos and on 28 March 2004 in Mexico (a Party to the WCT). The novel is then exploited without the author's consent in the USA (a Party to the WCT). Can the author claim protection for his novel in the USA on the basis of national treatment under the WCT? **17.32**

Indeed, apart from the starting point which is Article 3 WCT in combination with Article 5(1) of the Berne Convention, the solution corresponds to that in the Berne context.[67] Article 3 of the WCT in combination with Articles 3 and 4 **17.33**

---

the meaning of Art 20 of the Berne Convention, see Art 1(1) of the WCT and Reinbothe/von Lewinski (n 15 above) Art 1 WCT nn 8–11.

[61] The compliance clause in Art 1(4) of the WCT obliges Parties to comply with Arts 1–21 and the Appendix of the Berne Convention; para 17.161 below.

[62] Given the compliance clause, Art 3 of the WCT may even be considered superfluous; only the Agreed Statement may be useful, although it does not refer to all relevant articles: Ficsor (n 3 above), in particular C3.01, 05, 07.

[63] For an illustration of their application, see paras 17.32–17.33 below; Ficsor (n 3 above) C3.03. Phr 2 of the Agreed Statement on the term 'national' in respect of an intergovernmental organization takes account of the EC which is a Party to the WCT but has no proper nationality, so that nationality refers to that of the Member States. On the Berne principles, see paras 5.01 ff above.

[64] Hereon, see paras 17.151–17.152 below.

[65] Reinbothe/von Lewinski (n 15 above) Art 3 WCT nn 28, 29. On all exceptions to national treatment under the Berne Convention, see paras 5.40–5.53 above.

[66] para 5.09 above.

[67] paras 5.10 ff above.

of the Berne Convention (*mutatis mutandis*) apply in respect of the criteria of eligibility. Accordingly, A is eligible—although he is neither a national nor a resident of a WCT country—since he has simultaneously published[68] his work in a non-WCT (Laos) and a WCT country (Mexico).[69] His work is protected on the basis of Article 3 of the WCT in combination with Article 2 of the Berne Convention (*mutatis mutandis*). In parallel to the above solution in the Berne context, Mexico is the country of origin[70] and A can claim protection in the USA, a Party to the WCT and not the country of origin.

(2) WPPT

17.34   The WPPT does not entirely follow the principles of protection as laid down in the earlier treaties, namely the Rome Convention and the TRIPS Agreement. Unlike the WCT, the WPPT therefore does not apply the principles by analogy but specifies or modifies them in its Articles 4 (national treatment), 3 (general clause covering minimum rights), and 20 (no formalities). Only the Rome criteria of eligibility are applied by analogy.[71]

(a) Criteria of eligibility

17.35   **(i) General**   For the application of the principles of protection, the WPPT takes over the criteria of eligibility from the Rome Convention.[72] For this purpose, it uses the same legislative technique as the TRIPS Agreement: under Articles 3(1) and 4(1) of the WPPT, minimum rights and national treatment have to be granted to 'nationals' of other Contracting Parties, which are then defined in Article 3(2) of the WPPT by reference to the criteria of eligibility under the Rome Convention. The use of the term 'nationals' was necessary in the TRIPS Agreement, where references to different intellectual property treaties were required.[73] In the WPPT, however, the use of the words 'performers and phonogram producers' and a direct reference to the Rome Convention would have sufficed; the additional term 'nationals' is superfluous and has no proper function in the context of the WPPT.[74] In substance, there is no difference between both techniques of reference: performers and producers of phonograms

---

[68] In the meaning of Art 3(4) of the Berne Convention (*mutatis mutandis*).

[69] Art 3(1)(b) ibid (*mutatis mutandis*).

[70] Country of first publication under Art 3 of the WCT in combination with Art 5(4)(b) of the Berne Convention (*mutatis mutandis*).

[71] Art 3(2) of the WPPT and paras 17.35–17.40 below.

[72] For the Rome criteria in more detail than under paras 17.35–17.40 below, see paras 6.01–6.12 above.

[73] Art 1(3) phr 2 of the TRIPS Agreement, para 10.25 above.

[74] S Ricketson and J Ginsburg, *International Copyright and Neighbouring Rights: The Berne Convention and Beyond* (2006) 19.48, seem to have misunderstood the system under Art 3 of the WPPT, where they state that both nationality (in the ordinary meaning of the term) and the criteria of the Rome Convention must be fulfilled.

are covered by the WPPT, if they fulfil the criteria of eligibility under Articles 4 and 5 of the Rome Convention, respectively, were all the Contracting Parties to the WPPT Contracting States to the Rome Convention.

(ii) Performer Accordingly, a performer is protected in a Contracting Party of **17.36** the WPPT if her performance fulfils one of the following criteria.[75] First, if it takes place in another Contracting Party of the WPPT.[76] For example, where a violinist of any nationality (even from a non-Contracting Party) gives a recital in France (a Contracting Party) and a broadcast or recording thereof is then exploited in Belgium (also a Contracting Party), the violinist is protected in Belgium but not in France where the performance took place (indeed, the performer in this case would be protected in any other Contracting Party except France, where domestic law only applies).[77]

Secondly, she is protected if the performance has been recorded on a phonogram **17.37** which itself is protected under the WPPT[78] because (a) its producer is a national of another Contracting Party, or (b) the first fixation of sounds took place in another Contracting Party, or (c) the phonogram was first published in another Contracting Party. Where, in the above example, the performer claims protection in France and the performance in France is recorded by a producer who is a national of Belgium, the performer is protected in France.[79] The same applies if the recording is first published in Belgium,[80] or simultaneously in Canada (not a Contracting Party to the WPPT) and Belgium.[81] In the two preceding cases (performance in France, Belgian nationality of producer or first publication in Belgium), the performer may claim protection not only in France, but also in all other Contracting Parties except Belgium.[82] If the performance takes place in

---

[75] On these criteria of the Rome Convention applied here *mutatis mutandis*, see paras 6.02–6.07 above.

[76] Art 3(2) phr 1 of the WPPT in combination with Art 4(a) of the Rome Convention (*mutatis mutandis*).

[77] Art 3(2) phr 1 of the WPPT in combination with Article 4(a) of the Rome Convention (*mutatis mutandis*). See the corresponding example in the Rome context above, para 6.03. France is assumed to become a Contracting Party soon after the publication of this book.

[78] Art 3(2) phr 1 of the WPPT in combination with Art 4(b) of the Rome Convention (*mutatis mutandis*).

[79] Art 4(b) in connection with 5(1)(a) of the Rome Convention (*mutatis mutandis*).

[80] Art 4(b) in connection with 5(1)(c) of the Rome Convention (*mutatis mutandis*). See, however, that a Contracting Party may choose not to apply the criterion of publication, Art 3(3) of the WPPT in connection with Arts 5(3), 17 of the Rome Convention (*mutatis mutandis*); para 17.40 below.

[81] 'Simultaneous publication' equals 'first publication' and is defined through a thirty-day term, as in Art 3(4) of the Berne Convention, see Art 5(2) of the Rome Convention (here applying *mutatis mutandis*).

[82] She would be able to rely both on Art 4(a) and on Arts 4(b) in connection with 5(1)(a) or (c) of the Rome Convention (*mutatis mutandis*). Belgium does not qualify because it is the country of nationality/first publication rather than 'another' Contracting Party, Art 5(1)(a), (c) of the Rome Convention (*mutatis mutandis*).

Canada but the producer is Belgian or first publishes the recording in Belgium, the performer is protected in all Contracting Parties except in Belgium.[83]

17.38   In the above example, the criterion of fixation in another Contracting Party[84] is not fulfilled if the performer claims protection in France, because France is the country of fixation rather than 'another' Contracting Party. [85] This criterion only allows her to claim protection in a Contracting Party other than France.[86]

17.39   Thirdly, the reference in Article 3(2) of the WPPT does not exclude Article 4(c) of the Rome Convention, namely the criterion that a performance, not fixed on a phonogram, is carried by a broadcast protected under Article 6 of the Rome Convention. It is doubtful whether this criterion applies in the context of the WPPT, which itself does not protect broadcasts. Good arguments seem possible both in favour and against applying Article 4(c) of the Rome Convention *mutatis mutandis*.[87]

17.40   (iii) **Phonogram producer**   A phonogram producer is protected under any of the above-mentioned conditions (a) to (c) (nationality of producer, first fixation or publication in another Contracting Party).[88] Like the Rome Convention, however, the WPPT allows Contracting Parties not to apply either the criterion of first publication or of first fixation of the phonogram[89] or, under the conditions of Article 17 of the Rome Convention, to apply only the criterion of fixation.[90]

---

[83] See for the corresponding examples for the Rome context paras 6.04–6.06 above.

[84] Art 3(2) phr 1 of the WPPT in connection with Art 5(1)(b) of the Rome Convention (*mutatis mutandis*).

[85] Regularly, the fixation is made at the place of the performance (here, France); the possibility to fix the performance from a live broadcast or other communication will practically be without major importance to date, due to deficiencies in quality. If the fixation is, however, done in such a way in another Contracting Party than France, the performer then can claim protection in France.

[86] A Contracting Party may, however, choose not to apply the criterion of fixation, Art 3(3) of the WPPT and Art 5(3) of the Rome Convention (*mutatis mutandis*); para 17.40 below. For the concluding summary on how the example works in this case (Arts 4(b)/5 of the Rome Convention (*mutatis mutandis*)) in the corresponding Rome context, applicable also here, see para 6.06 above.

[87] Against: Ficsor (n 3 above) PP3.05; in favour: Reinbothe/von Lewinski (n 15 above) Art 3 WPPT n 6; most other commentators do not seem to address the problem.

[88] Art 3(2) phr 1 of the WPPT in connection with Art 5(1)(a) to (c) of the Rome Convention (*mutatis mutandis*); see also its Art 5(2) on simultaneous publication.

[89] Art 3(3) of the WPPT in connection with Art 5(3) of the Rome Convention (*mutatis mutandis*).

[90] Art 3(3) of the WPPT in connection with Art 17 of the Rome Convention for the purposes of Art 5 of the Rome Convention (*mutatis mutandis*). Art 3(3) of the WPPT also lays down how the relevant declarations must be made in the framework of the WPPT. On these possibilities under the Rome Convention, see paras 6.10–6.11 above; on the details of the application of Art 3(3) of the WPPT, see Reinbothe/von Lewinski (n 15 above) Art 3 WPPT nn 9–13.

(iv) Definitions in the context of eligibility   The relevant definitions of the   **17.41**
Rome Convention ('performer', 'producer of a phonogram', 'phonogram', 'publication') have not been taken over in respect of the criteria of eligibility but are
determined exclusively by Article 2 of the WPPT, which also includes the additional definition of 'fixation'.[91] Moreover, an Agreed Statement specifies that 'fixation' in this context means the finalization of the master tape only, since this
finalized fixation is the basis of exploitation and therefore important enough to
be an appropriate criterion of eligibility.[92]

As in the context of copyright, the question arose whether an exclusively online   **17.42**
'publication' would constitute a publication for the purpose of, in particular, the
criteria of eligibility. As in this context, online 'publication' is not covered by
'publication' under the WPPT.[93]

(b) National treatment

(i) Background   Under the Rome Convention, the scope of national treatment   **17.43**
is controversial.[94] Under the TRIPS Agreement, it is explicitly limited to the
minimum rights provided therein.[95] Article 4(1) of the WPPT is even more
explicit than the TRIPS Agreement by restricting the scope of national treatment
to the 'exclusive' rights specifically granted in the WPPT and the only remuneration right contained therein (ie the right to remuneration for secondary uses
under Article 15 of the WPPT).

Article 4 of the WPPT was one of the few Articles that required a vote because   **17.44**
delegations did not reach consensus. The underlying dispute reflected the different economic interests of the respective parties. Basically, the USA opted in favour
of an unrestricted scope of national treatment, except where a reservation regarding the remuneration right under Article 15 of the WPPT was made. This position corresponded to the interest of the USA as a major music exporter. To the
contrary, most other countries in the world that import more musical recordings
than they export had an interest in restricting the scope of national treatment as
far as possible. The EC and its Member States, Canada, and Switzerland submitted different proposals in order to achieve this aim, in particular with a view to

---

[91] Art 3(2) phr 2 of the WPPT.

[92] Agreed Statement concerning Art 3(2) of the WPPT. For more background, see Reinbothe/
von Lewinski (n 15 above) Art 3 WPPT n 14.

[93] Art 2(e) of the WPPT and related Agreed Statement; Reinbothe/von Lewinski (n 15 above)
Art 2 WPPT nn 17, 48, and 52, and para 17.139 below; for the problem of 'online publication' also
in the copyright context paras 17.151–17.152 below.

[94] See paras 6.27, 7.34–7.40 above

[95] Art 3(1) phr 2 of the TRIPS Agreement; see also para 10.34 above.

excluding remuneration rights for private copying from national treatment.[96] The Swiss proposal finally appeared to best achieve this aim. After numerous, unsuccessful attempts to bridge the gap between the Swiss proposal and the US position, the Swiss proposal was adopted by vote and became, subject to technical adaptation, Article 4 of the WPPT.[97]

17.45 **(ii) Scope of national treatment** Accordingly, national treatment does not extend beyond the exclusive rights explicitly provided under the WPPT (ie the performers' moral rights[98] and rights in unfixed performances,[99] as well as the exclusive rights of reproduction, distribution, rental, and making available of both performers and phonogram producers).[100] The economic rights are covered only in the form of exclusive rights rather than remuneration rights. For example, while the exclusive reproduction right is covered, any remuneration right for private reproduction is not.[101] In addition, the right to equitable remuneration under Article 15 of the WPPT on secondary uses of broadcasting and communication to the public is explicitly covered by national treatment. It had to be mentioned explicitly since, as a remuneration right rather than an exclusive right, it would otherwise not have been covered by the restricted national treatment under Article 4 of the WPPT.

17.46 A Contracting Party to the WPPT is thus not required to grant national treatment in respect of any right beyond those just mentioned, even if it provides such right under national law. With regard to the covered rights, national treatment extends to provisions on duration, remedies, and enforcement under the

---

[96] See the proposals in WIPO Docs CRNR/DC/32 (EC and Member States), CRNR/DC/44 (Canada), CRNR/DC/59 (EC and Member States following up on Canada's proposal) and the orally tabled Swiss proposal, Summary Minutes of Main Committee I, in WIPO (ed), *Records of the Diplomatic Conference on Certain Copyright and Neighbouring Rights Questions* (1996) 771, 772 (para 950).

[97] The vote showed a clear divide: eighty-eight votes were in favour of the Swiss proposal, two against (the USA and Thailand), and four abstained; on the details of the different proposals leading to the vote, see Reinbothe/von Lewinski (n 15 above) Art 4 WPPT nn 7–8; Ficsor (n 3 above) PP 4.02–4.06. The USA now pursues its aim bilaterally, see para 12.29/n 86 above.

[98] Even if moral rights are not 'exclusive' rights (ie property rights that can be transferred or licensed), it was understood that they would fall under the rights explicitly provided to be covered by national treatment, Reinbothe/von Lewinski (n 15 above) Art 4 WPPT n 13; less certain seem to be Ricketson/Ginsburg (n 74 above) 19.50.

[99] Art 6 of the WPPT.

[100] Arts 7–11 and 9–13 ibid.

[101] National laws, of the Continental European system in particular, in many cases beyond private reproduction compensate the loss of an exclusive right on the basis of a statutory limitation by granting a statutory remuneration right, see paras 3.59–3.61 above. Ficsor (n 3 above) PP 4.14 seems to be of a different opinion, though on the basis of somewhat vague and unclear arguments.

WPPT, including those on technological measures and rights management information.[102]

(iii) Exceptions to national treatment The only exception to national treat- **17.47** ment relates to the remuneration right for secondary uses under Article 15 of the WPPT.[103] To the extent that a Contracting Party makes a reservation permitted under Article 15(3) of the WPPT, the other Contracting Parties may apply material reciprocity instead of national treatment. Where, for example, a Contracting Party chooses to apply the remuneration right only to broadcasting but not to communication to the public, other Contracting Parties which provide a remuneration right for both kinds of uses are obliged to grant national treatment towards the first Party only in respect of broadcasting. The WPPT therefore corresponds to the Rome Convention as regards exceptions to national treatment.[104]

(c) Minimum rights

Like the Rome Convention, the WPPT provides for minimum rights. Admittedly, **17.48** its text does not explicitly state that Contracting Parties can provide for greater protection. In particular, Article 3(1) of the WPPT simply obliges Contracting Parties to grant the protection provided under the WPPT, and its Article 4(1) refers to 'the . . . rights specifically granted in this Treaty', without specifying that these are a minimum.[105] Yet, negotiating parties understood the protection as minimum protection, as confirmed by several clarifying Agreed Statements.[106]

The individual minimum rights are specified in Articles 5–15 of the WPPT. **17.49** Notably, for the first time in a major multilateral treaty, the economic minimum rights[107] are laid down for performers as exclusive rights rather than only the 'possibility of preventing' certain acts.[108] Yet, all rights except the live broadcasting right apply only to audio rather then also audiovisual performances.[109]

---

[102] Arts 18, 19, and 23(2) of the WPPT; on the scope of national treatment, see also Reinbothe/von Lewinski (n 15 above) Art 4 WPPT nn 12, 13.

[103] Art 4(2) of the WPPT.

[104] Art 16(1)(a) (iv) of the Rome Convention. The other case of material reciprocity under the Rome Convention relates to the protection of broadcasting organizations which are not covered by the WPPT; see for the Rome Convention paras 6.28–6.31.above. The TRIPS Agreement does not even provide for a remuneration right for secondary uses, so that national treatment also does not apply (Art 3(1) phr 2) and, consequently, an exception to national treatment is unnecessary. Yet, the same result is reached as under the Rome Convention and the WPPT.

[105] See the similar words by which Art 5(1) of the Berne Convention refers to minimum rights: '. . . the rights specially granted by this Convention'.

[106] Agreed Statement concerning Art 1(2) para 2, and both Agreed Statements concerning Art 15 of the WPPT.

[107] Except for the remuneration right under Art 15 of the WPPT.

[108] On the 'possibility of preventing', see paras 6.35–6.36 above; Reinbothe/von Lewinski (n 15 above) Art 6 WPPT n 3.

[109] For the background, see paras 18.01–18.07 below.

(d) No formalities

17.50 Finally, Article 20 of the WPPT introduces for the first time in a multilateral treaty dealing with neighbouring rights the unrestricted principle of 'no formalities' upon the model of the Berne Convention. Its interpretation may in principle follow that of the Berne provision.[110] It was adopted without major discussion. It simply states that the enjoyment and exercise of the rights under the WPPT shall not be subject to any formality. This is a step forward from Article 11 of the Rome Convention which allows specified formalities, and from the TRIPS Agreement which follows the Rome Convention in this respect.[111] Accordingly, formalities such as registration, deposit, or filing of phonograms, payment of fees, or use of the notice consisting of the symbol (P) cannot be required as conditions of protection. They may be required only as proof, facilitation to exercise rights, or for other purposes.[112]

D. Substantive standards of protection

(1) Parallel standards in both treaties

17.51 The following standards were negotiated in parallel for both treaties: the exclusive rights of reproduction, distribution, rental, and making available; the related limitations and exceptions; and obligations concerning technical protection measures and rights management information. Therefore, they are discussed together here.

(a) Reproduction right

17.52 (i) **Background** The exclusive reproduction right was one of the most controversial issues of the Diplomatic Conference: while this right was already contained in the earlier Conventions, digital technology raised new questions regarding the scope of the right.[113] In particular, delegations had different views on whether technical or automatic acts of reproduction were or should be covered by the reproduction right, and if so, to what extent limitations and exceptions should apply to them. Such acts of reproduction occur, for example, when using a computer program or during internet transmissions when reproductions that only last for microseconds are automatically made on cache or similar

---

[110] Art 5(2) phr 1 half-sentence 1 of the Berne Convention, see paras 5.55 ff above.

[111] See paras 6.32–6.33 above for the Rome Convention and para 10.39 for the TRIPS Agreement, and its Art 14(6).

[112] Reinbothe/von Lewinski (n 15 above) Art 20 WPPT nn 6, 7.

[113] See a very detailed presentation of earliest deliberations in WIPO on electronic reproduction up to the Diplomatic Conference 1996 in Ficsor (n 3 above) 3.26–3.122.

servers. Article 7 of the Basic Proposal for the Copyright Treaty was to clarify that Article 9(1) of the Berne Convention on the reproduction right covered not only direct and permanent, but also indirect and temporary reproductions, and that certain temporary acts of reproduction could be exempted under particular conditions.

This proposal provoked extremely strong reactions by lobbyists, in particular **17.53** criticism by representatives of the telecommunication industry, internet service providers, and users in the area of education and research. They basically objected to any text on the inclusion of temporary reproductions or called for a mandatory exception of such reproductions from protection. The telecommunication and provider industries were mainly concerned that they would become liable for acts of reproduction which occurred during the transmission over digital networks, where such transmissions between individuals were illegal.[114]

In contrast, governments that did not follow this position argued in particular **17.54** that Article 20 of the Berne Convention had to be complied with[115] and that distinction needed to be made between the scope of a right and its limitation on the one hand and questions of liability on the other. Their general approach was to refer the relevant industries to a solution in the framework of liability provisions, which, however, were not on the agenda at this Diplomatic Conference. They also pointed to the high risks for right owners through the possibilities of temporary reproduction. In respect of limitations, they considered unrealistic any agreement among more than 120 states about detailed, uniform, and mandatory limitations and exceptions.[116]

After numerous attempts to draft a text that would satisfy all Parties, no agree- **17.55** ment on any specific text on temporary reproduction as part of the Articles was achieved; only Agreed Statements in this respect were adopted, and this in part only upon a vote.[117]

---

[114] For their arguments in detail, see S von Lewinski and J Gaster, 'Die Diplomatische Konferenz der WIPO 1996 zum Urheberrecht und zu verwandten Schutzrechten' (1997) Zeitschrift für Urheber- und Medienrecht 607, 624–5; see also T Vinje, 'All's not Quiet on the Berne Front' (1996) EIPR 585, 588.

[115] On this argument, see para 17.57 below.

[116] For a more detailed presentation of the arguments, see von Lewinski/Gaster (n 114 above) 615–16.

[117] The fact that phr 2 of the Agreed Statement was adopted by majority does not 'reduce its binding force' (as suggested by A Françon, 'The Diplomatic Conference on Certain Copyright and Neighbouring Rights Questions' (1997) RIDA 2, 12); a text is adopted with the same binding force, whether on the basis of a vote by majority or by consensus. On the debates and votes at the Diplomatic Conference, see Reinbothe/von Lewinski (n 15 above) Annex to Art 1(4) WCT nn 9–13; Ficsor (n 3 above) 3.111–3.127.

17.56 (ii) **Contents of the right** Accordingly, the Articles of the WCT contain the reproduction right only on the basis of the compliance clause[118] which refers to Article 9 of the Berne Convention (reproduction right). Articles 7 and 11 of the WPPT, for lack of a compliance clause, contain the right of reproduction. They further specify it as 'direct or indirect' reproduction, thereby following the model of Article 10 of the Rome Convention,[119] and as reproduction 'in any manner or form', thereby following the model of Article 9(1) of the Berne Convention.[120] The reproduction right of performers is not subject to qualifications as known from the Rome Convention, such as fixation without consent.[121] Yet, like all other minimum rights of performers except the live broadcasting right, it is limited to performances fixed in phonograms or audio rather than audiovisual performances.[122] The reproduction right under the WPPT will have to be understood as also covering reproductions in modified form, following the understanding of delegates to the Diplomatic Conference 1996 as expressed in context with the proposed modification right.[123]

17.57 The parallel Agreed Statements concerning Article 1(4) of the WCT[124] and Articles 7 and 11 of the WPPT in their first phrases simply state in general wording that the reproduction right and its exceptions fully apply in the digital environment, in particular to the use in digital form. For the WCT, these words must be interpreted against the background of its nature as a special agreement in the meaning of Article 20 of the Berne Convention, which prohibits a restrictive interpretation.[125] Since Article 9(1) of the Berne Convention with its words 'reproduction . . . in any manner or form' is broad enough also to cover acts of reproduction of a very short duration, the WCT must not be interpreted as providing less protection.[126] Accordingly, it covers all acts of reproduction even where they are transient, technical, or incidental and made for the purposes of

---

[118] Art 1(4) of the WCT.

[119] On this specification, see para 6.61 above; Ficsor (n 3 above) PP7.03 und C1.49 considers this qualification as redundant in combination with 'in any manner or form'.

[120] On this specification, see paras 5.117–5.118 above.

[121] On Art 7(1)(c) of the Rome Convention, see paras 6.40–6.41 above; TRIPS did not already follow these restrictions.

[122] For the background, see paras 18.01–18.07 below.

[123] paras 17.153–17.154 below; Ricketson/Ginsburg (note 74 above) 19.56; Reinbothe/von Lewinski (n 15 above) ch 3 n 18.

[124] Since Art 1(4) of the WCT refers to Art 9(1) of the Berne Convention on the reproduction right, it is the appropriate Article as a reference point of this Agreed Statement.

[125] On Art 20 of the Berne Convention, see paras 5.250–5.251 above.

[126] Nevertheless, doubts could be raised whether extremely short-time reproductions are sufficiently stable so as to be considered as a form of fixation from which the fixed object can be perceived, reproduced, or otherwise communicated; on this condition, see Reinbothe/von Lewinski (n 15 above) Annex to Art 1(4) WCT n 14; on temporary reproduction, see Ricketson/Ginsburg (n 74 above) 19.56.

caching, browsing, or storing in electronic memories.[127] The necessary balance with the interests of users is left to the three-step test[128] which leaves sufficient flexibility for the provision of limitations and exceptions under national law.

In their second phrases, the Agreed Statements clarify that the storage in digital **17.58** form in an electronic medium constitutes a reproduction. The storage of works in a computer, if done 'in a form sufficiently stable to permit its communication to an individual', was already unanimously considered as a reproduction by a WIPO Committee of Experts in 1982.[129] Accordingly, the second phrases of the Agreed Statements reflect a common, traditional view.[130]

(b) Distribution right

(i) General remarks and contents of right While the Berne Convention, fol- **17.59** lowed by the TRIPS Agreement, provides for a distribution right only in the cine-matographic area,[131] and the Rome and Geneva Conventions do not provide any distribution right,[132] the WCT and the WPPT for the first time provide a general, exclusive distribution right at the multilateral level.[133] Its scope is restricted to the transfer of ownership (such as sale) and thereby deviates from a number of national laws under which the distribution right also covers forms of possession (such as rental and lending). Yet, the WCT and the WPPT provide a rental right separately from the distribution right.

Distribution is described as 'making available to the public . . . through sale or **17.60** other transfer of ownership' and covers, in particular, the putting of the object on the market for sale, donation, and barter. 'Distribution' refers only to the original and copies of works or fixed performances/phonograms (ie tangible objects such as books, CDs, and DVDs).[134] Thereby, the right is distinguished from the 'right of making available' which has been introduced in order to cover the diffusion of works in intangible form over the internet and similar networks.[135]

---

127 On temporary reproduction, see Ficsor (n 3 above) C1.50–C1.56.

128 Art 1(4) of the WCT in connection with Art 9(2) of the Berne Convention and Art 10 of the WCT, as well as Art 16 of the WPPT.

129 Second Committee of Governmental Experts on Copyright Problems Arising from the Use of Computers for Access to or the Creation of Works, (1982) Copyright 239, 245–6.

130 Reinbothe/von Lewinski (n 15 above) Annex to Art 1(4) WCT n 17; Ficsor (n 3 above) C1.51.

131 Arts 14 and 14[bis] of the Berne Convention in respect of cinematographic works and works adapted for cinematographic purposes; it has been argued that the Berne Convention also implicitly contains a general distribution right (para 5.131 above; Ficsor (n 3 above) 4.09 and 4.41); this view is not adopted here. For TRIPS, see its Art 9(1) referring to the Berne provisions.

132 The protection against distribution under Art 2 of the Geneva Phonograms Convention does not need to be implemented as an exclusive right, see para 4.66 above.

133 Art 6 of the WCT and Arts 8 and 12 of the WPPT, with Agreed Statements.

134 Confirmed by the relevant Agreed Statement.

135 Art 8 of the WCT and Arts 10 and 14 of the WPPT; on these, see paras 17.72 ff below.

17.61 (ii) **Implementation into national law**   The treaties do not prescribe any concrete way in which the distribution right must be implemented; they only require that the authors, performers, and phonogram producers can authorize or prohibit the described acts of distribution. Accordingly, national law can take over the wording of the treaties, or implement the right by the so-called *droit de destination*, which has been developed in France by jurisprudence on the basis of the reproduction right of authors.[136] It may also make the narrow distribution right of the WCT and WPPT a part of a broad distribution right, which in addition includes transfer of possession such as rental. In this case, the exhaustion of the distribution right must spare the rental right in order to comply with the exclusive rental right under both treaties. Some flexibility is also left in respect of the interpretation of the term 'public' which has not been defined, although the treaties would not allow an abusively narrow interpretation of 'public'.[137]

17.62 (iii) **Exhaustion of the distribution right**   At the Diplomatic Conference, the main controversy in the context of the distribution right related to the conditions of its exhaustion. Models for exhaustion chosen by legislators are in general (1) national exhaustion (ie exhaustion of the distribution right only if the object was distributed for the first time with the consent of the right holder within the national territory in question)—this choice corresponds in its effects to an exclusive importation right and prevents parallel imports; (2) regional exhaustion (ie exhaustion corresponding to the national exhaustion, but applying to an entire region instead of a national territory, as in case of the European Community);[138] and (3) international exhaustion (ie exhaustion of the distribution right upon the first act of distribution with the consent of the right holder anywhere in the world, so that parallel imports cannot be prohibited).

17.63 An importation right or, at least, the prohibition of international exhaustion, had been strongly favoured by some, in particular by the USA, on the grounds that such a strong right would promote (rather than impair) trade and allow the shaping of markets by territorial licensing. Other countries, in particular developing countries, Australia, Canada, and New Zealand opposed an importation right and the prohibition of international exhaustion, and favoured the possibility of parallel imports in order to promote free trade and consumer protection.[139]

---

[136] See thereon paras 3.56, 5.132 and n 243 above.
[137] Reinbothe/von Lewinski (n 15 above) Art 6 WCT n 10.
[138] On regional exhaustion in the EC, see Vol II chs 2, 6, and 10.
[139] On the arguments as expressed at the Diplomatic Conference, see Reinbothe/von Lewinski (n 15 above) Art 6 WCT n 6.

Since, after lengthy debates, support for an importation right or the prohibition **17.64**
of international exhaustion was not sufficient,[140] the choice of a model for exhaustion was left to the Contracting Parties; exhaustion is subject only to the following mandatory[141] conditions: exhaustion may take place only after the first sale or other transfer of ownership of the original or copy of the work, performance, or phonogram and only if such first sale has taken place with the authorization of the right holder.[142] In not specifying where this first sale must have taken place, the treaties leave the choice between national/regional and international exhaustion. If a Contracting Party requires for exhaustion in its territory or region that the first sale or other transfer of ownership takes place in this territory or region, it thereby prohibits international exhaustion.

The fact that 'nothing in this treaty' shall affect the freedom of Contracting **17.65**
Parties to choose the conditions for exhaustion also means that the exhaustion is not subject to the conditions under Articles 10 of the WCT and 16 of the WPPT. Accordingly, one cannot argue that conditions leading to international exhaustion would be detrimental to right holders' economic interests.[143]

Notably, exhaustion applies only to the original or the individual copy that has **17.66**
been put on the market. Consequently, after the first sale of a copy of a CD with the right holder's consent, only the right to distribute this particular copy is exhausted. Otherwise, the sale of the first copy of a new edition would take away the distribution right in respect of the yet unsold stock.

(c) Rental right

(i) **General principle: the TRIPS model** Two years before the adoption of the **17.67**
WCT and the WPPT, a rental right had been introduced for specified groups of beneficiaries in Articles 11 and 14(4) of the TRIPS Agreement.[144] This fact proved to be an obstacle to extending the rental right to authors of all kinds of works (rather than only of specified ones), as proposed in the Basic Proposal for the copyright treaty and supported by many delegations.[145] Finally, the views of most developing countries and other countries that did not want to go beyond

---

[140] See, however, the inclusion of an importation right in bilateral treaties concluded by the USA, and in the NAFTA, above, paras 12.10, 12.31, and 11.11; draft FTAA: para 11.31; CAN Decision 351: para 11.47.

[141] Contracting Parties can provide for additional conditions for exhaustion.

[142] Art 6(2) of the WCT and Arts 8(2) and 12(2) of the WPPT.

[143] Reinbothe/von Lewinski (n 15 above) Art 6 WCT n 14 for the WCT.

[144] See paras 10.64–10.79 above.

[145] Only works of applied art and buildings were exempted; the proposal corresponded to harmonized EC law (on the EC Rental Dir, see Vol II ch 6) and to Decision 351 of the Cartagena Agreement/Andean Pact and was therefore supported eg by the EC and also Peru, Summary Minutes of Main Committee I (n 96 above) paras 807, 841.

the TRIPS level prevailed. Also, a definition of 'rental' proposed for the WPPT was not adopted.[146] Instead, the word 'commercial' was added to characterize rental in both treaties, thereby following the TRIPS wording.

17.68 The rental right under the WCT and WPPT is modelled upon Articles 11 and 14(4) of the TRIPS Agreement in the following additional respects: the exclusion of the rental right for computer programs where they are not the essential object of the rental,[147] the impairment test in respect of cinematographic works,[148] and the grandfathering clause—even with the same date as under the TRIPS Agreement—in respect of existing systems of equitable remuneration, subject to the impairment test.[149]

17.69 (ii) **Clarifications as compared to TRIPS** A few clarifications were neverthe-less made as compared to the TRIPS Agreement. In particular, authors of works embodied in phonograms as well as performing artists are explicitly mentioned as beneficiaries of the rental right; both were much less clearly envisaged in Article 14(4) of the TRIPS Agreement.[150] At the same time, the grant of a rental right in both cases is conditioned by the phrase 'as determined in the national law of Contracting Parties', which was taken over from the TRIPS Agreement. The meaning of this phrase is not entirely clear; the ambiguity of the TRIPS Agreement may have been imported by this condition.[151] There are strong arguments in favour of the interpretation that the rental right must be granted to those authors and performers who, under national law, enjoy any rights at all in respect of phonograms.[152] Accordingly, where authors and performers enjoy a reproduction right or another right in respect of their works and performances when incorporated in a phonogram, they also would have to be granted a rental right under this condition.[153] Yet, some Contracting Parties seem to understand the provision as permitting the denial of the rental right to such authors and performers.[154]

---

[146] Art 2(f) of the relevant Basic Proposal. For the reasons, see para 17.150 below.

[147] Art 7(2)(i) of the WCT.

[148] Art 7(2)(ii) ibid.

[149] Art 7(3) ibid, Arts 9(2), 13(2) of the WPPT; on these elements in the TRIPS Agreement, see paras 10.67–10.70 and 10.79 above.

[150] Art 7(1)(iii) of the WCT and Art 9 of the WPPT; on Art 14(4) of the TRIPS Agreement and its ambiguous wording, see paras 10.72–10.77 above.

[151] Ficsor (n 3 above) C7.11, C7.12. On the different ways of interpreting TRIPS, see paras 10.72–10.77 above.

[152] Conclusion from Agreed Statement concerning Art 7 of the WCT phr 1; although there is no corresponding Agreed Statement concerning Art 9 of the WPPT regarding performers' rental rights, there are arguments in favour of the same solution, Reinbothe/von Lewinski (n 15 above) Art 9 WPPT n 13, Ficsor (n 3 above) PP9.02; Ricketson/Ginsburg (note 74 above) 19.58 have doubts.

[153] Reinbothe/von Lewinski (n 15 above) Art 7 WCT n 18, also for more arguments; similarly paras 10.72–10.77 above.

[154] Ficsor (n 3 above) C7.11 mentions 'several delegations' favouring the restrictive interpretation; see for the implementation of the WCT in eg Australia, C Creswell, 'Copyright Protection

The Agreed Statement concerning Article 7 phrase 2 of the WCT confirms the consistency of the WCT provision with the relevant TRIPS provision on the rental right of authors of works embodied in phonograms. Since the TRIPS provision is ambiguous, the Agreed Statement also may be read in two ways—so as to clarify the supposedly broad meaning of TRIPS with a view to include all kinds of authors, or as to adopt a supposedly restrictive interpretation of TRIPS for the WCT. Accordingly, different views are likely to subsist among Contracting Parties.

In addition, the WPPT has clarified that the rental right must be granted even **17.70** after an authorized distribution of the phonogram has taken place. Accordingly, countries that provide for a broad distribution right (including rental) and for its exhaustion after first sale, must exempt the rental right from the exhaustion. Already under the TRIPS Agreement and before, it has been clear that the rental right should be granted in respect of any act of rental, irrespective of any intermediate act of sale or other distribution; otherwise, the rental right would be deprived of its very value and purpose. This element, which was explicitly introduced only in the Articles of the WPPT, is simply of a clarifying nature.[155] Therefore, one cannot argue *e contrario* that the rental right under the WCT for authors (or even under the TRIPS Agreement) would have to be granted only until a broad distribution right was exhausted (namely, as a rule, until the object was sold or otherwise distributed).

A third clarification is laid down in the Agreed Statements concerning Articles 7 **17.71** of the WCT and 9 and 13 of the WPPT according to which the 'original and copies' referred to in these Articles exclusively mean tangible objects. Thereby, the application of these Articles to on-demand and similar uses is not permitted, even if the application of rental rights to such uses had been discussed at some point in time.[156]

(d) The right of making available

(i) General remarks and background   The exclusive right of 'making available' **17.72** for authors, performers, and phonogram producers is one of the centrepieces of

---

enters the Digital Age: The New WIPO Treaties on Copyright and on Performances and on Sound Recordings' (1997) Copyright Reporter 4, 13 (Creswell was the head of the Australian delegation at the 1996 Diplomatic Conference). Critical towards this interpretation: O Morgan, *International Protection of Performers' Rights* (2002) 189–90, and for the USA, where the authors of non-dramatic musical works can at least claim royalty payments under s 115(c)(3) of the Coypright Act (17 USC), see H Abrams, *The Law of Copyright* (2004, Release 10/06) § 5:179.

155 Reinbothe/von Lewinski (n 15 above) Art 9 WPPT n 16; it is not contained in the WCT or the TRIPS Agreement.

156 Reinbothe/von Lewinski (n 15 above) Art 8 WCT n 2; implementation of the on-demand right may still occur through a rental right at national level, ibid n 16.

both treaties which, for the first time in a large multilateral framework,[157] have thereby covered the offering and diffusion of works, performances, and phonograms on the internet and similar networks—a use which has turned out to be of high economic importance. From the beginning of discussions, governments expressed no doubt whatsoever about the need to cover this important use by an exclusive right; debates took place, in the framework of the Committees of Experts, mainly on the appropriate right to be applied to these uses. The application of the existing rights of broadcasting, distribution, rental, communication to the public, or even 'reproduction by transmission' was discussed, as was the introduction of a new kind of right.[158] Finally, a proposal by the EC with its Member States submitted in May 1996 was widely supported, then taken over into the Basic Proposal and, finally, adopted nearly without changes by the Diplomatic Conference. While on-demand uses are covered exclusively by the making available (rather than distribution, rental, or other) right under the WCT and WPPT, it was understood that Contracting Parties could implement this right in different ways at the national level by, for example, a right of broadcasting, distribution, or otherwise, as long as the substance from the Articles of the treaties were fully taken over.[159] This means, for instance, that a country which implements the making available right by a distribution right must exclude the exhaustion of the making available right.

17.73   (ii) **Contents of the right**   The success of the wording finally adopted may lie in the fact that it solves one of the major problems encountered with the concepts of 'communication to the public' and 'transmission to the public' when applied to on-demand transmissions. 'Communication/transmission to the public', like broadcasting and similar acts, are regularly understood as occurring simultaneously to the public in respect of a particular work, performance, or phonogram. On-demand and other internet uses, however, usually occur on an individual basis rather than simultaneously to the public. The making available right solves this problem without the need to specify or amend the term 'public' as traditionally understood in national laws. It is so defined that the covered act already starts prior to the actual transmission, namely with the offering or making available

---

[157] Beforehand, the NAFTA had already covered this right, see para 11.11 above; for bilateral treaties also including the right, paras 12.31 and 12.75 above.

[158] See for the different proposals of governments, 'Comparative table of proposals and comments received by the International Bureau', WIPO Docs of 10 January 1996, BCP/CE/VI/12 (paras 24–30) and INR/V/11 (in particular paras 38–42 and 65–8), and on governmental studies on digital technology in the USA, EC, and Japan Ficsor (n 3 above) 4.57–4.80.

[159] On this so-called 'umbrella-solution', see Reinbothe/von Lewinski (n 15 above) Art 8 WCT nn 6 and 16; Ficsor (n 3 above) C.8.06–C.8.23, referring also to different national ways of implementation.

works and phonograms.[160] This earlier act of offering works and phonograms for access does occur simultaneously to the public. The act of making available is understood also to cover the subsequent acts of individual access and transmission, if they take place.[161]

In sum, anyone who uploads a work or phonogram on a server in a way that **17.74** members of the public may access it, not only reproduces it but also makes it available in the meaning of Articles 8 of the WCT and 10 and 14 of the WPPT, and therefore at that point in time already needs the authorization of the right holders. In the framework of Peer-to-Peer networks where such uses regularly occur, authorization is mostly not sought. As a consequence, controversy has arisen regarding the appropriate means of enforcement. Also, suggestions of compulsory licences or other models have been made, though not always in compliance with international law.[162] A similar situation exists regarding platforms such as 'YouTube'.

In contrast to the distribution right, which is also characterized by the words **17.75** 'making available', the making available right refers only to works, performances, and phonograms in virtual rather than tangible form.[163]

The making available right applies only if works and phonograms are accessible **17.76** 'from a place and at a time individually chosen' by the members of the public. This requirement describes the typical situation of on-demand or similar access and excludes any communication of predetermined programs, because they do not allow members of the public individually to access a particular work or recording at a particular time.[164] Thus, not covered by the making available right are, in particular, webcasting or simulcasting of predetermined programmes over the internet, be it as original programmes or as simultaneous and unchanged retransmissions of traditional broadcast programmes over the digital network; pay-TV or pay-radio; pay-per-use services; multi-channel services; and near-on-demand services that repeatedly and in regular intervals broadcast particular works or recordings, such as the top ten of the music charts.

---

[160] In this subsection on the making available right, 'phonograms' are further understood as including recorded performances.

[161] Reinbothe/von Lewinski (n 15 above) Art 8 WCT n 17.

[162] For a synthesis of relevant issues of Peer-to-Peer uses, see S von Lewinski, 'Certain Legal Problems Related to the Making Available of Literary and Artistic Works and Other Protected Subject Matter through Digital Networks' (2005/1) e.Copyright Bulletin of UNESCO, 1–16.

[163] paras 17.59–17.66 above on the distribution right.

[164] For more details on this requirement, see Reinbothe/von Lewinski (n 15 above) Art 8 WCT n 20.

17.77 The term 'public' has been left to be defined at national level, as elsewhere in the Treaties; however, in order to guarantee an effective protection,[165] Contracting Parties may not choose an overly narrow definition of 'public'.[166] For example, a restriction of on-demand services to subscribers does not make the use a non-public one, because anyone who wants to gain access may do so upon subscription.[167]

17.78 The right of making available has been formulated in technically neutral terms, so that not only online uses are covered, but also uses carried out by satellite or other means.

17.79 **(iii) Relation to the communication right**   Under the WCT, the right of making available has been made a part of the right of communication to the public. Under the WPPT, it has been drafted as a right separate from the communication right. The reason for this difference is that performers and phonogram producers, unlike authors, traditionally have not enjoyed an exclusive communication right and were not envisaged to do so under the WPPT for traditional uses,[168] so that the envisaged exclusive making available right could not be made part of a (non-existing) exclusive communication right.

17.80 In any case, since the Treaties allow implementation of the making available right by any suitable right, as confirmed by the 'umbrella solution',[169] its relation to the communication right under the Treaties has no bearing on the choice of its systematic classification under national law.

17.81 **(iv) Agreed Statement**   The first phrase of the Agreed Statement concerning Article 8 of the WCT[170] may be explained against the background that online service providers claimed a safeguard against their liability for illicit acts of their users. It does not, however, respond to this claim. It only clarifies that the mere provision of physical facilities, such as cables, does not constitute a communication (including the making available), so that the mere supply of such devices cannot possibly be an infringement, even if others later make infringing uses through such devices. This is self-evident and corresponds

---

[165] See for this requirement Preamble of the WCT, Recital 1.

[166] On this term, see Reinbothe/von Lewinski (n 15 above) Art 8 WCT n 21.

[167] On the similar, regulated case of satellite encryption, see Art 2(f) of the WPPT and para 17.140 below.

[168] They enjoy a remuneration right rather than an exclusive right for the traditional acts of communication to the public, Art 15 of the WPPT and paras 17.126–17.130 below.

[169] Above, para 17.72 and n 159.

[170] It reads: 'It is understood that the mere provision of physical facilities for enabling or making a communication does not in itself amount to communication within the meaning of this Treaty or the Berne Convention.'

anyway to pre-existing law.[171] Yet, the Statement does not exclude any operator of online networks from potential indirect liability, namely for acts of making available works on these networks by third persons. Questions of liability have been excluded from the Treaties.[172]

The second phrase states that nothing in Article 8 of the WCT precludes a **17.82** Contracting Party from applying Article 11bis(2) of the Berne Convention on compulsory licences. It simply clarifies that Article 8 of the WCT specifies a minimum right rather than its limitation, and that Article 11bis(2) of the Berne Convention continues to apply, as confirmed by Article 1(4) of the WCT. Article 11bis(2) of the Berne Convention, however, relates to the rights covered under its Article 11bis(1) and therefore does not apply to acts of 'making available'.[173]

(e) Limitations and exceptions

The Berne and Rome Conventions provide for specific, permitted limitations and **17.83** exceptions (supplemented by a reference to national copyright laws under the Rome Convention). The TRIPS Agreement integrates these provisions and adds, for copyright, three general conditions known as the three-step test.[174] The WCT follows the approach of the TRIPS copyright provisions.[175] The WPPT takes over from Rome and TRIPS only the general reference to exceptions and limitations under national copyright law, to be applied to neighbouring rights,[176] and adds, for the first time in a major multilateral treaty,[177] the three-step test for neighbouring rights, thereby following the copyright provisions of TRIPS and the WCT.[178]

(i) WCT   In respect of the Berne rights, all of which have been integrated into **17.84** the WCT on the basis of the compliance clause,[179] the relevant Berne limitations (including the implied limitations[180]) apply in the first place.[181] If a national provision complies with these limitations, it then also has to comply with the

---

[171] See also para 10.10 of the Basic Proposal for the copyright treaty, WIPO Doc CRNR/DC/4; Ficsor (n 3 above) C8.24; Reinbothe/von Lewinski (n 15 above) Art 8 WCT n 22.

[172] See paras 17.53–17.54 above in context of the reproduction right.

[173] Ficsor (n 3 above) C8.05 also points at the condition that compulsory licences apply only in the countries where prescribed, so that they would not be permitted to apply to any future kind of non-interactive wireless global communication.

[174] Arts 9(1) phr 1, 14(6), and 13 of the TRIPS Agreement; paras 10.83–10.88 and 10.100 above.

[175] Arts 1(4) and 10 of the WCT.

[176] Art 15(2) of the Rome Convention; Art 16(1) of the WPPT.

[177] Art 1706(3) of the NAFTA precedes the WPPT in this respect, para 11.17 above.

[178] Art 16(2) of the WPPT.

[179] Art 1(4) of the WCT.

[180] On the implied limitations, see paras 5.199–5.204 above.

[181] These limitations also apply on the basis of the compliance clause of Article 1(4) of the WCT.

three-step test under Article 10(2) of the WCT.[182] As clarified by the word 'confine', a national legislator may provide limitations or exceptions only if they fulfil each of the three conditions. The provision sets the outer limits of what is permitted under national law as limitations and exceptions.

17.85 Similarly to Article 13 of the TRIPS Agreement, Article 10(2) of the WCT aims at preventing an overly broad interpretation of the limitations and exceptions of the Berne Convention.[183] Further extending limitations of Berne rights would not be permitted in the WCT merely because of its nature as a special agreement under Article 20 of the Berne Convention.[184] One may consider the additional conditions of the three-step test rather as a clarification, because the specific limitations and exceptions of the Berne Convention anyway would not allow a conflict with a normal exploitation nor an unreasonable prejudice to the legitimate interests of the authors.[185] At the same time, the scope of applicability of the Berne limitations is not reduced by Article 10(2) of the WCT.[186]

17.86 In respect of the minimum rights laid down exclusively in the WCT, rather than also in the Berne Convention (ie the rights of distribution (for all kinds of works), rental, and (in part) communication to the public/making available), it is only the three-step test that applies under Article 10(1) of the WCT. Also in this case, legislators may only provide for limitations and exceptions that fulfil all three conditions. Even if Article 10(1) of the WCT does not explicitly express such restriction, this interpretation is the only meaningful one: if further-reaching, broader limitations and exceptions were permitted, it would have been superfluous and meaningless to lay down any conditions for limitations at all.

17.87 The Agreed Statement concerning Article 10 of the WCT, in its first paragraph, applies to the entire Article and clarifies that Contracting Parties may carry forward and appropriately extend into the digital environment limitations and exceptions that are permitted by the Berne Convention, and may devise new ones. For example, the limitations and exceptions permitted by the Berne

---

[182] On the essence of the three conditions in the Berne and TRIPS context, see paras 5.175–5.186 and 10.83–10.87 above. These comments may, in principle, also serve as a guideline in respect of the WCT.

[183] Under the relevant Agreed Statement, the scope of applicability of Berne limitations and exceptions is not extended. J Reinbothe, M Martin-Prat, and S von Lewinski, 'The New WIPO Treaties: A First Résumé' (1997) 4 EIPR 171, 173. On the parallel situation under the TRIPS Agreement, see paras 10.83–10.84 above.

[184] Art 1(1) of the WCT. On Art 20 of the Berne Convention, see paras 5.250–5.251 above; Reinbothe/von Lewinski (n 15 above) Art 10 WCT n 24.

[185] ibid n 34, referring to P Sirinelli, 'Exceptions and Limitations to Copyright and Neighbouring Rights', WIPO Doc WCT-WPPT/IMP/1, of 3 December 1999, 45.

[186] This is confirmed by the related Agreed Statement, 2nd para.

Convention regarding the reproduction right can also be applied to electronic reproduction, subject to the three-step test, which anyway already applies on the basis of Article 9(2) of the Berne Convention. Also, new exceptions can be devised (for example, for the right of making available). In all cases, however, the three conditions of the three-step test must be fulfilled.

(ii) WPPT The WPPT does not contain a compliance clause, so that the limi- **17.88**
tations and exceptions of the Rome Convention are not incorporated into this Treaty. Instead, Article 16(1) of the WPPT allows Contracting Parties to provide the same kind of limitations or exceptions in respect of the rights of performers and producers of phonograms as provided under national copyright law. It thereby follows the model of Article 15(2) phrase 1 of the Rome Convention and the tradition in many national laws.[187] However, it does not take over phrase 2 of the provision, which prohibits compulsory licences that are not compatible with the Rome Convention. Accordingly, compulsory licences are not prohibited where they are allowed for copyright. This corresponds to the concept of the Continental European law according to which neighbouring rights should not enjoy broader protection than authors' rights. Yet, this new possibility of compulsory licences will hardly have an effect, because the relevant compulsory licences under copyright would be those for mechanical recording and broadcasting, which would have no, or a limited meaning for performances and phonograms:[188] the licence for mechanical recording does not have a meaning for performances and phonograms since it aims at allowing different interpretations of the same work; hence, it refers to a different situation. For the broadcasting licence, it could have a meaning only for live broadcasting, since recordings are covered by the remuneration right of Article 15 of the WPPT. In this respect, a compulsory licence would go against Article 22 of the Rome Convention for Rome members[189] and would therefore have to be interpreted as not permitted; in any case, applying the three-step test under Article 16(2) of the WPPT would probably lead to the same result.

Article 16(1) of the WPPT implies that any limitations or exceptions that go **17.89**
beyond those provided for copyright under the national law of the respective Contracting Party are not permitted. Otherwise, the entire provision would be superfluous and meaningless.

---

187 On that provision, see paras 6.67–6.69 above.
188 Arts 13 and 11bis(2) of the Berne Convention; assuming that all Contracting Parties will usually also be Berne Members, they will have to comply with these provisions for copyright.
189 On Art 22 of the Rome Convention, see para 6.78 above; Art 7(2) of the Rome Convention allows restrictions only after consent to broadcasting has been given, so that a compulsory licence regarding live broadcasting would mean less protection than under the Rome Convention.

17.90　In addition,[190] such limitations and exceptions must comply with the three-step test under Article 16(2) of the WPPT. Here, the word 'confine' again explicitly clarifies that limitations or exceptions that do not fulfil each of the three conditions must not be provided.[191] The Agreed Statement concerning Article 10 of the WCT applies by analogy to Article 16 of the WPPT.[192]

(f)　Obligations concerning technological measures and rights management information

17.91　The provisions on obligations concerning technological measures and rights management information[193] constitute novel provisions that were largely unknown beforehand in national and international law. Similar provisions regarding technical protection pre-existed mostly, if at all, with a very limited scope, as in Article 1707 of the NAFTA and Sections 296 ff of the UK Copyright Designs and Patents Act 1988 in respect of illegal decoding of satellite codes.[194] Unlike minimum rights, they do not grant any direct protection against unauthorized uses, but aim at indirectly protecting the minimum rights by flanking legal measures and thereby indirectly serve the enforcement of the minimum rights.[195] Further experience with technical measures and rights management information as well as their legal protection will be necessary before an overall assessment can be made as to their viability, consumer acceptance, satisfaction, and appropriate balance.

17.92　The WIPO Treaties do not oblige the Contracting Parties to impose the use of technological measures or rights management information; it is left entirely to the right holders or their representatives to decide whether to employ them, and if so, which ones to employ in which situations.

17.93　**(i)　Technological measures**　Most uses in the digital environment, such as reproduction and making available of works and phonograms, can easily be carried out by any user and can hardly be controlled without any particular mechanisms.

---

[190]　The view that Art 16(2) of the WPPT would not be cumulative to para (1) but apply alternatively (Morgan, n 154 above, 212) contradicts the wording which does not contain any restriction to apply para (2), and clearly contradicts the purpose, following the model of copyright, where the three-step test also applies as an additional safeguard for the application of specific exceptions and limitations.

[191]　For the essence of the three conditions, see in the Berne and TRIPS context, paras 5.175–5.186 and 10.83–10.87 above.

[192]　Agreed Statement concerning Article 16 of the WPPT; on the Agreed Statement concerning Article 10 of the WCT, see para 17.87 above.

[193]　Arts 11 and 12 of the WCT and 18 and 19 of the WPPT.

[194]　On the provision of NAFTA, see para 11.19 above. Also Art 7(1)(c) of the EC Computer Program Directive of 1991, Vol II ch 5.

[195]　On both provisions in more detail: Ricketson/Ginsburg (n 74 above) ch 15; on WIPO's work before and at the Diplomatic Conference, Ficsor (n 3 above) ch 6.

Therefore, right holders have employed technical protection, such as encryption or other devices which make it largely impossible to access, reproduce, or otherwise use works or phonograms. Such technical protection can, however, be circumvented by users who then may easily further distribute or make available both the now technically unprotected material and devices for circumvention. Therefore, technical protection alone is rarely sufficient to effectively protect works and phonograms in the digital environment. Consequently, with the advent of digital technology, right owners called for legal sanctions against the circumvention of technical measures in order to secure effective protection. Accordingly, the rationale behind the provisions on technological measures is as follows: copyright and neighbouring rights law remains the basis for protection. It is reinforced in the digital environment by a second layer of protection, namely technical protection measures. Since these measures alone are not considered sufficient, a third layer of protection has been introduced, namely legal remedies against circumvention of technical measures that protect copyright and neighbouring rights.

Given the lack of experience with legislation on technical measures in 1996, it is not surprising that the detailed provisions in the Basic Proposal were intensively discussed, even if few doubts were expressed regarding their principal necessity. In particular, among the controversial elements were the qualification of devices for circumvention (by their primary purpose, primary effect, or only by their purpose of circumvention), the acts (such as production and distribution of devices for circumvention) and services to be legally sanctioned, and the kind and conditions of legal sanctions. **17.94**

Finally, a rather short and general provision was drafted mainly by the different groups of interested stakeholders who probably had the best insight in technical and other relevant issues. Their compromise was taken over and adopted only with two minor changes by the governmental delegations who did not perceive a great manoeuvring space for modifying this proposal and, in addition, had to cope with time constraints. The adopted Article seems to be the first example of a provision in a multilateral treaty that was mainly drafted by the private sector and largely adopted at the governmental level.[196] **17.95**

Under Articles 11 of the WCT and 18 of the WPPT, sanctions need to be provided only against the circumvention of 'effective' technological measures. This condition aims at excluding sanctions where technological measures do not function properly or interfere with the normal functioning of equipment or services. For example, where the normal use of a video recorder automatically deactivates a technological protection measure, the user must not be subject to any sanctions **17.96**

---

196 See Reinbothe/von Lewinski (n 15 above) Art 11 WCT n 8.

for such activity. At the same time, 'effective' does not mean that the protection measure works at 100 per cent, because otherwise any provision on the circumvention would be meaningless.

17.97   Such measures must be used by authors, performers, or phonogram producers or, as is often the case, their successors in title, such as licensees.[197] The measures must be used in connection with the exercise of respective rights under the WCT and WPPT. Accordingly, both measures to control the protected uses directly (exploitation control measures) and indirectly (access control measures) are covered.[198] This link to the exercise of rights means also that the Treaties do not provide for any protection where works or phonograms in the public domain are technically protected and the protection measures are circumvented. In addition, such measures must be employed to protect uses that are not authorized by the right holders or permitted by law, in particular by a limitation or exception. For example, where a user circumvents a technological measure in order to make a copy for private purposes or educational purposes permitted under the relevant national law without the right holder's authorization, the WCT and the WPPT do not require Contracting Parties to provide for legal remedies against the circumvention; they clearly establish a link between copyright or neighbouring rights protection and the protection against circumvention. At the same time, Contracting Parties are free to provide for greater protection, since these provisions are minimum standards.[199] Indeed, many national laws provide for circumvention protection even regarding uses permitted by law.[200] It is highly difficult to find the right balance between adequate and effective protection—as required by the Treaties—and respect for national law limitations and exceptions, because devices cannot distinguish between permitted or non-permitted uses.[201]

17.98   Contracting Parties must provide 'adequate legal protection and effective legal remedies' against circumvention. One may well consider that legal protection is only adequate if it also sanctions, in addition to the circumvention itself, the preparatory acts such as the production of circumvention devices and their distribution, or services that facilitate or enable circumvention by third persons.[202] Also, circumvention devices must not only be those whose sole purpose is circumvention, but also those that are, for example, primarily

---

[197] On non-exclusive licensees, see in particular Ricketson/Ginsburg (n 74 above) 15.12.

[198] Ricketson/Ginsburg (n 74 above) 15.14–15.16; Reinbothe/von Lewinski (n 15 above) Art 11 WCT nn 18–19; Ficsor (n 3 above) C11.09.

[199] Reinbothe/von Lewinski (n 15 above) Art 11 WCT n 28.

[200] See eg Art 6(4) of the EC Information Society Directive 2001, which only exempts specific uses from the protection, Vol II ch 10.

[201] Ricketson/Ginsburg (n 74 above) 15.19.

[202] Reinbothe/von Lewinski (n 15 above) Art 11 WCT n 23; Ficsor (n 3 above) C11.12.

designed for circumvention.[203] In respect of the remedies, Contracting Parties have some leeway to choose the kind of remedy (eg under civil, criminal, or administrative law) and to determine the concrete level of sanctions. The remedies need only to be 'effective', which may be interpreted as expeditious and dissuasive.[204] This wording leaves some flexibility to strike the right balance between the interests of the parties involved.[205]

(ii) Rights management information Rights management information, as defined in Articles 12(2) of the WCT and 19(2) of the WPPT, identifies the right holders, the objects of protection, any holders of derived rights, and the terms and conditions of use, as well as any numbers or codes representing such information. It is protected when attached to a copy or appearing in connection with the communication[206] or making available to the public of a work or other subject matter. Such information can be manipulated by unauthorized third persons through deletion, modification, and otherwise. In addition, such manipulated information can be attached to works, performances, phonograms, or copies thereof, which themselves can be distributed or otherwise exploited[207] without authority. **17.99**

Both kinds of acts—manipulation and exploitation of works, performances, and phonograms with manipulated information—can induce, enable, facilitate, or conceal an infringement of a right where such information is used, for example, as a basis for licensing or for the calculation of royalties that are due to the right owner. Also, rights management information often interacts with technological measures. For example, it may indicate to a technical measure in a copying device how many copies, if any, are licensed to be made from a particular recording. If the indication 'none' is altered into 'an unlimited number' or any other number, the reproduction right of the right holder is infringed because the technical measure will consequently enable the indicated number of copies, an act contrary to the terms of the licence and therefore without authorization of the right holder. **17.100**

---

203 Ficsor (n 3 above) C11.12.

204 Reinbothe/von Lewinski (n 15 above) Art 11 WCT n 21 referring to Art 41(1) of the TRIPS Agreement.

205 For more details, see Reinbothe/von Lewinski (n 15 above) Art 11 WCT nn 17–23.

206 In the WCT, 'communication' covers both broadcasting and making available, Reinbothe/von Lewinski (n 15 above) Art 12 WCT n 24. This corresponds to the terminology in the WCT. The definition of 'communication' in the WPPT, however, excludes 'broadcasting' and 'making available', so that Art 19 of the WPPT, which mentions separately only 'making available', has to be understood as also covering 'broadcasting'; for the reasons, see Reinbothe/von Lewinski (n 15 above) Art 19 WPPT n 25.

207 In Art 12 of the WCT, broadcasting and communication to the public are mentioned separately, although communication under the WCT covers broadcasting; this may be understood as a clarification.

17.101   In order to fight against such indirect acts of infringement, Articles 12 of the WCT and 19 of the WPPT oblige Contracting Parties to provide 'adequate and effective legal remedies'[208] against anyone who manipulates such electronic information or carries out any of the above-mentioned subsequent acts, subject to different knowledge requirements. Again, Contracting Parties are free to determine the concrete legal remedies and to choose whether to provide them under civil, criminal, or administrative law. Yet, the remedies must be 'adequate'; accordingly, they must create a proper balance between the strength and consequences of the remedy on the one hand and the sanctioned act on the other. Also, they must be 'effective', namely, strong enough to deter potential infringers, so as to result in the enforcement of protection.[209] The Agreed Statement concerning Article 12 of the WCT[210] clarifies that the 'infringement' following the manipulation of rights management information or subsequent, related acts refers to the infringement not only of exclusive rights, but also of rights of remuneration.

(2) Standards only under the WCT

(a) *Substantive standards of the Berne Convention*

17.102   Article 1(4) of the WCT incorporates all substantive standards of protection under Articles 1 to 21 and the Appendix of the Berne Convention into the WCT as obligations of Contracting Parties under the WCT. Even if they have not been spelled out in the WCT but are only referred to, they have to be fully complied with under the WCT.[211] At the same time, Article 1(4) of the WCT does not oblige Contracting Parties to adhere to the Berne Convention. Unlike the similar 'compliance clause' of the TRIPS Agreement,[212] it does not exempt moral rights from this obligation.[213]

(b) *Computer programs*

17.103   The text of the Berne Convention does not explicitly cover computer programs as works; nor has its interpretation in this respect always been clear.[214] The TRIPS Agreement was the first major multilateral treaty to explicitly provide for protection

---

[208] Ficsor (n 3 above) C12.03 suggests that these words should be understood as 'adequate legal protection and effective legal remedies' under Arts 11 of the WCT and 18 of the WPPT.

[209] Reinbothe/von Lewinski (n 15 above) Art 12 WCT nn 12–14.

[210] It also applies by analogy to Art 19 of the WPPT, Agreed Statement concerning Art 19 of the WPPT.

[211] On these Arts, see above, ch 5 (except paras 5.252 ff). On their application in the framework of the WCT, see Ficsor (n 3 above) C1.21–C1.56.

[212] Art 9(1) phr 2 of the TRIPS Agreement, paras 10.52–10.54 above.

[213] This seeming inconsistency can be explained by the lack of an effective dispute settlement mechanism for the WCT, as opposed to the TRIPS Agreement; for this aspect in relation to the Berne Convention, see para 10.53 above.

[214] On the problem of interpretation, see paras 7.13–7.19 above.

of computer programs as literary works.[215] The fact that this occurred only two years before the WCT proved to be an obstacle to further improvement during WCT negotiation. Developing countries in particular preferred to take over the exact wording from Article 10(1) of the TRIPS Agreement and opposed any broadening of protection. Finally, the following compromise was reached: the wording of the TRIPS Agreement was slightly modified in Article 4 of the WCT, while an Agreed Statement confirmed that the scope of protection for computer programs under the WCT was consistent with Article 2 of the Berne Convention and on a par with the relevant provisions of the TRIPS Agreement. In addition, the general clause of TRIPS on the expression/idea dichotomy,[216] developed in the context of computer programs and only later separated as a general rule, was imported into the WCT[217] in order to accommodate the countries that were concerned about ensuring an equal protection of computer programs as in the TRIPS Agreement.[218] Accordingly, Article 4 of the WCT can be considered as a clarification of Article 10(1) of the TRIPS Agreement.

The WCT modifies the TRIPS wording in two aspects. First, the words 'shall be protected' (TRIPS) are replaced by 'are protected'. This means that computer programs have already been protected as literary works and that this provision is of a declaratory nature. Secondly, the protection of the WCT applies, in accordance with Article 2(1) of the Berne Convention, to computer programs 'whatever may be the mode or form of their expression' rather than only to the 'source and object code' (TRIPS) of the computer program.[219] This amendment includes both the source and the object code, and is open for additional forms that may emerge in the future.[220] **17.104**

(c) Databases

Discussions on the protection of databases resembled those on computer programs, again essentially because developing countries in particular were not ready to go beyond the scope of protection laid down for databases just two years earlier **17.105**

---

215 See on Art 10(1) of the TRIPS Agreement paras 10.56–10.59 above; not long before the TRIPS Agreement came into force, the NAFTA had already laid down the protection of computer programs (Art 1705(1)(a)); yet, NAFTA negotiations took place after the provisional conclusion of the TRIPS negotiations, see para 11.11 above.

216 Art 9(2) of the TRIPS Agreement, para 10.58 above.

217 Art 2 of the WCT.

218 Ficsor (n 3 above) C2.03–C2.04. Reinbothe/von Lewinski (n 15 above) Art 4 WCT n 5.

219 For the contents of Art 4 of the WCT (beyond the elements explicitly mentioned in the text) and Art 2 of the WCT, see comments on Arts 10(1) and 9(2) of the TRIPS Agreement, also applicable here in principle, paras 10.56–10.59 above.

220 Ficsor (n 3 above) C4.19.

in the TRIPS Agreement.[221] Also, the compromise was similar to that for computer programs: the wording of Article 10(2) of the TRIPS Agreement was slightly modified in Article 5 of the WCT, and an Agreed Statement on Berne consistency corresponding to that regarding computer programs[222] was adopted in respect of Article 5 of the WCT. The modifications in the WCT wording again concern the declaratory nature of protection of databases.[223] In addition, the seemingly broader term 'in any form' is used instead of 'whether in machine readable or other form'.

17.106   Otherwise, Article 5 of the WCT follows the wording of the TRIPS Agreement. In particular, the word 'compilations' rather than 'collections' (from Article 2(5) of the Berne Convention) is used.[224] Also, as in TRIPS, the protection is without prejudice to 'any copyright subsisting in the data or material' of the database. It would have been desirable to clarify, as proposed by Article 5 of the Basic Proposal, that the database protection is without prejudice not only to copyright in the contained material but also to 'any right' subsisting in its contents, such as rights of performers or phonogram producers whose recordings are contained in a database. Developing countries, however, insisted on taking over the TRIPS wording. Nevertheless, the 'without prejudice' clause must be read as referring to copyright only as an example, since this provision is not meant (and never has been so) to allow for database protection to prejudice any other rights subsisting in the database contents, such as performers' or phonogram producers' rights.[225]

(d) Right of communication to the public

17.107   The term 'communication to the public' has been used differently in different copyright and neighbouring rights treaties, and this often in deviation from national law terminologies, so that it may be difficult to ascertain the correct meaning for each treaty. The traditional communication right (as opposed to the making available right)[226] under the WCT has to be understood against the background of the communication right under the Berne Convention. The WCT incorporates the fragmentary set of Berne provisions on the communication right as its own obligation[227] and supplements it. It does so by providing the communication right without prejudice to specified Berne provisions on the

---

[221] See Art 10(2) of the TRIPS Agreement and comments hereon, paras 10.60–10.63 above. On the ambiguity of the Berne Convention which made such clarification necessary, see para 10.60 and Reinbothe/von Lewinski (n 15 above) Art 5 WCT n 13.

[222] para 17.103 above.

[223] The words 'shall be protected' were replaced by the words 'are protected'.

[224] On these terms, see para 10.63 n 129 above, and Reinbothe/von Lewinski (n 15 above) Art 5 WCT n 8.

[225] ibid n 15.

[226] paras 17.72–17.82 above.

[227] See the compliance clause in Art 1(4) of the WCT.

communication right.[228] Given this reference to Berne provisions, one will have to understand the WCT's term 'communication to the public' in the same way as under these provisions, subject to the WCT system of references.

The Berne provisions referred to in the WCT employ this term so as to exclude **17.108** the separate terms 'public performance' and 'public recitation' which refer to forms of direct presentation, often called 'public performance' under national law.[229] The WCT also does not refer to another form of direct presentation, namely 'communication to the public by loudspeaker'.[230] Even if the Berne Convention itself describes this latter form of direct presentation by the term 'communication', the WCT system of references shows that it excludes all forms of direct presentation from its communication right. Accordingly, there is no possible conflict between direct presentation and the WCT's communication right, so that a 'without prejudice' clause in this respect was not needed. Rights of direct presentation/public performance are covered under the WCT through the compliance clause, separately from the communication right.[231]

At the same time, the Berne provisions employ the term 'communication to the **17.109** public' to cover broadcasting, rebroadcasting, similar forms of wireless communication to the public, and retransmission by wire of a broadcast. Accordingly, there is little room left for a genuine meaning of 'communication to the public' in the WCT: forms of direct presentation are excluded, and most forms of remote communication are already covered by the Berne provisions. What is new under the WCT is, in particular, the original cable transmission of kinds of works for which the Berne Convention does not provide such protection,[232] retransmission by cable of such originated cable transmissions, and rebroadcasting and retransmission of a broadcast made by the organization that also emitted the original programme.[233]

The Agreed Statement concerning Article 8 of the WCT simply clarifies in its **17.110** phrase 2 that this Article does not affect the possibilities under Article 11bis(2) of the Berne Convention to provide for compulsory licences or similar restrictions of protection; Article 8 of the WCT lays down a minimum right but does not regulate the respective limitations and exceptions. Accordingly, Contracting

---

228 First part of Art 8 of the WCT referring to Arts 11(1)(ii), 11bis(1)(i), (ii), 11ter(1)(ii), 14(1)(ii), and 14bis(1) of the Berne Convention, paras 5.138–5.140 above.
229 See Arts 11(1)(i), 11ter(1)(i), 14(1)(ii) of the Berne Convention.
230 Art 11bis(1)(iii) of the Berne Convention.
231 Reinbothe/von Lewinski (n 15 above) Art 8 WCT n 11 for more detail.
232 Arts 11(1)(ii), 11ter(1)(ii), 14(1)(ii), and 14bis(1) of the Berne Convention include the cable transmission right only for musical and other specified kinds of works, paras 5.135–5.136 and 5.138–5.139 above.
233 Reinbothe/von Lewinski (n 15 above) Art 8 WCT nn 10–11.

Parties may, for example, retain a non-voluntary licence for the retransmission of broadcasts.

(e) Duration of protection of photographic works

17.111 Article 9 of the WCT was among the least controversial provisions at the Diplomatic Conference. It prohibits Contracting Parties from applying Article 7(4) of the Berne Convention, which allows for a shorter minimum duration for photographic works (twenty-five years from their making) instead of the general duration of fifty years *pma*. This discrimination of works of photography is rooted in the perception in many countries during the early years of the Berne Convention that photographic works would merit lesser protection than other works, not least due to the fact that they may be produced by a simple manual operation of pushing a button.[234] In national laws, this perception was often reflected in the grant of a shorter term of protection for photographic works than for works in general. The national laws were so diverse that agreement on a mere minimum duration for photographic works was possible only at the 1967 Revision Conference. To date, it is generally recognized that photography may mean much more than pushing a button and may involve at least as much creativity and merit as other kinds of works.

17.112 It is therefore only consequential that Article 9 of the WCT has assimilated the minimum duration for photographic works under the Berne Convention to the general one of fifty years *pma*. Accordingly, also the other general rules of Article 7 of the Berne Convention have to be applied to photographic works by Contracting Parties of the WCT. These are, in addition to the general duration, the rules on anonymous or pseudonymous works, the calculation of the term from 1 January of the year following the death of the photographer or the other events under Article 7(3) of the Berne Convention, the clarification that a longer term of protection can be provided, special rules for Contracting Parties which are bound only by the Rome Act of the Berne Convention, and the possibility of providing material reciprocity.[235] In addition, Article 7bis of the Berne Convention on joint works applies.[236]

17.113 Article 9 of the WCT has to be understood as a special provision prevailing over the reference to Article 7(4) of the Berne Convention in the compliance clause of

---

[234] Ricketson/Ginsburg (n 74 above) 8.48; para 5.224 above; on the protection of photographic works throughout Berne history, see eg Ficsor (n 3 above) C9.02–C9.08.

[235] See Art 7(1), (3) and (5)–(8) of the Berne Convention; paras 5.217, 5.220–5.221, 5.227–5.228, and 5.41–5.44 above.

[236] Arts 7(3), (5)–(8) and 7bis of the Berne Convention already applied beforehand to photographic works, though with the minimum duration of 25 years from the making of the work.

Article 1(4) of the WCT; accordingly, no conflict between both provisions exists.

Where a country provides for a shorter duration of protection of photographic **17.114** works and, upon accession to the WCT, has to prolong it in accordance with Article 9 of the WCT, the longer duration applies to existing photographic works as specified under Article 13 of the WCT in connection with Article 18 of the Berne Convention on application in time.[237]

(3) Standards only under the WPPT

(a) Moral rights of performers

(i) Importance and historical background of the provision Article 5 of the **17.115** WPPT is the first provision in a multilateral treaty to recognize performers' moral rights, namely the right of 'performership' or paternity, and the integrity right. A first proposal to include these rights in an international treaty goes back to the Draft Treaty submitted to the Conference of Samaden 1939.[238] When work on such a treaty was taken up after the Second World War, supporters dropped their claim to include moral rights into the Hague Draft when it turned out to be unacceptable for a number of delegations.[239]

The provision in the Basic Proposal for the 1996 Diplomatic Conference was **17.116** drafted upon the model of Article 6[bis] of the Berne Convention. This legislative technique of relying on an existing model familiar to governmental delegates may have facilitated agreement on the concrete wording.[240] In substance, the overwhelming majority of delegations agreed on providing moral rights for performers. Strong support for moral rights prevented the adoption of individual proposals to delete the provision or to limit the scope of rights for example to fixed performances. [241] Only one slight restriction of the right of performership was accepted in a compromise.[242] The envisaged restriction to musical performances[243] was even broadened to aural ones. The possible waivability of moral rights was opposed by most delegations; however, as part of a compromise, it was decided not to deal with this question in the text of the Article. Finally, countries for which the introduction of moral rights on the basis of the WPPT might have been difficult were satisfied by the transitional provisions of Article 22(2) of the

---

[237] para 17.164 below on Art 13 of the WCT.
[238] paras 4.55 and 6.60 above.
[239] Morgan (n 154 above) 195.
[240] For disadvantages of this approach, see para 17.123 below.
[241] For these and more rejected proposals, see Reinbothe/von Lewinski (n 15 above) Art 5 WPPT n 5.
[242] See the 'except where . . .' clause in the second half of Art 5(1) of the WPPT.
[243] Art 5 of the Basic Proposal, Alternative A.

WPPT under which it is allowed to apply moral rights only to performances occurring after its entry into force for that Party; from a pragmatic point of view, also the lack of an effective dispute settlement mechanism of the WPPT may have limited the opposition otherwise to be expected from certain countries.[244]

17.117   The discussions before and at the Diplomatic Conference reflected the prevailing view that moral rights may be particularly important in context of digital uses. The introduction of an integrity right for performers was even considered as sufficiently strong to respond to challenges provoked by the possibilities to digitally modify existing recordings. The integrity right was used as an argument to reject the need for the—also proposed—exclusive modification right for performers.[245]

17.118   (ii) **Scope of application**   Notably, moral rights under Article 5 of the WPPT are limited to live aural performances and performances fixed in phonograms. This restriction reflects the general controversy on the inclusion of audiovisual performances.[246] Aural is any performance which may be perceived by the human ear, including a musical one and any performance expressed by voice, such as the reading of a speech, reciting of a poem, or declaiming of any text. Even if the performance is not exclusively aural, such as the acting of an opera singer, moral rights can be infringed where the aural part of the performance is concerned, for example, where the performance by an opera singer on stage is made audible by a loudspeaker to an outside audience or through a live radio broadcast in an electronically mutilated form. Moral rights could also be infringed where the musical part of the performance is altered electronically during the performance. 'Live' is any performance which is not fixed on a phonogram or other carrier, such as a performance at a concert, even if it is broadcast, transmitted by cable, and simultaneously rebroadcast or retransmitted without having been fixed.[247]

17.119   (iii) **Right of performership**   Since the right to claim to be identified as the performer of one's performance is largely based on Article 6[bis] of the Berne Convention, comments may be limited at this point.[248] An important deviation from the Berne model is the exception from the performership right where the omission of the name is 'dictated by the manner of the use of the performance'. This exception is quite narrow, as indicated by the term 'dictated', which excludes any possibility of denying the performership right on the basis of standard practices, customary ways to identify performers, or arguments of simple practicability. The use of a performance by a large ensemble for radio broadcasting may be seen

---

[244] For such an approach of the USA under the TRIPS Agreement, see para 10.53 above.

[245] On that proposal, see paras 17.153–17.154 below.

[246] On this discussion, see paras 18.01 ff, in particular 18.02–18.07 below.

[247] Reinbothe/von Lewinski (n 15 above) Art 5 WPPT n 13.

[248] For a detailed presentation of the corresponding moral rights under Art 6[bis] of the Berne Convention, see paras 5.96–5.104 above.

as dictating the omission of the names of all performers, because the reading thereof would take a considerable part of the time available for broadcasting and would also not have a similar effect on the audience as a list of names available on paper. Nevertheless, broadcasters will be obliged to name all members of ensembles at least on request. The situation is different for leaflets of CDs or concert programmes where the omission of the names is not dictated by the manner of the use, as shown by a common, existing practice to list all names of performers even of large ensembles in such cases.[249]

Even if not explicitly stipulated, the performer may choose his real name, a pseudonym, or even anonymity. The right to be identified, however, does not include the right of a performer to object to any false attribution of a performance by a third person to that performer.[250] **17.120**

(iv) Right of integrity   The right of integrity relates to the performance rather **17.121** than, under Article 6bis of the Berne Convention, to a work, but otherwise follows the rules under the Berne Convention.[251] Relevant distortions, mutilations, or other modifications may include the change of speed of the recorded performance, its shifting to another pitch, the variation of the volume, timbre, or resonance of its sounds or, in the case of multitrack records, the mixing or remixing of tracks. Whether sampling is an infringement of the integrity right depends on the individual case and national law. Sampling is the extraction of individual sounds or a series of sounds from a recorded performance for insertion, possibly after modification, into a different recording. If the extracted part of the performance is important enough to constitute, under national law, a protected part of the performance (which may be doubtful in respect of individual sounds), the sampling constitutes a modification of the 'performance'.[252]

Unlike under the Berne Convention for works, a 'derogatory act in relation to . . .' **17.122** the performance does not infringe moral rights under Article 5 of the WPPT. Accordingly, if the performance is not modified itself but only presented in a context which may produce derogatory effects on the performance itself, the performer is not protected under the WPPT. Also unlike under the Berne Convention, the modification of the performance can be opposed only if it is prejudicial to the performer's reputation rather than also to her honour.[253] Accordingly, she does

---

249 Reinbothe/von Lewinski (n 15 above) Art 5 WPPT n 16; Ricketson/Ginsburg (n 74 above) 19.53 subsection (vi).
250 For these aspects, see also para 5.99 above, in the Berne context.
251 On the integrity right under the Berne Convention, see paras 5.100–5.104 above.
252 For more details, see Reinbothe/von Lewinski (n 15 above) Art 5 WPPT nn 20–1.
253 Ricketson/Ginsburg (n 74 above) 19.53 (vii) suggest that this may make the right more accessible to common law systems which regularly protect reputational interests. See also Ficsor (n 3 above) PP5.05.

not need to be protected if there is a possible prejudice to her honour. Yet, since this is a minimum right, national legislators may grant the integrity right even irrespective of any potential prejudice.[254] An actual prejudice is not necessary; the possibility that the modification causes a prejudice to the reputation suffices.[255]

17.123 (v) **Article 5(2) and (3) of the WPPT** The introduction of the Berne model regarding the minimum duration and exercise of moral rights after the death of an author into the context of the WPPT brings about certain ambiguities and shows that such legislative technique may not always be appropriate without adaptations. In particular, the minimum duration of performers' economic rights (determining that of moral rights) often may expire before the performer's death, in contrast to authors' rights. Article 5(2) phrase 1 of the WPPT seems to suppose that the duration lasts at least until the performer's death. One may therefore interpret this provision as setting a minimum duration for moral rights until the death of the performer, where the economic rights expire before he dies.[256]

17.124 Article 5(3) of the WPPT is a simple clarification, since remedies always follow the law of the country for which protection is claimed.[257]

(b) Rights of performers in unfixed performances

17.125 Article 6 of the WPPT lays down the performers' exclusive rights of broadcasting and communication to the public[258] of unfixed and as yet not broadcast (ie live) performances and the exclusive right of fixation[259] of unfixed performances. It largely follows the corresponding provision under the Rome Convention.[260] Unlike the Rome Convention and the TRIPS Agreement, however, the WPPT provides for exclusive rights rather than only for the 'possibility of preventing' certain acts.[261] In contrast, the WPPT is less protective than the Rome Convention as it limits the fixation and communication rights to the embodiment of

---

[254] Some countries like France and Greece do so, S von Lewinski, 'Neighbouring Rights: Comparison of Laws' in G Schricker (ed), *International Encyclopedia of Comparative Law: Copyright and Industrial Property* (2006) ch 5, 8.

[255] For more detail, see Reinbothe/von Lewinski (n 15 above) Art 5 WPPT n 25.

[256] For the arguments and a different possibility of interpretation, see ibid n 28; ibid n 29, also on further ambiguities under Art 5(2) phr 2.

[257] For the corresponding Art 6bis(3) of the Berne Convention, see para 5.106 above.

[258] For the definitions, see Art 2(f), (g) of the WPPT and paras 17.140–17.143 below; accordingly, even internet live transmissions of performances are covered by the communication right (Morgan (n 154 above) 160).

[259] Definition in Art 2(c) of the WPPT and para 17.138 below.

[260] Art 7(1)(a), (b) of the Rome Convention, paras 6.37–6.39 above; on the modified definitions, see paras 17.140–17.143 below. The broadcasting and communication rights under the TRIPS Agreement are worded less specifically, using only the words 'live performance' rather than the 'except-clause', paras 10.92–10.93 above.

[261] para 17.49 above. On the mere 'possibility of preventing' under the Rome Convention, see paras 6.35–6.36 above; also Art 14(1) of the TRIPS Agreement, para 10.91 above.

sounds, while the Rome Convention extends them to audiovisual fixations.[262] The live broadcasting right is the only one under the WPPT that covers not only audio, but also audiovisual and visual performances, as may be seen from the definition of 'broadcasting' in Article 2(f) of the WPPT.[263] The exclusive broadcasting and communication rights for live performances are supplemented by a remuneration right for broadcasting and communication on the basis of phonograms incorporating performances under Article 15 of the WPPT.[264]

(c) Remuneration right for broadcasting and communication to the public.

(i) **Main features**   Article 15 of the WPPT lays down a remuneration right for **17.126** performers and producers of phonograms for the use of commercial phonograms for broadcasting and communication to the public, following the model of Article 12 in combination with Article 16(1)(a) of the Rome Convention.[265] Yet, it reinforces the protection in the following respects: in principle,[266] both performers and producers of phonograms shall enjoy the right,[267] and also the indirect (rather than only direct) use for broadcasting and communication is covered; accordingly, the remuneration is due not only where the phonogram is used for a broadcast or played to the public in a discotheque (direct uses), but also where a broadcast made on the basis of a phonogram is rebroadcast (indirect use for broadcasting) and where such broadcast is played or otherwise communicated to the public (indirect use for communication).[268] For broadcasting, though, it seems that the qualification 'indirect' does not add any meaning, since the definition of 'broadcasting' in Article 2(f) of the WPPT, unlike that in Article 3(f) of the Rome Convention, covers also rebroadcasting. Therefore, it has been suggested that 'indirect' should be interpreted as referring

---

262 This limitation results from the definitions of 'fixation' and 'communication to the public' in Art 2(c) and (g) of the WPPT (paras 17.138 and 17.143 below) and has to be seen in context with the controversy about including audiovisual performances, paras 18.02–18.07 below; Reinbothe/von Lewinski (n 15 above) Art 6 WPPT n 7; Ficsor (n 3 above) PP6.04–PP6.07 discusses possible arguments for a broader interpretation. The fixation right under TRIPS is also limited to fixations on phonograms, see its Art 14(1) phr 1 and para 10.91 above; however, its live communication right extends to audiovisual performances, see para 10.93 above.

263 For the similar situation regarding the live broadcasting right under the Rome Convention, see its Arts 7(1)(a) and 3(f); para 6.38 above. For TRIPS, see para 10.93 above.

264 On this right, see paras 17.126–17.130 below.

265 On Art 12 of the Rome Convention, see paras 6.49–6.58 above.

266 Reservations are possible in both cases under Art 15(3) of the WPPT (Reinbothe/von Lewinski (n 15 above) Art 15 WPPT n 23) so that the result is similar, albeit subject to the need to declare a reservation.

267 Art 12 of the Rome Convention leaves a choice to the national legislators to grant the right only to performers, only to producers, or to both.

268 For the direct uses, see para 6.52 above on Art 12 of the Rome Convention; Reinbothe/von Lewinski (n 15 above) Art 15 WPPT n 21.

to the phonogram, so that the indirect use would mean the use of a reproduction of the phonogram.[269]

17.127   In addition, under Article 15(4) of the WPPT, the remuneration must also be paid for the use of phonograms that are 'published' only via the internet or similar networks, as opposed to those traditionally published for sale or other commercial purposes. While delegations could not agree on defining the term 'publication' in Article 2(e) of the WPPT so as to clearly cover 'online publication',[270] they wanted to cover phonograms 'published' online in Article 15 of the WPPT. Thereby, they wanted to ensure that the remuneration is also due where phonograms 'published' only online are used for broadcasting and communication to the public. Article 15 of the WPPT aims at compensating the use of a phonogram for broadcasting and communication, irrespective of how the phonogram was produced and put on the market. An equal treatment for both kinds of phonograms avoids a possible discrimination between different kinds of phonograms and a possible 'circumvention' of the payment obligation through the use of phonograms exclusively 'published' online.

17.128   (ii) **Agreed Statements**   The first Agreed Statement concerning Article 15 of the WPPT reflects more far-reaching proposals (even up to an exclusive right instead of the remuneration right for certain subscription services) that were however rejected by the overall majority of delegations.[271] Accordingly, the Agreed Statement has a political value rather than an independent legal value in expressing the higher ambitions of a number of countries; otherwise, it states the obvious, since the WPPT anyway grants only minimum rights and allows the provision of greater protection.

17.129   Likewise, the second Agreed Statement mainly has a political value. It too states the obvious for the particular case of folklore, namely that more far-reaching protection than under Article 15 of the WPPT can be granted at the national level. It clarifies that the right under this Article can also be applied to recorded performances of folklore, which in practice are usually not published for commercial gain and therefore not covered by Article 15 of the WPPT. Since the WPPT only provides for minimum protection, national laws may in any case provide that the

---

[269] Ficsor (n 3 above) PP15.04. This interpretation itself may, however, be subject to doubt since reproductions are arguably anyway covered by the provision, Reinbothe/von Lewinski (n 15 above) Art 15 WPPT n 20. On the reference to 'reproduction' in Art 12 of the Rome Convention, see para 6.52 above.

[270] para 17.139 below on the definition; see for the context of criteria of eligibility para 17.42 above, and paras 17.151–17.152 below.

[271] On the proposals, including that of the USA which seemed to be tailor-made to its national legislation, see Ficsor (n 3 above) PP15.07–15.10; Reinbothe/von Lewinski (n 15 above) Art 15 WPPT nn 8 and 13.

remuneration is due for the use of any kind of phonograms, whether or not commercial. The explicit reference to phonograms with recorded folklore, which are indeed extensively used for broadcasting and communication to the public in particular in developing countries, may be considered as a political signal pointing at the importance of folklore and the need of promoting its international protection.[272]

(iii) Reservations to the rights Article 15(3) of the WPPT largely follows **17.130** Article 16(1)(a) of the Rome Convention in allowing far-reaching reservations: Contracting Parties may declare that they do not apply the remuneration right at all; or that they apply it only in respect of certain uses, such as broadcasting, communication to the public, or certain kinds thereof; or that they limit the application of Article 15(1) of the WPPT in some other way, for example, by excluding certain groups of beneficiaries.[273] The need to reintroduce such possibilities of reservation seems to show that many countries are not yet ready to provide for such rights. A likely reason is that these rights may mean a financial burden on broadcasters and other relevant users, while they represent one of the economically most interesting rights for performers and phonogram producers. Similarly to the Rome Convention,[274] Article 4(2) of the WPPT allows Contracting Parties to apply material reciprocity towards another Contracting Party that has made a reservation under Article 15(3) of the WPPT.[275]

(d) Term of protection

Since the WPPT does not contain a compliance clause such as Article 1(4) of the **17.131** WCT, it was necessary to lay down a minimum term of protection. Following a worldwide trend towards a duration of fifty years for these neighbouring rights, provoked mainly by the phonogram industry in the years before the adoption of the TRIPS Agreement and reflected in its Article 14(5), Article 17 of the WPPT lays down the same period but with a slightly different calculation of the term: under the TRIPS Agreement, the duration starts from the fixation or the taking place of the performance; under the WPPT, it starts from the fixation, and for phonogram producers also from the publication where the phonogram is

---

272 On folklore protection, see ch 20 below; on the Second Agreed Statement, see Reinbothe/ von Lewinski (n 15 above) Art 15 WPPT n 19.

273 ibid n 23.

274 Art 16(1)(a)(iv) of the Rome Convention; Art 4(2) of the WPPT does not even require a reservation by the party that wants to apply material reciprocity; Reinbothe/von Lewinski (n 15 above) Art 15 WPPT n 7; Ficsor (n 3 above) PP15.06 does not seem to see similarities but differences.

275 For the other elements of Art 15 of the WPPT taken over from Art 12 of the Rome Convention, see paras 6.57–6.58 above (in the Rome context).

published; hence, in the latter case, it is potentially longer than under the TRIPS Agreement. Publication does not include online 'publication' in this context.[276]

(e) Definitions

17.132   Article 2 of the WPPT builds on the list of definitions under Article 3 of the Rome Convention. It partially extends or otherwise amends the previous definitions and adds the definitions of 'fixation' and 'communication to the public'.

17.133   **(i) Performers**   The definition of 'performers' has been extended in Article 2(a) of the WPPT to performers who perform 'expressions of folklore' rather than only literary or artistic works. Expressions of folklore are not considered as 'works' under copyright[277] so that performers of folklore so far have not been protected under international law. This addition stresses the importance of performances of folklore for the culture of many nations; it was inserted without any opposition. Also, the activity of 'interpreting' was added, as compared to the definition under the Rome Convention. It is of a clarifying nature only: the French and Spanish equivalents of the English term 'performers', namely 'artistes-interprètes ou exécutants' and 'artistas interprétes o ejecutantes', include the interpretative activity which now also has been explicitly mentioned in the definition.[278] It should be recalled that, although the definition covers actors and other audiovisual performers, the protection of the WPPT is limited to audio performances, except for the live broadcasting right.[279]

17.134   **(ii) Phonogram**   The Rome definition of 'phonogram' has been altered in two ways. First, the fixation 'of the representation of sounds' has been included in Article 2(b) of the WPPT, in order to take into account the possibility of fixing not only 'sounds' (that are audible) but also non-audible representations thereof. In particular, recorded sounds may be digitally modified and then directly fixed in the modified form without having 'sounded' in their modified version, or they may be produced by computers without any prior fixation of sounds. In these cases, only 'representations of sounds' are fixed. This addition to the definition renders it technically neutral and clarifies that the particular way of producing a phonogram (eg by a synthesizer) does not matter. The computer memory where the fixation is made constitutes the phonogram and is comparable to a traditional master tape from which copies are made.

---

[276] Art 2(e) of the WPPT and para 17.139 below. On online publication in this context, see Reinbothe/von Lewinski (n 15 above) Art 17 WPPT n 9.

[277] paras 20.07–20.09 below.

[278] For the different ways of distinguishing between interpretative and executive activities of performers, see Reinbothe/von Lewinski (n 15 above) Art 2 WPPT n 27.

[279] The rights are restricted to audio performances, due to indications such as 'aural performances' and 'performances fixed in phonograms' in the articles on rights; see para 17.125 above for the broadcasting right and paras 18.02–18.07 below for the background.

Secondly, phonograms have been distinguished from audiovisual fixations in a **17.135** different way. While Article 3(b) of the Rome Convention defines a phonogram as 'any exclusively aural fixation', the WPPT excludes from a 'phonogram' those 'in the form of a fixation incorporated in a cinematographic or other audiovisual work'. Accordingly, phonograms are also protected as such where they have been fixed in the context with images but where they are exploited separately, as with a soundtrack marketed as such. Where they have been fixed separately from images, they are phonograms; before they are incorporated into an audiovisual work, the related rights in the phonogram must be acquired. Where they are used afterwards independently from the audiovisual work, they are again phonograms, as confirmed by the Agreed Statement concerning Article 2(b) of the WPPT. Where they are incorporated in mere moving images—audiovisual fixations that do not constitute 'works' for lack of originality—they are likewise considered phonograms.[280]

(iii) **Producer of a phonogram** The definition of the 'producer of a phono- **17.136** gram' has also been modified as compared to the Rome Convention under which the person who, or the legal entity which, first fixes the sounds is the phonogram producer.[281] While this wording seems to imply that any sound engineer who actually carries out the fixation would be the phonogram producer, it has always been understood as meaning the person who, or the legal entity which, is economically responsible for the production of the phonogram.[282] Article 2(d) of the WPPT explicitly spells out this understanding by defining the phonogram producer as the person or the legal entity who or which takes the initiative and has the responsibility for the first fixation of the sound or its representations.[283]

The explicit mention of the word 'first' (fixation) clarifies that, in particular, **17.137** digital remastering of existing analogue recordings does not constitute a 'first fixation'. Therefore, those who digitally remaster a recording do not obtain separate protection in the remastered version; only the producer of the first, analogue recording remains protected for that recording, whether or not digitally remastered.

(iv) **Fixation** The definition of 'fixation' in Article 2(c) of the WPPT, not **17.138** contained in the Rome Convention, is largely self-explanatory. It covers embodiments of sounds or their representations, from which the sound or their

---

[280] On more detail of this complicated definition and the related Agreed Statement, see Reinbothe/von Lewinski (n 15 above) Art 2 WPPT nn 34–7; Ficsor (n 3 above) PP2.07–PP2.08; B Machuel, 'The Definition of "Phonogram" in the WPPT' in ALAI (ed), *Creators' Rights in the Information Society: ALAI Budapest 2003* (2004) 706 ff.

[281] Art 3(c) of the Rome Convention.

[282] W Nordemann, K Vinck, P Hertin, and G Meyer, *International Copyright* (1990) Art 3 RT n 12; see also paras 6.22–6.23 above.

[283] For more detail, see Reinbothe/von Lewinski (n 15 above) Art 2 WPPT nn 41–5.

representations can be made audible, reproduced, or communicated through a device. Examples are compact disks, sound tapes, and memories of computers such as hard disks or floppy disks. Like most other definitions, it does not cover fixations of images.[284] It is not limited to the finalization of the master tape.[285]

17.139   (v) **Publication**   The definition of 'publication' has been modified in Article 2(e) of the WPPT, as compared to the Rome Convention, only by requiring the right holder's consent to the offering of copies to the public; this requirement has been taken over from Article 3(3) of the Berne Convention.[286] The related Agreed Statement determines 'copies' to mean exclusively 'fixed copies that can be put into circulation as tangible objects'. It thereby excludes from the definition of 'publication' any act of making available phonograms for access online, since the phonograms in this case are offered only in intangible form rather than as tangible objects.[287] Consequently, the 'publication' exclusively online does not constitute 'publication' in the context of the criteria of eligibility[288] nor as the starting point for the duration under Article 17 of the WPPT, but only in Article 15 of the WPPT as explicitly provided.[289]

17.140   (vi) **Broadcasting**   The definition of 'broadcasting' has been altered in Article 2(f) of the WPPT, as compared to the Rome Convention, by inserting 'representations of sounds',[290] and by clarifying that satellite transmissions are also covered by the definition.[291] In addition, it has been clarified for encrypted signals that their transmission is also 'broadcasting' where the means for decrypting are provided to the public by the broadcasting organization or with its consent. Without this clarification, one might argue that encryption would hinder public reception so that 'broadcasting' would not take place. This second clarification follows the model of the EC Satellite and Cable Directive.[292]

---

[284] For the background, ie the controversy on the inclusion of audiovisual performances, see paras 18.02–18.07 below.

[285] *E contrario* conclusion from the Agreed Statement concerning Art 3(2) of the WPPT, see also para 17.41 above in the specific context of criteria of eligibility and Reinbothe/von Lewinski (n 15 above) Art 2 WPPT n 40.

[286] For the corresponding elements of the Rome and Berne Conventions, see paras 6.12, 5.33, and, regarding online 'publication', 7.31–7.33 above.

[287] For more arguments, see Reinbothe/von Lewinski (n 15 above) Art 2 WPPT n 48.

[288] para 17.42 above; Art 3(2) of the WPPT.

[289] Art 15(4) of the WPPT, para 17.127 above. On the discussion, see also paras 17.151–17.152 below.

[290] On this notion, see para 17.134 above.

[291] On a controversy regarding satellite broadcasting under the Rome Convention, see para 6.25 above.

[292] For Art 1(2)(c) of the EC Satellite and Cable Directive of 27 September 1993, see Vol II ch 8.

Unlike in the Rome Convention, rebroadcasting is not separately defined, but **17.141** considered as a form of broadcasting.[293]

In two notable respects, the WPPT follows the Rome Convention. First, its defi- **17.142** nition of 'broadcasting' refers also to the transmission of images and sounds, so that performers under the WPPT enjoy the live broadcasting right (unlike all other rights) also in respect of audiovisual performances.[294] Secondly, the defini- tion of 'broadcasting' is restricted to wireless transmissions, so that any form of cable-casting, be it an original cable transmission, cable retransmission, or wire- based web-radio, etc, is not covered by the definition of 'broadcasting'.

(vii) Communication to the public Yet, under the newly introduced defini- **17.143** tion of 'communication to the public', transmissions to the public by any medium otherwise than by broadcasting and, consequently, any kinds of wire communi- cation to the public, are covered, such as cable-casting, cable retransmission, live transmission of a concert over the internet, etc. 'Transmission' implies that the place where the sounds may be heard is at a distance from the place where the transmission originates. In order also to cover direct presentations for the pur- poses of Article 15 of the WPPT, the second sentence of the definition was added. It ensures that making sounds directly audible to the public constitutes 'commu- nication to the public'. Consequently, remuneration for communication to the public under Article 15 of the WPPT also has to be paid where sounds are played from a phonogram to a public that is present at the place where the phonogram is played, such as in a discotheque. 'Communication to the public', however, does not cover forms of making phonograms available online, as may be seen from the separate regulation of the making available right in Articles 10 and 14 of the WPPT (as opposed to the rights of communication in Articles 6(i) and 15 of the WPPT). Notably, the definition does not cover the communication of images, so that audiovisual performances do not benefit from the communica- tion right.

E. Enforcement provisions

While both the Berne and Rome Conventions include hardly any obligation **17.144** regarding the enforcement of copyright and neighbouring rights, Part III of the TRIPS Agreement for the first time in a multilateral treaty has laid down such obligations in a highly detailed manner.[295] The 'Basic Proposals' for the WCT and the WPPT proposed two alternatives: either the obligation to apply the

---

[293] Reinbothe/von Lewinski (n 15 above) Art 2 WPPT n 54; Ficsor (n 3 above) PP2.17.
[294] See para 17.125 above.
[295] paras 10.103–10.113 above.

TRIPS provisions by analogy, or the explicit inclusion of the adapted TRIPS provisions in annexes to the WCT and the WPPT.

17.145 However, none of these proposals was adopted because a number of countries opposed references in any form to the TRIPS provisions, even if they had already accepted those provisions as Members of the WTO/TRIPS Agreement. In particular, the USA no longer saw a need to include specific enforcement provisions into the WIPO Treaties after the successful conclusion of the TRIPS Agreement, and believed that the rights under the WIPO Treaties of 1996 would also be subject to the TRIPS enforcement provisions. Also, a number of developing countries preferred to deal with enforcement at the national level only, while the majority of countries opted in favour of including at least basic enforcement provisions; their importance as an element of any modern international copyright and neighbouring rights agreement, such as the new WIPO Treaties, was stressed in particular by the EC and GRULAC countries.[296] Finally, the agreed compromise consisted of inserting only a general provision into the WIPO Treaties.[297] It is identical *mutatis mutandis* with Article 41(1) phrase 1 of the TRIPS Agreement, which may serve as an interpretative guidance.[298]

F. Proposals that were not adopted

(1) The abolition of non-voluntary licences

(a) Background

17.146 Articles 13(1) and 11^bis(2) of the Berne Convention permit the provision of non-voluntary licences in respect of the right of mechanical recording of a musical work, and the broadcasting and communication rights under Article 11^bis(1). They were introduced in 1908 and 1928, respectively, in response to the fears by phonogram producers and broadcasting organizations that the relevant right holders would exercise the exclusive recording and broadcasting rights so as to negatively affect their activities.[299]

17.147 The International Bureau of WIPO, in preparation of the possible Berne Protocol, felt that such fears had proved to be unjustified and that, consequently, these

---

[296] For further detail and references, see Reinbothe/von Lewinski (n 15 above) Art 14 WCT nn 6–7.

[297] Art 14(2) of the WCT and Art 23(2) of the WPPT.

[298] Reinbothe/von Lewinski (n 15 above) Art 14 WCT nn 14–15, Art 23 WPPT nn 12–13. On Art 41(1) phr 1 of the TRIPS Agreement, see C Correa, *Trade Related Aspects of Intellectual Property Rights: A Commentary on the TRIPS Agreement* (2007) 410–12; D Gervais, *The TRIPS Agreement: Drafting History and Analysis* (2nd edn, 2003) 2.376.

[299] For the historical background, see para 5.193 above.

non-voluntary licences were no longer needed. Its proposal to delete both provisions in the framework of the possible Berne Protocol[300] was broadly welcomed, while a number of countries remained reluctant or preferred to abolish non-voluntary licences only for certain uses such as primary broadcasting as opposed to retransmission by cable.[301]

(b) Mechanical recording

At the Diplomatic Conference 1996, strong arguments were voiced in particular **17.148** against the abolition of the non-voluntary licence in respect of mechanical recordings. Delegates referred to the experience that authors seemed to be more efficiently protected by receiving remuneration under the statutory, non-voluntary licensing scheme, than on the basis of exclusive rights for which they could not bargain an equitable remuneration in buy-out contracts with publishers. Given the current domination of a few major record companies, the exclusive recording right was viewed as unable to fulfil its traditional function of providing authors with a certain negotiating power: consequently, remuneration rights under the non-voluntary licensing scheme were considered to benefit composers and text writers better than exclusive rights.[302]

(c) Broadcasting and communication

A proposal to abolish non-voluntary licences in respect of broadcasting[303] met **17.149** with less opposition; informal discussions resulted in a preliminary compromise on such abolition under certain conditions. In the subsequent formal meeting of Main Committee I, however, the Chinese delegation, later followed by other delegations, insisted on the need to maintain the non-voluntary broadcasting licence in order to better disseminate culture and ensure a fair remuneration to authors; also, Portugal pointed at the beneficial effects of such a non-voluntary licence for authors in particular 'now that situations of monopoly occurred frequently'.[304] Therefore, both proposals to delete non-voluntary licences were removed from the agenda by vote.[305] The argument by Portugal and others is notable against the background of policy discussions worldwide on the protection of authors in their

---

[300] See the WIPO Memorandum for the Second Session of the Committee of Experts on a possible Berne Protocol, (1992) Copyright 66 ff, 73 (paras 104–7) and 78 (paras 144–8).

[301] On the discussions in the Committees of Experts, see Reinbothe/von Lewinski (n 15 above) ch 3 nn 1–5.

[302] Summary Minutes of Main Committee I (n 96 above) paras 95, 96, 100, 103, and also 92, 98, 109, 112, and 114.

[303] Art 6(1) of the Basic Proposal was limited to the broadcasting and by intention did not cover retransmission and rebroadcasting within the meaning of Art 11bis(1)(ii) of the Berne Convention.

[304] Summary Minutes (n 96 above) para 874.

[305] For further refs, see Reinbothe/von Lewinski (n 15 above) ch 3 nn 7–10.

relation with publishers or other businesses, in particular where copyright contract law is not sufficient. It shows that in certain cases, an exclusive right in the hands of authors with a typically weaker bargaining position may be less beneficial for them than a compulsory licence with a statutory remuneration right.[306]

(2) Definition of rental

17.150 Following the tradition of the Berne Convention, no definition of rental was proposed in the Basic Proposal for the copyright treaty. In the proposal for the planned neighbouring rights treaty, however, 'rental' was defined as 'any transfer of the possession of a copy of a phonogram for consideration for a limited period of time'; 'for consideration' meant 'against payment of any fee'. [307] Since this would have included the activities of public libraries that impose lending fees upon users, the commercial nature of rental was preferred as a defining element. In the end, it was decided simply to qualify 'rental' by the word 'commercial' directly in the context of the provision on rental right rather than inserting a new definition. Apart from being more elegant, this solution had the advantages of being easily applicable also in the copyright treaty and of corresponding to the TRIPS wording.

(3) Online 'publication'

17.151 Article 3(3) of the Berne Convention which defines 'published works' does not clearly answer the question whether the making available to the public of a work exclusively on the internet constitutes publication under this definition.[308] Therefore, Article 3 of the Basic Proposal for the copyright treaty, in following the European Commission's suggestion at the last session of the Committee of Experts to address this problem,[309] defined the term 'publication' so as to cover online publication. Also, it specified that such publication should take place 'where the necessary arrangements have been made for availability of these works to members of the public'.

17.152 This definition would have been relevant in particular for the eligibility of authors for protection under the WCT,[310] the comparison of terms of protection,[311]

---

[306] On this aspect, see also para 3.60 above.
[307] Art 2(f) of the Basic Proposal (n 25 above).
[308] On the relevant problems of interpretation, see paras 7.31–7.33 above.
[309] Report of the Seventh Session, WIPO Doc BCP/CE/VII/4-INR/CE/VI/4 of 5 August 1996, 5 (para 10).
[310] Art 3 of the WCT in connection with Art 3(1)(b) of the Berne Convention.
[311] Art 1(4) of the WCT in connection with Art 7(8) of the Berne Convention and the term 'country of origin' which refers to first publication.

the application in time,[312] and the determination of the country of origin (and, consequently, the geographical area of application of the WCT, which extends only to Parties other than the country of origin).[313] However, this highly technical problem may have emerged too late so as not to allow sufficient time for discussion. Also, delegations may have assumed, in the course of deliberations, that the proposed determination of the place of online publication could have undesired implications on the questions of applicable law in the electronic environment and liability of online service providers. Therefore, the deletion of this proposal from the agenda seemed more appropriate than investing further time in discussion.[314]

(4) Modification right for performers and phonogram producers

17.153 The International Bureau of WIPO had proposed for the First Session of the Committee of Experts on the envisaged neighbouring rights treaty an exclusive adaptation right for performing artists and phonogram producers in order to respond to the widespread practice of digital modification of existing recordings and the subsequent combination thereof.[315] Concerns about any possible confusion with the meaning of 'adaptation' under Article 12 of the Berne Convention were subsequently taken into account by referring to 'modification' rather than 'adaptation'. Thereby, it was made clear that the adaptation of works was different in its nature from the modification of recordings. Yet, the proposal met with further objections, in particular the lack of need for such a right, given the potential of the reproduction right and of the performer's moral right of integrity. Not least, some delegations seemed to wish that the introduction of a modification right for performers and phonogram producers would constitute a further step on the way towards assimilating phonograms to works, not only in the copyright system but also under international law[316]—a wish that may have been a reason for many other delegations (in particular from author's rights system countries) rejecting this proposal.

17.154 At the Diplomatic Conference, opinions continued to be split. The widely felt unease about the vague scope of the new right, its implications for authors' rights, its relation to the reproduction right, and the above doubts resulted in the

---

[312] Arts 1(4) and 13 of the WCT in connection with Art 18(1) of the Berne Convention (through 'country of origin').

[313] Art 3 of the WCT in connection with Art 5(4) of the Berne Convention.

[314] For the discussion at the Diplomatic Conference, see Summary Minutes of Main Committee I (n 96 above) paras 325–35. For the approach chosen in the context of the WPPT, see para 17.139 above on the definition of 'publication'.

[315] Memorandum for the First Session of the Committee of Experts on the possible New Instrument, (1993) Copyright 142, 150, 152 (paras 48, 56(d)).

[316] Report on the First Session, (1993) Copyright 196, 220 (paras 105–9).

agreement to delete the proposed modification right from the agenda. The understanding expressed by one delegation that the reproduction right would also cover reproduction in a modified form did not meet with any objection.[317]

(5) *Sui generis* protection of databases

17.155 Proposals on two major issues were not adopted at the WIPO Diplomatic Conference 1996: those on the protection of audiovisual performances addressed in a separate chapter[318] and on the *sui generis* protection of databases. The Committee of Experts on a possible Berne Protocol, from its Fourth Session, had already discussed the possible inclusion of a *sui generis* protection for databases in an international agreement. In its Sixth Session in February 1996, the EC and its Member States submitted a proposal in this regard; around the same time, the EC had adopted the Database Directive harmonizing such a right.[319] At the Seventh Session, the USA submitted a corresponding proposal. General support and interest was shown also from African and Latin American countries, many of which, however, felt that further study was needed on this issue.[320]

17.156 The overall positive reactions of most delegations encouraged WIPO to submit a separate 'Basic Proposal' on *sui generis* protection of databases for negotiation at the Diplomatic Conference.[321] Its contents largely corresponded to those of the EC Database Directive and included elements from the US proposal and from discussions. In particular, it determined as the object of protection the substantial investment in the collection, assembly, verification, organization, or presentation of the contents of the database. Its maker was to be granted exclusive rights of extraction and utilization, subject to the three-step test. Alternative durations of either twenty-five or fifteen years after a specified event were also proposed, as well as the beginning of a new term of protection following a substantial change to the database if the change constituted a new substantial investment. The principles of national treatment and 'no formalities' modelled upon Article 5 of the Berne Convention as well as provisions on technological measures and enforcement of rights were included in the proposal.

17.157 Yet, time at the Diplomatic Conference 1996 was restricted, especially after around one-third of the available time had been used for procedural questions.

---

[317] On the proposal and discussions regarding the modification right, see Reinbothe/von Lewinski (n 15 above) ch 3 nn 15–18.

[318] See hereon, also regarding the discussions before and at the Diplomatic Conference 1996, paras 18.01–18.07 below.

[319] On the *sui generis* right under the EC Database Directive, see Vol II ch 9.

[320] On discussions during the Committees of Experts, see Reinbothe/von Lewinski (n 15 above) ch 3 nn 52–5, also for further references.

[321] WIPO Doc CRNR/DC/6 of 30 August 1996.

A clear priority was given to the treaties on copyright and on performers' and phonogram producers' rights, so that negotiations on the database treaty were not even opened. The reluctance to open these negotiations may have been reinforced by the developments which had taken place in the USA in the months preceding the Diplomatic Conference: interested circles, in particular from the academic branch, put into doubt the need and appropriateness of such kind of protection. They opposed it strongly, so that the support in one of the proposing countries had seriously declined. Consequently, the Diplomatic Conference only adopted a Recommendation calling for the convocation of an extraordinary session of the competent WIPO Governing Bodies in the three months following the Diplomatic Conference to decide on the schedule of further preparatory work on a database treaty.[322]

G. Framework provisions of both treaties

(1) Relation to other treaties

(a) WCT

Article 1(1) of the WCT incorporates an approach chosen from the earliest considerations, namely to adopt the WCT as a special agreement in the meaning of Article 20 of the Berne Convention rather than to envisage a Berne revision.[323] Accordingly, for those Contracting Parties of the WCT that are also Berne Union countries,[324] the provisions of the WCT must be interpreted in line with Article 20 of the Berne Convention, in particular by avoiding any interpretation of the WCT that would lead to a lesser protection than that granted by the Berne Convention.[325] This obligation may be relevant, for example, for the interpretation of the reproduction right under Article 1(4) of the WCT in connection with the related Agreed Statement.[326]   **17.158**

In addition, this provision clarifies that the WCT has no (legal) connection with treaties other than the Berne Convention, and that any rights and obligations under such other treaties are unaffected by the WCT. It was included in order to   **17.159**

---

[322] Recommendation concerning databases adopted by the Diplomatic Conference on 20 December 1996, WIPO Doc CRNR/DC/100, in: Records of the Diplomatic Conference on Certain Copyright and Neighbouring Rights Question, Geneva 1996, 97; see paras 22.01–22.04 below, on the subsequent fate of this issue.

[323] On the advantages of this approach (ie avoiding the required unanimity), see para 17.04 above.

[324] As of July 2007, all WCT Parties are also Berne members. Note that the EC is not eligible as a Berne member.

[325] For more details on Art 20 of the Berne Convention see paras 5.250–5.251 above.

[326] On the issue of the reproduction right, see para 17.54 above.

take account of concerns of developing countries that the TRIPS enforcement provisions and possibly even its dispute settlement mechanism could otherwise apply to the WCT and WPPT; in substance however, Article 1(1) of the WCT would not have been needed.[327] Even though these concerns were not legally justified, they reflected the urge felt to avoid any impact of the TRIPS Agreement. Accordingly, the TRIPS Agreement, the Universal Copyright Convention, and others are self-standing treaties that continue to be valid and unaffected in respect of the rights and obligations thereunder.[328] Also, their interpretation must remain independent, even where the same wording is used. For example, Parties to the WCT applying the three-step test of the WCT do not need to follow the interpretation of the three-step test of the TRIPS Agreement by a WTO panel.

17.160 Article 1(2) of the WCT contains the so-called 'non-derogation' or 'Berne safeguard clause', drafted upon the model of Article 2(2) of the TRIPS Agreement. It confirms that the existing obligations under the Berne Convention continue to bind the Contracting Parties of the WCT when such Parties are also Berne Members. It also confirms that the WCT does not derogate from obligations under the Berne Convention. This clause applies to obligations under any of the Berne Convention Acts that may be binding on individual Berne Members.[329] While the WCT does not derogate from Berne obligations, it does so from rights under the Convention. In particular, Article 9 of the WCT derogates from the right of Berne Union countries under Article 7(4) of the Berne Convention to apply a duration of only twenty-five years from the making of a photographic work.

17.161 Finally, Article 1(4) of the WCT contains the so-called 'compliance clause', corresponding to the same clause under Article 9(1) phrase 1 of the TRIPS Agreement.[330] Accordingly, all Contracting Parties to the WCT must comply with the substantive law of the Berne Convention, namely, its Articles 1–21 and its Appendix as interpreted under the Berne Convention, including implied limitations.[331] It does not mean that the Contracting Parties would have an obligation to adhere

---

[327] Ficsor (n 3 above) C1.02–C1.04.

[328] For more detail on the relationship between different treaties, see ch 24 (in particular paras 24.02–24.18) below, and Reinbothe/von Lewinski (n 15 above) Art 1 WCT n 12.

[329] *E contrario* conclusion from Art 1(3) of the WCT under which the 'Berne Convention' is meant to refer exclusively to the Paris Act only for provisions following Art 1(3) of the WCT. Only a few Berne Members today are still bound to either the Rome or Brussels Act, see para 4.47 n 122 above and 24.08 below.

[330] paras 10.50–10.51 above on the 'Berne-plus' approach. Art 1701(2) of the NAFTA similarly obliges the parties to 'give effect to the substantive provisions of' specified treaties, as do the latest Free Trade Agreements of the USA regarding the substantive provisions of the WCT and WPPT, paras 12.26–12. 27 above.

[331] Ficsor (n 3 above) C1.18. For an analysis of how Berne Articles apply as a part of the WCT, see ibid C1.21–C1.56.

to the Berne Convention; for the EC, this would not even be possible since the Berne Convention is open for accession only to countries. It simply means the incorporation of the substantive provisions of the Berne Convention into the WCT as WCT obligations. Unlike the TRIPS Agreement, the WCT does not, however, exclude from its application the provision of moral rights; this was not even seriously discussed.[332] The compliance clause (as all provisions following it) exclusively refers to the Paris Act of the Berne Convention, which accordingly represents the foundation to which the WCT has added supplementary elements of minimum protection.[333] These include the essence of most TRIPS provisions as well as additional ones. Accordingly, the 'Berne-plus' approach of the TRIPS Agreement has been supplemented in the WCT by certain TRIPS-plus elements.

(b) WPPT

Article 1 of the WPPT contains a non-derogation or 'Rome safeguard' clause in relation to the Rome Convention corresponding to that of Article 1(2) of the WCT. This clarification is particularly important where the Rome Convention provides for wider protection than the WPPT, as in the case of the performers' rights of communication and fixation of their live performances, which, under Article 7(1)(a) and (b) of the Rome Convention, are granted not only to audio but also to audiovisual performers. This wider obligation continues to be valid among Contracting States of the Rome Convention when such States are also Contracting Parties to the WPPT. While the WPPT does not derogate from Rome obligations, it does so from Rome rights of Contracting States. For example, Contracting Parties to the WPPT may no longer impose the formalities allowed under Article 11 of the Rome Convention.[334]   **17.162**

Article 1(2) of the WPPT on the relation to copyright protection reproduces by analogy the wording of Article 1 of the Rome Convention and therefore may be interpreted in the same way.[335] Finally, Article 1(3) of the WPPT contains, similarly to the WCT, a clause confirming the self-standing nature of the WPPT in relation to any other treaties.[336] 'Any other treaties' means here 'any treaties other than the Rome Convention'. Indeed, the connection between the Rome Convention and the WPPT is regulated for Rome members in Article 22 of the   **17.163**

---

[332] The main, political reason for which the USA did not (need to) request exclusion of moral rights, unlike under the TRIPS Agreement, is likely to be the lack of an effective dispute settlement mechanism under the WCT; for the TRIPS Agreement, see para 10.53 above.

[333] Art 1(3) of the WCT.

[334] Art 20 of the WPPT.

[335] On Art 1 of the Rome Convention, see paras 6.73–6.75 above. See also the Agreed Statement concerning Art 1(2) of the WPPT.

[336] The clause corresponds to that of Art 1(1) phr 2 of the WCT, see para 17.159 above.

Rome Convention, which corresponds to Article 20 of the Berne Convention on 'special agreements'. Even if this is not stated explicitly, the WPPT may be considered as a special agreement to the Rome Convention.[337]

(2) Application in time

17.164 Article 13 of the WCT makes applicable by analogy the provisions of Article 18 of the Berne Convention to the protection provided for in the WCT. Accordingly, the WCT applies in principle to all works existing and still protected in the country of origin at the time of coming into force of the WCT or of accession to it.[338] The same rules apply by analogy to the rights of performers and phonogram producers provided under the WPPT, with the possible exception of performers' moral rights, which may be restricted in their application to performances occurring after the entry into force of the WPPT for the relevant Party.[339] Accordingly, the WCT and WPPT have followed TRIPS in taking over the Berne model for copyright and neighbouring rights.

H. Administrative and final clauses of both Treaties

17.165 These clauses have been drafted in parallel in both Treaties and may be summarized as follows. For each Treaty, its continuing existence and application is guaranteed by its Assembly, which has to decide, among others, about the convocation of a diplomatic conference for the revision of the Treaty and the admission of any intergovernmental organization beyond the (already admitted) European Community to become Party to the Treaty.[340] The Assembly shall meet once every two years in ordinary session. In the case of votes, any intergovernmental organization that is a Contracting Party can vote, in place of its Member States, with a number of votes equal to the number of its Member States which are Parties to the relevant treaty. As soon as one Member State participates in the vote, the organization itself has no longer a right to do so, and vice versa. The administrative tasks concerning the treaties are performed by the International Bureau of WIPO.[341]

---

[337] For the reasons, see para 6.52 above. Ricketson/Ginsburg (n 74 above) 19.37; Ficsor (n 3 above) PP1.02–PP1.04.

[338] For the working of the individual rules under Art 18 of the Berne Convention, see paras 5.243–5.249 above; for TRIPS, see para 10.138 above; on its working in the context of the WCT, see Reinbothe/von Lewinski (n 15 above) Art 13 WCT nn 5–16.

[339] Art 22 of the WPPT; para 17.116 above, and, for the similar situation under TRIPS, paras 10.101–10.102; Reinbothe/von Lewinski (n 15 above) Art 5 WPPT n 5 and Art 22 WPPT n 16.

[340] Arts 15 of the WCT, 24 of the WPPT and 17(2), (3) of the WCT, 26(2), (3) of the WPPT.

[341] Arts 16 of the WCT and 25 of the WPPT.

The Treaties are open for accession not only to any Member State of WIPO, but **17.166** also to the European Community, after it declares its competence and enacts its own legislation binding on all its Member States in respect of matters covered by the relevant Treaty, and to be authorized to become a Party in accordance with its internal procedures. Accordingly, the WIPO Treaties are the first treaties on copyright and neighbouring rights[342] that have offered the EC the possibility to become a Contracting Party. The Treaties are also open to accession by any other intergovernmental organization such as the MERCOSUR, under the prescribed conditions.[343] The relatively high number of instruments of ratification or accession—namely, thirty—necessary for the entry into force[344] was claimed in particular by developing countries; this condition was fulfilled in the sixth year after the adoption of the Treaties, so that the WCT entered into force on 6 March 2002, and the WPPT on 20 May 2002. The Treaties are equally authentic in all six UN languages, namely, Arabic, Chinese, English, French, Russian, and Spanish.[345] The treaties may be denounced by notification.[346]

I. Assessment of the WIPO Treaties as compared to the Berne and Rome Conventions and the TRIPS Agreement

In general, the adoption of the WIPO Copyright Treaty and the WIPO **17.167** Performances and Phonograms Treaty may be considered a milestone in the development of international copyright and neighbouring rights law, and this for several reasons: as compared to the last revision of the Berne Convention in 1971 and to the Rome Convention of 1961, and even to the TRIPS Agreement adopted only two years before the WIPO Treaties, the minimum protection has been considerably raised, both in the traditional area and regarding latest technological developments to which the law has been adapted. Indeed, the WIPO Treaties of 1996 are distinguished by having addressed the challenges of digital technology and the internet at the very time when these started to become relevant in the field of copyright and neighbouring rights, and by having offered global solutions for these global challenges even before many national legislators could react to them.

---

[342] This was already possible in respect of the WTO/TRIPS Agreement, which, however, covers many more areas.
[343] Arts 17(2) of the WCT and 26(2) of the WPPT.
[344] Arts 20 of the WCT and 29 of the WPPT.
[345] Arts 24(1) of the WCT and 32(1) of the WPPT; regarding official texts, see para (2) of these provisions.
[346] Arts 23 of the WCT and 31 of the WPPT.

17.168 The timing of the WIPO Treaties of 1996 was also optimal as regards the generally positive attitude of delegations towards the needs of authors, performers, and phonogram producers; soon after 1996, user groups started a partly activist and quite vocal movement with a rather hostile approach towards strong copyright and neighbouring rights protection. In such an environment, it might have been very difficult, if not impossible, to adopt treaties with the contents of the WIPO Treaties of 1996.[347]

17.169 Finally, the adoption of the WIPO Treaties of 1996 is particularly remarkable because 127 countries were ready to agree, by consensus, on quite a detailed text granting a high level of minimum protection, and this even without any facilitating dynamics such as the 'package dealing' provided for in the GATT/WTO framework.[348] This shows that a revision of the Berne Convention by unanimity could have been possible.

(1) Progress[349] of the WCT as compared to the Berne Convention (1971)

17.170 The WCT incorporates the substantive law of the Berne Convention as a source of obligations under the WCT and ensures that the Berne law is not interpreted so as to reduce its protection.[350] The additional minimum standards of protection include, as mandatory objects of protection, computer programs to be protected as literary works and compilations of data which are not clearly covered by the Berne Convention (as opposed to collections of works). For minimum rights, the clarifying Agreed Statement on the reproduction right confirms its full application in the digital environment, including the storage in digital form in an electronic medium.[351] Additional minimum rights, as compared to the Berne Convention, are a general, exclusive distribution right beyond what has been provided in Articles 14(1)(i) and 14bis(1) phrase 2 of the Berne Convention in respect of works used for cinematographic adaptation and cinematographic works; an exclusive rental right in respect of computer programs, cinematographic works, and works embodied in phonograms; an extension of the right of

---

[347] On this movement, see S von Lewinski, 'International Copyright over the Last 50 Years: A Foreign Perspective' (2003) 50 J'l of the Copyright Society of the USA 581, 597 ff; the assumed difficulty to adopt treaties such as the WCT and WPPT in the years thereafter was expressed by J Reinbothe, M Ficsor, and other experts at a panel discussion on 25 April 2003 at the 11th International Intellectual Property Law & Policy Conference at Fordham Law School, New York.

[348] On package dealing, see paras 9.09 and 10.07 above.

[349] Since the Berne Convention and the WCT are treaties for the protection of rights of authors, 'progress' is used from their perspective. The fact that such an explanation seems necessary may reflect the changed environment between 1996 (when understanding an improvement in protection as 'progress' was not questioned) and today, when users might deny the logics and justification of this viewpoint. This remark also applies to subtitles (2) and (3).

[350] See Arts 1(4) and 1(1) of the WCT in connection with Art 20 of the Berne Convention.

[351] Agreed Statement concerning Art 1(4) of the WCT.

communication to the public in the traditional area to uses not covered by the Berne Convention (in particular original cable transmission of works other than dramatic, dramatico-musical, musical, literary works, and works adapted for cinematographic purposes as well as cinematographic works); and the exclusive right of making available works on the internet and similar networks, thereby covering a highly important kind of exploitation of works.

The mandatory adoption of the three-step test in respect of any limitations and exceptions aims at securing a sound level of protection against an overly broad interpretation of limitations and exceptions. The extension of the minimum duration of protection for photographic works to the general one of fifty years *pma* is an additional progress. Sanctions against the circumvention of technological measures that protect rights of authors, and regarding the manipulation of rights management information are to contribute to the better enforcement of rights in the digital environment; admittedly, it remains to be seen whether this will have positive effects for authors in the long term. Also the—albeit general—enforcement provision goes beyond the level of the Berne Convention. Finally, unlike the Berne Convention, the WCT is open to membership of the EC and other intergovernmental organizations. **17.171**

(2) Progress of the WPPT as compared to the Rome Convention

While the WPPT does not cover broadcasting organizations, it has considerably improved the protection of performers and phonogram producers. First, definitions have been updated: eg performers of folklore have been included; the definitions of phonogram producers and of a phonogram have been clarified; the possibility of fixing not only sounds but also digital and other representations of sounds has been taken into account in several definitions; the definition of 'publication' has been completed upon the model of the Berne Convention; and the definition of 'broadcasting' was clarified in respect of transmissions by satellite and transmissions of encrypted signals. In addition, new definitions of 'fixation' and 'communication to the public' have been introduced. **17.172**

The principle of national treatment has been defined in a clearer way than in Article 2(2) of the Rome Convention as regards its scope: it is clearly limited to minimum rights in the form of exclusive rights only, and to the remuneration right under Article 15 of the WPPT. It therefore does not apply to other remuneration rights such as those for private copying. The principle of 'no formalities' has been fully introduced. This is a step forward from Article 11 of the Rome Convention, which still permits specified formalities. **17.173**

In respect of performers' minimum rights, the WPPT has brought about enormous progress. First, it is no longer permitted simply to provide protection **17.174** through criminal law or similar means; rather, full exclusive rights must be provided.[352] Also, existing rights have been extended and a number of new rights have been introduced. The reproduction right is no longer subject to the conditions laid down in the Rome Convention and, in addition, it explicitly extends to indirect forms of reproduction and to acts of reproduction in any manner or form. An Agreed Statement also clarifies its application in the digital environment and to the storage in digital form in an electronic medium. Yet, the reproduction right (as all rights newly provided in the WPPT) and the rights in unfixed performances (except live broadcasting) do not cover audiovisual performances and thus are more limited than the Rome Convention, despite its Article 19. The newly introduced rights are the two basic moral rights, namely, the right to be identified as the performer of a particular performance and the right of integrity of the performance; and the new economic rights, namely, the exclusive rights of distribution, rental, and making available of fixed performances. The remuneration right for secondary uses of phonograms for broadcasting and communication to the public has been extended, as compared to Article 12 of the Rome Convention, to indirect uses (in particular rebroadcasting, and playing to the public of a broadcast made on the basis of a phonogram), and to phonograms which have been published exclusively online. Also, both performers and phonogram producers must be granted the remuneration right in principle. Yet, as under the Rome Convention, this (extended) protection may be made subject to different reservations.

17.175   Phonogram producers are granted, in addition to the reproduction right already covered by the Rome Convention, the exclusive rights of distribution, rental, and making available to the public, as well as the just-mentioned, extended remuneration right for secondary uses for broadcasting and communication to the public.

17.176   For both performers and phonogram producers, this level of protection is also safeguarded by the application of the three-step test to any limitations and exceptions. The minimum term of protection of twenty years under the Rome Convention has been extended to fifty years. As in the field of copyright, the obligations concerning technological measures, rights management information, and enforcement constitute additional elements of protection. The rule of the WPPT on its application in time is more generous than Article 20 of the Rome Convention because it also covers the performances and phonograms existing at the time of entry into force or accession, under the conditions of Article 18 of the Berne

---

[352] On the meaning of 'the possibility of preventing' certain acts under the Rome Convention, see paras 6.35–6.36 above.

Convention (*mutatis mutandis*). Finally, like the WCT, the WPPT is open to membership of the EC and other intergovernmental organizations.

(3) Progress of the WCT and WPPT as compared to the TRIPS Agreement

The substantive standards of the WCT and the WPPT are also considerably **17.177** higher in comparison with the TRIPS Agreement. The WCT has brought about certain clarifications in respect of computer programs and databases as well as to the scope of the reproduction right in the digital environment. It clearly goes beyond the TRIPS level as regards the exclusive rights of distribution and communication to the public,[353] including the right of making available. The exclusive rental right for 'authors of works embodied in phonograms' is provided more clearly than in Article 14(4) phrase 1 of the TRIPS Agreement. Also, the minimum duration of the protection of photographic works of fifty years *pma* and the obligations concerning technological measures and rights management information go beyond the TRIPS level. Last but not least, the WCT does not exclude moral rights from its application.

In respect of performers' and phonogram producers' rights, progress of the WPPT **17.178** is even more significant: additional rights provided for performers under the WPPT are the moral rights, as well as a number of economic rights that must be exclusive rights rather than protected under criminal or similar law only. The reproduction right has a more clearly defined scope, and the exclusive rental right is phrased more clearly than in Article 14(4) phrase 1 of the TRIPS Agreement; yet, the live communication right is more limited in the WPPT since it does not include audiovisual performances. Additional rights under the WPPT for performers and phonogram producers are the exclusive rights of distribution and making available online, as well as the remuneration right for secondary uses for broadcasting and communication to the public. The obligations concerning technological measures and rights management information are additional elements of protection.

The term of protection for phonogram producers is potentially longer under the **17.179** WPPT: where the phonogram was published within fifty years from fixation, the duration under the WPPT is calculated from the end of the year of its publication rather than from the fixation only.

---

353 These rights are covered by the TRIPS Agreement via the Berne compliance clause of its Art 9(1) only in a fragmentary way.

(4) Résumé

17.180 Overall, the Treaties have successfully reacted to challenges by new technologies and adapted international protection accordingly. Their minimum level of protection is clearly higher than that of the preceding multilateral treaties.[354] At the same time, it is worth noting that quite often, models from existing treaties have been followed, and this not only within the same area. For example, the WPPT has taken over models or elements from the Berne Convention regarding moral rights, the definition of publication, the specification of the reproduction right, etc. Soon after 1996, the substance of the WCT and WPPT was considered for inclusion, en bloc, into a future version of the TRIPS Agreement—an idea no longer pursued in the current environment.[355] Instead, recent bilateral treaties of the USA include the substantive standards of the WCT and WPPT as minimum obligations. Accordingly, the WIPO Treaties 1996 are making their 'careers' also via the vehicle of such agreements.

---

[354] See also the tables comparing the level of protection in the major treaties in the field in ch 23 below.

[355] On this environment, see paras 25.27–25.33 below; for an allusion to this idea based on Art 71(2) of the TRIPS Agreement and ventilated among governments, see Ficsor (n 3 above) C1.07.

18

THE PROTECTION OF AUDIOVISUAL PERFORMANCES

To date, audiovisual performances (ie performances which may be or are fixed on **18.01** a visual or audiovisual medium), are hardly protected in multilateral treaties. Like other performances, they are not protected as works under any copyright treaties.[1] In addition, their protection under the Rome Convention was largely excluded following insistence by the USA, which, however, never acceded to the Convention.[2] The TRIPS Agreement covers audiovisual performances only in respect of the rights of live broadcasting and communication to the public; for other rights, it is limited to performances fixed on phonograms.[3] Finally, recent attempts by WIPO to achieve an international protection for audiovisual performances have failed, and little hope seems left to reach this aim in the near future. The lack of a meaningful international protection is exceptional: in all

---

[1] On initial ideas to consider performances as works of adaptation and to include them in the Berne Convention, cf paras 4.50 ff above.

[2] Art 19 of the Rome Convention makes inapplicable the minimum rights of the Rome Convention for performers once they have agreed to incorporate their performances into a visual or audiovisual fixation, see paras 6.46–6.48 above. E Ulmer, 'The Rome Convention for the Protection of Performers, Producers of Phonograms and Broadcasting Organisations—Part III' [1963] 10 Bulletin of the Copyright Society of the USA 219, 242.

[3] Art 14(1), (4) of the TRIPS Agreement; see also paras 10.91–10.93 above with further references.

other important areas of copyright and neighbouring rights covered at the national level, international protection has been achieved. The reasons for this lack of international protection may be better understood when analysing the discussions and experiences made at the WIPO Diplomatic Conferences of 1996 and 2000, and thereafter.

A. The WIPO Diplomatic Conference of 1996

(1) Different proposals

18.02   Already before the Diplomatic Conference of 1996, governmental experts did not agree on whether to include audiovisual performances in the envisaged treaty, which was tentatively called a 'Possible Instrument for the Protection of the Rights of Performers and Producers of Phonograms'.[4] While the USA wanted to limit the treaty to musical performances, most other countries preferred to cover all kinds of performances.[5] Therefore, the Basic Proposal (ie the text on the basis of which negotiations at the WIPO Diplomatic Conference 1996 took place[6]) offered the following alternatives: the coverage of only musical performances, the coverage of all kinds of performances, or the principal coverage of all kinds of performances combined with the possibility for Contracting Parties to declare a reservation with a view to applying the treaty only in respect of sounds/musical performances.[7] Although the third alternative seemed to offer sufficient flexibility to satisfy every delegation, indeed the USA was not satisfied with the proposed possibility of a reservation, and it could not even agree to a subsequent proposal by the EC and its Member States for more diversified reservations instead of a comprehensive en bloc reservation.[8]

---

[4] J Reinbothe, M Martin-Prat, and S von Lewinski, 'The New WIPO Treaties: A First Resume' (1997) 4 EIPR 171, 175; see also the comparative table of proposals by Member States for the fifth session of the WIPO Committee of Experts on a Possible Instrument for the Protection of the Rights of Performers and Producers of Phonograms (so-called 'New Instrument'), WIPO Doc INR/CE/V/11 pp 8–10 ff.

[5] See the US proposal and proposals of other governments, in particular of the EC and its Member States and Latin American states in the comparative table (n 4 above).

[6] Basic Proposal for the Substantive Provisions of the Treaty for the Protection of the Rights of Performers and Producers of Phonograms to be Considered by the Diplomatic Conference, WIPO Doc CRNR/DC/5; on the Basic Proposals for the three different treaties at the 1996 Conference, see paras 17.10 and 17.12 above.

[7] Art 25(1) of the Basic Proposal (ibid); its alternatives C and D had to be combined with alternatives A and B appearing in all relevant Articles of the Basic Proposal.

[8] WIPO Doc CRNR/DC/32 and Summary Minutes of the Main Committee I in: WIPO (ed), *Records of the Diplomatic Conference on Certain Copyright and Neighbouring Rights Questions* (1999) paras 471, 472.

Instead, the USA submitted a proposal that contained a package of entirely new **18.03** provisions which, if adopted, would have allowed them to agree to the coverage of audiovisual performances.[9] This package included the exclusive rights of fixation, reproduction, distribution, and making available for all kinds of performers but excluded moral rights, the modification right (for performers and phonogram producers) and, for audiovisual performers, the rental right. In addition, it contained a provision on the free transferability of all exclusive rights under the treaty, including those of audio performers—an element which the USA had already tried to achieve in the TRIPS negotiations not only for performers' but also for authors' rights, though without success.[10] A key element was the mandatory rebuttable presumption of transfer of all performers' rights under the new treaty to the producer of the audiovisual fixation upon the mere consent of the performer to the fixation. Also, a choice of law rule referred to the law of the Contracting Party which was most closely connected to the contract, in the absence of a contractual agreement on the applicable law. In addition, the so-called 'implementation clause' was to allow Contracting Parties to determine the way of implementation including, in particular, collective bargaining agreements under labour law rather than exclusive rights for performers. This clause would have allowed the USA to continue its domestic system while leaving open the question how performers who contributed to a foreign film would be protected in the USA. Finally, a broad scope of national treatment (which was rejected by the overall majority of negotiating parties)[11] was proposed for all, including audio performers. The USA was ready to agree to the protection of audiovisual performances only if the entire package was accepted by the other delegations.

It is no surprise that many of the proposed elements were contrary to the interests **18.04** and positions of the majority of delegations, such as the exclusion of moral rights and rental rights, the broad national treatment even beyond the audiovisual performances and, primarily, the provisions of free transferability, choice of law, and the mandatory presumption of transfer of rights to the producer.

(2) Background to different positions

This split of positions reflected the different systems of protection as well as the **18.05** economic interests of the USA on the one hand and of most other countries in the world, in particular those of the European Continental system, on the other hand. In the USA, the protection of audiovisual performers is mainly based on

---

9 WIPO Doc CRNR/DC/34 and Summary Minutes of the Main Committee I, ibid paras 465–8.

10 On free transferability, see S von Lewinski, 'Copyright in Modern International Trade Law' (1994) 161 RIDA 4, 57 and paras 11.18, 12.13 above.

11 paras 17.45–17.46 above.

collective bargaining contracts in the framework of labour law. As a rule, any person (including foreign) who wants to act or otherwise perform in an audiovisual production with a US producer must be a member of a trade union, such as the Screen Actors' Guild and is thus protected by its collective bargaining agreements. Likewise, as a rule, US producers are permitted to employ actors only if they are members of a guild. Therefore, the guilds are continuously growing and have a sufficiently strong bargaining power to negotiate reasonable conditions under their collective bargaining agreements. Their power is reinforced by their right to strike—an extremely powerful right because it has the potential for huge economic consequences with even only one day of strike in the film industry. Individual actors are allowed to negotiate higher royalties and better conditions. Actors in foreign productions to which US labour law does not apply do not enjoy such protection when the films are exploited in the USA.[12]

18.06 To the contrary, in countries following the European Continental system, audiovisual performers are, as a matter of principle, treated in the same way as audio performers because any discrimination between different kinds of performers is not perceived as justified. Indeed, the merit of a performance is the same irrespective of the medium of its fixation. From a performer's point of view, it is not intelligible why she should be protected where her musical performance is recorded on a phonogram but not where images are added thereto or the performance is broadcast by television or fixed by audiovisual means.[13] Therefore, audiovisual performers just like audio performers enjoy exclusive rights in these countries under the system of neighbouring rights protection. Protective provisions on contract law[14] also apply. Presumptions of transfer of rights to the producer have been introduced in many countries; yet, these are often subject to restrictions or specific conditions such as the payment of an equitable remuneration.[15] At the Conference of 1996, most governments, however, did not want to be obliged internationally to continue to provide for presumptions of transfer, especially if not accompanied by certain safeguards in favour of performers.

---

[12] On the system of collective bargaining agreements in the USA, see N Reber, *Film Copyright, Contracts and Profit Participation* (2000) 208 ff; for a comparison of the US and Continental European systems, see S von Lewinski, 'The Protection of Performers in the Audio-Visual Field in Europe and the United States' in H Hansen (ed), *International Intellectual Property Law & Policy* (Vol IV, 2000) 96-1–96-14.

[13] See also para 6.47 above.

[14] See on this Continental European concept paras 3.70–3.72 above.

[15] On presumptions of transfer, see eg S von Lewinski, 'Legal Presumptions of Transfer of Rights of Audiovisual Performers in Selected European Countries' in S Martin (ed), *Mélanges pour Victor Nabhan* (Les Cahiers de Propriété Intellectuelle, *Hors série*, 2005) 275–88; see also Art 2(5) and (7) EC Rental Rights Directive 1992 (on this Directive, see Vol II ch 6).

(3) Outcome of the Diplomatic Conference 1996

After intense discussions, including bilateral talks between the USA and the EC **18.07** and its Member States which nearly arrived at an informal basis for a possible compromise, the prevailing view among European and other non-American performers and most governmental delegations was that such a compromise, which would comprise a mandatory rebuttable presumption of transfer, would have potentially weakened the position of performers more than the complete exclusion of audiovisual performances from the treaty. It was feared that such a compromise would result in a treaty for film producers rather than for performers, and that it would have strengthened, in particular, the already dominant US film industry, not least given the additional elements of the possible compromise.[16] Therefore, no protection seemed better for most delegations than such a compromise. Consequently, the topic was no longer pursued at the Diplomatic Conference. At the same time, the strong regrets of this outcome in particular by the EC and its Member States, and African and Latin American countries is reflected in a resolution which was adopted by the Diplomatic Conference 1996 stating that the work on this issue was to continue with a view to the adoption of a protocol to the WPPT before the end of the year 1998.[17]

B. Activities between 1996 and 2000

After 1996, work continued in the WIPO Committee of Experts on a Protocol **18.08** Concerning Audiovisual Performances, followed by the Standing Committee on Copyright and Related Rights.[18] Discussions in these Committees allowed the delegations to extensively exchange views on the different positions among delegations, and to test new proposals and drafting options. Yet, the basic positions did not change. In particular, the EC and other European delegations, and African, Latin American, and Caribbean countries continued to favour, in compliance with the Resolution of 1996, the adoption of a protocol to the WPPT because it was most closely to follow the provisions of the WPPT and not to include any article regarding the transfer of rights. On the other hand, the USA and a number of Asian countries opted for an entirely independent treaty which would deviate from the

---

[16] J Reinbothe and S von Lewinski, *The WIPO Treaties 1996* (2002) 475 f; S von Lewinski, 'The WIPO Diplomatic Conference on Audiovisual Performances: A First Resume' (2001) EIPR 333, 334.

[17] WIPO Doc CRNR/DC/99.

[18] The Committee of Experts met in September 1997 and June 1998 (WIPO Docs AP/CE/I/4 and AP/CE/II/9) and the Standing Committee in November 1998, May 1999, November 1999, and April 2000 (WIPO Docs SCCR/1/9, SCCR/2/11, SCCR/3/11, and SCCR/4/6).

WPPT in many respects, including the transfer of rights.[19] By 1999, all relevant issues had been clearly identified. Even if deliberations did not point at a possible compromise, a decision to proceed to a Diplomatic Conference, after major hesitations and several postponements, was finally taken in April 2000.[20]

C. The Diplomatic Conference 2000

18.09   The Diplomatic Conference on the Protection of Audiovisual Performances was convened by WIPO from 7 to 20 December 2000, in Geneva. Two weeks were available to negotiate the envisaged treaty as a left-over from the 1996 Diplomatic Conference. Negotiations were based on the 'Basic Proposal' prepared by the Chairman of the Committee and published on 1 August 2000.[21]

(1) The least controversial provisions

18.10   The least controversial provisions of the Basic Proposal were those on the exclusive rights of performers in their unfixed performances and their exclusive rights of reproduction, distribution, rental, and making available of fixed performances; limitations and exceptions; the term of protection; obligations concerning technical measures and rights management information; formalities; reservations; and enforcement of rights.[22] It was also provisionally agreed that the related agreed statements would be taken over from the WPPT by analogy. In respect of the rental right, the so-called 'impairment test' continued to be controversial. It had been introduced in Article 11 of the TRIPS Agreement regarding cinematographic works in order to accommodate needs of the USA,[23] but not in Article 9 of the WPPT.[24] Yet, in particular the EC and its Member States were ready to compromise so that the impairment test was kept in the provisionally agreed version of Article 9 of the Basic Proposal.[25]

---

[19] On the discussions in the WIPO Committees after 1996 and before the Diplomatic Conference of 2000, see Reinbothe/von Lewinski (n 16 above) 476–8.

[20] ibid 478 (n 32).

[21] The Basic Proposal for the Substantive Provisions of an Instrument on the Protection of Audiovisual Performances to be Considered by the Diplomatic Conference (WIPO Doc IAVP/DC/3 of 1 August 2000) was prepared by the Chairman of the Committee; see also the Basic Proposal for Administrative and Final Provisions of the International Instrument on the Protection of Audiovisual Performances to be Considered by the Diplomatic Conference (WIPO Doc IAVP/DC/4 of 22 September 2000) which was prepared by the International Bureau.

[22] Arts 6–10 and 13–20 of the Basic Proposal.

[23] See paras 10.67–10.69 above.

[24] Art 9 of the WPPT includes the impairment test only in context with pre-existing systems of remuneration rights, see Reinbothe and von Lewinski (n 16 above) Art 9 WPPT n 17.

[25] Text of Draft Articles and Draft Agreed Statements provisionally adopted at the Diplomatic Conference on the Protection of Audiovisual Performances, Geneva, 7–20 December 2000, WIPO Doc IAVP/DC/34; von Lewinski (n 16 above) 333, 336–7.

A comparatively easy agreement *ad referendum* was also reached on a few other **18.11** issues which were relatively uncontroversial, namely on the relation to other conventions and treaties[26] and on the beneficiaries of protection.[27] The controversy on the relation of the new treaty to the WPPT, that is whether it should be a protocol to the WPPT or a self-standing treaty, was finally transferred to the administrative and final clauses. Article 1 of the Basic Proposal as provisionally agreed simply contained the non-derogation clause in respect of the WPPT and the Rome Convention and was also otherwise based on the model of Article 1 of the WPPT.[28] The designation as a protocol or a treaty was considered less important than the actual legal link of the new treaty to the WPPT to be laid down explicitly in the final and administrative provisions; in the end, however, no agreement was reached on this issue in the framework of these provisions.[29]

Regarding the beneficiaries of protection, the EC and other European delegations **18.12** preferred to adopt only the nationality rather than also the habitual residence of the performer as a possible point of attachment. They wanted to avoid backdoor protection through this additional criterion which would allow a country not to become a party to the new treaty and therefore not to be subject to international obligations in this field, while its nationals could benefit from protection in the Contracting Parties by establishing habitual residences in these countries. The USA and other delegations, however, wanted to broaden the circle of beneficiaries. The EC and its Member States again acquiesced so that provisional agreement was reached on both points of attachment.[30]

(2) The most controversial issues

The most controversial issues were the definitions (in particular that of 'audiovisual **18.13** fixation'), moral rights, the rights of broadcasting and communication to the public, and, in particular in this context but also in general, national treatment, as well as application in time and the broader issue of transfer of rights. These issues were all legally or politically linked. A provisional, tacit agreement was reached *ad referendum* without discussion regarding all issues except for the transfer of rights which was finally not resolved. This partial agreement, however, has to be considered against the background of the overall aim to adopt an entire package, namely the envisaged treaty on audiovisual performances. Since the issue of transfer remained unresolved, the provisional agreement on other controversial

---

[26] Art 1 of the Basic Proposal (n 21 above).
[27] Art 3 ibid.
[28] However, it stated a non-specified connection with the WPPT in Art 1(3).
[29] von Lewinski (n 16 above) 338.
[30] von Lewinski, 'International Protection for Audiovisual Performers: A Never-Ending Story? A Resume of the WIPO Diplomatic Conference 2000' (2001) 189 RIDA 3, 23–5.

issues can hardly be considered as a continuing position of the respective governments.

(a) Definition of audiovisual fixations

18.14 First, the proposed definition of 'audiovisual fixation'[31] was drafted so broadly that it could have overlapped with the definition of 'phonogram' under Article 2(b) of the WPPT, depending on the interpretation of the latter provision which, representing a compromise, could vary. Since the new treaty on audiovisual performances was likely to grant performers in relation to producers a less advantageous position than did the WPPT, the performers had an interest in maintaining the broadest possible scope of application of the WPPT. This interest was particularly strong in view of the possibility that producers could concentrate on producing musical recordings supplemented by visual elements in order to benefit from the potentially more producer-friendly provisions of the new treaty. A Solomon solution was reached by the draft of an agreed statement according to which the definition of audiovisual fixation would leave without prejudice the definition of 'phonogram' under Article 2(b) of the WPPT.[32] Accordingly, this definition of a phonogram would have remained unaffected even in its broadest possible interpretation.

(b) Moral rights

18.15 Secondly, in respect of moral rights, the Basic Proposal had been based on Article 5 of the WPPT.[33] Yet, it severely reduced the applicability of the integrity right by exempting any modifications consistent with the normal exploitation in the course of an authorized use of the performance.[34] The controversy essentially dealt with the extent to which the integrity right would be acknowledged; in particular, the USA tried largely to exclude its application by sanctioning 'customary practice' or 'standard industry practice' (under which disregard of integrity interests is indeed widespread). On the contrary, the EC with its Member States and others preferred a strong moral rights protection. Provisional agreement was finally found in a compromise which seemed vague enough to allow quite different ways of interpretation.[35]

---

[31] Art 2(c) of the Basic Proposal (n 21 above).

[32] Von Lewinski (n 16 above) 336.

[33] On Art 5 of the WPPT, cf paras 17.115 ff above; it is based on Art 6[bis] of the Berne Convention and covers the rights of paternity and integrity.

[34] Art 5(1)(ii) of the Basic Proposal (n 21 above).

[35] Von Lewinski (n 16 above) 337.

(c) Broadcasting and communication rights and national treatment

Thirdly, the rights of broadcasting and communication to the public regarding   **18.16**
fixed performances in context with national treatment was highly controversial.
Article 11 of the Basic Proposal provided for an exclusive right which could be
replaced under national law by a right to equitable remuneration. Both the exclusive
and the remuneration right were made subject to reservations similar to those
under Article 16(1)(a) of the Rome Convention regarding the secondary uses of
commercial phonograms.[36] Accordingly, this provision did not lay down any
strict minimum standard. Yet, its inclusion was considered important because
the right would be covered by national treatment. In particular European
performers wanted to exclude national treatment regarding these rights as far as possible. They argued that they would hardly benefit, for example, from simultaneous
cable retransmission rights in the USA, due to particular infrastructural problems
whereas US and other foreign performers could fully enjoy the highly developed
services of European collecting societies. After discussion of further proposals,
the following provisional compromise was adopted: material reciprocity was
introduced in respect of the exclusive and remuneration rights under Article 11
of the Basic Proposal and in the context with the possible reservations under
Article 11(3) of the Basic Proposal.

In respect of national treatment in general, the situation was similar to that under   **18.17**
the WPPT, so that provisional agreement was also reached here on a limited scope
of national treatment according to the model of Article 4 of the WPPT.[37]

(d) Application in time

Article 22 of the WPPT, which served as a model, in principle made the treaty   **18.18**
applicable to existing performances.[38] Article 19 of the Basic Proposal did not
entirely follow this model but allowed Contracting Parties not to apply the
economic rights to existing performances, in combination with the possibility of
other Contracting Parties to apply material reciprocity. Instead, the EC and its
Member States wished to be able not to apply the moral rights to existing
performances, thereby following the model of Article 22 of the WPPT. Yet, a
number of other countries wanted to be able not to apply both economic and moral
rights, hence the entire protection, to existing performances. The provisional
compromise was then concluded on the basis of the Basic Proposal. Accordingly,

---

[36] cf para 17.130 above.
[37] Art 4(1) of the provisionally agreed text; von Lewinski (n 16 above) 336–7; on Art 4 of the
WPPT, cf paras 17.43 ff above.
[38] For Art 22 of the WPPT which itself followed the model of Art 18 of the Berne Convention,
and on the possibility of limiting the moral rights to future performances, see para 17.164 above.

Contracting Parties could have chosen to leave economically unprotected the entire repertoire existing at the time of entry into force of the envisaged treaty.[39]

(e) Transfer of rights

18.19 As at the 1996 Diplomatic Conference, the issue of transfer was the most controversial one—and again, in the end, it could not be resolved. The Basic Proposal offered the following alternatives: (i) a mandatory rebuttable presumption of transfer of all exclusive rights under the treaty to the producer—an alternative which had already been rejected in 1996;[40] (ii) a mandatory rebuttable presumption of the entitlement of the producer to exercise the exclusive rights under the treaty, once the performer has consented to the audiovisual fixation of his performance—an alternative which was so close to the first one that had already been rejected in 1996 that its chances for adoption were not strong; (iii) no provision, so that the issue would be left to national law—an alternative which could have accommodated most countries' needs but would certainly not have satisfied the USA, which had from the beginning insisted on dealing explicitly with the issue of transfer in the envisaged treaty; and (iv) a rule on applicable law in respect of the transfer of performers' rights to the producer on the basis of a contract or by operation of law.[41] In essence, this fourth alternative would have allowed a country to apply its domestic rules regarding transfer or entitlement of rights in respect of the exploitation of its films worldwide. This would have been inconsistent with the law in many countries and could have distorted the consistency within domestic systems of international private law.[42]

18.20 Extensive negotiations resulted in the conclusion that the controversy did not relate to terminology but to substance. On the one hand, a majority of countries would have preferred or at least accepted not to deal with this question at all in the treaty. Yet, they were ready to adopt a provision on the applicable law regarding contractual transfers. At the same time, they rejected such provision regarding any transfer by operation of law.[43] On the other hand, the USA, in particular, insisted that statutory transfer provisions (such as the work-made-for-hire rules) of the law of the country where the audiovisual production was made would be explicitly recognized to apply 'extraterritorially' in the country of exploitation. By these means, the USA wanted to centralize all worldwide rights in the hands of

[39] On application in time, see also von Lewinski (n 16 above) 338.
[40] Reinbothe/Martin-Prat/von Lewinski (n 4 above) 175.
[41] Alternative G of Art 12 of the Basic Proposal (n 21 above).
[42] eg Summary Minutes of Main Committee I, WIPO Doc IAVP/DC/37, para 442.
[43] See the proposal by the EC and its Member States in particular, WIPO Doc IAVP/DC/12 which made the relevant Agreed Statement subject to mandatory provisions in the law of the country for which protection was claimed and left it without prejudice to international law; see also von Lewinski (n 16 above) 339.

the film producers and thereby reach the same aim as envisaged by means of a mandatory presumption of transfer or entitlement of exercise in favour of the producer. The USA showed that reaching this aim was crucial for them and would alone trigger their interest in adopting the treaty. It became clear that such a treaty would serve the USA as a means to guarantee the transfer of performers' rights to the producer worldwide and thereby to facilitate the exploitation of films in favour of producers. It was clearly not in the interest of the rest of the world to thereby further strengthen the US film industry, which was already dominating the world market. This consequence as well as the inappropriateness of including international private law rules in a neighbouring rights treaty on only one specific aspect made it impossible for the majority of delegations who were concerned about performers rather than producers to accept a treaty with such a rule.[44]

(3) The outcome of the Diplomatic Conference

Although it would have been realistic and, under the rules of procedure, possible **18.21** to adopt a treaty without a transfer clause by a majority vote, the Director General of WIPO made successful efforts to avoid any vote (which would have mainly isolated the USA). This procedure could certainly be explained by political reasons and it corresponded to WIPO's traditional and fundamental aim of inclusiveness. At the same time, it raised doubts as to its appropriateness, in particular since a vast majority of countries seemed to be ready to adopt the treaty without a transfer clause. Accordingly, it seemed realistic that international protection of audiovisual performances would finally be achieved and also widely recognized.[45] In fact, however, the only outcome of the Diplomatic Conference of 2000 was a declaration that was read by the President of the Conference in the Plenary as follows: 'The Diplomatic Conference notes that provisional agreement has been achieved on 19 Articles and recommends to the Assemblies of the Member States of WIPO, to be held in September 2001, that they reconvene the Diplomatic Conference for the purpose of reaching agreement on outstanding issues.'[46] Accordingly, the Diplomatic Conference could be resumed in principle

---

[44] Von Lewinski (n 16 above) 338–9; from an American point of view, see R Oman, 'The Protection of Actors' Rights: The U.S. Perspective', in ALAI Hungary (ed), *Creators' Rights in the Information Society: ALAI Budapest 2003* (2004) 911 ff; on the formal discussions on the issue of transfer at the Diplomatic Conference, see Summary Minutes of Main Committee I (n 42 above), in particular paras 428–75; eg India stated that it was confused seeing 'a right of producers introduced', ibid para 433; also n 42 above.

[45] On such doubts, also in respect of the future of treaty-making in intellectual property already at a time when developing countries had not yet voiced fundamental opposition to enhanced protection, von Lewinski (n 16 above) 340.

[46] Reinbothe/von Lewinski (n 16 above) 485 in n 96, later published in the Summary Minutes of the Plenary, WIPO Doc IAVP/DC/36 para 96.

with a view to finding a compromise on the remaining issues. Yet, this prospect was not overly promising. Chances to resolve the remaining issues seemed limited. Also, the provisional agreement on the title, the Preamble, and the 19 Articles (Articles 1–12(1) and 13–19) was only adopted *ad referendum* and would most probably have to be renegotiated together with the remaining issues, namely the question of transfer/applicable law, administrative and final provisions regarding the link between the new treaty and the WPPT, and the number of necessary ratifications for the entry into force.[47]

D. Developments after 2000

18.22 At its session in September 2001, the WIPO Governing Bodies considered that it was too early to resume negotiations on a treaty on audiovisual performances, and the Chairman of the General Assembly proposed to retain the issue on the agenda and to encourage the parties to inform the Standing Committee on Copyright and Related Rights on any progress in the discussions.[48]

18.23 Subsequently, informal contacts continued, and WIPO initiated and published a number of studies: first, a survey on national protection of audiovisual performances in ninety-eight Member States of WIPO prepared by the Secretariat in cooperation with its Member States;[49] secondly, studies on audiovisual performers' contracts and remuneration practices in Mexico, the United Kingdom, and the USA,[50] and in France and Germany;[51] thirdly, studies on the transfer of rights of performers to producers of audiovisual fixations. The studies on transfer dealt with the substantive law regarding performers' rights, in particular the rules on transfer of their rights, as well as with the private international law rules in this context. The main study covered the relevant multilateral treaties and the law in France, the USA and, on the basis of separate studies, in Egypt, Germany, India, Japan, Mexico, and the United Kingdom.[52]

---

[47] Von Lewinski (n 16 above) 340.

[48] See the full statement of the Chairman of the WIPO General Assembly on this occasion in Reinbothe/von Lewinski (n 16 above) 485 (in n 97).

[49] WIPO Doc AVP/IM/03/2 Rev 2 of 25 August 2005.

[50] Study by K Sand, WIPO Doc AVP/IM/03/3A.

[51] Study by M Salokannel, WIPO Doc AVP/IM/03/3B.

[52] See the main study by J Ginsburg and A Lucas, WIPO Doc AVP/IM/03/04 Add of 12 May 2004 following an earlier version with the same document number of 2003; study on Mexico by JR Obón León, WIPO Doc AVP/IM/03/4A Rev; on the United Kingdom by H MacQueen and C Waelde, WIPO Doc AVP/IM/03/4B; Egypt by H Bodrawi, WIPO Doc AVP/IM/03/4C; Germany by S von Lewinski and D Thum, WIPO Doc AVP/IM/03/4D Rev; India by P Anand, WIPO Doc AVP/IM/03/4E; and Japan by M Dogouchi and T Ueno, WIPO Doc AVP/IM/03/4F.

All these studies were presented and discussed at two ad hoc informal meetings **18.24** organized by WIPO outside the Standing Committee on Copyright and Related Rights on 6 and 7 November 2003, and 17 November 2004.[53] It was mainly the studies on transfer of rights that clearly showed, as also perceived by the audience, the high degree of complexity and diversity of national solutions, in particular regarding the private international law issues. Consequently, most participants had the impression that it would not be advisable to address these complex issues in any possible future treaty on the protection of audiovisual performances. The main study on transfer of rights also made clear that, given the diversity of substantive law, any treaty provision on applicable law would fail to resolve essential difficulties.[54] Yet, even the harmonization of substantive law regarding performers' rights (in particular regarding the transfer of rights) did not emerge from the studies as a realistic approach. Finally, contractual stipulation of the applicable law is not a viable solution for all issues to be dealt with, since at least some of them are governed by substantive law and cannot be regulated by contractual stipulations on the applicable law.

At the above informal meeting of November 2003 at WIPO,[55] where different **18.25** presentations by actors and independent producers were made, the Screen Actors' Guild (USA) announced a change of its position. Beforehand, including at the 2000 WIPO Diplomatic Conference, the Screen Actors' Guild had agreed with the US producers, for certain returns, to opt for a transfer clause. At the above meeting, it announced it would join the position of the actors in the rest of the world and go along with the adoption of a treaty without any clause referring to the transfer of rights to producers.[56] This change appeared to open up a new possibility to relaunch the stalled discussions on a treaty on audiovisual perform-ances. However, it seems that the US government so far has not been in a position to endorse this point of view against its producers, and that WIPO continues to favour the consensus principle. If the US government were in a position to do so, the adoption of a treaty on audiovisual performances would seem likely,[57] particularly since the rest of the world has continued to prefer a treaty without any transfer clause, or at least could well go along with such a treaty. Currently, informal talks continue.

---

[53] 'Ad hoc informal meeting on the protection of audiovisual performances' 6–7 November 2003; 'Information meeting on the protection of audiovisual performances' 17 November 2004.
[54] See the study by Ginsburg and Lucas (n 52 above) 6–7, presenting potential options for treaty solutions with their respective disadvantages.
[55] See n 53 above.
[56] Oman (n 44 above) 915 alluded to that change of position already before the November meeting.
[57] After the general attitude of at least certain developing countries in international intellectual property negotiations became much more reserved from around 2004 on, the prospects may how-ever be less positive, even if developing countries in 2000 strongly promoted a better protection of audiovisual performers.

Unless a fundamental change of position on one of the sides occurs, the adoption of such a treaty will remain very unlikely. The fact that this issue has been controversial since the adoption of the Rome Convention and that several, intensive attempts to bridge the gap, even in the particularly dynamic situations of two Diplomatic Conferences, have failed seems to suggest that the possibilities for a compromise have been exhausted, at least for the time being.

19

THE PROJECT OF A TREATY ON THE PROTECTION OF BROADCASTING ORGANIZATIONS

A. The launch and development of discussions on the protection of broadcasting organizations in WIPO

(1) Initial activities

(a) The lack of broadcasting organizations in the WPPT

The most recent neighbouring rights treaty, the WPPT, did not follow the Rome **19.01** Convention and the TRIPS Agreement in their coverage of broadcasting organizations.[1] One of the reasons is certainly that it emerged from the call to better protect phonograms and their producers at the international level; performers, whose performances are often incorporated into phonograms, were natural allies for protection. Broadcasting organizations, however, are no such natural allies; rather, their interests are often in conflict with those of phonogram producers and performers. Consequently, their inclusion could have complicated negotiations

---

[1] Art 13 of the Rome Convention and ch 6 (eg paras 6.24, 6.63–6.66) above; Art 14(3) of the TRIPS Agreement and ch 10 (eg paras 10.33 and 10.96–10.97) above.

on the WPPT. In addition, just before the WIPO Committees started their work, TRIPS negotiations had shown the difficulties in agreeing on minimum standards for the protection of broadcasting organizations: different national law backgrounds had proved to be a stumbling block for a meaningful protection in the TRIPS Agreement.[2] Nevertheless, some delegations during Committee of Experts' discussions suggested including broadcasting organizations in the later WPPT, but they did not find sufficient support to extend the mandates of the Committees accordingly.[3]

(b) New initiatives

19.02 Already at the last session of the Committees before the WPPT was adopted in 1996, the Philippines proposed the convocation of a forum on the international protection of broadcasters' rights, the purpose of which was to assess the need for new international norms; this proposal was met with a positive reaction by the Director General.[4] Subsequently, claims for better international protection of broadcasting organizations were forcefully relaunched at two international WIPO symposia in April 1997 in Manila and in February 1998 in Cancun.[5] In panel discussions at the Manila Symposium, governmental and non-governmental participants addressed different issues regarding the protection of broadcasting organizations, such as the existing international law; new challenges for broadcasters as owners of neighbouring rights; broadcasters as users of works and other materials; the rights of satellite broadcasting, cable redistribution, and communication to the public by cable; as well as internet transmissions.[6]

19.03 At the end of the Manila Symposium, the responsible Assistant General of WIPO sensed that governmental delegates wished to start an international norm-setting process regarding the protection of broadcasting organizations, and he encouraged them to submit proposals to WIPO.[7] The Symposium of Cancun

---

[2] For the weakness of the TRIPS protection in Art 14(3), see para 10.97 above.

[3] Sweden and Norway claimed a balance between the three neighbouring rights, see Anon, 'Committee of Experts on a Possible Protocol to the Berne Convention for the Protection of Literary and Artistic Works, First Session, Report' (1992) Copyright 30, 45 paras 41, 45; several delegations suggested inclusion of broadcasters' protection, eg Anon, 'Committee of Experts on a Possible Instrument on the Protection of the Rights of Performers and Producers of Phonograms, First Session, Report' (1993) Copyright 196, 198 paras 11, 12 (Ecuador, Austria).

[4] Report of the February 1996 sessions of both Committees, WIPO Doc BCP/CE/VI/16-INR/CE/V/14, paras 266–8; earlier in the session, it had claimed the extension of the terms of reference of the Committees, ibid, para 35.

[5] WIPO (ed), *WIPO World Symposium on Broadcasting, New Communication Technologies and Intellectual Property* Manila, April 28–30, 1997 (1998) 1, WIPO Publication 757(E); *WIPO Symposium on Copyright, Broadcasting and New Technologies for Countries of Latin America*, Cancun, 16–18 February 1998, WIPO Doc OMPI/DA/CUN/98.

[6] Conference Proceedings, ibid; for a resume of discussions, see M Ogawa, *Protection of Broadcasters' Rights* (2006) 76–91.

[7] Conference Proceedings (n 5 above) 114.

concluded with a declaration according to which the existing international protection was insufficient and in need of updating, especially in light of new technologies. The declaration suggested starting work on a possible international treaty in the framework of a WIPO Committee of Experts.[8] Subsequently, in March 1998 the governing bodies of WIPO approved coverage of the protection of broadcasting organizations by the biennial programme budget for 1998–9.

(2) Development of work in the Standing Committee of WIPO

(a) Initial sessions

In its first session in 1998, the newly established Standing Committee on Copyright and Related Rights (SCCR) discussed the protection of broadcasting organizations only to a limited extent, given its primary focus on the protection of audiovisual performances—one of the yet unresolved issues of the Diplomatic Conference 1996. Yet, the Committee recommended that the matter of broadcasting organizations remain on the agenda and be dealt with in regional consultations, and that the International Bureau invite participants to submit proposals or views on the topic.[9] At the Second and Third Sessions of the SCCR in May and November 1999, submissions (including some in treaty language) by governments and non-governmental organizations were discussed, though only by general remarks.[10] Most of the proposals drafted in treaty language closely followed the WPPT model and included even more extensive rights.[11] Since the Fourth Session of the SCCR was entirely devoted to audiovisual performances in order to prepare the Diplomatic Conference 2000,[12] it was only at the Fifth Session in May 2001 that a more substantive discussion on broadcasters' issues began, and only at the subsequent sessions that discussions focused on key issues such as definitions, objects of protection, and rights to be granted.[13]

19.04

---

[8] Reprinted in the submission of the International Association of Broadcasting (IAB) in WIPO Doc SCCR/2/6 p 21 para 6.

[9] Report on the First Session of the SCCR in November 1998, WIPO Doc SCCR/1/9 of 10 November 1998, para 204(c).

[10] The submissions are contained in WIPO Docs SCCR/2/5 (EC and Member States, Japan, Switzerland), SCCR/2/6 and Add (non-governmental organizations of broadcasters, authors, performers, and the Digital Media Association), SCCR/2/7 (Mexico), SCCR/2/8 (UNESCO), SCCR/2/12 (Cameroon), SCCR/3/4 (Argentina), SCCR/3/5 (Tanzania); see also the reports on regional meetings in WIPO Docs SCCR/2/10 Rev (Central European and Baltic States) and SCCR/3/6 (Asia and the Pacific), and the Reports of both Sessions, WIPO Docs SCCR/2/11, paras 119–57 and SCCR/3/11, paras 87–121.

[11] Notably, the proposal of Switzerland, ibid, on a 'Protocol' to the WPPT, and proposals by broadcasters' organizations.

[12] On that conference, see paras 18.09 ff above.

[13] For the Fifth to the Seventh Sessions, see WIPO Docs SCCR/5/2–4 (proposals by Kyrgyzstan, Sudan, and Japan), SCCR/6/2 and 3 (EC and Ukraine) and SCCR/7/7 (Uruguay) and reports in Docs SCCR/5/6, SCCR/6/4, and SCCR/7/10.

(b) Proposal on webcasters

19.05 At the Eighth Session in November 2002, the USA—previously not a strong promoter of broadcasters' rights[14]—surprised delegates with its proposal to provide protection not only for traditional broadcasting and cable-casting organizations but also for webcasters.[15] Ironically, this new proposal proved to be a burden on the subsequent discussions for a number of years, most of the other delegations rejecting the inclusion of webcasters as premature, while the largely isolated USA conveyed the message that it was not interested in a treaty on broadcasters' rights without the coverage of webcasters. This situation remained even after the Chair had proposed different ways of dealing with webcasters, including a non-mandatory protocol to the planned treaty on broadcasting organizations.[16] Participants were only able to avoid a deadlock at the Fourteenth Session in May 2006 when the USA, though reluctantly, accepted the Chair's proposal to split traditional broadcasting from webcasting, and to deal only with traditional broadcasting and cable-casting at a possible diplomatic conference; they proceeded with the understanding that webcasting would be reincluded in the SCCR discussions if the General Assembly did not recommend the preparation of a diplomatic conference for traditional broadcasting and cable-casting organizations.[17]

(c) Scope of protection

19.06 Besides the issue of webcasters, another major development during discussions in the SCCR concerned the scope of protection to be granted to broadcasting organizations. A number of proposals, such as the Swiss one, contained very extensive lists of exclusive minimum rights, including exclusive rights of simulcasting[18] and of decryption of encrypted broadcasts. Yet, a growing number of governmental delegates and representatives of non-governmental organizations preferred a much more restricted scope of protection in order to reduce the conflict of interests with right owners in the contents of broadcasts and to focus on protection against piracy. Different models for this anti-piracy approach were proposed, such as the US proposal under which, in respect of certain post-fixation rights, mere rights to prohibit should be provided, with no possibility to grant licences (as opposed to full exclusive rights) and the similar Canadian

---

[14] For this attitude in the TRIPS context, see para 10.97 above; Ogawa (n 6 above) 83.

[15] WIPO Doc SCCR/8/7 and, refined, SCCR/9/4.

[16] WIPO Doc SCCR/12/5 prov; the other two proposals were the inclusion of webcasters into the treaty, in combination with a reservation; and the inclusion of webcasters on the basis of an 'opt-in by notification' clause.

[17] Report of the Session, WIPO Doc SCCR/14/7/prov, paras 286 ff and, for the USA, 346 in particular. Such re-inclusion later took place, cf para 19.11 below.

[18] On simulcasting, see paras 19.15 f below.

suggestion to grant post-fixation rights only where the fixation was made without the authorization of the broadcaster or within a permitted limitation.[19] This approach was connected to the claim that broadcasting organizations should only be protected for their signals but not for the content carried by them, which is already protected by the rights of authors, performers, and phonogram producers. From the outset, certain developing countries had opposed any protection that would interfere with the rights of authors and others in the contents of the broadcasts; they pointed to widespread practices of broadcasting organizations, particularly those in Africa, not to respect the existing rights of authors and neighbouring rights owners.[20]

(d) The way towards an envisaged diplomatic conference

Desiring some progress towards a diplomatic conference, the Chairman tried to streamline the discussions since 2004 by means of a consolidated text that would show the areas of agreement and disagreement.[21] At the same time, those who preferred a limited scope of protection became more vocal. In addition, certain developing countries, in particular India and Brazil, started to voice fundamental doubts about the maturity of a possible treaty and the appropriateness of numerous provisions, including provisions on circumvention of technological measures and a fifty years' duration; they pointed to the need to balance protection and adapt it to the level of development in developing countries. Their doubts likely also reflected a broader political strategy, namely to generally slow down norm-setting procedures in the WIPO, the WTO, and other international organizations; this strategy became manifest in the SCCR in June 2004 when these countries focused discussions on procedure more than on substance. Yet, at the Session of November 2004, other developing countries, in particular those from Latin America and Africa, seemed to change their previously doubtful basic position regarding the maturity of a diplomatic conference and expressed their hope that controversial issues could be settled and a treaty be concluded as soon as possible.[22] **19.07**

Following the weak recommendation made at the SCCR's June 2004 Session,[23] the 2004 General Assembly did not go further than indicating that it could **19.08**

---

[19] WIPO Doc SCCR/10/5 paras 22, 44, 47, 49 for the Canadian proposal, and WIPO Doc SCCR/9/4Rev at 5–6 and the Report of the Session, WIPO Doc SCCR/9/11 paras 25, 54, 66 for the US proposal.
[20] The summary of interventions only makes an allusion to such statements, eg in WIPO Doc SCCR/5/6 paras 38–9, 93; SCCR/6/4 paras 99, 141.
[21] The consolidated text was first submitted for the 11th Session in June 2004, WIPO Doc SCCR/11/3.
[22] For an overview of discussions at the SCCR meetings up to the 11th Session in June 2004, see Ogawa (n 6 above) 92–112.
[23] Report on the Session, WIPO Doc SCCR/11/4 para 146 A.

approve a diplomatic conference at its next Session in 2005, but it could not set a date for a diplomatic conference.[24] The 2005 General Assembly then decided that two more meetings of the SCCR would be needed in order to enable the General Assembly in 2006 to recommend the convening of a diplomatic conference. In the SCCR Session of November 2005, a general tendency towards a possible treaty with a lower level of protection was promoted, especially by developing countries; Brazil and Chile submitted new proposals including general public interest clauses, the primacy of cultural diversity protected under the UNESCO Convention on Cultural Diversity, detailed provisions on limitations and exceptions, the defence of competition, and the abuse of intellectual property rights with an adverse effect on competition.[25] These new proposals, supplemented by others in the Session of May 2006,[26] broadened rather than focused the discussions, and gave more reasons for those developing countries that had been doubtful about a diplomatic conference further to stress the need for additional meetings.

19.09 The General Assembly 2006 finally agreed to convene a diplomatic conference in November/December 2007 with a view to concluding a treaty that would be limited to the protection of broadcasting and cable-casting organizations in the traditional sense, and negotiated on the basis of the Draft Basic Proposal elaborated in the SCCR.[27] However, this decision was subject to agreement on a revised version of this Proposal as a basis for negotiations at the diplomatic conference. Such agreement was to follow a signal-based approach and relate to the objectives, specific scope, and object of protection; in addition, it was to be achieved in two special sessions of the SCCR in 2007,[28] as was required by developing countries, which argued that the matter was not yet ripe for a diplomatic conference and that further discussions in additional sessions were needed before a final decision on a diplomatic conference could be made.

19.10 The last draft text submitted as a non-paper to the SCCR's second Special Session was not only based on a signal-based approach but also quite limited in scope, as mainly demanded by developing countries. Yet, despite major efforts and transition to informal sessions, delegations still could not agree on a text; it seems that a general political unwillingness rather than substantive issues was decisive for this outcome.[29] In particular, one could observe that leading developing

---

[24] Thirty-first (fifteenth extraordinary) Session of the WIPO General Assembly in September 2004, Report, WIPO Doc WO/GA/31/15 (2004), paras 51 and 56.

[25] WIPO Docs SCCR/13/3 and SCCR/13/4.

[26] Peru, WIPO Doc SCCR/14/6; Colombia, SCCR/14/4.

[27] Revised Draft Basic Proposal, WIPO Doc SCCR/15/2.

[28] WIPO Doc WO/GA/33/10 para 107.

[29] For a similar impression already at the 2006 General Assembly, see the remark by Croatia, WIPO Doc WO/GA/33/10 para 99.

countries, such as Brazil and India, deployed different strategies as, for example, the submission of proposals that would dilute discussions and likely meet opposition of leading industrialized countries, and that would result in controversies between them and the USA in particular. These strategies and controversies might be among the first signs of a political reaction to US bilateralism and unilateralism. At the same time, it is notable that the issue of broadcasters' protection did not seem to be a North–South issue.[30]

Given the lack of agreement at the second Special Session of the SCCR, the issue   **19.11** of the protection of broadcasting organizations was not promoted to a diplomatic conference, but moved back to the agenda of the SCCR. Yet, any future agreement or progress in the SCCR seems even less likely than before, since the highly controversial issues of webcasters and simulcasting will be included again,[31] and because the motivation to proceed with the matter of broadcasting organizations is likely to remain very low given the experiences over the past nine years.

B. Overview of the main issues discussed as possible contents of a broadcasters' treaty

Since current chances for progress towards a broadcasters' treaty are relatively   **19.12** low, this subsection only briefly presents the main elements of the Revised Draft Basic Proposal (RDBP) for the WIPO Treaty on the Protection of Broadcasting Organizations of July 2006 and the non-paper submitted to the SCCR in its second Special Session in 2007; these documents were the last discussed in 2007.[32] The RDBP is based on proposals made by delegates since the Second Session of the SCCR and on discussions within this Committee. It contains a number of alternatives where major differences between delegations' views exist. In principle, the RDBP in major parts resembles the WPPT. Therefore, the following analysis focuses on issues that are specific for broadcasters.

---

[30] At the 2006 WIPO General Assembly, of the delegations that took the floor in formal session, those in favour of a diplomatic conference in 2007 were the EC, Japan, Croatia and the Group of Central European and Baltic States, Norway, as well as Nicaragua, Mexico, El Salvador, Pakistan, Mongolia, Kyrgyzstan, Ukraine, Azerbaijan, China, Russia, Singapore, Morocco, Macedonia, Kenya, and subject to certain conditions, Nigeria on behalf of the African Group, Algeria, Honduras; Indonesia proposed postponement to 2008. The following delegations considered a diplomatic conference in 2007 premature or otherwise unwanted: USA, India, Uruguay, Chile, Canada, South Africa, and Venezuela; ibid, paras 74–104.

[31] On this concession to the USA in the SCCR, see para 19.05 above. On simulcasting, see para 19.15 f below.

[32] WIPO Doc SCCR/15/2 Rev; non-paper on the WIPO treaty on the protection of broadcasting organizations of 20 April 2007, <http://www.wipo.int/edocs/mdocs/sccr/en/sccr_s2/sccr_s2_paper1.doc>.

(1) Principles of protection

19.13 Delegates discussed relatively little on the principles of protection, namely national treatment, minimum rights, and 'no formalities'. For national treatment, the RDBP offers three alternatives: full national treatment according to the Berne model, and limited national treatment according to both the TRIPS model for neighbouring rights[33] and the WPPT Article 4 model.[34] Reciprocity is proposed as an alternative where a country limits the rights to a mere right of prohibition.[35] Due to its economic and political impact, national treatment usually is not a candidate for resolution before a diplomatic conference.

19.14 The principle of 'no formalities' was copied from Article 20 of the WPPT (and, indirectly, from Article 5(2) of the Berne Convention).[36] Since formalities are uncommon for broadcasting organizations, this Article would seem to have minimal impact, if any.

(2) Right owners and objects of protection

(a) Overview

19.15 The following five groups of right owners and objects of protection have been discussed during SCCR meetings: broadcasters in respect of their 'traditional' broadcasts (transmissions over the air for direct reception by the general public) and for their signals prior to broadcasting; cable-casting organizations in respect of their cable-casts; organizations that perform simulcasting for their simulcasts (simultaneous real-time streaming of traditional broadcasts and cable-casts); and webcasting organizations for their webcasts. The two last-mentioned, internet-related objects were excluded from the scope of application of the proposed treaty, following persistent opposition by all but one delegation.[37]

(b) Simulcasting and webcasting

19.16 Simulcasting is generally understood as the simultaneous broadcasting and streaming over the internet, or the simultaneous dissemination of a broadcast over different transmission systems, such as a radio broadcast of the sound of a

---

[33] Art 3(1) phr 2 of the TRIPS Agreement, see para 10.34 above.

[34] On Art 4 of the WPPT, see paras 17.43–17.46 above. The non-paper (Art 6) only contains the Berne and WPPT models.

[35] Art 8 Alternative FF of the RDBP; on the distinction between full exclusive rights and 'rights to prohibit', see para 19.29 below.

[36] Art 21 of the RDBP and Art 11 of the non-paper. On Art 20 of the Berne Convention, see paras 5.250–5.251 above.

[37] para 19.05 above; Art 6(4) of the RDBP. They are back on the SCCR agenda, para 19.11 above.

TV programme.[38] Delegates did not see any need to vest simulcasting organizations with a separate protection for their simulcasts.

Like simulcasting, 'webcasting' is not yet defined under international neighbouring rights law but may be understood as the transmission of audio, video, or other data files by 'streaming' technology. Streaming can be real-time (or live) streaming[39] and on-demand streaming.[40] In any case, the user must individually request transmission;[41] accordingly, unlike traditional broadcasting, webcasting is a point-to-point transmission over the internet, activated by the user. As for the internet in general, such transmissions may occur by wire or wirelessly. **19.17**

There are strong arguments to assume that under the Rome Convention and the TRIPS Agreement, webcasters are not protected. In particular, 'broadcasting' is defined in Article 3(f) of the Rome Convention as transmission 'for public reception' and understood as simultaneous transmission to members of the public; therefore, it is likely to exclude point-to-point transmissions at the request of the user. In addition, where webcasts are carried out by wire, they are not protected because 'broadcasting' under these treaties is limited to wireless transmission.[42] **19.18**

Delegates altogether rejected the proposal to protect webcasters in respect of their webcasts as premature, mainly because the need for protection was not proven and because experience was lacking in the field. Japan convincingly illustrated this position by analysing a number of issues that raised many questions requiring further study.[43] **19.19**

(c) Traditional broadcasting and cable-casting

(i) Wireless broadcasts The inclusion of the other three groups of right owners and objects of protection has not met with comparable opposition. In respect of traditional wireless broadcasts, the proposal aims at remedying the weaknesses of the definition of the Rome Convention by clearly covering satellite broadcasts,[44] even for encrypted signals according to the model of Article 2(f) of the **19.20**

---

[38] WIPO Doc SCCR/7/8 para 57; another example is the simultaneous relay of the broadcast on a cable, broadband, or mobile telephone system, see W Rumphorst, 'The Broadcasters' Neighbouring Right: Impossible to Understand?' (2006) July–September e-Copyright Bulletin of UNESCO 1, 5.
[39] In this case, data is distributed by a server without creating an intermediate file.
[40] In this case, the data is first stored in a file before the user can access it.
[41] This characteristic is also described as 'pull technology'; for a presentation of webcasting/streaming, see WIPO Doc SCCR/7/8 paras 47–56.
[42] See also WIPO Doc SCCR/9/9 paras 14, 15.
[43] WIPO Doc SCCR/9/9.
[44] This question was quite controversial when satellite broadcasting became possible; today, though, the Rome Convention is generally interpreted as covering satellite broadcasting, see para 6.25 above.

WPPT.[45] For clarification and in order to reassure those delegations that opposed any mentioning of 'computer networks', the proposed definition explicitly excludes transmissions over computer networks from the term 'broadcasts'.

19.21 **(ii) Pre-broadcast signals** Signal piracy—the unauthorized interception of pre-broadcast signals[46] on their way from the transmitting station to a satellite, or from a satellite to a relay station—is quite frequent. Yet, broadcasting organizations are not protected in this respect under the Rome Convention[47] or under the TRIPS Agreement. The Brussels Satellite Convention includes such protection, though not necessarily by a neighbouring right.[48] The RDBP proposes such protection, but leaves open the means of protection since delegations disagree on whether to protect pre-broadcast signals by neighbouring rights or otherwise, such as by telecommunication law.[49]

19.22 **(iii) Cable-casts** When the Rome Convention was adopted, cable-casting was not yet a viable technology. The Convention, followed by the TRIPS Agreement, is therefore limited to the protection of broadcasting organizations that carry out wireless transmissions. Today, it is widely recognized that organizations that use cable instead of wireless means in order to transmit programme-carrying signals should be protected alike.

19.23 The RDBP defines 'cable-casting' upon the model of the definition of 'broadcasting', including the aspects of encrypted signals and exclusion of transmissions over computer networks.[50] The basic distinction between broadcasts and cable-casts is the way of transmission by wireless means and by wire, respectively. Many national laws use the same term both for wireless broadcasting and cable-casting by wire, so that the inclusion of cable-casts widely corresponds to existing national law.[51] In parallel to the protection of broadcasting organizations, cable-casters are protected only for cable-originated transmissions rather than cable retransmissions.[52]

---

[45] As compared to Art 3(f) of the Rome Convention, it also adds, as in the WPPT, 'representations' of sounds and images and describes more accurately that the transmission is 'for the reception by the public' rather than 'for public reception', Art 5(a) of the RDBP. See also Art 2(a) of the non-paper which reflects the signal-based approach.

[46] Signals that occur before the entire transmission or broadcast to the public has taken place.

[47] Pre-broadcast signals are not 'for public reception' as required by the definition in Art 3(f) of the Rome Convention.

[48] On the Brussels Satellite Convention, see paras 4.70–4.74 above; see Art 2 of that Convention.

[49] Art 16 of the RDBP: 'adequate and effective legal protection' against the acts corresponding to minimum rights for broadcasting organizations; similarly: Art 8 of the non-paper.

[50] Art 5(b) of the RDBP, as compared to Art 5(a), and para 19.20 above.

[51] eg EC Rental Rights Dir of 19 November 1992, Art 6(2), see Vol II ch 6; S von Lewinski, 'Neighbouring Rights: Comparison of Laws' in G Schricker (ed), *International Encyclopedia of Comparative Law: Copyright and Industrial Property* (2006) ch 5, 1, 20; see Art 6(3) of the RDBP.

[52] Art 6(4)(i) ibid and Art 3(4)(i) of the non-paper.

(iv) Definitions of broadcasting and cable-casting organizations While the **19.24**
Rome Convention does not define broadcasting organizations as right owners,
the RDBP does define broadcasting and cable-casting organizations by partly
following the definition of the producer of a phonogram under the WPPT and
by adding specific elements for these organizations. Accordingly, a 'legal entity'
must take the initiative and have the responsibility for the transmission as well as
for the assembly and scheduling of the content of the transmission.[53]

(v) Signal versus content protection Regarding the object of protection— **19.25**
broadcasts, cable-casts, and pre-broadcast signals—a fundamental debate took
place throughout the SCCR's work on whether the protection would refer only
to the signals or to additional elements, such as the contents. This discussion was
provoked by proposals for an extensive list of minimum rights that would also
cover uses *post*-fixation. Many delegations and content owners argued that protection in respect of post-fixation uses would no longer concern the signal but
only the content, and should therefore not be provided for broadcasting organizations. Accordingly, the General Assembly 2006 mandated the SCCR in 2007
to agree on a finalized Basic Proposal 'on a signal-based approach'.[54] Discussions
in January 2007 aimed at clarifying that the protection would relate only to the
broadcast (to be defined as the programme-carrying signal used for transmission
by the broadcasting organizations), and that the treaty would not give rise to protection in the programme's content itself; the non-paper has clearly followed this
approach.[55]

In many cases, broadcasting organizations may be able to rely on derived rights **19.26**
of authors and neighbouring right owners in the contents in order to fight piracy.
Yet, such protection may be insufficient where rights have not comprehensively
been transferred. Also, for lack of international protection, they cannot rely on
rights that would be vested in them as film producers for their own productions.
Furthermore, in important cases, such as sport programmes, the content is often
not protected by copyright or related rights, so that they cannot rely on derived
rights. This situation may explain the call by broadcasting organizations for broad
protection beyond the signal and beyond the regular justification for protection,
which is the investment made in the broadcasting activity.

Indeed, the provision of post-fixation rights seems contradictory to a mere signal **19.27**
protection, because the signal no longer exists after fixation. Even if one considers

---

[53] Art 5(c) of the RDBP; only the first part of this definition is contained in Art 2(c) of the
non-paper, and for broadcasting organizations only.
[54] The mandate extended to two special sessions of the SCCR, WIPO Doc WO/GA/33/10
para 107.
[55] See, in particular, the definition of 'broadcast' in Art 2(a).

the investment of the broadcaster as justification for protection, it is very doubtful whether any use of a fixed broadcast refers to the investment in the transmission (the 'broadcasting') and the scheduling of a programme. Rather, post-fixation uses would seem to concern achievements related to the contents, such as the production of a film or the recording of a phonogram.

19.28 Even a protection that would be limited to signals cannot, however, avoid a conflict of interest with content right owners who will not be able to exercise their rights by authorization if broadcasters prohibit the relevant uses. Even a safeguard clause similar to Article 1 of the Rome Convention would not change this situation. While content owners do not object to such restrictions to the exercise of their rights for uses directly related to the signal or the broadcaster's investment, they do so for uses post-fixation, such as distribution of video copies or making available on demand of fixations of their works and other achievements incorporated in a broadcast.

(3) Minimum rights

19.29 The discussion on the signal as the object of protection is therefore directly related to the scope of minimum rights. Generally, unlike those in favour of exclusive rights, many delegations opted for a mere protection to fight 'piracy', understood as the 'theft' of signals.[56] Some delegations proposed, as an alternative to exclusive rights, mere 'rights to prohibit' post-fixation uses. Such rights would not allow the right owner to grant licences; yet, the above conflict of interests with content owners would remain. This alternative to an exclusive right is included in the RDBP, together with yet another alternative of an exclusive right with the option to declare in a notification to apply only the right to prohibit.[57]

19.30 The list of post-fixation rights in the RDBP (reproduction, distribution, transmission following fixation, and making available) is shorter than an earlier text discussed in the SCCR, which also included the exclusive rights of decryption of encrypted broadcasts and rental of fixations of broadcasts. As regards prefixation, the RDBP includes the exclusive rights of retransmission (including rebroadcasting, and retransmission by wire and over computer networks), fixation, and communication to the public (defined as making the transmission audible and/or visible in places accessible to the public)[58] if the communication is made against payment of an entrance fee. Many delegations opposed in particular any form of transmission over computer networks, such as simulcasting.

---

[56] 'Piracy' is not a legal term and is not defined in any neighbouring rights treaty.
[57] Alternatives O, HH, Q, II, KK, S, and LL in Arts 12–15 of the RDBP.
[58] Arts 9, 11, and 10; definition in Art 5(e) of the RDBP; see the more limited definition of retransmission in Art 2(e) of the non-paper, and the lack of fixation and communication rights.

The non-paper only covers exclusive rights of retransmission and deferred transmission.

(4) Limitations and other restrictions of protection

In respect of limitations and exceptions, one alternative corresponds to Article 16 **19.31** of the WPPT, which refers to permitted limitations and exceptions under national copyright subject to the three-step test. Other alternatives suggested by certain developing countries provide, in different forms, lists of specific permitted limitations and exceptions in combination with the three-step test.[59]

Some developing countries also proposed quite sweeping provisions, for example **19.32** on the unlimited freedom of contracting parties to promote access to knowledge and information, to curb anti-competitive practices, to promote public interest in important sectors, to protect and promote cultural diversity, and on the obligation to take adequate measures to prevent the abuse of intellectual property rights.[60] One of the main controversies in the special sessions of 2007 related to these provisions, in particular their placement either in Articles of the text (as proposed by the *demandeurs* and reflected in the RDBP), or in the Preamble (as reflected in the non-paper).

(5) Other minimum standards

While the minimum duration under both the Rome Convention and TRIPS **19.33** Agreement is twenty years, the RDBP provides for a fifty years' duration. Many proposals by delegations simply copied the fifty years' duration from the WPPT. With time progressing though, a growing tendency emerged towards twenty years as the appropriate minimum duration.[61]

Similarly, the WPPT provisions on technological measures and rights manage- **19.34** ment information were copied into many proposals at the beginning but later strongly opposed by a number of delegations.[62] The basic provision on enforcement, copied from the WPPT, was not, however, subject to major opposition— indeed, much more detailed enforcement provisions already bind the TRIPS Members.[63]

---

[59] Art 17 of the RDBP; Art 10 of the non-paper is based on the WPPT model.

[60] Arts 2–4 of the RDBP.

[61] Art 18 ibid includes both alternatives, and the non-paper does not include any provision on the duration.

[62] For the different alternatives in the RDBP, see its Art 19; Art 9 of the non-paper contains a streamlined version.

[63] Art 24 of the RDBP and the identical Art 14 of the non-paper.

(6) Framework provisions

19.35 Regarding the application in time, little discussion has taken place on the proposal to apply Article 18 of the Berne Convention *mutatis mutandis*—again, this is in part a copy from the WPPT. The WPPT has also been the model for one of the three alternatives for Article 1 on the relation to other conventions and treaties; the others are shorter non-derogation clauses in relation to the Rome Convention and in relation to any other copyright or related rights treaty.[64] Administrative and final clauses largely follow the WPPT model and have not been discussed.

C. Résumé

19.36 In comparison with the preparations for the 1996 Diplomatic Conference and even for the 2000 Audiovisual Diplomatic Conference, preparations for the broadcasters' treaty took place in a much less enthusiastic atmosphere. The rights of broadcasting organizations have not been backed by equally strong promoters. In particular, the USA has never shown a genuine interest in the protection of broadcasting organizations; it is not a Contracting State of the Rome Convention and was behind Article 14(3) phrase 2 of the TRIPS Agreement, which largely eliminates the obligation to protect broadcasting organizations.[65] Indeed, at the Manila Symposium, which launched the initiative of a broadcasters' treaty,[66] the USA was the only country wishing 'to take no action'.[67] The EC and its Member States already provided for a quite high level of protection and promoted the initiative, though with less enthusiasm than the initiatives for the 1996 and 2000 Conferences. Developing countries at the beginning were rather critical towards a treaty on broadcasting organizations; they prioritized international protection for audiovisual performers and pointed at the frequent disrespect of authors' rights and related rights in the broadcast contents by broadcasting organizations in their countries.

19.37 A new obstacle to progress emerged when the USA presented its own proposal, including the protection of webcasters as an essential element without which the USA did not seem to be ready to conclude any treaty on broadcasting organizations, while the rest of the world considered this idea as clearly premature. Although this problem was later provisionally resolved by its removal from the agenda of a possible diplomatic conference, a new one appeared when certain

---

[64] Art 23 of the RDBP and the identical Art 13 of the non-paper; Art 1 of the RDBP.
[65] para 10.97 above.
[66] paras 19.02–19.03 above.
[67] Ogawa (n 6 above) 83.

developing countries such as Brazil and India, seemingly as part of an overall political strategy, succeeded in considerably slowing down the process towards a diplomatic conference. Eventually, even the compromise option of a treaty with a very limited 'anti-piracy' approach did not find sufficient support for the convening of a diplomatic conference. As stated above,[68] chances for the conclusion of a treaty on the protection of broadcasting organizations seem to be rather low for the foreseeable future.

---

[68] para 19.11 above.

20

PROTECTION OF FOLKLORE

A. Introduction: the issues at stake

For a long time, indigenous peoples[1] have sought respect and protection for their **20.01** folklore or traditional cultural expressions.[2] They consider that folklore belongs to the particular community from which it emanates, as confirmed by their customary laws, while Western intellectual property systems largely to consider that folklore is part of the public domain. The resulting conflict is evident: Westerners and other outsiders, in relying on Western laws for legality, have regularly used folklore without asking for consent from and without sharing the benefits with indigenous peoples. Thereby, Westerners affect the economic and non-economic interests of indigenous peoples whose customary laws recognize these interests;

---

[1] On this term, which is not defined in this book, see P-T Stoll and A von Hahn, 'Indigenous Peoples, Indigenous Knowledge and Indigenous Resources in International Law' in S von Lewinski (ed), *Indigenous Heritage and Intellectual Property* (2nd edn, 2008) 8 ff.

[2] The terms 'folklore' and 'expressions of folklore' are used in this book as synonyms for 'traditional cultural expressions' and do not mean to imply any negative connotations. Discussions in the WIPO Intergovernmental Committee (see paras 20.36 ff below) have shown that the term 'folklore' is perceived negatively only in some parts of the world but even preferred over 'traditional cultural expressions' in other parts. WIPO therefore uses both terms simultaneously. The term is not defined in this book; many definitions have been proposed in different contexts. On the term and definitions of 'folklore', see A Lucas-Schloetter, 'Folklore' in von Lewinski (ed), n 1 above, 342 ff.

yet, these laws do not apply to outsiders. Consequently, indigenous peoples have claimed protection at national and international levels.

20.02 The specific challenge in resolving this conflict is rooted in the underlying, basic differences between the Western and indigenous cultures. At the risk of improperly generalizing, some of these differences are highlighted here to facilitate the understanding of current discussions on the protection of folklore. First, Western cultures are predominantly individualistic, as opposed to community-driven indigenous cultures. For example, expressions of folklore are usually community owned and may, under customary laws, be subject to the custody of particular persons, clans, or other groups of an indigenous community, or may only be used in a particular way by designated members thereof. Accordingly, rules on exclusive responsibilities and privileges in the context of community obligations usually apply instead of Western-style property rights and broad concepts of freedom of expression.

20.03 Secondly, Western cultures are based on writing, fixation, and—consequently in the field of law—legal security on the basis of written law. In contrast, indigenous cultures are oral. For example, folklore, just like traditional knowledge in a narrow sense,[3] is passed on orally from generation to generation, often for a long period of time. The oral character promotes the dynamic nature of indigenous cultures; for example, folklore is usually not static but part of the living heritage and, hence, is subject to continuous, small changes produced in the course of using it. Also, customary laws are regularly not written down and, hence, quite dynamic. Thirdly, indigenous peoples have a holistic world view where everything is interrelated rather than being looked upon separately in distinctive categories, such as folklore and traditional knowledge.

20.04 Fourthly, the arts in Western societies have a primarily entertaining function and represent an economic factor. In contrast, folklore (just like other elements of living heritage) is meaningful for every aspect of life of indigenous communities. It may express and renew relationships of members of indigenous communities with their land, other living beings, themselves, the community, and even their spiritual ancestry.[4] Accordingly, it plays an essential role for their identity, their self-determination, and thus possibly even for their survival. Indigenous peoples' claims for control over the disposition and interpretation of their folklore must be considered in this context in order to understand their fundamental importance. At the same time, the context of these claims with the self-determination

---

[3] Traditional knowledge in the broad sense also covers folklore, in the narrow sense only knowledge in non-artistic, technical, agricultural, medicinal, and similar areas.

[4] For the Australian Aborigines eg J Cowan, *Mysteries of the Dreaming: The Spiritual Life of Australian Aborigines* (3rd edn, 2001) 38 ff, 68 ff, 124 ff.

right and the aim for recognition of sovereignty renders discussions on protection of folklore even more difficult, given the potential impact on broader, delicate issues such as land rights within existing relations between states and indigenous peoples inhabiting them.

These features of folklore show that claims for control are largely rooted in non-economic interests, such as, and especially, interests regarding sacred and secret expressions of folklore and protection against unauthorized non-customary uses that may be highly offensive or have other, negative non-economic effects. In addition, authenticity interests have led to claims for protection against making available non-authentic, copied expressions of folklore as authentic ones. Finally, economic interests in sharing the benefits from exploitation of folklore are often asserted to be protected on the basis of either an exclusive right, or a right to give consent, or a statutory remuneration right.[5]   **20.05**

Following discussion in the late 1970s to the mid-1980s, the topic of folklore protection re-emerged at the end of the 1990s in the context of claims for protection of traditional knowledge and genetic resources. It re-emerged in response to increased exploitation by outsiders and, on the side of indigenous peoples, as a consequence of enhanced awareness of the disadvantages of exploitation, improved self-organization, and more efficient representation of indigenous peoples within international organizations. This chapter sets out the possibilities of protecting folklore under existing laws, summarizes the past attempts to achieve international protection in the field, and presents the current status of discussion within the leading organization in this respect, WIPO. As is evident from the copyright focus of this book, the chapter does not deal with other, even if highly important, aspects of folklore, such as its preservation.[6]   **20.06**

B. The existing possibilities for protecting folklore

(1) Direct protection of folklore

To date, it is widely acknowledged that expressions of folklore as such (as opposed to works based on them) cannot be protected by copyright, due to the different nature of expressions of folklore as opposed to works protected under copyright.[7] In particular, one usually cannot ascertain an individual author or individual co-authors because expressions of folklore are constantly evolving through   **20.07**

---

[5] Lucas-Schloetter (n 2 above) 341–2 for the different interests at stake.
[6] On the different UNESCO conventions on cultural heritage dealing with such aspects, see ibid 418 ff.
[7] For a detailed analysis of the reasons see ibid 381 ff.

collective participation—they are 'living' heritage rather than works created at given times by individual persons. Even where an individual author has been involved at the outset of a particular expression of folklore, his creation only becomes 'folklore' after having been subjected to the change and continuous development by the community.[8] Applying other concepts, such as the concept of anonymous works, does not remedy the problem of lacking authorship, in particular because the duration of protection usually would have been expired for a long time.[9]

20.08   Indeed, the limited duration of copyright is one of the most important obstacles for applying copyright to folklore. Since, consequently, most of the existing folklore is considered under copyright to be part of the public domain, another obstacle arises: the required originality can relate only to the continuous, small changes that constantly modify folklore. Such changes, however, usually do not fulfil the requirements of originality, even where these requirements are very low, as is typical in countries adhering to the copyright system. Even if, in an individual case, such changes were protected by copyright, then the scope of protection would be limited to such changes, and the main thrust of the expression of folklore would remain unprotected by copyright.

20.09   In addition, copyright protection is not available in countries of the copyright system (as opposed to the author's rights system), under which fixation of a work in material form is regularly required, because folklore is usually passed on orally from generation to generation rather than written down or otherwise fixed. Even if folklore is fixed, say for the purpose of preservation, it will continuously change through its use and, after some time, deviate from the expression that was fixed, so that the fixation requirement would not be fulfilled in respect of the subsequent versions of the expressions of folklore.[10]

20.10   Design law, similarly to copyright, regularly does not protect folklore due to failure to fulfil novelty and originality requirements.[11]

---

[8] K Puri, 'Preservation and Conservation of Expressions of Folklore' (1998) 32/4 Copyright Bulletin of UNESCO 15.

[9] In particular, Art 7(3) phr 4 of the Berne Convention allows countries to terminate protection of anonymous works when one can reasonably presume that the author has died more than 50 years ago. Also, the rule that the publisher indicated on the work is deemed to represent an author will regularly not result in the desired protection for the community.

[10] For more details, see S von Lewinski, 'The Protection of Folklore' (2003) Cardozo Journal of International and Comparative Law 747, 757–9.

[11] Lucas-Schloetter (n 2 above) 397–8.

(2) Indirect protection of folklore

(a) Copyright and neighbouring rights

Expressions of folklore may be protected indirectly by copyright and neighbouring **20.11** rights where individual works are based on folklore and where folklore is fixed or performed. First, individual works created on the basis of folklore are protected if they fulfil the general conditions, such as originality. For example, adaptations of expressions of folklore by contemporary aboriginal artists are regularly protected. The same applies to translations. The scope of protection in these cases, however, does not extend to the folklore used, but is limited to the adaptation—the individual creative additions—or translation by the author. Accordingly, the underlying expressions of folklore remain unprotected by copyright and can be used by any third author of a new work without authorization either by the author of the adaptation/translation or by the owners of folklore.

Folklore is also protected indirectly by copyright where it is included in a database **20.12** or other collection, if either the arrangement or the selection of the material constitutes an intellectual creation.[12] The scope of protection is limited to the arrangement or selection of material and does not extend to the collected material itself. A similar situation exists in respect of certain fixations: a person who makes a photograph of a traditional design acquires a copyright in the photograph (rather than in the design itself) and can prohibit or authorize the use of the photograph. A person who makes a sound recording of a traditional song—a phonogram producer—acquires a neighbouring right or, in countries of the copyright system, a copyright in the recording itself (rather than in the song). The same applies where a person produces a documentary film of a traditional dance.

Finally, under many laws, as also required by the WIPO Performances and **20.13** Phonograms Treaty,[13] performers of expressions of folklore (as opposed to performers of works only, as under the Rome Convention) have to be protected. Accordingly, musicians and dancers of folklore in particular enjoy protection; yet, such protection relates to their performances rather than to the performed folklore. Hence, they cannot prohibit anyone from singing a traditional song, but only from recording and further using their performance.

---

[12] Most copyright laws today extend such protection to collections of material beyond works and can therefore cover collections of folklore; for an important step in international law in this regard, see paras 10.60–10.63 above.

[13] On Art 2(a) of the WPPT, see para 17.133 above.

(b) Other intellectual property rights

20.14 Adaptations of folklore may be protected as designs, when they are registered and fulfil the general conditions of design protection. Protecting adaptations as designs has the same effects and consequences as for adaptations under copyright.[14]

20.15 Trademarks, geographical indications, and unfair competition may afford some protection. Trademarks may be particularly useful in the form of collective marks and, as a special form thereof, certification marks, since collective marks correspond to the collective nature of traditional cultural expressions by allowing an association to be the right owner. In addition, the association does not need to have an industrial or commercial establishment. By forming such associations, indigenous communities are therefore enabled to register collective marks.

20.16 Collective marks (like trademarks in general) do not directly protect folklore: indigenous communities cannot prevent others from reproducing and distributing goods that incorporate their folklore, but only from using the mark in connection with these goods. Accordingly, collective marks that indicate the identity and commercial origin of goods protect the authenticity thereof. Indigenous communities who market their own goods with a collective mark may enjoy an advantage on the market, because the mark allows consumers to distinguish authentic products from similar ones that are imitated by persons from outside the indigenous communities.

20.17 Certification marks or guarantee marks may serve the interests of indigenous communities even better, since they additionally guarantee certain characteristics of the respective goods vis-à-vis the public, such as certain quality standards or specific ways of manufacture according to the traditions of a community. The quality standards and other characteristics are specified and controlled by the association with which the certification mark is registered. In practice, many indigenous peoples have already used collective marks with a view to decreasing the market for imitations made by outsiders.[15]

20.18 Geographical indications likewise do not protect folklore itself against unauthorized uses, but identify it as having its origin in a certain geographical region or other part of a specific territory. Accordingly, they also serve authenticity needs, though in respect of the geographical origin of folklore.

---

[14] paras 20.11 ff above and 20.24 ff below; Lucas-Schloetter (n 2 above) 397–8.

[15] See for the Maori Made Mark (Toi Iho) for Maori cultural expressions, WIPO Doc GRTKF/IC/4INF/2 of 25 November 2002, nos 79 ff; for marks of Australian aborigines and Iroquois, WIPO (ed), *Intellectual Property Needs and Expectations of Traditional Knowledge Holders: WIPO Report on Fact-Finding Missions on Intellectual Property and Traditional Knowledge (1998–1999)* (2001) (WIPO publication 768 E) 73, 213.

To some extent, rules of unfair competition may provide protection, namely **20.19** where commercial transactions involve goods incorporating folklore, and where a competition relationship exists between the indigenous community and a person who commercializes folklore. In particular, undisclosed folklore may be well protected against disclosure by the protection of undisclosed information under Article 39 of the TRIPS Agreement, and by the protection against disclosure of confidential information in civil law countries or breach of confidence in common law countries. On this basis, secret expressions may be prevented from being made available to the public, or—if so desired—can be commercialized under know-how licences.

Finally, a number of countries have introduced *sui generis* protection for folklore. **20.20** This protection is either outside or inside copyright acts, and deviates to some extent from copyright principles.[16] It seems, however, that at least the latter protection rarely function properly in practice.[17]

(c) Protection outside intellectual property.

In brief, cultural heritage legislation regularly aims at the identification, documentation, preservation, or promotion of cultural heritage, but does not provide **20.21** indigenous peoples with the right to control uses of their heritage, including folklore.[18] While these aspects are fundamentally important, they are beyond the intellectual property focus of this book.

International human rights law to date is of little help, given its individualistic **20.22** approach and vagueness. These deficiencies do not apply to the United Nations Declaration on the Rights of Indigenous Peoples, which was adopted by the UN General Assembly on 13 September 2007 against the votes of Australia, Canada, New Zealand, and the USA after twenty-two years of debates: it establishes a number of human rights for indigenous peoples, and includes Article 31 on the right to maintain, control, protect, and develop their traditional cultural expressions. However, the Declaration is legally non-binding. It is nevertheless quite important for its high political and symbolic value. National constitutions and national laws that specify the rights of indigenous communities in respect of their land and cultural heritage may be better suited to protect folklore.[19]

---

[16] For solutions outside copyright acts (Panama and the Philippines), see W Wendland, 'Intellectual Property and the Protection of Cultural Expressions: The Work of the World Intellectual Property Organisation (WIPO)' in W Grosheide and J Brinkhof (eds), *The Legal Protection of Cultural Expressions and Indigenous Knowledge* (2002) 101, 115 ff; inside copyright acts, see Lucas-Schloetter (n 2 above) 371–80.

[17] Wendland (n 16 above) 115.

[18] For examples, see Lucas-Schloetter (n 2 above) 418 ff.

[19] On the UN Declaration, see ibid; examples ibid 438–9.

20.23 A quite important means of protection is the customary law of indigenous communities. It often regulates the conditions for use of folklore in many respects.[20] Yet, it regularly does not apply to outsiders and is therefore of limited use.[21] Different ways of integrating customary laws into *sui generis* laws seem promising, for example, by excluding 'customary uses' from protection and designating the beneficiaries of protection—traditional owners—by reference to those who are custodians under customary law.[22]

(d) Résumé

20.24 As a rule, folklore itself is not protected by classical intellectual property rights. Where folklore is indirectly protected by copyright, neighbouring rights, or design law (for example, where it is adapted, collected, performed, or fixed in a phonogram, film, or photograph), it is in practice typically anthropologists, musicologists, or other outsiders rather than community members who would enjoy rights to prohibit or authorize uses of such derived products. Indigenous communities could even be excluded from using the protected products and might therefore have an interest in 'defensive protection' against such rights in the derived products; for example, by a positive *sui generis* protection of their folklore against such uses.[23] For adaptations and performances, it is more likely, however, that community members will in fact benefit from such indirect protection since indigenous peoples more often adapt and perform their own folklore than they would record it or collect it in databases.

20.25 Another problem of indirect protection may arise where an indigenous artist enjoys copyright in an adaptation/translation of folklore because this right may conflict with customary rules that usually provide for a different kind of privileges, such as custodianship in the used folklore itself. Within an indigenous community, it seems however that a solution could be found on the basis of customary law.

20.26 Unfair competition rules may provide for limited protection only in a competitive context. Trademarks and geographical indications may protect the mere authenticity interest. Cultural heritage laws usually focus on preservation and documentation rather than on protection against unauthorized uses. Customary laws are usually

---

[20] Examples ibid 411 ff.

[21] S von Lewinski, 'Final Considerations' in S von Lewinski (n 1 above) 505, 514, also on other disadvantages from a Western point of view.

[22] For examples, see the 'Regional Framework for the Protection of Traditional Knowledge and Expressions of Culture' adopted by the Secretariat of the Pacific Community, Model Law of 2002, ISBN 982-203-933-6; the latest WIPO proposals (paras 20.39–20.40 below) and for a discussion von Lewinski (n 21 above) 515–6.

[23] ibid 511–13.

not applicable to outsiders of communities. *Sui generis* laws seem not to have functioned properly in practice. Therefore, new provisions are currently being developed, in particular in WIPO.[24]

C. Past attempts to achieve international protection of folklore

(1) The Berne Convention

The first notable attempt to achieve international protection of expressions of folklore was undertaken at the 1967 Stockholm Revision Conference of the Berne Convention. At that time, most former colonized territories had become independent states and started to represent their own interests as developing countries. They were the countries to raise and strongly support the issue of folklore, although it was not a pure North–South issue given the presence of indigenous peoples not only in developing but also in industrialized countries such as Australia, New Zealand, Canada, and the USA. At first sight, the inclusion of folklore in an international treaty protecting authors' works did not seem unjustified, because both were productions in the literary and artistic fields that are covered by the Berne Convention. Also, the Berne approach may have been chosen for the pragmatic consideration that an existing treaty with large membership would save countries the difficulty of adopting a separate treaty. **20.27**

At the same time, delegations were aware that folklore was different from authors' works: the proposal by India[25] to include 'works of folklore' in the non-exclusive list of literary and artistic works of Article 2(1) of the Berne Convention, although supported by many delegations, was not adopted, especially following doubts by Australia on whether the Berne Convention (based on the protection of individual, identifiable authors) could apply to folklore (which did not involve identifiable authors). Instead, the proposal to add a new paragraph (4) to Article 15 of the Berne Convention was adopted. **20.28**

This provision deliberately did not use the word 'folklore', given the difficulties of definition.[26] Instead, folklore was described as 'unpublished works where the identity of the author is unknown, but where there is every ground to presume that he is a national of a country of the Union', thereby taking into account that **20.29**

---

[24] paras 20.39–20.40 below.
[25] See Records of the Intellectual Property Conference of Stockholm 1967, Vol II (1971), 1152/ paras 126, 127.
[26] Yet, the main field of application of this new provision was supposed to be folklore, ibid 1173/ para 252; see also 918/para 1509.2.

folklore is usually unpublished and does not have any identifiable author or group of authors, while one can relate a particular expression of folklore to a specific geographical area. Yet, the provision was still based on the concept of individual authorship; the mere possibility of designating a competent authority to represent the author and protect and enforce his rights in the Berne Union did not sufficiently take account of the particularities of folklore. This may have been one of the main reasons why the Berne approach was not successful; indeed, only India has designated such authority.[27]

(2) WIPO model provisions

20.30   Consequently, a new approach was chosen: the inclusion of provisions on folklore in non-binding model laws[28] such as, at first, the Tunis Model Law 1976.[29] It was designed to assist developing countries in drafting their own copyright laws in general. Accordingly, the provisions on folklore represented only a minor part of the Model Law. They addressed folklore by specific rules, including a definition of folklore, the provision that fixation would not be required, and an unlimited duration of protection.[30] Such provisions were much better adapted to the particular characteristics of folklore than the Berne solution and were indeed implemented in a number of national laws. Yet, they demonstrated some deficiencies; for example, the collective nature of folklore was not taken into account.[31]

20.31   Not long thereafter, at the request of the WIPO Governing Bodies in 1978, a WIPO/UNESCO Committee of Governmental Experts discussed folklore, and in 1982 adopted the 'Model Provisions for National Laws on the Protection of Expressions of Folklore against Illicit Exploitation and Other Prejudicial Actions' to assist national legislators.[32] These Model Provisions chose a *sui generis* rather than a copyright approach. They defined the subject matter of protection, the

---

[27] Lucas-Schloetter (n 2 above) 351. For more details, see M Nordmann, *Rechtsschutz von Folkloreformen* (2001) 25 ff.

[28] On model laws by WIPO, see in general para 15.14 above.

[29] Tunis Model Law on Copyright with a commentary drafted by the Secretary of UNESCO and the International Bureau of WIPO, (1976) Copyright 165 ff. It was adopted by the Committee of Governmental Experts of UNESCO and WIPO in Tunis, 23 February to 2 March 1976. See Lucas-Schloetter (n 2 above) 443–5.

[30] In particular see s 1(3) in connection with s 6, s 18(iv), s 5[bis] and s 6(2) of the Tunis Model Law (n 29 above).

[31] See also Nordmann (n 27 above) 28 with references.

[32] (1982) Copyright 278 ff. On the Model Provisions, eg P Kuruk, 'Protecting Folklore under Modern Intellectual Property Regimes: A Reappraisal of the Tensions between the Individual and Communal Rights in Africa and the United States' (1999) 48 American University Law Review 815 ff; M Ficsor, 'Indigenous Peoples and Local Communities: Exploration of Issues Related to Intellectual Property Protection of Expressions of Traditional Culture ("Expressions of Folklore")', ATRIP paper GVA/99/27, 7–12; and Lucas-Schloetter (n 2 above) 445–8.

acts subject to authorization by a competent authority or community, and the exceptions to such rights of authorization. They laid down the obligation to indicate the source of any identifiable expression of folklore, and contained other provisions, for example, regarding enforcement, protection of foreign folklore, and the relationship with other forms of protection.

(3) Draft treaty

The Model Provisions 1982 had been conceived as a first step on the way towards   **20.32** international protection. Consequently, in December 1984 a WIPO/UNESCO Group of Experts discussed a draft treaty based on the Model Provisions 1982 and on national treatment.[33] Although the Group, in principle, recognized the need to establish an international legal framework for the protection of folklore, it raised a number of concerns. For example, the Group considered it difficult to identify expressions of folklore to be protected in other member countries. Also, in respect of expressions of folklore that could be found in several countries, workable mechanisms of dispute settlement were missing. As a result, the perceived legal uncertainty as to the scope of the international obligations under the proposed treaty was a stumbling block on the way to its adoption. Eventually, most participants considered the adoption of an international treaty premature and recommended first gaining experience with the protection of folklore at the national level, in particular following the Model Provisions 1982.[34] After this discouraging result, international ambitions faded away for a long time.

(4) The recent relaunch of debates in WIPO

Only in the framework of preparations for the 1996 WIPO Treaties[35] did the   **20.33** topic of folklore reappear. The plan to negotiate a treaty on the *sui generis* protection of databases at the 1996 WIPO Diplomatic Conference in addition to the later WCT and WPPT[36] may have provoked the perception by developing countries that the new treaties, in particular the database treaty, would primarily benefit industrialized countries. Developing countries tried to establish a link between a possible database treaty and a possible international instrument for the protection

---

[33] Group of Experts on the International Protection of Expressions of Folklore by Intellectual Property; Draft Treaty for the Protection of Expressions of Folklore against Illicit Exploitation and other Prejudicial Actions (1984), reprinted in (1985) Copyright Bulletin of UNESCO 34 ff (para 9.19 no 2) and in (1985) Copyright 47 ff (with comments). See Lucas-Schloetter (n 2 above) 448–50.

[34] See the report on the meeting, (1985) Copyright 40 ff, in particular para 14.

[35] WCT and WPPT; von Lewinski (n 10 above) 755.

[36] Eventually, the third Draft Treaty was not even opened for negotiations at the 1996 Diplomatic Conference, mainly due to lack of time, see J Reinbothe and S von Lewinski, *The WIPO Treaties 1996* (2002) ch 3, n 57, and para 17.157 above.

of folklore. Consequently, the WIPO Committee of Experts preparing the 1996 WIPO Treaties recommended in February 1996 to WIPO's Governing Bodies that an international forum be organized to explore issues concerning the preservation and protection of expressions of folklore, the intellectual property aspects thereof, and the harmonization of different regional interests.[37]

20.34 As a result, WIPO and UNESCO organized a forum in Phuket in April 1997.[38] The forum concluded with the adoption of an 'action plan' to be submitted to the competent organs of UNESCO and WIPO. The suggestions were quite ambitious: not only were regional consultations to take place, but also a Committee of Experts was to be established in cooperation with UNESCO in order to 'complete the drafting of a new international agreement on the sui generis protection of folklore . . . in view of the possible convocation of a Diplomatic Conference, preferably in the second half of 1998'.[39] Obviously, this plan was too ambitious.

20.35 Not much later, WIPO was faced with the related topics of genetic resources and traditional knowledge, already addressed in the 1993 Convention on Biological Diversity and in other international fora.[40] Among its initial activities in relation to these topics were, in 1998, a joint study with UNEP (United Nations Environment Programme) on benefit sharing[41] and fact-finding missions.[42] Subsequently, when setting the agenda for the Diplomatic Conference for the Adoption of the Patent Law Treaty to take place in May/June 2000, the WIPO was challenged by claims to include certain aspects regarding genetic resources in favour of indigenous peoples.[43] The inclusion of such a controversial topic would have considerably burdened the planned treaty negotiations. Finally, the WIPO successfully opposed such claims; yet, continued pressure to discuss genetic resources and traditional knowledge resulted in the establishment of the Intergovernmental Committee, which then also covered folklore.

---

[37] See the report on the meeting, WIPO Doc BCP/CE/VI/16-INR/CE/V/14, para 269.

[38] See a collection of the contributions and other material submitted for the forum in UNESCO Publication No CLT/CIC/98/1 and WIPO Publication No 758 E.

[39] UNESCO/WIPO (ed), *World Forum on the Protection of Folklore* (1998) 235.

[40] Art 8j of the Convention of 29 December 1993, 31 ILM 818. On other international fora, see eg Stoll and von Hahn (n 1 above) 35–45.

[41] A Gupta, *WIPO-UNEP Study on the Role of Intellectual Property Rights in the Sharing of Benefits Arising from the Use of Biological Resources and Associated Traditional Knowledge—Study n° 4* (2004) (mandated in 1998).

[42] The fact-finding missions also covered folklore and resulted in a report (n 15 above). See also W Wendland, 'Intellectual Property, Traditional Knowledge and Folklore: WIPO's Exploratory Program' (2002) 33 IIC 485, 488.

[43] Also on other activities in this context, see von Lewinski (n 10 above) 749.

D. The Intergovernmental Committee of WIPO

(1) Overview of the Committee's work on folklore

The WIPO Intergovernmental Committee on Intellectual Property and Genetic **20.36** Resources, Traditional Knowledge and Folklore held its first session in May 2001; most recently, the eleventh session took place in July 2007.[44] From the outset, a number of tasks have been discussed and are, in part, already realized. First, information gathering has been essential. Unlike in other fields of intellectual property, where knowledge is widespread or at least easily accessible, there was relatively little updated, systematized information available on folklore and the related topics in 2001; also, this topic seemed new for many delegates, even if they were experts in intellectual property. In this context, the WIPO secretariat accomplished extremely useful work by collecting and reviewing information on national experiences with existing protection,[45] drafting session documents with substantial amounts of information (including information on the current forms of available protection and terminological issues),[46] and mandating case studies[47] for the purpose of exchanging information and as a basis for better-informed deliberations on the relevant issues.

Secondly, WIPO has provided legal and technical assistance to Member States **20.37** and their indigenous peoples and communities or regional organizations in respect of the establishment, strengthening, and more effective implementation of systems and measures for the legal protection of expressions of folklore. On this basis, WIPO has assisted in, for example, the drafting of the Regional Framework of the Pacific Community, and it continues to work in other regions.[48]

Thirdly, possibly the most important task is controversial and relates to legislative **20.38** activities. The early proposal to update the 1982 Model Provisions[49] did not

---

[44] Sessions took place in May 2001, December 2001, June 2002, December 2002, July 2003, March 2004, November 2004, June 2005, April 2006, November/December 2006, July 2007, see WIPO Docs GRTKF/IC/1–10 (with further subdivisions, including reports of the sessions), <http://www.wipo.int/meetings/en/topic.jsp?group_id=110>. On the initial sessions, see in detail Wendland (n 16 above) 112 ff.

[45] Questionnaire to governments: WIPO Doc GRTKF/IC/2/7.C; responses and summary: WIPO Doc GRTKF/IC/3/10; also Wendland (n 16 above), 115 ff.

[46] <http://www.wipo.int/meetings/en/topic.jsp?group_id=110>.

[47] For studies and similar publications by WIPO, see <http://www.wipo.int/tk/en/publications/index.html>. A mandated study on customary law is currently being prepared.

[48] n 22 above.

[49] para 20.31 above.

reach a consensus among delegates of WIPO.[50] The preparation of an international treaty or other legally binding instrument on the protection of expressions of folklore (and traditional knowledge) has been discussed and is included in the current mandate. Yet, from the beginning of the Committee's work, a split between developing and industrialized countries became visible: developing countries have been urging the Committee to work towards the ultimate goal of adopting a treaty,[51] while industrialized countries, in particular the USA, have vigorously opposed such work. Several times, it was therefore difficult to agree on the mandate of the Committee which must be renewed periodically.[52] The General Assembly has so far not excluded any outcome of the work, so that work on a treaty is covered by the mandate.[53] The fierce opposition of industrialized countries to any binding instrument in the field has led to their refusal even to discuss the articles submitted by the WIPO secretariat, which, however, clearly stated that the language (proposed articles and commentaries explaining their contents one by one) was without prejudice to the legal nature of any possible legal instrument, such as a model for national or regional legislation, or, if desired, for an international instrument of any kind, be it binding or non-binding.[54]

(2) The latest proposals

20.39   These articles were part of a document elaborated for the seventh session and revised for the eighth session by the Secretariat at the request of the Committee to develop an overview of policy objectives and core principles for the protection of expressions of folklore.[55] The document reflects the Committee's work since its establishment and draws on past consultations by WIPO. It contains draft policy

---

[50] According to established WIPO practice, WIPO therefore did not pursue this task; for the task No 2, see WIPO Doc GRTKF/IC/1/3, annex 4 and IV, for the report: WIPO Doc GRTKF/IC/3/17 para 294.

[51] See in particular the African group's proposal of 2003 to present a treaty to the General Assembly during the 2004/2005 budget biennium, Report of the Fifth Session, WIPO Doc GRTKF/IC/5/15 paras 175, 123, and 48.

[52] eg during the Eighth session, it seemed that developing countries would agree to renew the mandate subject only to stipulating the aim to elaborate a treaty, to which industrialized countries were strictly opposed. Eventually, the Committee could agree only to recommend to the General Assembly renewing the mandate 'to continue its work . . .' without specification of the kind or aim of the work, WIPO Doc 'Decisions adopted by the Committee, June 10, 2005—Intergovernmental Committee on Intellectual Property and Genetic Resources, Traditional Knowledge and Folklore, Eighth session, Geneva, June 6 to 10, 2005' para 9, <http://www.wipo.int/meetings/en/details.jsp?meeting_id=7130>.

[53] See the most recent decision on the mandate by the General Assembly 2005, WIPO Doc WO/GA 32/13 of 5 October 2005, paras 166–202.

[54] On these Articles, see paras 20.39–20.40, fn 55 (Doc 8/4) below. On the outlook for future options, see paras 20.41, 20.42 below.

[55] WIPO Docs GRTKF/IC/7/3 and, for an outline of the policy options and legal mechanisms for folklore protection, GRTKF/IC/7/4; revised version: WIPO Doc GRTKF/IC/8/4 (repr in the annexes to Docs GRTKF/9/4 and GRTKF/10/4).

objectives (common general directions for protection, such as to recognize the value of and promote respect for folklore); general guiding principles to ensure consistency, balance, and effectiveness of substantive principles (such as balance and proportionality, and respect for customary use of folklore); and specific substantive principles (ie the essence of protection in form of articles with explanations).

The draft articles concern similar matters as would be covered by copyright **20.40** norms, such as subject matter and beneficiaries of protection, acts of misappropriation/scope of protection, exceptions and limitations, term of protection, and the principle that no formalities shall be required. Yet, they deviate from copyright in many respects, thereby taking into account particularities of folklore. While a detailed analysis would go beyond the scope of this chapter,[56] a number of points are highlighted. The definition of folklore is quite comprehensive by even including signs, names, and symbols. It requires the expression to be characteristic of the community's cultural and social identity and cultural heritage and to be used by or within the community in accordance with its customary law. It thereby reflects the justification for protection, namely the importance of folklore as living heritage for a community. Consequently, the draft also proposes linking the duration of protection to the continuous fulfilment of these requirements; similarly, beneficiaries are only those communities for which an expression of folklore is living heritage. Protection against misappropriation is proposed in form of necessary prior and informed consent (for registered expressions), a remuneration right, and rights similar to moral rights; customary uses are excluded from protection. An agency is offered for assistance in managing rights. In sum, these articles are currently among the most advanced models for protection of folklore, in particular since they reflect the desire to take account of the specific needs and the customary laws of indigenous communities.

E. Outlook

The split between developing and industrialized countries regarding the aim of a **20.41** treaty[57] led, in December 2006, to a potential deadlock, which was successfully avoided by an agreement to first discuss a number of substantive issues of

---

[56] For details, see the explanations in WIPO Doc GRTKF/IC/8/4 and comments by delegations on the preceding version in Doc GRTKF/7/15 paras 65–99 and in subsequent session reports; see also S von Lewinski, 'Adequate Protection of Folklore: A Work in Progress' in P Torremans (ed), *Copyright Law: A Handbook of Contemporary Research* (2007) 207, 217 ff.

[57] para 20.38 above.

protection rather than the proposed articles.[58] This compromise may still be useful as a step towards the ultimate aim of a treaty. At the same time, regional agreements and national laws should be developed and implemented in practice in order to eliminate concerns that there is not yet abundant evidence for the proper functioning of protection systems as drafted by WIPO. WIPO has successfully begun to assist such development in the South Pacific,[59] Africa,[60] and elsewhere.

20.42 Finally, one may wonder why industrialized countries show so little readiness to even talk about the possibility of a binding treaty. After developing countries have been very cooperative in the past regarding classical intellectual property treaties from which often they do not themselves gain as much as they have to give, it would seem appropriate for industrialized countries to now develop the same sense of cooperation—all the more since any treaty, if ever concluded, would probably bring about relatively small economic 'losses' for them but would, at the same time, bring about great profits in terms of good will, greatly needed today.[61] Possibly, what is still needed is the sincere readiness to listen to the other side, and to try to understand and accept the existence of different world views and concepts of property—put simply: mutual respect.

---

[58] WIPO Doc 'Decisions of the Tenth Session of the Committee' of 8 December 2006, para 8(i), under <http://www.wipo.int/meetings/en/details.jsp?meeting_id=11222>.

[59] para 20.37 and n 22 above.

[60] The African regional organizations OAPI in autumn 2007 adopted a regional instrument largely based on the first WIPO draft (n 55 above), Lucas-Schloetter (n 2 above) 465–7, also on the similar draft of ARIPO.

[61] paras 26.02 ff, 26.13 and 26.14 below.

21

THE WIPO DEVELOPMENT AGENDA

A. Background	21.01	C. Main contents of proposals	21.06
B. Subsequent activities	21.03	D. Outlook	21.11

A. Background

General politics increasingly influence the expert bodies of international entities, **21.01** such as the Specialized UN Agency WIPO. One major, recent political movement aims at generally strengthening developing and least developed countries (LDCs)—an approach considered necessary not least in order to diminish the negative consequences of globalization in these countries. Notably, in September 2000 the General Assembly of the UN adopted the United Nations Millennium Declaration, which contains eight millennium development goals to improve the situation in developing countries and LDCs.[1] Many other actions, declarations, and developments towards such improvements followed in this and other international organizations; for example, the current WTO Doha Round adopted the 'Doha Development Agenda' in November 2001; and the World Summit on the Information Society addressed the so-called 'digital divide' and similar issues.[2]

Against this background, Argentina and Brazil submitted to the WIPO General **21.02** Assembly 2004—around the same time when certain developing countries started a general political agenda in WIPO, WTO, and other international organizations to demonstrate their potential impact[3]—a proposal 'for the establishment of a development agenda for WIPO'.[4] With later support by twelve

---

[1] <http://www.un.org/millenniumgoals/background.html>; on globalization, see its para 5.

[2] On the World Summit on the Information Society, which took place in Geneva in December 2003 and in Tunis in November 2005, and on its outcomes, see <http://www.itu.int/wsis/index.html>. More activities regarding development issues are mentioned in WIPO Doc WO/GA/31/11 Annex p 1.

[3] paras 19.07 and 19.37 above.

[4] WIPO Doc WO/GA/31/11. It is notable that already in 1961, Brazil had also submitted to the UN General Assembly a Resolution for development, though limited to patent law, see A Menescal,

other developing countries, this self-identified 'Group of Friends of Development'[5] essentially proposed that the development dimension be better implemented into WIPO's work. In reaction to this proposal, the General Assembly decided not only to organize an international seminar on intellectual property and development,[6] but also to convene intersessional intergovernmental meetings in order to examine this and future similar proposals.

B. Subsequent activities

21.03   Subsequently, three intersessional intergovernmental meetings were organized in 2005. Participants discussed not only the above proposal but also proposals submitted by the USA, Mexico, the United Kingdom, Bahrain (co-sponsored by ten additional Arabic countries), and another UK proposal; an African proposal was not discussed for lack of time.[7] The International Bureau itself highlighted its own development cooperation activities in a separate document.[8] Discussions were quite general and often related to industrial property law; basically they were limited to exchange of views.[9] In light of these proposals, the subsequent WIPO General Assembly 2005 decided to constitute a Provisional Committee that would follow up on the intersessional meetings in order to accelerate and complete the discussions on proposals on the WIPO Development Agenda.[10]

21.04   During four sessions in 2006–7, the Provisional Committee discussed old, revised, and new proposals.[11] In order to structure the discussion on the many proposals, the Chair prepared a set of clusters of like-oriented proposals. Since no consensus on substance was reached until June 2006, the subsequent WIPO

'Changing WIPO's Ways? The 2004 Development Agenda in Historical Perspective' (2005) 8/6 Journal of World Intellectual Property 761 ff.

   [5] WIPO Doc WO/GA/31/11 Add: Bolivia, Cuba, Dominican Republic, Ecuador, Egypt, Iran, Kenya, Peru, Sierra Leone, South Africa, Tanzania, and Venezuela; see also the more elaborated proposal in WIPO Doc IIM/1/4.

   [6] This seminar took place on 2 and 3 May 2005 and was co-organized by UNCTAD, UNIDO, WHO, and WTO. It dealt with many issues under the two general themes 'IP and Public Policy' and 'IP and Development', WIPO Doc ISIPD/05/INF/1 Prov, see <http://www.wipo.int/meetings/en/details.jsp?meeting_id=7523>.

   [7] For these proposals, see WIPO Docs IIM/1/2, IIM/1/5, IIM/2/2, IIM/2/3, and IIM/3/2.

   [8] WIPO Doc EDS/INF/1.

   [9] Report of the First Session: WIPO Doc IIM/1/6; Report of the Second Session: WIPO Doc IIM/2/10; Report of the Third Session: WIPO Doc IIM/3/3.

   [10] Provisional Committee on Proposals related to a WIPO Development Agenda; WIPO Doc WO/GA/32/13 para 146, also for further discussions in this context.

   [11] See, for example, the revised African proposal, IIM/3/2 Rev; proposal by Chile, WIPO Doc PCDA/1/2, Colombia (WIPO Doc PCDA/1/3), USA (WIPO Doc PCDA/1/4), Argentina and the 'Group of Friends' (WIPO PCDA/2/2), and Kyrgyz Republic (WIPO Doc PCDA/2/3). For the four sessions, see <http://www.wipo.int/ip-development/en/agenda.html>.

General Assembly 2006 renewed for one year the mandate of the Provisional Committee in order to further discuss in depth and in a structured way the then 111 submitted proposals. It also mandated the Committee to narrow down the proposals in order to avoid repetition or duplication, to separate actionable proposals from mere declarations of general principles, and to note proposals that relate to existing activities of WIPO.[12] In its 2007 sessions, the Provisional Committee succeeded in narrowing down the proposals to forty-five without leaving out any substantive issues.[13]

In its June 2007 session, it finally recommended by consensus that the General **21.05** Assembly adopt these proposals for action, immediately implement nineteen of them, and establish a Committee on Development and IP that would replace the Provisional Committee and the Permanent Committee on Cooperation for Development Related to Intellectual Property as well as develop a work programme for implementation of the adopted recommendations, monitor the implementation, and discuss intellectual property and development-related issues; the General Assembly adopted these recommendations on 28 September 2007.[14]

C. Main contents of proposals

The individual proposals are categorized under the following main topics: tech- **21.06** nical assistance and capacity building; norm-setting, flexibilities, public policy, and public domain; technology transfer, information and communication technology, and access to knowledge; assessments, evaluation, and impact studies; and institutional matters including mandate and governance.

From the proposals, only a few illustrative examples are mentioned here.[15] In **21.07** respect of technical assistance, an important desire is that WIPO's legislative advice take into account the special needs of developing countries and the different levels of Member States' development, and comprise the use of flexibilities contained in the TRIPS Agreement; other proposals recommend that WIPO put particular emphasis on the needs of small and medium-size enterprises and institutions dealing with scientific research and cultural industries; assist Member States in developing infrastructure and in setting up national strategies in

---

[12] WIPO Doc WO/GA/33/10 para 66, where the different clusters for discussion at the two meetings in 2007 are also set out.

[13] WIPO Doc PCDA/4/3 Annex I.

[14] For the complete list of recommendations, see WIPO Doc PCDA/4/3 para 76.

[15] For the entire list of the originally 111 proposals, see the Report of the WIPO General Assembly (n 12 above); on the list adopted in 2007, see n 13 above.

intellectual property; and assist Member States in dealing with intellectual property-related anti-competitive practices.

21.08 Norm-setting should recognize the different levels of development of Member States, support a 'robust public domain' and facilitate access to knowledge, take account of flexibilities offered by intellectual property treaties, and reflect a balance between benefits and costs for developed and developing countries. WIPO's working documents for norm-setting should address links between intellectual property and competition, as well as, notably, 'safeguarding national implementation of intellectual property rules'. The original Brazilian proposal more clearly refers to the right of countries to implement international obligations 'in accordance with their own legal systems and practice'.[16] This special attention to national implementation, which is often lost under bilateral treaties with the USA,[17] might reflect the wish of countries to keep their sovereignty regarding the way in which treaties are implemented into national law. Prior to new norm-setting activities, WIPO should conduct informal, open, and balanced consultations. In addition, the process on the protection of genetic resources, traditional knowledge, and folklore should be accelerated.

21.09 Furthermore, a yearly review and evaluation mechanism for assessment of WIPO's development-oriented activities is recommended, as well as studies to be conducted on intellectual property and development, and on related topics. In addition, WIPO is requested to intensify cooperation on intellectual property-related issues with other international organizations, and to enhance measures to ensure participation of civil society in WIPO activities.

21.10 The proposals recommended for work on the WIPO Development Agenda cover all areas of intellectual property and are generally quite broad, open, and vaguely formulated—a fact that has facilitated agreement on the recommendation among delegates.

D. Outlook

21.11 Ultimately, the WIPO Member States will have to decide how to formulate and implement these proposals and what consequences they should have. Discussions due to start in the new Committee in 2008 might carry on for quite some time, especially when considering the political nature of the Development Agenda; also, it may be more difficult to agree on a concrete implementation of these

---

[16] WIPO Doc WO/GA/31/11, Annex at 4, referring to the corresponding flexibility granted under Art 1.1 of the TRIPS Agreement.
[17] paras 12.31, 12.41, and 14.20 above, for example on the US–Australia FTA.

proposals than it was to agree on the broad list of forty-five proposals in 2007. In any case, since the new Committee will cut across the different areas of WIPO's mandate, any particular recommendation by the Committee will have to be adopted by the General Assembly and redirected to the competent committee, such as the SCCR, for questions of copyright and related rights.

On the one hand, the proposals on the table do not seem revolutionary; they refer **21.12** to issues that have been among WIPO's main concerns throughout its existence: for example, WIPO has always offered technical and other assistance and taken account of the needs of developing countries in other ways, such as within the procedures at diplomatic conferences.[18] On the other hand, the adoption of these proposals could be meaningful where issues such as competition practices may only now be clearly within WIPO's mandate. In addition, they may reflect the wish of Member States to more strongly redirect WIPO's focus to development issues; this is particularly true for the area of norm-setting, where developing countries have felt bullied to adopt the TRIPS Agreement and even higher standards in regional and bilateral trade agreements, and this in conjunction with unilateral measures. The initiative for the WIPO Development Agenda might thus be viewed as a reaction to these pressures, and as a signal to other countries to stop this tendency. It may also reflect the wish of developing countries to demonstrate a certain power as players on the international scene—a power that in recent years has already been experienced in several WIPO committees and even beyond WIPO.

---

[18] These WIPO procedures allow for more transparency and equal chances than those of the GATT/WTO, see on this aspect para 9.09 above and para 25.15 below.

22

ADDITIONAL ISSUES DISCUSSED IN
WIPO AFTER 1996[1]

A. *Sui generis* protection of databases

When in early 1996 the EC adopted its Database Directive, which included *sui* **22.01**
generis protection,[2] and submitted to WIPO its proposal for a treaty on *sui generis*
protection of databases,[3] reactions by other delegations were sufficiently positive
so that the Chair of the Committee was mandated with the preparation of a Basic
Proposal for a database treaty. Yet, during the short period between the submission of the proposal and the Diplomatic Conference in December 1996, support
by those other delegations largely faded away due to users' concerns; in addition,
no time was left at the Conference for negotiation on the Basic Proposal. As a
result, the Diplomatic Conference simply adopted a Recommendation to convoke an extraordinary session of the WIPO Governing Bodies during the first
quarter of 1997; the session was to decide on a schedule of further preparatory
work for such a treaty.[4]

At an extraordinary session in March 1997, the General Assembly of WIPO and **22.02**
the Assembly of the Berne Union decided that only an information meeting was

---

[1] Audiovisual performances, broadcasting organizations, folklore, and the WIPO development
agenda are separately covered in chs 18–21 above. For database protection before and until the
Diplomatic Conference 1996, see paras 17.155–17.157 above.

[2] Dir 96/9/EC of the European Parliament and of the Council of 11 March 1996 on the legal
protection of databases, in particular Arts 7 ff; Vol II ch 9.

[3] WIPO doc BCP/CE/6/13.

[4] On *sui generis* protection for databases during the Committees of Experts up to the 1996
Diplomatic Conference, see paras 17.155–17.156 above.

to be convened for database protection, while the other unfinished issue left over from the 1996 Diplomatic Conference—audiovisual performances—by contrast was to be discussed in a Committee of Experts.[5] Accordingly, an 'Information Meeting on Intellectual Property in Databases' took place in September 1997 in combination with the first session of the Committee of Experts on a protocol concerning audiovisual performances. The meeting primarily served to exchange information regarding the need for protection; discussions were based on WIPO documents about existing legislation and information received from WIPO Member States[6] rather than on the Basic Proposal for a Database Treaty prepared for the 1996 Diplomatic Conference.

22.03   Many delegations did not deny a need for *sui generis* protection; yet, statements of most delegations stressed the importance of public interests such as research and education[7] and thereby reflected the strong user concerns that were already visible in the second half of 1996.[8] The Meeting called for further information to be collected and distributed by the International Bureau.[9] In 1998, the *sui generis* protection of databases was put on the agenda of the then newly established Standing Committee on Copyright and Related Rights (SCCR). Work within the SCCR and in regional group meetings[10] showed that controversy subsisted between those favourable to a *sui generis* protection and those concerned about free access and public interest. Many delegations considered it premature to conclude a treaty in this field, and requested the International Bureau to present a study on the economic impact and consequences of database protection, in particular in developing and least developed countries.[11] A number of studies were

---

[5] WIPO Doc AB/3X/4 para 20; for a more detailed presentation of discussions in WIPO after 1996 until the Third Session of SCCR in November 1999, see J Reinbothe and S von Lewinski, *The WIPO Treaties 1996* (2002) 489–91.

[6] WIPO Memoranda in WIPO Docs DB/IM/2, DB/IM/3 and DB/IM/3Add; see also submissions by the World Meteorological Organization, WIPO Doc DB/IM/4, and by UNESCO, WIPO Doc DB/IM/5.

[7] Report of the Information Meeting on Intellectual Property and Databases, 17–19 September 1997, WIPO Doc DB/IM/6 Rev 4 ff and, for statements at the debate, Annex II.

[8] para 17.157 above.

[9] Report (n 7 above) 4–5, para 12.

[10] eg Consultation Meeting for Central European and Baltic States, WIPO Docs SCCR/2/10 and SCCR/2/10 Rev; for African countries: WIPO Doc SCCR/3/2; for Asia and the Pacific: WIPO Doc SCCR/3/6; and for a group of Central and Eastern European countries: WIPO Doc SCCR/3/10.

[11] Report on the First Session of the SCCR, WIPO Doc SCCR/1/9 para 204(b)(ii)/p35.

then submitted to the SCCR at its Seventh Session in May 2002.[12] These studies evoked little discussion.[13]

While the work of the SCCR until 2000 focused on the planned treaty on audio-visual performances and therefore devoted limited time to the *sui generis* protection of databases, interest in this topic remained low even after the Audiovisual Diplomatic Conference 2000. The situation might have changed if the USA had joined the EC in introducing such protection at the national level, but despite several attempts, it did not succeed. The absence of major driving forces (in addition to the EC) in favour of the treaty and the lack of interest in the *sui generis* protection of databases even after submission of the above-mentioned studies led several countries to propose removing this topic from the agenda of the SCCR. Due to the opposition of the USA, the EC, the Russian Federation, and Romania, the Committee instead decided at the Ninth Session to address database protection only every other session.[14] After similar discussion at the Eleventh Session, it was decided to again include the topic on the agenda of the Thirteenth Session and thereafter at appropriate intervals at the request of interested delegations.[15] After a very short discussion at the Thirteenth Session,[16] the topic has no longer been addressed in the SCCR, and there is currently no indication of any new initiative for a database treaty.

B. Other topics

(1) The search for new topics

The issue of possible new topics for the SCCR emerged for the first time in 2001—at a time when the plan of the audiovisual performers' treaty had lost

22.04

22.05

---

12 Y Braunstein, 'Economic Impact of Database Protection in Developing Countries and Countries in Transition' WIPO Doc SCCR/7/2; S El-Kassas, 'Study on the Protection of Unoriginal Databases' WIPO Doc SCCR/7/3; T Riis, 'Economic Impact of the Protection of Unoriginal Databases in Developing Countries and Countries in Transition' WIPO Doc SCCR/7/4; P Vandrevala, 'A Study on the Impact of Protection of Unoriginal Databases on Developing Countries: Indian Experience' WIPO Doc SCCR/7/5; Z Shengli, 'The Economic Impact of the Protection of Database in China' WIPO Doc SCCR/7/6; A López, 'The Impact of Protection of Non-original Databases on the Countries of Latin America and the Caribbean', WIPO Doc SCCR/8/6; see also a similar study by the EC and its Member States, 'The Legal Protection of Databases', WIPO Doc SCCR/8/8 and a proposal by Kenia, 'Protection of Non-original Databases', WIPO Doc SCCR/9/2 and SCCR/9/2/Corr.

13 Report of the Seventh Session: WIPO Doc SCCR/7/10 paras 12–23; Eighth Session: WIPO Doc SCCR/8/9 paras 12–15.

14 Report of the SCCRs Ninth Session in June 2003, WIPO Doc SCCR/9/11 paras 10, 22; 130(e).

15 Report of the Eleventh Session, WIPO Doc SCCR/11/4 Annex III p 2.

16 Report of the Thirteenth Session, WIPO Doc SCCR/13/6 paras 186–93.

momentum after the failure of the 2000 Diplomatic Conference, and when the accomplishment of the other major project, the planned treaty on broadcasters' rights, was considered realistic for the then foreseeable future.[17] Accordingly, some might have felt that an early search for new topics would be appropriate. At the same time, not all topics were planned to be addressed in the SCCR; some of them would rather be envisaged for studies, symposia, information meetings, and the like.[18]

22.06 At the Seventh Session, Mexico proposed studies on representatives[19] of internet service providers, applicable law regarding international copyright and neighbouring rights infringements, voluntary copyright registration systems, and resale rights. Hungary proposed studying ownership of multimedia products and issues of private international law, namely choice of forum and choice of law; Russia suggested work on digital rights management and ownership in the digital environment; the USA added economics of copyright; Sudan, like Hungary, proposed the collective management of copyright and related rights; and certain NGOs mentioned limitations and exceptions.[20]

22.07 At the Eighth Session, the International Bureau submitted a document that described the topics mentioned by delegations. It suggested discussing the priority of possible topics for future SCCR work, though not necessarily work towards norm-setting. Delegations showed interest in many of the topics in the document and expressed different priorities.[21] Some also reminded the Committee that the unfinished issues of audiovisual performances, broadcasting organizations, and *sui generis* protection of databases should be addressed and solved first.[22]

(2) Work on new topics

(a) Liability of internet service providers

22.08 On the liability of internet service providers, which was left out of the WCT and WPPT,[23] WIPO had already organized a workshop in 1999 and included the issue in the programme of the WIPO International Conference on E-Commerce

---

[17] For the Sixth Session, see Report, WIPO Doc SCCR/6/4 paras 170 ff; for the optimistic estimation by the Chair that a diplomatic conference on a broadcasters' treaty might already be convened in 2004, see Report of the Eighth Session, WIPO Doc SCCR/8/9 para 125.

[18] ibid para 104.

[19] Original wording in all three available languages; probably referring to 'responsibility'.

[20] Report of the Seventh Session, WIPO Doc SCCR/7/10 paras 132–45.

[21] The issues are described in WIPO Doc SCCR/8/2.

[22] For the reactions of delegations, see Report of the Eighth Session (n 17 above) paras 103–23.

[23] para 17.54 above.

in 1999 and 2001.[24] In 2005, it organized a seminar on copyright and internet intermediaries where discussion took place on issues such as the broadening of the definition of internet intermediaries to include peer-to-peer services and internet portals such as YouTube, as well as the issues of notice-and-takedown procedures, regulatory perspectives, and future policy directions.[25]

(b) Private international law

Especially with the internet, questions of private international law have become **22.09** very important and complex, such as the question of what law applies to an act of making available works on the internet—an act with global effect. On this topic, WIPO organized three worldwide symposia in 1994 and 1995 and established a 'Group of Consultants on the Private International Law Aspects of the Protection of Works and Objects of Related Rights Transmitted through Global Digital Networks' in December 1998.[26] It included an overview of the issues of jurisdiction and applicable law in its Primer on Electronic Commerce.[27] In January 2001, it organized a forum on private international law and intellectual property.

When new attempts were made to relaunch the aim of a treaty on audiovisual **22.10** performances, WIPO presented a number of mandated studies on the substantive and private international law rules concerning the transfer of performers' rights in audiovisual works in selected countries and, on this basis, a general study.[28] Discussions on these studies in November 2003 and 2004 revealed the high degree of complexity with these issues and may have thus discouraged Member States and the WIPO Secretariat from taking additional initiatives in this field.

(c) Economic importance of copyright and related rights

In respect of the economic importance of copyright and related rights, in 2002 **22.11** WIPO organized a working group of economists to prepare a study that was

---

[24] For the 'Workshop on Service Provider Liability' 9–10 December 1999 in Geneva, see WIPO Docs OSP/LIA/1–3; for the electronic commerce conference, see 'International Conference on Electronic Commerce and Intellectual Property' 14–16 September 1999 in Geneva, WIPO Docs WIPO/EC/Conf/99/SPK/4ff, in particular 15-A, <http://www.wipo.int/meetings/en/details.jsp?meeting_id=3834>, and WIPO Second International Conference on Electronic Commerce and Intellectual Property of 19–21 September 2001 in Geneva, WIPO Doc WIPO/EC/Conf/01/SPK/1ff, <http://www.wipo.int/meetings/en/details.jsp?meeting_id=4390>; for a short stock-taking, see also 'Primer on Electronic Commerce and Intellectual Property Issues', WIPO Doc WIPO/OLOA/EC/PRIMER of May 2000, paras 132–5 and 137. For further WIPO conferences and seminars on electronic commerce, see <http://www.wipo.int/meetings/en/topic.jsp?group_id=21>.
[25] <http://www.wipo.int/meetings/en/2005/wipo_iis/program.html>.
[26] WIPO Docs GCPIC/1 and 2 (studies by A Lucas and J Ginsburg).
[27] n 24 above, paras 37–79.
[28] For refs, see para 18.23 above.

published in 2003 and that envisaged harmonizing the methods for measuring the economic importance of copyright and related rights. It summarizes existing experiences and indicates practical instruments for future surveys in order to establish a basis for comparison.[29]

(d) Collective rights management, registration, and other new topics

22.12 Collective rights management was addressed at the 1997 WIPO 'International Forum on the Exercise and Management of Copyright and Neighbouring Rights in the Face of the Challenges of Digital Technology' in Seville, Spain,[30] and at other conferences, including those of electronic commerce in 1999 and 2001.[31]

22.13 In respect of voluntary registration of works and of other subject matter, in November 2005 the International Bureau submitted a document on national laws that was based on a questionnaire responded to by twelve countries.[32] It perceived some advantages in voluntary registration, such as prima facie evidence of the subsistence of copyright;[33] especially in the digital context and most recently in the context of 'orphan works' (ie works for which the author cannot be located), registration has been considered useful. No discussion on this issue took place.[34] Other proposals by Member States for new topics, namely the resale right and ownership in multimedia products, have not been pursued.[35]

(e) Implementation of the WCT and the WPPT

22.14 In the context of the implementation of the WCT and the WPPT, many Member States felt the need for exchange of information, in particular on the legal protection of technical measures—an area where most did not yet have any experience.[36] Similarly, finding the right balance between the new rights and the users' interests in the digital environment was a challenge for many WIPO Members. The International Bureau assisted countries in these matters by organizing workshops and conferences.[37] Already before the entry into force of the WCT and the

---

[29] 'Guide of Surveying the Economic Contribution of the Copyright-Based Industries', WIPO Doc SCCR/10/4 (also WIPO Publication no 893(E)).

[30] WIPO Publication no 756(E).

[31] n 24 above. Also numerous seminars and workshops on this topic are notable, <http://www.wipo.int/meetings/en/topic.jsp?group_id=155>.

[32] Thirteenth Session of the SCCR; WIPO Doc SCCR/13/2.

[33] WIPO Doc SCCR/8/2 para 13.

[34] Report on the Thirteenth Session, WIPO Doc SCCR/13/6 paras 184–5.

[35] On these issues, see WIPO Doc SCCR/8/2 paras 14–15 and 16–18. The other topic proposed, the protection of folklore (ibid paras 35–8), had in the meantime been taken on by a new Intergovernmental Committee, see above paras 20.36 ff.

[36] For a number of questions, see WIPO Doc SCCR/8/6 para 22.

[37] WIPO Workshop on Implementation Issues of the WCT and the WPPT in December 1999, WIPO Doc WCT-WPPT/IMP, see in particular nos 2 and 3 (studies by A Strowel and D Marks/B Turnbull and the above conferences on electronic commerce 1999 and 2001 (n 24 above).

WPPT, the workshop on implementation issues of these treaties dealt with exceptions and limitations; it was based on a detailed study by Pierre Sirinelli.[38] In April 2003, WIPO submitted an important study by Sam Ricketson, which dealt in particular with exceptions and limitations under the Berne and Rome Conventions, the TRIPS Agreement, the WCT, and the WPPT. In addition, the study analysed the three-step test as it applies to specific uses and as it is implemented in US, EC, and Australian law.[39] After the entry into force of the WCT and WPPT, WIPO compiled a survey on Member States' provisions for their implementation.[40] It also published a study on 'current developments in the field of digital rights management', which was revised after pronounced criticism for being inaccurate and subjectively reflecting an industry's point of view.[41] Another study concerned 'automated rights management systems and copyright limitations and exceptions'.[42]

(f) Exceptions and limitations

In a different context, the topic of exceptions and limitations—this time, for **22.15** purposes of education, libraries, and disabled persons only—was reiterated in November 2004 when Chile suggested it for the SCCR's Agenda.[43] All delegations that took the floor were from developing countries and generally supported this proposal; yet, Chile did not clearly answer the question concerning the ultimate aim of such discussions: should it be a mere exchange of information on experiences in this field or should it be a norm-setting exercise?[44] In the following session, continued discussion showed different views on limitations and exceptions; for example, Benin and Morocco stated the need to ensure that right holders' interests were not harmed by exceptions, and many others also mentioned the

---

[38] WIPO Doc WCT-WPPT/IMP/1 of 3 December 1999; see also the WIPO conferences on electronic commerce of 1999 and 2001 (n 24 above).

[39] WIPO Study on limitations and exceptions of copyright and related rights in the digital environment, WIPO Doc SCCR/9/7.

[40] WIPO Doc SCCR/9/6 with Parts I–III of the Annex, and WIPO Doc SCCR/9/6 add 1 of 25 April and 11 July 2003, respectively; on the interest in issues concerning the implementation of the WCT and WPPT, see Report of the Sixth Session (n 17 above) para 170.

[41] Report of the Tenth Session, WIPO Doc SCCR/10/5 paras 62, 67; for the revised version, see J Cunard, K Hill, and C Barlas, WIPO Doc SCCR/10/2Rev, which described current digital rights management technologies and the present legal framework in international treaties, the USA, the EC, Australia, and Japan; it also dealt with the practical implementation of digital rights management systems and discussed policy issues.

[42] N Garnett, WIPO Doc SCCR/14/5.

[43] Twelfth Session of the SCCR, WIPO Doc SCCR/12/3 which does not contain any further substance. The topic of this proposal reappears in the Development Agenda, see paras 21.04, 21.08 above.

[44] For the short discussion, see the Report in WIPO Doc SCCR/12/4 paras 11–31.

three-step test as a limit, while others spoke in favour of users' interests. A related information meeting in context with the SCCR focused on such limitations.[45]

22.16 Generally welcome was a proposal that WIPO initiate a survey of national laws to serve as a basis for future recommendations on any need for changes to national laws or international treaties.[46] Chile then submitted a more substantial document specifying its own proposal by indicating three areas of possible work for the SCCR: the identification of national models and practices concerning exceptions and limitations; an analysis of exceptions and limitations needed to promote creation and the dissemination of developments stemming therefrom; and the establishment of agreement on exceptions and limitations as a minimum in all national laws.[47] This document was not discussed. The subsequent SCCR sessions dealt exclusively with the more pressing issue of a possible treaty on broadcasting organizations; however, an in-depth 'study on copyright limitations and exceptions for the visually impaired' was submitted to the SCCR, though not discussed.[48] The WIPO Secretariat continues to analyse this aspect of limitations and exceptions, for example, in respect of existing national laws.

(g) Enforcement

22.17 As another notable activity, WIPO has established an Advisory Committee on enforcement; it held its first session in June 2003.[49] It covers all areas of intellectual property. It has no mandate for norm-setting.[50] A special projects division within the International Bureau was set up for enforcement, as was an electronic forum for easier exchange of information.[51] Valuable documents, for example, on the experience of civil law litigation or administrative remedies in different countries in respect of intellectual property, have been made available in the context of the Advisory Committee.[52]

---

[45] <http://www.wipo.int/meetings/en/details.jsp?meeting_id=9462>, meeting of 21 November 2005.

[46] See the Report, WIPO Doc SCCR/13/6 paras 17–54.

[47] WIPO Doc SCCR/13/5.

[48] WIPO Doc SCCR/15/7, study prepared by J Sullivan; see also the Information Meeting on Digital Content for the Visually Impaired, organized in context with the Tenth Session of the SCCR, <http://www.wipo.int/meetings/en/details.jsp?meeting_id=5035>.

[49] See the conclusions by the Chair, WIPO Doc ACE/1/7 Rev.

[50] ibid para 4.

[51] IPEIS—Electronic Forum on Intellectual Property Issues and Strategies.

[52] See the WIPO Docs ACE/2 and /3 (with subnumbers), <http://www.wipo.int/meetings/en/topic.jsp?group_id=142>.

C. Outlook

As this chapter shows, valuable work can be done not only as part of norm-setting **22.18**
activities, but also beyond. One may presume that in the years to come, the
SCCR and other relevant committees may primarily present a forum for discussion and exchange of information on new challenges in the field of copyright and
neighbouring rights and related national experiences; in particular, if the topic of
limitations and exceptions should become a priority, as seems possible not least
in context with the WIPO Development Agenda, then one may well expect
that norm-setting will not be the immediate goal of deliberations, and even any
agreement on soft law will be highly difficult to achieve.

Part IV

OVERALL RÉSUMÉ AND OUTLOOK

23

COMPARATIVE TABLES OF THE CONTENTS OF THE MAIN INTERNATIONAL COPYRIGHT AND NEIGHBOURING RIGHTS TREATIES

The following tables for the main copyright and neighbouring rights treaties **23.01** present a 'big picture' of the rules and elements of protection through their juxtaposition and thereby aim at facilitating their understanding in a broader context. The tables may be useful to clearly visualize developments over time as well as the strong tendency to build on the relevant earlier treaties. In combination, the tables may be of benefit for the reader who is interested in a comparison of the individual elements of protection and provisions under copyright and neighbouring rights. The tables are necessarily rudimentary; the preceding chapters should be consulted for details.

A. Copyright

Element of Protection	Berne Convention (BC) (Paris Act 1971)	TRIPS Agreement (1994)	WIPO Copyright Treaty (WCT) (1996)
Principles of protection	• *national treatment:* Art 5(1)/(4) • *Exceptions to national treatment:* Arts 7(8), 2(7) phr 2, 6, 14ter (2), 30(2)(b) phr 2 • *minimum rights:* Art 5(1)/(4); Art 19 • *'no formalities':* Art 5(2)	• *national treatment:* Art 3(1) phr 1 • *Exceptions to national treatment:* Art 3(1) phr 1 with reference to exceptions under BC • *minimum rights:* Art 1(1) phr 1, 2; Art 1(3) phr 1 • *'no formalities':* Art 9(1) phr 1 with reference to Art 5(2) BC • *most-favoured-nation treatment:* Art 4, with safeguards for exceptions to national treatment under BC (Art 4 phr 2 (b)) • *criteria of eligibility as under BC:* Art 1(3) phr 2 with Arts 3, 4 BC • for the three first-mentioned principles also: compliance clause Art 9(1) phr 1 with reference to relevant Arts of BC	• *national treatment:* Art 3 with reference to Art 5(1)/(4) BC • *Exceptions to national treatment:* Arts 3 and 1(4) with references to exceptions under BC • *minimum rights:* Art 3 with reference to Art 5(1)/(4) BC • *'no formalities':* Art 3 with reference to Art 5(2) BC • *criteria of eligibility as under BC:* Art 3 with reference to Arts 3, 4 BC • in all cases also: compliance clause Art 1(4) with reference to relevant Arts of BC
Protected works	• Arts 2, 2bis(1), 14bis (1) phr 1	• Art 9(1) phr 1 (compliance clause) with reference to Arts 2, 2bis(1), 14bis BC • plus Art 10 (computer programs, databases)	• Art 3 with reference to Arts 2, 2bis (1) BC • Art 1(4) (compliance clause) with reference to all BC provisions, including Art 14bis • plus Arts 4, 5 (computer programs, databases)

Scope of protection of work	• 'expression' in Art 2(1) implies the same content as Art 9(2) TRIPS	• Art 9(2) idea/expression dichotomy	• Art 2 (corresponds to Art 9(2) TRIPS)
Right owner	• author (not defined; arguably only a natural person), Art 2(6) et al • successor in title, Art 2(6) • cinematographic work: Art 14bis(2), (3)	• Art 9(1) phr 1 (compliance clause) with reference to Arts 2(6), 14bis(2), (3) BC 'authors and their successors in title', Art 11	• Art 3 with reference to Art 2(6) BC; • also: Art 1(4) (compliance clause) with reference to Arts 2(6), 14bis(2), (3) BC
Moral rights	• Art 6bis and explicit safeguard in other provisions, eg Art 11bis(2) phr 2	• excluded from application of compliance clause, Art 9(1) phr 2	• Art 1(4) (compliance clause) with reference to Art 6bis BC and safeguard provisions
Economic rights	• *reproduction* in any manner or form: Art 9(1), (3) • *translation, adaptation/alteration*: Arts 8, 12 • *public performance, communication to the public* (except acts under Art 11bis) of dramatic, dramatico-musical, musical, and literary works: Arts 11, 11ter • the preceding four rights (except translation) also in the specific context of cinematographic works: Arts 14(1), (2), 14bis(1) phr 2 • *broadcasting, communication of broadcast*: Art 11bis • *distribution* in context with cinematographic works: Art 14(1)(i), 14bis(1) phr 2; arguably also in context with seizure, Art 16	• the *same rights* as under BC: Art 9(1) phr 1 (compliance clause) with reference to relevant BC provisions • plus: *rental right* (with limitations) regarding computer programs, cinematographic works, and (arguably) phonograms: Arts 11, 14(4)	• the *same rights* as under BC: Art 1(4) (compliance clause) with reference to relevant BC provisions • plus: *rental right* (with limitations, similar to TRIPS) regarding computer programs, cinematographic works and works embodied in phonograms: Art 7 • *distribution right* for all kinds of works: Art 6 • large *communication right* including '*making available*', complementing the communication right of the BC: Art 8

Element of Protection	Berne Convention (BC) (Paris Act (1971)	TRIPS Agreement (1994)	WIPO Copyright Treaty (WCT) (1996)
Limitations and exceptions	• certain uses of public lectures for informatory purposes: Art 2bis(2) • reproduction in general: Art 9(2) • quotation: Art 10(1) • illustration for teaching: Art 10(2) • certain uses of works on current events: Art 10bis(1) • incidental use of works when reporting on current events: Art 10bis(2) • ephemeral reproduction: Art 11bis(2) phr 2, 3 • compulsory licences: broadcasting (Art 11bis(2)) and (second and further) mechanical recordings (Art 13) • implied exceptions and limitations (*de minimis* kind and regarding the translation right)	• the same limitations and exceptions as under BC: Art 9(1) phr 1 (compliance clause) with reference to relevant BC provisions; includes implied exceptions and limitations • plus: additional application of three-step test to Berne rights, and separate application to TRIPS-right (rental): Art 13	• the same limitations and exceptions as under BC: Art 1(4) phr 1 (compliance clause) with reference to relevant BC provisions; includes implied exceptions and limitations • plus: additional application of three-step test to Berne rights: Art 10(2) (including Agreed Statement), and separate application to WCT- rights: Art 10(1)
Duration of protection	• general duration: 50 years *pma*: Art 7(1) • specific durations for cinematographic works, anonymous and pseudonymous works, photographic works and works of applied art, works of joint authorship: Arts 7(2)–(4), 7bis • moral rights: Art 6bis (2)	• same as under BC: Art 9(1) phr 1 (compliance clause) with reference to relevant BC provisions, except for moral rights (phr 2) • specific duration for works for which term is calculated on a basis other than the life of a natural person (mainly corporate works): Art 12	• same as under BC: Art 1(4) (compliance clause) with reference to relevant BC provisions • but assimilation of duration for photographic works to the general duration: Art 9

Enforcement provisions	• seizure: Art 16 • procedural minimum (presumption of authorship, etc): Art 15	• same as BC: Art 9(1) phr 1 (compliance clause) with reference to relevant BC provisions • extensive set of provisions on general obligations, civil and administrative procedures and remedies, provisional measures, border measures, and criminal procedures: Part III (Arts 41–61)	• same as BC: Art 1(4) (compliance clause) with reference to relevant BC provisions • general clause: Art 14(2), corresponding to Art 41(1) TRIPS
Technical measures and Rights management information	• no regulation	• no regulation	• Arts 11,12
Application in time	• in principle, coverage of existing, protected works: Art 18	• 70(1) (past acts not covered) • for covered works, same as BC: Art 70(2) phr 3 and Art 9(1) phr 1 (compliance clause) with reference to Art 18 BC • Art 70(5) (no application of rental right in respect of already purchased originals or copies)	• same as BC: Art 1(4) (compliance clause) with reference to Art 18 BC
Dispute settlement between contracting states	• referral to ICJ: Art 33 (binding *ante hoc* declaration)	• special dispute settlement mechanism: Art 64 with reference to Arts XXII, XXIII GATT 1994 and DSU	• no provision (general rules of public international law apply—possibility of referral to ICJ if parties accept its jurisdiction); draft WIPO dispute settlement treaty 'on ice'

B. Neighbouring Rights

Elements of Protection	Rome Convention (RC) (1961)	TRIPS Agreement (1994)	WIPO Performances and Phonograms Treaty (WPPT) (1996)
Principles of protection	• *national treatment*: Art 2 • *exceptions to national treatment*: Art 12 with Art 16(1)(a)(iv) (remuneration for secondary use of phonograms) and Art 13(d) with Art 16(1)(b) (communication right for broadcasting organizations) • *scope of national treatment* is controversial, Art 2(2): unlimited or, likely, restricted to level of minimum rights • *minimum rights*: Art 2(2); • *formalities*: limited formalities for phonograms permitted, Art 11 • *criteria of eligibility*: Arts 4, 5 with reference to 6	• *national treatment*: Art 3(1) phr 1 • *exceptions to national treatment*: Art 3(1) phr 1 with reference to exceptions under RC • *scope of national treatment* restricted to minimum rights under TRIPS: Art 3(1) phr 2 • *minimum rights*: Art 1(1) phr 1, 2; Art 1(3) phr 1 • *formalities*: same as under Art 11 RC: Art 14(6) phr 1 • *most favoured nation treatment*: Art 4 with safeguards for exceptions to national treatment under RC (Art 4 phr 2(b) and for restricted scope of national treatment, Art 4 phr 2 (c)) • *criteria of eligibility as under RC*: Art 1(3) phr 2 and 3 with Arts 4, 5, and 6 RC	• *national treatment*: Art 4 • *exceptions to national treatment*: Art 4(2) (similar to Art 16(1)(a)(iv) RC) • *scope of national treatment* limited to minimum exclusive rights and remuneration right under Art 15 • *minimum rights*: Art 3(1) • *'no formalities'*: unlimited principle of 'no formalities': Art 20 • *criteria of eligibility as under RC*: Art 3(2), (3) with Arts 4, 5, and arguably 6 RC

Subject matter and right owners protected	• *performances by 'performers'*: Art 3(a), but strongly limited protection for audiovisual performers: Art 19 • *phonograms*: Art 3(b) made by 'producers of phonograms': Art 3 (c) • *broadcasts by broadcasting organizations*: definition of 'broadcasting' in Art 3(f)	• no definitions • *performances by performers* on phonograms only (except broadcasting and communication rights): Art 14(1) • *phonograms* made by their *producers*: Art 14(2) • *broadcasts by broadcasting organizations*: no strict (if any) obligation of protection: Art 14(3)	• *performances by 'performers'*: Art 2(a): definition like RC plus performers of expressions of folklore; audiovisual performers: only live broadcasting right (Arts 6(i) and 2(f)) • *'phonograms'* made by *'producers of phonograms'*: Art 2(b), (d) (difference to RC: delineation from audiovisual fixation; producer as person with initiative and responsibility for production; inclusion of 'representations of sounds') • *broadcasts by broadcasting organizations*: not covered; plan for new WIPO treaty with little perspective
Moral rights	• none	• none	• moral rights (modelled on Art 6bis BC) for performers: Art 5
Economic rights	• *performers*: only 'possibility of preventing' instead of exclusive rights; • live broadcasting and communication to the public: Art 7(1)(a) • fixation: Art 7(1)(b) • reproduction under certain conditions: Art 7(1)(c)	• *performers*: only 'possibility of preventing' (like RC); scope of rights similar as RC (live broadcasting and communication to the public; fixation; reproduction (same conditions as in RC by reference in Art 14(6)): Art 14(1); in addition, arguably also rental right: Art 14(4)	• *performers*: full exclusive rights: • live broadcasting and communication, fixation: Art 6 • reproduction: Art 7 • distribution Art 8 • rental (similar to TRIPS: 'as determined in the national law of Contracting Parties'): Art 9 • making available: Art 10

Elements of Protection	Rome Convention (RC) (1961)	TRIPS Agreement (1994)	WIPO Performances and Phonograms Treaty (WPPT) (1996)
	• remuneration for broadcasting and communication to the public of commercial phonograms: Art 12 (subject to reservations, Art 16(1)(a));	• no remuneration for broadcasting or communication to the public of commercial phonograms (such as Art 12 RC);	• remuneration right for broadcasting and communication to the public of commercial phonograms (even including 'indirect use' unlike in Art 12 RC): Art 15 (but reservation possibilities: Art 15(3)
	• *phonogram producers*: exclusive right of reproduction: Art 10 • remuneration right for broadcasting and communication to the public of commercial phonograms: Art 12 (subject to reservations, Art 16(1)(a)) • *broadcasting organizations*: exclusive rights of • wireless rebroadcasting: Art 13(a) • fixation: Art 13(b) • reproduction under certain conditions: Art 13(c) • communication to the public of television broadcasts made in places accessible to the public against payment of entrance fee: Art 13(d) (with reservation, Art 16(1)(b))	• *phonogram producers*: exclusive right of reproduction: Art 14(2) • exclusive rental right: Art 14(4) • no remuneration right as under Art 12 RC • *broadcasting organizations*: scope of rights similar as RC: exclusive rights of • wireless rebroadcasting • fixation • reproduction (same conditions as in RC by reference in Art 14(6)) • communication to the public of television broadcasts (same conditions as in RC by reference in Art 14(6)) • however: no strict obligation, see above under 'subject matter and right owners protected': Art 14(3) phr 2	• *phonogram producers*: exclusive rights: • reproduction: Art 11 • rental: Art 13 • distribution: Art 12 • making available: Art 14 • remuneration for broadcasting and communication to the public of commercial phonograms, even for indirect use, unlike in Art 12 RC: Art 15 (but reservation possibilities in Art 15(3) • *broadcasting organizations*: not covered

Limitations and Exceptions	• four cases (private use, reporting of current events, ephemeral fixation, teaching and research): Art 15(1) • plus same limitations as under national copyright law: Art 15(2)	• same as RC: reference in Art 14(6) phr 1	• same limitations as under national copyright law: Art 16(1) (similar to Art 15(2) RC) • in addition: three-step test: Art 16(2)
Duration of protection	• for all groups: 20 years • *performers*: calculation after fixation (Art 14(a)) or after performance (for performance not incorporated in phonogram), Art 14(b) • *phonogram producers*: calculation after fixation, Art 14(a) • *broadcasting organizations*: calculation after broadcast: Art 14(c)	• performers and phonogram producers: 50 years, broadcasting organizations: 20 years • *performers, producers of phonograms*: like RC: calculation after fixation or performance: Art. 14(5) phr 1 • *broadcasting organizations*: like RC, calculation after broadcast: Art 14(5) phr 2	• performers and phonogram producers: 50 years; broadcasters not covered • *performers*: calculation after fixation: Art 17(1) • *producers of phonograms*: calculation after publication or, failing such publication within 50 years from fixation, after fixation: Art 17(2)
Enforcement provisions	• none	• extensive set of provisions on general obligations, civil and administrative procedures and remedies, provisional measures, border measures and criminal procedures: Part III (Arts 41–61)	• general clause: Art 23(2) (corresponding to general clause of Art 41(1) TRIPS)
Technical measures and Rights management information	• no regulation	• no regulation	• Arts 18, 19

Elements of Protection	Rome Convention (RC) (1961)	TRIPS Agreement (1994)	WIPO Performances and Phonograms Treaty (WPPT) (1996)
Application in time	• no prejudice to rights acquired before entry into force: Art 20(1) • no protection of pre-existing performances, phonograms, and broadcasts: Art 20(2)	• Art 70(1) (past acts not covered) • for covered performances and phonograms, in principle, protection for pre-existing subject matter: Art 70(2) phr 3 with Art 14(6) and analogous application of Art 18 BC • for broadcasting organizations: general rules apply: Art 70(2) phr 1, (3), (4) (in principle, protection of existing or protectable subject matter, but no restoration of protection where protection has expired) • Art 70(5) (no application of rental right in respect of already purchased originals or copies of phonogram)	• in principle, protection for pre-existing subject matter: Art 22(1) (analogous application of Art 18 BC) • but possibility to apply moral rights for performers only to performances occurred after entry into force: Art 22(2)
Dispute settlement between contracting states	• referral to ICJ: Art 30 (binding *ante hoc* declaration)	• special dispute settlement mechanism: Art 64 with reference to Arts XXII, XXIII GATT 1994 and DSU	• no provision (general rules of public international law apply—possibility of referral to ICJ if parties accept its jurisdiction); draft WIPO dispute settlement treaty 'on ice'

24

THE RELATIONSHIPS BETWEEN
DIFFERENT TREATIES

A. Introduction

As demonstrated in the preceding chapters, copyright and related rights are cur- **24.01**
rently covered by a multitude of treaties, including treaties that specifically deal
with these matters and broader treaties that cover intellectual property among
different areas of trade or investment. Even treaties with no or quite unspecific
provisions on copyright and related rights may have an impact in this field of law,
such as treaties on human rights and cultural diversity. In addition, treaties that
cover intellectual property may be multilateral, regional, and bilateral agreements. Accordingly, it is important to clarify different aspects of the relationship
between these treaties as well as the jurisdictional competence.

B. Relation between treaties

(1) The relevant rules

(a) Specific rules

Specific treaty provisions on the relation with other treaties in the same field have **24.02**
become a standard element in treaties on copyright and related rights, not least
given the increased number of treaties in the field. They take precedence over
general rules, such as Article 30 of the Vienna Convention on the Law of Treaties
(Vienna Convention) on the application of successive treaties; these rules are of a
mere residuary character, that is, they only operate in the absence of specific treaty

provisions.[1] Examples of specific rules in the most important copyright and related rights treaties are presented below.[2]

(b) General rules

24.03 Even if specific rules will mostly apply in the field of copyright and related rights, the general rules on relations between treaties are briefly presented here. Different kinds of relations between successive treaties may exist. First, the second treaty might consist in a termination of an earlier one, if all parties to the earlier one give their consent.[3] Secondly, the second treaty might be interpreted as a revision of the first one for the parties of the first one. Yet, a revision under general public international law requires unanimity, subject to specific rules in the treaty; possible procedural rules of the first treaty may also have to be fulfilled. Thirdly, the second treaty might implicitly terminate or suspend the application of the first treaty, again upon the condition that all the parties to the first treaty conclude the second one on the same subject matter.[4] Fourthly, the temporary suspension of the application of the first treaty by agreement between only some of the contracting states is possible, though subject to a prescribed procedure.[5] Finally, the new agreement between two or more of the parties of a first agreement may constitute a modification of the first agreement, if further conditions are fulfilled.[6] In the field of copyright and related rights, all of these rules are unlikely to apply.

24.04 Rather, Article 30 of the Vienna Convention on the application of successive treaties relating to the same subject matter will usually govern the relationship between different copyright and related rights treaties, subject to specific rules in these treaties. This provision applies to all treaties concluded after the entry into force of the Vienna Convention[7] and, because its rules are customary international law that is simply codified in this provision, they also apply to earlier treaties.

24.05 Since all treaties generally are of equal rank, potential conflicts between subsequent treaties must be solved according to criteria other than hierarchy. Essentially, Article 30 of the Vienna Convention applies the chronological criterion by including the rule *lex posterior derogat legi priori*, according to which the subsequent treaty prevails.[8]

---

[1] IM Sinclair, *The Vienna Convention on the Law of Treaties* (2nd edn, 1984) 97 ff.
[2] paras 24.07–24.20 below.
[3] Art 54 of the Vienna Convention.
[4] Art 59 ibid.
[5] Arts 58 and 65 ibid.
[6] Art 41 ibid.
[7] Art 4 ibid.
[8] It is controversial, though, whether and to what extent Art 30(3) of the Vienna Convention includes this general rule of customary international law, see WH Wilting, *Vertragskonkurrenz im*

The *lex posterior* rule only applies in case of a conflict between two treaties. **24.06**
Whether and to what extent such a conflict exists has to be ascertained by treaty
interpretation—often a very difficult task. In the case of a potential conflict, the
rule of *lex specialis* is often applied to avoid a conflict where the subsequent treaty
is simply more specific but not incompatible with the earlier one.[9] Only if the
interpretation shows that a conflict remains, will it regularly be the later treaty
that prevails under the *lex posterior* rule. Overall, these basic rules may seem clear
and easy to apply; yet, it is noteworthy that the meaning of 'conflict' and the
application of these rules are controversial in many respects in public international law doctrine.[10]

(2) Specific examples

(a) Universal Copyright Convention (UCC)

The UCC regulates its relation with the Berne Convention,[11] in particular by **24.07**
excluding its application to UCC countries that are also Berne Union countries
for works that have a Berne Union country as country of origin; this rule aims at
ensuring the application of the Berne Convention with its higher level of protection between Berne Union countries that are also UCC Members.[12] The UCC
also regulates its relationship with multilateral or bilateral conventions between
American Republics and with previously existing multilateral or bilateral conventions.[13] The TRIPS Agreement and the WCT, which both cover the same
subject matter as the UCC, namely copyright protection, do not regulate their
relationships with the UCC. An analysis shows that only the TRIPS Agreement
and the WCT respectively apply between two countries that are both Members
of the UCC and either of the TRIPS Agreement or the WCT.[14]

Völkerrecht (1996) 78–9 ; this provision reads: 'When all the parties to the earlier treaty are parties
also to the later treaty but the earlier treaty is not terminated or suspended in operation under article
59, the earlier treaty applies only to the extent that its provisions are compatible with those of the
later treaty.' On the relation between subsequent treaties, see Sinclair (n 1 above) 96–8. On the lack
of a priori hierarchies of sources of international law, see J Pauwelyn, *Conflict of Norms in Public
International Law* (2003) 94 ff, and on *lex posterior* 96, 361 ff.

[9] W Karl, 'Conflicts between Treaties' in R Bernhardt (ed), *Encyclopedia of Public International
Law* (Vol IV, 2000) 935, 937–8. On this and other conflict-avoidance techniques, see Pauwelyn
(n 8 above) 385 ff, 240 ff.

[10] eg Wilting (n 8 above) 78 ff, in particular 88; E Vranes, 'The Definition of "Norm Conflict" in
International Law and Legal Theory' (2006) 17/2 European Journal of International Law 395 ff;
Sinclair (n 1 above) 96–8. Pauwelyn (n 8 above) 164 ff on 'conflict'.

[11] Art XVII and the related Appendix Declaration.

[12] For details, see S von Lewinski, 'The Role and Future of the Universal Copyright Convention'
(2006) October e-Copyright Bulletin UNESCO 1, 2–3.

[13] Arts XVIII and XIX of the UCC.

[14] For the argumentation in detail, see von Lewinski (n 12 above) 3–6.

(b) Relation between different Acts of the Berne Convention

24.08   Any Revision Act of the Berne Convention constitutes an independent treaty, which only binds those Union countries that have joined it by ratification or accession. Accordingly, Union countries may be bound by different Revision Acts. Since newly acceding countries can only accede to the latest Revision Act of 1971, and since most countries today have joined the 1971 Act, Article 32 of the Berne Convention on the relations between countries that adhere to different Acts is currently relevant only for the remaining ten countries that are still bound by the Rome and Brussels Acts. The basic rule of Article 32 corresponds to the general rule of public international law that countries can only be bound by those treaties that they joined. Accordingly, the relation between a Union country that adheres to the Brussels Act and another one that adheres to the Paris Act is governed by the latest Act to which both are parties.[15] A similar rule is contained in Article 30(4)(b) of the Vienna Convention.

(c) Relation between the Berne Convention and the TRIPS Agreement or WCT

24.09   **(i) Non-derogation clauses**   Both the TRIPS Agreement and the WCT contain non-derogation clauses,[16] under which Berne obligations of Berne Members that are also TRIPS- or WCT-parties continue to exist between them. Consequently, for a country that is party of both the Berne Convention and the TRIPS Agreement or the WCT, the rules of the Berne Convention and the other treaty apply cumulatively. This is possible without a conflict. Indeed, since the Berne Convention provides for minimum standards, the higher minimum standards of the TRIPS Agreement and the WCT are not in conflict: just like any Berne country may unilaterally decide to provide for more protection, Berne Union countries may agree among themselves to do the same. Even if some might see a conflict between the Berne Convention and the higher level treaties in the prohibition of parties of the TRIPS Agreement and the WCT to rely on the lower standards of the Berne Convention, this result is permitted by the Berne Convention because it explicitly allows for greater protection.[17] Where the TRIPS Agreement provides for less protection, as is the case for moral rights, both treaties can still apply cumulatively, since the TRIPS Agreement also includes minimum standards and does not prohibit application of this higher level among Berne members.

---

[15] For the specific rule regarding a country that becomes party to the Paris Act without having been party to the earlier Acts and a country party to an earlier Act, see Art 32(2) of the Berne Convention. On Art 32 of the Berne Convention, see S Ricketson and J Ginsburg, *International Copyright and Neighbouring Rights: The Berne Convention and Beyond* (2006) 17.69–17.77.

[16] Art 2(2) of the TRIPS Agreement and Art 1(2) of the WCT; on the latter, see J Reinbothe and S von Lewinski, *The WIPO Treaties 1996* (2002) Art 1 WCT nn 14–15.

[17] Art 19 of the Berne Convention; Art 20 safeguards and promotes even higher-level protection.

(ii) 'Special agreements' For Berne Union countries, both treaties addition- **24.10** ally constitute 'special agreements' in the meaning of Article 20 of the Berne Convention. This is explicitly stated in the WCT[18] and is also true for the TRIPS Agreement, though not explicitly stated.[19] Accordingly, the TRIPS Agreement and the WCT must be interpreted as either providing for more extensive rights or containing other provisions not contrary to the Berne Convention.

At first sight, it may appear that the TRIPS Agreement is inconsistent with Article **24.11** 20 of the Berne Convention in that it excludes moral rights from the compliance clause of its Article 9(1), which obliges TRIPS Members only to comply with the other substantive law provisions of the Berne Convention. Yet, the TRIPS Agreement does not derogate from the Berne obligations, so that in line with the purpose of Article 20 of the Berne Convention, the protection between Berne members is not lowered; the exclusion from the compliance clause only has the effect of preventing the application of the dispute settlement procedure under the TRIPS Agreement.[20]

(d) Relation between the TRIPS Agreement and the WCT

Article 1(1) phrase 2 of the WCT determines its relationship with treaties other **24.12** than the Berne Convention: it has no (legal) connection with such treaties nor is it to prejudice any rights and obligations thereunder.[21] Accordingly, parties of both treaties continue to be bound by obligations and to enjoy rights under both of them. In other words, they coexist and are not considered to be in conflict. Indeed, since the TRIPS Agreement provides for minimum protection, any treaty with stronger protection such as the WCT is not in conflict with it.[22]

---

[18] Art 1(1) phr 1 of the WCT; Reinbothe/von Lewinski (n 16 above) Art 1 WCT nn 8–11. On Art 20 of the Berne Convention, see paras 5.250–5.251 above.

[19] It fulfils the criteria of a 'special agreement'; see also M Ficsor, *The Law of Copyright and the Internet* (2002) C1.11; WIPO (ed), *Implications of the TRIPS Agreement on Treaties Administered by WIPO* (1996), WIPO Publication no 464 (E) para 17.

[20] Ricketson/Ginsburg (n 15 above) 6.136–6.137 argue that the exclusion under the TRIPS Agreement does not lead to a lower protection for Berne members because the Berne Convention does not include an effective dispute settlement mechanism; yet, even if the Berne Convention had such mechanism and therefore a greater protection than the TRIPS Agreement, the non-derogation clause would safeguard the Berne protection for Berne members. See also Ficsor (n 19 above) C1.15, also pointing to the possible reduction of protection under cross-retaliation; D Gervais, *The TRIPS Agreement: Drafting History and Analysis* (2nd edn, 2003) 2.89–2.90.

[21] On this provision, see ibid Art 1 WCT nn 12–13.

[22] For a similar reasoning regarding the relation between the Berne Convention and the TRIPS Agreement or the WCT, see para 24.09 above.

(e) Relations between treaties in the field of related rights

24.13 **(i) Non-derogation clauses**   Relations between treaties in the field of related rights are principally similar to those in copyright. First, a non-derogation clause is provided both in Article 2(2) of the TRIPS Agreement and Article 1(1) of the WPPT in respect of the Rome Convention. Accordingly, the rules under the Rome Convention and each of the other treaties coexist and apply cumulatively. As in copyright, this is possible without conflict as far as minimum standards allow for the application of higher standards.

24.14 **(ii) 'Special agreements'**   Secondly, both the TRIPS Agreement and the WPPT may be considered 'special agreements' in the meaning of Article 22 of the Rome Convention, which corresponds to Article 20 of the Berne Convention. Although they do not explicitly mention this relation, they fulfil the conditions of Article 22 and therefore must be interpreted as providing more extensive rights or containing other provisions that are not contrary to the Rome Convention.[23] At first sight, one may have doubts whether these conditions are fulfilled where the TRIPS Agreement and the WPPT do not provide for protection contained in the Rome Convention or provide for a lower level of protection, such as regarding broadcasting organizations, audiovisual performances, and in some other instances.[24] Yet, this may be regarded as consistent with Article 22 of the Rome Convention, since the non-derogation clause in line with the purpose of Article 22 prevents lowering of protection among the contracting states to the Rome Convention that continue being obliged under the higher level of the Rome Convention.[25]

24.15 In principle, the same reasoning could be applied to the scope of national treatment, if one interprets the Rome Convention as providing for an unrestricted scope. In that case, the limited scope of the TRIPS Agreement and the WPPT would not lower the Rome protection between Rome parties, due to the non-derogation clause. Yet, it seems that the explicit and intended restriction of national treatment to the level of (exclusive) minimum rights in the TRIPS Agreement and the WPPT was understood as reflecting the Rome national treatment in clearer wording; this wording is also best brought in harmony with the

---

[23] For this and more reasons regarding the WPPT, see Reinbothe/von Lewinski (n 16 above) Art 1 WPPT n 12. However, for a controversy regarding membership as a condition, see para 6.78 above.

[24] Slight differences exist in respect of audiovisual performers and the remuneration right for secondary uses, which is not contained in the TRIPS Agreement but also not a strict obligation under the Rome Convention where a reservation under Art 16 is allowed; broadcasting organizations are not covered by the WPPT and not fully by the TRIPS Agreement; on these differences, see paras 10.144 and 17.172 above.

[25] For a more specific reason regarding categories of right owners not covered by the subsequent treaty, see Reinbothe/von Lewinski (n 16 above) Art 1 WPPT n 12.

conditions of Article 22 of the Rome Convention if interpreted as the view of the parties to be in line with the scope of national treatment under the Rome Convention. This would mean that the Rome Convention already contains a restricted scope of national treatment and is simply specified in the TRIPS Agreement and the WPPT; no assumption can be made that the parties to the TRIPS Agreement and the WPPT that consciously drafted these restrictions deliberately wanted to disregard the conditions of Article 22.[26]

(f) Relation of bilateral and regional trade treaties with other treaties

Bilateral and regional trade agreements that cover copyright and related rights **24.16** today often contain non-derogation clauses in respect of other treaties in the field to which the parties adhere.[27] Accordingly, the same principles as elaborated above apply.[28] In addition, they usually contain the obligations to comply with the provisions of the main multilateral treaties as a minimum and to adhere to them.[29] Accordingly, they build on these treaties, and to this extent can hardly be in conflict with them, so that their cumulative application is possible. Likewise, those bilateral and regional agreements that are more detailed than the multilateral treaties mostly build on the earlier provisions or provide for additional, stronger protection. In both cases, there is no conflict between the treaties, for the same reasons as elaborated above.[30]

A conflict may arise where, for example, the TRIPS Agreement has granted tran- **24.17** sitional periods in favour of developing and least developed countries in order to allow them smoother adaptation to the required standards. This aim cannot be reached where a later, bilateral agreement requires the implementation of the same or even stronger standards by the developing or least developed country within a shorter period.[31] One will have to analyse all relevant provisions of the later agreement in order to ascertain whether there is a conflict; this might not be the case, for example, where parties reaffirm their rights and obligations with respect to each other under the WTO Agreement—including the right to benefit from such longer transitional period.[32] If a direct conflict is considered to exist, the *lex posterior* rule in principle gives priority to the subsequent agreement, so that the shorter period applies.

---

[26] On national treatment under the Rome Convention, see also paras 7.34–7.40 above.
[27] Para 12.28 and n 81 above.
[28] Para 24.09 above.
[29] On such obligations, eg paras 11.09 and 12.26–12.27, 12.50, and 12.78 above.
[30] Para 24.09 above.
[31] This case is different from the above case where minimum protection is provided in the earlier treaty, so that countries may provide for more protection; transitional periods for developing countries here were, however, meant to be a maximum of what could be demanded from developing countries that were to be protected against demands for sooner implementation.
[32] eg Art 1(2) of the US–Jordan Free Trade Agreement, see para 12.27 above.

24.18 Where investment treaties or investment chapters of trade treaties include copyright and related rights, they usually provide for unrestricted national treatment.[33] By contrast, national treatment in the classical copyright and related rights conventions is subject to exceptions and restrictions, as specifically provided therein; in addition, it only covers those right owners who are eligible for protection under the criteria of these conventions.[34] In order to assess, in the absence of any specific rule, whether there is a conflict between the broader national treatment under the investment treaties and restricted or further specified national treatment under the copyright and related rights treaties, one has to take into account the rule of *lex specialis*; since investment treaties or chapters of trade treaties and their national treatment clauses apply to many different areas of trade rather than specifically to copyright and related rights, and since the provisions on national treatment in the copyright and related rights treaties are more specific regarding the scope of national treatment and exceptions thereto, the rule of *lex specialis* will usually result in the absence of a conflict, because the general rule of national treatment under the investment provisions is simply specified in the copyright and related rights treaties, which therefore remain applicable.

24.19 The same result is reached for the relation between the non-discrimination rules under human rights treaties and the more specific provisions on national treatment in copyright treaties;[35] the same is true for the relation between rules on authors' rights as well as freedom of expression in human rights treaties and the more specific provisions on authors' rights and limitations of their rights in favour of the general public in copyright treaties; these broadly conceived human rights, which first need to be balanced between themselves, can hardly be a sufficient basis even for any precise indication on how to interpret the relevant rules of copyright treaties.[36]

---

[33] eg the US Model BIT (see paras 12.18, 12.19/n 53 above) provides for national treatment without referring to exceptions; in the earlier Model, intellectual property was excluded, see UNCTAD (ed), *National Treatment: UNCTAD Series on Issues in International Investment Agreements* (1999), UNCTAD/ITE/IIT/11 (Vol IV) at 45 and, generally, 12. For the draft MAI, which was not adopted due to fierce opposition by European and other non-US countries, see S Ercolani, 'The OECD Multilateral Agreement on Investment (MAI) Project: The Possible Consequences of Including Intellectual Property' (1998) EntLR 125 (128 on national treatment), and M Haedecke, 'Urheberrecht als Investitionsschutz? Das Urheberrecht im geplanten multilateralen Investitionsabkommen (MAI-Abkommen)' (1998) GRUR Int 631 (633–4 on national treatment).

[34] For the Berne Convention, see the exceptions to national treatment in paras 5.40–5.53 above; for related rights, see paras 6.28–6.31 above; for the TRIPS Agreement, para 10.36, and for the WCT and WPPT, paras 17.31 and 17.47 above.

[35] For an in-depth analysis, see S von Lewinski, 'Intellectual Property, Nationality, and Non-discrimination' in WIPO (ed), *Intellectual Property and Human Rights* (1999, repr 2000; WIPO Publication no 762(E)) 175, in particular 191–5.

[36] ibid, edited transcript of discussion at 202.

C. Jurisdiction

Where the same or a similar rule under different treaties may apply to the same **24.20** situation between the same countries, the question of the choice of forum arises. This situation today is ever more likely to occur in general[37] in the field of copyright and related rights, given the proliferation of treaties that include the same or similar obligations and, at the same time, provide for their own dispute settlement mechanisms, especially in the trade context.

For disputes under copyright and related rights treaties, the International Court **24.21** of Justice (ICJ) is usually competent, irrespective of any explicit reference to the ICJ. In particular, the references of the Berne and Rome Conventions to the ICJ simply mean that the parties to the conventions *ex ante* subject themselves to the jurisdiction of the Court,[38] while disputes under other treaties without a similar reference, such as the WCT and the WPPT, may also be submitted to the ICJ under its Statute for clarification of a provision, if the other party agrees.

Since countries have never made use of this procedure (and probably will not do **24.22** so in the foreseeable future), the practically more important question on jurisdiction relates to the dispute settlement mechanisms available under the TRIPS Agreement on the one hand and bilateral and regional trade or investment agreements on the other. Most of the bilateral and regional agreements provide for their own dispute settlement mechanism, usually based on the model of the WTO mechanism. Some of them regulate the relationship with the WTO Dispute Settlement Understanding (DSU), and they do so in different ways: often, the complaining party has the choice, until one forum is chosen;[39] under other treaties, it seems that the parties can be forced to settle their disputes under the bilateral agreement rather than the WTO, if the parties cannot agree on a single forum.[40]

---

[37] For this phenomenon in general, see Y Shany, *The Competing Jurisdictions between International Courts and Tribunals* (2003).

[38] Arts 33 of the Berne Convention and 30 of the Rome Convention; see paras 5.257, 6.79, 8.23 above.

[39] eg the agreement between Korea and EFTA states, see A Ziegler, 'Dispute Settlement in Bilateral Trade Agreements: The EFTA Experience' in L Bartels and F Ortino (eds), *Regional Trade Agreements and the WTO Legal System* (2006) 415–16; also NAFTA follows this solution and further specifies the rule where a third party wishes to have recourse to the NAFTA, while the complaining party has selected the WTO procedure, see Art 2005 of the NAFTA and K Lee and S von Lewinski, 'The Settlement of International Disputes in the Field of Intellectual Property' in FK Beier and G Schricker (eds), *From GATT to TRIPS: The Agreement on Trade-Related Aspects of Intellectual Property Rights* (1996) 278, 321–2.

[40] Art 77(2) of the EFTA States–Mexico Agreement; Ziegler (n 39 above) 416.

24.23 In general, it seems that countries tend to prefer the WTO dispute settlement mechanism to those of regional and bilateral trade agreements.[41] Therefore, situations will be rare where a dispute settlement body under a bilateral treaty would interpret TRIPS-identical provisions or WTO law incorporated into the bilateral agreement. Consequently, the question of how such interpretation may in fact influence a WTO panel, if the same issue later arises between other countries in the framework of the WTO, might be of little practical relevance. In any case, since the competence of dispute settlement bodies is limited to the relevant treaties, no interpretation by one dispute settlement body would bind a body of another treaty, even if the provisions have the same wording in both treaties.

D. Résumé

24.24 Overall, the multitude of treaties may lead to difficult questions on their applicability between countries that are parties to several treaties and regarding disputes on the same issue, as well as difficult questions in respect of the choice of forum, especially where no regulation is provided. In respect of the relation between treaties in the field of copyright and related rights, it seems that their cumulative application is the rule, be it because of non-derogation clauses or also because no conflict between the relevant rules arises. Yet, even ascertaining the presence of a conflict on the basis of treaty interpretation may be difficult in individual cases. If a conflict actually arises, then the above-described rules and procedures to resolve resulting disputes apply.

---

[41] For regional trade agreements, see W Davey, 'Dispute Settlement in the WTO and RTAs: A Comment' in L Bartels and F Ortino (eds), *Regional Trade Agreements and the WTO Legal System* (2006) 343, 344, and 349 ff.

25

OVERALL ASSESSMENT OF THE DEVELOPMENT OF INTERNATIONAL COPYRIGHT AND NEIGHBOURING RIGHTS PROTECTION

A. Introduction

In the beginning, there were thirty-two intra-German bilateral treaties. Then **25.01** came the creation of the Berne Convention by ten, mostly European countries. Today, about 120 years later, there are four major multilateral treaties that cover copyright protection, five major multilateral treaties that cover different neighbouring rights, and a multitude of bilateral and regional trade or investment treaties that cover both areas, as well as several treaties on general issues, such as human rights or enforcement aspects,[1] which have an impact on copyright and neighbouring rights. International protection of copyright and neighbouring rights today has a largely worldwide coverage. International law up to the latest treaties has largely succeeded in adapting the protection to the requirements of technical and other developments. This chapter focuses on some of the notable aspects of mainly more recent developments.

---

[1] eg Art 14 of the UN Convention on Jurisdictional Immunities of States and their Property of 2004.

B. Selected Aspects

(1) The challenging and dynamic life of the Berne Convention

(a) *Fragmentation among Member countries*

25.02   When the founders of the Berne Convention in 1886 agreed on its first text, they felt the historic importance of this event and the enormous potential for development of the Convention towards the envisioned universal protection of authors' rights. Given the aim of the widest possible application of the Convention, challenges were foreseeable. Indeed, the ten initial countries that adopted the Berne Convention were at a similar state of development and had the same, basic views regarding the need to protect authors in their works—a situation that would not subsist in the case of much wider application. Challenges first arose upon the first revision conference in 1896, when the required unanimity for a revision was not reached and, instead, a split situation emerged between Berne Members that were parties to the Additional Act, or to the Interpretative Declaration, or to both. At the 1908 conference, it was then possible to revise the Berne Convention only because Members could declare reservations to be bound only by the earlier, 1886 text, either entirely or in specific points. Also new Member Countries were admitted to accede to the 1886 version instead of the 1908 version; an ongoing fragmentation thus had to be accepted as a reality. The situation of a Berne Union with split membership of different acts has continued until today, although from 1948, new countries had to accede to the latest adopted revision act, so that more fragmentation was avoided and enhanced unity was reached.[2]

(b) *Potential loss of a major Member and slow-down at the Brussels Conference*

25.03   A later, smaller challenge was the threat of Great Britain together with its dependent territories to leave the Berne Union, unless retorsion against backdoor protection in non-Union countries was permitted. This problem was solved by the adoption of the Additional Protocol of 1914.[3] A more important challenge was the increased influence of user industries, the general public, and developing countries that were opposed to extensive copyright protection and slowed down progress for authors' rights at the Brussels Conference.[4]

---

[2] Art 28(3) of the 1948 Brussels Act for accessions from 1 July 1951, and Art 34(1) of the 1971 Paris Act.

[3] para 4.11 above.

[4] para 4.16 above

(c) Potential dilution by non-creative subject matter

A different kind of challenge was the claim to internationally protect neighbour- **25.04**
ing rights. In line with several national laws, under which protection of performers and phonogram producers was initially granted on the basis of authors' rights,
proposals were made as early as in 1908 and 1928 to include neighbouring rights
into the ambit of the Berne Convention. However, at the Brussels Conference,
plans for the adoption of Annexes to the Berne Convention on neighbouring
rights were revised so as to clearly distinguish between authors' rights and neighbouring rights, and to pursue neighbouring rights' protection in a different
forum.[5] Loading the Berne Convention with these matters could have weakened
its operation for authors' rights and diluted the conceptual difference between
authors' rights and neighbouring rights.

(d) Potential split between treaties in The Americas and the Berne Union

Another major challenge to the Berne Convention's underlying aim of universal **25.05**
protection was the separate development of international protection in the
Americas on the one hand and in Europe and beyond on the other hand, which
took place in the first half of the twentieth century. In the mid-1940s, when several inter-American conventions were followed by the 1946 Washington Convention, a world split into two different systems of international protection
became a real threat. Consequently, the Berne Union countries first tried to find
various common solutions, such as a general agreement replacing the existing
ones, but later encouraged a separate, independent solution through the Universal Copyright Convention, which would meet the needs of American countries
to provide for lower protection than under the Berne Convention, and at the
same time would allow Berne Union countries to adhere to this other Convention. Thereby, the idea of universality was realized.[6]

(e) The North–South conflict as a problem for revisions by unanimity

Subsequently, the 1967 and 1971 Revision Conferences faced a major chal- **25.06**
lenge—or even crisis—to the Berne Convention, when developing countries
strongly asserted their own interests by calling for compulsory licences and similar restrictions of protection in their favour, and industrialized countries first
refused to ratify the 1967 Revision Act. The compromise finally adopted with
difficulties by the necessary unanimity at the 1971 Paris Conference enabled
industrialized countries to ratify the Paris Act while it prevented developing
countries from denouncing the Convention. Yet, the North–South conflict
had shown that unanimous decisions on specific minimum standards among

---

[5] para 4.57 above. For a similar development for phonograms in 1991, see paras 17.05–17.06
above.
[6] paras 4.34, 4.35 above.

countries at quite different stages of development would continue to be very difficult.

(f) 'Competition' through trade fora

25.07 About another twenty years later, the Berne Convention and the WIPO as its administering organization met a different kind of challenge, which was rooted in the experience of 1967/1971 and the resulting abstention from initiatives for treaty-making. Leading industrialized countries had lost confidence in the possibility of adopting another revision of the Berne Convention in the WIPO framework, although this was felt to be needed. Consequently, they chose the GATT as a forum to adapt international copyright and neighbouring rights protection to the new challenges of technology and worldwide piracy. In 1991, when the conclusion of the future TRIPS Agreement seemed realistic,[7] the inherent threat to the importance of the WIPO as the leading international organization in the field became manifest.

25.08 Although there is no proof of a causal link, it was notably at this very point in time that WIPO started to hold meetings of a Committee of Experts on a possible protocol to the Berne Convention. The solution they found to escape the unanimity requirement was the choice of a 'special agreement', which did not need to be adopted by all Berne Union countries—a solution previously avoided to escape refragmentation. It was also around the same time that WIPO elaborated a Draft Treaty on dispute settlement in respect of treaties administered by the WIPO in order to remedy the deficiencies of the existing system and thereby respond to the needs of Member countries.

25.09 Yet, these initiatives were too late to hinder a shift into the trade framework; WIPO might have avoided the GATT approach, and the resulting 'competition' with the later-formed WTO, if it had started these initiatives much earlier. Indeed, when the Dispute Settlement Draft Treaty was ready for adoption in 1994, WIPO decided not to further pursue this plan, essentially because a major player, the USA, considered it unnecessary in view of the then newly available dispute settlement mechanism under the WTO. This decision equally meant a setback for the WIPO, since the WTO/TRIPS Agreement now remains the only agreement (apart from other trade agreements) under which copyright and neighbouring rights provisions can be effectively enforced—including those of the Berne Convention, though through trade glasses.

25.10 By contrast, the WIPO in 1996 succeeded not only in adopting two treaties by unanimity (the WCT and the WPPT), but also in adapting the protection

---

[7] The Agreement was provisionally concluded in December 1991, para 10.22 above.

standards for authors, performers, and phonogram producers to the latest challenges of digital technology—challenges not even conceived of two years earlier in the WTO, when the TRIPS Agreement hardly amended the old Berne and Rome standards of 1971 and 1961.

In addition, the Berne Convention gained profile from this challenge through **25.11** trade law, because its substantive law provisions were included as a minimum obligation into the TRIPS Agreement as well as into most bilateral and regional trade agreements that covered intellectual property. Likewise, most parts of the WCT and the WPPT are included in many bilateral and regional trade agreements. In addition to compliance obligations, most of these trade agreements oblige contracting parties to adhere to the Berne Convention, the WCT, and the WPPT.

Accordingly, the Berne Convention (as well as its Special Agreement, the WCT, **25.12** and the WPPT) has not only been able to avoid marginalization, but, to the contrary, has even gained influence and membership.[8] Indeed, the Berne Convention has experienced the strongest boost in its 'career' through the incorporation of its substantive law into the TRIPS Agreement and into bilateral and regional trade agreements. Moreover, the WIPO has even gained influence on the implementation of the TRIPS Agreement into national laws by providing technical assistance on the basis of the WIPO–WTO Cooperation Agreement.[9] In sum, WIPO embraced the trade threat and largely turned it into a success story.

(2) The inclusion of copyright and neighbouring rights into the trade framework

While the reasons for the inclusion of intellectual property into the trade frame- **25.13** work and an assessment of the trade approach have already been elaborated above,[10] some of the aspects and consequences of the trade approach are further highlighted at this point. In short, the trade approach has enormously increased the number of countries bound by international copyright and neighbouring rights obligations, has increased the level of internationally available protection, has increased the enforceability, and has increased the similarity of national provisions. These effects are due to the link of intellectual property with other trade areas; it is these other areas that may be more important for countries that otherwise might not have agreed to such international obligations. Accordingly, these countries' needs for market access or trade liberalization in areas other than

---

[8] para 10.146 above.
[9] para 15.19 above.
[10] See the entire ch 9; and paras 14.02 ff above.

intellectual property have been played for the benefit of intellectual property industries in industrialized countries.

25.14 Especially in relation to the USA, many other countries have agreed to introduce specific intellectual property standards in ways that may not leave sufficient flexibility for implementation into the local legal system; they also have accepted standards that seem inappropriately high when considering their state of development[11]—a decision often made to avoid possible unilateral trade measures. The price to be paid for such aggressive trade policy is resentment, reluctant enforcement, and a negative image not only of the USA but also of copyright and neighbouring rights protection as such, because it is perceived to be exclusively imposed for the benefit of foreigners and as a matter to be rejected for this reason alone. These negative perceptions usually prevail over the perception of potential economic benefits gained for the relevant country from the respective trade agreement in other trade areas. Also, the recent political agenda of certain developing countries in international organizations may be a consequence of such practices.[12]

25.15 Another weak point of the trade approach is the negotiation procedure regarding the TRIPS Agreement as well as bilateral and regional trade agreements. The procedure of the GATT has been described as lacking transparency and as inherently disadvantageous mainly for developing and least developed countries with their typically weaker negotiation power but favourable to industrialized countries, as is often reflected in positive results for their industries.[13] In respect of bilateral and regional trade agreements, the imbalance of negotiating powers is often even more pronounced; in addition, negotiations are usually behind closed doors and negotiation proposals are not made available to the public, so that interested parties may have limited, or selected access and possibilities for asserting their interests. Where such negotiations are combined with national approval or ratification procedures that allow for little parliamentary debates, such as the US 'fast-track' procedure, the entire exercise is even more questionable.

25.16 As another effect of bilateral treaties in particular of the USA (and of separate lobbying activities), specific standards desired by US industry have been and are continuously set in countries around the world—mainly in developing countries with their typically weaker bargaining position, which usually does not allow them anything other than to accept these standards. This procedure is often initially unnoticed in countries not subjected to US bilateral treaties (or to separate

---

[11] On these aspects, see paras 14.11, 14.16 above.
[12] paras 19.07, 19.37, and 21.02 above.
[13] P Drahos, 'BITs and BIPs: Bilateralism in Intellectual Property' (2001) 4/6 Journal of World Intellectual Property 791 ff.

lobbying in foreign countries), such as European countries, or if noticed, it remains a *fait accompli*. The effect is that at a certain point of time, these standards are established in the laws of a majority of countries of the world, so that the remaining countries come under pressure to adopt them too. Similar dynamics could already be noticed in the 1990s in respect of the protection of computer programs and databases and are currently about to appear in respect of the duration of performers' and phonogram producers' rights and other issues.[14] Accordingly, this not very democratic procedure of negotiating trade agreements even seems indirectly to restrict the freedom of third countries to legislate according to their own views.

It is difficult to ascertain whether the trade approach has changed the way in **25.17** which copyright is applied. Admittedly, the TRIPS Agreement excludes moral rights from its application and, consequently, is limited to economic rights. Yet, moral rights continue to play an important role in countries where they were already provided. They are simply excluded from the WTO dispute settlement procedure and, in that respect, weaker than economic rights that principally can be internationally enforced through this mechanism.[15]

It is also difficult to ascertain whether the inclusion of intellectual property into **25.18** the TRIPS and other trade agreements strengthened multinational enterprises more than smaller right owners, or whether this development is due to the increased economic importance of copyright and neighbouring rights' goods on the market. In any case, it seems that the biggest companies can best benefit from the increased protection worldwide, resulting in increased media concentration and harsher competition that leads to rigorous business practices focused on one-sidedly optimizing profits without sufficient regard to the individual authors who create works and, in part, to consumers who demand access to works. Also, it may sometimes appear more profitable and thus more attractive to businesses today to take the risk of disregarding the law in certain cases.[16]

The domination of ever growing but fewer multinational companies at the same **25.19** time bears the risk of reducing cultural diversity and the access of consumers to a broad variety of works.[17] Another aspect remains to be evaluated, namely whether

---

[14] S von Lewinski, 'Negotiation Methods and Role of Lobby Groups' in ALAI (ed), *Exploring the Sources of Copyright, ALAI Congress, 18–21 September 2005, Paris* (2007) 154, 168.

[15] There are, however, limits to such enforcement, as demonstrated by the WTO case on s 110 US Copyright Act, see paras 10.52–10.54 above.

[16] Indeed, this currently occurs at the state level, where the compensation to be paid by the USA for violation of the TRIPS Agreement has been criticized to be far below the value of money to be paid if the USA complied with the TRIPS Agreement; para 10.132 above.

[17] Such developments are strongly criticized in respect of the Recommendation of the European Commission regarding online music licensing, see eg European Parliament, 'Report on the Commission Recommendation of 18 October 2005 on collective cross-border management of

the inclusion of copyright and neighbouring rights into trade agreements, in combination with effective dispute settlement mechanisms, will result in a more trade-oriented interpretation of copyright and neighbouring rights provisions. So far, in the ten years of its operation the TRIPS dispute settlement mechanism has only brought one panel report in the field of copyright and neighbouring rights, so that any trade influence through dispute settlement will probably remain limited, even if, in principle, interpretation that takes into account the trade objective of the TRIPS Agreement might in certain cases lead to slightly different argumentation and possibly different outcomes than might interpretation under a classical convention.

(3) Main players

25.20 The roles of different players in international copyright and neighbouring rights have changed over time. From industrialized countries, two players are highlighted here: the USA and the EC. From developing countries, no selection is made, but they are covered as a group.

(a) The USA

25.21 For most of the time of its copyright history, the USA played a rather defensive, passive role in the field of international copyright, when it was not ready to accept international obligations, or later did so only to a limited extent as a Member of the UCC.[18] Its role fundamentally turned proactive in the mid-1980s, as evidenced by its adherence to the Berne Convention in 1988 and, in the same year by the launch of the trade approach on the basis of its 1988 Trade Act.[19] As one of the effects of its increased influence combined with its push for recognition of elements of the copyright system in the world, the fight between the author's rights and copyright systems got accentuated and became more visible as a major source of problems in initiating or adopting international treaties. As regards the trade approach, the USA became one of the driving forces and was in many respects the first and only country to propose certain provisions for inclusion in the TRIPS Agreement, such as those on protection of computer programs and those on rental rights.[20] As regards trade measures and agreements, it continues to act more systematically and intensively than other countries. Its role in WIPO

---

copyright and related rights for legitimate online music services (2005/737/EC),(2006/2008(INI)', <http:www.europarl.europa.eu/oeil/file.jsp.id=5303682>.

[18] W Patry, *Patry on Copyright* (2007) § 23:1 ff, on the history of US participation in international copyright law.

[19] For more detail, see S von Lewinski, 'International Copyright over the Last 50 Years: A Foreign Perspective' (2003) 50 J Copyright Soc USA 581, 588 ff.

[20] paras 10.56–10.57 and 10.64 above.

is likewise important,[21] even if other countries have become important counterparts.

(b) The EC

Exactly in the same year as the USA proactively entered the international copy- **25.22** right scene, the EC took first steps towards harmonization of copyright laws within the EC. The consequence of harmonization was the transformation from concurrent to exclusive competence for the EC (as opposed to the Member States) in areas beyond the trade context where it was already competent. The background for the harmonization activities was an economic one: the goal to achieve the internal market by 1992, as required by the Single European Act of 1986.[22] As a consequence, since the mid-1980s the EC has usually spoken with one voice and thereby become an important counterweight to the USA.[23] The emergence of the EC brought new dynamics to international negotiations. The USA and the EC were generally seen by others as the leading forces; at the same time, this new situation showed that the North was not always unified in its views. Relations became more complex than the previous North–South conflict. With the growth of the EC from twelve Member States in 1988 to twenty-seven in 2007, the EC has gained political strength.

(c) Developing countries

Developing countries have also changed their role over time. From the time of **25.23** their independence, developing countries have sought compulsory licences and other limitations of exclusive rights in their favour in order to take account of their developmental state and needs. The compromise of the 1971 Paris Act of the Berne Convention did not correspond to their initial demands, and the compulsory licences have only been applied to a limited extent. Even if they may have positive effects on the willingness of right owners in industrialized countries to grant licences under preferential conditions, these effects are difficult to ascertain. As current discussions in the framework of the WIPO Development Agenda suggest, more could be done to facilitate utilization of works from industrialized countries in developing countries.

For a long time, developing countries did not forcefully claim more privileges **25.24** than under the Berne Convention's Appendix. After the experience of the GATT-TRIPS negotiations and their outcome, as well as other experiences with

---

[21] cf eg its rather impeding role at the Dispute Settlement Draft Treaty (para 16.05 above) and at the Audiovisual Performances Conference, paras 18.20–28.21 above, as well as its initiating role for the WCT and WPPT, see para 17.09 above.

[22] For more detail, see von Lewinski (n 19 above) 592 ff.

[23] ibid 593–4.

industrialized countries in the trade arena, many developing countries showed frustration and felt disrespected. As a consequence, developing countries now demand more attention for their needs, such as is reflected in the WIPO Development Agenda; also, certain developing countries in particular started a political agenda that has led to the slow-down of negotiations in different international organizations and thereby has shown their potential power[24]—even if this procedure may not be useful for them, when industrialized countries consequently shift to unilateral measures and bilateral treaty negotiations.

25.25 Maybe a new thought in context with the needs of developing countries is useful here. Certainly, developing countries depend on protected works and phonograms less than on patented inventions from industrialized countries to advance their own development. In particular, developing countries usually have their own, rich culture; one may doubt whether their prosperity or level of development would increase if they listened to mainstream Western music or watched commercial movies from industrialized countries. Rather, what they need for their development in the cultural field is a working infrastructure and the technical and financial capacities to produce and market high-quality movies and other products in order to become competitive exporters of their own cultural goods and actually better benefit from international protection.

25.26 Several countries have shown that this is possible without benefiting from broad compulsory licences in the field of copyright: for example, India has blossoming movie and computer industries, Nigeria's different film industries have been labelled 'Nollywood',[25] and Egypt produces a high number of movies. Where foreign works in developing countries are protected and are more expensive than local works, the lack of compulsory licences may even lead to the strengthening of local culture and local right owners that enjoy the competitive advantage of being less expensive. For example, the Indonesian musical collecting society has higher revenues for local works than for foreign works.[26] The situation may have to be differently considered for educational material; yet, limitations for educational purposes may anyway be provided according to the general rules.

(4) The user movement

25.27 Proponents of a recent, notable movement that is becoming global have started to voice their views in WIPO's and other meetings at the international level, and

---

[24] eg paras 19.07, 19.37, and 21.02 above.

[25] Anon, 'The Nollywood Phenomenon' (2007) June WIPO Magazine 8.

[26] W Ramelan, 'Karya Cipta Indonesia: Copyright Collective Management' in EPO (ed), 'EU-ASEAN Symposium on Copyrights and Neighbouring Rights: Proceedings' (2004), slides 6, 8, and 10.

to claim a new balance between copyright and neighbouring rights on the one hand and individual users' interests on the other. They have initiated a highly emotional, often aggressive debate. The user movement appeared for the first time in 1996 in the context of the planned WIPO Treaty on the *sui generis* protection of databases.[27] After the EC had introduced such protection without major opposition, the same idea met with vigorous opposition in US academic and other user circles to the extent that the US delegation would probably not have been able to strongly support such protection at the WIPO Diplomatic Conference 1996; in the end, negotiations on a WIPO Treaty on the *sui generis* protection of databases were not even opened, also due to lack of time. After the movement became visible there, it then spread to the rest of the world and seems now to be mainstream in academic circles across many countries; the number of non-governmental organizations in WIPO that represent the public interest has proliferated since 1996.

Calls for greater 'access to information', though, are not new in principle: already   **25.28**
at the 1884 Diplomatic Conference for the Berne Convention, access to knowledge was debated.[28] Also at the inception of the Universal Copyright Convention, these claims were particularly strong; in the end, however, expert knowledge was able to convince the promoters of access to knowledge of the justification of a certain level of copyright protection.[29]

Today's movement seems to have deep roots in the direct contact of individual   **25.29**
users with copyright uses that were previously performed only by publishers, broadcasters, or other professionals. The internet allows users to perform such acts, for example where they participate in peer-to-peer networks or upload works for access on their personal homepages. Many users have become accustomed to the actually free availability of works on the internet, and it may therefore be particularly difficult to explain to them that authors' works are also protected on the internet. This applies all the more where users find confirmation in their beliefs through each other in the framework of blogs or other internet fora, and thus will feel sufficiently justified in their beliefs on free access. As a consequence, one-sided opinions that are expressed beyond any legal or policy-making considerations and that are often based on emotions rather than expertise and objective, balanced reasoning, may gain weight and become, for their followers, a 'truth'.[30]

---

[27] para 22.01 above.

[28] M Ficsor, *The Law of Copyright and the Internet: The 1996 WIPO Treaties, their Interpretation and Implementation* (2002) n 5.06; for the 1948 Brussels Conference, see para 4.16 above.

[29] Indeed, UNESCO's first programme in the field of copyright which included a universal convention reflected its focus on education and science and the view that copyright would be an obstacle to free circulation of information—a view that was later revised, Anon, 'La Première Conférence Générale de l'UNESCO', (1947) Droit d'auteur 4–5.

[30] For more details, see von Lewinski (n 19 above) 597–604.

25.30   Language is a strong tool for this movement and is often used in a misleading, manipulative way. An example is a 'Civil Society Coalition' that only represents users rather than also other members of civil society, such as authors and artists, or even the free access to 'information'—a legitimate demand, as long as information is understood as in the Berne Convention, namely as mere facts that are anyway not protected. Where, however, this legitimate demand is understood as covering protected works, such as music, the concept of copyright would be completely undermined. Similarly, the book title *The Future of Ideas*[31] seems to suggest that this future is endangered by copyright, while ideas never have been protected by copyright. Most recently, the words 'transformative use' have been invented,[32] with an unclear meaning—possibly to circumvent the technical terms of copyright and to suggest that a use which is subject to the author's authorization, such as adaptation, would not fall under these terms.

25.31   Many arguments used in the debate, such as and in particular the human right of freedom of expression, are often used in a biased way. It is notable that even some academics and international institutions seem to overlook the fact that authors' rights are also human rights and that a balance between those has to be found.[33] This balance indeed has been inherent in copyright protection from its inception; for example, ideas have never been protected and works must fulfil certain criteria, such as originality, in order to be protected; in addition, protection is limited in time and rights are restricted through limitations and exceptions in favour of the general public. Accordingly, it is a matter of fine-tuning and continuously adapting these parameters to new factual circumstances rather than questioning the entire system of protection.[34] Such a balance has been struck within

---

[31] L Lessig, *The Future of Ideas* (2001).

[32] *Gower's Review of Intellectual Property* (2006) 66 ff.

[33] Even the UN Sub-commission on the Promotion and Protection of Human Rights in its Resolution 2000/7 of 17 August 2000 (Resolution E/CN.4/SUB.2/RES/2000/7) had to be criticized because it opposed freedom of expression to authors' rights without noting the human rights quality of authors' rights, see S von Lewinski, 'Opinion by the Max Planck Institute' (submission to the Sub-commission, summarized in the Report of the Secretary General on Economic, Social and Cultural Rights—Intellectual Property Rights and Human Rights, UN Economic and Social Council, Doc no E/CN.4/Sub.2/2001/12 of 14 June 2001, p 17, <http://www.unhchr.ch/huridocda/huridoca.nsf/AllSymbols/95A1F896BC21CBA9C1256A9A005A49C3/$File/G0114202.doc?OpenElement>). In particular among US academics, it has become fashionable to debate human rights and intellectual property with an exclusive or dominant focus on freedom of speech (or, in Europe, of expression) in order to call for a different balance with authors' rights. Often, language is used so as to contrast human rights with copyright or other intellectual property rights and thereby suggest the latter rights are not human rights, eg A Brown, 'Human Rights: In the Real World' (2006) J'l of Intellectual Property Law and Practice 603, eg at 607 ('where human rights and IP conflict').

[34] R Anderson and H Wager, 'Human Rights, Development, and the WTO: The Cases of Intellectual Property and Competition Policy' (2006) 9/3 J'l of International Economic Law 707, 724, 725; pointing at differences between US law and Continental European Law, von Lewinski

the existing copyright and neighbouring rights treaties; their provisions are more specific than the very general Human Rights Treaty provisions. Consequently, it will hardly be possible to draw any concrete conclusion from the balance between authors' rights and freedom of expression in human rights treaties for any concrete interpretation of the more specific copyright treaties. The *lex specialis* rule will usually lead to the absence of a conflict between both treaties.[35]

Fine-tuning of the balance between the rights of authors and neighbouring rights owners and the interests of users has been among the tasks of copyright legislatures and judges throughout copyright history; where protection is felt to have been extended too far in individual instances, an informed debate should be the appropriate tool to address these instances. **25.32**

(5) Technical progress

The internet has probably played a major role in the user movement; it has brought about new kinds of uses and enforcement problems, as well as challenges to the principle of territoriality that are currently addressed by private international law. These certainly are major problems, some of which have already been addressed, and will continuously require adaptation of law and practice. Whether the internet presents an unmanageable challenge to copyright and neighbouring rights protection and thus is fundamentally different from earlier technical developments remains to be seen. It seems that to each generation, its own situation always looks most dramatic and different from anything that came before. For example, while our generation is overwhelmed by the internet, twenty-five years earlier it was 'in the field of using works that the scientific and technological *revolution* has brought the most decisive changes for copyright'.[36] Regardless, through the WCT and the WPPT, international law responded with potentially global standards immediately after the internet was perceived as a global problem for copyright and neighbouring rights, and thereby offered a basis for national legislators to cope with this challenge. **25.33**

(n 19 above) 597, 601; P Goldstein, 'Copyright's Commons' (2005) 29/1 Columbia J'l of Law and the Arts, 1, 2 ff.

[35] para 24.19 above; courts have generally rejected the direct reliance on international treaties in national law cases, where users had argued on the basis of human rights treaties, see eg G Karnell, 'Copyright Protection under Human Rights Control, in particular of Works not Disseminated to the Public' (2004) 10 World Intellectual Property Report 23 ff; H Cohen Jehoram, 'Copyright and Freedom of Expression, Abuse of Rights and Standard Chicanery: American and Dutch Approaches' (2004) EIPR 275 ff.

[36] M Ficsor, 'Disquieting Report from the Maginot Line of Authors: Technological Progress and Crisis Tendencies in Copyright' (1982) Copyright 104, 106; emphasis added.

C. Résumé

25.34 Looking back at the fathers of the Berne Convention and their original aim—or dream—of universal protection for authors, one may wonder whether they would consider today's circumstances as coming much closer to it or even achieving this aim. At least at the surface, it may seem that we have come quite close to universal protection: the current laws of most countries in the world adhere to the principles of national treatment and minimum standards and provide for very similar standards of protection, be it as a result of the widespread acceptance of the Berne Convention and its successor treaties or also as a result of bilateral and regional agreements as well as unilateral trade measures. Even if the Berne fathers thus might be satisfied at first sight, they would also recognize certain, possibly less appreciated aspects.

25.35 For example, it is doubtful whether it is appropriate to use different trade tools to impose quite high standards of protection upon countries that are at a low stage of development; the setbacks of this approach have been elaborated above.[37] In addition, they might dislike the intrusion of elements of the copyright system into international law that was largely built on the author's rights system, as reflected in the Berne Convention. In this context, the potential weakening of the individual author as opposed to exploitative businesses due to the focus on trade and economic aspects of copyright would certainly not correspond to the initial (and today still valid) motivation of the Berne fathers to achieve worldwide recognition of the rights of individual creators.[38]

25.36 On another thought, today's situation may also show that an idea or concept, such as the recognition of authors' rights in their works, may be born out of a specific culture and not easily be transferred to other cultures where different concepts existed from the outset (such as Asian cultures, where it was often an honour for a master to be copied rather than a violation of his 'rights').[39] We can see today that the penetration of such ideas may take quite some time and may not be obvious; under this surface, differences will continue for a long time. This is also evident from practice of moral rights in countries of the copyright system; even where they provide for moral rights, the understanding is quite different from

---

[37] paras 14.20–14.23 above.

[38] eg the Swiss invitation to the first Diplomatic Conference in 1884 spoke of the 'work of the genius of man', the rights of the writer and artist, and supported the idea of the predecessor of ALAI (ALI) for an international convention—with ALAI having been founded by Victor Hugo, focusing on individual creators and having had a strong influence on the Berne Convention, see J Cavalli, *La Genèse de la Convention de Berne pour la protection des œuvres littéraires et artistiques du 9 Septembre 1886* 163 in n 18.

[39] para 3.04 above.

that in countries of the author's rights system. Finally, this observation seems to confirm that the initial idea of a fully universal protection was too idealistic; since law is a reflection of ideas, values, and concepts rooted in societies and their cultures, a certain degree of diversity of approaches (as, in particular, between the author's rights and copyright systems) will—and should—remain under the surface of a high similarity among copyright norms.

26

OUTLOOK: PROSPECTS FOR THE DEVELOPMENT OF INTERNATIONAL COPYRIGHT AND NEIGHBOURING RIGHTS LAW

A. Another crisis?

Where are we today, and what can be expected for the development of inter- **26.01** national copyright and neighbouring rights law in the near future? When looking at the recent past, one may observe a fundamental change of atmosphere at the international level: the success of the adoption of the WCT and WPPT in 1996 was generally felt as a zenith for the protection of authors' rights and neighbouring rights; enthusiasm was so great that soon thereafter, the idea of adopting both agreements en bloc within the TRIPS Agreement[1] was considered. A meaningful protection of authors and neighbouring rights owners then was still an unquestioned goal and considered a good thing to achieve. Only a few years later, such a statement would no longer be undisputed, and no one would seriously think of incorporating the standards of the WCT and the WPPT into the TRIPS Agreement (although, ironically, the same result is meanwhile being reached through bilateral trade agreements and other trade measures). The user movement and the growing opposition by developing countries in the multilateral fora have changed the general situation.

---

[1] On this possibility, see para 10.140 above.

26.02 After 1996, attempts to adopt multilateral treaties in the field of neighbouring rights have not met with success. Does this mean that multilateral treaty-making is no longer possible in this field of law? The first post-1996 plan for a treaty put on ice was the Draft Treaty on the protection of audiovisual performances. For this plan, one has to consider that very particular circumstances from the outset have prevented the adoption of international protection: already in the framework of the Rome Convention 1961, protection for audiovisual performers was largely excluded; also the TRIPS Agreement and the WPPT did not introduce such protection. The root of problems, namely the gap between the systems of protection in the USA and in the rest of the world, has always subsisted and hindered the adoption of international protection as long as the USA participated in the negotiations. Accordingly, the failure of adopting a treaty on audiovisual performances is not necessarily a sign of a general crisis.

26.03 This may be somewhat different regarding the draft treaty on the protection of broadcasting organizations. Yet, one has to note that enthusiasm for such a treaty has always been much lower than that leading to the adoption of the WCT and the WPPT. A need for such protection was less strongly perceived, and many developing countries as well as the USA did not show a strong interest in the matter at the beginning. When the USA later showed interest in protecting webcasters, the rest of the world was not ready to address this new phenomenon through international norms. Subsequently, leading developing countries (in particular, Brazil and India) strengthened their opposition to such a treaty, even without webcasters, seemingly as part of a general political agenda that was also pursued in other international organizations such as the WTO; delegates who were often well trained in US and British universities applied their knowledge and strategies now in the same way as delegates of major industrialized countries had done before, resulting in what could be called a power-play or bullying show with respective exposure of muscles; the latter aspect too often tended to prevail over the discussion on substantive issues. In the end, agreement among all delegations on a basic proposal for the planned diplomatic conference became unachievable. Where it seems to be more important to find out who is the winner of the game and thus may have a better starting position in the next game, the situation may not be propitious for future negotiations.

26.04 A similar scenario prevails in respect of WIPO discussions on the protection of folklore, where discussions are fruitful as long as the question of a possible treaty is not at stake. In this case, industrialized countries oppose even the acknowledgement of any substantive outcome of the Committee work and reject the idea of an international treaty.[2] The recent success in context of the WIPO Development Agenda may not necessarily be seen as a sign for more constructive dynamics, since the delegates simply agreed on a set of vaguely drafted issues to be discussed in a future committee, while there was not yet any question of treaty-making.

Consequently, can we speak of another crisis in international copyright and **26.05** neighbouring rights law? Even if one tends to do so, this will not be the end of international copyright and neighbouring rights protection or further developments in the field. The Berne Convention and other treaties have survived many crises,[3] and chances are good that this will remain so in the future. Indeed, talking about a 'crisis' or even the end of copyright always seems to have been popular— maybe every generation needs its own copyright crisis and likes to speculate about the endangered future of copyright.[4] Against this background, 'crisis' might be the wrong word, all the more so since it is normal that after a major, successful effort to improve international protection, such as occurred with the WCT and the WPPT in 1996, a time without treaty-making follows—and should follow— as happened after 1971 when WIPO started the 'guided development' period. Even in the past, multilateral treaties were only concluded in longer intervals. Yet, some industrialized countries felt the urge for further treaty-making and plan to negotiate among themselves an Anti-Counterfeiting Trade Agreement (ACTA) as a leadership agreement outside any formal structure, on TRIPS-plus enforcement provisions, best practices and international cooperation. After adoption, it is planned to persuade other countries to join the Agreement.[5]

---

[2] Report of the Eleventh Session of the IGC, WIPO Doc GRTKF/11/14, see in particular decision no 8(v) to ask the Secretariat only to make a 'factual extraction..., consolidating the view points and questions of Members...'; also paras 20.38, 20.41, and 20.42 above.

[3] For a summary of challenges, often called 'crises', see paras 25.02–25.12 above.

[4] For references to crises, see W Goldbaum, *Verfall und Auflösung der sogenannten Berner Union und Übereinkunft zum Schutz von Werken der Literatur und Kunst* (1959) (author's translation: 'Decline and Dissolution of the So-Called Berne Union and Convention on the Protection of Literary and Artistic Works'); after 1967, eg E Ulmer 'The Revision of the Copyright Conventions in the Light of the Washington Recommendation' (1970) IIC 235 ff; at the beginning of the 1980s, see M Ficsor, 'Disquieting Report from the Maginot Line of Authors: Technological Progress and Crisis Tendencies in Copyright', (1982) Copyright 104 ff, with many references to crisis-related articles; in the early1990s: E Traple and J Barta, 'Is the Berne Convention Undergoing a Crisis?' (1992) 152 RIDA 3 ff; for even later, see P Geller, 'Intellectual Property in the Global market Place: Impact of TRIPS Dispute Settlements' (1995) 29/1 The International Lawyer 99, 100 ff.

[5] The USA, Japan, the EC, and Switzerland were initial proponents, joined by further (also developing) countries interested in strong IP protection, see eg a discussion paper by the Australian government, <http://www.dfat.gov.au/ip/ACTA_discussion_paper.html; <http://www.ustr.gov>, press release of 23 October 2007; <http://www.iipa.com>, reaction of 23 October 2007 (press archive).

B. The way ahead

(1) Consolidation

26.06 Still, there are other ways to usefully promote international copyright and neighbouring rights protection. The present time should be used for absorption of the newly introduced standards, for proper implementation, for experience with them, and possibly for correction or adaptation where practice shows deficiencies or imbalances in what has been achieved. In addition, especially regarding developing countries, more groundwork should be done, including focused training; assistance in establishing the necessary infrastructure, such as collecting societies or enforcement mechanisms, in order to allow developing countries' authors to benefit from the provided protection; and awareness raising for authors about best ways to assert their rights, as well as for users about respect for the value of protected culture in their countries and the need of authors to survive from their work. Major efforts are needed in many developing countries to create a legal market in the first instance; all too often there, authors still cannot even publish their works due to a lack of publishing houses or producing companies, nor do they have any other means to market their works so as to earn a living as authors.

26.07 Only a good working and appropriate system of protection may be credible enough to make copyright and neighbouring rights protection work at all and to create confidence with authors that such protection may support local authors rather than simply being imposed by major foreign countries for the benefit of foreign authors.[6] Only a good working and appropriate system of protection may also convince users that protection allows for more diversity and quality of creation, and that the access to such diversity suffers where creation is not sufficiently protected and respected. In addition, legal advice to governments on intellectual property legislation, whether performed by WIPO staff or any others working in technical assistance programmes, should take account of the local needs and factual situations by using the permitted flexibilities under international law as regards, in particular, limitations and exceptions.

26.08 WIPO has already taken this approach, for example, in respect of audiovisual performances. After the unsuccessful 2000 Diplomatic Conference, the WIPO proceeded to lay very useful groundwork, such as specialized training and assistance for the establishment and operation of collecting societies in the field. Similarly, WIPO staff members have been assisting *demandeur* countries in drafting national or regional norms on the protection of folklore on the basis of a

---

6 This latter perception indeed prevails with authors of many developing countries, as expressed on different occasions to the author of this book.

fruitful dialogue. Such activities are currently more important than further attempts at treaty-making.

(2) Balancing against other aspects

Especially in the trade framework, the concentration on trade aspects should be **26.09** balanced against other aspects; one should focus attention on remedies against the negative effects of the trade approach. In particular, one-sided economic approaches and tendencies towards more media concentration best benefit multinational enterprises and need a rebalancing in favour of other values that are justified as well. Among the remedies, competition law and policy should obtain a greater role in fighting media concentration; as a result, greater diversity among media companies may be beneficial to authors through a greater choice of independent companies as contracting partners, and it may be beneficial to users through possibly more diverse choices of goods on the market. More competition could also to some extent indirectly help to rebalance the typically unbalanced situation between (weaker) individual authors and their (stronger) publishers or other contracting partners; as a consequence, authors might negotiate and obtain better revenues from their creations.

A better, direct way to reach this aim of strengthening the individual author in his **26.10** relation to media companies would be the provision of rules protecting authors in their contractual relations with such companies (as in countries of the author's rights system).[7] So far, international law does not include such rules; rather the USA has been pushing in its trade agreements for the opposite result. In the current situation, and even if the general atmosphere for treaty-making were positive, it would however seem utopian to hope for the inclusion of such rules into international treaties. Individual authors usually do not have strong enough lobby organizations or sufficient financial means for effective lobbying to realistically compete with lobbying by media companies at the international level.[8] The situation might improve for authors where major powerful companies would give way to a multitude of smaller companies. Even if this aim then still seems utopian, it may be worthwhile to promote activities in this direction and to try the seemingly impossible, not least to render the justification for protection more credible again.

---

[7] paras 3.70 ff above.

[8] Although several NGOs representing individual authors are admitted (eg the Creators' Rights Alliance, European Visual Artists, European Writers' Congress, Federation of European Audiovisual Directors, European Scriptwriters in Europe, CISAC, <http://www.wipo.int/members/en/organizations.jsp?type=NGO_INT>, only few (as compared to other NGOs) appear in meetings (eg at the 15th session of the SCCR, only the Creators' Rights Alliance, ALAI, and the Portuguese Society of Authors represented individual authors, while forty-seven other NGOs represented other interests).

26.11   On a somewhat related point, the issue of cultural diversity should be honoured, including in the trade context. Indeed, cultural diversity presupposes an adequate protection of creators who need an income from their work in order to continue to create, as well as fair market structures that allow creators to get their works distributed or otherwise made accessible to the public at all, and this for the final benefit of users. Experience, for example, in Canada has shown that the quota for local production resulted in a blossoming of local culture, which is now much more exported; beforehand, it did not even have a realistic chance to become known to a larger public. In international relations, collecting societies' social and cultural funds as practised in countries of the author's rights system[9] should be acknowledged in their important functions for the welfare of authors and for cultural diversity rather than rejected on a purely economic, property-rights-based approach.[10] The possibilities of the internet may to some extent help unknown artists get an audience, but this may not be generally sufficient. The urge for the recognition of cultural diversity as a value to be protected and maintained against dominating mainstream cultural products and against the 'diktats' of international trade[11] has recently resulted in the adoption of the UNESCO Convention on Cultural Diversity.[12] Yet, the Convention does not derogate from other treaties to which the Parties are parties, such as the WTO Agreement,[13] so that it will probably have greater political than legal effects. Indeed, since its adoption, cultural diversity is referred to in many recent official documents on copyright or neighbouring rights[14] and reflects the widely perceived need to protect cultural diversity. At the same time, some players, especially developing

---

[9] para 3.75 above.

[10] Similarly, European Parliament, 'Report on the Commission Recommendation of 18 October 2005 on collective cross-border management of copyright and related rights for legitimate online music services (2005/737/EC)(2006/2008(INI)', <http://www.europarl.europa.eu/oeil/file.jsp?id =5303682>, mainly recital I, and statement 6, 10th recital.

[11] A Dorion, 'La Convention sur la diversité des expressions culturelles et la propriété intellectuelle: panacée ou placebo?' (2007) 19/1 Les Cahiers de le propriété intellectuelle 321, 322, referring to E Brooks, 'Cultural Imperialism vs Cultural Protectionism: Hollywood's Response to UNESCO Efforts to Promote Cultural Diversity' [Spring 2006] Journal of International Business & Law 5, 112.

[12] Convention of 20 October 2005; it entered into force on 18 March 2007; see <http://portal. unesco.org/en/ev.php-URL_ID=31038&URL_DO=DO_TOPIC&URL_SECTION=201. html>; notably, the USA had largely opposed the Convention but was defeated in the end.

[13] Art 20(2) of the Convention: 'Nothing in this Convention shall be interpreted as modifying rights and obligations of the Parties under any other treaties to which they are parties'; see also Art 20(1) on mutual supportiveness of provisions in other treaties.

[14] See, in particular, the European Parliament's report on the European Commission's recommendation on online music licensing (n 9 above), where cultural diversity is mentioned throughout the document; see also the proposals by Brazil and other countries in the framework of the Draft Treaty on the protection of broadcasting organizations (paras 19.08, 19.32 above; Brazil, WIPO Doc SCCR/13/3 Corr, Annex pp 2–3 (Art [y]), and Peru, WIPO Doc SCCR14/6 Annex pp 2–3).

countries, seem to view cultural diversity as a possible argument to reduce copyright protection—an approach that must be considered a misunderstanding.[15]

C. Copyright and neighbouring rights in the mirror of general developments

While trade liberalization has brought about overall economic prosperity in most **26.12** countries,[16] negative consequences for copyright and neighbouring rights of a one-sided trade approach should be remedied in particular by means of competition law, promotion of cultural diversity, improvement of the situation of individual authors, and an appropriate, fine-tuned rebalancing of rights with justified user interests; this approach, which takes account of aspects other than trade, would be in line with recent demands in the WTO to take account of other areas, such as environmental protection and minimum standards for workers under labour law.[17] Even without a crystal ball, it is safe to say that global movements of civil society (understood in the broadest sense, including in the field of copyright not only users but likewise authors and artists), which have expressed some of these latest desires and trends, will exercise a stronger influence on global developments than before. Indeed, copyright and neighbouring rights law has left the niche of experts, with all the accompanying positive and negative consequences— the positive one of more democratic influence, and the negative one of less knowledge-based discussions.[18] This development towards a possibly stronger influence of global movements may be one of the consequences of globalization, being a reaction to the global influence by multinational companies; it may have to be seen in context of discussions on 'global governance', understood as the increasing loss of influence of national sovereignty of states in exchange for supra- and international organizations where NGOs and multinational companies participate as part of a world civil society in decision-making.[19]

---

[15] T Desurmont, 'Considerations on the Relationship between the Convention on the Protection and Promotion of the Diversity of Cultural Expressions and the Protection of Authors' Rights' (2006) 208 RIDA 2, 4 and, referring to the Brazilian proposal (n 13 above) as an example for the view of developing countries, 8 ff.

[16] PT Stoll and F Schorkopf, *WTO-Welthandelsordnung und Welthandelsrecht* (2002) nn 3–5.

[17] eg the 1994 Ministerial Decision created the WTO Committee on Trade and Environment, and the Doha Development Agenda includes negotiations on trade and environment; the Doha Ministerial Declaration 2001, paragraph 8, reaffirms the Singapore declaration regarding core international labour standards and takes note of ILO's work on the social dimension of globalization.

[18] For the negative consequences, see P Goldstein, 'Copyright's Commons' (2005) 29/1 Columbia J'l of Law and the Arts, 1, 2 ff, who speaks, eg, of the need for public education, and flawed notions being used.

[19] On global governance, see JS Rosenau, 'Governance, Order and Change in the World' in JS Rosenau and E-O Czempiel (eds), *Governance without Government: Order and Change in World Politics* (1992) 1, 4 ff.

26.13 Yet other developments in the field of copyright and neighbouring rights seem merely to reflect general political and social phenomena. In particular, the gaps between the rich and the poor seem to grow, both at the domestic and the international levels, leading to more aggressive behaviour on the market; the prevalence of economic versus legal arguments in decision-making—be it in the framework of legislative activities and other norm-setting, or in context of decision-making within (mainly multinational) companies; less bargaining power of those who are already in a typically weak position (such as individual authors); and more short-sighted egoistic behaviour without due regard to the concerns of the other side, such as in relations between individual authors and media companies, and between individual users and powerful right owners, or even between powerful and less powerful right owners of the same kind, for example within collecting societies.

26.14 In general, and in the field of copyright and related rights in particular, the different groups of societies need less rigid confrontation and more dialogue. The willingness to listen to the other side and honestly to take into account their arguments has decreased so as to impede the dialogue that is necessary to cope with the current challenges. In this context, it will also be necessary for some to renounce widespread populist, sometimes even demagogic, behaviour and rhetorical or manipulative language as well as cliché suggestions and instead to proceed to objective, informed, and de-emotionalized discussions which alone have the potential properly to address today's challenges. Those who publish and otherwise communicate on issues of copyright and neighbouring rights have a responsibility to clarify the law and basic concepts of copyright, even if this may not be popular, in particular to those who call for 'access to information' but mean rather free entertainment, and who certainly have access to copyright literature, but who seem not interested in using this access in order to recognize the basic principles of copyright.[20] Maybe this book can offer a small contribution in this regard. Only once debates have regained sufficient expertise and more respect for the other side can a more constructive situation—domestically and internationally—be reached.

---

[20] Goldstein (n 18 above) 2 ff deplores the inaccurate perception of copyright and the lack of basic knowledge thereon, and proceeds to the necessary clarification of basic notions of copyright.

INDEX